LETTERS FROM FOREST PLACE

A Plantation Family's Correspondence

1846–1881

Letters from Forest Place

A Plantation Family's Correspondence

1846–1881

Edited by

E. Grey Dimond

and

Herman Hattaway

University Press of Mississippi
Jackson

To
Louise "Mimi" Parmele Johnson,
Lettie's granddaughter,
who preserved these letters and who recalls first-hand accounts
of the days when the Watkins family measured its well-being
in carriages and cotton

Copyright © 1993 by the University Press of Mississippi
All rights reserved
Manufactured in the United States of America

96   95   94   93   4   3   2   1

The paper in this book meets the guidelines for permanence and durability of
the Committee on Production Guidelines for Book Longevity of the Council on
Library Resources.

Library of Congress Cataloging-in-Publication Data
Letters from Forest Place : a plantation family's correspondence,
    1846–1881 / edited by E. Grey Dimond and Herman Hattaway.
        p.   cm.
    Includes index.
    ISBN 0-87805-653-X
    1. Plantation life—Mississippi—Carroll County—History—19th
century.   2. Carroll County (Miss.)—History.   3. Watkins family—
Correspondence.   4. Carroll County (Miss.)—Biography.
5. Mississippi—History—Civil War, 1861–1865.   I. Dimond, E. Grey
(Edmunds Grey), 1918–   II. Hattaway, Herman.
F347.C3L48   1993
976.2'633—dc20   93-25041
                                                            CIP

British Library Cataloging-in-Publication data available

A British visitor to Mobile, Alabama wrote, "People live in cotton houses and ride in cotton carriages. They buy cotton, sell cotton, think cotton, eat cotton, drink cotton, and dream cotton. They marry cotton wives, and unto them are born cotton children."

Emory M. Thomas,
The Confederacy as a Revolutionary Experience

CONTENTS

PREFACE

More than ten years ago, we became aware of a treasure trove of letters written by the Watkins family of Carroll County, Mississippi, and carefully preserved by a descendant, Mrs. Louise (John H.) Parmele Johnson of Austin, Texas. Mrs. Parmele's daughter, Eugenia (Mrs. Clifford J.) Richards of Houston, Texas, captured our interest by showing us a trickle of letters; as we responded, she kept revealing more of the letters until we finally realized there was an entire story to be told. With the permission of Mrs. Johnson and Mrs. Richards, we have selected letters that provide a coherent theme, that tell what plantation life was like—its satisfactions and its burdens. Putting their letters into a book has not been labor because of the pleasant support of these Watkins descendants.

The letters are valuable not only because they are well crafted and fun to read, but because they reveal a great deal about the writers. In many ways they tell a love story. Beyond that, they delineate much about the ongoing lives of one particular slave-owning family in antebellum and Civil War-era Mississippi. The bulk of the material was written to and/or by women, and the collection doubtless will be welcomed by that growing number of scholars who recently have been so meaningfully developing and enriching the field of gender studies. Too, portions of some of the letters were either written or orally dictated by various slaves, so the collection will be of interest to students in black studies. Lastly, the letters and the "cast of characters" therein will be a delight, and a useful tool, for genealogists.

E. Grey Dimond
Herman M. Hattaway
University of Missouri–Kansas City
December 8, 1992

INTRODUCTION

The Watkins letters provide the reader with an apolitical, unrehearsed, unself-conscious glimpse at the multitude of moments that make up a lifetime.

The letters intimately describe plantation life in the Deep South during the Civil War era. Thus, they also describe slave life. With no attempt to hide this reality behind euphemisms, the editors have retained the words and language of the Watkins family, especially the Watkins women. The word "slave" essentially does not appear. The word "negro" was used to describe race. The person to whom a task was assigned was spoken of as "family servant." Those who did not work at the home and in family chores were "field hands."

A stranger reading the letters would not always know if the person referred to was a plantation owner or a slave. The same sentence might say, "Mary is very sick, Mama is better." Only the family would know Mary was the plantation owner's daughter and Mama was the slave baby–nurse, but we, as editors, have tried to clarify this sort of thing.

The letters give a good sense of the physical and emotional burden borne by Mrs. Watkins as she went about her tasks: cutting out the clothing for her servants, assigning and moderating their work, attending to their well-being and medical needs. When the doctor made one of his frequent extended trips, his wife's responsibility for a corps of a hundred people, in a rural setting, was increased.

The story of Carroll County is the story of the South—the moving in of the whites and their slaves as new land became available, the years of wealth and abundance, the devastation of property and the loss of male descendants in the Civil War, the years of Reconstruction bringing the proud families down, and the young people moving out and on to careers, not on the land, but in the professions. The Watkins letters make those years intensely human as they report the daily life of the plantation and tell of the girls going on to school, to romance, to husbands.

There is an inclusion of the slaves into the family; that slaves are property and not family is made real when they are hired out, given away, sold. The frequency of illness and death made it an accepted truth, as constant as the seasons. Death came so often that mention of it flows through the letters as regularly as remarks about guests.

The letters do not move swiftly; they cover over dramatic events with the tedium and slow pace of daily life. The story of the Civil War is told as it happened, not on the battlefields, but to the burdened population, including events so small that the size of the action is brought down to the question of whether a hog can be slaughtered to feed the slaves. Young men who grew up as friends go away and die, and another dies, and another, as the letters maintain their slow pace of recitation, fitting the deaths in as a part of normal expectations.

The story of Lettie and of her growing up, her rebelliousness, her unapproved marriage, the sustained parental hostility, the reconciliation, and the grandchildren transcends time or place. Lettie was eight years old when the family came to Carroll County; Mollie was born within a year (February 22, 1844). The sequence of letters covers their growing up, their schooling, their romances, and Lettie's children.

The Watkins plantation, Forest Place, was six miles east of Carrollton and four miles west of Middleton; the nearest neighbor was Magnolia, the plantation of Edmunds Grey Whitehead.

The census of 1850 identifies Thomas A. Watkins, age forty-eight, living on 1,500 acres of land with his wife Sarah, age thirty-six, Letitia, fifteen, and Mary, six. Readers may get a sense of the size of this estate if they know that a mile square of land comprised 640 acres, and that the Watkins property encompassed approximately 2 1/2 of these square miles.[1]

The neighbor, Edmunds Grey Whitehead, is identified in the 1850 census as age forty-four and his wife, Martha Jennet, as age thirty-two; their children, Elizabeth, thirteen; Virginia, eleven; William, seven; Grey, four; Thomas, two; and Emma, three months were all born in Carroll County.

Doctor Thomas Alexander Watkins was born October 30, 1802, in Georgia. He graduated from the University of Georgia (then Franklin College) and obtained his medical diploma from the University of Pennsylvania. He began the practice of medicine at age twenty-three, in

---

1. William W. Whitehead of Wilkinson County, Mississippi, took up homesteads #1152 and #1153, sec. 22, township 18N, range 5–#, 1833. On the same day, homestead #1161, west 1/2 NW 1/4, sec. 23, township 19N, range 5E, was taken up by Edmunds Grey Whitehead of Holmes County, Mississippi.

Thomas A. Watkins's land was all in township 19, range 4E, and the homestead piece was in sec. 23: east 1/2 of SW 1/4, and the SE 1/4 and NE 1/4, and east 1/2 of the NW 1/4.

1825, at Courtland, Alabama. He also had a drugstore. At age thirty-two, in 1834, he married Miss Sarah Epes Fitzgerald, a young lady of twenty. Their first daughter, Letitia Ann, was born a year later, March 21, 1835. In 1843, after eighteen years of practice, the doctor moved his family— Letitia was eight years old and Sarah was pregnant—to Carroll County, Mississippi. The move overland was probably made by ox wagons and carriages. By the fall of 1843, the doctor was settled on his place receiving shipments of goods coming in by steamboat on the Yazoo River at Williams Landing.[2] He was a Mississippian from age forty-one, in 1843, to age sixty-four, in 1866.

Their second and last child, Mary (Mollie) Early Watkins was born February 23, 1844. The doctor never practiced again; for the next twenty-six years he was a planter, managing the affairs of a 1,500–acre plantation.[3]

The family home was within walking distance of the Edmunds Whitehead home, the same Whitehead who was the presiding officer over the founding of the county ten years earlier. The county road joining Carrollton and Shongalo passed by the two homes, with Middleton being the nearest "urban" settlement.

To understand the Watkins letters, one must understand one small part of the South, Carroll County, Mississippi.

Scattered throughout the area, in Carroll County and Montgomery County, is evidence of the past: large handsome homes, those that have survived because of owners who cherish them, and great old trees planted near the homes by someone who cared and who had the time, the desire, the taste, the wherewithal to live in a grand style. Who were they, where did they go, and where did they come from? How could this scruffy, hilly, red clay land generate, create, sustain what must have been elegant living? Cattle now grazing where once the field hands tended the cotton illustrate the truth about the poor land.

By the 1820s the growth and power of the young United States made life difficult for Indians living east of the Mississippi River. A military man and politician, Andrew Jackson understood the will of the western frontiersmen, and his campaigns made him a popular folk hero and finally president. During his presidency, the Indian Removal Act of 1830 forced the settlement of most of the Indians into the area now forming Oklahoma.

2. Williams Landing was the original settlement on the Yazoo River; eventually the site became Greenwood, Mississippi.

3. His earliest land purchase was October 9, 1843, and additional land was purchased in 1844, 1846 and 1853.

The Choctaw Indians occupied two-thirds of what is now Mississippi, but by 1831 they were forced into a surrender under the Treaty of
Dancing Rabbit Creek.[4] The United States Senate ratified the treaty on
February 25, 1831, and the resettlement of the Choctaws across the
Mississippi River began. This was the third cession of land made by the
Choctaw (1805, 1820, 1830) and when combined with the cession by
the Chickasaw in 1832 made up the major dominion now known as the
state of Mississippi. Northern Mississippi in 1830 was an Indian wilderness. There were about twenty-three thousand Choctaws in the region.

On December 23, 1833, the Mississippi state legislature[5] authorized
Edmunds Grey Whitehead, James Collins, Titus Howard, Absalom Her-
ring, and William Collins to organize Carroll County, almost in the
center of the newly ceded land. The county was named in honor of
Charles Carroll of Carrollton, Maryland, a signer of the Declaration of
Independence.

Early on, several families from southeast Mississippi, all closely related, came to Carroll County. These were the families of Edmunds Grey
Whitehead, Hugh Davis, Robert Davis, William W. Whitehead, John E.
Palmer, and Dr. J. C. Calhoun. The Davis brothers, the Whitehead brothers and Judge Palmer settled near Middleton, while Dr. Calhoun and
family stopped near Blackhawk. Soon, new settlers also came from Virginia, North Carolina, Georgia, Alabama, and Tennessee.

The enthusiasm of Edmunds Grey Whitehead and his brother William for the new land was evident. When the northern Mississippi land
was opened for purchase between October 1 and December 1, 1833,
they bought 13,557 acres between them.

The first police board meeting of Carroll County was March 11, 1834,
at the home of George W. Green, where the town of Carrollton is now
located. At the April 16, 1834, meeting, the board ordered that the
county seat be called Carrollton.

In addition to Carrollton, the early towns were Middleton, Shongalo,
Blackhawk, Coila, McCarley, and Teoc.

Middleton's location, north–central Mississippi in the hills above the

---

4. Arthur H. deRosier, Jr., *The Removal of the Choctaw Indians* (Knoxville: The University
of Tennessee Press, 1970), 116–28.

5. On December 23, 1833, Governor Hiram G. Runnels signed into law the act of the
Mississippi legislature creating sixteen counties from the land acquired at Dancing Rabbit
Creek. In 1831, 1832, and 1833, the new counties were surveyed and marked off from south
to north in townships and from west to east in ranges. A township was six sections square
(thirty-six square miles) and each section was divided into sixteen forty-acre subdivisions.
The board of police was the county government.

Delta country, was considered healthy and relatively free of the fevers of the low rich lands of the Delta. The Delta, which included the Yazoo River lowlands as well as the major area of the Mississippi, began about forty miles west of Middleton. As schools, physicians, and owners of land deep in the Delta sought the cooler hill country, Middleton became a cultural center. This considerable community included hotels, taverns, doctors, a tanning factory, shoe factory, cabinet shop, clock shop, general stores, sawmills, carriage factory, and several churches. Middleton grew to 2,900 people and was incorporated in 1840.[6]

The board of police meeting made as a first order of business the laying out and building of roads. Two of these crossed at the Little Log Store, a trading post. This Little Log Store was at the junction of the Carrollton and Shongalo Road and was at first called Oxford, then Bowling Green; finally, the name Middleton was adopted because the town was halfway between Shongalo and Carrollton. Carrollton remained the legislative base and the site of judicial and regulatory functions. Middleton became the education, social, and mercantile center.[7]

The business part of the town was built around a square which measured 250 feet on each side. On the south side of the square were located two doctors' offices, a cabinet shop where furniture was made, and a shoe factory where shoes were made to order by measurement. Two general merchandise stores were on the west and two on the north side. In 1839, Colonel O. J. Moore and Peter Gee arrived from Virginia and established the Big Store, the second-largest store built at Middleton. Men's suits were made and tailored to order. Another clock shop was opened in 1836 where clocks could be repaired for the newly arrived settlers who needed their timepieces regulated after a long and strenuous journey.

The Middleton Hotel, a large two-story building, was on the east side. This building was one of the town's attractions; there was a daguerreotype photographer shop on the upper floor and a town hall for entertaining and traveling shows on the ground floor.

Near the east side of the square was a blacksmith's shop and carriage factory where closed carriages called barouches, as well as small and large coaches, carriages, and wagons were made to order. A row of law offices was east of the blacksmith's shop and carriage factory. There was a newspaper published around 1843 titled *The Family Organ*.

6. Mrs. O. K. Gee, Sr., *History of Middleton Carroll County, Mississippi* (Winona, Miss.: Lowry Printing Co., 1961), 3.
7. Ibid., 3, ff.

About three miles west of Middleton was located a mill that made wool into rolls of batting ready to be spun. A three-story flour mill and a cotton mill were built northwest of the town. North of Middleton was a tanning yard where leather was put into a lime solution and then soaked in a vat filled with water and bark taken from the red oak trees. John O. Young and his family owned the tanning yard.

The Watkinses and their nearby neighbors and friends, the White-heads, owned plantations about four miles due west of Middleton, near the main road joining that town and Carrollton.

Cotton was hauled through Middleton from the eastward counties of Choctaw and Chickasaw to Greenwood,where it was loaded onto the riverboats that regularly moved down the Yazoo to Vicksburg; there it was put onto the big Mississippi River steamboats.

From an early time Middleton had two prominent schools: the Judson Institute and the People's Academy. The Judson Institute became the Middleton Female Institute, and People's Academy became the Middleton Male Academy.

In 1841, Middleton was one of seven candidates for the location of Mississippi University. This movement was bitterly opposed by the local schools and was defeated by two votes.

Middleton was also considered as a suitable location for the capital of Mississippi, but this, too, was voted down. In 1850, the possibility of a railroad coming through Middleton began to be discussed, and the people living there said that if that happened the town would be ruined. Colonel Moore, who owned the Big Store in town and whose plantation was several miles east of Middleton, offered a right–of–way through his plantation and a location for the depot.

In 1858, the railroad was started, and at the same time Colonel Moore had his area surveyed and laid out for a town to be called Winona. When the railroad was completed in 1859, east of Middleton, the merchants began to move their businesses to the new town.

By the time in 1859 when the town of Winona celebrated the joining of the north and south line of the railroad, Middleton was finished. Only some tumbled-down gravestones in the midst of an almost impenetrable wilderness of thickets, brush, and trees can still be found. Middleton is gone, totally.

The movement of the white Americans and their slaves into the county brought the population to 10,481 in 1840; 18,491 in 1850, and 22,035 by 1860. In this 1860 population, 12,616 were slaves, leaving the whites as a minority of fewer than 10,000.

Cotton was the driving force of the economy. On prime land, a top field hand could produce five bales. With a bale weighing four hundred to five hundred pounds, a single laborer in the field yielded approximately two thousand pounds of cotton in a season. Middle-quality land, which would better describe Carroll County, would average twelve hundred pounds (three bales) per field hand. The primary concern was not yield per acre, because land was limitless and the limit on production was manpower for this labor-intensive crop.

On the Watkins land, if fifty able field hands were used, the year's yield would have been one hundred and fifty bales, adding up to sixty thousand pounds.[8] Therefore, the wealth of a plantation owner was not necessarily in the land's cash yield but in the ownership of the land, home, implements, livestock, and slaves. Morison cites the value of a "prime field hand 18–25 years old": five hundred dollars in 1832, thirteen hundred dollars in 1837, eighteen hundred dollars in 1859. A family owning one hundred slaves of varying ages, sex and skills easily had an investment of one hundred thousand dollars in a readily marketable product. On the day the Civil War ended, this value became zero.

8. Samuel Eliot Morison, *The Oxford History of the American People* (New York: Oxford University Press,1965), 504–505.

MAPS

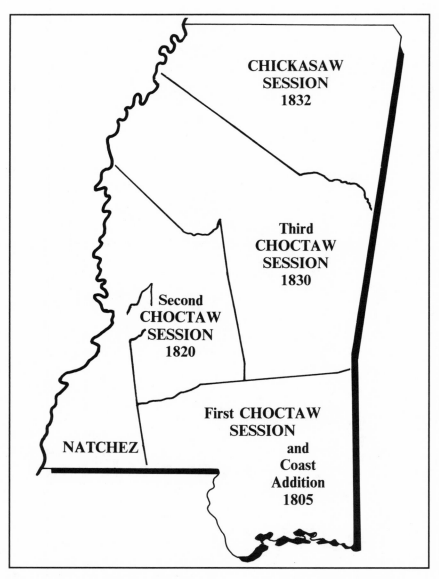

The accession of Indian land in the formation of Mississippi. Carroll County was formed in the Third Choctaw Session.

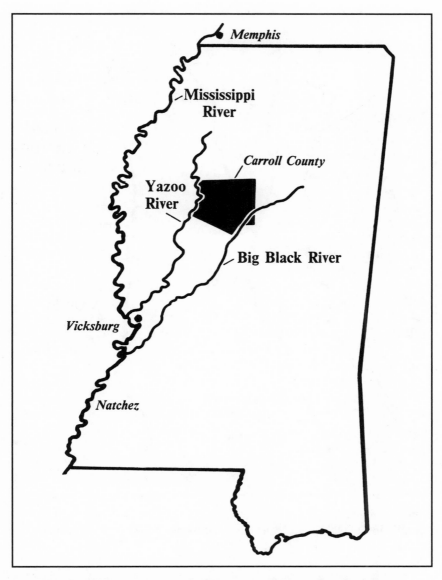

The location of Carroll County (slightly expanded for illustration). It occupied the high land above the delta of the Mississippi and Yazoo Rivers. Early access was by boat up the Yazoo from Vicksburg.

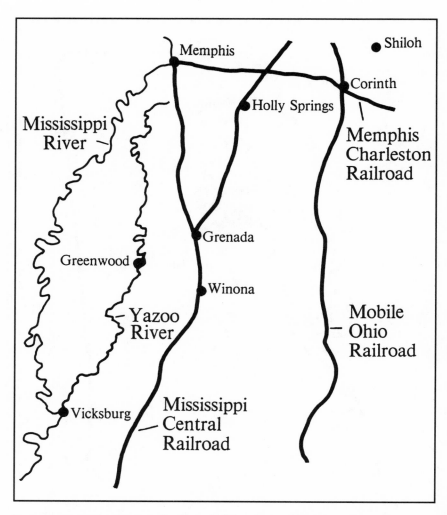

Routes of travel: rivers and railroads. The three railroads—Mississippi Central, Mobile Ohio, and Memphis Charleston—were major targets in the war.

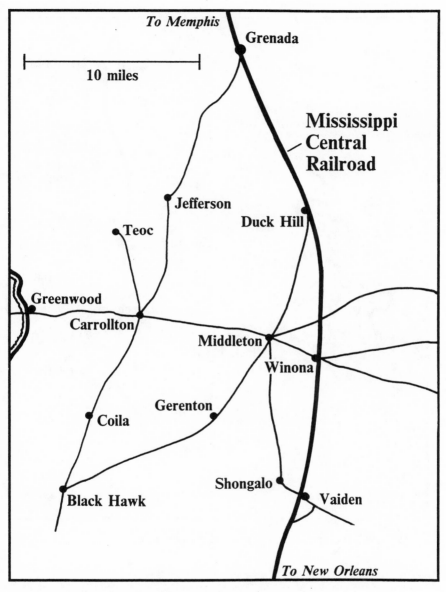

The major towns and railroad at the outbreak of the war.

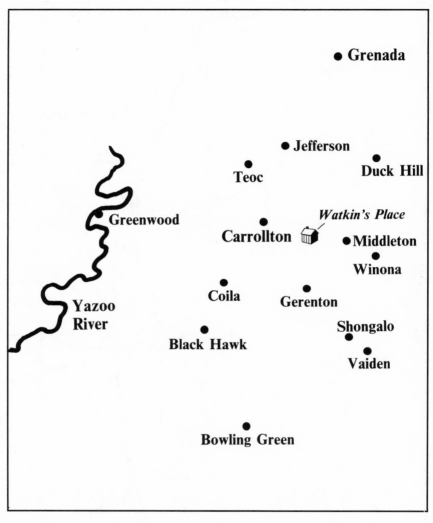

Dr. Watkins's plantation and the world about it as discussed in the letters.

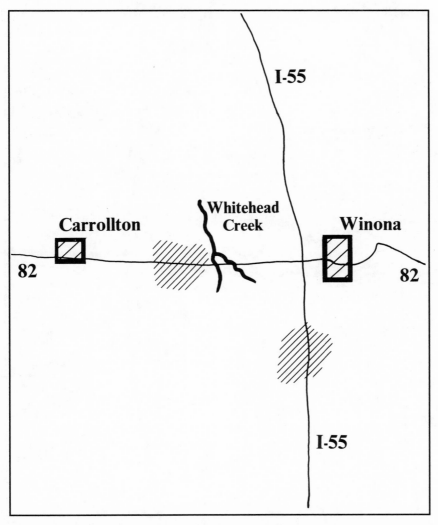

The present-day highway (82) and interstate (I-55) and their relationship to our story. The upper shaded area represents Watkins's Forest Place and E. G. Whitehead's Magnolia; the lower shaded area locates W. W. Whitehead's Hazelgreen.

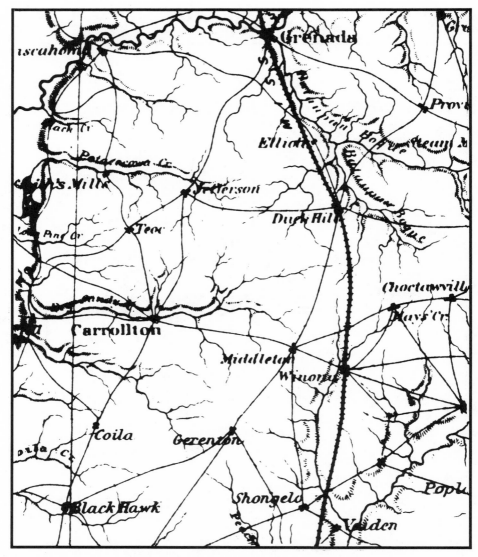

Rivers, creeks, roads, railroad, and towns. (From a Civil War map, Williams Landing, Carroll County, 1833–1983, Williams Landing Sesquicentennial, Inc., 1983.)

The Watkins Family Settles in Mississippi

I

Pre-War Letters
1846–1861

The setting for the letters begins with the Watkinses' move from Alabama to Carroll County in 1843. Included were the family, the slaves, and the livestock. Early family notes record the shipping of two hogs from Alabama to Forest Place at the time of the family's move. The invoice, dated December 4, 1843, reads: *"Two live hogs in boxes. The Boat is not responsible in case they should die."*

The animals were shipped from Alabama on the Tennessee River to the Mississippi River, down to the mouth of the Yazoo River at Vicksburg, up the Yazoo to Williams Landing [now Greenwood], and, finally, by wagon to Carrollton and to the Watkins plantation.

In November 1844, the doctor ordered from New Orleans a 246-pound barrel of the *"best old sugar"* at 6.75 cents a pound and a bag of Java coffee, 125 pounds, 14.5 cents a pound.

On December 24, 1844, the doctor ordered:

1 barrel whiskey
1 barrel apples
1 barrel flour
1 barrel sugar
1 barrel molasses
1/2 barrel of fish
2 kegs of oranges and spice

The agent wrote at the bottom of the invoice, *"cotton is selling very low, 3 1/2 to 5 1/2 (cents) . . . and but little prospect of an improvement. We send you acct. sales for 6 bales cotton at 6 cents to your credit $168.09. . . ."*

From New York, Dr. Watkins subscribed to Blackwoods' *Edinburgh* magazine, two dollars per year, and in 1845, he ordered from a New York stationer and bookstore:

Thiers' *Napoleon*
Wandering Jew

Lee's Campaign
Parry's Expedition
Wesley's Sermons
one ream of letter paper
one pack of visiting cards
Total cost, $12.09
sent by ship Arkansas to New Orleans

Evidence that Dr. Watkins was not an experienced cotton planter comes from the following exchange, dated March 18, 1846. The doctor wrote Dr. Ewing, a neighbor:

March 18, 1846
Sir:
Please let me know what day I shall commence planting cotton? Also when to commence hauling out the seed for planting? Please state how many half shovel plows will be enough for me? My corn that was first planted is coming up nicely. The bearer of this has an ink stand and pen sent with him by me so that you can easily write an answer to my interrogatories in the field or anywhere else.

Dr. Ewing replied, on the bottom of Dr. Watkins's letter:

I think I would not plant cotton before the last days of this month or the first day of April unless the weather is very fine. Some five or six days previous to the planting will be soon enough to haul out and five half shovels will do very well.
This [is written] in the field and I hope will be satisfactory. I have just finished planting 60 acres of corn . . . on my new ground.
Your frd.
Dr. Ewing

CHAPTER ONE

"My duty as a mother"

With the move from Alabama, Dr. Watkins ended his practice of medicine and devoted himself full time to the task of being a planter. After a two-year period in Mississippi, he sold some of the books from his medical library to a prominent local physician, Dr. D. M. Lipscomb. The Watkins family settled comfortably into the social fabric of the area, and—typically for their class and era—enjoyed visiting and being visited by other planters and by relatives. A cascade of cousins begins to appear, as mentioned in the correspondence.

At the age of thirteen, the Watkinses' eldest daughter, Lettie, was placed in the Reverend F. G. Smith girls' seminary in Columbia, Tennessee, matriculating for the fall term in 1848. Her interesting letters home tell about her travels and her daily activities. Although she was far away, the doctor maintained strict supervision of her conduct. And Mrs. Watkins commenced what would become the constant thread of her life—long, newsy letters to her daughters. The letters to Lettie at school, as well as those from her, reveal much about what life was like on the Watkinses' Carroll County plantation in the late antebellum period.

Lettie's coming home for the summer was a major concern, but because the family's spendable cash was limited and because the doctor insisted upon extreme measures of decorum (limiting the means by which she might travel), in 1849 she was denied permission to make the trip. This rendered her tearful and distraught for a time—indeed she became homesick—but her pleas long went unheeded, until at last, (we do not know how), she got home. And she did not return to the school in Columbia. She transferred to Captain Binford's school in Grenada, Mississippi, just north of Middleton. There she remained until 1851, when she switched to a school in Middleton.

4 May 1846
Hazelgreen

Dr. Thomas A. Watkins

Dear Sir:

Yours of yesterday's date was handed me per boy, as also the kind letters to your friends in Tenn. and Ohio for which please accept my thanks. The blue grass seed I will procure and ship for you as requested. I shall not purchase any mules or horses, other than those we shall use—were I buying for myself, it would give me pleasure to attend to your wishes.

I retain the horse my boy will plow, for little sons to ride to my brother's. He will send him over this morning. I calculate to reach Lexington about the last of this month, where we will probably remain until the 10th of July and expect to return home from the first, to the middle of August. I shall be pleased to receive a letter from you during my stay in Ky.

Very respectfully,
your friend, etc.
W. W. Whitehead

26th June 1846
Lexington

Dr. Thomas A. Watkins

My Dear Sir,

After a somewhat protracted travel, we reached this place on the 28th ultimo. Our trip, taken altogether, proved a pleasant one, no accident of any importance having occurred, and the travel proving of decided benefit to Mrs. Whitehead's health, which is much improved. We find Kentucky a most beautiful country, and could have made our stay here very agreeable, but for the situation of our little son, whose affliction caused our visit to this place. Immediately upon our arrival, I placed him under the charge of Dr. Dudley,[9] who

9. Abraham Flexner, *Medical Education in the United States and Canada* (New York: Carnegie Foundation for the Advancement of Teaching, 1910), 49.

"Benjamin Dudley, son of a poor Baptist preacher, dissatisfied with the results first of his

put him on a course of diet, and on yesterday, at eleven o'clock, operated, and took from him a Stone, about 2 inches long and nearly or quite an inch in diameter—I cannot describe to my dear sir, my feelings, when the Dr. with his attendants arrived at our boarding house to perform the operation, and trust in God, it may never be my fate again to have to submit to such a trial—none but a parent who has realized it can conceive the feelings which I experienced during the operation, which lasted (from the time he was tied on the table, until the stone was taken out) about two minutes. The little fellow bore it with great fortitude, not having complained loud enough to be heard in an adjoining room, during the time. The Dr. was to see him this morning, and thinks he is doing very well—indeed he has suffered less since the operation, than we could have expected. He has some fever this evening, but that was to be expected as a matter of course. I trust in two or three weeks he will be able to travel, when we shall set out for home. I find Dr. Dudley a very intelligent and pleasant gentleman, and am much pleased with him. In this department of surgery, he is certainly the greatest man in the world. He tells me this is the 189th case in which he has operated for stone, without losing a single patient from the knife—four only, of the number having died, and from other causes.

We came by Columbia, Tenn. on our way up, where we placed our daughters at School.[10] We spent 5 days there, found Mr. Smith (the Rector of the Institute) a very polite gentleman, who gave me every opportunity to witness the plan upon which the School is conducted; and I am free to say, it fully met my expectations—there are nearly 200 young ladies in the institution, taught by upwards of 20 teachers, male and female, and everything seems to be managed according to the strictest system. The young ladies look remarkably healthy, and appear to be very contented and happy. On the whole, I do not think I could have made a better selection in a school.

I presented the letter you were kind enough to send me to your friend Col. Trotter whom I found a very interesting gentleman. We spent one evening at

---

apprenticeship, then of his Philadelphia training, hoarded his first fees, and with them subsequently embarked temporarily in trade; he loaded a flatboat with sundries, which he disposed of to good advantage at new Orleans, there investing in a cargo of flour, which he sold to the hungry soldiers of Wellington in the Spanish peninsula. The profits kept Dudley in the hospitals of Paris for four years, after which he came back to Lexington, and for a generation was the great surgeon and teacher of surgery in the rough country across the Alleghanies"

10. The girls being placed in school were Martha Louisa Whitehead, born Carroll County, November 27, 1837, and her older sister, Mary Whitehead, born in 1830. The boy undergoing surgery to have a stone removed from his bladder was evidently William Whitehead, born in 1834.

his house, and were very kindly treated, both by him and Mrs. Trotter, whom we also found an intelligent and most agreeable lady.

I handed Mr. John Bull of Louisville $2 on yesterday to purchase your blue-grass seed. I was told they would cost 75 cents to a dollar per bushel. The seed of the new crop were not gathered as I came up, and I was advised not to purchase the old. Mr. B. will ship them to William Porterfield and Co., Vicksburg, with instructions to re-ship per first boat to McConnell & Brothers, Greenwood. He will enclose you the Bill of Lading per mail. I think of nothing else at present, worth writing.

Mrs. Whitehead unites in our kindest respects to Mrs. Watkins.

> Believe me very truly
> Yours, etc.
> W. W. Whitehead

P.S. I shall be pleased to hear from you. If you write, address to Columbia Tenn. as we shall leave before your letter could reach there. WWW

> 9th July 1846
> Middleton

Doctor Watkins

Dear Sir:

Your note of the 7th inst. was rec. and to avail myself of your offer, in regards to your library, I have to state that I have most of the works named in the catalogue. There are however several works named which I do not possess and which I would be pleased to have—particularly:

> Velpean's Surgical Anatomy
> Hall on Female Diseases
> Percivals' Medical Ethics
> Abernethy's Works

I would like for you to send the books named above, with the prices annexed, by my boy and to allow me the privilege of returning them this week—if I should not be satisfied—I should like very much to possess your Medico Chirurgical Review, and if it is not too much trouble, I would be pleased to learn the price at which you estimate it, and no. of volumes you have!—but candor obliges me to apprise you that unless you put it very low, I have no idea I shall buy it—

But if you can afford it as low as I bought the American Journal in Philadelphia, I should like to get it.

> Respectfully yours,
> D. M. Lipscomb

28 February 1848

Dr. T. A. Watkins: (per your Boy)

Dear Sir:

Your polite note of this morning asking myself & family to spend the day with you on Wednesday next, has just been handed me; unless something more than I now know of takes place to prevent, we will do ourselves the pleasure of visiting you on that day.

Respectfully,
Your Obedient Servant
E. G. Whitehead

October 21, 1848
Columbia, Tennessee

Dear Mother,

I am now sit down to tell you about what I have seen since I started from home. The first day we started from home we stayed at cousin Dick Townes. He married cousin Betty Lee. Her father was William Lee that used to live at the cross-roads. I like them very much. Mother, you must go to see them. I stayed the next night at cousin Patsy Powell's. Tell Semira [*slave*] that I saw her grandmother and she was well. I stayed one night with Mrs. Thompson and she said that Doc Thompson had four children. We stayed at very good houses nearly every night. One night Papa asked for some water to wash his feet and what do you reckon they brought the water in? Here came two negro boys with an urn of water and papa would not wash his feet in it.

We are at Mr. Wingfield's now. I like them all very much. We went to Nashville in the stage last Saturday and we stayed at the Suwanee House and they had silver forks. Aunt Prudence and Uncle Bob Watkins are living in Nashville. I saw cousin Mary Sanders and children and cousin Sarah Foster and cousin Louisa Harris. She has two children, and I saw Mr. Ethlebert McMahon and Joe Parrish. They came to the Suwannee to see me.

Sarah Sherrod is in Nashville, but I did not see her. I went to the Penitentiary and I went to the paper mill and they had the most rags I ever saw in my life, and I went to the printing office and I went to the Roman Catholic Church and they had an organ in the church; they had candles burning. I will tell you all about them some other time. I saw the Penitentiary and all the things in Nashville. Mother, I would have written to you before now but have been waiting to go to Nashville before I wrote.

We went to a wedding Thursday night. Mrs. Wingfield's niece Miss Frierson was married to Mr. McCune, a young man from Nashville. Tell Mary [*sister*] I am going to send her some candy and she must give all the negro women some and tell them I sent it to them. Tell Mary I am going to send her a heap of things. Tell America [*slave*] that I am going to send her a candy heart. Mother, I am going to send you something too. Mr. McMahon said that he heard from Uncle Billy's not long before he left and they were all well. I have so much to write that I can't think of all now.

This is written very bad but I can't write it over. I am going to start to school Monday. Give my love to all the negroes and accept my best love for yourself Mother. I forgot to tell you that Dandridge Epes[11] was condemned to be hung next December. We stayed four days in Nashville.

I remain your affectionate daughter,
Letitia A. Watkins

October 23, 1848
House of Mr. Wingfield

Miss Letitia A. Watkins
Columbia Female Institute
Columbia, Tennessee

My Dear Daughter:

It rains so that I cannot start home this day. For the present you will study none of the ornamental branches but music on the piano. When Mr. Smith will permit, you may visit the houses of Messrs. S. D. Frierson, Bradly Mayes, Albert Wingfield, & W. I. Dale. Mrs. Dale will call to see you and you must go & see her. Mr. & Mrs. Dale are particular friends of Mr. Whitehead and I am anxious that you should become acquainted with them.

You must obey strictly the rules and regulations of the "Columbia Female Institute" and be *very* polite to all those that have the management of your education.

Probably in a month or so I may wish you to study the French language and some other of the ornamental branches.

I wish you to show this letter to Mr. or Mrs. Smith.

Your affectionate Father,
Thomas A. Watkins

---

11. A relative whose misbehavior, although obviously substantial, is unknown to the family.

*PEOPLE'S LINE . . . LOUISVILLE, NASHVILLE & NEW ORLEANS
TELEGRAPH*[12]
COLUMBIA OFFICE

*The following communication was received at this office at 4 o'clock P.M.
minutes, October 31st.*

Dated: Holly Springs, 1848

Miss L.A. Watkins
Columbia

Dear Daughter,

Please send word by Mr. Smith how you are and how you are satisfied.
I am well.

Your affectionate Father,
Thomas A. Watkins

Please answer immediately paid in Holly Springs.

November 7, 1848
Carrollton, Mississippi

Miss Letitia A. Watkins
Columbia, Tennessee

My Dear Daughter,

I received your affectionate letter with pleasure. My attention has been so much taken up with the sick negroes that I could not compose my mind to write. Abram*[13] and his two daughters* have been very sick. Abram is yet in the house. Doctor Geren had to attend them. Chloe* is very sick; Dr. Geren has been attending on her for two weeks. I am afraid she will not recover.

Martha* had a daughter this night week. It is very small. They are both well.

Your father got home yesterday and brought us some fine apples. Mary [daughter, age four] is very much pleased with her doll and the other things that you sent her. I am obliged to you for the presents you sent me. Mary sometimes cries when we are talking about you and says she wants her sister to come home. The weeks appear very long to me since you left. If it was not the great anxiety I have for you to have a good education, I could not bear with your being from me for such a length of time.

My dear child, you must attend closely to your studies and strive to learn

12. By 1843, Washington was linked by telegraph with Baltimore. By 1848, Mississippi was reached.
13. In this letter, for orientation, an asterisk has been placed by each slave's name.

fast. Obey and be polite to your teachers. Do not show your temper at any time. Be kind to your schoolmates. Be neat in your dress and do not wear your stockings with holes in them.

I have been to Mrs. Jenkins' and Mr. Delap's once since you left here. Mrs. Jenkins and Mary have been over once to warp a piece of cloth. Susan has been in town for a week. Green Jenkins and Mr. Fort have got back. Green does not like Texas. Fort rented a place for next year in Texas. Mrs. Geren came with Dr. Geren to see me yesterday. That is most every body I have seen. I have at last received a letter from Brother William. He mentioned his wife had the congestive fever and Joe's Tom.* Milly's* baby died with the croup.

Your father has just returned from town. He received your dispatch by telegraph. We are glad to hear you were well and satisfied. Margaret Palmer has gone back to Marion. I believe I have written you all the news I know. You must write to me very often. I am always anxious to hear from you. Patty*, Becky* and Henrietta* send howdy to you.

Your affectionate mother,
Sarah E. Watkins

P.S. You sent one of your chemises back with your papa's clothes.

P.S. Write if you have gotten your winter dresses and if they are made or making. Your father says you must get Mr. Smith to get you a bandbox.

December 1, 1848
Carrollton, Mississippi

Miss Letitia A. Watkins
Columbia, Tennessee

My Dear Child,

I received your affectionate letters last evening. I am very uneasy and much distressed to hear of your indisposition and am afraid you were more indisposed then you would let me know of. My dear child, I wish you were at home so I might attend to you. I have been uneasy about you ever since I got your first letter. It is wrong to believe in dreams. I dreamed last week you were sick and night before last of being at the Institute and seeing all the girls except yourself. Your papa dreamed you had a pin down your throat.

I do not think sleeping in a room without fire will injure your health. It is very injurious to sleep in a room with as wet a floor as you mentioned in your letter. Your father says he will write to Mr. Smith about it. I hope you have recovered your health by this time. You must have caught that breaking-out by sleeping on some dirty bed in traveling.

Mr. John McMahon was to see us week before last. He said he heard from

Uncle Billy's just before he left Alabama. They were all well. Emma Swoope goes to school in Tuscumbia. Virginia is staying at home. Mary is very fleshy. Your cousin Cynthia's health has improved. Harriet McMahon has lost her daughter. Mrs. Billy Elliot and Robert Jorden are dead. Miss Fanny Bently is married to Mr. Houston living in Courtland. Charles Barker that kept tavern this side of Moulton got killed by the bursting of a boiler on the steamboat. Orren Davis is keeping tavern at Walker's old stand on the road to Columbus.[14]

You wish to know how Mrs. Farmer's health is, I do not know. I send butter to her every week. Joe said the family was well last Tuesday. It is Mrs. McLane who is a relation of Mrs. Nat Neal's that your papa wrote about. I went to Carrollton shopping last Tuesday, that is the only time I have been from home since you left here. Abram* has not recovered his health sufficiently to go out to work yet. Chloe* is recovering. She is not well enough for Hannah* to leave her yet. She has had a very black tongue. Patty* has to cook on account of Hannah having to stay with Chloe. America* got some candy and the candy heart. She was very much pleased with it. She keeps it in my drawer. Your cactus I have in my room, the others are in the kitchen cellar. Your two pigeons are living and are very tame. Mary as usual is out playing. I cannot get her to stay in the house without whipping her. Your father says you can have two teeth plugged [*cavities filled*]. He has written to Mr. Smith about it, his letter will go with mine.

You must write in a short time whether you have been changed to a more comfortable room and if all the girls have to dress without fires. If they do, you must not think hard of it that you have it to do. There are not many boarding schools that girls are allowed to have fires in their rooms. Your stockings are thinner than you have been in the habit of wearing in the winter—that may be one cause of your keeping with a cold. You had better wear two pair. You can wear your white under your black stockings. I noticed your number in the last Guardian. All of your marks 7. I am pleased to see they are no lower but you must try and get better marks particularly in deportment and neatness. It would be mortifying to me to see an ought against you.

Oh dear child I feel more sorrow than can be expressed at being parted from you. The time appears more like years than months since you left home. I am anxious for you to have a good education. It is the only reason why I can bear with being separated from you. Do my dear child try and learn as fast as you can. Do not speak ill of your teachers, be very respectful to them and you will gain their esteem. Do not be ill-natured to your schoolmates and do not say any thing against one girl to another. Always think twice before you speak once. Treat Miss Watkins kindly, do not make any remarks about her coldness

14. All news about their former home, Courtland, Alabama.

to you. She is a stranger to you; therefore, you cannot expect her friendship more than any other girl's.

Mr. Holt intends teaching a female school at Blackhawk next year. I hope when you receive this letter you will be enjoying good health. I am fearful that breaking out will leave ugly scars on your face. You must write to me if it does. I shall be very uneasy until I hear from you. You must be certain to write soon and let us know if you have a better room. Sally* and Henrietta* send their love to you. If you are not able to write you must get some one to write for you. I will be miserable if I do not receive a letter from you next week.

Your affectionate Mother,
Sarah E. Watkins

To Letitia Watkins:

December 29, 1848
Carrollton, Mississippi

Letitia Watkins
c/o Reverend F. G. Smith
Columbia, Tennessee

My Dear Daughter,

Your welcome favor of 16th inst. came to hand about three days ago. We were—as we always are—truly glad to hear from you. We hope you will write often, as it affords us pleasure & improves you. I am glad that Mr. Smith has removed you from that damp room; had it not to have been done I would have removed you from school.

I wonder you do not write me sometimes, in answer to my letters. Is it because I criticize too much your writing, spelling, etc? All I do is for your own good.

Give my best respects to Mrs. Smith, also to Mr. Wingfield's family.

William Whitehead had a great dining party at his house on Christmas day—Miss Carroway & Miss Terry & Mrs. Terry were at it. The young persons danced there for a day or two. Your Mother went to the dining and came back same day: I did not go as I had a bad headache.[15]

I have heard of no other frolicking during Christmastime. I was much mortified that Mrs. Terry did not come by & see us.

You wrote some time ago that you wanted to know which Mrs. McLean was dead. I cannot as yet tell you as I have not been to Middleton since 1st November. Mr. Thomas Saunders of Carrollton died a few days ago.

---

15. The doctor's headaches recur in the letters. He probably suffered from migraine.

You wrote us that Miss Ann Bowen kindly offered to make your Mother a bead bag. Please thank her for the offer & you must get some silk & beads for the purpose. If Mr. Smith has none, & he will let you, you may get them at the store of Mr. Dale. You must write word whether the dentist has done anything to your teeth. Mr. Richard Anderson, the gentleman that you wrote about is the uncle of Miss Ann Watkins of Huntsville, Ala. You must not say any thing against him, he is a very respectable man & has no enemies. I am afraid that you & your Cousin Ann W. [*Watkins*] are not so very friendly. I am sorry if you have had any falling out.

You have improved in letter writing & I am glad of it. Still there may be corrections made in your letters. You put "Columbia, Tenn." in right place, but then you commence the letter too low down on the page. You should write Dear Mother etc. etc. near the top. Commence two lines below the "Columbia, Tenn."

You spelt some few words wrong; though there has been great improvement in Spelling.

You should spell "wear uniform" instead of ware uniform. You should spell "knit a bead bag," not nit. Miss Bowen would not like to have nits about her head. Spell "raisins" not rasans. Spell "congregation," not congrigation.

You will soon write a very fine nice letter. If you could only see how pretty a letter Miss Fanny Eggleston can write.

Give my respects to your cousin Ann Watkins. Your Mother says that she will write you in answer to your letter, very soon. The next time I write I will write you some more about the Grecians etc. etc. Poor Sam & Frederick Sherrod have lately died. They were brothers of Major Felix Sherrod.

> Your affectionate Father,
> Thomas A. Watkins

> January 13, 1849
> Carrollton, Mississippi

Miss Letitia A. Watkins
Care of Reverend F. G. Smith
Columbia, Tennessee

My Dear Child,

I received your letter this day week. Sickness in the family prevented me from answering it sooner. Your father received one from Mr. Wingfield at the same time. I am glad to hear that you are in good health and enjoyed yourself Christmas at his house.

I was at a dining at Mr. William Whitehead's Christmas and enjoyed myself very pleasantly. Mrs. Terry, Miss Terry and Miss Carroway were there. Dr. Bibb and his brother escorted the two young ladies. Mrs. Terry promised me to spend the next night with us. She did not come. Mary Whitehead's health is very good. She looks better than I have ever seen her. Mrs. Farmer and Mrs. Parmele send a great deal of love to you and say they often talk about you and wish to see you. They miss you mightily. Mrs. Farmer's health is better than when you left but has not recovered entirely, she has a sore on her arm yet. She has had old Mrs. Lum attending of her. Mrs. Phillips is keeping house. Mr. Phillips or Farmer, I do not know which, is living at Mr. Holt's lot. Mr. Simmons has moved to Mr. Young's lot, and Dr. Geren is living at Mr. Phinney's lot. Adelaide Geren is going to school at Captain Binford's. Mrs. Purnell, Tom Purnell's mother, died last month.

Mary is begging to let her write. I tell her to wait until I am done then she may write. She is very well and just as bad and lively as she can be. Martha*, Henrietta,* and Siah* have the measles very bad. Day before yesterday, Ritter* was so sick I was afraid she would die. She and Martha are better today. Joe* and America* were very sick the first week, they are better. They have a breaking-out, I expect it is the measles. Salsbury,* Else* and Abram* are sick. I sent for Dr. Geren day before yesterday to see Henrietta,* he had gone to see his mother that was sick and did not come until a few minutes ago. I think she needs the cook more than a physician today.

Dr. Geren says the cholera is fifty miles from Greenwood on Honey Island. There was a man sick at Greenwood that had every symptom of the cholera. Mr. Neal that lives there says it was not the cholera. It has been reported that it was at the Point. I am sorry that you are uneasy about the cholera. I do not think you have any cause to be. You must put your trust in God, he can protect you in one place well as another.

I wish you could be with me always. I am never happy when you are from me. My dear child, I want you to have a good education. You cannot get one by being always at my side. You may think hard of me now but you will see it is for your good when you complete your education. You want to know if I am going to see you this summer. I cannot go this year. Times are hard, we made a short crop this year and I do not think Sam and Bill [16] would hold out to carry me there and back home. I would like very much for you to come home in the vacation if your papa would agree to it. You know that is as he choses, not me.

Your papa started last Tuesday week to Alabama. I hope he will not push my dear beloved Uncle for what he is owing him. I feel trouble about it, do not mention it to no one. I sent your chemise with my candy orange enclosed

16. Horses

in it by General Pillow.[17] Write to me if you have gotten it. Why did you want to know if Dick Anderson was uncle to Miss Watkins? He is her mother's brother. He is a very respectable gentleman. I am afraid you have said something about him you ought not.

Fred and Sam Sherrod died with the winter fever last month. Mary sends her love to you and says she wants you to come home and I must tell you that Frank* can say "Mary," "Baby," "Mama." America* says she is very much obliged to you for the candy heart, that it is the prettiest thing she ever had. The women say I must give their love to you every time I write, they are always anxious to hear from you. Sally* has a very bad pain in her hip. She can scarcely get along. You must excuse my mistakes. Mary troubles me so much I cannot write without making them. It has been raining most all day and she cannot go out to play. Mr. Hemingway has had a negro child and Jim* that he got from Collins Hemingway to die with the measles. I must stop and let Mary write. She says, "Mother, you will not let me write none."

> Your affectionate mother,
> Sarah E. Watkins

P.S. That scribbling is Mary's writing. She says you will be glad to get a letter from her. Give my respects to your friend Miss Bowen.

> February 14, 1849
> Carrollton, Mississippi

Miss Letitia A. Watkins
Care of Reverend F. G. Smith
Columbia, Tennessee

My Dear Child,

I received your affectionate letter yesterday. It put me in good spirits to hear from you and to hear that you stood so good an examination. Nothing on earth can give me more pleasure than your doing well. I think you are at a very good school, you must apply yourself closely to your studies and improve all you can. You wrote to know if I did not think you have improved in writing. I think you have improved a little. You write a very sensible letter for the short time you have been writing them.

Your father got home from Alabama last Sunday two weeks. He left our relations well. Mrs. Bledsoe got a fall from her horse and broke her leg. I could not hear much news from your papa. He says he did not force Uncle Billy to pay him. Uncle Billy offered him Milly,* her two children and Polly* baby. He

---

17. General Gideon J. Pillow, a Carroll County planter.

did not take them. They did not make more than six bales of cotton last year and nearly out of corn. Brother speaks of selling the place. We did not make but forty-eight bales. The corn crop turned out better than was expected and not well at that.

Delap is the overseer this year, he gets along very well with the negroes. Ned* has taken the negro woman Delap hired from Kimbrough's estate for a wife, she has two children. Mary, Semira* and Chloe* have just gotten well of the measles. Mary was not as sick with them as the negroes, she broke out last Saturday week. Yesterday is the first time she has been out of the house. She has a cold and her eyes are inflamed yet. She is at Patty's* house now playing with the children. Salsbury* says I must give his respects to you and tell you he has been almost dead with the measles. He is better today. Harry Ann* had a boy last Monday night three weeks, she has been very sick since. She is mending. Martha's* child is named Milly.* It is not as pretty as Siah.*

I forgot to write you Mrs. Jerry Roberson had a baby this Fall. The Yazoo River is higher than it has ever been known to be, it is up to where you saw those wild geese. Everybody that travels along there has to give a dollar to be carried across in a ferry boat to the landing. That is the only way to get to Mr. Roberson's—go to the landing and take a steam boat down as far as his house. The Point is all overflowed.

Mr. Fort has had a room put up at Mrs. Jenkins', his family will live there until the Fall. He speaks of going on to Texas with his hands. I have not seen Mrs. Jenkins nor the girls in a long time. Mrs. Jenkins told me to give her love to you. I forgot it when I wrote you before. Your papa received a letter from Mr. James Watkins lately. His family was well and he was getting more reconciled to Texas. He says it is a fine country for cotton. Your papa saw your Uncle Robert at Uncle Billy's. He is doing no better. Old Mrs. Hemingway died Sunday night. I do not know whether Morrison is teaching school or not. The people of Middleton spoke of getting another teacher. I heard he told them if they did he would have a school in opposition to their's. I reckon he could not make up a school if there was another teacher. Write to me how you like your teachers and if the teacher that died was your music teacher.

Your father went from home Sunday to attend Mr. Pinchback's sale of negroes in Holmes County. I am expecting him back this evening.

Mary says can you read her writing, if you can she will write to you. Henrietta* sends her love to you and says the measles did not kill her. She has gotten well. Dr. Geren came to see her the day I wrote to you before. I wrote you that Ritt*[18] had gotten so much better that she stood more in need of the cook than a doctor.

18. Henrietta, Ritter, Ritt are all the same person.

February 15th—Your father got back last evening. He was at Major Terry's and Mrs. Eggleston's. Both families inquired very particular about you and send their respects to you. Mrs. Eggleston says if you come home this summer you must go to see her. Elisa Terry speaks of visiting Nashville in July, she says if she does, she will call on you. Mrs. Terry says Miss Carroway is to be married in a few weeks and we must go to the wedding. Guess who she is going to marry?

The Yazoo River is so high that it is up to Alfred Roberson's door. They have had to move out of their house to some negro cabins higher up. Mrs. Roberson had to take up her shrubbery and put it in barrels and carry it off. James Watt bought a lot in Greenwood. He has to go from his house to his store on horseback on account of high water.

Yesterday morning was very pleasant until twelve o'clock. It clouded up, turned cold and last night it snowed a little—not enough to stay on the ground. This morning is very cold. It is the first morning I have seen frozen milk this winter. My peas and cabbage plants are just up. The daffodils, heart-ease and your single hyacinths are in bloom and some of the peach trees. The day after I wrote to you about your pigeons, the white pigeon was missing. We never have found out what became of it. Polly pigeon is here yet and very tame. The apples your father brought when he came from Tennessee are just gone, most of them were limber twigs.

I am sorry you could not get the silk and beads for Miss Bowen to knit the bag. Give my respects to her and tell her I am much obliged to her for her kind offer. I am afraid it would be giving her too much trouble. Enclosed you will find some seals. Give Miss Bowen half, let her take choice of them. Lettie, I am writing with a gold pen—everything that shines is not the best. This letter is written so badly I am shamed to send it.

Jenkins had a dance at his house Christmas. They had Miss Frances Ross and the Estels at it. Mrs. Jenkins was at Mr. Fort's.

Your yellow hen raised six chickens. I sent them to Middleton this week and sold them to Mr. Phillips for six bits. Mrs. Phillips sent me word she would come to see me. Mrs. Farmer's health is so bad she cannot leave her.

Find out which of the girls from Yazoo, Holmes and Lafayette Counties are coming home this summer by water. If any of them are coming that will be the way for you to come home. If you do not come that way, you cannot come at all. Sally,* Patty* and the rest send their love to you.

Your affectionate mother,
Sarah E. Watkins

February 20, 1849
Carrollton, Mississippi

Miss Letitia A. Watkins
Columbia, Tennessee

My Dear Daughter,

Your affectionate letter of 10th inst. came to hand this day. Of all letters that I ever received it gave me the most satisfaction. You have improved in penmanship & diction. But what gave me & your Mother such inexpressible delight, was the very favorable account given of you by Miss Ann Bowen. You do not know how to appreciate a parent's feelings when they hear such flattering tidings of their children. A present of one thousand dollars would not have pleased us as much as the few lines of postscript to your last letter written by Miss B. All I am afraid is that her partiality to you may make her see things in a more favorable light than they are in reality. However let us hope for the best & be very thankful that you have friends that can appreciate your merits. I know you can learn—that you have the capacity—& that you can, by care & diligence be among the first in your several classes. As to your good conduct & moral deportment I have never had any fears. Give our respects to Miss A. B. & tell her that her postscript will keep us happy for many months.

Unless times get too hard & money too scarce, I think you can come home during summer vacation—provided you can accompany some of the young ladies who live in Yazoo, Holmes, Yalobusha, LaFayette, or this county. It is too far to come or send after you, but if you can find any of the young ladies of the above named counties coming home, I will provide so that you can accompany them & I will take you home from their residence. Even if you can get with any of the girls as far as Holly Springs I will go up there for you. But if you come home you must not think of quitting the Institute—you must go back to resume your studies on 1st of September. One reason that I am disposed to let you come home, during vacation, is that I hear such favorable accounts of your good conduct, & your rapid progress in your studies. If I hear bad news of you hereafter—which I by no means expect—then you cannot come home.

I have not much news to write you concerning your acquaintances & friends here. Since I wrote you last I have visited Mrs. Terry & Mrs. Eggleston. They all & their daughters join in sending love to you. Mrs. Terry and Mrs. Eggleston & all made many inquiries concerning you. Miss Fanny Eggleston says that we may get as many squabs from her for you as we want. Almost all of her mother's family were sick last summer after we left.

Miss Mary Carroway & Algernon Bibb will be married about 6th of next

March. He is younger than his brother, deaf Dr. Bibb. I expect that we will be at the wedding. Mr. Bibb is a nephew of Aunt Prudence Watkins & a distant relative of Miss Ann Watkins at the Institute.

I would have sent some oranges from New Orleans but I thought that Mr. Smith would not let you have them—being afraid of the Asiatic Scourge [*perhaps cholera?*]. I would still order them from New Orleans for you did not the same reasons still exist. I hope that Mr. Smith will let you read the "Saturday Courier." I have ordered it to you & it will come to you in about a week or ten days. If he will not let you take it out you must let me know.

I am told that Colonel LeFlore of this county will send one or more of his daughters to the Institute in March & if I can get a chance, I will send you by him your "Merry's Museum" & your neck handkerchief that your Aunt Emily sent you. You saw his daughter and granddaughter at Major Terry's.

I am sorry that the cholera is at Nashville. I hope that it is not fatal & that the very cold weather will make it entirely disappear. By the by last Saturday night—17th instant—was one of the coldest nights ever felt in this part of the country. Some of our ink bottles, pitchers, & vinegar jugs were ruined by their contents freezing. Your mother & Baby enjoyed themselves very much in eating frozen milk. Every time they took any they said, now if Lettie was only here how glad we would be, so she might get some.

You must write often, it gives us great pleasure to hear from you. Give our best respects to Mr. & Mrs. Smith. I am highly pleased that Mrs. Smith is so good to you. I hope you will visit Mrs. Dale as soon as you can even if to stay a very short time. When you see any of Mr. Albert Wingfield's family, give my respects to them.

How I do wish you could be with us at the wedding at Major Terry's.

I enclose a copy of a letter you must transcribe & send to Uncle Joel Early—Greensboro, Georgia. He would be highly pleased to get a letter from you.

Your affectionate Father,
Thomas A. Watkins

March 9, 1849
Carrollton, Mississippi

Miss Letitia Watkins
Care of Reverend F. G. Smith
Columbia, Tennessee

My Dear Child,

I received your affectionate letter day before yesterday. It was a great relief to my feelings. Not receiving a letter from you sooner caused me to be uneasy about you. I had seen the death of Miss Hays announced in the Memphis paper that made me more uneasy about you. I do thank my God that he has been so merciful in restoring you to health as the winter is gone. You must be prudent and take care of yourself, do not do anything that will make you sick. Miss Carroway was married Wednesday night to Algernon Bibb. We were at the wedding. The bride was sick in the evening. Dr. Mathews gave her an emetic, she got well enough to be married, and do her share of dancing. She was dressed in a swiss muslin robe, she had a lace scarf across her head the ends to hang down each side and a wreath of flowers on her head. Miss Elisa Terry and Martha Whitehead were the bridesmaids. They were dressed in swiss muslin.

There were about a hundred people at the wedding, all enjoyed themselves very much. Some of the ladies and gentlemen sat up until day dancing. We would have staid until today if we had not been afraid it would rain and make the road bad. I must write you a little joke on your papa. He was sitting by Mrs. Whitehead and a lady dressed in white. Mrs. Whitehead got up he saw the lady's dress down on the floor. He took it to be Mrs. Whitehead's handkerchief. He picked it up and called Mrs. Whitehead and was about to tell here there was her handkerchief when he found out his mistake.

Mrs. Terry requested me to give her love to you. Mrs. Dr. Farmer, Mrs. Holt, Mrs. Ware, her son Ben and Ellen McCray were at the wedding. Ellen has grown very much. She had her hair fixed up like a grown lady. She is going to school to Mr. Holt in Blackhawk. Mrs. Ware has three children, the youngest six months old. Mr. Leflore's son was married last month to Miss Newman, the young lady we saw at the camp meeting with the red jacket on. Her sister was married the same night to Mr. Davis. The widow McCarroll attempted to kill herself lately by cutting her throat with a razor. She first took laudanum and throwed it up. She said she was tired of living.

Mrs. Estel had a big quilting last week, the young folks danced all night. Mr. Fort has gone to Texas with his son James and his negroes. His wife and daughters are living at Mrs. Jenkins'. Miss Temperence spent a night and day with me last week. I gave her a root of your single blue and double white hyacinth.

Mary [*sister*] sends her love to you and says she is very glad to get a letter from you, if she could write she would answer it. She often speaks of plays you and she used to have and wishes you were here to play with her. I told her just now that you said you had not received a line from her. She said, "Mother did I not spark in your letter?" She is pestering me to let her write to you. Sometimes when she hears your papa and myself talking about you she says, "Everything is Lettie, Lettie. Don't care for nobody but Sister." She says I love you better than I do her and all the negroes love you the best.

If you need stockings you must buy them from Mr. Smith. If you cannot get a piece from the lady that made your dress, you had better buy enough to mend it.

Give my respects to Miss Bowen, tell her I read her letter with a great deal of pleasure. I am afraid she flattered you in writing so much in your praise. I do want to see you more than tongue can express. The time appears like years instead of months that we have been apart. The measles are yet in the family. Hannah is sick a little and Harry Ann. Sally, America, Ritt and Martha send their love to you.

I will enclose the invitation we got to the wedding in this letter and in that you will see some gilt paper cut in flowers. The cake was dressed with these.

Your affectionate mother,
Sarah E. Watkins

P.S. I have not received a letter from Alabama since October. You were born 21 of March 1835. Mary alluded to the scribbling she did in one of my letters to you that she calls the spark.

March 26, 1849
Carrollton, Mississippi

Miss Letitia A. Watkins
Columbia, Tennessee

My Dear Child,

I received your letter yesterday, it was a great relief to my feelings to hear from you. When I do not get a letter from you at the expected time it makes me uneasy thinking you are sick. I am truly sorry to hear you and Mrs. Stovall do not agree. You are under her protection and must be obedient to her. Treat her with respect and you will gain her esteem. Never speak back to her when she reproves you for doing anything she does not like—if she tells you not to put your stockings on sitting on the bed or your bonnet box on the bed, you should not do it. You must be advised by her as if she was your mother and not wish to have your own way. If you are sick and wish to lie down, ask her permission to do so. Do not think I am scolding you; it is my duty as a mother to give you advice. I am very glad you wrote to me about your difficulties with Mrs. Stovall.

Your papa received a letter from Mr. Smith two weeks ago. He gave you a very fine character. He mentioned you had gained the hearts of all. Your father was so much pleased to hear it, he sent the letter to Uncle Joel. I hope you will keep you your good character and deportment. When you receive letters or anything from home you must always acknowledge the reception.

Write to us if you have received the "Saturday Courier" and your cravat you wrote to be sent you, we sent it by mail.

We had a dining Friday week. Mrs. Terry, Miss Terry, Mr. Bibb and lady, Mr. William and Edmunds Whitehead's families, Mrs. Parmele, and Ellen Palmer. Mr. Shephard, Mr. Trousdale, and Broadwell were the young gentlemen. Mrs. Terry's family and the Miss Whiteheads staid all night and danced at night. We went to Mr. E. Whitehead's last Wednesday and to Mr. William Whitehead's last Thursday. Mrs. Terry, Mr. and Mrs. Bibb spent the night with us Friday and left Saturday morning for home. Miss Terry intends staying at William Whitehead's a month or two; she and the girls have promised to come here shortly to go fishing and have a fish fry. I do wish you could be here to go with them. Your papa has been fishing four times this Spring and caught a good many.

The people in Middleton and around are trying to raise subscription to have a large school. There was a basket dinner given at the Presbyterian Church and some speaking last Tuesday in Middleton to raise money for the school. Another dinner will be given tomorrow at the same place and for the same purpose. Miss Mory and Miss Billings are teaching school at the academy. Lizzie and Virginia Whitehead are boarding at Mr. Phillips' and Mrs. Phillips teaches them.

Mrs. Farmer is in very bad health. William Farmer was married this month to Miss Mary Mathews of this county. Yesterday two weeks Lucy Ann Caperton ran away from preaching in Middleton and went to Parson Neal's and married Mr. Rowe, a brother of Mr. Wolfe's.

Mary[19] pesters me so much I can scarcely write. She is at this time working at my back and fretting to go to Harry Ann's house to play with the children. She sends her love to you and says she misses you mightily. Your papa says you must write if you have written to Uncle Joel and write if you have received those seals I enclosed in my letter to you and Miss Bowen.

Sam Horse carried us to the wedding at Major Terry's and back home. Soon after he was worked to the gin[20] and ploughed and was taken lame. I am afraid he never will be well again.

Mrs. Davis sends her love to you and says when Eveline improves in writing, she shall write to you. Mary and Martha Whitehead send their love to you and say you must write to them. Mrs. Terry, Mrs. Bibb, and Mrs. Parmele send their love to you. Mrs. Green Bledsoe has a daughter. Patty sends her love to

19. Mary has just become five years old.

20. Evidence of Dr. Watkins's progress as a cotton grower comes with his order of a brand-new cotton gin, May 16, 1849, from Mr. E. Carver and Co., East Bridgewater, Massachusetts. The cost was $240.00.

you and says she missed you helping her about the cake for the dining. All the servants about the house send their love to you down to America and Chloe.

Your affectionate mother,

Sarah Epes Watkins

P.S. Give my love to Miss Bowen; tell her I will take it as a favor if she will reprove you whenever she sees you doing wrong.

March 31, 1849

My Dear Daughter:

Your favor of 10th inst. came to hand on yesterday. As usual I was highly delighted to get a letter from you.

It always cheers us up when we get any good news from you & your letters when received are generally a subject of pleasing conversation in our family for a day or two, when they contain news of your being well & doing well.

Your mother has written you lately & I presume has given you all the news. I do not recollect of anything that has occurred since her letter has been sent.

I enclosed to you a letter to Uncle Joel which I hope you have transcribed & sent to him. I do want you to treat my Uncle Joel with great respect, for he has been a Father to me & never can I forget him & I do not want any of my family to forget him.

I am glad that the American Courier has come to hand. I ordered it some time ago for you. I hope Mr. Smith will not object to your receiving it & reading it at spare intervals.

I was so well pleased with the favorable reports that I got concerning you that I wrote Mrs. Smith a letter of thanks for her kind deportment towards you. I also sometime ago wrote to Miss Ann Bowen. You must not ask them if I have written them; but if they have mentioned to you that they have received any letters from me, you will please inform me when you write again.

I have sent up by letter your Aunt Emily's little shawl which I hope you have received long ere this.

You can come home after the examination if either of the young ladies that you mentioned are coming home then in the stage or by steam boat. Should they come home by private conveyance of course you could not impose so much as to request of them to take you along. You must write me & let me know in time if you can go with either of the girls after the examination.

Major Terry was at my house this day. He has rented out the place where you visited his family. He has moved to a place near the Yazoo valley.

Miss Eliza Terry has been & is now staying at William Whitehead's.

Poor Mrs. Phinney & daughter have returned to their place in Middleton & it is said they are without money, bread, or meat. The neighbours are sending them things to live upon. I am a going to write to McConnell to send them flour, meat, etc. to the amount of Sixteen dollars. I know your tender heart & I expect you will almost cry when you hear of their destitute condition.[21]

William Whitehead & others are making great efforts to get a Young Ladies Academy in Middleton. About seven thousand dollars is subscribed but that is not near enough. If we could get a good school & have Mrs. Armstrong at the head of it I would like to have you go to Middleton. But such events are not probable & so you must content yourself to be educated at Columbia— that is the school for you.

My wife went into the garden this morning & brought out two strawberries & one pea hull near full of grown peas.

The measles are nearly through at my house & we have had no deaths as yet.

You must write soon & let me know your arrangement about coming home; but there is no chance for you should the girls come home in their own carriage. Give my respects to Mrs. Smith & to Miss Ann Bowen. Your mother also sends her respects to Miss Bowen.

Our strawberry vines are very full of blooms & we will have many strawberries. Mrs. William Whitehead's family have promised to come & eat some when they ripen.

Your affectionate Father,
Thomas A. Watkins

The Judson Institute, which represented the first appearance of Baptists in educational work, was built around a manual labor plan. The institute faltered and later became nondenominational. It was finally converted into the Middleton Female Academy. Lettie and Mollie were each there at one time.

These schools were the boardinghouse type and drew patronage from all over this section of the state. The female academy had an enrollment of one hundred to one hundred-fifty students. The curriculum included the classical languages, English and composition, mathematics, chemistry, astronomy, history, philosophy, and physical education. Each school had a music department. Students often boarded with town families.

---

21. Albert Finney died at Pt. LeFlore, four miles above Williams Landing. He was on his way home from New Orleans, contracted yellow fever, and died, leaving the family penniless.

April 25, 1849

My Dear Child,

Your letter the 6th of April to me and the 9th to your father was received last week with pleasure. Your letter the 14th of April was received last Sunday.

Your papa has been gone to Alabama over two weeks. He promised me to go and see you before he returns home. He has bought Milly, her two children, and Polly baby from Uncle Billy.

Mary has just come out of the garden with her hand full of strawberries, the largest one she says I must put in my letter and send it to sister. We would have a great many strawberries if it was not for the birds, they eat them before they are ripe. We had a very heavy frost the 15th of this month. It killed everything that could be injured by it. Several farmers were very forward with their crops. They have been compelled to replant their cotton and corn. We had not more than sixty acres of cotton up, all the seed of that had not come up. Uncle Vivion says it is a better stand now than it was before the frost. There was a fine rain evening before last and yesterday, Mr. Delap says since the rain the corn has improved, he does not think he will have to replant. I did not have many vegetables up, my peas were old enough to eat—the frost injured them. I have 23 little turkeys and some hatching. I have about 50 little chicklings. Your favorite yellow hen that staid at Hannah's house quit there and has been missing sometime. Your other good hen has behaved badly. She was setting in the henhouse, she quit her nest and whipped the other hens off their nests. She did not hatch but three chickens. You have such bad hens I do not think they will make you a fortune. Your hyacinths looked beautiful this spring. They had finished blooming when you wrote for me to enclose one in my letter. I often think of you when I go in the garden and wish I could hear the sweet singing of the mockingbird we used to listen to last year.

Elisa Terry, Mary and Martha Whitehead staid with me this night two weeks on their way to Maj. Terry's. If it was not for work and reading I would be very lonesome. I seldom see anyone or hear anything. My poor horses are worked most to death. Tom has been very lame and Bill was ploughed 'till he had the "reels." They have to stop ploughing him. Felton is sold and your papa has to ride Bob.

I have not been to preaching but once this year.

Mr. Phillips started to Ala. last week for Mrs. Oliver.[22] Margaret Palmer will return home with them. Her health is bad. I do not hear anything about Elizabeth and Virginia Whitehead going to Columbia. They board at Mr. Phillips'

22. The first Mrs. Oliver was the Phillipses' daughter.

and go to school to Miss Maury and Miss Billings [*in Middleton*]. It is said they have forty pupils. Morrison spoke of going to California, he has changed his notion. The last I heard of him he was teaching singing school in Middleton. Mrs. Dr. Saunders died last Saturday in Middleton. She had been sick several weeks, I believe she lost a baby the week before she died. Mrs. Jones that lived at John Purnell's died the 10th of inst. month. Mary Jenkins is going to school to Miss Rosco in Carrolton. The young ladies of the school intend having a coronation the first of May. Your sister says I must tell you "howdy" and give her love to you and says she wants to see you mighty bad. If she knew when you were coming she would run up to the big road to meet you. She says I must write just as she tells me.

When I read the part of your letter that you said you would be the best child that ever was if you could come home, she said, "Sister tells a story, she would not be the best." I am afraid you will be disappointed in coming home this summer. I am so anxious to see you. You must not anticipate too much on coming home. If you should be disappointed it will not be so hard with you. You have improved very much in your writing. Do you compose your letters yourself or get someone to assist you? Patty sends her love to you and says she is glad to hear that you are improving. She is as anxious for you to be at home as you are to come. All the house servants send their love to you. Mary is standing by me with Martha's child in her arms begging me to give the child's love to you and says it can play with her. Frank, VanBuren, and Siah and walk and talk a little. Tom can stand alone, Harry Ann's child is named Amos. Henrietta was taken sick night before last, I think it is chills that is the matter with her.

Enclosed I send you some of my hair and Mary's that you wrote for.

Give my love to Miss Bowen.

Your affectionate Mother,
Sarah E. Watkins

July 7, 1849
Holly Springs, Mississippi

Miss L. A. Watkins
Columbia, Tennessee

My Dear Daughter:

I start this day for home. I have been waiting here two days for you. It is a sore disappointment that I do not see you, & your Mother will immensely regret that you cannot come.

I have heard that Mrs. Moore will not come home in some time. You must stay at Mr. Wingfield's in vacation.

I will write you fully on my return home. You should have written to me at this place.

It is now too late for you to come with Mrs. Moore.

Your affectionate Father,
Thomas A. Watkins

July 8, 1849
Columbia, Tennessee

Mrs. Sarah E. Watkins
Carrollton, Mississippi

My Dear Mother,

You all must write to me for I have given up all hopes of going home with Mrs. Moore. She is going to the Springs where Mrs. and Mrs. Smith are. The day that I heard she was going to the Springs I cried almost all morning. I am very sorry indeed that she has declined going. I was very much disappointed. I expected to have much pleasure at home this summer. Oh dear Mother, just to think if I do not see you this vacation, I will not see you and sister until twelve months more and perhaps never again. I think you all ought to take me home while you have the opportunity, perhaps you will never have it again. Some of us may die before another twelve months roll around and I think while we are all well you all might send or come for me. I almost know that Papa will come to see me before another vacation. Mother, please beg Papa to come for me—tell him I say please for my sake to come and take me away from this place. I will be willing to come back next session but I am not willing to stay anywhere in Tennessee during vacation. I never will be happy until I see you all once more. I think as I have stayed contented here this long, Papa might come for me. Tell him I say please to come Mother, beg him to come. I can study so much better next session, but if I stay here all this time I will be completely worn out by the time the session commences. I will study so hard next session if you all will just let me come home. Do beg Pa to come for me. I know he will come to see me next session so he had as well take me home where I can see you all and then not come to see me. Oh mother, I would give anything to go home sweet home. Tell Pa to take some of my five hundred dollars for him to come here and carry me home and back here. I would give anything in the world that I have got except America[23] and I could not give her away. But if Pa had have given her to me he might have her back again, but as she was given to me by the one that she was, nobody shall have her.

23. Lettie's grandmother's will, November 19, 1840, read: "I give to my granddaughter, Lettie Ann Watkins five hundred dollars and Sally's child viz. America."

I am going out to Mr. Wingfield's tomorrow. Ask Pa if I will stay or board out there. Tell him that I would not like to stay out there that long as I did not have an invitation to spend the vacation out there or even if I had, I would not like to stay on there so long without making them a nice present or paying board. Beg Papa to come for me.

I heard Eugenia Harris is going to be married the first of month and I believe it too. Her father has not come for her yet. She is down in Hickman County this State and is going to be married down there. It has been raining very hard today. Tell Pa please to come for me. This is written so much better than I generally write. I expect you will think that I did not write it but I surely did. Give my love to Pa and sister and to all. Kiss dear sister for me. Tell Pa please come after me. Good bye.

I remain your affectionate child,
Letitia A. Watkins

P.S. When you write, direct your letters to the care of A. Wingfield. If you do not I will not get them. They will go down to the Springs. Pa, please please please come for me. I am almost crazy to see Mother, Sister and you and home and all the servants and everybody. The old gin house, the spring, the field—I want to see them all. They are all dear to me. Everybody in Tennessee are afraid to eat any kind of vegetables for fear of the cholera which I expect will be here before long as it is spreading in the country around Nashville. Please come for me and take me out of the place a little while if no longer. Do come and take me to my sweet home. L.A.W.

July 16, 1849
Carrollton, Mississippi

Miss Letitia A. Watkins
Care of Mr. A. M. Wingfield
Columbia, Tennessee

My Dear Daughter,

You no doubt have received my letter written while I was at Holly Springs. We all are very much disappointed that you have not been with us this summer, but it cannot now be helped. It is out of my power to come after you. You must content yourself at my friend Mr. Wingfield's until school commences again.

Your letter of 8th inst. was received on yesterday. If you want any clothes you must get such as you want at Mr. May's or Mr. Dale's store on a credit & I will pay sometime this year for them. You can ask Mrs. Wingfield to tell who will be a good hand to make the clothes up for you & when they are done, you can pay the seamstress out of some of the money that you get from Mr.

Dale. When you employ a seamstress you must find out exactly what she charges before you set her to work for you. You will find Mr. & Mrs. Wingfield as kind as persons can be to you & you must obey them strictly & be very polite to them & kind to their children. Give my best respects to Mr. & Mrs. Wingfield & tell them I am under many obligations to them for their kind treatment to you.

If Mary Wingfield goes shopping with you & she fancies any dress in the store that will cost about five dollars, you may get it for her & make her a present of it.

I think Mrs. Moore has treated us very badly. She had no business to promise you unless she knew that she could comply. She has made you feel very bad & made me go all the way to Holly Springs. I never want to have anything to do with her. If she had not have promised you, it is probable that you could have come home with some other person.

If you are taken with a bowel complaint you must not let it run on, but take some cholera medicine immediately & if that does not stop it you must send for Dr. Frierson or Dr. Hay & if they cannot be got you must send for someone else.

Mr. Wingfield will tell you what is the best medicine for stopping the bowel complaint that brings on the cholera.

Mrs. McConnell died about 1st of this month.

Your affectionate Father,
Thomas A. Watkins

P.S. All your friends here join in sending love to you. Your mother will write you shortly. T.A.W.

July 23, 1849

My Dear Beloved Child,

I received your letter of the 8th yesterday week and of the sixth last Saturday. I am very much grieved at your not coming home and am truly sorry that you were disappointed in coming home. I cannot describe my feelings when your papa came back from Holly Springs without you.

You must not continue to grieve about home. It is so much better for you to be at a good school than to go to those little schools that are always breaking up. I am always uneasy about you, nothing could induce me to be separated from you if I was not so anxious for you to be well educated. Your papa says if you were to come home now he would not send you back. He would send you to school at Capt. Binford's. They have a very good teacher in their family.

I hope you will enjoy yourself at Mr. Wingfield's until your school commences and then you must study hard, do not let your mind be too much on home. Mr. Brown of Grenada said you could have come with him if he had known it. His daughter goes to the Methodist school in Columbia.

I expect you have received your papa's letter he wrote to you what to do about getting your clothes and having them made. Why do you not want to get uniform for the summer, if it is a rule of the school you ought to conform to it. Your papa says you may have three dollars of the money Mr. Dale has of his. The times are mighty hard. Do, my dear child, try to take care of your clothes well as you can. I went to Middleton this day week to see Mrs. Oliver. She had left that morning for Alabama. I spent the day with Mrs. Farmer. Her health has improved, she is in the family way. She told me to give a great deal of love to you for her. Mrs. Phillips went as far as the river with Mrs. Oliver.

All of your friends say they are sorry you did not come home. I spent the day with Mrs. E. Whitehead last Thursday. All of Mr. Davis[24] family was there except Evve [*Eveline*]. Mrs. Davis said Evve would write to you on the next Saturday. I like Mrs. Davis very much. It is said that James Bryant and Temperance Fort are to be married. They are waiting for Mr. Fort to come from Texas. His family is expecting him soon to come and carry them to Texas. Mr. Wadlington's Ned died last week, he was sick five or six weeks. Mrs. Wadlington had a son last week. There was a picnic dinner given in Middleton and a cotillion party the Fourth of July. There was a dance at Patty's last Saturday night. Your papa expects the Miss Egglestons here next week. I am afraid we cannot have anything cooked fit for them to eat. He has commenced having the house white washed today. I am sitting in the shed room and will have to sleep in here tonight.

There has been a great deal of rain for the last two weeks, it is very cloudy at this time. I have had the worst luck raising chickens I ever had. Something killed seven hens in the henhouse last week. Your white hen with the top crown was one of them, she had two chickens. I have not seen them since. Polly pigeon went away several weeks ago. Daniel and Simon say they saw her last week at the gin house. I was very glad to see Aunt Letty's[25] letter to you. It is the first time I have heard from them since the Dr. came from there. You must write to Aunt Letty shortly. I have come to the conclusion that none of them care for me as they will not write to me; Mary sends her love to you and says she is mighty sorry you did not come home. She cried when I read your letter to her.

All the servants send their love to you and say they are sorry you could not come home. Ritt and Elsie wished Mrs. Moore would die with the cholera

24. Brother of Mrs. William Whitehead.
25. Uncle Billy's wife, in Alabama.

for disappointing you. Dr. Dandridge, Mr. and Mrs. Bridges had a fight lately. Bridges accused Dandridge of telling a lie. Dandridge attempted to strike Bridges and Mrs. Bridges throwed a chair at him. Mary wants me to enclose a small rag doll in my letter to you. She has her candy man and woman and candy star yet. She is anxious to eat the star. We cook tomatoes like you had them last year with molasses, only we cut up the tomatoes and put a cup of molasses and a tablespoonful of butter. You must write me what kind of clothes you get and how much you have to give for the making of them. Give my respects to Mr. and Mrs. Wingfield. Tell them I am very much obliged to them for taking care of you. I hope I may have it in my power to return their kindness.

Your affectionate mother,
Sarah E. Watkins

February 9, 1850

My Dear Child,

I have not received a letter nor heard a word from you since you left me. What is the reason you have not written to me? I am very anxious to hear from you.

Abram got home last night[26] and went in his house before anyone saw him. There was great joy with us all to see him. He says he left all well at Uncle Billy's. They had not moved when he left. The house was not finished. Brother hired some poor men to work on them. They eat more than they work. It would be a pleasure if it was in my power to assist my beloved Uncle, Aunt, and Brother. Hannah's sister Sally is sold (to a negro trader, he has taken her to New Orleans), and her daughter Mary was sold before she was and gone to Texas.

Lizzie and Ginny Whitehead came to spend the night with you the day after you left here. They would not stay as you were not here. I have not been to see Mrs. Whitehead yet. She has a daughter about four weeks old.

Mr. McLemore went to Memphis and it is said he came back with the smallpox. His child has died with it. Mrs. Farmer has been very ill for twelve days. She was better yesterday but not able to turn herself over. I have not seen anybody since you went away last Saturday. Mary [*daughter*] fell at the kitchen chimney, struck the back of her head against a block and cut a gash nearly an inch long. When she heard your Papa tell me to cut the hair off the place she was very much frightened. She said, "Will I die?" She is as bad as ever. It seems like Patty will never finish spinning the yarn for your

---

26. From Alabama—he had journeyed there for the doctor, traveling alone the whole trip.

gloves. She has been sick with the colic. She has been working in the garden, she is put out in the field today. Uncle Vivion has been sick all the week. Sally, Henrietta, and America send "howdy" to you. Mary joins me in love to you. Give my respects to Capt. Binford's family and Miss Holmes. You must write soon.

Your affectionate Mother,
Sarah E. Watkins

P.S. Mrs. Estel's old Danny came in just now and said, "Mistress, I have not eat no flour bread so long, can't you give me a little piece?" I went to get him a biscuit. He whispered to Sally to know if he could get some milk. SEW

March 19, 1850
Carrollton, Mississippi

Miss L. A. Watkins
Grenada, Mississippi

Dear Daughter,

Your favor of 7th inst. come to hand on the 15th & the one of the 15th was received this day.

I have sent to New Orleans for all the music ordered by you. I think it will arrive here in about three weeks from this time. I also ordered a fine bonnet for your Mother, which I expect will come along with the music.

Your mother & myself are highly delighted that Miss Barksdale & Miss Binford will accompany you home when I send for you. You must without fail bring them along with you. I shall send the carriage for you & the young ladies in about two weeks—say Thursday, 4th of April.

I sent by mail lately a letter from Eutaw, Alabama[27] to you, which I hope has come safe to hand. Your Mother says that you must bring home with you a piece of the gingham that she gave you to make yourself a bonnet. She only wants a small piece—just enough to piece the belt in your sister's dress. I saw the storm that you said kept you from sleep. We felt none of its effects here, but I knew that the weather was very bad where it passed along for I never saw such quick & constant flashes of lightning in my life.

Give our best respects to Captain Binford's family—also to Miss Holmes. Tell her that I am very sorry that she will so soon take her departure for New York. Tell her that we shall be much disappointed if she does not come home with you.

Your affectionate Father,
Thomas A. Watkins

27. Home of Mr. Oliver.

April 20, 1850
Carrollton, Mississippi

Miss Letitia A. Watkins
Care of Captain Binford's
My Dear Child:

I send you your two dresses, one chemise and four handkerchiefs. Thinking your body might not fit, I would not sew it on nor the sleeves in. You can get Mrs. Rose to finish it and let me know what she charges, I will send you the money to pay her when we send for you. We will send your music. Your Papa will send the bill and Captain Binford can see what the music is worth that the ladies take.

I am anxious to send your things tomorrow. It is raining so much today I am afraid the weather will not admit of it. You have to be careful in wearing your pink dress, it fades very ugly when washed. I received my bonnet. It is not pretty for such a high price. It is open straw trimmed with ostrich feathers on each side and white ribbon and artificial flowers inside.

I was at Mr. E. Whitehead's Thursday, Lizzie and Virginia are at home. Mr. Holt expects to commence school shortly. It is said the smallpox is yet in Blackhawk. Your father got a letter from Dr. Hall last week. He wrote that both of his carpenters, James and George, were drowned the week before he wrote. Mary sends her love to you and says you must make haste home, she wants to see you. She asks me to write a letter for her to you. I promised her I would but she has gone to sleep. Your Papa has been sick with a headache yesterday and today.

Let me know how your body fits. If it does not suit, you must have it altered. Give my respects to Captain Binford's family and Miss Holmes.

Your affectionate Mother,
Sarah E. Watkins

Dear Daughter,

The weather has been so bad all the week we could not send your things to you. It is said Elisa Terry is to be married shortly to Mr. Prince, a cousin of her brother-in-law. If you have finished your linen sleeves send them. Your linen is done all to the sleeves. Elsie came home yesterday. She is just starting back. She says I must tell you howdy. Enclosed you will see the bill for the music—hand it to Captain Binford. Do my dear child, behave to your teacher, do not show your temper.

Your affectionate Mother,
S.E. Watkins

[Note: Attached to this letter is a bill from E. A. Tyler, No. 39 Camp Street, Dealer in Fine Watches, Jewelry, Silver Ware, Spectacles, Perfumery, Fancy

Goods, & C. &C. The bill is from New Orleans, dated March 26, 1850 with an additional heading at the top of the bill: "Agent for the sale of Piano Fortes, of the Best Manufacturers, also Sheet Music. Thirty-two pieces of music were purchased for a total amount of $5.70."]

May 15, 1850
Carrollton, Mississippi

Miss Letitia A. Watkins
Care of Captain John A. Binford
Grenada, Mississippi

My Dear Daughter,

I received your letter last evening and was very glad to hear from you. I am always pleased to have you with me but am sorry your school will be out so soon. You ask to have your daguerreotype taken. Your Papa says I must write he has no money to throw away. He expects the man is a northern abolitionist. If he was a southern man and settled at some place and followed that as his trade, he would have no objection. You must wait 'till you go to Nashville or some other place and have it taken. I would like very much to have your likeness but you know if your Papa is opposed to it I cannot have it taken.[28]

I received a note from Brother last evening. His wife had a son the 20th of April. The family was all well. Daniel Devine is dead. Major Robert H. Watkins has sold his home place and the negroes on it to James Saunders. He is living there. His other land and negroes he has sold to his two sons and he has moved to Nashville. His health is very bad.

A most disastrous fire broke out in Huntsville lately consuming the buildings on two squares and a half. Mr. William Hemingway has moved. Collins Hemingway has moved to William Hemingway's old place. Mrs. C. Hemingway has had a baby since she has come to this neighborhood. Mrs. Neal has a baby. Mary Jenkins has been in Carrollton two or three weeks. I have had fifty little turkeys, they keep dying up. I wish you would inquire of someone how to raise them. Your Papa has employed a man by the month to attend to his business. He is to be here tonight [*evidently an accountant*].

I do not know any news to write. Your Papa has had the headache for three days. Tell Mrs. Rose I am very much obliged to her for her kindness in making your dress. I think fifty cents is too little for making it. You ought to insist on her having more pay than that. Be sure and thank her politely for her goodness. Give my respects to Captain Binford's family and Miss Holmes. Mary

---

28. It is revealing of the doctor's feelings that he would not tolerate one whom he suspected to be an abolitionist, even to photograph his daughter.

sends her love to you and says you must make haste and come home. Henrietta sends howdy to you. She has had the colic one or two days and just getting over it. She took six pills, pepper and laundanum yesterday. I have made some mistakes, you must look over them.

Your affectionate Mother,
Sarah E. Watkins

Home, June 7th, 1850

Miss Letitia A. Watkins
at Capt. Binford's
Mississippi

My Dear Daughter,

The rain and a grassy crop prevented us from sending for you on yesterday. I presume that a delay of one day will make but little difference with you—especially as you are in such fine and agreeable company.

Doctor Smith, the Rector's brother, has lately married a fine intelligent lady and they are boarding at Bridges' Tavern in Middleton. He came out lately to see us and I told him that you would call and see him and his wife when you passed through Middleton on your way home. You must on no terms fail to call and try to get them to come out home with you in the carriage. Dr. Smith inquired very particularly about you and he would be very much mortified if you did not call a few minutes at Bridges' Tavern to see him and his lady.

It may be that at the time you call they may be absent at Church or some other place—if so, leave your card. Enclosed I send you two cards. You can leave the one I have written on, or if you do not like the style, you can write on the other one and leave it with Mrs. Bridges or some intelligent servant, in case Dr. S. and wife are not at the tavern.

I hope Miss Margaret, the interesting Miss Margaret Binford will accompany you home and stay some time and go with us down to Mrs. Eggleston's. I shall take you down there in a few days after you get home.

The water is too high to fish at Mr. Robinson's lakes. It is probable that it will be some time before any fish can be taken by the hook from them.

Semira has a very fine son. He is near two weeks old.

Your affectionate Father,
Thomas A. Watkins

P.S. Our best respects to Capt. Binford and family and to Miss Holmes.

CHAPTER TWO

"We think you can do better"

Lettie's reaching adolescence and her lively interest in members of the opposite sex caused discord in the Watkins family. Although enrolled in a school in Middleton, apparently she boarded with the William H. Phillips family during the fall of 1850 and the early spring of 1851. Her sudden discovery of boys (she was then sixteen) was followed by what her father regarded as the paying of too much attention to beaux, especially one John Stevens (who was a merchant in Middleton, working with James Parmele). So the doctor decided to move Lettie to a school in Holly Springs, Mississippi—the Reverend G. W. Sill's Academy.

Lettie finished her schooling at the conclusion of the spring term in 1852 and returned home to live. For the next several years, 1852–54, she was one of the "belles of Carrollton." She seemed constantly to be visiting or going to parties. She had many admirers among the young men in Carroll and surrounding counties. Family tradition has it that she received *eighteen* proposals of marriage by the time she was *eighteen years old*. A considerable collection of "flowery" letters from beaux, still in the family, but—for the most part—not included here, supports this claim.

Dr. Watkins wanted Lettie, his adored and lovely firstborn, to marry eventually into a family he considered "good enough," but in this he was to be sorely disappointed. Sometime during the second half of 1852, Lettie met her husband-to-be, a handsome young lawyer just home from the University of Virginia, William Martin Walton. Not knowing the

Walton family, or anything about it, the doctor was most disapproving of the young man as a suitor for his daughter. But before he left Carrollton to practice law in Austin, Texas, young Will Walton asked Lettie to marry him, and she agreed, secretly. Despite her father's vigorous disapproval, the two young people, Lettie, eighteen, and Will, twenty-one, carried on a secret correspondence through 1853.

During this time Dr. Watkins took Lettie to the World's Fair in New York City, to introduce her to society and to help her "forget" Mr. Walton. Then, in January 1854, after all was prepared in Austin, Will returned to Carroll County. In the face of bitter opposition, he and Lettie were married on February 9, 1854, at Forest Place, the Watkins home. Dr. Watkins refused to attend the ceremony. Afterwards he told them never to return.

April 4, 1851
Carrollton, Mississippi

My Dear Lettie,

I received your welcome and affectionate letter last evening. Oh! it gave me so much pleasure to hear from you. I had just arrived here when Brother came to supper. He brought your letter. I am now boarding at Mr. Money's. I am very well pleased at present. Fannie and Bettie Ewing, Bill Patton, James Smith, Brother and myself are boarding here. I room with Martha Compton, the oldest. I think she is one of the sweetest girls I ever saw. Mary Ann Latham and Mary Cardle are going to school here. I am not all alone, no. But alas! if you were here I would be happy. Oh! yes, Buck is living here too. He is reading medicine under Doctor Askew.

Lettie, today is Friday and I am not going to commence school until Monday. All the girls are gone and I am alone writing to one as near and dear to me as a sister. Oh! I have just returned from Brother's store. He does not keep dry goods but groceries and all kinds of candy and everything that you can think of that is good to eat. I got my pockets so full I was ashamed to go through town. I do wish you were here with me.

Hugh McKenzie was here last night. We stay in the parlor until we get ready to go to bed. I am very sorry Mrs. Phillips is getting so tight with you all, but Lettie, it is for your own good. I do think you do very wrong to allow the young gentlemen to go with you when you know it is against Mrs. Phillips' wishes. Lettie, I would advise you not to allow them to go with you when they ask you, just say to them that it is against the rules of your boarding house and that you did not think it would be right for you to allow it while you stayed with them. Then they could not get angry with you but would think a great deal more of you. Lettie, although you are older than me, I do not think it is wrong for me to advise you. You must not get angry with me for what I have said to you. Have you sent that album back that John gave you? I hope you have sent it back. I heard one of the young men at the fair bought you a doll and gave it to you and then one of them stole it from you and you ran all over the house hollering, "Where's my doll, where's my doll?" until you caught Bill Witty and got it. Is that so or not? I hope it is not.

Well, Lettie, I do not know what else to write. I believe I am out of something to write. When I commenced, I thought I could write two or three sheets but I cannot think of anything more to write. Mother has been very sick for the last week but she is getting well now. That was the reason I did not come down here before yesterday. I will commence studying French Monday. Oh! don't you pity me? It is so hard. I do dread it so much. I wish you would come to the party here next Tuesday night. It is to be a conversation party at the Academy in Carrollton. I would be so glad to see you. We have got a good many new scholars in school this session. We had a party the first day. We will have some four or five more next session. When you write tell more for goodness sake how many scholars you have got. I heard the other day you had fifty, but I do not think that can be true as you had only forty-two when I was there. Old Simon Stovall like to have taken my head off the other day because I was coming here to school. I do wonder if he thought that would do me any good.

Lettie, I must come to a close. Excuse this short letter and mistakes and write soon and write all the news you can think of.

> I remain as ever your affectionate
> friend,
> Octavia Simmons

> April 9, 1851
> Carrollton, Mississippi

Miss Letitia A. Watkins
Middleton, Mississippi

My Dear Child,

Get up all your things and put them together so they can be got when sent for. Your Papa went to Carrollton yesterday and came home full of anger. He said you shall not go to school in Middleton again and you shall not go to the dancing school if Middleton sinks. He will not tell me his reason for taking you away, I expect some busy body is the cause of it. Do not forget to give Miss Campbell her rings you have on.

> Your Affectionate Mother,
> Sarah E. Watkins

May 30, 1851
Carrollton, Mississippi

Miss Letitia A. Watkins
Care of Reverend G.W. Sill
Holly Springs, Mississippi

My Dear Beloved Child,

Your Father returned home yesterday. It gave me pleasure to receive your letter. I received one from dear Aunt Letty the same time which doubled my pleasure.

Oh, my dear child, how soon my joy was turned to grief when I read the letter you wrote to Sarah Campbell in which you sent your love to John Stevens and said it would always would be a pleasure to hear from him. Lettie, did I think I had raised my daughter with no more prudence than to be sending her love to a young man, particularly when it is said she is to be married to him.

Lettie dear child, how could you deceive a poor broken hearted mother? A mother that has bestowed most of her earthly affections on you, that has idolized you. All the world could not have made me believe you love John Stevens. You told me you respected him as a gentleman, that he never had addressed you. You told me you did not keep anything from me except what the girls told you in confidence. If he has any idea of addressing you, you could not encourage him more than by sending your love to him. If he has given you no reason to believe that he has an idea of you, it must give him a contemptible opinion of you having the boldness to send your love to him. Is it not enough to make your father think the report true?

He broke open your letter you wrote to Miss Campbell and read it. He has not delivered her your letter, he is perfectly right not to send it to her. He says he does not know what to do with you and if you marry Stevens he will have nothing to do with you and you should not come in his house. He has lost all confidence in you. From his ways towards you at times you thought he had no love for you. You were mistaken. He has shown his love in indulging you to everything you have asked of him. He has been to a great deal of trouble and expense in educating you. It is your duty to look over his eccentric ways and be conformable to his wishes. It is very provoking to a father after he has taken so much trouble with his daughter for her to love a man beneath herself in every respect.

I did think it was an enemy that informed your Papa of that report. Since I have seen your letter to Miss Campbell, I believe he was informed of it from a pure motive. I cannot but think you would disgrace yourself in marrying Stevens. He is beneath you and your family in every respect. What can a young girl of sixteen in the bloom of life, that has every prospect before her to make her happy, have to do with such a man as Stevens.

I am afraid I have not discharged my duty towards you in some respects. I have let my love for you blind me too much to your faults. The confidence I placed in you made me more indulgent to you. Your temper has distressed me more than any fault I have ever seen in you until now. I am so distressed my heart is fit to burst. I can hardly write for crying. No one but a mother knows my feelings. Can it be possible that you have placed your affections on a man of no higher standing in society? He is not your equal in any respect. You need advice, you need the watchful eye of a mother more now than when you were nine years old. I thought what caused your unhappiness was your Papa hearing of that report and preventing you from attending the parties in Middleton. If that is all your are unhappy about, do cheer up and do not grieve yourself to death about nothing. From your letter to Miss Campbell, it must be love that is distressing you and making you look like the devil before day.

If it is that, more the shame that you should let your young mind be tortured with such idle passion. Take the advice of a mother who feels more for you than can be expressed. Apply your mind to your studies, try to improve yourself, be more aspiring in your associations, always make yourself agreeable in company, keep in the first circle of society and malicious stories will not be told of you. It is my duty as a mother to advise you. Be more prudent how you write or speak. Never do you send your love to a man again. My dear child, be very particular how you act, the least blemish can ruin a girl's character forever. It would kill me for your character to be ruined. For your own sake, for the sake of your little sister and your poor broken hearted mother, never disgrace yourself.

Write to me as soon as you receive this letter, write with candor and let me know what is the cause of your unhappiness. If there is confidence to be put in a human being, I cannot think you would marry Stevens. Say in your next letter to me if you would or not. If you were to marry him or any other man that is as much your inferior, I would turn my back upon you forever.

I expect it will make you very unhappy to hear that your Papa read your letter. You have brought your unhappiness on yourself by your own imprudence. You cannot blame him for believing that report when he has seen what you have written.

I know so well what affect grief has on you. You must not grieve yourself sick about it. Let this scrape be a warning to you. Do, my dear child, govern your temper. Do not get in a rage when you read this. It is for your good and the love your parents have for you is why they take so much interest in your welfare. I shall feel uneasy until I hear from you. I have not seen anybody nor heard any news since you left here. I miss you very much. Your Papa told me he heard you perform on the piano. He said you performed well, he admired your singing.

Aunt Letty wrote very little news. They were all well except herself. She has sore eyes and risings. She wrote that Mary Swoope had joined the Presbyterian church. Susan Watkins is married to Acklin, Milton Watkins married Acklin's cousin. Mr. Watkins is well pleased with the matches. Sarah Moseley that was is dead and left a child a few days old. Aunt Letty says she has not heard from us since last winter. She certainly did not receive your letters. James Davis brought you a ticket last week to a party in Middleton. The party was last night. Be certain to write to me as soon as you get this letter. Mary joins me in love to you and says she is obliged to you for the candy you sent her.

Your affectionate Mother,
Sarah E. Watkins

June 9, 1851
Carrollton, Mississippi

Miss Letitia A. Watkins
Care of Reverend G. W. Sill
Holly Springs, Mississippi

My Dear Dutiful Daughter,

I received your affectionate letter written the 3rd of June last week and one on the 6th inst. yesterday which was very gratifying to our feelings. Our confidence is perfectly restored in you since receiving your letter. You must not give yourself any more unhappiness about it. I did not think you would marry Stevens or any other man as much as your inferior as he is. But seeing the way you wrote to Sarah, I did not know what to think about it and knew it was my duty to write you and find out the truth about it.

If it was not the care we have for you we would not trouble ourselves so much about your marrying. It is the great love we have for you why we are so solicitous about you.

Your Pa says that he doted on you and wished to do a good part towards you but when he read that letter it soured him mightily. Since he has seen your letter, he has become reconciled and told me to write that he has confidence in you. This scrape will be a good lesson and a warning to you to be more particular how you write and act hereafter. When you receive this letter I hope it will give peace to your mind and make you a cheerful, happy girl again. Last night your Papa asked me if you danced with Stevens at the Carrollton party. I had to tell him you danced one set with him. He remarked, "You tried to keep it from me like you did that report. If you had have told me of the report it would have prevented all this trouble." I do hope all this talk about nothing is ended forever. When you are unhappy it makes me so.

The commencement[29] comes on the 16th and 17th of July. Your Papa says he will try to be there and wants to know if you can meet him there. If you go one or two days before it comes on, it will make no difference. You could stay at the tavern. My dear child, be very particular who you go with and what company you keep. This is such a malicious, envious world, things are so apt to be said to injure your character. If you go in the stage, do not be too conversant with strange men. You should never converse with any man that you have not been introduced to by a respectable person. The man you wrote about that traveled in the stage with you, he must be a bold daring puppy to act in the way he did with you. Such a character would seduce a girl if he could. Always be cautious of such fellows. Never suffer a man to put his hand any where about you, nor to be holding your hand. Most men are deceiving creatures. Never be too familiar with any man. Not that I think you would be imprudent in any way but you are young and thoughtless and all girls need advice of older persons about such things.

Your Papa wrote to Mr. Sill not to let you receive any letters but those that has his seal on them. I am sorry he has deprived you of that pleasure. Do not take it to heart. He carried the presents to Octavia [*Simmons*] you sent her. The book for Sarah is here yet, I forgot to send it to her last week. I reckon it will be sent in the morning.

Marion Simmons is very ill in Carrollton. Mrs. E. Whitehead spent the day with me last Thursday. She told me that Miss Norman who boarded at Mrs. Smith's ran away with Mr. Lilly and went to Mr. Gould's and married him. A Miss Martin came to the barbecue in Middleton given to Jeff Davis[30] Saturday week and ran off and married some man. I don't know who he was.

We had a rain Saturday and yesterday for the first time since April to do any good. The crop was suffering very much for the want of it.

America has just come in with a bowl of raspberries and a few strawberries. I wish you had them. I do miss your company and want to see you very much. Hannah says you must recollect what she told you, now you are in

29. The commencement at the University of Mississippi, Oxford, Mississippi. The president, Augustus B. Longstreet, was a Watkins family friend, and the doctor enjoyed attending commencement.

30. In 1851, Jefferson Davis campaigned for the governorship and was defeated. Ten years later Jefferson Davis would be president of the Confederacy. At the time of this letter, Davis was a U.S. senator, in the lead among those persons who were disillusioned, by now, with the Compromise of 1850 — and was canvassing Mississippi in behalf of the gubernatorial candidacy of John A. Quitman, who was trying to heap defeat upon the so–called "submissionists," i.e., those who were soft on the state rights issue. See William C. Davis, *Jefferson Davis: The Man and His Hour* (New York: Harper Collins, 1991), 213.

trouble is the time to pray. I hope you will be out of trouble when you receive this letter. I pray you may think more about your sinful soul and prepare for a better world. Ritt sends howdy to you.

Write often, I am always anxious to hear from you.

Your affectionate Mother,
Sarah E. Watkins

Cousin Elisa Cunningham is dead. S.E.W.

October 15, 1851
Carrollton, Mississippi

Miss Letitia A. Watkins
Holly Springs

My Dear Beloved Child,

I arrived home Sunday evening, found all well except America and little Simon. Chloe had been sick enough to call in a physician. They are all well now but Simon, he is better. I got to cousin Patsy Powell's last Thursday and staid until Saturday morning and came from there to Dick Towne's. Your Papa left me two miles from cousin Patsy's and came on home. I liked my visit very much and would have staid longer but was so anxious to get home.

There are two Miss Hastings going to school at the college from Yalobusha; cousin Patsy told them if they did not go to the same school with you that they must go to see you and get acquainted with you. Judge Clayton from near Holly Springs staid here Sunday night. Some of his family may call on you. He said he would like for you to visit them. Mr. and Mrs. Alfred Roberson came here Monday morning and left this morning. I sent butter to Mrs. Phillips' yesterday by Abram. She and Mrs. Parmele send me word to give their love to you. Mrs. Phillips is sick. Mrs. Parmele's son Jack is dead. Ed Wellons went to Tennessee this summer and died there.

I am very sorry your letter from Martha Watkins and the Miss Watkinses were broken open by your Papa and read. He asked me who did Mary Susan refer to H.B. I told him I did not know. You ought to write to the girls to be particular what they write to you about as your letters have to be seen.

I hope you are more contented this session then you were last. Do my dear child place your mind on your studies and improve yourself and try to please your teachers in every respect. Write to me soon. I am anxious to hear from you. The week appears like a month since we parted.

Prince [*slave*] ran away the week before your Pa went to Alabama. He has not come in yet. Don't say nothing about it when you write to me.

Your affectionate Mother,
Sarah E. Watkins

October 16, 1851
Carrollton, Mississippi

Miss Letitia A. Watkins
Care of Reverend G. W. Sill
Holly Springs, Mississippi

My Dear Daughter,

Your favor of 11th inst. just at hand. We were all glad to hear from you & that you were so well contented. Study hard & you will not have time to be unhappy. You must try hard & improve the time you have yet to go to school.

I have given Mr. Sill permission that your correspondence be unrestricted.

I do not wish you to write Miss Campbell often & if I know of your writing to or about J.S.[31] I & my family will cease our correspondence with you. I am very decided upon that subject.

Please write us often; we are always pleased to hear from you.

Your mother has some large sweet potatoes that she is very anxious to send you, but I fear that she will have no opportunity.

Your affectionate Father,
Thomas A. Watkins

November 7, 1851
Carrollton, Mississippi

Miss Letitia A. Watkins
Care of Reverend G.W. Sill
Holly Springs, Mississippi

My Dear Child,

Your Papa received your affectionate letter last week. He would have answered it. I told him I would write you. I have been waiting to hear some news to write you. I attended preaching at the Methodist church in Middleton Sunday and heard Mr. Morrison preach a very good sermon. Aunt Mary Cobbs was baptised by Mr. Green, the Methodist preacher. I saw Mrs. Parmele, Sarah Campbell and Eveline Davis. Eve told me to give her love to you. I asked S. Campbell if she received the letter you wrote her directed to Greensboro. She said she did.

Dr. Smith is keeping house. He lives in the Judson Institute and teaches school in one room and music in another. Miss Edmundson is the only assistant teacher in the school. Dr. Smith teaches music himself. Rebecca Davis

---

31. The doctor continues his objection to John Stevens.

boards with them. Mrs. Phillips has only two girls boarding with her: Sarah Campbell and Miss Witty. One of S. Campbell's brothers died this summer.

Your Papa says he has permitted you to write to whom you please. He does not want you to correspond with Sarah Campbell, she will be writing about J. Stevens to you. Be on your guard who you write to and what you write about. Your Pa said it made him mad for you to complain so much in your letter. He don't think you would be contented in heaven. Do not say anything about what I write you that he says to me. In your next letter write me what you are studying. Do try to study hard and improve your mind all you can.

I spent the day with Mrs. E. Whitehead Wednesday. Lizzie and Ginny go home to school every morning in Middleton. Eve Davis goes to school at Mr. Burrows. Lettie, the devil is to pay here today. Bird[32] and your Pa are searching in the negroes' houses. They have found a pack of cards in Glasgow's house and one big potato. It makes me so nervous I can scarcely write. Prince has not come home yet. I do not know what they can be searching for unless it is for him.

I dined at Mr. Southworth's yesterday. Mrs. Southworth is anxious for you to visit her when you return home. Temperence Fort is married to a widower by the name of Reynolds living near Mr. Fort's, cousin to Mrs. Ransom.

There is to be a party in Grenada tonight. Mary and Martha Whitehead are going to it. You wrote to know if Mr. and Mrs. Roberson were traveling or visiting. They were visiting Mr. Gaden's family, Mr. Booth's and our's. The Campbellites and Methodists are disputing with each other in Middleton. The Campbellite preacher went to the Methodist preacher in the congregation and told him when he called up a mourner not to tell him to get down and pray but tell it to rise and be baptized. From that they commenced a controversy and it is said there was as much stamping of feet and applauding as if they had been at a theater or some such place.

I wish I could have a way to send you some potatoes and ground peas. America was sick when we were in Alabama and has been sick most ever since I got home. She is in at work today. She says I must tell you howdy. Sally and Ritt send howdy. Ritt says I must write you that she saw Bill Witty and he had more hair on his mouth than anybody she ever saw.[33] You must write often. I am always anxious to hear from you.

Your affectionate Mother,
Sarah E. Watkins

32. The overseer.
33. Moustache?

December 15, 1851
Carrollton, Mississippi

Miss Letitia A. Watkins
Care of Dr. Cummings
Holly Springs, Mississippi

My Dear Daughter,

We are well & no news to relate you. Dr. Hall is now on a visit to us. He is lively & fat.

Mr. William Whitehead's daughters & wife have lately been to see us. We are expecting Miss Fanny Eggleston up on a visit this winter.

You must study hard & learn all you can; if you wish me to purchase for you a piano; but I am not certain that I can. We are anxiously looking for a letter from you.

The principal object in writing you is to get you to try & visit our friend Mrs. Martin during Christmas. I presume Mrs. Moore would make some arrangement to go with you there. It is your duty to do so if you can. Mrs. Martin has been kind to you & it would be paying respects to her & tell her that I & your mother always think of her with great gratitude.

Mr. Mason's family is another family that you might visit if you are properly invited.

My best respects to Mr. & Mrs. Clapp & Dr. Cummings' family.

I sent you lately five dollars by mail which I presume has ere this reached you. Baby wants "to go to school at Holly Springs with sister."

Your affectionate Father,
Thomas. A. Watkins

December 24, 1851
Holly Springs, Mississippi

Doctor Thomas A. Watkins
Carrollton, Mississippi

My Dear Father,

Your most welcome letter of the 15th instant came duly to hand last week, and also the one of the 17th last Sunday. We have had two snows here this winter. Neither of them were an inch deep. It snowed Monday and it is so very muddy now that I am afraid to go out at all. I attended the party last night and of course I do not feel very well today. It was given by Clark the dancing master. We danced up over a store. All the *big folks* were there. I danced every set but two or three. I missed those through choice.

I expect Mr. Sill will give us a week holiday. If I could only see you all during that time I would be so happy. Mrs. Cummings' brother is here. He is very fine looking and one of the most intellectual gentlemen of his age I ever met with. I danced several sets with him. He has flattered me a great deal. He seems to be a perfect gentleman.

Mr. Donaldson married Jennie Watson. She is very pretty. I have seen her daguerreotype. Martha Anderson (a niece of Mr. Richard Anderson's) invited me to spend my Christmas at her house, but I fear the inclemency of the weather will prevent my doing so. Mr. Clapp has invited me to spend some of the holiday at his house. I intend going there as soon as the roads get dry enough. If I have an opportunity I will also go to Mrs. Martin's.

Papa please excuse all the mistakes as I am not very well and much fatigued from last night's dissipation. Give my love to Mother and ask her why she does not write to me. Surely she has not forgotten that she has a daughter away from her. Does Dr. Hall tease Baby as much as he did me?

I remain as ever yours truly,
Letitia A. Watkins

P.S. Have you paid Clark yet? It is about ten dollars, but I missed six lessons therefore I would not pay him but eight.

January 14, 1852
Carrollton, Mississippi

Miss Letitia A. Watkins
Care of Dr. Cummings
Holly Springs, Mississippi

My Dear Beloved Child,

I received your affectionate letter last Friday, it gave me pleasure to hear from you. As you had just had your teeth plugged the day before you wrote, I have felt uneasy about you. I have heard of one or two ladies having the lockjaw from a tooth being plugged that caused their death. I have seen nobody and heard so little news I hardly know what to write about. The cold weather has frozed up my ideas. We have had a plenty of frozed milk for two mornings. Mary [*now eight years old*] is sitting by me eating frozed buttermilk sweetened. I must tell you how she served me one day this week. She went to the bucket of milk and skimmed all the cream off. She said she thought it was frozed buttermilk until she was eating the last mouthful, it eat so good she found it was cream. She has been very industrious the last month or two. She has knit her Papa and John Smith a pair of coarse yarn gloves, Abram a pair of galluses and now knitting herself a pair of gloves.

Dr. Ewing has brought his daughters home from Columbia. One of them was very sick while there. Nature stopped on her that caused her sickness. Lettie, do be very particular at such a time. A little imprudence at such a time might cause your death.

Mr. Parmele has broken up his store. They auctioned their goods off. Mr. Connerly intends having a store in Middleton. He has got the storehouse that Parmele and Farmer had. It is said that Simon Stovall is about to go broke, he has given a deed of trust on twenty-five of his negroes. It has been reported that him and Miss Edmundson were to be married. Mr. Sill sent your Papa his account for your board and tuition. He sent your marks for the months enclosed with it. And wrote that your Pa had a right to be pleased with your deportment and diligence this session. He wrote that all of the teachers speak well of you. It pleased me very much to hear you are getting along so well and hope you will continue to do so. Still charged for a month and a half board for you and charged for your tuition from the commencement of the session. Your Papa has written to him about it and says if he does not deduct it you shall not go to school to him. Don't say nothing about it.

Your Pa says I must write you that you spelt street wrong in your letter to me. Mary joins me in love to you and says as I do she wants to see you mightily bad. I am like a child always counting the months to see how long before the time for you to come home. Your Papa says he has sent after some letter stamps. They will not be here in 12 or 15 days. Sally, Ritt and America send howdy to you. America is sewing on your chemise. She has chills every week yet.

                                        Your affectionate Mother,
                                        Sarah E. Watkins

                                        January 30, 1852

Letitia Watkins
c/o Dr. Cummings
Holly Springs
Dear Lettie:

Your papa received your letter of the 24 last evening. We were very glad to hear from you. I am afraid your mind is more on beaux than your studies. Do, my dear child, remember this is the last year you have to go school. Apply yourself diligently to your studies. Do not have beaux in your head until you quit school. You cannot attend to your studies and beaux at the same time.

If you think the gentleman you wrote about has any idea of addressing you, do not be too familiar with him, give him no encouragement; if you have partiality for him, do not show it. Do not be so easily fascinated with every man that pretends to love you. They are deceptive creatures.

When your papa read your letter he said, "Lettie is such a fool." He said to me, 'You think Lettie has any notion of that man?' I told him I reckon not; he said if thought so he would bring you home. You have given him something to talk about a long time.

But enough of this chit chat. You had rather hear how we are going on here. Well, Lettie, Christmas is over and it was the worst Christmas I ever spent. I have seen nobody, I have been at work all the time. Bird is here for another year [*overseer*], Jesse is hired at Mr. Eccles' again next year. John Smith is hired out at the steam mill, London is hired to Mr. McBridge, the rest of the negroes will stay at home. I wanted to hire Glasgow out but your pa would not agree to it.[34] To keep peace I let it go so.

Do try to be as saving as you can, don't buy anything but what you really need. Your pa tells me about his being in debt and throws up to me the many servants that stay about the house. If the bad management of the overseer does not break him there is no danger of my few servants doing so. America staying about the house is a great eyesore to him. She is most always sick with chills. She has not been well two weeks at a time since I came home.

You ask in your letter if I have forgotten if I have a daughter from me, why I have not written. No, that can never be forgotten by me you are always utmost in my mind. The reason I have not written is your papa writes to you so often that I thought it useless for me to write as I had so little news to write you.

There was a party at Mr. Brown's in Carrollton Christmas and one in Middleton last Friday night at the old Female Academy.

Mrs. Phillips' negro man Elic died week before last. Mr. Farmer has sold his plantation to Dr. Lipscomb. They will all live together in town next year.

Mr. W. and E. Whitehead families were here four weeks ago. Mary Whitehead told me I must write you that several gentlemen inquired about you at the party she was at in November at Grenada. She said they wanted to know when you will be at home. Your Pa told her he did not know your fame had reached that far. (I cannot write today without leaving out words and making mistakes, you must excuse me.)

It is said Dr. Holeman is a beau of Margaret Binford's and a lawyer went to see her mother Christmas. She says Octavia speaks of going to school in Middleton next year.

Your papa says why do you ask if he has paid Clark? Have you heard he has not or heard anyone hint such a thing? He says he has paid him and has

---

34. Glasgow belonged to Mrs. Watkins by inheritance from her parents; she was perhaps interested in hiring him out in an effort to get some personal pocket money.

Clark's receipt for it. He paid him a ten dollar gold piece when we were at Holly Springs.

Your papa has one of his bellowing headaches today. It has been raining all day.

Dr. Hall left Saturday week, he has fattened and looks old. He did not plague Mary as he used to do you. He said he wonders if you would quarrel with him now like you used to. He told us Charles Sherrod was to be married to Susan Billups the next week after he left home.

Mary joins me in love to you. She is very anxious to see the toy you have for her and to know the color of the horse. Patty sends howdy to you and says you must not take up with any thorny poor thing. Martha and Henrietta send howdy. Hannah is sick. You must write to me oftener, do not wait for me to answer your letters. I will write frequently if your pa does not.

Your affectionate Mother,
Sarah E. Watkins

February 23, 1852
Carrollton, Mississippi

Miss Letitia A. Watkins
Care of Dr. Cummings
Holly Springs, Mississippi

My Dear Child,

Your kind feeling letter was received last evening with pleasure. It is very consoling to have an affectionate daughter to comfort and sympathize with a distressed mother. Oh Lettie, I am so distressed about the death of my dear fatherly uncle [*Uncle Billy*]. The announcement of his death came so unexpected it had the same effect on me that it did on you. It gave me a sick headache in a short time. Mr. William McMahon wrote to your papa of the death of my beloved uncle the day he died. He wrote that he had the jaundice. I received a letter from Brother written the same day informing me of his death. He died the ninth of this month, five minutes before seven in the morning in full hopes of a blessed hereafter. That is a great comfort to me to hear that he was prepared to die. It would be too hard for as good a man to be lost. Brother said his funeral would be preached to next day at eleven or twelve o'clock by Mr. Thompson, a Baptist preacher that was with him in his sickness. He prayed for him and conversed with him about religion. Brother wrote that he died with the liver disease. My dear motherly aunt. I do feel so much for her and wish I could be with her to try and comfort her in her distressed situation. I know her distress is so great no one can comfort her. I hope and pray the Lord will enable her to bear with the loss of her affectionate and loving husband. I wrote to brother to tell our beloved aunt it would be a pleasure to me if she will live with us. Dear Uncle Billy was taken sick the 30th of January. Do not be uneasy about me. I will try to bear with the death of my dear uncle but how hard it is to do. I loved him as much as I could have loved a father—he has been a father to me. I would like to have you with me, but it is better for you to be at school than here where you could not enjoy yourself. I do want to see you more than can be expressed and am anxious for the time to arrive when we will meet again.

Your Papa received a letter from Aunt Sarah Early last week. She told him to tell you that Mary Wingfield was spending the winter in Georgia and is quite a pretty girl. He was in Middleton today and saw Octavia Simmons. She had just come in to school. She sent us a very pretty steel bag for you. It will be sent with your chemises. They will be ready to send as soon as they are washed. I expect to go to Carrollton tomorrow if it is a good day to get some mourning and will try to get some linen edging to put on your chemise. I had put a ruffle on the neck of one before I got your letter. If you do not like it you can take it off. You asked how much your account was at Mason's. It was fifty-five dollars. I think you were extravagant in giving five dollars for a handkerchief. You ask if I think your dress is pretty, I reckon it is right pretty in the dress. I can't tell so well by the piece. You must take care of it, it is such a delicate color it will soil very quickly.

You remember Miss Austin you saw at Fisher's wedding with Mrs. Gayden? She is expected to have a child shortly. Is it not awful to think of a girl disgracing herself in that way. I had rather a daughter of mine should be burnt alive than to act in that way.

Abram's health is about the same, he seldom lies up, his swelling is no better. All are well except little Abram and Martha. She is grunting. I expect she is about to increase her family.

I am sorry you would not attend your examination. People will think it was for the want of sense why you did not want to be examined.

Mary joins me in love to you. Sally, Ritt, America, Hannah and Patty all send howdy to you.

Your affectionate Mother,
Sarah E. Watkins

Feb. 24th—Martha had a daughter last night. S.E.W.

March 2, 1852
Carrollton, Mississippi

Miss L. A. Watkins
Holly Springs, Mississippi

My Dear Daughter:

Your favor of 22nd ult. came to hand this day—contents noticed. It by mistake was sent to Middleton & Abram brought it home this day. Your Mother sent a package to Carrollton to be sent you by first safe chance. It contains some clothes & Miss O. Simmon's [*Octavia*] present to you; all of which I hope will reach you in safety. The package has your name on it. Care of Capt. Eppes. So when you think it arrives you can send to his tavern for it.

You wrote about marrying. When you quit eating ginger cakes & read through the spelling book, you will then have time enough to think about marrying.

I am glad you think so little of Tom Purnell.

Mr. Tom Bingham our former overseer was only last Friday killed by his negroes & his body was then hid in the creek. His residence was 10 miles west of Carrollton.

Dr. Saunders formerly of Middleton will shortly marry Miss Rebecca Davis. I presume all the neighborhood news is fully told you by Miss O. Simmons who writes you often.

Colonel Strong has sold his place to a North Carolinian & I hope he will move away.

Dr. Cummings knows Colonel Strong.

You write your words too small. They are so small they are hardly legible. If you had directed my letter in a larger hand probably it would not have been sent to Middleton instead of Carrollton.

I am sorry that Mrs. Clapp did not get some of your oranges & raisins. Go & see her often & give my very best respects to her family.

I and Baby go fishing every fair day.

Your affectionate Father,
Thomas A. Watkins

March 12, 1852
Carrollton, Mississippi

Miss Letitia A. Watkins
Care of Dr. Cummings
Holly Springs, Mississippi

My Dear Daughter,

Your favor of 7th inst. just at hand. I generally write short letters & to the purpose. A gentleman of the description mentioned in one of your late letters would not, *would not* suit the taste of your father or mother. The matter has been talked over in my house & we think you can do better.

With regard to the jewelry you wrote for, we will write you more fully hereafter & let you know about giving you money to purchase it. All the books mentioned by you shall be purchased & ready for your perusal when you quit school. I am truly glad that you have a taste for reading. I never knew you to ask for a book before. You have heretofore asked for sugar toys, looking glasses, earrings, fine shoes, head dresses & oranges. A person is not fit to keep good company unless the mind is well-stored with useful information. Intelligent people are always in request & their company desired.

I have some very fine books & will get any you may name.

You must cultivate a taste for reading & then you will have an invaluable source of pleasure within yourself.

I have sent up by stage care of Capt. Eppes a bundle containing some clothes & Miss Octavia Simmon's present to you. When they arrive please be sure to inform us of it. When money, in fact, anything is sent you & received, be sure always to advise the sender that such & such came to hand.

Enclosed I send you five dollars—also some letter stamps. You should put them on almost all letters. Let me know if you have bought much at Messr. Masons' this year. They are clever men & I had rather you deal there than at any other place. The five dollars is for you to purchase music, etc.

Your letter contained Mr. Harris' receipt to Dr. Cummings for the sum of twelve dollars & 50 cts.

Please write me when the half-session expires. I presume it will be about 20 of April.

Mr. Clapp complains that you do not visit his family often enough. They are of the upper tendom[35] & the society of such as his & family should be courted.

We cannot hear from Aunt Letty. Your mother wrote & gave her invitation to come & live with us.

---

35. Upper 10 percent socially.

No news concerning your acquaintances worth relating. I presume Miss O.S. keeps you posted up on that subject. Write often. We are always glad to hear from you.

Dr. Cummings has recently written me a letter concerning you & if you knew all the good things he has said of you, you would go crazy. So I will not tell you for I want you to keep what little sense you have. Please give my best respects to Dr. C. & his family.

Your affectionate father,
Thomas A. Watkins

March 21, 1852
Carrollton, Mississippi

Miss Letitia A. Watkins
Care of Dr. Cummings
Holly Springs, Mississippi

Dear Daughter,

I shall visit North Alabama & intend taking Holly Springs in my route. You may expect me about next Friday or Saturday. The unsettled condition of the estate of the late Captain William Fitzgerald[36] calls me to Alabama.

We are all well & hope that you are not married yet & also that you let that subject occupy none of your thoughts.

Your mother & sister join in sending love to you.

Your affectionate Father,
Thomas A. Watkins

April 4, 1852
Carrollton, Mississippi

Miss Letitia Watkins
Care of Dr. Cummings
Holly Springs, Mississippi

My Dear Beloved Child,

I received your affectionate letter last evening with pleasure. I am so glad to hear you that you are coming home with your Papa; if you do not come, I will be so disappointed. I reckon you think I write you very seldom. It is not that I do not think of you. You are seldom out of my mind. I seldom see any body or hear any news and always have so much work to do that keeps me from writing often. Mary is a perfect tomboy wildcat—she runs out and tears

36. Uncle Billy, who had secured a loan from the doctor by mortgaging certain slaves.

up her clothes, gets as dirty as the little negroes. She is growing up like a wild, uncultivated weed. She says, "Pa troubles me, Mother troubles me, and when sister comes home, she will be troubling me. I don't know what to do." She says, "When I tell sister good night I won't kiss her. She has a pin in her mouth and sticks it in my lips."

I could not have sent for Octavia last Friday. Abram was white-washing the parlor and other parts of the house. I will send for her next Friday if she will come out. I will be very glad to have her company. I am so low spirited, I am no company for no one.

I received a letter from dear Aunt Letty last Sunday. The family was well. She will not come to live with us. She mentioned that Brother will not agree for her to leave him and her situation compels her to be there. Uncle Billy was owing your Pa five hundred dollars and the interest for it for three years. I hope he will have more feeling for my dear distressed Aunt then to call on her for pay now.

The letter you saw in your Pa's trunk from you to me, I sent it to Aunt Letty. Your pa said it was such an affectionate letter he requested me to send it to Aunt L. to see.

The tatting on your sleeves came off of a linen piece your Aunt Mary gave me for Baby before she was born. I put a piece of linen edging in your steel bag. If you did not like the ruffle you could take it off and put on the edging.

I have not heard from Mrs. E. Whitehead since she was here before Christmas. I want to go to see her but our carriage is in Carrollton to be sold. I have no way of going. I did not hear of Mr. Phillips' derangement until week before last. He does not get any better. Mr. Bird told me this morning he heard that he was confined—it made him so much worse he had to be let loose.

I was looking for Mrs. Palmer and Mrs. Parmele here last week. They did not come. Ritt saw Mrs. Parmele last Sunday in Middleton—she told her she wanted to see me but she wanted to see you worse. Mrs. Jenkins and Susan were here in February. I have not seen them since. Mrs. William Hemingway has been to see me at last.

Your Papa was not mad at all about what you wrote him. He said such a match would not suit: you poor, the man poor, it would not do at all. He said he reckoned it was the dentist that fixed your teeth as he could not hear anything about the bill. I hope you would be more aspiring than to place your affection on a dentist.

I gave your Pa a list of what to get if he goes to New Orleans. I am keeping my New Orleans bonnet for you to dress when you come home. I wish you would get me a pretty mourning ribbon to dress it and two black neck ribbons. I will enclose Mary's measure for a pair of shoes. She needs a pair of nice shoes.

You must excuse mistakes and bad writing. I can't write for making them and my pen is very bad. As Abram is going to Carrollton tomorrow, I have violated the Sabbath in writing today. I feel bad about it, it is the reason I can't write no better. Mary has just come in hollering, "Mother, who are you writing to? Chloe caught two fish." I asked her if she had been fishing. She would not answer me. She says you must bring her the jar your pickle is in. Frank says he wants Miss Lettie to come home to give him candy out of her pocket. I told your Papa to let you have ten dollars of the money he owes me. You must be a mighty good girl for it. Mary has lost her earrings. I want a pair of plain gold ones for her. Mary joins me in love to you, Ritter and Chloe send howdy to you.

Your affectionate Mother,
Sarah E. Watkins

Write soon.

April 11th, 1852
Holly Springs, Mississippi

Doctor Thomas A. Watkins
Cincinnati, Ohio

My Dear Father:

Your most welcome letter to Mother and myself came to hand last Monday. I should have answered before now, but have not had time before today. I have nothing of importance to relate but as you requested me to write to you, I shall endeavor to write a few lines.

I have studied very diligently and practiced hard ever since you left. The idea of going home has enlivened my imagination and enabled me to grasp my studies with more vigor than when I thought I had to pour over the *dry things* for the next three or four months.

I received a letter from Mother last week. She says she is very glad that I am going home. All was well when she wrote. Dr. Cummings says he cannot let his daughter go with us to New Orleans. She is very anxious to go and I should be very much pleased to have her with me. Very few girls have such a kind Father as I have and one who takes so much interest in letting them see something of the world.

I do not see the use of people having money if they do not intend to enjoy it. I believe Mr. Cummings would let his daughter go with us if he was not too stingy.

Judge Clayton called to see me last week. He was going to Carrollton and he came to see if I had anything to send home. Mr. Strictlin is married to Miss

Thompson. Dr. and Mrs. and Miss Cummings were very much pleased with you. They think I have a *mighty* good Father. I hope you will get back here time enough for us to go to New Orleans. I think you mentioned in your letter that Virginia Swoope had written to me. If she has, I have not received the letter. I cannot think of anything else to write.

Your affectionate daughter,
Letitia A. Watkins

April 19, 1852
Middleton, Mississippi

Miss Letitia A. Watkins
Care of Doctor Cummings
Holly Springs, Mississippi

My Dear Child,

I received your kind letter last week. Very unexpectedly last night I received the letter you sent me of your Pa's. I was very glad to hear from him, but was so disappointed when I saw it was not from you. Why did you not write one or two lines in it to me, about yourself?

Octavia did not come out last Friday because she was going home. I will send for her next Friday if she will come out. Semira Estel was married to Joe Money yesterday morning. Mary and Susan Jenkins were her waiters. Tom Estel escorted Mary Jenkins home in his buggy last evening. Ritt saw them when she was coming home from preaching in Middleton. She said Mary Jenkins had on a pink braish dress with three or four tucks in it. Rebecca Davis is married to Dr. Sanders.

Miss Woods, sister of Mrs. Isham Scruggs, was married lately to Atlas Johnson. Bird says the day after they were married old man Johnson gave them a *chunk* of a dinner. When the bride's parents started home from the dinner, she bursted out in a great boohoo cry and cried so much her father told her husband to get their horses and carry her back home with them. She has been staying there ever since. That is the way you will do if you be so unfortunate as to ever marry.

Mr. Jack Farmer went to Blackhawk last Friday week, was taken sick, and died last Saturday. Mr. Phillips got a horse last Monday unbeknown to any one, went off, he was pursued in a day or two, and carried back home.

You think you will have a new carriage to ride in, but I think your pride will have to be lowered down to ride in the old one. It is not sold yet and no probability of it being sold. I have wished often in the last three weeks that I could ride on horseback. I want to visit some of my acquaintances. There is always some obstacle in the way when I feel like going. Poor me, I am sorrow's child. I hope you will have more enjoyment in life than I have or ever did have. Girls think if they can get married their happiness is completed. I can tell them their troubles have just begun. My motto is remain single, live at your ease and do as you please.

Mary sends her love to you and says she wants to see you and wants you to come home so she can get some good things to eat. She teased me so much to have a custard that I had to make Ritt make one. It is just done. I wish you were here to eat some of it. Martha sends howdy to you and says you must buy Siah a harp, Charlotte a doll and Milly a toy and she will pay you what you give for them when you get home. I told her I would not write to you for her, that money was not so plentiful with you. Henrietta sends howdy to you. I had about as many strawberries today as your Pa could eat at one time for dinner.

Write soon. I am very impatient for the time to arrive for you to come home.

> Your affectionate Mother,
> Sarah E. Watkins

April 20, 1852
Irving House
New York

My Dear Daughter—

I have bought the carriage & a pretty one it is. I have also bought a beautiful summer mourning dress for your mother. The carriage & piano[37] will be shipped in about ten days, & about the middle of June, if we have good luck, they both will be at our house. I start in the morning for Niagara Falls. I expect to be in Holly Springs in about ten days from date. I bought also the books you gave me a memorandum for.

Please send this to your mother.

> Your affectionate father,
> Thomas A. Watkins

37. Dr. Watkins's travels took him to New York City, where a piano and new carriage were acquired. In 1916, the huge four legs from the piano were used for making a library table. In 1968, two of Lettie's great granddaughters "divided" the table, and each has a sideboard with two of the 1852 piano legs.

June 24, 1852
Hazelgreen

Dr. Thomas A. Watkins
At Home

Dear Sir,

Your very kind note of yesterday's date was handed me by your boy and in reply will say that in case you can furnish one horse, I think I can so arrange it that my daughters will accompany Miss Letitia to Oxford.[38] I dislike giving you so much trouble, but would not feel safe in risking one of my carriage horses since they ran away with the carriage.

Should Mrs. Whitehead's health permit, I will take great pleasure in accompanying you myself.

Very truly
Yours, etc.,
W. W. Whitehead

February 21, 1853
Austin, Texas

My Dear Lettie,

Yes, I was much disappointed in not receiving a letter from you at Pulaski. But knowing you as I do, placed the reason as emanating from valid cause. I gave directions to B.W. Esq.[39] to forward on my last note to you immediately. You were absent I believe. Were you not?

And you have been to a party. I hope you enjoyed yourself. Nothing can more alleviate the pain of separation than to know that dear L is comparatively happy. Have you received no letter from me save the one from Vicksburg since I left? I wrote to you two from Pulaski. The mails are so irregular and conveniences so bad that it is almost certain nothing through the P.O. will arrive in the proper time. Perhaps they may never arrive. But now I have no apprehension but what we may correspond uninterruptedly. The Postal arrangements are very correct and straight from here to N.O. and from there to C.

You remarked that my D-type [*daguerreotype*] is not so handsome as I am. Why is that? Is it not merely my shadow? Each line—feature—and linament is placed and traced with the accuracy of sunlight. But perhaps it is because

38. Oxford, the home of the University of Mississippi, was a popular focal point for the planters, especially at commencement time.
39. Ben Wellons, Judge Wellons's son and Will Walton's friend.

I wore those *whiskers*. You do not think that I finished shaving. Thought that I had better *taste* than to wear the *goatee*. Oh! dear L, do you detest the thing so much that their unredeeming qualities cannot be reclaimed, even by him who hears them? I told the "*Scapegrace*" of a *Typist* that it made me look as though I wore "hair on my chin." But he said "no" the picture would look unnatural if the shadow were not there. When I first saw the "*locket*" after it was finished, it seemed to have a *beard*. But it was not so. It is the shade of the chin. Look close dear L, and you will see that it is as I say. I cannot blame you for thinking it were as you wrote. Yes, I do in truth have more *taste* than to wear such a thing. So do not be alarmed, you shall never see me with one on! No, never. You could not *love me* half so well. Oh! dear Lettie, do not talk of halving our love. It is holy—true—and *sublime*. Change it and thin air is the consequence. Love the less I cannot. Love the more tis impossible. For with the deepest affection of the soul and the fullest powers of the mind do I love thee.

No, I am not mad with you. Nor will I be, so long as reason holds her doubtful sway upon the throne of my mind. What I could be mad with you for is inconceivable. If it were so, you know I would tell you. But you further know that I will never so do. For good reasons too. That is, I'll never be mad with you. I knew that Mr. Young[40] was somewhat *moonstruck* with your appearance. He saw that there was something behind the scene with us, not yet acted. I did not think he would discover as much, but so he did. He attempted in that blunt offhand manner to joke me when returning to town the day we left. But surely I cooled all his fears upon the then interesting subject of your *love*. And he too made none the wiser by it. I somewhat admire the tenacity with which Mr. Barksdale pursues. You did right in answering his letter I suppose. Of course, you wrote in positive terms. There is no necessity to negotiate with one upon such a subject, when your *love* is given to another. I know you will pursue the wiser course in all such matters. At least I shall ratify all things done in the premises and sustain them too by the proper means. Barksdale seems really anxious. Sent a servant did he? Wanted to ride with you up to G [*Grenada*]?—Well! Well! I would give something right handsome to have that time with you. Would it not be a treat to meet for even a short time? Mr. Young thinks that you are no longer "*free*." I know not what he calls freedom. But if to love when and where we please be freedom, then you have it in the fullest sense. You love me. You have seen good so to do. You see proper to continue so to do. Is not that freedom? I'm *free*. Free to love you and you alone. I would love none other. Though we are not permitted to consummate our love by the final action, owing to opposition from a very

40. Young and Barksdale, old boyfriends.

potent quarter, yet we can love—love continuing forever. I have no doubt myself but what we will marry—none in the world. My whole soul is bent upon that. My future hopes are based upon it. Do not despair! I know you will view all things in a reasonable light. We are both young. The world—the future is all before us. Perhaps happiness is there hidden in some unknown spot. There is an oasis in every desert. A healing balm for every wound. Let our watchword be "patience and constancy." The clouds which obscure our horizon will fade away. The sun of love will spring out in all the glorious effulgences of native youth. And then dear L, a long and happy life together must be the consequence.

I much admire the friendship of Miss Mary [*Whitehead*] as it is exhibited in our behalf. I never knew her before. I was almost an entire formal acquaintance of hers until the night before we came to you. Will you be so kind as to return my compliments and respects. Confidence which I have placed in her I feel confident is in safe and secure hands.

So far as it being easy to have gotten a *"Lady,"* there I know not. I never observed any evidences of easy conquest. It all matters little now, as I saw proper to love you and have a confession of reciprocation. You know we all have certain indescribable and undefinable preferences. There is something about you which did suit and now suits my fancy—and that so well too, that none other can suit half as well.

Yes, you may call me *Will* if you wish. I am tired of cold Mr. *Walton.* Don't it look so formal? Is not all formality done away with between us? Yes, call me Will, dear Will. I will call you dear Lettie at all hazards. "What in the world did you ever love me for you ask?" Why, *goodness alive,* good taste—what else could have prompted me? Do you think that I could pass dear L by and not love her?

Do not even let your own inward and most secret thoughts whisper forgetfulness! You do not, nay you cannot, believe that I will forget you. That were one of the impossibilities. I have no fear that you will either neglect or forget me. You must have been convinced of my love entirely—or else yours would have never been confessed. Is it not so dear L? Ah! I know it.

You think that I would not be willing to live in Mississippi for your sake. Now dear L, you know I offered to throw all this Texas notion to the wind, if we were married. I should have remained in Mississippi all the time.

But when our union was opposed by parents—duty to myself—duty to you—duty to all concerning or relating to us in any way, bid me to proceed upon this trip. In another letter, I will detail to you some of the many advantages consequent to you and myself (if we are married) from this move on my part. You know that I would be willing to live and die with you at any given place—if to live at any given place were placed as the obstacle to our union. For your sake, I can and will do many things. When I come back, all things will be arranged for your home. When you consent to marry me, notwithstanding all opposition or the consent of your parents is obtained, then we will select our home. That will be with you mostly—after you are fully informed as to the advantages of each action. I know your good sense will always do me justice. At least I fear nothing on that score. If Mississippi can afford you more happiness, you know my wish for your welfare and peace of mind will prompt the proper action.

Why did I attempt to kiss you? Why, just because, I wanted to do so. I love Thee so, and then not kiss you. I wish I were in reaching distance now, I would learn you who would attempt the second time. Why did you not let me kiss you on the lips? Answer me that will you?

You asked if I cried at parting—yes, I cried, but twas not from the eye. The heart bled—the soul wept. All my better nature dropped in sadness. When, oh when, will we meet again? You alone shall be the summoner to your side—bid me return and see my bride—I come upon the wings of joy and gladness. When will you tell me to return? In the spring of '54 I have set for the longest time. It will not be later than October before I will be so situated as to take you home. Yes, take you dear Lettie to my home—and then our homes will be the same. Will not that be joyous? To live amid your smiles (through this otherwise, black, and inhospitable world) will be an Elysium upon earth.

I wish I had gone to the Judge's with you now too. But a few hours with you pass away so soon that I can hardly note it down. Yes, I came to Texas by land. I had never been the land route and thought I would like to see the inland country. I thought for a long time that I would come by Judge W. [*William Whitehead*] then but knew that it would be late before I could get there—and that being the evening you intended to return, I feared we might miss one another. And then too, the meeting was bound to be short—perhaps it is well that we met not. 'Twould all be the same now.

I will send at convenient times during our correspondence all the notes I took on the way. I shall write every week. You must do the same. Who was it who asked you at the party if I was an admirer of yours? I believe no one knows in Carrollton of our engagement except Ben Wellons and Miss Mary Whitehead. I was compelled to disclose to B.W. in order to secure our correspondence. Then we will let it remain dark 'til our consummation day. I do not think we have anything to fear from B.W. He will assist correspondence or anything, but never disclose to living being.

Judge Wellons was not sick when I left. He was well and hardy. I love the old man. Fatherly care he has exercised over me. He cried as a child left by its mother when Brother and myself left. He loved us as his own sons. May his grey hair rest in peace when he is called away.

I hope you may enjoy yourself at Grenada. Ruinzi [*a novel*] ends very sadly. I told you of that before. But he lived a glorious life. Filled with high deeds of noble daring and scenes of excitement. Surrounded by danger at all times, he braved them all and died to save his country but failed. Well, so it is with all things. We rise to fall. "We bloom today, tomorrow die." But let us make the most of life. Twill soon be over.

I arrived here last evening. After being on the way very nearly 6 weeks. Though I can be at your side in 9 days by crossing the Gulf—by way of New Orleans. When I return, I shall come that way. I do not know that you will receive this before your return from the South.

I want all your face and features. Do not have on any Bonnet. I want all thy lovely face. If I could get an answer from you before you leave, I should meet you in New Orleans. If you get this before you leave, write me about the time you will be there and where you will stop. If we can understand one another, we will meet there.

Would it not be better for us to correspond through Miss M.W. instead of B.W.? Would it not be safer from discovery and would you not receive them more regularly?

I shall hire out my negroes until October when I will place them on a farm and put them to work. I have a good house in Austin now. But of course will have one built in the country if you prefer it. This is beautiful country. Around the city and through it flourish evergreen, Live Oak, and Cedar. Oh! we can be so happy here. Will you come and live with me? Undying love shall by thine. Write each week! I will surely. Be sure and send your D-type from New Orleans.

Yours as ever in love,
Will

March 6, 1854
Carrollton, Mississippi

Mrs. Lettie A. Walton
Austin, Texas
Care of Mr. William Walton

My Dear Child,

I received your letter last Thursday and was very glad to hear from you. I have nothing interesting to write you. I have seen very few people since you left. Mrs. Echols spent the day with me the Sunday after you left. The next

Friday Abram went for Baby, came back without bringing her and said she was sick and not well enough to come out. I went in for her the next morning expecting to find her quite sick. When I got to McWilliams' she had gone to Mrs. Smith's. I went there for her. When we got down to the street that turns to go to Mrs. Smith's, the horses got frightened at the group of men that was standing at the stores. I thought the carriage would turn over. I said somebody stop the horses. Someone came up and took hold of them. John Stevens[41] and Bill Witty came to the carriage. I got out and Mr. Stevens walked with me to Mrs. Smith's. I felt so hurt at the horses acting so and I all alone.

There was a letter received from Mr. Jones[42] yesterday. He mentioned that Brother had five spasms and they turned to the palsy. He lost the use of one side and it affected his speech and mind. He is recovering slowly.

Mr. Baskerville Vaughn is dead. Your Papa got very angry at seeing Mr. Walton's writing on the back of your letter. He said if it was not for the respect he had for me, he would have throwed it down and stamped it. He says if he sees any more of his writing, he will not take it out of the [post] office. He told me to write you to direct your letters you write me to Middleton. That he does not want to see none of your letters. He will not carry nor bring them, he never wants to hear from you, and if you and Mr. Walton were to come in his house, he would kick you both out if he died directly afterwards. He says he never will forgive you for the way you acted in deceiving him. He says he was not for your marrying so much for riches, he wanted you to marry in a respectable family.

Oh Lettie, you have made a kind father angry and destroyed the happiness of a heartbroken mother. I never can get over my grief—it will carry me to my grave. What helps to distress me more was my knowing of your being engaged and keeping it a secret from your Papa. I shall forever reproach myself for permitting you to go on as you did. It was so imprudent of me as a mother to suffer you to correspond with one that I was opposed to your marrying. If I had known that you would marry without our consent I would not have kept it secret from him. I used all the influence I could to break it off but could not.

Lettie, when you first left me it distressed me almost to death that I had not told your Pa and knew you were expecting Mr. Walton. The love I had for you and you wishing me not to tell him prevented me from telling him. He asked me the week after you left if I knew it. I had to tell him I did but you

41. The same John Stevens who had been Lettie's early beau.
42. Dr. Watkins's kinsman, Col. Richard Jones of Courtland, Alabama, father–in–law of "Fighting Joe" Wheeler, cavalry general of Confederate War fame.

told me in confidence and I could not tell him. My mind was relieved in a great degree after I told him that much.

There is one thing I hope he will not find out how you got your letters. I would not have him to know that I knew of your receiving any. He has asked but I turned it off some way. He thinks you got them from Middleton. There are so many busy people, I am afraid he will find it out.

My dear child, you have acted wrong. You ought not to have treated your Pa as you did. You deceived him too much. It distresses me so much the way my beloved child has gone. I never can enjoy your company again. It almost kills me to think of it, that my child could leave her mother and love another better. You are always in my mind. My distress is great, but your Pa being so angry with you makes it greater. It is my prayer to God that you may do well and become a Christian and if we never meet in this world may we meet in heaven.

Mary sends her love to you and says you must write to her. Poor child is very much grieved at your marrying and going away. Henrietta sends her love to you. Don't show my letters. Direct your letters to Middleton.

Your affectionate Mother,
Sarah E. Watkins

CHAPTER THREE

A Long Road toward Reconciliation

Lettie, now Mrs. William Walton, has moved to Austin, Texas. She and her new husband departed Greenwood by riverboat, which took them to New Orleans, where they boarded a ship for Galveston. From there they went up the bayou by boat to Houston and then travelled by stagecoach to Austin.

Lettie's father's anger dominates much of the correspondence that immediately ensues. That the mother had known of the secret engagement, and that a secret courier had been used to avoid the father's eye, fueled his anger—and his pain. Lettie immediately made an effort to reach out to her father and make amends, but he was recalcitrant. It took rather a while for Lettie fully to realize the depth of his intransigence.

In spite of her husband's attitude about Lettie's marriage, letters were frequently exchanged between Mrs. Watkins and her older daughter. They contain much detail concerning the social circuit that the Watkinses enjoyed.

Mary, the younger of the Watkins daughters, begins to be a correspondent. Her writing efforts are impressive considering her tender age. Also they reflect the gloom that often prevails at the Watkins home. The hurt that the father feels continues. But it soon becomes evident that almost all of the family friends, including the Whiteheads, are supportive of Lettie and her husband. More and more, it is Mary, the remaining daughter at home, who dominates the parents' thoughts.

Meanwhile, the ice eventually begins to break, and the Waltons—by the spring of 1856—will be reconciled with the Watkinses. Mrs. Watkins closed one of her letters to Lettie with a cordial greeting to young Mr. Walton. Will in turn seized an opportunity first to write to Mary ("Baby," Lettie's sister) while she was visiting Courtland, Alabama, for otherwise the doctor would have been expected to intercept the letter. The Watkins family previously had lived at Courtland, and there at this time Mrs. Watkins's brother, Col. William Fitzgerald, lay grievously ill. Will then also wrote to his mother-in-law at Courtland, and she responded after her return home.

We learn, too, of major tragedies that now befell Mrs. Watkins's close relatives. Her brother, William, succumbed to his illness, and he left his wife, Mary, deeply in debt. Mrs. Watkins's sister, Aunt Letty, who, newly widowed herself, had been living with the William Fitzgeralds, also was in dire financial straits, and she was soon forced to sell her slaves. Thus, the state of well-being for the slave-owning class could be tenuous.

March 8, 1854

Austin, Texas

My Dear Father,

We arrived in this place last Sunday. It took us five days to come from Houston here. We are now staying with a very fine family by the name of Glasscock. He is a nephew of the Glasscock who married Mrs. Hudson. Austin is a very pretty place everyone says very healthy. Judging from the looks of it I should think it was. Oh! Pa, the lands are so rich here and were you to see them you would never be contented to live on those poor hills in Mississippi. The land immediately around Austin is selling very high, but I am told that fine land can be got here for two & half & three dollars an acre. The two Mr. Waltons[43] have some of their hands on a farm (about half mile from the city) in partnership with the two Mr. Marshalls from Mississippi (brothers-in-law to General Acey) of Yalobusha Co. I am going to live there as soon as I can get my things ready to furnish a room. Old Mrs. Marshall will keep house.

I am very busy sewing. I have gotten a set of furniture for eighty dollars. The Mr. Waltons have six of their hands employed in the brick mason business. They have twenty-two negroes and four or five thousand acres of land here. So you see Pa, we have a plenty to begin with. They have a very nice

43. The two Mr. Waltons were her husband, William M. Walton, and his brother, George Lowe Walton.

house and lot here but George rented it out before we got here. I do not wish to keep house this year any how.

The land on this size of the Brazos River is the finest I ever saw anywhere. It is not swamp land on this side. It is just as black and rich as it can be but I am told it is sickly. The greatest objection I have to Texas is there is too much prairie and timber is rather scarce in places. Come over Pa and look at the land; if a man can't make a fortune here he never can anywhere. I am delighted with my new home, if I am blessed with good health I will be willing to spend the remainder of my days here. We have limestone water to drink—it does not agree with me. The water or something has given me the dysentery very bad though I have not been confined to my bed.

A man came from Houston in the hack who was sick all the way. It has proved to be the measles that he had. I am very much afraid I will have them. Now Pa if you wish to make money come to Texas—come to look at the land anyhow. Excuse me for writing with a pencil but there is no ink about the house—I was in a notion to write this evening. Tell Mother to *pick her geese good* and save the feathers for me for I cannot get any here. I tell you a feather bed is a rarity here in this county.

Flour is fourteen and fifteen dollars a barrel. Milk and butter is very scarce but it is nothing but carelessness for they have fine grass and plenty of water, the muskeet grass grows all about here and the prairies look like wheat fields. Coming from Houston here sometimes I could get nothing to eat but ham, fried eggs, corn bread, and something intended for coffee.

Write often—tell Mother and sister to do the same. My love to all.

Ever your affectionate daughter,
Lettie A. Walton

P.S. Oh! If I only had one cold drink of water from our spring I would feel better. This water does not quench my thirst—the more I drink the more I want.

March 20, 1854
Austin, Texas

My Dear Sister,[44]

What is the reason you nor Mother have written to me? It has been nearly six weeks since I left you and not one word have I heard from you all yet. You will scarcely think this is your sister's handwriting but, dear Baby, you must excuse the writing for I am sick in bed with the measles. It has been a week tomorrow since I took them. I traveled three or four days in a hack with a

---

44. Mollie was ten years old when Lettie wrote her this letter. Lettie was nineteen.

man that had them. I have not been very sick much of the time. I think by acting by the Dr.'s direction I will be up in a day or two. I am so hoarse that no one can distinguish anything I say across the room. Oh! how often I have wished to be near Mother during my sickness—so many little things she would think of I could get there that is not to be had here.

When I was first taken sick there was not a bit of flour to be had in Austin. I have everything very nice now but I do not feel like eating. I have not eaten a mouthful in two days. Will went to kill some birds for me this evening, maybe I can eat some tonight. Will is just as kind and attentive to me as Mother could be, he gets up all times at night and waits on me. Baby, no matter how much *others* speak against him you continue to love him. Stand up for your sister, honey. I have got the best husband in the world and if I am satisfied, other people ought to be too.

Oh! Baby, did you cry after I left you that day at school? What did all the girls say about my marrying and what did those who saw Will say about him? Write often sister and tell me everything. God bless your dear sweet little soul, I did not know how much I loved you till I left you.

Give my best love to my dear mother. Tell her to write often and not to let the prejudice of others cause her to neglect her child. My eyes are sore and I am lying down so you must excuse bad writing.

My love to Ritt, America, and all. Tell Ritt to write to me. Goodbye—goodbye. Answer immediately.

Your affectionate sister,

Lettie Walton

P.S. Will killed some very nice birds for me last evening. I ate a leg of partridge for supper. I am a good deal better today and think I will be well enough to dress tomorrow. Goodbye sister, be a good child and mind your mother. March 21st L.A.W.

April 4, 1854

My Dear Child,

I received your affectionate letter of the 13 inst. today, and received one from you over two weeks ago; I did not answer it as I had no news to write. I expect you have received one from your unhappy mother in this time.

We started from home this day week and went to Mr. Avery's the first day and the next to Mrs. Eggleston's. The family appeared very glad to see me. They inquired after you and requested me to give their love to you. We dined one day with Mrs. C. Eggleston. Mr. Sessions' family, Mrs. Judge Murry and her daughter from Natchez and Mrs. Mead dined there that day. We went to Mr. Walton's last Saturday evening, attended church in Lexington Sunday and left Mr. Walton's [45] Monday. Staid last night at Mrs. Kennedy's and came home today. She is very much distressed about Eugene, he has not returned from Florida and she has not received a letter from him in some time. She got a letter from a gentleman in Vicksburg that had been with Eugene at Tampa Bay and said he had been very sick.

Mrs. Kennedy is very anxious for your Pa to become reconciled to you. She spoke in the highest terms of Mr. Walton from what she had heard of him to your Pa. Her talking done no good. He says you deceived him so much and Mr. Walton wrote such an insulting letter to him that he never will forgive you. I have not heard him say anything about receiving your letter. He says I must write you to direct your letters to Middleton, that he does not want to see them.

You say you don't think you were wrong to marry Mr. Walton. You were very wrong to marry any man that we were opposed to. Your parents had been too kind to you for you to treat them as you did. I can't blame your Pa for being angry with you. You did treat him ill. You say I must not be distressed at his not wanting you to visit his house. My dear child, how can I keep from being distressed? It is enough to kill me but to save my feelings, I hope you never will come to his house. I can't write for crying.

If you come next winter it would give me both pleasure and grief. You would not be welcome here, and the roads will be so bad I can't go to see you unless you stay near enough for me to walk. I would walk several miles to see you. You ask if I have forsaken you. No, my dear child, I have not. But you forsook your poor Mother when you married and went off as you did. I can never get over my distress. At times I am so short breath from grief that I have to bring a long sigh to get my breath. Oh Lettie, we loved you too well for you to bring sorrow on us as you have done. I never walk in the garden without thinking of you and think if you were prepared for death I had rather visit your grave than for you to have acted as you did. I try to console myself by thinking you did not love me, or you would have taken my advice and not married so contrary to our wish. When you become a mother you will then know the feeling a parent has for a child. Your Pa has been too good to you for you to treat him with contempt. You should always speak with respect of him for the many favors he has done for you. He says he loved you not wisely but too well. He says now he has not one spark of affection for you. I don't think he ever will be reconciled to you. He is always speaking against you to me, that makes me more distressed. I often wish I could be out of his company to prevent my hearing him talk about you. He says you married in such a low

45. This Mr. Walton probably is a distant relation of Lettie's husband but was evidently not close to their family.

family after he had given himself so much trouble for you. He says he will not place his heart on Mary, perhaps she may turn out better.

The piano is advertised for sale.

Miss Wade was very glad to see us and would have come home with us if she had not been going to New Orleans shortly. I like her very much. She looked better than I ever saw her. She went to Jackson this winter. Her friend Miss Hooker invited her down to her wedding, she was her bridesmaid. There was a gentleman by the name of Dotson came home with her. I do not know if she discarded him or not. I think Dr. Hudson has addressed her. She was very much surprised when she heard of your marriage. She said she could not believe it when she first heard it.

Eldon Field killed a man by the name of Honeycutt in Lowndes County and ran off. The Governor has offered three hundred dollars reward for him.

Mrs. E. Whitehead had a daughter last Monday week.[46] Salsbury's wife had one Sunday. Adelaide Geren is very sick, not expected to live.

I have got a bonnet and two caps and a bonnet for Mary from New Orleans. Mine is fine straw dressed with white satin ribbon. Mary's is straw dressed with blue ribbon. I am sitting in your room writing. Everything in it reminds me of you. The happy hours we have been together in it will never be again. I have not seen Baby since Sunday week. She does not like to stay at home since you been gone. I tell her I think it is hard neither of my children loves me well enough to want to stay with me. She says she loves me but she has so much fun with the girls.

Write me what you wrote to your Pa and what did he write to you. Ritt sends her love to you and says Mrs. Parmele's Hannah is married. Jesse and all the house servants send their love to you. It is too troublesome to write all their messages. Are you boarding at a public house? Mrs. Echols told me to give her love to you. (Direct your letters to Middleton.)

Your affectionate Mother,
S. E. Watkins

Mary Watkins writes her sister, Lettie, in Austin, Texas:

Dear Sister,

I received your kind letter yesterday and was very sorry to hear that you had the measles. I could not keep from crying when I read your letter. I cried myself sick when you went away. I would a great deal rather be sick than for you to be sick, so far off from us. I expect you will be very much surprised to

---

46. The baby died in May 1857 of scarlet fever.

hear that Miss Evvie Davis is married to John Stevens.[47] They were married last Sunday morning, in the Baptist church. I do not know if her parents were willing or not. Her waiters were Miss Sarah Smith, Miss L. [*Lou*] Gee, Miss Elizabeth Taylor, Martha Jane Palmer. A great many people went to church to see her married. Pa, mother and myself went. Elizabeth and Virginia White-head were to have been her waiters but they would not attend.[48]

Where were you going from when you caught the measles? Are you board-ing out or keeping house? I am so glad Mr. Walton treats you kind, for not a soul in this world loves their sister better than I do you. I did not know my lessons for two or three weeks after you left us. Everyone that heard you were married was very much surprised. I never was so surprised in all of my life.

Sister, if you had died, home could not be more sad. If I ever missed anyone in my life, I miss you. Sister, you ought not to have married and gone so far from us where we never can go to see you.

L. Lockhart sends her love to you and says you must write to her. Miss Octavia Simmons has not been to see us since you have been gone. Sister, I would tell you to come to see us but pa says he never wants you to come into his house. He is so angry with you he says he will never forgive you.

I have not any news to write to you. Mother joins me in love to you, and she says she has written to you twice. Ritt, America and all of the negroes send their love to you. Good-bye, dear sister.

Your Affectionate Sister,
Mary E. Watkins

P.S. Ritt says Mrs. Phillips' Phyllis is married to a man who has had five wives. Mr. E. Whitehead's Mourning borrowed her breast pin three weeks ago to get married and the man had just asked for her. She says the girls marrying up so fast that it makes her feel three years older. She hardly ever uses her [*Ritt's*] crutch. She can walk a great deal better since you left. If she could see you she says she would tell you more than she can write you about. There was a party in Middleton last night.

Sarah Watkins to Lettie, April 26, 1854:

My Dear Child,

I received your affectionate letter last Friday and was very glad to hear from you. I was uneasy about you when I heard you had the measles, and am afraid your health will not be good again.

---

47. Time has resolved the importance of John Stevens. He married the niece of Mrs. Wil-liam Whitehead.

48. They were first cousins of the bride, and parental influence against the marriage must have been strong.

We intended going to the Messrs. Roberson's [*down river from Greenwood, Mississippi*] this week. I put up my clothes Tuesday expecting to go yesterday. It looked so much like rain we put off going until this morning. It is as cloudy today. We will defer going. I have so little news to write I thought I would delay writing until I returned from the river. As you want the receipt for making cough drops, I had better write.

I was at Judge Whitehead's last week. Mary Whitehead was sick in bed. She took cold sitting up with Adelaide Geren. Judge Whitehead and the girls inquired about you. Lettie, you must write to Mary. She is a true friend to you.

Judge Whitehead spoke in the highest terms of Mr. Walton. He said he would write to him in a few days to get him to attend a claim he has against someone in Texas. I have not heard of but one person speaking against him except your Pa and that was a lady talking to Abram. She said if she was your Pa and me she never would forgive you for treating us so that you went off with nothing.

I was to see Mrs. E. Whitehead one week before last. She has a daughter. I told her that your Pa was not willing for you to come to his house. She told me to tell you to go to her house, that her doors should be open for you.

Your Pa says if you have independence you will not come here. I don't want you never to come to his house. You know how he is. I could not enjoy myself with you if you were to come here. I told Mr. Walton when we parted that he must let you come to see me. I did not think at that time your Pa would oppose your visiting his house but he says he never wants to see you nor hear anything from you. When we receive your letters we have to keep them concealed from him. He says he would move anywhere so Mary can be raised in a better circle. He says he will not put his heart on her and maybe she will turn out better than you have. Do not think, my dear child, that I do not want to see you. Oh yes, I had rather see you than anybody in the world. I wish I could be with you always.

You say it is not worth while to grieve for spilt milk. (That is true.) But my grief is carried from something greater than can be compared to spilt milk. If you had have died I could get over it. It would have been the hand of providence. But to take yourself from me as you have done, it has given me more unhappiness than I ever had in all my life. I would not grieve if I could help it, but a Mother that loves her daughter, as I love mine, can't prevent grieving under such circumstances.

You could have lived single six years before you would have been an old maid. Don't say you were obliged to marry, people will think you had a passion for man. It is a pleasure to have a husband that loves you and one that you can confide in. I hope your husband's love will be lasting and you both may do well. I think he had rather you would not have married him, your parents being so opposed to it and you worth nothing and could do nothing.

Learn to do all you can about domestic affairs from Mrs. Marshall, it will be a great service to you. Is she not Mrs. Lacy's mother? Is lawyer Marshall that was said to be a beau of Elisa Terry, her son? Did not she and her husband part? You ask what your Pa says about the way you all left that business with Wellons. I have not heard nothing about it.

Jerry Roberson has lost eight negroes with the measles. Mrs. Martha Prince's husband is dead, killed himself drinking.

Mary is taking music yet. Her Pa says he is going to stop her from taking after this session. She is learning so well. I have had one cry about her stopping. She has your music book and can play "Wait for the Wagon" and "St. Anna Retreat." She said you would laugh at her letter and did not want to send it. I made her send it. She loves you dearly.

I have not received a letter from Ala. since last August and have not heard from Brother since before I wrote you last. Your Pa received a letter from William Watkins. He said he, Dr. Shackleford and Mrs. Shackleford are going to Texas next month to look at the country. Judge Palmer, his two sons, Mr. Conley and some others started to Texas last week. I went to Carrollton last week shopping. I wish you were here to fix the bodice of my dresses.

Henrietta walked to Mr. Echols' last Sunday. She sends her love to you. Hannah, America and all send love to you. Ritt says write her the name of your servant that you keep to wait on you.

Your affectionate Mother,
Sarah E. Watkins

Receipt for cough drops:

> One dram of gum arabic
> One ditto of licorice
> One ditto of antimonial wine
> 58 drops of laudanum
> One ounce of water

Dissolve the gum arabic and licorice in
warm water and pour it into the wine and
laudanum. A tablespoonful a dose for a
grown person twice or three times a day.

Lettie receives a letter from her mother that was begun on May 15, 1854. The theme of depression continues and the letter carries over to June 2, but she concludes with a cordial greeting to the new husband.

My Dear Child,

Your letter written the 9th of April was received yesterday week. I have little to write you but grief. I received a letter from Aunt Letty last Sunday week. She wrote me that my poor dear Brother was very low. She did not think he could live long and I must go up soon as I could. He has been confined to his bed since Feb. He has spasms at the change and full of the moon. I expect every mail to receive a letter mentioning his death. If he was prepared to die I could bear with it better. He is such a sinner and now his mind is not in a situation to prepare for death. His wife has a son named Henry. Moses is dead and old Mr. Jolly.

Mr. E. Whitehead's family, Judge Whitehead and Mary and Martha dined with us Thursday.[49] Mary rode on horseback going from here to Mr. Whitehead's. Her horse wanted to catch up with the buggys that were along. She thought he was running away with her, she jumped off and fell on her face in the road near Mrs. Jenkins'. She hurt her head, shoulder and hip but no bones were broken. I heard from her yesterday. She was in bed but better. I wish everybody was like the Whitehead family. Would there not be pleasant living with us all.

From the way you write this world is a heaven to you. I pray it may continue so. When I was first married I thought myself happy for ten months, at the end of that time my happiness ceased. No happiness for me. You have destroyed what little happiness I did have.

Mary has just come home and Octavia Simmons has come. I have to stop writing.

June 2nd—Dear Lettie, I commenced this letter two weeks tomorrow. As Octavia wrote you from here, I deferred writing until now. Yesterday week we went down to Greenwood and staid a night with Mrs. Watt. The next day we went on the steamboat to G. Roberson's. Sunday evening we went to A. Robersons' and staid until Thursday morning. We came back on the boat to Mr. Watt's and yesterday we came home. Octavia went with us. She is gone home this morning in our carriage. Laura Watt returned from Columbus last week. She has quit school. Mr. Watt has sold his place and most of his negroes. His family is living with Mr. Gunn.

I saw Mr. Conley on the boat on his way home from Texas. He told me he was introduced to Mr. Walton and he saw one of his negroes. He stuttered so that he could not understand what he said. Mrs. G. Roberson lost her youngest child with the measles. Mrs. Southworth has a daughter. Her mother died with the yellow fever in Vicksburg. Semira Money died last Monday week with

49. Judge William Whitehead's wife, Elizabeth Davis, died January 23, 1854.

a congestive chill. I heard from Brother last week, he was better. I don't think I will go to Alabama before September.

I got two valentines from Middleton post office for you. One was just verses written and the other from Oxford is very pretty. It is on satin with a looking in the middle and verses written on the blank paper. Camilla Kennedy told me her brother Tom sent it to you.

Don't have a bear for a pet, they are such dangerous ugly things. Ritt says if you keep it you will have a baby like it. Do have it killed. Ritt, America and all the negroes send their love to you.

Give my respects to Mr. Walton.

Your affectionate Mother,
Sarah E. Watkins

P.S. June 4th Mary received your letter last week and says she will write you shortly. She don't like you showing her letter to Messers. Walton. Martha Jane Palmer and Tine Lockheart came home with Baby Friday, they are gone to Mr. Echols' this evening. Jenny mule was got for Tine to ride, she started off walking. Martha Jane and Mary rode John. They said they would take it turn-about in riding.

Mr. and Mrs. Conley and Mrs. Palmer dined here yesterday. Our carriage was sent for Mrs. Summerville to come here. Mr. S. was expecting his brothers and would not let her come. Mr. Conley is very much pleased with Texas, he expects to move there.

This is a lonesome Sunday evening. I do wish you were Lettie Watkins now and was here with me. I would be so happy but that happiness I can never enjoy. Everybody I hear speak of you is anxious for your Pa to be reconciled to you. From the way he talks about you to me I am afraid he never will. I pray to God the time will come when his heart will be changed. You must become a Christian and if we can't live together on earth let us meet in heaven where parting will be no more.

I am sorry you have become such a slave to snuff that you have to use tobacco. Oh Lettie, my child, give up that abominable practice of using snuff. To see a lady with tobacco in her mouth looks so lowlife. Do keep up the character of a refined lady. It is useless for me to advise you. You will not take my advice. When Mary does anything I don't approve of I say to her "like Lettie." She tells me she will write you that when I get angry with her I throw you up to her. I am determined to keep her under my thumb if I have to chain her to my bedstead. There will be no danger of men turning her a fool. She will not be pretty—if she continues to learn as fast as she does now she will be intelligent. Her Pa will not love her as he did you. The way you have acted towards him makes hard for poor Baby. You did not care who you put in the fire so long as you kept in the frying pan. As I can't see you I will not quarrel with you. Good bye. S.E.W.

Don't show my letters to Mr. W.

August 15, 1854
Austin, Texas

Miss Mary Watkins
Courtland, Alabama

My Dear Mary,

Your sister received your letter written after you arrived at your uncle's two or three days ago. She was very glad to hear from her dear little sister, her mother, and all her good and kind relations. You gave her much joy when you wrote that her uncle Bill[50] was getting better—she loves him mighty good.

In this same letter you request me to write to you. It is with pleasure that I embrace the opportunity and shall be pleased to write to you a long time. You are very kind to me to want me to write when your Pa hates me so very bitterly. But maybe, after a while, when he knows me better and sees me prospering in the affairs of the world he will not look upon me in so bad a light and then, Baby, your sister can come to your mother's house again and be happy. She loves you all mighty well and is sorry for any of you to have trouble. This world has a great deal of care and sorrow in it. We must all act the best we can and we will be happy.

I have been thinking all the year that Lettie would be back to see you all this winter but she does not know now whether she will come or not. I want her to come for I will do everything in my power to make her happy. I will work hard to indulge her, for if I were not willing to do that, Baby, I would never have married her. I love her, Baby, better than all the world besides. She is so good, kind and affectionate that everybody loves her who knows her.

She went in the country the other day to see a distant relative of mine and left me at home. In two days I went after her. We were so glad to see one another. This is the longest time we have been from one another since we were married.

About the first of next month we are going to see some of her relatives who live about 30 miles from here. They are Mr. James C. Watkins and his family. Your cousin Martha will be there. She is married now and lives about

---

50. Sarah Epes Fitzgerald had one brother, William Fitzgerald. He is the uncle referred to here. He was born December 20, 1810; married Mary Bledsoe; and died October 1, 1854 in Lawrence County, Alabama.

100 miles from this place. We anticipate a great deal of pleasure then. There is going to be a Camp Meeting there and Lettie and I are going to attend.

Dr. Jack Shackleford and his lady have been out here. They went to see Mr. Watkins. I suppose they have returned home by this time. They are very kind people from all I can learn.

Baby, Lettie and I are mighty happy together. I have to work all the time but it makes me healthy and glad to see Lettie when I come at dinner and night. I would much rather be poor and work hard and be happy than to live any other way. You may rest satisfied that your Sister is happy. She would not change her life and condition with anybody.

Now, Baby, you must be very kind to your mother and father. They have no child but you now, and they are getting old [*Mrs. Watkins had just turned forty*] and will need all your attention and will be happy to receive little kindnesses which you will be able to give. You must study your books and learn fast and be a smart young lady. Your parents will be good to you if you will be kind and obedient to them. All the love they had for you and Lettie together will be given to you. Lettie has made them sorrow and melancholy. It cannot be that they will love her like they love you and will love you if you do right and never give them cause to discard you.

I am sorry that I was the cause of any sorrow either to your mother or father but unfortunately I have trespassed so that they will never forgive me. It is true that I was not rich and did not have a chance like a great many other young men but it is all passed now, and it is no use to talk about it.

Write when you receive this and I will be ready to answer.

I am very truly your friend,
Wm. W. Walton

September 2, 1854[51]

My Dear Child,

I received your affectionate letter written July 3rd since I have been here. As Mary had written to you and Mr. Walton, I delayed writing. Mary received a letter from you lately. She commenced very determined to answer it. She wrote about a page; she can't steady herself long enough to finish it.

I have had several of my acquaintances to see me since I have been here. I have no way of returning their calls. Mr. Campbell keeps the Chylibeate Springs. Several families from the valley board with him, it is three miles from here. There was a party out there last night, it is the third one that has been

---

51. Lettie's mother writes her from Mountain Home, Alabama. Sarah and Mary had gone to see about Sarah's brother, Col. William Fitzgerald; his sister is Aunt Letty. "Uncle Billy" was Capt. William Fitzgerald, Aunt Letty's husband.

given there lately. The gentlemen carry the school girls in their buggys to them from the Institute.

Aunt Letty has but one boarder. She is Martha McGhee, her parents live near Moulton, Alabama. They were very well acquainted with Mr. Walton's grandfather[52] and his family. Cousin Patty Leigh was married last month to Cousin Paschal Ligon. They were married early in the morning and came to his father's. Her sister Mrs. Burleson died in June in child bed. Her infant died since. Mrs. Dr. Jenkins died last month with milk leg. Bob Elliot and his wife have parted. We heard she stabbed him week before last. Property was the cause of it. The root of all evil.

Brother is not as low as he was last winter. He is yet very sick. I don't think him as well now as he was when I came here. He has been able to put on his clothes and lie on a bed in the passage. For the last two weeks he has not been able to leave his bed. The Dr. thinks he has dropsy in his head. He seems to be in his right mind but he can't call nothing by the right name. He knows everybody but can't call their names except Aunt Letty's, his wife's, mine and some of his children's. He has had two spasms since I have been here. It was the most distressing sight I ever saw. He is always uneasy for fear of having one, he is so much afraid of dying. Poor Aunt Letty has so much trouble. It distresses me that it is not in my power to assist her in her difficulties. Lucinda was sold last month. Mr. Acklin bought her and sent her to his mother's near Huntsville.

Mary received a letter from her Pa this week. He wrote that Judge Whitehead had gone to Tennessee to marry Miss Arnold, one of the teachers of the Middleton school.[53] Adelaide Geren is dead. Conley has moved to Greenwood to merchandise. John Stevens had gone there to be a clerk for him. Judge Palmer and his children are going to move to Texas this fall. It is reported Jimmy Davis and Mary Buchanan is to be married and Dr. Holeman to Miss Bennett.

Your Pa wrote to Baby that he was very glad to see she showed some affection for him, that her sister never did, and he was done with her forever. You ask me if I never talk to your Pa to get him reconciled to you. My dear child, if I were to say anything to him in your favor, it would do no good but make him mad with me. He says the same of you that you do of him. If you loved your parents you could not have gone off from them as you did. I frequently shun his company to keep from hearing him talk about you. It is so distressing to me the way he talks about you. He says he will never forgive

52. George Walton and his wife, Rebecca Isaacs.
53. The judge's first wife died January 23, 1854. He and his second wife, Martha Arnold, had five children; three survived to adulthood. Martha's brother, Charles, married the judge's daughter, Mary.

you. Mr. Jones and Mrs. Paul Watkins say they want to see him to talk to him about being so opposed to you and try to get him to be friendly with you. Mr. Jones says he has written to him about it and he intends writing again. From what he has heard of Mr. Walton, he has a very good opinion of him. Aunt Letty says she was not opposed to your marrying so much against the wish of your parents. What she has heard of Mr. Walton she thinks you have married a very worthy gentleman. She thinks he must be a gentleman as everybody speaks well of him. She is glad you married the one you love and thinks him worthy of you. She is anxious for you and him to come see her. She says she wishes you were here to eat some pig. If she had any way to send it she would have one roasted and send it to you. She says you must write to her.

Mrs. Bledsoe, her sons, John and Henry, expect to move to Texas next month.

I expect to go home the last of this month. Your Pa wrote to Mary that I must write to him when I get my visit out. He will meet us at Aberdeen or Lagrange, Tenn. I hate traveling by myself. When I marry again I will marry a gentleman that loves me enough to go with me as seldom as I visit.

You must have patience with your maid. It is not the most whipping that does good if she has not the knowledge to do anything. You can't learn her by whipping. You must govern your temper. I know how you are. She is young, you can't expect a child to do as a grown person, particularly one that has not been taught to do things as you want them done. I carried America with me to Mrs. Eggleston's and Mr. Roberson's. She done very well. Ritt begged so hard to come with me. I had to bring her. She has mended very much. She sends her love to you . . . Becca has miscarried since I left home.

The family joins Mary and myself in love to you and Mr. Walton. Tell Mr. Walton I received his letter and will answer it.

Joe Ayers was a white man working at old Stevens and got a child by Winney Stevens. I asked Mrs. Whitehead to send your letters to me if any came to Middleton.

> Your affectionate Mother,
> Sarah E. Watkins

November 9, 1854
Middleton, Mississippi

Mr. William Walton
Austin, Texas

Esteemed Sir:

I hope you will not take it amiss my not answering your respectful letter before this. When I received it I was staying with my beloved sick brother whose situation was so distressing to me I could not compose my mind to write you. Your letter was received with a great deal of pleasure and would have been answered before this time if I had not met with an accident on my way home from Alabama. The stage turned over and I got badly hurt. I was detained at Oxford three weeks and just got home last Sunday. You say as a mother you know I have good and sufficient reasons to condemn you and despise you. No, Mr. Walton, I do not despise you. I respect you as the husband of my daughter. I must be candid and acknowledge I was opposed to Lettie marrying you. Lettie knew my objections and can tell you, I expect she has told you, I could not be willing for my daughter to marry any gentleman that her father was so much opposed to. Lettie could not have married a gentleman with a purer character than yourself. Every person speaks in the highest praise of you. I showed your letter to several of my friends, all that read it said it showed you were a man of sense and advised me to write you a friendly letter. I was disposed to write you a very friendly letter without their advice.

If my husband would become reconciled to you and Lettie and suffer her to visit his house, I would be happier. As it is I never can be happy to be deprived of my dear child, perhaps for life. She can't come to see me and it will never be in my power to visit her. It is enough to break any mother's heart. When you and Lettie become parents you will know the feeling a parent has for their child. I hope you and Lettie will continue to live happy with each other and prosper in temporal and spiritual welfare.

Please tell Lettie I started from Alabama the first day of October. My poor brother was taken worse an hour after I left him, he had a spasm and then revived and would answer questions that were asked him and begged Aunt Letty not to leave him. He told her he was very sick from his head to his stomach and would die. He had two more spasms and died at 12 o'clock. When I parted with him that morning I had no idea he would die that day. I think being distressed parting with me caused him to have spasms. They were so severe he was too weak to bear with them. If he had been prepared to die, I could bear with it but he was a sinner.

My aunt's letter mentioning brother's death was received here while I was at Oxford. I did not know of my brother's death until yesterday. Her letter was handed me by Dr. Watkins. I am here alone, no husband, no child to grieve with me. Mary is at school in Middleton.

Give my love to Lettie, tell her I am very anxious to hear from her. She must write soon, I will write to her shortly.

Accept my love for yourself.

Your affectionate mother-in-law
Sarah E. Watkins

Edmunds Grey Whitehead, the nearest neighbor to Dr. Watkins, asks for a little neighborly help:

March 8, 1855

Dear Sir, if you will not want to use your carriage tongue for the next ten days, it will oblige me very much to have the use of it. I started this morning for Holly Springs and got near Carrollton when a treetop fell near me and frightened my horse and the mules very much, and the Boy caught the hind wheel of my buggy with his carriage and made a perfect smash of the wheel and broke the carriage tongue. If you can loan yours, please let the Boy bring it over with him.

I have also to apologize to you for taking the liberty of asking your old man Abram to assist my Boy to get the buggy over to Town. I hope it will make no difference. He came up immediately after the accident occurred.

Respectfully yours, etc.,
E. G. Whitehead

Mother to Lettie:

June 1, 1855

My Dear Child,

I received your letter written May 1st this dayweek and the one written in April three weeks. I have been busy making Mary a swiss muslin dress for the examination that prevented me from writing you before now. I am very sorry your health is so bad. I think if you could go to a mineral spring and use the water it would cure you of the mange. Your being unwell I expect is caused from weakness. It was three or four months before I was well after the birth of you and Baby. I took quinine and vitrol[54] mixed together three times a day. My afterbirth was pulled away, a piece of it as large as a hen's egg came from me the next day. A piece of skin like a gut as long and big as my finger hung

---

54. Probably vitriol of iron, iron sulphate, helpful for anemia.

down several days. Patty cut it off with the scissors. Your Pa said it was one of the watery tags that hang to the womb. Martha says she had a pressure below and was unwell for three months after the birth of her last child.

Cream and parsley stewed together is good for sores, try it when you have that breaking out, if it does no good it can't do no harm. If you have no cream, fresh butter without salt will do. The flies are so troublesome I can scarcely write. We have had two good rains in the last three weeks which will help the crops very much. Crops and everything has been suffering for rain. I never did see as warm weather in May. We have had only one small mess of straw-berries this year and cherries enough for one tart. We have had raspberries for three days. I wish you were here today to eat raspberries and simblins[55] for dinner. There are two cucumbers on the vine large enough to eat. If you were here you might eat them. I am saving them for dear Baby tomorrow.

What luck have you raising chicklings. As usual I have very poor luck, I have very few. I had great many turkeys hatched, several of them have died.

I have taken Glasgow from that man. He is living here, I believe he wanted to come home to live. He has found out that he lives as easy here as any-where else.

I received a letter from Aunt Letty. She had been very sick and was still feeble and was in a great deal of trouble. Joe and Peggy was sold to the doctor. Aunt Letty hires them from him. Robin was to be sold in three weeks. She don't think he will sell for much. Dr. Watkins wrote to Mr. Jones if he does not sell too high to buy him for him and Aunt Letty can hire him. The negroes she sold to pay the debts the court has decided that the title is good only for her life time and they are liable to be sold after her life time. She said she needs a friend. She can't keep anymore than the law allows her. From her letter I can't understand whether the negroes she sold had been returned to her or not. All of Tillie's family were sold but Martha and Nancy and Sarah. I don't know of them being sold. It distresses me very much that it is not in my power to assist my Dear Aunt that has been a mother to me. The last time I wrote her I asked her come to [*sic*] and live with us. I think she hates to leave Brother's children and will not quit them if she can help it.

Mr. Davis you spoke of, I saw him once at Uncle Billy's. He boarded there a short time. I think he was editor of a newspaper in Columbus the year we lived there. His is the man Hannah's sister Sally told us cursed Brother so much. He said he loaned him money and Brother went off without paying him. He was not at my wedding that I know of. Is he related to Mr. Walton's father or mother?

Paul Watkins has bought the tar springs and will live at them soon as he

55. Simlins are round squash with a scalloped edge.

can have them fixed. His daughter, Amelia Antoinette Mumford died in Memphis last winter.

Judge Palmer carried his son John to the lunatic hospital in Jackson as deranged. He came back two weeks ago and is running at large; before he was carried to Jackson he went into Ory's office one night where some men were gambling, stoled Ory's money and went to his father's plantation near Middleton. The money was missed. The men went out to the plantation after John and made him give up the money. One of the negro men, seeing the men after John, went to town to inform his master of it. Judge Palmer started out there and met the men returning to town. It is said not to be the first money he has stolen. He stole some from Mr. Conley. Judge Palmer looks more serious, the rest of the family looks the same.

I dined at Judge Whitehead's in April, went to Maj. Hawkins' in the evening and staid until the next evening. I like Mrs. Hawkins very much. She said I remind her of you. Maj. Hawkins said you were a general favorite, he liked you and Mr. Walton. Why is it you are liked and nobody cares for me?

E. Whitehead has built near the school house that Elizabeth Jenkins taught school at and has moved to it. They have but three rooms. I believe he intends having another house built.

I am very anxious to see you and your child but am glad you will not come this summer. The river has been so low that the boats could not get up from New Orleans. So many accidents befall the steamboats it is dangerous to be on them.

Corn is scarce with good many of the farmers and sells at a dollar and a half a bushel. Flour sells at $14.00 a barrel. It would be a pleasure to me to visit you. It is out of my power, my dear child, to go so far as Texas. I have not the means to carry me there and back. I have heard no more about Booth and his wife going to Texas. I do wish you would get Mr. Walton to move nearer so I could go to see you. I have dreamed twice lately of being with both my children. Oh, I was so happy but when I waked it was all a dream. Will those dreams ever be realized? I am afraid not in this world, I pray it may be in heaven. I would have my likeness and Baby's taken for you if I could meet with an opportunity. I would like very much to have yours, Mr. Walton's and your sweet baby's.

Why don't you write to Mary Whitehead. She is a true friend of yours. You must write to her. Baby was sick last week with a cold. She was not well Tuesday when she went to school, she will come home to night. She is so much company for me.

Several of the negroes have had diarrhea it seems to be a disease going through the family. My eyes are sore from sewing. I have joined the church.

Lettie, do quit using snuff, it will kill you. I was so glad [*when I*] thought you had quit. If you were to smell Ritt's breath it would incense you so much against it you would stop using it. Her breath smells like duck dung. Tell Will he must not buy any for you. Make you angry about it and you will quit. Give my love to Mr. Walton and kiss your baby for me every day.

Abram's health is about the same as when you left. Sally, Ritt, America and all send their love to you.

Your affectionate Mother,
Sarah E. Watkins

Write soon.

Sarah writes again on June 3, 1855, sending this with the June 1 letter.

June 3, 1855

My Dear Lettie,

I attended Methodist church today in Middleton. Saw Mrs. Phillips and Mrs. Farmer. Mrs. Phillips asked me why I did not visit her. I told her I seldom went from home. She said she could come to see me but she did not like to go where she did not feel welcome, that she was surprised when she heard Dr. Watkins had anything against her or her family, that she did not think I was unfriendly to them. I told her I thanked her for her kindness to you. Envy was the cause of it all. She said she did not suspect anyone of telling anything to him about her, she knew she had given no cause.

I told her it would not do to take everybody for a friend that smiled in her face. She proposed for us to meet at Judge Whitehead's someday and have a talk. She spoke very affectionately of you. Said all her family, black and white, liked you.

Mrs. Farmer's health is better. Wash Rowe is in jail in Carrollton for selling whiskey to negroes.

Mary went back to school this morning. I am very lonely. This is the time I have the blues. If you were to see your poor mother you would be astonished to see how old and ugly she looks. Going on into today I asked Baby if my cap looked well in my bonnet. She said yes, but there are a plenty of gray hairs showing. I remarked to her I had grief and trouble enough to make me gray. It is said old Mrs. Hill is dead.

America is sick with diarrhea not dangerous, Hannah is too.

Your loving Mother,
S. E. Watkins

The mother writes Lettie again July 4, 1855:

My Dear Child,

I received your letter of May 20th over three weeks ago: I did not wait for news that is something I seldom hear, but for a little time to answer it.

The examination [*school exam for Mary*] in Middleton was last Tuesday, Wednesday and Thursday. We attended every day. I staid Thursday night to the concert; Mary bore a very good examination. She has staid ahead of her classes. She is not pretty. If she continues to learn as fast, she will be intelligent. That is preferable to beauty. She is sitting by me making a dress for Milly. I have to stop writing now and then to show her. This is the worst time I could chose to write. The negroes have their barbecue today. I am annoyed by them for they keep coming in for something to barbecue.

We have just eaten the first ripe watermelon we have had this summer. I wish you were here to eat some of it. I have had some ripe muskmelons, there are no early apples nor peaches. Ritt says our early apple trees are dead.

I saw Octavia Simmons the last day of the examinations. I was so glad to see her. I had the pleasure to read a letter from you she received that day. It put me in better spirits to hear your health was improving.

Your Pa did not know of your having a baby until the reception of your last letter to me. I asked him if bathing was good for a falling of the womb, he said it was and asked who had that. I told him you had it and had not been well since the birth of your child and told him the age of it. He says inject often with red oak tea with alum in it. It is very good for it. Much exercise nor traveling is not good for it. He says the warm climate is the cause of that breaking out you have. He commenced blaming you for going off and I stop talking to him about you. He thinks Miss Wade done badly and says you done worse.

Mr. McDonell was here lately, he was just from Texas. Pa asked him if he saw or heard from you or Mr. Walton, he said to me it was the first time he had inquired about you all and it was just curiosity when he did inquire. McDonell said he inquired for all of you of Mr. Chandler, he told him you were living eight miles from Austin. Mr. Chandler regrets very much Mr. Walton not liking the profession of law better and is quitting the practice. She said he was a smart man and if he had continued with them in a few years he might have one of their places if they should go out, that he can make more by law in three years than by farming in the ten years. Your Pa said it was a great faux pas for him. He says it will be (*the same as happened to*) Judge Wellons: he will spend his property and . . . he will come to nothing. I hope Mr. Walton will do well and they will see that they are mistaken in their prediction.

Lizzie and Ginny Whitehead returned from Holly Springs last Saturday. I spent the day with them yesterday at their father's. Oh, what a happy family they seemed to be. I did wish I was happy as they looked to be. My heart string is broken and never can I expect happiness in this world. Elic McCarroll and A. Keys went to Mr. Whitehead's Monday and staid until last evening. Mr. Keys is as handsome as ever. Baby played [*the piano*]. I have something sweet to tell you. Keys was playing cards, he turned round two or three times and looked at her as if it reminded him of the past.

I dined at Judge Palmer's Thursday. I heard him say that E. McCarroll told him he brought Mr. Keys with him and he was worth *20,000* dollars. Palmer said he is of a good family too.

Sarah Smith starts today to visit her Uncle Dr. Smith. She will not teach music in Middleton anymore. It is thought her and Eugene Kennedy will be married. It is said Lou Gee is engaged to Dr. Taylor, some say to Bill Witty.

There is to be a party in Shongalo tonight and a ball in Carrollton. Baby has a ticket to the ball, it is the first time she has had. She is anxious to go to it and wishes she could dance. She says ask Mr. Walton why he did not write her a composition and send it for the examination. She slipped off one of your compositions and gave it to one of the girls.

Mrs. Bird [*overseer's wife*] had a son last week. Semira had a son two weeks tomorrow. Becky like to have had one in the field yesterday, her water broke. Nancy had to lead her home. She is doing well today. Most all of the negroes have had it [*falling of the womb*]. Martha says blackjack bark made in a tea and inject with it is good for falling of the womb. Abram sends howdy to you and is very much obliged to you for the dollar. He say he will try to keep it always.

Mary says you must write to her. She joins me in love to you and Mr. Walton. Kiss the baby for us. Baby says be sure to come to Miss. next fall if you can't come before. All the negroes send their love to you.

Your affectionate Mother,
Sarah E. Watkins

P.S. What was Mrs. G. Walton's maiden name?

My Dear Child,

The last letter I received from you was written the 24 of July, I wrote you the day I received it. I had sealed my letter before it came. I have not heard from you since I received Mr. Walton's letter. Why don't you write? It makes me uneasy not hearing from you. I sent for Baby, Friday, [*Mary is boarding in Middleton and attending school*] and looked with great anxiety for her to come and expected a letter from you. I was disappointed in both. It was nearly dark when Jesse got back. I went to the gate expecting to see her. It looked so much like rain she would not come. She came home two weeks ago through a very hard rain, the wind blew very hard. She said it most blowed her off the mule. She out-rode Mingo that went of her, when she got to the gate she got straddle and opened it.

I walked that same day to Mr. E. Whitehead's and spent the day there with Mrs. Hawkins, Mrs. Foulks & Octavia Simmons. They were coming home with me in the evening. It rained so I had to stay all night. Mrs. Hawkins was uneasy about her children she left at home. She was afraid they were in the bad weather going from school. I was very sorry I could not get them to come home with me the next day. Mr. Whitehead brought me home in his buggy. Baby took Siah behind her and came over to Mr. Whitehead's the next morning. We all thought she was a lady riding up.

Octavia has fallen off and looks paler, she is pretty. I like Mrs. Hawkins and Mrs. Foulks very much. Mrs. Foulks told me to write you to come to Miss. that you could come to her house & I could go there & be with you & we could enjoy each other's company to ourselves if we wish it, that she has a large house. Mrs. E. Whitehead says you must come, she will have room for you. I told them what I had written you about coming. They said I ought not to have written to you in such a way.

I am very anxious to see you. The yellow fever is so bad the way you would come I can't advise you to come while that is raging. I grieve so much about you at times it gives me a shortness of breath. You know now the feeling a mother has for her child as you are a mother. I love my children too much. I often wished I had become angry with you before you married, maybe it would have prevented you from giving me so much sorrow. Lizzie & Jenny Whitehead staid all night with me last night week. Some beaux came to their father's & Mrs. Whitehead sent for them soon after dinner this day week.

Sarah Smith is married to Eugene Kennedy, his health is very bad. It is said Tom Purnell is to be married to Camilla Kennedy next winter. Fanny Nelson was married at prayer meeting one Wednesday night to Mr. Dismuke. Mrs. Judge Whitehead has a son two weeks old. Laura Whitehead has gone to Somerville, Tennessee to school.

Your Papa has been gone to Tennessee three weeks, I am expecting him home every minute. Amos sprained his ankle, his walking on it inflamed it and caused it to rise. Dr. Sanders has been out three times to see him. He opened it the last time he came. I never saw so much matter run out of a place. He can't walk on it yet.

Joe came to me just now with one side of his face swollen for something to rub it. Bird made Joe lie on a log & whipped him last month. Saturday he talked of taking his [*Joe's*] breeches down & whipping his behind. If he had done it, I would have insulted him.

Our corn crop is good, the drought injured the cotton some, 22 bales have been sent off. By selling the old corn this spring we commenced using new corn last month. I have not tried the potatoes yet. We made fine Irish potatoes. You done badly in raising chickens from fifteen hens. I raised very few, I lost most of my best hens. I have turned out several pullets and roosters for next year. Lynn Hemingway sent me a half Shanghai rooster & pullet. I have a full breed Shanghai rooster that was hatched here. I have raised ten guinea fowls & 2 turkeys, 3 goslings & a few ducks.

We have some very large apples, I wish you had them, they rot on the trees. There were very few peaches here.

Baby did not go the party in Carrollton. John Steven & Evve [*Davis*] are living at her father's. Baby gave your composition to Julia Gary. She read it at the examination. Baby did not have one, she was not compelled to have one. Ann Bailey is to be married to West Gary & Tom Bailey to Mary Barrow next month.

Harry Ann had a boy last Oct. named Mitchell. Else has a boy named Robin, Becky has one named Charles, Semira has one named Willy. Polly is in the family way. I am out of pens, my pen is so bad I can hardly write. My back aches, I must stop. Kiss your sweet child for me. Give my love to Mr. Walton. All the servants send love to you & say they want to see you & your child.

Your affectionate Mother,
Sarah E. Watkins

P.S. At the examination someone stole Mr. Walton's likeness[56] from Baby. She cried & was mighty distressed about it Write soon. Did Will Patton marry a widow?

In the months following the death of Elizabeth Davis Whitehead in January 1854, to September 1855, Judge Whitehead remarries and has a new son. The judge's daughter, Laura, has gone to Somerville, Tennessee, to school.

A short note to Dr. Watkins on November 17, 1855:

Dear Sir,

We are obliged to you for kind invitation to let the girls spend the evening with you, but fear it may not be in their power to do so. We got notice yesterday that we would have some company today ourselves, and should they come, will not leave before tomorrow.

---

56. When Will Walton went to Austin in January 1853, he had his "likeness" made in Vicksburg, put in a locket, and sent to Lettie. It was found; Eugenia Richards has it today.

Should the weather prevent their coming in today, I will send them over this evening.

Respectfully yours,

E. G. Whitehead

Mrs. Watkins writes her daughter Lettie:

January 12, 1856

My Dear Child,

Time has passed off swiftly since I wrote you. I will comply with my promise and delay no longer writing you. I often think I will do this piece of work then write to Lettie when I finish it; something prevents me.

We have the longest spell of cold weather I have seen in this State. It sleeted the day before Christmas some, and Christmas it sleeted and snowed. It was so slippery we could scarcely walk for falling. I slipped once and caught around a plum tree. Baby laughed mightily at me. Yesterday the ground was slippery. I don't know whether it rained and froze or sleeted. Last night and this morning it snowed. The snow is most shoe deep.

I expect Baby will have fun today with the girls snowballing. Three of their teachers were coming home with her last evening. The weather was too bad to send for them.

We were invited to Mr. McWilliam's to a dining Christmas, bad weather prevented us from going.

I can't write today for making mistakes; do excuse them.

Judge Whitehead had a party night before Christmas. Jud Echols gave one last Tuesday night. James Bryan is living at Collins Hemingway's place. He gave one last week. We were not invited to none of them.

Mary Whitehead was here in November. She told me to write you if you did not send her a beau she would marry a widower this year. It is such a pity some girls can't marry when they want to.

It is said Mildred Petty went deranged about Peter Woods; she died last fall. Hulda Petty was married one Sunday last month to a Mr. Peck. James Woods is married to Miss Couch, Ann Bailey to West Gary. I heard Mrs. Davis wrote to Mary Jenkins to put on a calico dress the next day after she married and go to work, that she never should be recognized by any of her family. Anna told Jimmy her ma told her not to talk to his wife, but she intended to talk to her as much as she pleased.

Mrs. Hale had a baby November twelve months. She is about to have another.

Bird is overseer for Mr. E. Whitehead this year. He had not been there over a week, our negroes say he commenced whipping the men. He had one boy tied [*for*] whipping him. Two of the boys ran him out of the field with clubs, he ran to his house and sent for Mr. Whitehead. The two boys ran away; I have not heard of their being caught.

Jesse, Ned, John Smith, and William are hired at the stagehands. Prince to Atlas Johnson, Mingo to Gant, Susan to some man across big Sand [*Creek*]. Milly's children are here at home. She is hired to a poor man near Mullins. I am sorry for her. There is a single man named Pentecost overseeing here this year. Your Pa says he will pay me or give me a draft on New Orleans after the first of February for 40 dollars to you for America's hire. Last year's draft can be sent in a letter.[57] If it is money, how must I send it to you? Write me what you will hire America to me for this year. She is not worth more than 40 dollars, she can't do any hard work. She has grown to be a very likely looking girl. I tell her if you were to see her you would want to take her.

Mary Wingfield is married to a Mr. Martin. She is living neighbor to Mrs. Branch, Babe Watkins that was, in Arkansas. Mrs. Branch informed her of your marriage. Ellen Wingfield is dead.

Baby received your letter written December 6th last week. She wrote you in November or December. She commenced a letter to you Christmas night, wrote a few lines, got tired, and stopped.

I have dreamed often lately of seeing you and kissing your sweet baby, and he looked so pretty.

How does cousin Betty Townes like living in Texas? Give my love to her.

Mrs. Flournoy's mother was a half-sister to Mrs. Early that died at our house and cousin to Mrs. Hawkins of this county.

Why do you think you have no warm friends in Texas? Don't the people seem to like you? I wish you all would move to Mississippi so I could go to see you.

Mary Newland and Virginia Whitehead has told two or three times to give their love to you, when I write I would forget it. The negroes send their love to you. I can't take the trouble to write their messages to you.

My back hurts me too bad, my feet are cold—it makes me most sick. I am sitting in the dining room. The Dr. is in my room with headache.

We have made a hundred and 13 bales of cotton and are not done picking yet, and a good corn crop.

Give my love to Mr. Walton; kiss your baby for me every day.

> Your affectionate Mother,
> Sarah E. Watkins

57. America was inherited by Lettie, but both America and Mrs. Watkins wanted her to remain at Forest Place—thus this offer of compensation. Later an exchange was made, leaving America with Mrs. Watkins and sending "Missouri Aunt Sally" and her daughter Catharine to Lettie.

CHAPTER FOUR

Twilight of Tranquility

Grandchildren, as one might have expected, softened the hardness of Dr. Watkins's heart. Will Walton and Lettie had a son, Newton Samuel Walton, born in Austin, Texas, on March 12, 1855. In April 1856, Lettie, again pregnant, went back to Mississippi with little Newton to visit. First she stayed at the home of one of her parents' neighbors, but then Dr. Watkins relented and sent his carriage for her.

The Waltons' second son, Early Watkins Walton, was born at the Watkins home in Carroll County, Mississippi, on September 1, 1856. The young mother and her two infant sons continued to visit in Mississippi until the late fall, when they departed for Galveston. There, Mr. Walton met them and saw his new son for the first time.

More voluminous, and newsy, correspondence ensues. Much detail concerning slave life is recounted therein. Most interestingly, sometimes the slaves themselves append personal comments onto the Watkins-Walton letters.

Mary, meanwhile, commences school. In the fall of 1857 she matriculated at the Reverend Chevalier's Holly Springs Female Institute. After one year there, Dr. Watkins, apparently finding the Holly Springs school inadequate, transferred Mary to Patapsco Female Institute at Ellicotts Mill, Maryland, near Baltimore.

September 6, 1856
Carrollton, Mississippi

Mr. Wm. M. Walton
Dear Sir:

You must excuse me for not answering your letters; I have been so busy I had very little time to write. Lettie writes so often I thought it useless for me to write you.

Lettie had a fine boy last Monday night at seven o'clock. They are both doing well. She had a headache yesterday, she is quite well today, she has had no fever. She has propped herself up in bed and writing a few lines to enclose to you, she says. I believe, if I do not prevent her, she will write a long letter. I am very anxious for her health to be recovered entirely and look like she used to before marriage. It takes Lettie, Aunt Clara and myself to attend the baby at night. We are all awkward nurses and he is a cross child at night. I am very glad my dear child is with me and I have it in my power to wait on her and attend to her baby during her confinement. I am sorry the time is drawing near for us to part again. Do move to Mississippi near enough for us to visit each other often. It would be such a great pleasure to Lettie and myself.

Newton is a sensible, good looking boy. He has fattened very much in the last week or two. I can't get him to love me. I love him dearly. Mary has had a long vacation, she will commence going to school next Monday. Newton is very fond of her, he will miss her very much for carrying him in mischief. I think Lettie has her hands full, two babies at the same time to attend to will keep her busy. She will have to give Newton up to you to manage. She will spoil him too much. She will be like me, so devoted to her children that she cannot see when they need correction. Newton is easily governed now, but his disposition may change as he grows older. If he takes after his mother, he will be very self willed.

Mary joins me in love to you and says you must answer her letter soon. When you write to me direct your letter to Middleton.

Your Sincere Friend,
Sarah E. Watkins

Sarah writes to Lettie, back in Austin, on December 28, 1856:

My Dear Child,

I received your affectionate letter this day two weeks. I would have answered it immediately; Mary needed her dresses so much I have not had time to write. I sat up one cold night until two o'clock trying to get her green deliane done for her to wear the next day at Judge Palmer's.

Miss Eldridge came home with her when she came from school and stayed until Monday. Mary went to Middleton with her, and Martha J. Palmer came out here with her.

There have been a good many storm parties[58] this month and some are going to be next week. Mary attended one at Colonel Moore's[59] and one at Mr. Baker's. We were stormed Friday night by the people of Middleton and Shongalo, some few were from Carrollton. They were invited and Lynn and Margaret A. Hemingway. The young people danced all night, most of us sat up until day. I had a week to prepare for it. I did wish you were here to assist me about the cake, and now I wish you and dear Newton were here to eat it. I had better luck with it than I expected. Martha Jane Palmer and Minerva Bennett came Thursday and dressed the cakes. Mrs. Palmer and the girls set the table. We could not get but two dozen oranges, we had a few raisins and almonds and a pound or two of candy. The table looked very nice. We are invited to a storm party at Judge Palmer's next Thursday night. I am very anxious to attend it to see if they will have a nicer set table than mine was. Octavia Simmons was here. She had been at Mr. E. Whitehead's all week.

Reed Simmons and Nancy came here Friday evening. Octavia Simmons was dressed in the silk Mr. Hawkins gave her and the cape was trimmed with pink ribbon you saw her have. Mary wore her silk. I got Mrs. Rowe to make the body and sleeves. The body is made like her white dotted swiss and the sleeves has two puffs. I am much obliged to you for the patterns. The basque is too shortwaisted for Mary. The side bodice look like they are to be stitched on instead of sewing them in a seam. Do you know which way they ought to be done?

There has been an excitement in Carrollton about the negro rising. Several were taken up and I believe some are in jail. Daniel was taken up, he says for selling whiskey to negroes but it could not be proven on him. He has been here all through Christmas. Negroes are kept very close at home, none permitted to go off without a pass. Mrs. Phillip's Deb and one of Thomas' negroes was accused of burning Mr. Henry's cotton. They were taken to Carrollton, it could not be proven on them. It is said Henry's own negroes burnt it.

Mrs. Judge Collins died soon after you left here. Dr. Hudson's wife died lately. Dr. Hudson was going from his wife's burying, he got down to open the

58. A storm party was a gay explosion of young people descending upon an unexpecting family. One can assume, however, that the host family usually had some warning.

59. Col. O. J. Moore settled in Carroll County east of Middleton and owned the land where Winona was founded. He came from Virginia with kinsmen Peter Gee, Thomas Gee, and William Gee. His eldest daughter married J. T. Lay, a businessman from Grenada, shortly before the war. The second daughter, Laura, married Davie B. Turner in 1860. Peter Gee and Col. O. J. Moore had a mercantile business in Middleton.

gate and the horses ran off with his child and nurse in the buggy. The tongue of the buggy hit a tree. The nurse saw he would fall out, she throwed the child back. It liked to have killed the nurse, the child did not get hurt.

The day after Joe and Abram went with you it rained all day, so much they had to stay at Neal's until Tuesday morning. Neal charged four dollars and 20 cents for the time they stayed after you left. Your Pa says he will take pay out of America's hire. Let it go so. I will pay you the $4 and 20 cts. along in the year. Your Pa says he will send you a draft for America's hire in February. Write me what you will charge for hire of America next year.

I do want to see you all so much, I miss you and the sweet children a great deal. Don't let Newton forget his grandmother. Kiss him and the baby for me every day. I was very glad to receive your letter and hear you had arrived safe to New Orleans. I am very anxious to hear from you. I do hope you all arrived home without any accident. Write to me soon and often. Mary joins me in love to you and Mr. Walton. Kiss the children for us. Write what you have named the baby. Be sure to have Early in its name. Sally sends howdy to you and Aunt Clara and a heap to say about Newton. I can't remember it to write. All would send some word if they know I was writing to you. As it is Sunday you must put up with a short letter. My pen is so bad I cannot hardly write. Mary speaks of writing you tomorrow. Who did you give that long-bodied dress of Newton's to and the fifth one of your skirts to? Hannah and America have found out I am writing to you all and say kiss Newton and Johnny[60] for them. Tell Clara howdy for me.

Your Affectionate Mother,
Sarah E. Watkins

On March 11, 1857, the mother writes to Lettie:

My Dear Child,

Your most welcome letters of February 1st and 19th to Mary and myself were received last Saturday with a great deal of pleasure. It made me feel cheerful to hear your health had improved so much and dear Newton was getting rosy. No one but a mother can tell the feeling a mother has for her child. I regret to this hour that I was not a more affectionate child to my mother, but I loved her and would have sacrificed my happiness in any way to please her.

Mary and her Pa started two weeks tomorrow to New Orleans. The road was so bad they went on horseback to Greenwood. When they got there, there was no boat. They went the next day to Sidon. Abram says that Baby

---

60. A name had not yet been chosen; "Johnny" was temporary.

stayed all night at Mr. Poindexter's [*the Poindexters farmed in the Sidon area*] and your Pa went to Mr. J. Roberson's and Saturday Baby was going with Mr. Poindexter's family to Mr. A. Roberson's to dinner. The two Mrs. Kennedys and Tom Kennedy were going to New Orleans with them. They stopped at F. Pleasant's in Greenwood. I have not heard when they took a boat to New Orleans. Mary will be sent off to school sometime this year. Her Pa has not determined yet where he will send her.

Narcissa Wells was married this morning two weeks to Ad Booth. Minerva Barrow is married to Joshua Bailey, they are going to California. Miss Eldridge was one of her waiters. Mary Arnold [*Whitehead*] has been very sick since the birth of her child. She is staying at Mr. E. Whitehead's on account of the measles being in her Pa's family. Mrs. Whitehead and a negro woman has to suckle her baby. Her breast rose. I expect to go to see her tomorrow if the weather is good and I am well. I reckon I had the colic night before last and have not felt well since. As it is ten o'clock at night and my eyes are weak, I will stop writing. Ritt is sitting fast to sleep.

March 12th. Today was so cold I did not go to see Mary Arnold. Icicles were hanging from the water bucket today. Ritter brought in a frozen turkey egg this morning. The peach trees were in bloom. I am afraid we will not have any peaches. My peas, cabbage, lettuce and radishes are up. April is the time to plant ground peas. Your large onions I reckon will be good to eat. They will have seeds or buttons this summer. Some people break out the middle stem that is going to seed if they don't want them to go to seed. I think mine rotted when I broke the stem out. When you have them worked don't hill the earth up around them, it will prevent them from bulbing.

I am so glad you are living in the country this year. I hope you will live more comfortably. This is dear Newton's birthday. If he was with his grandmother she would have had a cake made for him. Whose pocket does he search now? The negroes and I were delighted to hear you had received your box. Sally dreamed you had got it. Has Aunt Clara got her things? They are always pitying her for leaving them.

The measles are in several families near here. It is said one of John Purnell's daughters has it at Dr. Ewing's and another one has it at Henry Purnell's. That one at Henry Purnell's was expected to die last Sunday. Mrs. Judge Whitehead, Martha Young, Mary Davis, and Mrs. Somerville [*James Somerville, lawyer*] are all in the family way.

Else had a girl in January. She says it is named Mary Ann. Harry Ann is getting better. Have you seen or heard from Cousin Betsy Townes since you returned? My old schoolmate Mrs. Newell, have you heard from her?

Jennie Whitehead and Emma stayed with me Saturday night before last until Sunday evening. Jennie sends her love to you. I heard Aunt Mary Cobbs wanted to marry old Mr. Thomas and Mrs. Phillips prevents her.

Two weeks ago there was a storm party at Major Hawkins'. It is said there was dancing all night. It was Baby, Jeff McLemore was talking on about.[61] Don't let her know I have told you but they are nothing but little children. Do pray Lettie, don't write to her about beaux. I am afraid she will think of them sooner than she ought. Tom Kennedy came here one evening, she had gone up with Becky after the cows. When she came back she dressed up in a summer dress to make her appearance before him as if she thought he would notice whether she had on a domestic or muslin. Alfred Roberson's oldest son was here last night two weeks. He is a sensible gentleman and very pleasant manners.

Ritt says I must tell you that Hannah is grandmama. It is said that William had a child at Coule where he is hired. Daniel wife's child is said to be a white one. Sally, America, Ritt send their love to you, the children and Clara. Sally is still grunting with her jaw.

I will send Aunt Letty's daguerreotype with this letter. Give my love to Mr. Walton, kiss the dear children for me and tell Newton to smack his sweet mouth for his grandmother. I dreamed of kissing him and he smacked his mouth so sweetly. Tell Aunt Clara howdy. Write soon and often.

Your Affectionate Mother,
Sarah E. Watkins

P.S. I am obliged to you for the sleeve pattern. I expect it is dressy. I hope you received the basque pattern I sent you.

Sarah writes to Lettie again on May 15, 1857. The doctor has become serious about buying land in Arkansas and moving there.

My Dear Child,

Mary received your letter last Monday. We were very glad to hear from you all. I began to feel uneasy about you as it had been over a month since you wrote to me. Mary and her Pa started last Tuesday to Little Rock in Arkansas. Your Pa said perhaps he might change his notion when he gets to Memphis and visit his relations in Alabama and Georgia. They will be gone three or four weeks. I think he is going to look for land in Arkansas. He seems to be determined to buy land somewhere. Mary[62] carried with her to have made in Memphis one silk, one organdy muslin, one grenadine and expected to have

---

61. The first mention in the letters of Mary's (Baby's) future husband.
62. At thirteen, Mary has become a young lady.

a traveling dress made there. I am sorry Mary is gone, but mighty glad to get those dresses off my hands to make. I have a blue and white jaconet, a purple and white lawn and two purple and white muslins to make for myself. The muslins were 25 cents a yard to wear every day. Shirts that we commenced making last September, Ritt is now making the last one and the bosom of the first is wearing out. I am trying my best to get out of work. I made Sally last week make two bedticks, two bolsters and eight pillow ticks and filled them up out of the old cases. She has commenced making my undershirts. I don't reckon she can see to sew them nice.

For two weeks the weather has been very pleasant. Our crops is tolerable good. The cotton is large enough for hands to cut it out. I have had only two messes of peas, the first mess the ninth of May. We have had strawberries twice. I wished you had them. I have not been in my garden this week, I don't know how the vegetables are looking. It rained, thundered, and the wind blew very hard last night. I was afraid we were going to have a storm. It blew down the wheat very much. I hope it has not injured it. We ought to be very thankful to God that we have a plenty of corn and meat when some people about here have very little of either. It is said corn will be as scarce as it was some years ago about here.

Milly, Susan and John S. stay at home this year. Jesse, Ned and William are hired at the same places. London is hired out to Mr. Bamburg, he lives about six miles from here. Today the two negro men that killed Hale are to be hung. One of the women was cleared. The other woman has to be tried over next fall. Vivion, Joe, Abram, Sally, Patty and Martha are gone to Carrollton to see the men hung. Your Pa said none of the others were to go. Harry Ann has been out to work this week, she is always with a pain. She has to cook for the children. I hear her tongue in the kitchen now. She cooks today because Patty is gone. John W.[63] is doing jobs at home for awhile. Major Neill was here lately to hire him. He is going to have a house built. He inquired about you and said you were a favorite of his. He spoke in the highest terms of Mr. Walton. I thanked him for his kindness to you. He said he done no more than he thought I would do for his daughter. He said some told him that it would break the friendship between him and your Pa but he does not think it has. He said him and your Pa were agitated. He believes that he was the most so. Your Pa was not here when he came. I would not have him to know that Major Neill talked to me about it. He is so strange in his ways, such little things set him against anyone.

Mrs. Estell told your Pa that Brother's wife [*Mary, a widow since October 1, 1854*] is going to be married to a poor man. She wrote to her brother Green

63. John Watkins was the carpenter-slave.

asking his advice about it. He wrote to her to go ahead. She is expecting her down here, then she is going back and get married and move down here. I hate for my brother's children to be raised in such a mess. Aunt Letty wrote me that she thought if John Barbee were to court her (that is sister) she would marry him.

Mrs. E. Whitehead's baby [*the baby of April 1854*] died Tuesday evening with the scarlet fever. I attended the burying Wednesday evening. Her two youngest children were very sick with it. As the disease is contagious, I was afraid to go to the burial. Mrs. Whitehead has been a friend to me. I ventured to go over as she sent to let me know it. I did not go close to the children, was in the room only a few seconds and had a glimpse of one of them. I am very sorry I can't go to see them but as I could do no good there is no use of my risking life and my families. Mrs. Phillips was there. She is such a good and useful lady to the sick. I saw her at church last Sunday. She told me to write you that Mrs. Parmele thought very hard of you for not writing to her since your return to Texas. Mrs. Farmer's health is worse than it has been since she was first taken sick.

I can't write today for making mistakes. I don't know what is the matter with me. I had a small mess of peas for dinner today. Did you not tell me if cabbage were not primed they would head sooner? I have bad luck with my goslings, ducks and turkeys. From over 30 turkeys I have only fourteen. The rats took 12 one day out of the turkey house. I do wish you lived in a plentiful country. You would enjoy life so much more. Does Mr. Walton make enough by his profession to induce him to live in that hard country? Does he hire out any of his negroes this year? How is your green dress made that you can't alter it. If it can't be altered, were I in your place, I would wear the skirt with a black basque[64] or white spencer.[65] I am sorry you did not take that black and white berge of mine you said you want. I have not had a lady to visit me since before I last wrote you. I don't go no where, I can't expect people to come see me. I do want to see you and your dear children so much. If you all were with me now, I am alone, it would be such a great pleasure to me. If we were to ask your Pa what is good for Newton's cough he would recommend cough drops like he makes.

I received a letter from Miss Fanny Eggleston last Monday. She inquired when I heard from you and how you were getting on and if there is any hope of your returning to Mississippi and requested to be remembered to you when I write.

Give my love to Mr. Walton, kiss the sweet children for me every day and

---

64. A tight-fitting woman's blouse or bodice.
65. A woman's short, fitted jacket, usually waist length.

talk to Newton about his grandmother. Can Early crawl? How many teeth has he? Tell Aunt Clara howdy. Ritter, America, Hannah and Martha send love to all. Alfred is most always with a cold, he is a large child. Ritter sends love to Aunt Clara. I will enclose a gold dollar in this letter for you. Write soon.

Your Affectionate Mother,
Sarah E. Watkins

To Letitia Walton from Sarah Watkins:

June 8, 1857
Carrollton, Mississippi

My Dear Child,

I have received two letters from you dated 10th and 14th of May. I expect you received one from me about the time I got your last. Mary and her Pa have not returned home yet. I received a letter from him Saturday written the 25th ultimate. They were at Little Rock staying with their cousins, Judge George C. Watkins and Dr. Robert Watkins principally. Your Pa writes he is much pleased with his relations and never saw people more friendly and hospitable than they are. He and Baby first stopped at the hotel. They all called to see them. They were going to start to the Hot Springs in a day or two and spend a few days there and would come home in three or four weeks. They have been gone four weeks tomorrow. I am expecting them home every day.

I have had a very lonely time. Margaret Ann Hemingway stayed two days and a night and Miss Polly Iva stayed one night with me. That is all the company I have had. Last Wednesday I spent the day at Mr. Hemingway's, yesterday two weeks I was at a quarterly meeting [*church*] at Bluff Spring.

Yesterday I heard Mr. Pittman preach in Middleton. He is yet battling with the Campbellites.[66] I saw Mrs. Phillips and Mrs. Farmer. They told me to give

66. People in the frontier areas were attracted to religious shouting, singing and fervent prayer, all aimed at the idea of personal conversion. Revivals and camp meetings were both religious and social.

"Campbellites" was an early popular alternative name for the Disciples of Christ. The movement was formed by Scottish Presbyterians Barton W. Stone, Thomas Campbell, his son, Alexander, and Walter Scot. The Campbellites caused much controversy and provided competition for converts. In their early years they were ardent "restorationists," i.e., they were restoring the purity (and unique correctness) of the original first-century Christian church. They insisted upon baptism by full immersion. Hence, they clashed with Baptists, though the differences were but slight, and with the Methodists, because they could not agree that other

you a great deal of love for them. Mrs. Farmer's health is very bad. She don't look like she is long for this life. Mrs. Parmele started to preaching was taken sick and went back home.

None of Mr. E. Whitehead's family had the scarlet fever but the three youngest children. I am anxious to visit Mrs. Whitehead but cannot for fear of catching the fever. Judge Whitehead has had one negro to die and his overseer's child with it.

I received a letter from Aunt Letty written the fourth of May. She wrote that Brother's son Thomas died the morning before at half past eight o'clock with the flux. From what she wrote, he must have been sick over a week. His death distressed her very much. She says she will miss him so much, she don't know what she will do. He could go and get her anything she wanted and add it up and settle it up as well as any man.

It is thought your Aunt Mary will marry Barbee's son. She was at Barbee's when Tom was sick. Aunt Letty says he would not agree for her to send for her nor a doctor but she would send for a doctor. I reckon she put off sending for a doctor too long. I think she ought to have sent for his mother. I expect Aunt Letty thinks she does not care for her children as she is always going off visiting and leaving them when she ought to stay at home and work for them. Visiting would be no pleasure to me if my children were in rags because I would not make clothes for them. I feel sorry for her if she was not with Thomas when he died. No one that has not been a mother can tell the feeling a mother has for her child. I think I love my children more devotedly than most mothers and what little pleasure I am permitted to see with them. When you were a sweet little girl, the idol of your parents, I then was happy but was not sensible of the happiness. I was enjoying and looking forward for happiness, anticipating so much pleasure to be enjoyed with you when you became grown. Just as my happiness were about to be realized, came the monster worse than death and blasted all my happiness. It makes me shed tears while I write to think of it. I will take Mr. Walton's advice and look on the bright side and not always on the dark and maybe things will come right after a while. I pray that you and him may become Christians and help me in my feeble prayers to pray that we may see the day that we can enjoy each other's company in this world with pleasure.

Your Pa tries to delight in Baby but I don't think he loves her like he did you. He tells her he used to love children but he don't care much for them

---

forms of baptism were even valid at all, hence Campbellites could not accept that Methodists were Christians. See Martin E. Marty, *Pilgrims in Their Own Land* (Boston: Little, Brown, 1984), especially 174, 197–98, 201.

now. I tell her not to be head strong like you were. You asked why your Pa will not become friendly with you. You know he often told you if you were married against his consent, he would never have anything to do with you. That is the only answer I can give you. As it is a disagreeable subject to me to write about, I will drop it.

George Savage is living at Little Rock. He is now on a visit to Texas. Your Pa says the society of that place is very fine and if I were there I would not exchange that place for any other. There are moral people, good schools and fine churches. He says if I were as willing as he is, we would move to that State. You know he has his way in everything. It would not surprise me if we were to move to that state. This place is so worn out. We will be compelled to get land somewhere but we have very good luck on this place. We have plenty of corn and meat. I hear of it being scarce with several people in the country. Our crop is good considering the backwardness of the season. America has just come in with a small mess of raspberries. I wish you had them. The birds destroy them mightly. The plums are not ripe yet. My garden is doing tolerably well, my onions are very pretty. My turkeys has done badly. I have not got twenty young ones. Ritter says I have three hundred chickens. They are scattered about so much, I can't see many of them.

Your Pa traveled in the stage and on the car to Memphis with Dr. Lott from Austin. He said he is a partner of Dr. Steel's. Do you ever hear of Eggleston Townes or his sisters, Mrs. Grey and Mrs. Leigh? Mr. Kirkwood died last week. He was on his way home from the Hot Springs, got to his son-in-law's and died. Ritt has a very bad boil between her right arm and breast. It broke yesterday but is paining her today. She sends her love to you, the children, and Aunt Clara. Martha, America, Sally and Hannah send love to all. Martha and Sally says tell Aunt Clara that she promised to write to them. Alfred got to a gourd of lye last week and had all his mouth swollen up from it. Yesterday he trod in hot ashes and burnt the bottom of his feet enough to prevent him from walking.

I will have my likeness and Baby's taken the first opportunity I have. I reckon Aunt Clara knows Turner's Burt, Sunday before last his wife's funeral was preached. Yesterday, he was married in church at Bluff Springs to Mr. E. Whitehead's Harriet.[67] Chloe was her bridesmaid. Kiss the children for me every day. Tell Newton he must be a good boy. Write soon and often.

Your Affectionate Mother,
Sarah E. Watkins

67. Marriages between slaves on neighboring plantations were frequently arranged. Many of one family's slaves might have been with the family for generations and be interrelated. Often, fixed days for visitation were set by the owners.

Mary adds the following short note to Sarah's letter:

Miss Lettie A. Walton
Austin, Texas
Dear Sister,

As mother is writing I will enclose a few lines. Isabella Wadlington that used to be has a fine son. Tell Brother William to write me a composition for next June on a mother's love, I fear he will forget it and therefore shall tell him in time.

Give my love to Mr. Walton. Kiss Newton for me. Write soon, both of you. Good night.

M.E.W.

P.S. Mary wrote this in a hurry. Her Pa called to play on the piano for him. She had to fret about it first. S.E. Watkins.

To Letitia Walton from Sarah Watkins:

July 30, 1857
Carrollton, Mississippi

My Dear Child,

As I had written to you just before receiving your last letters, I did not answer them immediately. I have sad news to write. Our dear beloved Aunt Letty is dead [*less than three years after the brother's death*]. She died the sixth of this month at eleven o'clock at night. She was confined to her bed four or five weeks and only the two last weeks she seemed seriously ill. My kind loving friend Cynthia Swoope was the first to write informing me of her death. She wrote me the eighth of the month a very consoling and sympathizing letter. She wrote that she had just returned from a visit of several weeks to her daughter's when she heard that Aunt Letty was very ill. After one day's rest she ordered her carriage and started for Mountain Home. But alas, she was too late! Closed forever were those eyes that had ever beamed with affection. Silent that voice that ever bid her welcome. The hand that had so often grasped hers with the warmth of friendship lay by the side of that inanimate form, cold, motionless, dead. Her features were as placid as if in sleep—as if she had just laid down to take an hour's repose. She says she was not shrouded but dressed in black with the cape and cap I worked for her many years since and which she had put by for the occasion. She was told that she spoke with great calmness of death and gave directions how and where she wished to be buried. Still her heart clung with undying love to those dear orphan children of Brother's—her strongest tie to earth. She had been more than a mother to them and it was hard to leave them.

On the day of her death she did not converse only once or twice. She called Sister's name but did not say anything when Sister asked her what she wanted or if she wished her to do anything. The minister too was there and nothing that kind hearts could do was left undone. Cynthia's letter is beautifully written. It is equal to any sermon—I wish you could see it.

I received a letter from Mr. Cooper, the minister that was with Aunt Letty during her sickness. He said he wrote by the request of Aunt Letty. He mentioned what time she died. He preached her funeral at three o'clock the evening she was buried. He mentioned the words of the text and the hymn sung on the occasion was partly of her own selection. He says her disease was an obstinate irritability of the stomach, the smallest quantity in the stomach produced vomiting. He thinks she was rational to the last. He said her last words were, "Mary, Mary, poor Mary," and then seemed perfectly exhausted. He does not write whether he thought her prepared to die or not. I received a short note from brother's wife informing me of Aunt Letty's death. Sarah Ann wrote two days before Aunt Letty's death telling me of her illness.

If I had heard of her illness in time I would have gone up to see her. In her last letter to me she said she would like so much to see me once more. If we could have seen each other again I could bear with her death so much better. I anticipated being with her in September. The disappointment is so heartbreaking but I know it is wrong to murmur at the will of God. His will must be done. He deals in love and mercy with all his creatures. That what he does is always best, his time is the right time. Let us not think of her as in the cold grave but raise our thoughts above to heaven to the right hand of God and behold her there freed forever from suffering. Those five last lines are taken from Cynthia's letter.

Mr. Joe Keys was taken sick at Mr. McLemore's and died there last Sunday night. Mrs. Sturdivant's oldest child died this month with scarlet fever. Mrs. Norwood was married lately on a Sunday to Dr. McClure. Ellen Butt is married to Summerfield Fox. Mrs. Judge Whitehead has a black-haired daughter [Alberta]. Mary Arnold did not go to Wells, her health has improved. Her child has the whooping cough. She is staying with Martha Young; Martha is expecting to be confined. Mrs. Baskerville Vaughn is married to Judge Graham, the man that hired Prince and Else. Tom Purnell bought a new carriage and a match of horses. Him and his wife [Camilla] were going from Major Hawkins' and just as she got in the carriage the horses got scared and ran off, broke the carriage all to pieces, and hurt Mrs. Purnell very much but none of her limbs were broken. She is in the family way.

I visited Major Hawkins', Judge Whitehead's and my Shongalo acquaintances last week. Saw Tom Purnell and his wife at her mother's. She has not
entirely recovered. Tom P. does not look as well as he used to. He has sold
his plantation on the river to Major Hawkins and the place he is living on to
somebody else. Mrs. Kennedy sends a great deal of love to you. Mrs. Pleasant
said she never has seen you but knew Mr. Walton's parents.[68] She sends love
to you both.

I am going to try to go to see Mrs. Simmons this fall. Don't say nothing
about my going there in your letters to me. Mary is invited to a party at Roger
Wells's next week. She is anxious to go. I do not think her Pa will let her go
to it.

I expect to go to Carrollton tomorrow to buy my mourning for poor Aunt
Letty. Cousin Patsy Powell told me that Dick Townes left half of his property
to Judge Townes's children and made his wife promise to leave them her part
at her death. Why do you want to know how he made his will? Five of the
negroes have dysentery but they are all better today. I have had some ripe
watermelons this week. Baby and I wished today you were with us. We said
to each other, "Dear Newton, how he would enjoy it." Baby joins me in love
to you and Mr. Walton. Kiss the dear children for us. The negroes send love
to all. Enclosed I send you a gold dollar. It is nearly night, I must stop
writing.

Your affectionate Mother,
Sarah E. Watkins

On October 8, 1857, the first letter is sent to Mary Watkins, who has
gone to school at Reverend Chevalier's Holly Springs Female Institute.
The letter is sent care of Reverend M. Chevalier, now principal of the
school in place of Reverend Sill. Lettie had gone there earlier.

The mother writes:

Last week I received a letter from you and your sister at the same time.
Her's was written five days before yours. It gave me such a pleasant feeling to
receive a letter from both of my dear children . . .

The tribe of little negroes have come in with chinquapins.[69] Some of them
say they are for you. I had to quit writing to get some biscuits to pay for them.
They remind me of hogs after corn. Once or twice when I had been from home

---

68. William Walton, Lettie's husband, lived in the Shongalo area, now Vaiden, Mississippi,
as a child.
69. Nuts from a small oak that produces a sweet, edible acorn.

and come back, they went to meet the carriage and looked in to see if you were in it.

Judge Longstreet [*president, University of Mississippi*] was here last week. He spoke in Carrollton this day last week, Saturday in Middleton, and this week at Shongalo. There was a barbecue to be given for him at Shongalo tomorrow. Tomorrow he is to speak at Black Hawk. Your Papa left home today to meet him at Black Hawk and get him to go with him to Mrs. Eggleston's.[70]

Mrs. Edmunds Whitehead and Mrs. Whitehead, their daughters, and Miss Hines spent the day with me last Wednesday. From what I heard I think Jennie and Tom will be married this fall. I would not say it out of my family, but it frets Jennie's people talking so much about her being engaged. I heard that Lizzie was engaged but did not hear to whom. I do not think she is. I plagued her about it. She says it is not so. She said, "Tom just told you I was engaged to A. Keys as a blind." I have not heard of Keys[71] visiting Jennie. [*Nothing came of these rumors—Lizzie married William Oliver in 1860.*] It is said that John Watkins is going to be married and Mrs. Hawkins is going to Carolina to his wedding.

. . . Your Pa says you must not buy anything but what you actually need, that you can buy a cloth and a worsted dress. Have the dress made, and charge the making of it to the merchant you deal with. Don't get a costly cloth. Notice that it is not moth-eaten. Get someone with taste to assist you in choosing the things. . . . Your Pa says date your letters. He says you write a very good letter. . . . P.S. Miss Phelps, 14 years old, was married to Mr. Gouch week before last.

To Letitia Walton from Sarah Watkins:

October 24, 1857
Carrollton, Mississippi

My Dear Child,

I received your kind letter of the 10th of October yesterday. I was very glad to hear from you all. After hearing Newton was sick I felt uneasy about him, and am sorry to hear that he has not recovered his health. I hope him and Mr. Walton have recovered by this time.

I received a letter from Baby last week. She said she had been very sick with the croup, she could scarcely get her breath. Mr. Chevalier was frightened about her, he thought she had the scarlet fever. He sent for a physician to her. She said she thought that she was going to die. Her cold was very bad

---

70. Eggleston descendants still live in Carrollton, though the Eggleston family of these letters lived near Lexington, Mississippi.

71. The son of a physician, Dr. Joseph M. Keys, whose plantation was west of Coila.

when she wrote but she said she would soon be well and I must not be uneasy about her. I can't help being uneasy. I am always uneasy about you both, particularly if I do not get a letter for some time.

Just now someone said a barouche[72] was coming. I was certain a lady was in it. I jumped up and put away my writing. It was Judge Longstreet. He was invited in the bedroom so I will continue writing. Mr. McDonald came here soon after dinner. I am fixing up a box of ham, cakes, puddings, biscuits and ground peas to send Mary tomorrow by the stage. I do wish you and dear Newton had some of the cakes. I have a dish of boiled peas, I wish you were here to eat them with me.

I spent the day with Mrs. E. Whitehead. Tuesday, Judge Whitehead's family were there and Tom Kennedy. I think Tom and Jennie Whitehead will be married. It has been reported so a long time. I don't know that it is so.

Major Watt has declined moving to Memphis. Mr. Summerville's lot is advertised for sale. He spoke of moving to Memphis. Mrs. Summerville thinks if he would leave his associates that he would become temperate so I heard. It was reported this summer that they had parted. He got to drinking and she went to her brother's and staid a few weeks and then she and Mr. Summerville went to Alabama. I don't like to tell such things unless I know the truth of it. Do not say nothing about it. Mr. Sturdivant is moving to the swamp to live. I looked for Mrs. Sturdivant and Octavia to see me last week but they did not come. Mrs. Hawkins is in very bad health.

I am sorry Mr. Walton[73] sold his negroes. A person seldom does well when they sell their patrimony. I am more desirous for him to do well then any man in the world. Was he obliged to sell on account of debt? You will miss Aunt Clara. Poor Newton, did it not distress him for her to leave him. I would be afraid to stay in the country alone with hired negroes. I have never heard what was done with Aunt Letty's things. I wrote to Sister to know what had become of them. She would not answer my letter. Harry Ann has been sick most a week like she was last winter. Moses is sick with a pain in his side.

October 25th—I could not finish my letter last evening. Judge Longstreet left this morning in our carriage, he will go in it as far as Randolph Leigh's. Mr. McDonald has just left. They have disagreeable weather for traveling. It drizzled rain most of yesterday and this morning. I think we are going to have cold weather. I heard the wild geese flying by and the little negroes saying, "Do you see the wild gooses?" Old Mr. Harry Burt is dead. Mrs. Solon Sykes is in bad health. I am expecting Miss Meady and Mary Eggleston next week. I

---

72. A four-wheeled carriage with a half-cover that can be raised or lowered over the passengers; the driver is uncovered. Four passengers are seated, two facing forward, two to the rear.

73. Lettie's husband. This is a misunderstanding. They were not sold.

have less fine work to do than I have had in three years. I have got all the negroes' winter clothes cut out except the women's dresses. Have you received the third dollar I enclosed in my letter before the last I wrote? Do you never see nor hear from cousin Betsy Townes? I heard Mr. Judge Townes was very much pleased with Texas. You can write on a piece of paper and let me know if you received the dollar. Give my love to Mr. Walton. Kiss the children for me every day. The negroes send howdy to all.

Your affectionate Mother,
Sarah E. Watkins

To Mary from Sarah Watkins:

October 24, 1857
Carrollton, Mississippi

My Dear Child,

Your letter of the 10th inst. was received last week. I was very sorry that you had been so sick. I am very thankful to God that he spared your life. I hope you have entirely recovered and will keep well. My dear child take care of yourself, don't be imprudent and don't do what you know will make you sick. What could have given you such a bad cold? Perhaps your shoes and stockings are too thin. Do not suffer your feet to keep cold. Provide yourself with thick shoes and stockings: you have been in the habit of wearing thicker stockings every day and that might have caused you to have been sick. If your feet are not warm enough you had better get six pair of black worsted hose to wear during the winter. I am always too uneasy about you. I think of you and your poor sister day and night with a troubled mind. I waked up one night, I expect it was the time you were sick, with such a troubled feeling about you it almost made me sick.

I have a ham boiled, some ginger cake and pound cake and citron puddings made to send you and some ground peas. We will have them put in a box and send it to Carrollton to be carried by the stage. Baby, don't make yourself sick eating them and do not eat late at night. It might give you the colic. I saw the death of Mr. Reeves announced in the paper last week, it said he died with the cramp colic in two hours after he was taken.

I am very much pleased to hear that your teachers think so much of you and that you are well pleased with the school. I hope you will act in such a way as to gain their esteem all the time.

I received a letter from your sister yesterday written the 10th of this month. She said Newton had been very sick since she wrote last. He was mending slowly. Mr. Walton was sick. He has sold all his negroes but one man, Denmark, to his brother, George Walton.[74] Mr. Walton has hired a negro woman with one child. I think he was wrong to sell his negroes.

I spent the day at Mr. E. Whitehead's last Tuesday. Mrs. Judge Whitehead, Laura and Tom Kennedy were there. I told Jennie you said she must invite you to her wedding. Mrs. Whitehead says I must tell you that she will take that part on herself, that she will let you know in time. They will not tell me but I think Jennie and Tom will be married. Tom said that his mother had not received a letter from Ophelia since she left home. It made her uneasy about her for fear she was sick.

Mr. Pittman has resigned preaching in Middleton. A man by the name of Leigh is expected to be the minister of the Baptist church in Midddleton. The school at Middleton has more scholars than it had last session.

The music teacher is pretty. She is said to be a widow from Memphis. I saw her at church last Sunday. I thought she was a school girl. I reckon you know that M.E. Davis is at school in Carrollton. I expects she writes to you. She can inform you of more news than I can. Mr. Sturdivant is moving to the river. He has very rainy weather to move in. Abram heard two weeks ago that old Mrs. Holt that lives at Judge Collin's was dead. Harry Ann is sick like she was in the winter. Moses is sick. I do not hear the little negroes say very much about you but the grown ones very often talk about you. They would send some message if they knew I was writing. Which class are you in? What are your studies? I do not remember the name of the gentleman and lady from Holly Springs that visited Lizzie and Jennie. Just as the table was cleared off, Mr. McDonald came. I have not seen him yet. Dinner is preparing for him. He is sitting in my room and my bed as usual tumbled by your Pa. I am sitting in your room without a fire, it is right cool. Write often, I am always anxious to hear from you.

Your affectionate Mother,
Sarah E. Watkins

P.S. Ritt and Hannah send howdy. Hannah says you must not find fault of your things, that she tried to have them nice. I had to make Ritt make the puddings. Patty was not well enough to make them. She had a pain in her stomach. She is better now. Write me how the ladies have their silk dresses made. I may get me a black silk. I want to know how to make it. S.E.W.

Tilla says she wish she was with you when you get your box—that she

---

74. The slaves had not been sold. He sent them with his brother, George, who needed them on his plantation in Louisiana because he, Will, was not farming and needed only town servants. The servants were all inherited from their father. One man, Denmark, stayed in Austin and Major Walton gave him property to live on near Austin after the war. Denmark's "hired-out" earnings helped support Lettie and her children during the war.

knows you would give her some of the things. I have cut out all the negroes' winter clothes except the women's dresses. I will cut them next week.

Oct. 25th—Judge Longstreet left here this morning. We sent your box with him as far as his house at Oxford and then it will be carried on the railroad to Holly Springs. Your Pa says you must write directly when you receive the box. He will be anxious to know about it. Be sure to write. You must not delay writing.

To Mary Watkins from Dr. Watkins:

> November 30, 1857
> Carrollton, Mississippi

Miss Mary E. Watkins
Holly Springs, Mississippi [75]

My Dear Daughter,

Your kind and affectionate letter of 26th inst. is just at hand—contents noted. Miss Meady Eggleston and her sister Mary left here a few days ago. They say they enjoyed themselves very much while here. They and my family spent one day at Mr. Edmunds Whitehead's—one day at Judge Whitehead's— one day at Dr. Stansbury's in Carrollton and one day at Judge Wright's near Carrollton. The way we made the champagne bottles pop at our house and at Dr. Stansbury's and at Judge Whitehead's was truly amusing. At the house of the latter gentleman, a great many bottles were opened. He gave a very fine and nice dinner and so did all the abovenamed persons—except the undersigned.

If you have got any one dollar bills your only chance to get them off will be to get some of your merchants or Mr. Chevalier to send them to Memphis and do the best they can with them. One dollar bills pass in Tennessee but not in this State.[76] Your merchants and Mr. Craft and Mr. Chevalier are trading men and they get off the dollar bills to much better advantage than yourself.

I shall have some business above Holly Springs a few days before Christmas and if the weather is good and I am well, I will go up and of course I will call and stay a day or two with you. If the weather is bad you need not look for me. I shall be up about Saturday or Sunday before Christmas. If you find that you will need a little pocket money you can write me word.

---

75. Reverend Sill had been principal when Lettie was there. Tuition for Mary, September through February, was sixty dollars.

76. This would have been "bank note" currency, or some similar privately issued unofficial paper money. The United States at this time had no paper money issued by the national government.

Your mother and myself will on tomorrow call on young Dr. Hawkins and his wife, who are now staying at his father's. A few days ago Mrs. Dr. Vaiden and her sister and Miss Mary Pleasants called and stayed a day and night with us. We were truly glad to see them. Mrs. Vaiden is truly a nice lady.

I see some errors in your letter—not however more than I could expect of a girl of your age and experience. Sometimes your punctuation is not the best and at other times you commence a sentence with a small letter instead of a capital. Your spelling is very good, which is a very important matter. Nothing looks worse in writing than bad spelling.

I am much pleased at your determination to, "attempt to be an accomplished lady and gain the love and esteem of all with whom you are acquainted."

If I go up to Holly Springs, your mother says she will send you something in the way of eatables.

When you write to any person, put their name at the commencement of your letter as I do.

Your affectionate father,
Thomas A. Watkins

P.S. Always sign your name to any instrument of writing in a larger handwriting than the other part of the writing, as I have done—also always write plainly the name of the town, village or P.O. where you write from and the date. TAW

P.S. I hope your teeth are not seriously injured to as to give you much pain. TAW

P.S. Please write me where to find your visiting cards. We have looked for them but cannot see them anywhere. TAW

To Letitia Walton from Sarah Watkins:

December 2, 1857
Carrollton, Mississippi

Mrs. Lettie A. Walton
Austin, Texas

My Dear Child,

I received your welcome letter of the 11th ult.[77] last week. I am sorry to hear of you and your family being indisposed and am grieved at you having the mange again. It makes me low-spirited that you cannot have good health. Do be careful of yourself and try to get cured of that troublesome disease.

---

77. "Ult.": abbreviation for ultime vit., in the previous month—in this case, November 1857.

The Miss Egglestons left here this day week. They had quite an agreeable time while here. Some company visited them and I went with them to return their visits. We spent a day at Mr. E. Whitehead's and the next day at Judge Whitehead's. Monday week spent a day at Dr. Stansbury's. Saw Mrs. Jack Leflore and Mrs. Harris there. Mrs. Leflore got a prize at the fair in Grenada for a vest made out of swan skin. She chose a gold thimble.

Tuesday week we dined at Judge Wright's. He lives two miles from Carrollton and is a partner of Mr. Helm's and married a cousin of Mr. Helm's. Mr. Helm was the only beau that visited the ladies while they were here. Yesterday your Pa and myself called on John Hawkins and his wife at Major Hawkins'. We spent the day there and was after dark getting home. Mrs. Hawkins is very pretty and a very pleasant lady. She is about your size, has fair skin, black hair, and blue eyes. She said she never was far from her mother before and is not homesick at all and is very much pleased with the country. Mrs. Hawkins is very much pleased with her daughter-in-law. I think Major Hawkins is too. John looks very boyish. He has got some beard growing out. He has not an intelligent look. His Pa outshines him now in looks. I expect he is a very steady gentlemanly youth and will be better looking when he gets his growth. He and his parents asked about you.

Mrs. Hawkins is expecting Mr. Simmons at her house next Saturday to attend Camilla Purnell's funeral at Shongalo next Sunday. She died happy and did not care to live only on her mother and husband's account. She had five doctors with her. Forceps were used to take the child from her and they gave her ergot to increase the pains. They said the pains did not work right. They went up in her stomach and she had spasms and blindness. She had her child Friday and did not know it until Monday. She died the next Thursday. Mrs. Hawkins says her lungs were very much affected and she thinks that caused her death.[78]

Mary Arnold is staying at her father's [*Judge William Whitehead*] 'til after Christmas next year. She expects to live on her farm that her Pa gave her. She looks very thin. Her boy is a large, good looking child. Mrs. Petty that lives in Carrollton and her daughter were riding in a buggy and the horse ran way with them and hurt them very much. Lately, the daughter, Sally Petty has died. Mrs. Vaiden, Mrs. Herron and Mary F. Pleasants was to see us last week. Miss Sally Vaiden died this fall.

I wish I could see dear Newton with his breeches on. I expect he looks very sweet. I hope he will continue to be stingy and when he gets old so he will have something to live on that will keep him from the frowns of the world.

---

78. Probably today we would call this toxemia of pregnancy and readily treat the basic problem of hypertension.

I have a plain black silk dress to make. I dread fitting the basque.[79] We received a letter from Baby this week, she was well. Ritt is sick today with her old pains and a boil in her nose. Semira is sick a little. She is lusty. It is most dark, I must stop and give out supper.

It is after supper. Miss Meady E. [*Miss Eggleston*] requested me to give her love to you when I write. Fanny Tab is in the family way. Dr. Hudson's child died this fall. I am obliged to you for the magnolia seed. When is the time to plant them? You ought to take more pains in writing. You used to write a pretty hand. Read whenever you have the least opportunity, such books as will improve your mind. Do not bury yourself alive because you are married. For the sake of your children seek good society. Do not let them associate with the low-breed people. Do not spoil your children. No one can love or esteem a spoilt child. I saw a very bad little boy two weeks ago. His mother could not have much peace for him. I thought, "Were you my child when I got home I would take off your breeches and give you a good tuning. The next time I write to Lettie I will write her not to spoil her children."

The fire popped, it made me jump and made that blot. It has just been a year since you left here. The time seems so very long since you and the dear children left me. I do want to see you all so much. I hope in course of time we will live nearer each other so we can see each other oftener. To know that you are doing well would be a great comfort to me. Write soon and often. It is such a relief to my poor heart to receive letters from you. Give my love to Mr. Walton. Kiss the children for me. I wish I could send them a Christmas present. Hannah and America send love to you and the children.

Your affectionate mother
Sarah E. Watkins

Again on December 28, 1857, Mrs. Watkins writes Letitia:

December 28, 1857
Carrollton, Mississippi

Mrs. Lettie A. Walton
Austin, Texas
My Dear Child,

This day five weeks I received a letter from you dated November 12th. Oh why my beloved child have you not written to your mother before this? Not hearing from you in such a long time causes me to spend a sad Christmas.

---

79. *Oxford Unabridged*: "the continuation of a lady's bodice below the waist, sometimes fitted with pockets."

Your Pa went to Holly Springs to meet Robin [80] and saw Baby. He says she has grown very much and looked very well. She concluded to come home with him but gave it up. She had made such a large store account she said what it would take to bring her home would help to pay off her accounts. She has not been to Holly Springs five months yet and her account is a hundred dollars or more. That is more than you would have spent in a year. Her Pa does not seem to care about it. He is as fond of her as he used to be of you. She expects to spend Christmas with her schoolmates, the Miss Johnsons. They live in Tipah County, twenty miles from Holly Springs. I think Baby is seeking religion. The letter before the last she wrote me she said, "I hope the next time I write, I can write that I have given my heart to the blessed Creator." I do pray that I may see my dear children as true Christians and when we are done with the trouble of this world we may have a place in heaven where parting and grief will be no more.

Robin got here the day before Christmas. He came all the way on the railroad and stage by himself. By the Dr. going to Memphis, he did not meet him. He got here the day after Robin. Robin says none of Aunt Letty's things have been sold but her secretary. Sister sold that for seven dollars to Mrs. Turyan. I feel very gloomy that some of the negroes have to be hired out. There is a man here now to hire John Smith. Poor John, he is a good negro but his master [Dr. Watkins] don't like him. My children and my negroes keep my heart constantly aching.

Virginia Whitehead [81] was married to Tom Kennedy last Wednesday night. Laura Whitehead [82] and Ophelia Kennedy [83] were her bridesmaids and Albert Keys and Mr. Maddox were his bridesmen. Tom and his company came here and dressed. There were a good many people at the wedding. Octavia Simmons was there and looked pretty as any girl there. Tom Purnell was there and looked very sad. Mrs. Phillips and her daughters were there and told me to give their love to you. Mrs. Parmele thinks hard of you for not answering her letter. Do write to her, they are your sincere friends. Mrs. Phillips says you must come to Miss. next year, that she will have a place for you at her house. Jane Sykes was married last Tuesday night to Dr. Austin of Grenada. It is said he is dissipated. Paul Watkins is married to a widow.

Robin says brother's wife is courting Barbee. He don't think B. is courting

---

80. Robin was one of the William Fitzgerald "Uncle Billy" slaves. When he died, Robin had to be sold to pay debts, and Dr. Watkins bought him but left him with Aunt Letty for her lifetime. Upon her death, Robin came to the Watkins home.

81. Daughter of Edmunds Whitehead.

82. Daughter of Judge Whitehead.

83. Sister of Tom Kennedy.

her. She would leave her children at home with him [*Robin*], Tilla, and Sarah and go off visiting several days. Mr. Wise of Moulton [*Alabama*] is guardian for the children. They have not got Becky and Abby back who were sold during Aunt Letty's life. Abby is in Texas with Mr. Masterson. Robin says she has a husband at Mr. Eggleston Townes's and he spoke of buying her. I am afraid the children cannot recover those negroes. They both have a child.

Your Pa says when he sells his cotton and gets everything fixed that he will give a draft on New Orleans to pay for America's hire for this year. Write me what you will hire her for next year. Your Pa requests me to ask you if you have heard of a gentleman living in Texas by the name of Hon. Julius C. Alford and wants you to inquire if he is living in Austin. He says if he is you must go to see him and make his acquaintance. He and your Pa was raised as boys together in Green County, Georgia. He was a member of congress and distinguished himself in the Florida war against the Indians.[84] He used to be called the "War Horse of Troup County, Georgia." The Dr. met with Mr. Alford's nephew in Memphis, Mr. Cone, and he told him that his uncle was living in Texas.

Judge Longstreet[85] is going to take charge of the college at Columbia, South Carolina. Cousin John Powell was here week before last. He spoke very much in your praise and said he would like to become acquainted with Mr. Walton. He told me that Judge Townes said that Mr. Walton is a very intelligent man. It made me feel proud for my son-in-law to be complimented so highly by one that is capable of judging. I do crave to hear his name sound aloud as a distinguished lawyer. Lettie, times are mighty hard.[86] Don't be extravagant, take care all you can for your dear children. It is my prayer to God that you and your family may prosper in this life both in spiritual and temporal concerns. I have spent a very dull time this Christmas, have had no company. I did not care to have any as my dear children can't be with me. Give my love to Mr. Walton and kiss the dear, sweet children for me every day. America and the rest of the servants send love to you. Write soon and often. I am so anxious to hear from you all.

Your affectionate mother,
Sarah E. Watkins

Tell Newton to kiss you for me.

---

84. Although the Third Seminole War had commenced earlier in this year, Sarah undoubtedly is referring to the much larger conflict, the Second Seminole War (1835–42).

85. Judge Augustus B. Longstreet. Letitia's third son was named George Longstreet Walton for him. The judge was the president of the University of Mississippi and later president of the University of South Carolina.

86. The depression following the Panic of 1857.

To Mary Watkins from Sarah Watkins:

December 28, 1857
Carrollton, Mississippi

My Dear Child,

I have just finished a letter to your dear sister. I will now write to you. My memory is so bad I cannot remember whether I have answered your last letter.

Your Pa got home Friday. He told me you had grown in height very much and looked well and came near coming home with him. I want to see you very much but am glad you did not come as you would have only a short time to stay with us and had bad weather to come in and maybe had to go back. I hope you are enjoying yourself this Christmas. We have a dull time. I feel very low-spirited. My dear children being from me and some of the negroes are to be hired out. I have not heard from my poor child Lettie, it makes me very sad.

Robin got here the day before your Pa did. He said Brother's family were well. Virginia Whitehead and Tom Kennedy were married last Wednesday. Laura Whitehead and Ophelia Kennedy were her waiters and Albert Keys and Mr. Maddox were his bridesmen. Tom came here and six gentlemen with him to dress. There were a good many people at the wedding. Mary E. Davis and Laura Moore were there. Mary E. Davis said she had not received a letter from you in several weeks. Several of us sat up all night because it was too dark to drive home. Jane Sykes was married to Dr. Austin of Grenada last Tuesday night. It is said he was dissipated.

I was surprised at your account being so much at the stores at Holly Springs. My dear child, do not be extravagant. The times are mighty hard. Don't get no more than you actually need. Your Pa is spoiling you as much as he spoilt Lettie. I think he is very proud of you and he frequently speaks of you. It is a great comfort to me to hear that you are progressing finely and thought so much of by your teachers. You must keep up your good character with them. I am pleased that you have an idea of religion. My dear child, do not be persuaded that you have religion, be convinced by your own feelings that you have it before you make any profession. Do not join the church without your Pa's consent. I don't think he wants you to join until you become older. I would rejoice and do pray that my children may become true Christians. Mrs. Chevalier told your Pa that you had not had your monthly courses[87] since you left here. If it does not make you sick you need not be

87. Menstrual periods.

uneasy about it. If it makes you sick let me know it very soon. It is most dark, I must stop. Write soon. None of the servants know I am writing to you. They would have some word to send.

Your affectionate mother,
Sarah E. Watkins

P.S. The money I sent you in the black silk bag is what I received for your six ducks and six chickens. I hope you are not prevented from writing to your poor sister. If you are, you ought to beg your Pa to let you write to her. Judge Collins' daughters will be at home in February. Mrs. Conley has a boy two or three weeks old.

William has come home, he is very large. He is to stay at home this year. Hannah is distressed about Isham and Chloe. Isham is hired at the stage stand and Chloe to Green Woods. Robin, John Smith, and Melia are to be hired out. Those that were hired out last year will be hired out again next year. I have had one cry about it today.

Let me know how you spent your Christmas. You have never informed me which class you are in. Do you think you can graduate in two years? Robin says Sarah Ann got the prize at school. I am pleased to hear it. SEW

To Mary Watkins from Sarah Watkins:

January 18, 1858
Carrollton, Mississippi

My Dear Child,

I wrote you last week. We received your affectionate letter of the 11 inst. Saturday. I feel so uneasy about you having a pain in your side that it induces me to write to you again requesting you to write me more particularly about the pain. What do you think is the cause of the pain, do you have fever with it? What side is it in? I am afraid it is your not having your monthly courses is the cause of it. Buy a bottle of Radway's Ready Relief and rub your side with it and take some of it. The bottle costs a dollar. Take some of your own money and get it and I will send you a dollar in place of it. Let me know if you get the Radway. If you do not use that, put a mustard plaster on or warm, dampened ashes or a corn meal mush. Take a ginger tea or a black pepper dram. Keep your feet warm, do not expose yourself in the cold. Do you have the pain every day and how long does it last? I do wish you could be at home until you get well of it. Your Pa thinks the pain is not very severe and does not say what ought to be done for it. You know how he is, anyone must be very ill before he thinks they need doctoring. I wake in the night thinking about you with such a troubled feeling for fear you are suffering for the want of attention. My poor heart is forever troubled about my dear children. I do wish they could be with me always. I put my trust in God and pray he will hear my prayers and protect them in this life and prepare their souls for heaven.

Your Pa says I must tell you he does not want you to join the church, he rather you would wait until you are old enough to know what you are about. I think myself, you ought not to be too hasty in joining the church. Have you embraced religion? Do you know that your soul has been truly regenerated? People are so often deceived and think they have religion when they have none. If you are a Christian, I rejoice to hear it and pray you may hold out faithful.

I am sorry you and Mrs. Chevalier can't agree. Bear with her, do not saucy her, don't talk back to her, the less you say to her when she scolds you the better you will come off by it. Try and keep up your good character with them.

You asked what gentlemen came here with Tom Kennedy: Alfred and Frank Keys, Maddox, John Sturdivant, Durram, Herron, and Augustus Pleasants. They did not go from here until after dark. As I wanted to go before night, I went off and left them here. Tom Kennedy sent me word I need not wait for them as they would be late going to Mr. Whitehead's. I will tell you a secret you must not tell it. They brought spirit with them to drink. Frank Keys got so drunk he had to stay here after the others were gone until he got sober enough to go. He got Glasgow to go with him and drive his buggy to Mr. Whitehead's for him. The servants say Albert Keys hated it very much and asked them not to tell me about it. He said his brother was not in the habit of drinking. America says I must tell you that John Sturdivant said he is going to wait for you, that Miss Mary has so many darkeys.[88]

I can't write without making mistakes, you must look over them and not follow my example. Directing your last letter you spelled *Thomas, Thosum*, and in dating it you put it 1857 instead of 1858.

I made my silk a basque, trimmed it with narrow fringe, the sleeves are made with two large puffs and open at the bottom. Miss Eggleston gave me the sleeve pattern. Write as soon as you receive this letter. I am very anxious to hear from you. The servants send their love to you.

Your affectionate mother,
Sarah E. Watkins

If you are sick and cannot write, get someone to write for you. Let me know exactly how you are. Your Pa named Polly's baby Polly Early [*slave baby*].

88. Meaning Molly had many slaves to inherit.

To Letitia Walton from Sarah Watkins:

February 6, 1858
Carrollton, Mississippi

My Dear Child,

I received your affectionate letter of January 14th last Sunday with delight to hear that you all are in good health and you were in fine spirits and you were enjoying yourself in the pleasures of life. But my child, the worldly pleasure you enjoy will do for this life. Your poor soul, what will become of that? In an hour when you think not the Lord might call you away. Do seek God and become a Christian. Then you will have real happiness in this world and be prepared to meet your Savior in heaven. If we cannot live together in this world, let us try to be Christians that we may live together in heaven forever. Do not be the cause of your husband giving up his religion, encourage him to hold out faithful and God will bless him.

Mary wrote me that sometimes she thinks she has religion and then she has has a doubt but she knows some of her sins are pardoned. Her Pa don't want her to join the church. He thinks she does not know what she is about and if she was to attend a party she would dance. I think she had better not be too hasty in joining. If she is truly regenerated she would know that all of her sins are pardoned, not some of them.

There is to be a party the eleventh of this month in Carrollton called the bachelor's party. Lizzie and Laura Whitehead spent the day here this day two weeks. They told me that there had been storm parties at Mr. Folke's, Mr. Simmons' and Mr. McKinsie's the week before. The road was so bad that Judge Collins' carriage with four mules to it stuck in the mud going to Mr. Simmons' party. There has been very little cold weather here this winter but it rained enough to make the roads bad. It snowed last Thursday evening if the ground had not been wet, it would have been deep enough to stay until now. I have not commenced gardening yet, but will as soon as the ground is dry enough. Have you a garden on the place you are living at? Had you no woman that you dried up your lard yourself?

You say that Mr. Walton is in easier circumstances than he has been since you were married. He may be less in debt. How can he be in easier circumstances when he has sold all of his negroes and yet owes two thousand dollars? Did it take all of his negroes sold to pay for his debts? Was he owing his brother anything when he sold him his negroes? My reason for inquiring is your Pa and I was talking about it a short time before I received your letter. He said he thought he had heard that Mr. Walton was owing his brother George. I told him that he was not owing him and that you had written me that he was not compelled to sell his negroes. Do not let Mr. Walton know my inquiries. He might think I am too inquisitive about his affairs. I will give you one hundred dollars for America this year. I received a letter from Sarah Ann Fitzgerald lately: she wrote me that Tilla and her children would have to be sold at March court to pay her Pa's debts. He was owing 1,000 dollars. She said her mother had gone to Courtland [*Alabama*] a few days before she wrote to get a place to board at, she intended to break up keeping house.[89]

I am very sorry for her and the children particularly. Sarah Ann's letter was written and spelt badly. I wrote her to get her teacher to instruct her and Letty in writing letters.

Mr. Harris staid here one night last week. He inquired about you. Asked how many children you have. Asked if Mary would be as good looking as Miss Lettie. I told him I did not think she will be as good looking but she was fonder of school than you were.

Give my love to Mr. Walton. Kiss the children for me. Tell Newton to kiss you often for me. Whip that temper out of Early. Aunt Letty said I had very high temper when I was a baby. I have enough now and say too much for my good.

Sally says kiss Newton for her. I asked her if you must kiss Early too, she said yes but she loves Newton best. Sally, Hannah, Abram, America and all would if they knew I was writing to send love to you and the children. They are anxious to know if you hear from Aunt Clara and how she likes her home.[90] I reckon you wish you had her and some of the rest back. I have written this letter in a hurry to send by Abram this evening. Write soon and often. I am always anxious to hear from you all and do hope and pray you all may do well and make a fortune yet. I like to forget to tell you Mr. Sam Watkins of Petersburg wrote your Pa that Uncle David Williams died suddenly Christmas day with a stroke of paralysis.

Your affectionate mother,
Sarah E. Watkins

The work of the plantation went on and the doctor and his factor kept supplies coming in. An order of April 1858 gives a view of what was brought in (and required money).

89. Sarah Ann Fitzgerald was Mrs. Watkins's niece, daughter of her brother, Thomas. Thomas had inherited slaves from his mother. Tilla may have been the child of one of these. The family seemed to be in very straightened circumstances following the deaths of Uncle Billy, Aunt Letty, and brother William.

90. Aunt Clara was the Walton slave who was baby nurse for Newton and accompanied Lettie and little Newton on their trip to Mississippi in 1856. She and the other Walton Negroes, except for Denmark, went to Louisiana to work on George Walton's plantation there.

10 sacks	coarse salt [pickling and preserving]
3 sacks	fine salt
1 barrel	rock salt
1 can	sperm oil [lamp]
1/2 box	candles
2 dressed	deer skins
2 tanned	skins
42 pair	russet shoes [shoes for slaves]
4 coils	rope
4 hanks	twine
5 pieces	Kentucky bagging [for cotton bales]
3 bottles	castor oil
3 bottles	sweet oil, sometimes used as skin lotion
1 bottle	spirits turpentine
1	tongs
2 ounce	opium
1 ounce	quinine
6 pounds	white wax
1 pound	salt petre

and in June, a less plebian order was placed:

1 basket	wine
1 box	cognac brandy
1 malt	coffee

To Letitia Walton from Sarah Watkins:

April 5, 1858
Carrollton, Mississippi

My Dear Beloved Child,

I received your affectionate letters written the 21st February and 6th March. As I expected you would come, I delayed answering them. I have almost given you out and I will not put off writing any longer. I want to see you and the children very much and will be very much disappointed if you do not come. I anticipated seeing so much happiness with my dear children and grand children next July and August it seems that my anticipation is blasted in having you and your children with me as the time has past that you expected to come. I am very sorry that you are disappointed in coming. What could prevent you from coming?

Patty [*slave*] came in just now. I told her I was writing to you. She said give my love to her and tell her for God's sake come along. I said to her perhaps you were in the family way. She said for that reason I want her to come where she can be taken care of and not stay there for them doctors to kill her. Octavia wrote me a note and sent it by John Smith yesterday inquiring about you, if you had come and when did I hear from you last, that she had not heard from you in a long time. She wrote very affectionately about you. She is at Mr. Hawkins'. I went to church in Middleton yesterday. I saw Mrs. Phillips and her daughters. Mrs. Parmele inquired about you and said she intends writing to you shortly. Mary Arnold is in bad health and in the family way. She is under the Dr.'s practice. Mrs. E. Whitehead had a son Saturday week, she was very sick at the birth of it. I was to see her last Friday evening, she was doing well. I spent the day at Mr. Hemingway's Saturday. Mrs. Hemingway was not as well as usual. Margaret Ann's health is very bad. She looks as badly as her mother. Major Hawkins' family dined with us the 12th of March. I promised Mrs. Hawkins to carry you to see her when you come as soon as you get rested. She was prevented from coming sooner by her children having the whooping cough. If you were here now you could have fine times fishing, they bite well. The Dr. caught several messes last week.

My garden is very backwards. The weather has been good for four days. I hope it will continue so. I have only eighteen little chickens and several hens sitting. The peas you had for dinner, were they this year's growth? Early must be a hearty boy to eat so much salad. Your Pa paid to Judge Whitehead the twenty-fourth of March the money I owed you. The amount was ninety-five dollars. He paid him one dollar interest on it which made ninety-six dollars Judge Whitehead received from him.

I received a letter from Baby last week. She was well and very anxious to come home. She says it seems that June will never come for her to come home. Semira [slave] had a daughter the 21st of February. Your Pa named it Jane, after his sister. I know so little news I have nothing to write that would be interesting to you.

Give my love to Mr. Walton. Kiss the children for me. Tell Newton to kiss you for me every day. The negroes send love to you and say you must come, they want to see you and the children. Come my dear child if you can, I am so anxious to see you and the children.

Write soon.

Your affectionate mother,
Sarah E. Watkins

To Letitia Walton from Sarah Watkins:

April 26, 1858
Carrollton, Mississippi

My Dear Child,

Your very welcome letter the 9th April was received with a great deal of delight Saturday night. You cannot imagine how uneasy I had been about you for the last week. Saturday night week just before I went to bed I saw an account in the Memphis paper of the steamboat in Fall City exploding her boiler just as she was leaving New Orleans and seven or eight people were killed and several injured. I was afraid you and your children were on it and had gotten destroyed. I went to bed, had a cry, and before day and all day Sunday felt sick and did not feel well until I received your letter. Oh, it was such a relief to me to know that my beloved child and grandchildren were not lost. When I think of it I feel like saying glory to God. Mr. Simmons had sent me word by Abram that Octavia had gotten a letter from you saying you expected to start in two or three weeks. Octavia staid with Mrs. Neill last week. Ritter [*slave*] saw her at Maj. Neill's Sunday week. She sent me your letter by Ritter. I intended going to Mr. Simmons' this evening but it has been so cloudy and cold all the morning that I declined going until tomorrow if the weather is good. It has been disagreeable and changeable weather for April. I have had strawberries enough for my dinner twice or three times. They were not quite ripe. The peach trees are full of peaches. I will have peas shortly.

Your Pa started to Arkansas last Thursday week. He seems determined on that State. Land is selling so high I think he will not buy any there. I have a lonely time by myself and wish you and your sweet children were with me. I hope it will not be long before I have the pleasure of having you all with me. Your health must be good to be able to carry Newton on your back. You are wrong to strain yourself in that way, it might cause you to have falling of the womb again. My health is good with the exception of my back that is always hurting me.

I had the steel trap set in the peahouse to catch the rats. It caught a cat by the tongue and cut it off. Ritter brought it to show me and it made my back hurt me to look at it. I had to turn off from it. Mr. Pentecost [*overseer*] was taken sick one night last week. He is confined to his house yet but not dangerously sick. Harry Ann [*slave*] has been sick a week today. I don't think she is sick much, now she has a pain in her side and had a blister put on it today. I have twenty-four little turkeys and about eighty little chickens. This is very bad weather on them. It is really a chilly day. I am sorry to hear of cousin

Mrs. Stith's death. I have heard before of Stith's unkindness to her. Has Eggleston Townes moved back to Alabama yet? The times are so dull. I have not been from home nor seen nobody since I wrote to you last. I do not know any news to write you. I want to see you all very much and hope we will have the pleasure of meeting soon. Give my love to Mr. Walton and kiss the children for me and tell Newton to kiss you every day for me. America sends love to you and the children and says you must come on. All the servants would send their love if they knowed I was writing.

Write soon and often.

> Your affectionate mother,
> Sarah E. Watkins

April 29th:

I started to Mr. Simmons' Tuesday, half after eleven o'clock and came back home last evening. Mrs. Simmons appeared so glad to see me. Octavia and Martha Fox had been all day on the creek fishing. They got back late in the evening. Octavia heard I was there and a lady came with me. She thought it was you. She was disappointed to find it was not so. I was very much pleased with my visit. Mrs. Simmons is such a pleasant lady and Octavia is a sweet girl and gets prettier every day. They are very anxious for you to come. We talked about you a great deal. Nancy seemed glad to see me and sorry for me to come away. She is so brisk for one of her age.

It is said that Albert Keys is engaged to be married to Miss Maddox, a pretty girl, her father married the widow Gaden. Mrs. John Hawkins is in the family way, so said. April 30th. I spent today very pleasantly at Mr. E. Whitehead's. It is said that Tom Purnell is courting Miss Maddox, the same lady that A. Keys is said to be engaged to. Some people think T. Purnell and Octavia will be married. It is said Major Cothron is pleased with Octavia. Mary F. Pleasants is married to Dr. Stuart. He lives in Sidon. There is some talk of Margaret Sykes coming to Mississippi next fall. Until lately Dr. Sykes opposed her bringing her children, he said she might come but he would not come nor let the children come. He has consented for the children to come with her and he will come with her to New Orleans. SEW

To Letitia Walton from Sarah Watkins:

> June 14, 1858
> Carrollton, Mississippi

My Dear Child,

I received your affectionate letter of the 18th of May two weeks ago and would have answered it immediately if I had not written to you a short time before. I am very sorry you were disappointed in coming. As this is the fourteenth of June and you have not come yet, I have given you out. Baby will be here in two weeks. How happy I would be if both of my children would get here the same day. I dined with Octavia Simmons at Judge Collins' yesterday. We went there from preaching. Octavia said she had not received a letter from you since February. She thought you were expecting to come was the reason you had not written to her. I did not have an opportunity to ask her about Major Cothron. I advised her not to marry an old man. She asked me why not. I told her I would hate to see her married to an old man. I don't think it is so about Tom Purnell courting Miss Maddox.

Brother's wife came to her brother's, G. Bledsoe, yesterday three weeks. She brought her youngest son with her. She was there a week before I heard of her being there. We sent for her the day after I heard she was there. She came and staid two nights and two days and said she would come back the next Sunday. She did not come and I have not heard from her since. She spoke of going back to Alabama last week but said if she got a letter from her daughter saying all was well, she might perhaps stay longer. She says Tilly and her children were not sold, that she forbid the sale of them. She, sister and her two youngest children board at Mr. Barbee's, the other children board at Mountain Home [*Alabama*] and go to school.

Semira was very sick last week. Friday we were afraid she would die. She had severe pain in her stomach and nothing she took would stay in her stomach and she had the hiccough. She is a great deal better now and I hope on the mend. There has been very hard washing rains lately. They have washed these old hills mightly and injured our cotton crop but not worse than other people's. I have the most backward garden I ever did have. It is disheartening to work at it. It makes me almost willing to move to a new country. Nothing but the high price of land prevents your Pa from moving to Arkansas.

Mr. E. Whitehead's family spent a day with me last week. I have not seen Jennie since she was married. Emma Kennedy is sick and has been expected to die with typhoid fever. Mrs. Hemingway's mother is to see her. I do wish you lived where I could go to see you, it would give me so much pleasure to visit you. I do want to see you all so much. I am afraid it will be a long time before I can have happiness to see you and your dear children. Do my dear child, strive to be a Christian and if we cannot enjoy ourselves together in this world, let us try to live together in heaven where parting will be no more and pleasure will be forever. I try very hard to walk in the path of rightousness and hope the Lord will hear my feeble prayers for myself and family and give us prepared hearts for heaven.

Give my love to Mr. Walton and kiss the children for me. America sends love to you all and says you must come.

Your affectionate mother,
Sarah E. Watkins

To Letitia Walton from Sarah Watkins:

October 7, 1858
Carrollton, Mississippi

My Dear Child,

It frequently happens that I write to you a few days before receiving a letter from you. For that reason I delay answering your letters directly. It has been some time since I received your letter of the 27th ult. I have been so busy getting Mary's and her Pa's clothes in order for them to go off I could not have time to write. They started this evening. They will stay in Carrollton tonight and take the stage in the morning to go as far as Water Valley [*Mississippi*] and then take the car and go on perhaps to Tuscumbia and Florence [*Alabama towns*] and then come back to a place this side of Tuscumbia (I don't know the name of the place) to meet Mr. Todd and his daughter Lucy. Mr. Todd wrote to your Pa to meet him at that place and they are going on to Arkansas to look at the land and buy land if they like. Mary will not go with them to Arkansas. She will return to Holly Springs to school. She left home very cheerful, she did not cry. I came very near it, I feel very sad about her leaving me but as it is for her good, I bear it with fortitude. She had two chills [*malaria?*] last month and two this. I hope she will not have no more. She told me to give her love to you and tell you she would write to you when she gets settled at school. She received your letter of the 22nd ult. on the 5th of this month. It is glorious news to me my dear child to hear that you have made a start for heaven. I pray you will be a sincere Christian and hold out faithful. Do not despair and give up trying. God will hear the prayers of those that ask in faith. Be willing to forsake all your sins, give your soul to God and he will make you a Christian.

There has been [*church*] meetings at several places about here. I have not heard of any revivals. There is to be a quarterly meeting at Sissiley's mill Saturday and Sunday. I do not expect to go as Abram has to start Sunday to Arkansas with the buggy and one of the carriage mules. I am afraid to drive any of the other mules. Salsbury drives the carriage very well. He has a boil on his knee at this time.

There has been more sickness here for two months than we ever had before. Most all the servants have been sick and are sick with chills and fever. Some of them get well and take them again. One week there were eighteen sick. They would be taken sick two and three a day. Siah has been very sick he has been in three weeks or more. He is not strong enough yet to go out to work. I put Milly out to work last week. She and the baby are the only two of Martha's children that have not had chills. Ritter was taken with a chill yesterday while she was packing up Mary's clothes. She has been taking quinine today. She took the last spoonful tonight. She said thank God all gone, she says it gripes her. She has just taken a dram to relieve her. Sally, Hannah, Glasgow, Tom, Tave, and Alfred, are the only sick ones at this time. Sally and Hannah have been very sick. Glasgow says he is going out tomorrow if he is as well as he is today. I think by tomorrow all of them will need the cook more than a doctor.

I had a chill and fever Saturday, took quinine Sunday and it made me very sick at my stomach. I am very well now except my back that is hurting me at this time. I make so many mistakes that I will quit writing for tonight.

The 8th—My dear child, night has come again. I spent today with Mrs. E. Whitehead. Lizzie was just about to get on her horse to go to Mrs. Phillips'. She had promised Mrs. Phillips to go and assist her about some work. Mrs. Phillips, Mrs. Farmer, Eppie Oliver, and Julia Parmele expect to start to Alabama tomorrow. Mrs. Phillips has been sick several days and was sick in bed today. Mr. Oliver[91] sent his buggy and horses and hired a rockaway[92] and horses at five dollars a day for them to go. Mrs. Phillips intends leaving Eppie at school in Tuscaloosa.

I received a letter from Siah[93] informing me that he would repair my mother's grave for eight dollars. In the letter he said he wished I would write to someone to see to Brother's children. It appears that they are at a loss for a mother. It appears that their mother is banished from all society. I cannot understand why he writes in that way about her.

Your Pa says he had relations named Harris. Buckner Harris had some relation named Early Harris. I reckon the preacher is some of that family.

No new cases of sickness here today. Hannah and Glasgow are not as well as they were yesterday. Middleton has not improved any. The stage comes through there from Water Valley and goes on towards Shongalo. I want to see you all very much but would not have you to risk the yellow fever to come. It is thought that Nat Neal died with the yellow fever. He had been to Vicksburg.

91. Mr. Oliver was Mrs. Phillips's son−in−law. Eppie Oliver was his daughter. When widowed by the death of the Phillips daughter, he married Elizabeth Whitehead, Edmunds Whitehead's eldest child.

92. A rockaway was a four−wheeled carriage, open at the sides, with two or three seats and a standing top.

93. Siah was probably a Fitzgerald servant back in Alabama where Sarah's mother was married.

Give my love to Mr. Walton and kiss the children for me. It is very dry and dusty, yesterday it turned cold and this morning there was a frost. Have you seen the comet?[94] Ritter and America send their love to you.

> Your affectionate mother,
> Sarah E. Watkins

Write soon.

From Sarah to Lettie:

> October 26, 1858
> Carrollton, Mississippi

My Dear Child:

Your letter of the 23rd ult. was received last Saturday two weeks. My beloved child, it made me feel very happy to hear that you had embraced religion. I pray to God that you may hold out faithfully and never turn back to this sinful world. The Christian has many temptations, crosses and trials to contend with; you must pray to the Lord to enable you to bear with the many difficulties you will have to meet with and strive to live it as a Christian. In your prayers remember your poor mother who needs the prayers of the righteous.

I wrote you Mary had started to Holly Springs to school. However she has gone to Patapsco school near Baltimore. Your Pa was taking her with him to meet Mr. Todd and his daughter near Tuscumbia. He met with Bishop Green on the car the other side of Holly Springs and found out that Bishop Green was on his way to Baltimore. He got him to take charge of Mary and she went with him to Baltimore and he carried her to Patapsco school. Your Pa says Mary was willing to go. He got home Saturday from Arkansas. He nor Mr. Todd did not buy land. Your Pa offered a man twenty thousand dollars for his place, he would not take it and he asked twenty-five thousand for it. Your Pa met with Bishop Green when he was coming home and received a letter from him that he wrote when he was in Baltimore. He said Mary arrived safe without any accident. We have not received a letter from her yet. I was very much surprised and grieved when I received a letter from her Pa informing me of Mary's going off to Patapsco. If she is satisfied I will be glad that she is gone there. The school at Holly Springs have not the same teachers and a young man for their music teacher. I would object to that.[95]

Ritter has a rising in the same place that she had it four years ago when we were coming from Alabama. It commenced rising Thursday night. She kept

---

94. Donati's Comet, first seen in 1858 and due to reappear in 2098.
95. Young, male, unmarried music teachers were considered especially risky contacts.

up until last Monday week. She has since suffered a great deal with it until last Friday since that time she has been better. I sent for Dr. Griffith to see her last Thursday, he opened the rising before it was ripe and stuck it very deep which makes the place very sore at this time. She is well now all to that soreness and weakness. From the quantity of blood she discharged I think it must have been broken inside.

The negroes continue to have chills. Hannah has not come out yet; I don't believe she is sick only weak. Becky was taken sick last week. I have Semira cooking, she does tolerable well for a new hand. I wish I was like you, could go and cook to suit myself. My flour is indifferent. I reckon that is the reason Semira can't make good biscuits. I told her to get Patty to show her how to make a biscuit and when they came in they had so much soda in them they were not fit to eat. I searched over my old receipts and looked in the cookery books to find a receipt for making soda biscuits but could not find one. Write me how you make soda biscuits. How much soda do you put to a quart of flour? Every lady ought to learn to cook if she don't have it to do herself, it is a great help to her to know how to cook and then she would never be bothered about having a cook that did not understand cooking. I have never had a good cook and I never had no one to show me how to cook and I never had the turn to go in the kitchen and learn. I am sorry for it now.

Alfred Robinson died the 10th of this month. Judge Collins' ginhouse was burned down lately, it is supposed to contain forty or fifty bales of cotton. I do want to see you all very much but would not have you to risk the yellow fever to come. America sends her love to you and says I must tell you she is getting healthy that she has not had the chills yet. Sally and Martha send love to you and the children. Martha says what did you take to cure you when you had the colic and it would go off by the way of your bowels? She is affected in the same way. Give my love to Mr. Walton and the children and kiss the children for me. Tell them they must be good boys and not let you have to whip them.

> Your affectionate Mother,
> Sarah E. Watkins

November 1st, 1858
Carrollton, Mississippi

My Dear Child,

Why have you not written to me? Not receiving a letter from you makes me very uneasy fearing you are sick. I was very much surprised and grieved when I received a letter from your Pa saying he had sent you to Patapsco to school. Since he has returned home and told me about the school at Holly

Springs, I think he acted wisely in sending you to Patapsco. I hope you are well pleased and doing well. Do my dear child be attentive to your studies and obedient to your teachers. You have only two years to go to school, try and make good use of your time. It will make me proud to have a well-educated and accomplished daughter. Your Pa is very anxious to get a letter from you. He says if you are not contented to be there it will make him mad.

He received a letter from his sister Jane Hillyer, last week. She said she had just written to you and would go to see you in a few days and if you need her attention, she and her family would do the same for you as she would for her own child. If you are ever very sick, let her know it. Write to her and be affectionate to her and she will be kind to you. Your pa says if you want any pocket money, ask Mr. Archer to give you five dollars. Ask Mr. Archer to get you what dresses you need for the winter or give you money to get them. He says you can go to Washington City when you have an opportunity if you want to go, that he will not mind the expense of your going.

I spent the day with Mr. E. Whitehead the day after you left. I went to preaching in Middleton yesterday. Mr. Neiler preached. Very few people were at preaching. Preaching was at the Christian church. Coming home I passed Colonel Moore's carriage. The girls bowed to me as they passed. Judge Collins' daughters stopped to invite me home with them when they got to their road. Betty has come home. They inquired very particularly about you. Betty and Mollie looked pretty. The negroes have chills yet. Ritter has been very sick with a rising in the same place she had of four years ago. Dr. Griffith had to open the place. She is well enough to come in to sewing this morning for the first time in two weeks.

I received a letter from Lettie Saturday, three weeks. She wrote that she had embraced religion. It made me feel very happy. I pray she may hold out faithful and gain a rich crown in heaven. Baby, take care of yourself, don't do nothing imprudent that will make you sick. I will be always uneasy about you. I pray God will hear my feeble prayers and take care of you and permit us to meet again next summer. Abram, I believe, is going to town. I hope he will bring a letter from you. We are so anxious to hear from you. Ritter and America and Martha send love to you. Martha says I must tell you she has a very sore eye. Several of the negroes have and have had sore eyes. Alfred has a shaking chill.

Your affectionate mother,
Sarah E. Watkins

P.S. Abram has returned from the office and brought no letter from you. What can be the matter? If you are ever too sick to write get someone to write to me for you. It would relieve my feelings so much to receive a letter from you. I am so uneasy about you.

To Letitia Walton from Sarah Watkins:

December 20, 1858
Carrollton, Mississippi

Mrs. Lettie A. Walton
Austin, Texas

My Dear Child,

Your affectionate letter of the 15 ult. was received last Thursday two weeks. I have been very busy cutting out negroes' clothes and drying up my lard that has prevented me from answering your letter and I thought you would be here before you would receive a letter from me. I received a letter from Baby the same time I received yours and Pa got one from her last night. She is getting on very well and very much pleased with the school. We received her reports of grade for studies and deportment. All her marks were the highest number, 300, except music that was 298. We are proud of her and I think she will be an intelligent lady and good looking when she is grown. Judge Hillyer has been to see her and wanted her to go home with him[96] Her teacher was away and she could not go without his consent.

I was at preaching at the Baptist church in Middleton yesterday. Going on I met Octavia Simmons going to Judge Collins'. There was a gentleman in the carriage with her, I suppose he was her relation, Mr. Simmons. She asked me about you. I told her I was expecting you every day. She said that she is going to Carolina week after next and she must come back to spend the winter with you. She and Sarah Collins came to church. Lettie, I do believe from my heart Octavia is engaged to be married. After preaching I asked her who was going with her to Carolina and she said a relation. I asked his name, she said Simmons. I asked her if she was going to be married. She said not now. I asked who it was to and if it was to that relation, she said no, it was not to him. I begged her to tell me who it was to. She said she could not now. My curiosity and anxiety is raised to know if it so and who to. I hope not to Major Cothron, he is too old and ugly for such a pretty girl.

Mrs. Phillips has returned from Alabama. I saw her yesterday. She inquired about you and said I must let her know when you come and that she wants to see you. Margaret Sykes has been to Mississippi over two weeks. Dr. Sykes came with her as far as New Orleans. He speaks of buying a sugar plantation in Louisiana. William Whitehead [*son of Edmunds Whitehead*] is to be married to Sally Tyson the 22nd of this month. Mary Arnold [*daughter of Judge White-*

96. Judge Junius Hillyer's wife, Jane, was Dr. Watkins's sister. He was a senator from Georgia.

head] is in very bad health. She has gone to a water doctor[97] in Winchester, Tennessee. Laura Whitehead went with her. I went to Carrollton last month shopping and to have my likeness taken for you and Baby. The artist was sick, I could not get it taken. Since that time the weather has been bad. It seems that I can never get it taken.

It commenced raining last evening and is raining today. Chills has not entirely quit our negroes yet. Every week some of them have chills. Yesterday week Polly's Moses had a chill and while the fever was on him he had a fit. The doctor bled him and at night gave him a dose of calomel. He discharged a worm since then and he is well. That is the second fit he has had this fall, I expect worms is the cause of his having them. I had about three chills this fall. My health is very good at this time. If I could only be blessed with happiness as I am health, what a happy woman I would be.

We all have trials and crosses and mine are not greater than I should bear. I pray God will enable me to bear with mine that when I die I may wear the crown in heaven. I pray you are still enjoying religion and will hold out a faithful Christian and if we cannot live together in this world, we may in heaven where parting will be no more. Give my love to Mr. Walton and kiss the dear children for me. I am anxiously looking for you and the children every day. Ritter and America send love to you all. All the servants would if they knew I was writing.

Write soon and often.

> Your affectionate mother,
> Sarah E. Watkins

97. Mary Arnold was suffering from water retention and probably what now would be called toxemia of pregnancy.

CHAPTER FIVE

"Will I ever enjoy that much happiness again?"

The second Watkins daughter, Mary, spent the three ensuing school years (1858–60) at the Patapsco Female Institute, near Baltimore, Maryland. She acquired much polish and grace, as is illustrated by the marked progress she makes, over time, toward being an accomplished correspondent. Too, her parents took much pride in her consistently high marks and in her popularity.

The years were trying ones for the doctor and his wife. Although the national sectional controversy seems to have attracted only a scant amount of attention, closer to home they suffered numerous tragedies. Much sickness occurred and death visited often. Many acquaintances and slaves died. Compounding the losses in slaves, a large amount of livestock, especially mules, perished. But the doctor still had the wherewithal to buy more, which he did. The cotton still grew and the carriages still were available, for the most part, whenever Mrs. Watkins wished to go on a visit or attend some church function. (She revealed in one letter to Mary, however, that the Watkinses themselves received but few callers at their home: "On account of your father's eccentricity, I have to live so aloof from everybody that very few people feel welcome to come here.")

Lettie and her brood, in Texas, add another dimension to the family concerns. Although reconciled—to a degree—the Watkins family was still strained over the state of affairs that existed, one so different from any previously envisioned as acceptable by the strong-willed and self-centered doctor. Lettie's mother sometimes said that Lettie had been "too pretty" for her own good; that her great beauty had been a mixed blessing, bringing temptations that would have been better avoided.

December 27, 1858
Carrollton, Mississippi

Miss Mary E. Watkins
Patapsco Female Institute
Ellicotts Mill, Maryland

My Dear Daughter,

Your welcome and affectionate letter of 15th inst. was received on yesterday. You have improved very much in your manner and style of conducting your correspondence. However, you go to improve.

On 22nd. inst., William Whitehead and Miss Tyson were married. Mrs. E. G. Whitehead sent to your mother some of the wedding cake. I enclose two parcels of it to you. One is for you and the other is for the girl in school you love best. I do not think the cake is of any consequence for that young lady, but I want her to know that I like any person whom you love. When you write again you must tell me to whom you gave the cake. Tell me also if you visited your Aunt Jane during Christmas—also if you have seen cousin Anderson Watkins.

Your sister arrived here this day about 5 o'clock p.m. in company with her two children. They are all well. We are having a dull Christmas here, but I hope you have had a lively time at Washington. Your mother and sister send love to you. Please excuse this short letter.

Your affectionate father,
Thomas A. Watkins

To Dr. Watkins from a carriage maker in New York:

February 7, 1859
William T. Worrall
with Wm. McDonald
Manufacturer of
CARRIAGES, HARNESS, & c.
Repository
No. 26 Beckman & 18 Spruce St.
New York

Doctor Thomas A. Watkins
Carrollton, Mississippi

Dear Sir:

Your welcome letter came duly to hand and contents noted. I shall be happy to sell your friend Mr. E. G. Whitehead, anything he may need in my line, for a N. Orleans Acceptance payable next February. I should recommend No. 44 to him for its superior comfort and elegance, besides the novelty of the style. Buggies such as I sold you, are now nearly out of date. Fashion, remorseless tyrant that she is, has made that style so antiquated that there are no buyers for it now. I can find him a very fine affair like No. 44 for $200 with a good set of harness. I mailed Mr. Whitehead one of my books, from which he can select any style that pleases him. I shall be delighted to hear from you at any time.

I remain Sir,
Your friend
Wm. L. McDonald
Worrall

To Mary Watkins from Letitia Walton:

March 15, 1859

My Own Sister,

It has been a long time since we heard from you or received a letter from you. Pa received a letter from Mr. Archer last week and also your report with which we were all very much pleased. It is indeed gratifying my sister to see that you obtained the highest mark for everything.

It pains me to say that Pa is still confined to his bed though he is able to get up and go out and has been able to do that all the time—still he is too weak to sit up long. Mother and Pa both requested me to write to you. Pa is too feeble to write and Mother is compelled to stay with him all the time. He does not like for either of us to be away from him and particularly mother—he does not like for her to go out of the room.

Pa is very much changed, my sister, and loves me and my children now. I have talked a great deal to him about religion and last night he said he believed he was a Christian. Oh! You cannot imagine the unspeakable joy those words gave me. I felt as happy as when I professed religion. He says that he intends doing a good part[98] by me and my children and he said it was all made up between us now but when you write *be sure* to say nothing about that as his mind may not have been right when he said it, time can only tell how true it is. His mind is very much affected and caused from distress at losing his mules and one of the carriage horses *died* before it had been here a week. The other one ran away with the plough—was in great danger of cutting himself to pieces and killing Glasgow. Glasgow fell down while the horse was running and kicking—though he held on to him and thus prevented any accident.

Mr. E. Whitehead comes to see Pa every day or two. Judge Whitehead and Tom Kennedy have been once. Mr. Hemingway comes often—has staid two nights with Pa. He seems to do Pa more good than anyone else. You have no idea what an intelligent man Mr. Hemingway is. He has an extraordinary mind. He gets Pa engaged in conversation and Pa almost forgets his malady. He is a good man and I shall always love him.

Pa is better this morning and I sincerely hope he will soon be well. When you write—write nothing that can possibly disturb him as the least thing racks his mind. He loves you very much and talks a great deal about you. I asked him if he did wish you to come home and he said "No, it would only distress the child and she had better stay there." He is much better than he has been and he is not dangerously ill now so do not distress yourself sister—but attend to your studies and improve yourself as fast as possible.

The peach trees are done blooming here and are beginning to have large leaves. The hyacinths are blooming. It is right cold this morning—but if it gets colder we will have roses in a few days.

The children have fattened as much since they have been here. Newton is as plump as a little shoat [*little pig*].

I believe I told you that Jennie Kennedy has a *little daughter. It is a perfect scrap.*[99] Margaret Palmer Sykes has another son born since Jennie's.

Amos was rolling and groaning with the colic a while ago, with that exception, all the servants are well. Joe Eggleston came home during the fever. America sends *howdy*. Goodbye my dear sister. I am so anxious to see you

---

98. I.e., to recognize her adequately in his will.
99. Camilla (Minnie) Kennedy, born February 18, 1859, married H. M. Vaiden, Jr., 1882.

and glad the time is fast approaching (if the Lord is willing) for us to meet again. Write often.

Your devoted sister,
Lettie Walton

P.S. 17th—Pa has told me several times lately that he has become reconciled to my marriage and that he wants me to have as much of his property as you get. You may speak of it when you write if you wish.

June 3, 1859
Carrollton, Mississippi

Miss M. E. Watkins
Ellicotts Mill, Md.

My Dear Child:

Your very nice and well written letter of the 5th ult. was received the 23rd ult. A letter from you is always made much over by us all. I am so sleepy and dull I have scarcely energy to write. We have not been from home nor seen nobody lately to hear no news to write that will interest you. Your Pa expects to start for you in the morning, that is the most pleasant news to me that I can write. I do rejoice that I will have the pleasure of seeing my dear child in a few weeks. He intends stopping in Alabama and other places before he goes on to Patapsco.

Martha is sick this week with the fever that prevented him from starting yesterday. She is better today. Ritter was married last Sunday week at church to Maj. Neill's Jackson. She has had chills this week. She is at work today but not very well. The weather is very warm and dry. This morning I thought we would get a good rain and the clouds passed by. Some of the little negroes are sitting near the gate singing a very mournful tune. We had a good mess of strawberries for dinner today. Your Pa said he wishes he could carry them to you. The plums are ripe. Lettie and her boys go to the orchard to get them every evening. Newton goes to sleep in the evening when he lies down. He says to his mother wake me up when you go to the orchard.

I have no work to do for myself. I want to go to Carrollton to buy me a dress. I have no way to go because the carriage wheels are out of repair—the mules cannot be stopped from plowing to carry it to Carrollton to have the wheels fixed. I do wish I was able to have carriage horses and driver of my own so I could go when I please. As it is when I want to go there is always an obstacle to prevent me from going.

Don't make your Pa think you are not anxious to come home. It would make him sorry that he went for you. I know you will be glad to come. Lettie and I am so anxious for you to come. Lettie unites with me in love to you and says she wants you to make haste home. Ritter sends her love to you. All the servants would if they knew I was writing. Write soon, your letters are slow coming.

Your affectionate mother,
Sarah E. Watkins

P.S. Your Pa says I must tell you that he will visit with you after commencement before he starts home.

To Mary Watkins from Sarah Watkins:

November 2, 1859
Carrollton, Mississippi

Miss Mary E. Watkins
Patapsco Institute
Ellicotts Mill, Md.

My Dear Child,

I received your affectionate letter of 22nd inst. yesterday. It's useless to express the pleasure it gave me as it is always a pleasure to receive letters from my dear children. I expect before this you have received a letter from me. I am very lonely but sick negroes and a plenty of work prevent me from being lonesome. Dear Lettie and her family started to Texas Monday week. Mr. Walton came Thursday to Mr. Whitehead's and stayed until the morning they started.[100] I spent the day with him at Mr. Whitehead's Saturday. He walked with us far as the overseer's old house when we came home in the evening.

Your Pa left home yesterday. He said he was going down on the river fishing and will be gone until Saturday or Sunday. The weather has been quite cold several days but not cold enough for snow. It is very dry and dusty. It has been pretty weather for gathering the crop. We will make a very good crop of corn and cotton. The negroes come in most every day with chills. There are only seven sick at this time. Sunday week Lucinda had a chill. Tuesday evening she was speechless and did not speak until Wednesday morning. She cannot sit up yet. She has congestive fever. Martha's Milly is very sick this morning. I had to stop writing to go to see her. It makes me so uneasy when the negroes are sick and I do not know what to do to relieve them.

I went to preaching last Sunday at the new church near the place where Ritter was married at. It is called Chestnut Hill. There were more common

---

100. Lettie and the children were back in his good grace, but even after a successful visit and with the husband making the long journey from Austin, Texas, Dr. Watkins would not accept him.

folks at it than I knew was in the neighborhood. Fire was made in a large iron pot in the church. The meeting was to continue several days. Octavia Simmons is to be married the seventeenth of this month to Dr. Merriwether. Lizzie Whitehead, Ellen Purnell, Fanny Smith and Sarah Collins are to be her bridesmaids. She will be married in the morning and leave her father's. She will have only her waiters and some of her relations to attend her marriage. Lettie would have been at it if she had staid until the time.

Mrs. Ewing's mother died last week. Miss Lolla Shaw was married last month to Mr. Boling of Kansas City, Mo., November 4.

Early Wednesday evening, Mrs. Eggleston, Miss Fanny Eggleston, and Fanny Cook Jones came and they left this morning. They had been up to Yalobusha visiting. This morning only four negroes are sick. Lucinda is mending and able to sit herself up in bed. Milly has dysentery that makes her sick. I do not think her dangerous. Write to me if you have dyspepsia [*indigestion*] now. Have you had any chills since you left home? Do my dear child be prudent. Don't do anything to injure your health. America sends love to you and says you must write to her. Henrietta sends love to you. Charlotte says I must tell you howdy and says she wants to see you mighty bad. Your Pa says you may go to Washington Christmas. You can tell Mr. Archer that we have written to you that you may to go Washington City, Christmas. Write soon and often.

Your devoted mother,
Sarah E. Watkins

Lettie to Mollie:

November 7, 1859
Concordia Parish, La.

You have doubtlessly heard that my husband has been near father's. I insisted on his going there because I thought perhaps if the people of Carroll could see him some of the slanderous reports would cease and I did not wish to travel alone . . . While he was there I did hope that Pa would become reconciled to our marriage and treat him as a son. But no—he still persists in doing wrong.

December 16, 1859
Carrollton, Mississippi

Miss Mary E. Watkins
Patapsco Institute, Maryland

My Dear Daughter,

I concluded to write you though I have no news to write about except the death of our poor old man London. He was taken sick in Middleton and I brought him home where he lingered about a week. His disease was pneumonia or inflammation of the lungs. He got nearly well and then relapsed and died on 9th inst. His death has affected me a great deal and makes me very low-spirited.

. . . Tell Mr. Archer that we are very much pleased at the quarterly report of you, sent us by him. I hope you will continue to get the best of marks. You are sent to the best of schools at a heavy expense and your friends hope and expect much from you. You must continue to obey the laws of your school and always treat your teachers with great respect. They can have great influence in making you respectable and in giving you a good name. If you do bad it will make me descend in sorrow and in tears to the grave.

. . . It is raining and I expect much bad weather this winter. You must take care and not take colds and not let your crinoline put you so close to the fire during your visits as to be scorched and probably burned up.

> I am, dear daughter,
> with great respect,
> your affectionate Father,
> Thos. A. Watkins

To Mary Watkins from Sarah Watkins:

> December 28, 1859
> Carrollton, Mississippi

My Dear Child:

I received your affectionate letter of the 7 inst. the 20th of the month and could not answer it immediately but sent the composition the first opportunity and hope you will receive it in time. We are having a very dull Christmas, everybody looks dull and sad. Death has again visited this place and taken off one of the most valuable servants. My poor Glasgow[101] was taken with a chill at night last Friday week and died last Thursday evening with pneumonia. He had a pain in his stomach and shortness of breath. The day he was taken was a very cold, raining, sleeting and snowing day. He was in most of it of his own accord as he brought a very heavy hog on his shoulder that he had helped to kill from the spring. I think he strained himself that caused his sickness.

I had a chill Sunday morning and fever all day and night. I feel better today than I have felt since Sunday morning. The negroes still have chills. I hope you are enjoying yourself finely. Your Pa and I are uneasy for fear going to Washington will make you sick. There has been a good deal of cold freezing

---

101. Mrs. Watkins had inherited Glasgow from her father and mother. Today, we would think he had a myocardial infarction.

weather. The icehouse is nearly full of ice. I wish you would be here next summer to drink ice lemonade. You will be so much better off than if you were here to be having chills. If you spend your vacation in Virginia you will have pleasure and ice too. You complain of my not writing to you oftener. It has not been convenient for me to write often. If your Pa does write to you the oftenest it is not because he loves you any better than I do. He has more time to write and sometimes when I am about to write he writes, then I put off my writing for another time.

I heard there was to be a party at Mrs. McIntire's, Mrs. George's, Mrs. Barnes' and Mrs. Key's. Richard Whitehead [*a son of Judge Whitehead*] went up to Lagrange, Tennessee several days ago to marry Mary Conkey.[102] I received a letter from Lettie last Thursday. She had just got to Austin. She and her family were well. I have not seen but one lady since I came from Mrs. Eggleston's and she was Miss Giving. She came to Middleton to see about buying the old Seminary. Your Pa saw her and found out from her that she was acquainted with my relations in Florida and brought her in his buggy to see me. She knew the old maiden cousin Mary and Fanny Fitzgerald. When you write to cousin Betty Irby give my love to her and ask her if Uncle Freeman Fitzgerald's daughter, Virginia, married a son of cousin Edmund or cousin William Irby and ask her if cousin Frank Fitzgerald's wife is not a daughter of cousin William Irby.

Write very soon. We are anxious to hear from you. The servants don't know I am writing as they would send love to you. I have not made cake nor had a turkey for Christmas. Cousin Henry [*Watkins*] is in Carrollton. He has not been to see us since he left here. He expects to stay in Carrollton next year.

Your affectionate mother,
Sarah E. Watkins

To Letitia Walton from Sarah Watkins:

December 28, 1859
Carrollton, Mississippi

My Dear Child,

Your welcome letter was received last Thursday. I am very glad to hear that you and your family arrived safely to Texas. There has been so much very bad and cold weather here it made me very uneasy about you. You have, I expect, received a letter by this time from me. I wrote to you about London [*slave*] being here sick. He died last Friday morning two weeks. He was thought out of danger, could walk about some in his house and was taken

---

102. The daughter of Dr. Z. Conkey of Oxford, Mississippi.

with a chill Wednesday and had one Thursday in the day. Thursday late at night Prince thought he had another, I reckon death had struck him. He died very hard.

Glasgow was taken with a very hard chill in the night last Friday week and died last Thursday evening with pneumonia. He had a pain in his stomach and shortness of breath most all the time. He breathed like the mules with the glanders. It was not known that he was dying until he breathed his last breath. Polly thought he was dying. I think he strained himself bringing a very heavy hog from the spring. He done it of his own accord. It rained, snowed and sleeted Friday week, he was in most of it.

I send you a draft for America's hire this year. Write me what you will hire her for next year. I cannot give you more than one hundred dollars for her as what money I have made by selling butter is my dependence now for paying for her and if your Pa hires her he is not willing to give more than one hundred dollars for her. Please write soon and let me know if you will hire her to me for a hundred dollars or have her hired out for more.

Sally suffers more than she ever did with her jaw. She has not attended in my room for over a week. I had a chill Sunday morning and a fever all day and night, it made me quite sick. I feel better today than I have felt since Sunday morning. Grief I expect was the cause of my sickness. Oh my dear beloved child, I wished for you so often to have your good nursing and to soothe my troubled mind and grieved heart. This is a very dull Christmas with us. I have seen nobody and have not made any cake nor killed a turkey. The negroes are not as merry as they generally are at Christmas.

It is said that Richard Whitehead has gone to Lagrange, Tennessee to marry Mary Conkey. Mrs. McIntire, Mrs. George, Mrs. Keys, and Mrs. Barnes, I heard intended to give a party this Christmas. Mr. Hemingway was here Saturday. He told me about the parties. He said to me that Mr. Walton had been slandered in Carrollton. That Major Cothron and Mr. George said they saw him and the Major said he talked and told Mr. Walton about the report and from what Mr. Walton said to him, convinced them the report was not true. Mr. Hemingway said he would liked to have seen Mr. Walton. He did not know he was in the neighborhood until you were starting away.

Lynn [Hemingway] got home last Saturday week, brought thirty ponies Semira says. He got to Sidon and several of them got away from him. He got them all to three. Collins Hemingway's daughter is married. I have not seen any of Mr. Whitehead's family since you left here. Mr. Whitehead had gone to New Orleans a week ago. Mrs. Estel has bought Mr. Blunt's place. The negroes have chills yet. I feel uneasy about you all yet. I am afraid traveling so much in the cold will cause you all to be sick. Did you get your trunk? Give my love to Mr. Walton and the sweet children. Kiss the children for me and tell them

I want to see them very much. They must kiss you for me every day. Write very soon and be sure to send us a receipt for draft. Hannah sends howdy to you. She has been sick several days with headache and chill. America sends love to you and the children.

> Your devoted mother,
> Sarah E. Watkins

To Mary Watkins from Sarah Watkins:

> January 19, 1860
> Carrollton, Mississippi

My Dear Child,

Your last letter we received from you was dated the 9th of December. It is a month tomorrow since I received it. What is the matter my dear child that you have not written to your parents that love you so dearly? If it was not for the irregularity of the mails, we would be very uneasy about you. I have had so much grief and uneasiness for the last six weeks that it has affected my nerve and mind so much I can scarcely write. Your Pa is so distressed at the negroes dying and so much sickness, he says he has not the heart to write to you.

Jesse was taken sick last Saturday. He was very ill Sunday and Monday and is yet sick but we do not think him dangerous now. Melia came in day before yesterday with the earache and fever. He is sick this morning with headache and some fever. Ritter's husband, Jackson, has been very sick with typhoid fever. Green Woods hired Chloe again this year. This morning a man came to see if she was here, said she had run away. Chloe has come since. I did not see her. Ritt told me Patty persuaded her to go back to Woods.

Your Pa had gone to Carrollton. He has just got back and brought no letter from my children. It has been four weeks today since I received a letter from my dear child Lettie. Cousin Henry intends assisting in teaching school in Carrollton another session. He has not been out to see us since he went to Carrollton. This night week there was a party given at Ware's hotel to Richard Whitehead and his bride. We were invited to it. We do not feel like going to parties. I have not heard anything from it. They had a very rainy evening for it. I have not been from home since I came from Mrs. Eggleston's, not even to preaching. No one has visited us except Mr. Hemingway. He was here a short time one day not long ago. Major Neill[103] and Tom Purnell called here to see Jackson.[104] He was taken sick here but had been able to go home the day they

---

103. Maj. G. F. Neill, local citizen and state senator.

104. Slave from another plantation married to Ritter. It was not unusual for slaves who were married to be at different locations and to have fixed visiting periods.

came to see him. Major Neill was going home with T. Purnell. It is reported that Lizzie Whitehead is engaged to be married to Mr. Oliver (Eppe's father).

I do wish I had some news to write to you. I hear nothing, know nothing and see nothing for that reason. I have nothing to write. Do write soon and let us hear from you. How and where did you spend Christmas? Ritter and America send their love to you.

> Your affectionate mother,
> Sarah E. Watkins

P.S. Sam MacLemore [*Jeff McLemore's brother*] is married to Miss Gipson, John Davis' niece.

January 21st. Your letter of the 10th inst. was received last evening. You cannot imagine how much rejoiced your parents were to receive a letter from their dear child. It put your Pa in a better humor than I have seen him in for several weeks. He has been so unfortunate in the last twelve months in losing mules and negroes that he does not want you to be extravagant. He says we have lost about six thousand dollars worth of property in the last year.

Last Wednesday two weeks in the morning William came to your Pa and said he was sick. He was sick himself and did not think any more about William being sick. Thursday he went to Carrollton. After he had been gone some time Isham came by the yard and told me William had a headache and wanted your Pa to bleed him. When your Pa came back from town about two o'clock I was attending to my lard out in the yard and did not think to tell him. Prince went to see him in the evening and found him speechless. He died the next day.[105] Uncle Vivion said he talked with him at dinner, he did not think him so sick. We think he had a congestive chill. Negroes are always coming in with chills and that made us more careless attending to him.

To Letitia Walton from Sarah Watkins:

> January 27, 1860
> Carrollton, Mississippi

My Dear Child,

I have been waiting an answer to my letter from you before I wrote you again. It seems that I am never to get a letter from you. It has been five weeks yesterday since I received one from you. I am out of patience and write to inquire what can be the cause of your long silence. Perhaps it is the irregularity of the mails and you may be complaining in the same way of me.

It has been a very cold disagreeable winter until the last week, the weather

---

105. Another slave, probably with a cerebral hemorrhage.

this week has been mild and suitable for gardening until this morning. It is cold enough to kill hogs. We are having our second killing today. Our first killing of hogs was three weeks last Tuesday. The weather was very cold. William helped to kill hogs Tuesday. Wednesday they came to your Pa and told him that he was sick. Your Pa had a headache and did not see him anymore. Thursday morning he went to Carrollton and forgot he, William, was sick. About eleven o'clock Isham came by and told me that William said he wanted his master to go and bleed him that he had a headache. I was attending to my lard and it was so cold I did not think to go to see him as they have chills and headaches so often. The Dr. came from town at two o'clock. I neglected telling him that William had sent for him to bleed him. Late in the evening Prince came by Hannah's house, went in and found William speechless. Prince came to the yard and told me. I had the horn blowed for the Dr. He had walked to the field but came in a short time and went to see him. He said his pulse was good and thought it was a deceit. I did not think until after supper that anything was the matter with him. He died Friday this day three weeks. He never came to his speech. Uncle Vivion said he talked to him at dinner and he did not think him so sick. I think he had a congestive chill.

Last Saturday two weeks Jesse was taken very sick and for three days he was as ill as anybody could be to recover. Close attention from your Pa and a good nursing saved him. He is mending but not able to leave his house. Martha was taken night before last with the colic. She had a fever and diarrhea all day yesterday. Siah has chills. Melia has been sick over a week, she is well all to weakness. There are always from four to five negroes sick here. Always coming in with chills. Jackson [*Ritter's husband*] was taken with a chill here in the Christmas and using his head he got well enough to go home the third ultimate and relapsed a week after he left here. He had typhoid fever and he is getting well. Ritter went to see him Sunday before last Sunday. Mr. Little died with typhoid fever last month.

Mrs. Hemingway spent the day with me Wednesday. She is the only lady I have seen this winter. She told me she heard Mrs. McIntire gave a party Christmas. The ladies were dressed in calico. Mrs. McIntire's was so long she tore it off before at the tail in dancing. She throwed the piece out at the window and danced on afterwards until some of the ladies persuaded her to change her dress. Paten told Ritt that Mr. McIntire got drunk and fell out of the carriage in the mud flat on his back. Mrs. McIntire had him put to bed.

A party was given this month at Ware's Hotel to R. Whitehead and his bride. We were invited. We did not feel in the spirit of going to parties. The evening was very rainy. Today was the first time I have seen any of Mr. E. Whitehead's family since you left here. Tom W. [*Whitehead*] came over to bring his dogs to catch some hogs for us. I have not been from home since I came from

Mrs. Eggleston's in November. Your Pa saw Ellen Finney in Middleton this week. She and her mother were staying at Judge Collins'. They want to get a school. They have been living in Arkansas teaching school. Miss Given from Florida has bought the Seminary in Middleton and intends commencing a school in February.

Jan. 28, 1860—As I have to attend to my lard this morning, I cannot write a long letter. The sick are doing well this morning. None of them can be called sick but Jesse. Your Pa is on the bed with a headache, not a very bad one. Give my love to Mr. Walton and the dear sweet children. Kiss the children for me and tell them they must be good children. I do want to see you all very much. Ritter and America send their love to you all. Write soon and often.

> Your devoted mother,
> Sarah E. Watkins

To William Walton from Sarah Watkins:

> February 3, 1860
> Carrollton, Mississippi

Mr. William M. Walton
Austin, Texas
Dear Sir,

Your very welcome letter of the 17th ult. was received the 28th of the month with many thanks for informing me of the illness of my dear child [*a miscarriage*]. Her sickness grieves me very much and would almost derange me if you had not have written that she was thought out of danger. I hope and pray that she was recovered by this time but cannot help feeling uneasy about her fearing she will be imprudent and not take care of herself as she ought to. I was very sorry to hear of dear sweet Newton's sickness. I hope the dear child has recovered. Not receiving a letter from Lettie in such a long time, I was uneasy about her. I am very superstitious about dreams and I had some dreams about her that made me uneasy. Cousin Henry Watkins staid here night before last. He told me he received a letter from you. He has quit the school in Carrollton on account of there not being scholars enough to have an assistant teacher. He intended to take that car [*train*] at Winona yesterday and go to Memphis and from there to Little Rock in Arkansas if he did not get a school in Grenada. Dr. Watkins went to the same depot yesterday to go to Memphis or New Orleans, I don't know which. He was ready to start last Tuesday. John Watkins [*slave*] cut his foot with the ax right bad just at the time. He put off going on that account until yesterday. Today John is sick with a pain in his head and side.

Woman Milly came in this morning with a chill and a little negro, Paten, was taken sick today. We have so much sickness that my mind is never easy, particularly when the Dr. is away. It makes my heart beat to hear the negroes coming to the door, expecting to hear some of them are very ill. Miss Laura Jane Blunt was married last night to Mr. Duke, Mr. E. Whitehead's overseer. They had a large wedding. Charles Estel will give them a complimentary party today or tonight.

Wednesday and Thursday the weather was very cold. Today is a very mild pretty day. I hope it will stay so until I can have some gardening done. I have not been from home this winter and see so few people that I seldom hear any news.

I am very anxious to hear from Lettie and Newton. Give my love to her and the children and tell her to write soon if she is not able to write, you must write for her. Accept my best wishes for yourself.

Your affectionate mother-in-law
Sarah E. Watkins

P.S. The Carrollton paper says that the Mississippi Central Railroad is completed. The last rail was laid and the last nail driven on last Tuesday. There was a large assemblage of people present. The President, Chief Engineer, Directors, participated in the work. The locomotive called for our highly esteemed citizen and representative in the State Senate. Major G. F. Neill was the first to pass over the completed road.

To Mary Watkins from Sarah Watkins:

February 10, 1860
Carrollton, Mississippi

Miss Mary E. Watkins
Patapsco Female Institute
Ellicotts Mill, Maryland

My Dear Child,

Your very affectionate and welcome letter of the 22nd ult. was received the 8th of this month. I received one from your dear sister at the same time. She had been very ill. She was taken with the flu the first of January and about the 15th or 17th of the month she miscarried after suffering very much. Her letter was written the 21st of last month. She wrote that she was sitting in bed writing and had put on her dress that day. She said she was gradually mending but was very weak and poor. She put postscript in her letter that evening and wrote that she put on a hoop skirt and her dress that evening and walked outside the yard. I think she was very imprudent for doing so as she had just left her bed. Mr. Walton wrote me about Lettie's sickness. He thought her out of danger when he wrote. Newton was sick with the flu at the same time. He has recovered.

I sent the composition you wrote to me to send you in a short time after receiving your letter in December. Cousin Henry staid here last Wednesday night week. He went back to Carrollton the next morning to pack his trunk and intended starting that day to Memphis and from there to Little Rock in Arkansas if he could not get a school in Grenada. The male school has become so small in Carrollton that it does not justify employing an assistant teacher. He liked Carrollton very much. He said he enjoyed himself at the parties this winter in Carrollton very much.

I am glad you were permitted to see Judge Watkins and his son. Your Pa would have disliked it very much if you had not have seen them. Tell Mr. Archer that his accounts for you have been received. Your Pa left home before they came and he is expected to be gone some weeks. When he returns home he will attend to them. From one of the accounts it seems that you had a doctor to attend you the 16th and 18th of November. What was the matter with you?

Your Pa left home last Thursday week. He expected to go to Memphis and perhaps to New Orleans. I don't know which end of the railroad he took when he started off on the car. He was about to start two days before he did and just at the time John W. cut his foot with the ax. It was bleeding profusely and he thought it best to put off going a day or two. Since he left, John has been quite sick. I sent for Dr. Griffith to see him Monday, he did not think him dangerous and said John had neuralgia in his head. He is better today. Yesterday and today is the first time there has been so few sick in a long time. Jessie is recovering, he came to the kitchen today for the first time since he was taken sick. He is not able to do any work yet.

I have been confined at home all this winter with so much sickness and bad weather. I have not seen but one lady this winter. Mrs. Hemingway spent a day here about two weeks ago. Laura Jane Blunt was married to Mr. Duke last night week. They had a big wedding. Charles Estell was to give them a complimentary party the day or night after. Mr. Oliver gave them a dinner this day week. Mr. Duke is Mr. E. Whitehead's overseer. Dr. Griffith told me that Mary Sanders and Dick Love is to be married the 15th of this month. It is said that Dr. Griffith is a beau of Laura Moore's. If it is so, I reckon you know it.

I wish very much you could come home next summer and spend your vacation. I don't think your Pa will agree to it on account of your health. He will think coming home to stay might give you chills. That would be my only objection to your coming. I will rejoice when your school days are over and you can stay at home and be a comfort to your parents in their old age if it is the will of our heavenly Father to spare us to see that time. I often think of the happy time I spent with my beloved children last summer and think will I ever enjoy that much happiness again in being with my dear children at the same time? Nothing could add more to my temporal happiness than to have my children with me always. Your mama[106] says she was mighty afraid you would take cold going to Washington and it would make you sick. Your Pa and I were uneasy about you too. John[107] says please find out where his sister Mima and all her children are living and with whom are they living. I received a letter from Sarah Ann lately. She wrote that her mother was married the first of Jan. to Mr. Cathren of Memphis. Sarah Ann expects to go to Florence to school in March and board at cousin Wm. Leigh's. Ritter and America send their love to you. America says you did not say love to her in your letter. She says you must write to her. Your Pa will have to let you know about having your clothes made at the Institute when he comes home. Abram has just brought a nice welcome letter from you dated the 28th ultm. I am very much pleased to hear of your acquitting yourself well at the examination. I expect you merited the praise Mr. Archer gave you. Write often. You can't imagine what a pleasant feeling it gives me to receive letters from my dear beloved children.

Your devoted mother,
Sarah E. Watkins

P.S. Give my respects to cousin Matte Mathews.

To Mary Watkins from Sarah Watkins:

March 6, 1860
Carrollton, Mississippi

Miss Mary E. Watkins
Patapsco Female Institute
Ellicotts Mill, Maryland

My Dear Child,

Your affectionate letter of the fifth ult. to your Pa was received last Tuesday two weeks. I was very much pleased with your report and also to hear that you acquited yourself well at the examination. Your mamma says that you will be a queen. Your Pa read your letters with delight and often reads them over a second time and says I will read my Baby's letter again. He is very proud of you and loves you dearly. He left here four weeks yesterday. I have

---

106. "Mama" refers to the slave who cared for Mary when she was a baby.
107. John was a Watkins family servant (slave). Probably his sister, Mima, had become property of one of Dr. Watkins's sisters, perhaps Aunt Jane Hillyer.

not heard from him since he left Winona. I don't know whether he went to Memphis or New Orleans. He expected to go to both places.

I received a letter from Mr. Walton last week, it was written the 17th of February. He wrote that Lettie's health was far from being good. He had carried her and the children out in the country thinking it would improve her health. I believe I wrote to you about her sickness the last time I wrote to you. I hope and pray she may recover her health and live for the sake of her dear children. No one but a mother knows my feelings for my poor dear child.

I must congratulate you at being sixteen. I did intend having a birthday cake made for you. I went to Mr. Hemingway's and spent the day and did not think of it being your birthday until I returned home in the evening. Margaret A. Hemingway spent the day and night with me last Sunday. It is said that she and Gus Pleasants are to be married shortly. Mrs. Whitehead and Lizzie spent the day here Wednesday week. Lizzie promised to come over night this week. This is Friday and she has not come yet. Mary Sanders and Mr. R. B. Love were married the 16th of February. One or two parties were given to them in Carrollton. Betty Ewing was married at five o'clock in the evening Tuesday week to Dr. Tyson of Tennessee. She did not have a large wedding. They left for Tennessee the next day. I was at church in Middleton the 2nd Sunday in February. I saw Laura Moore. She inquired about you and said she had not had a letter from you in some time. Col. Moore keeps entertainment. It must be disagreeable to Mrs. Moore. Last Monday for the first time in six months all the hands were out at work but the next day Ned came in sick with chills, he has got well. Tom has been in two or three days, little Simon came in this evening with a pain in his side. Robin last Monday had a large heavy stick of wood on his shoulder. Just as he got the kitchen door with it he was taken with the cramp in his leg and fell down and hurt his leg so badly that he has not been able to cook or do anything since. Wednesday morning Else's Robert had the ax cutting and cut his leg to the bone. Old Mrs. Burt died last month.

I was busy today and put off writing until tonight. I expect you are like I am about wondering why you do not get a letter from me. I don't know what prevented me from writing to you last week. There has been so much sickness here that it kept my mind always disturbed. I would forget when I wrote to you last. I will try and let it not be so long before I write to you again.

Ritter sends her love to you. She is sitting with her sewing in her lap, she is gone to sleep. America sends love to you. She is sleep too. You must write often.

Your affectionate mother,
Sarah E. Watkins

P.S. If you can buy your clothing as cheap at the Institute as in Washington, I don't think your Pa will object to your buying them at the Institute. You had better write to him again shortly and know of him where he rather you should get them.

To Letitia Walton from Sarah Watkins:

March 16, 1860
Carrollton, Mississippi

Mrs. L. A. Walton
Austin, Texas

My Dear Child,

I received your very affectionate letter of the 1st inst. this week and two from Baby at the same time. It afforded me great pleasure to hear from my dear beloved children and was a great relief to my feelings to hear that you had recovered your health and was improving in flesh. I hope you may keep healthy and look as well as you did when you were here last fall. It is a great consolation to me to hear that Mr. Walton is getting on well in his pecuniary affairs and hope you will soon have a comfortable home and make a fortune for yourselves and your smart boys. I have seen no boys to equal them in sense and beauty. I received Mr. Walton's letter of the 14 ult. about two weeks ago and was much obliged to him for informing me how you were. I would have answered it if I had not been very busy ever since. I think writing to you at this time will do as well, as my letter will be more interesting to you than to him.

Baby said in her letters that she was well and is anxious to come home this summer.[108] We are very willing for her to come and think she will come home and spend the vacation and return to Patapsco in the fall and the next summer come home a graduate. Oh, how proud it makes me feel to think of it. By that time I hope I will have the pleasure to have you and your dear children with me and that would add greatly to my happiness. I often think will I ever have my children with me at the same time again. I pray to God that we may meet and enjoy that blessing.

Your Pa returned home Wednesday week. He had been to Little Rock and St. Louis.[109] Dr. Montgomery's daughter came with him. She is staying at Mr. E. Whitehead's. Mr. Whitehead's family wrote to her for her to come to Lizzie's

108. Mary spent the summer of 1860 visiting Sarah Epes Watkins's kin in Virginia: the Williamses, Irbys, Fitzgeralds, Epeses, etc., especially in Nottoway County.
109. The doctor was sorely tempted to sell out in Mississippi and move the family to Arkansas. He was unable to find just the right circumstance. Texas and Arkansas were attractive, especially to those in the hill country of Carroll County, who were seeing the land being exhausted and eroded.

wedding. I don't know when the wedding is to be. The Dr. and I spent the day at Mr. E. Whitehead's last Friday. Nothing was mentioned about the marriage to any of us. Margaret A. Hemingway was married last night to Gus Pleasants. They had very few at it besides the waiters. None of the neighbors were invited that I know of except Mrs. Brian and her niece, Miss Shackleford. Mrs. Brian assisted in baking the cake and it was commenced making Monday week.

Margaret Ann [*Hemingway*] came to see me last Sunday two weeks and staid until Monday morning. She told me in confidence that she would be married on the 15th inst. Abbey Eubanks and Miss Gabe Barnes were her bridesmaids and Joe Gee and Al Smith were his. Mrs. H. sent my cake pans and preserve dishes just now that she borrowed and sent me a bundle of cake. I wish Newton and Early had most of it. The servant that brought it said the bridal pair had gone to a dining given them at Mr. Frank Pleasant's today. I made the sleeves of three chemises and stitched on one yoke and two bands for her and made the skirt of her second day's dress. I will send you a sample of her dress in this letter. Don't you think I had done enough to deserve an invitation? I did not expect one. I would like to have seen the table and how she looked. Ritter told me her wedding dress was tarlton trimmed with very wide blond lace on the body and sleeves, a white artificial wreath to wear on her head, and a very long tarlton veil with several rows of narrow ribbon put round it. The veil was to be put on the back of the head and hung down to her ankles. Ritter saw the dressing when she carried the work over that I had done.

Bettie Ewing was married to Dr. Tyson of Tennessee last month. Mary Sanders to B. B. Love. Mr. and Mrs. Burt that we saw at Mr. Whitehead's are dead. Mr. Burt died in two weeks after his wife. Mr. B. and the only two grown negro men he had died with pneumonia and several of his negroes has been sick and his daughter Ann. His daughter, Mrs. Pratt, is expected to die. Joe Money's wife had a child lately, she has the dropsy very bad. John Hawkins' other child, Mrs. Nunry, has one and the sore on her nose has got well. Mrs. T. Jones has a baby. Mr. Lytle that we saw at Judge Collins' party is the one that died this winter. He had a brother to die in this county a year or two ago. Mrs. Phillips has had several sick in her family lately. Mrs. Parmele has been sick with falling of the womb brought on by her imprudence. She carried a pail of water from the spring to the house that caused it. There was no need of her carrying it, there was two women at the spring that could have carried it to the house. Take warning and don't you be lifting heavy things. Martha Parmele and Caro Dennis is sick. Mr. Parmele sent here last Sunday to get some ice for Martha. He wrote that she had not cleared of fever in several days and there were four cases of typhus fever in his family. I have not heard from there since the ice was sent. Mr. Parmele's health is not good, he has had hemorrhage of the lungs. His negro Bettie that did belong to Mrs. Farmer died lately.

Ritter got a letter from her sister, Melia lately. She mentioned the death of Mrs. Dora Shackleford and Mrs. William McMahon. Mr. Pierce has bought Peggy. I think I wrote you that Brother's wife [*Mary*] was married to Mr. Cathren of Memphis the first of Jan. Mary Wingfield that was is dead. She left two children. Her husband has sold out in Arkansas and moved back to Tennessee [*the Wingfields were friends Lettie visited when she was in school in Columbia, Tennessee.*]

Jesse had winter fever, he got well and went out to work two weeks ago. Day before yesterday he had a chill, he is not sick much at this time. We are all well today. You and Baby both complain of my writing so seldom. I will try to write oftener. When I write or sew much it makes my back hurt me. My memory is so bad, I forget which I wrote to last, you or Baby when I write. I use the sewing bird and like it very much and prize it highly for your sake.

I sent by your Pa for a bonnet, four caps and two collars and two pair of undersleeves. He got them in St. Louis and got Mrs. Montgomery to choose them. The bonnet is plain straw dressed with wide blue ribbon, a rush inside and pretty blue flowers. It is a neat bonnet, plenty fine for my age. I told him not to get a costly one. The caps are made of tulle on black bobinnet and two are trimmed with white ribbon and one with white wide ribbon and narrow purple ribbon. The fourth cap has white bobinnet with frills on it and the crown and the frills are worked with cotton floss and that cap can be washed, it has no ribbon on it. The strings are wide, made of bobinnet and worked around. I wish I had six such caps, they would do to wear at home and to the neighbors. The collars are large. He brought me a lawn dress,[110] double skirt. The collar is brown and white, the 18 yds. came to $5.00. He brought me a shawl, black and white. It is not very thick but does mighty well to wear in the spring and fall. Dr. Montgomery sent Lizzie [*Whitehead*] a beautiful silk. It is black colored with two very wide flounces, colored black and lilac. Her father bought her a very pretty silk in New Orleans this winter. He gave thirty-six dollars for it. The color of that is blue and white with narrow flounces with pink and green flowers in it.

Ellen Conley made choice of her bonnet. It is very pretty, very white chip with small white feathers and flowers on it and flowers inside of it.

I fixed the remedy the next day after I got your letter and gave it to Sally to

---

110. A fine material resembling cambric, often linen or silk.

take. She has suffered very much for two days with pain in her head and jaw. Yesterday and today she has kept in her bed. The weather has been cold this week that makes her jaw worse.

Give my love to Mr. Walton and the children. Kiss the children for me. Tell Caroline [*slave*] howdy, America and Ritter send their love to you all. Write often, I do want to see you all so much.

Your affectionate mother,
Sarah E. Watkins

To Mary Watkins from Sarah Watkins:

March 17, 1860
Carrollton, Mississippi

Miss M. E. Watkins
Patapsco Institute Md.

My Dear Child:

Your very interesting letters of the 24th ult. and the 7th inst. was joyfully received last Tuesday. I received one from dear Lettie written the first of March which added to my joy to hear from both of my beloved children and learn that they were well and doing well. Lettie wrote that she was quite well again and getting some flesh on her bones. She wrote to me that you wrote to her that you still have dyspepsia. I am afraid you do not take enough exercise and are imprudent in your diet. Your Pa is willing for you to come home this summer. I hope very much you may come. Your Pa came home last Wednesday week and brought me a straw bonnet trimmed with wide blue ribbon and blue artificial flowers inside. Some very neat caps, two pair undersleeves and two collars, a lawn dress with double skirt and a shawl, black and white, suitable to wear this time of the year. He was at Little Rock and St. Louis. Dr. Montgomery's daughter came home with him from St. Louis. She is staying at Mr. E. Whitehead's.

Margaret A. Hemingway was married 15th of this month to Gus Pleasants. None of the neighbors were invited except Mrs. Brian and her niece, Miss Shackleford. Mrs. Brian assisted in baking the cake and setting the table. There were very few at it besides the waiters. Joe Gee and Al Smith were his waiters and Abbey Eubanks and Gabe Barnes were her's. Mrs. Hemingway sent me a bundle of cake when she sent my preserve dishes and cake pans home that she borrowed. I wish you had some of it. Your Pa has eaten heartily of it. His appetite is very good and he is fonder of a dessert than I ever knew for him to be. He wants a dessert every day. That is too often to suit my convenience. This time of the year the eggs are needed for setting. The cows are decreasing in milk and it takes eggs, butter and milk to make most desserts. I have no fruit to make pies or tarts except preserve fruit. I have very bad luck with my hens, a mink killed four one night and came the next night and killed one hen that was setting and then I had to break up another that was setting to keep it from killing her. Another setting hen disappeared suddenly. I think a possum caught her and two little chickens. Abram had a plank trap in the garden that he made to catch rabbits. The possum was caught in it. I have thirty young chickens, I hope to raise a plenty for you to eat this summer. I miss Lettie finding turkey and guinea nests for me. She was fond of going out to hunt them last year when she was here. She is too energetic of a lady to be buried down in such a place as Austin.[111] Your mama came to the door and told me that two ladies and a man was coming. I had to stop writing until this evening. It was Miss Montgomery, Emma and William Whitehead. William went on to the creek fishing. They walked over. Emma was taken sick on the way and had a chill soon after she came. William heard she was sick and went home and brought the buggy for them and carried them home just now. For dessert for dinner today I had a very nice preserve cherry roll and sauce and some of the wedding cake.

Miss Montgomery and your Pa walked to the creek and caught a few fish, they were not gone long. Charlotte and Lettie [*slaves*] went with them. Lettie slipped off of the end of the log and got her feet wet. Miss Montgomery laughed at Lettie's falling and Miss Montgomery slipped down the bank.

Lettie is going out to work Monday. Charlotte told me that she wants to go to the field to work. I will not put her out yet a while, I need her to do little jobs about the yard. Sally has been in bed most of this week with pain in her jaw and head. Every day most some of the negroes come in with a chill. Jesse had one this week and he is not entirely well. Alberta had one yesterday and Moses came in today with one. Sickness is so light to what it has been here this winter that I feel very thankful. You and Lettie complain of my not writing oftener so I will try to do better. You must write often. It is always a pleasure to us to receive a letter from you.

Your Pa received a letter from Judge Hillyer. He wrote that you were an honor to your parents and anyone that is connected to you. It is very gratifying to me to hear you praised so highly. Ritt and America and Patty send a heap of love to you. America says you must write to her.

> Your affectionate mother,
> Sarah E. Watkins

111. An interesting remark to read a century and a quarter later, considering the changes in the destinies of Middleton and Austin.

Sunday evening, March 18, 1860

I attended the Baptist church in Middleton today and heard Mr. Pittman preach. Saw Mrs. Palmer and she said Octavia was having chills. This was her well day [112] but she left her in bed. I saw Bettie and Mollie Collins and Laura Moore. Mollie Collins inquired about you. I told her you were coming home this summer. She said, "Oh: I am so glad."

I have seen Laura Moore twice lately and she did not ask when I had heard from you. She has a cousin with her, Miss Moore from Baltimore. She is a pretty girl. Mollie Collins and Bettie looked pretty today. Lizzie Barrow was at church and looks as fat as a shoat. Mrs. Martha Jane Gary was there dressed in a black silk made low neck and a black lace mantle on. I wore my thick cloak for fear of sitting in the cold church would give me a chill. Your Pa ate his dinner and walked off before I got back from church. I am all alone and no one is in the yard. The negroes are singing a most doleful tune at Patty's house and it makes me uneasy fearing the Dr. will come in and hear them. You know he don't allow them to meet and sing and pray together. [113]

March 26, 1860
Carrollton, Mississippi

Miss Mary E. Watkins
Ellicotts Mill, Md.

My Dear Daughter,

Your esteemed and welcome favor of 16th inst. was received on yesterday, contents noted. Your mother at the same time received yours of 10th inst. We all of course were very glad to hear from you.

We are this evening going to Miss Lizzie Whitehead's wedding. She married Judge Oliver of Alabama. There have been many Carroll County girls married this season. Mr. Samuel Hart's daughter was a few evenings ago married to a silver smith in Carrollton by the name of Tustin. Miss Margaret Hemingway was married a few days ago to Mr. Pleasant.

There have been some deaths also. The father of Dr. Holeman died lately and also some others that you did not know. Mr. Bailey, the father of the Bailey that married Miss Barrow died lately in California.

Such clothes as you need you can have made at the Institute. You can come home this summer. I wish you would inquire of the Miss Pulliams and

112. Undoubtedly malaria, which characteristically has fever and chill days interspersed with well days.

113. A prohibition reflective of the uneasiness felt by the slave owner during the last of the antebellum period.

others of the St. Louis girls if they will come home in the summer. I would like for you to come home that way and I could meet you in St. Louis. It might be that they would go by the way of Niagara Falls, which would be a pleasant trip for you. If you come to St. Louis you will have a fine view of the Illinois prairies. In May or June I will write you all about your journeys and the way you could come home.

You spell Miss Fearn's name wrong. It is Fearn, not Phern. You can tell her that she is as respectably connected as any person in Alabama. I have known Dr. Thomas Fearn of Huntsville, Alabama for thirty years. He is her father or uncle. He is a superior man in every sense of the word. He is honorable, talented and probably the best physician that ever was in Alabama. He is the father of Mrs. Barry whom you saw in Oxford at the Commencement. You can tell her also that I am under many obligations to her uncle, Mr. George Fearn of Jackson, Mississippi. Last fall I attended the Fair at that place and as every hotel and boarding house was full, I had no place to stay. Mr. George Fearn found it out and he took me to his house and treated me as well as if I had been General Jackson or Mr. Buchannon.[114] It is not often that we meet with as kind gentlemen as Mr. F. His family is a very nice one. He is a widower and has several sons and daughters that live with him. I wish he would come up and see Miss Fanny Eggleston. Miss Green of Jackson knows Mr. Fearn and family. You can write me if Miss F. is a daughter of Dr. Thomas Fearn of Huntsville or of Dr. Lee Fearn of Mobile.

If she is of the latter she knows our relative, Mrs. LeVert[115] of that city. You ask me if I know that Watkins of Jackson, Mississippi. I do know them and they are just as fine, clever persons as you will find anywhere. I visited them while I was in Jackson last fall and I became very much attached to them. They are relatives of ours. Dr. Miles S. Watkins is the father of that family. I would like to know if Dr. Sykes's daughter and Mrs. Bradley's daughter go to your school. They are of the very most respectable families. Miss Bradley is a granddaughter of Governor Thomas Bibb of Alabama. The Bibbs are very talented. I have a book at home that gives a history of that family. Many of them are very wealthy.

I believe I have written you all the news that I now can recollect about.

Bishop Green will be at my house on the 14th of April and preach in Carrollton on the 15th. Miss Fanny Eggleston and sister have promised to come and visit us at that time. My respects to cousin Martha Matthews and to the Miss Pulliams because Mr. Perry, their step-father, was so kind to me at

114. President James Buchanan.
115. Mrs. LeVert was the great-granddaughter of George Walton, a signer of the Declaration of Independence. George Walton's sister was Dr. Watkins's grandmother.

St. Louis. You may, if you choose, read to Miss Fearn what I say about her family, also to Miss Sykes and Miss Bradley what I say about their families.

Your affectionate father,
Thomas A. Watkins

P.S. The railroad is now completed and we can hear the steam car whistle every day.

To Mary Watkins from Sarah Watkins:

April 4, 1860
Carrollton, Mississippi

Miss Mary E. Watkins
Patapsco Institute, Md.

My Dear Child,

Your very welcome letter of the 10 ult. was received Monday week and one of the 23rd ult. was received this evening with delight to hear from my beloved child that she was well and getting on so well in her studies. How can a mother help being proud of such a daughter.

A letter came today from Mr. Archer to your Pa. He mentioned that you were in excellent health and doing well in your school duties and that he thinks you will do credit to yourself, to your father, and to your state. Your Pa is not at home. He left last Sunday morning and took the car to Winona. I don't know whether he is gone to Alabama or St. Louis. He said he would try to get back by Saturday week. Bishop Green is expected here on that day. He wrote to your pa if he would send his carriage to the depot for him at the time that he would come here. He is to preach in Carrollton the 15th of this month. Your Pa invited Mrs. Eggleston's daughters to come up to see the Bishop and I believe he has written to Major Hawkins' family inviting them to come here on that day. Miss Fanny wrote to him that they would come if it is convenient for them to leave home. Mrs. Eggleston was sick when Miss F.E. wrote.

I saw Miss Sarah Reed at Lizzie Whitehead's wedding. She told me Mrs. E. [*Eggleston*] had gotten well and Miss Senora Eggleston had married her cousin Mr. Mead that is several years younger than herself. I expect your Pa wrote you that Lizzie Whitehead was married the 27th of March to Judge Oliver. We were at the wedding. She did not have as large of a wedding as Jennie had. The neighbors, their relations and a few young people were at it. Phil Palmer spoke to me at supper. I did not recognize him. He said to me, "Why you don't know me, do you?" And I replied, "No, I do not. Phil Palmer is it not?" He has grown so tall and quite good looking. Martha Jane Gary was there too. Octavia P. asked if you would be at home this summer. I told her you would and she said she would be glad to see you.

It is night and Ritter and America are sleep. Ritt has waked up and is rubbing her eyes and says, "I can't see good now." She has commenced knitting. Her eyes are half open and her face with a frown. The frogs and a lonesome cricket are serenading me. They are rejoicing at the warm weather. It is too warm for me to have a fire tonight. It is bedtime, I will quit writing. I do not like to sit up by myself. Just now the tongs fell, it made me jump. The door is open and I heard something walking in the passage, I looked towards the door and there stood one of our puppies looking in at me with her white face and shining eyes.

5th, Morning is come with the appearance of rain. I want to go to Carrollton tomorrow to call on Mrs. Richard Whitehead and to go shopping. I sent by your Pa for an organdy muslin and a summer silk. I have not made my lawn he brought me. I am waiting for Miss Montgomery to come here and show me how to make it. She sent me word that she would come next week. She is at Judge Whitehead's this week. Mr. Pentecost heard last Sunday that Laura Whitehead was to be married. He said he saw Eugene Whitehead giving out something at church that looked like tickets. He did not hear who she was to be married to. I expect it is a false report.

I received a letter from Lettie Monday week the same time I did yours. She wrote that her health was very good and her complexion better than it has been for years. I see no ladies I think prettier than my sweet darling Lettie. Oh, she had better never to have been pretty. That pretty face has caused her an unhappy life from the time she was sixteen until the present time. She says she has a good husband. I expect he is a loving, kind husband and exerts himself to discharge his duty towards his family. That sad face of hers shows deep seated sorrow in her heart caused from her self-willed disposition in not taking the advice of parents that loved her and made too much of an idol of her. If she had married to please your Pa, what a happy family we would now be. Take warning my dear Baby from your poor sister's course and never bring unhappiness on yourself and parents as she has done. I love her dearly. Her Pa never will have much affection for her again, I fear. It makes my heart ache to hear him speak against her. You act with so much prudence and good sense that I do not think you will grieve your parents and break their hearts by disobeying them or acting imprudently in any way. We're very proud of you and love you as sincerely and devotedly as parents can love a child and look forward to seeing a great deal of happiness with you. From the way you wrote, I think you are more inclined to go to Virginia than to come home. Your Pa and I will be glad for you to come home. I think he expects for you to come home. I will leave it to you and him to decide. I am very anxious to see you. I have declined the idea of going to Virginia this summer. Home suits me best and I don't expect my relations care to see me and I would not like to trouble them to send me in their carriage from one place to another.

Cousin Henry Watkins is teaching school in Little Rock, Arkansas. He gets forty dollars a month and his board. Martha and America send their love to you and say you must come home. Martha says Alberta can talk. Ritter sends love to you. Sally suffers a great deal with pain in her jaw. She is not able to attend in the house. Patty is well and just finished making my soap. I am making a purple muslin dress with a double skirt for Else. I will be very busy sewing for a while so you must not expect many letters from me shortly as I have to write to you and Lettie too. You know I am slow at everything I do. If I could write sensible letters like you, I would not mind writing. I ought to write to Lettie today. My back is weak, writing much makes it hurt. I must put off writing to her for another time.

Write soon and often.

Your affectionate mother,
Sarah E. Watkins

P.S. Abram has just returned from town. He heard there is to be a large party at Judge Whitehead's tonight. Your letter was not sealed.

To Letitia Walton from Sarah Watkins:

April 10, 1860
Carrollton, Mississippi

Mrs. L. A. Walton
Austin, Texas

My Dear Child,

Your very welcome letter of the 14th ult. was received yesterday two weeks and ought to have been answered before this, but it has not been convenient for me to do so until now. Two letters were received from Baby at the same time and I have received one since. She was well and said she was uneasy about you as you were sick the last time you wrote to her. In the winter she wrote to us that she had rather come home this vacation than go anywhere else. From the way she wrote in her last letter I think she is inclined to go to Virginia. She wrote, "Please write me immediately and state exactly what you all prefer my doing next summer. Although I had said that I rather go home in vacation yet I will recall it and leave everything for you all to decide." We had concluded for her to come home this summer. I am willing for her to do as she pleases about coming. Her Pa has not seen the last letter, I don't know whether he will consent for her to go to Virginia instead of coming home. He left home a week or more. I expect him back this week.

Bishop Green is to be here next Saturday. Abram is to carry the carriage to Winona for him to come here. Major Hawkins' family we expect to dine here on that day. Bishop Green is to preach in Carrollton next Sunday. The Misses Egglestons may be here too as they were written to come. Miss F. Eggleston wrote that they will come if it is convenient for them to do so. Miss Senora Eggleston is married to her first cousin, Mr. Meade. She is several years older than he is. Lizzie Whitehead was married to Judge Oliver the 27th of March and left for Alabama the 29th, they went by New Orleans. There were not as many people at her wedding as there were at Jennie's. Their relations, neighbors and a few young people were invited. Miss Montgomery, Laura Whitehead and Sallie Collins were her waiters and Mr. Gorden, Mr. Weir and Shawl Stevens were the bridesmen. Octavia Merriwether came up to her Pa's the day before the wedding and heard it was to be and came to it without any invitation. Octavia looked as happy as if she had just dropped from the skies. She looks more like a married lady than you do. I told her so. Her face is not so full and she was paler than she used to be. Mr. Hugh Davis told me to write that we believe Octavia was off.[116] Octavia said what makes you think so. I put my finger on her face and said, "From the looks of that." She says she has one of the best husbands.

Mrs. Kennedy told me to give her love to you and to tell you that you promised her to carry your husband to see her when he came and you did not do it. She was at the wedding. She had on a black silk with three double skirts with narrow fringe around them and one row of velvet inch wide and two rows of velvet about that not quite as wide. The sleeves were open up high with a cap on them. The sleeves were lined with white Persian[117] and ribbon quilled in them like your silk sleeves.

I saw Mrs. Richard Whitehead. She said she would be very glad to see you. I expect to call on her shortly. There was a party at Judge Whitehead's last Thursday night. I expect it was given to Miss Montgomery. Miss Lizzie Hines' nephew came last Saturday to carry her to live with his parents in Missouri. She expected to start yesterday. He came here expecting to meet her as she had written to him to meet her here. I don't know why she wrote for him to meet her. She had not been here since last November, twelve months, until Sunday, she walked here the hottest time of the day to get me to send her and her baggage to the depot. I told her I could not take the liberty of sending her. She had too much weight for our carriage and our mules were busy ploughing. I told her the track puffed[118] from Carrollton to Winona and that

116. Pregnancy?
117. A thick silk fabric formerly used for linings.
118. The train. Evidently a feeder train, from Carrollton to the main line in Winona.

could take her and her baggage too. I felt very sorry for her and would have sent her. I thought your Pa would say there was the hack, why could she not take it? She staid a very short time here. She said she asked Mr. Whitehead to send her. He told her he could not do it. Poor woman, I hope she will arrive safely at her sister's and be blessed with a comfortable home.

Mrs. Gooch, Mrs. Jim Woods' mother, died last week. She had pneumonia and was getting well and taken with chills and died. Mr. White the mantua-maker's[119] husband died last week in Carrollton. Old Mr. Holeman is dead.

I don't think I ever felt as warm weather in April as there is this April. If it was not that the wind is constantly blowing we would suffer with heat. It is very dry and rain is needed badly. Yesterday morning I intended going to Carrollton and it was so cloudy I would not go, and as it is court week, I did not like to go at such a public time by myself.

I got a letter from Sarah Ann[120] lately. She said the man her mother married is named Kettering, living in Memphis and that she don't know anything about him.

My peas are in bloom, I have lettuce and radishes, snaps up. I made Ritt trim and work the rose bushes and flowers in the garden this spring. I have got a new fence around the old garden and I have four turkeys setting and about seventy little chickens and six goslings. Ritter has not found but two guinea nests yet and one of them she can't get any eggs from. I told her today if you were here you would have found more. That if I was as successful as you in finding eggs I would go myself and hunt them. I tried the receipt you sent me for Sally the next day after I received it. It made her so sick she had to stop using it. She suffers a great deal. She got Paten to cup[121] her in the temple and it eased her for a while. She had the toothache that day and had the tooth pulled out. Since then she walked over to Mr. Hemingway's and got him to cup her. I don't see that it relieved her any. Yesterday she said her tongue hurt her. She is making the negroes shirts of her own accord. I don't make her do nothing. Becky is pregnant that caused her sick stomach.

You advise me to go to Virginia this summer, I had rather stay at home. I don't like to travel. My health is good all to a weakness in my back. Writing and sewing makes that hurt. I will be busy for awhile so you must not expect

119. Dressmaker.
120. Daughter of Mary Fitzgerald, the Alabama sister–in–law. The stepfather was named Cathrin, not Kettering.
121. A medical treatment using one or more small cups, often of glass, in which was placed a wisp of cotton soaked in alcohol. The alcohol was lighted and the cup pressed over the ailing part. The flame burned up the oxygen in the cup and a suction was produced that caused a reddening and congestion of the area beneath the cup, and a "drawing" out of the cause of the pain was assumed. Cupping is essentially nonexistent in the United States today; however, it is used in much of the world and with considerable patient satisfaction.

for me to write to you often until I get some of my work done. Give my love to Mr. Walton and the children. Kiss the sweet boys for me.

P.S. Newton has the sweetest mouth I ever kissed except my mother's and my children's. The gnats disturb me and I can't write as I ought to. I went to Bluff Springs last Sunday to church. It reminded me of the day that you and Baby and cousin Henry and myself went there to preaching and wished I could have the same pleasure of enjoying the company of my children. Cousin Henry is teaching school in Little Rock and gets forty dollars a month and his board. Hannah was at Captain Wood's Sunday. She says Captain Wood and Mrs. Wood told her to tell me that a gentleman, an acquaintance of theirs, was there lately from Texas and told them that he saw you and Mr. Walton a short time ago and that Mr. Walton was doing well and spoke very highly of him and said you were a very nice dressy lady and very good company. Mrs. Wood said if she had been well and had have known that I would have been at church, she would have gone to church to tell me about it. She said she spoke mighty well of you to the man. I did not hear his name.

Ritter and America send love to you all. Ritt says tell Caroline that she is glad to hear she is doing well and she must continue to do well.

Your affectionate mother,
Sarah E. Watkins

To Mary Watkins from Sarah Watkins:

April 28, 1860
Carrollton, Mississippi

Miss M. E. Watkins
Patapsco Institute, Md.

My Dear Baby,

I am very busy but must take time to write to my darling child. I am making my summer dresses and just finished an everyday purple muslin dress last evening and have two gingham dresses to make. My pretty lawn with double skirt—I do not know how to make the body and sleeves as I want it made fashionable.

Lucinda has come in with one egg and six little negroes with her. Don't you think it a costly egg if I have to pay seven for one egg? I had given the cold biscuits to Robin to stuff a wild turkey gobbler for dinner that Mr. Pentecost [*overseer*] killed yesterday. He killed a turkey hen Monday. I wish all my family was here today to eat dinner with me I could give them turkey, peas, citron pudding, pound cake and a few strawberries and very nice lettuce and some beets. I have not had any peas and beets cooked yet. I have been looking for Mrs. E. Whitehead and Miss Montgomery to see me all the week. I waited for them to come before I had any for your Pa to come home. None of them has come and it is Saturday.

I heard the stage horn just now as it passed along the road. I think perhaps the Dr. is in it and will walk from the road home. He left home four weeks tomorrow to go to St. Louis or Alabama, I have not heard from him since he left home. He said he would try and get back to meet with Bishop Green.

I sent the carriage to Winona for the Bishop this day two weeks. He came by Mrs. Phillips' and staid a while and got here between eleven and twelve o'clock. Staid a short time after dinner and went on to Carrollton to preach that night. I went to Carrollton to hear him preach Sunday. He preached in the courthouse. There were several people to hear him. Mr. Holstead the Episcopalian minister from Holmes City assisted him in the services. The Bishop confirmed George Wellons and Miss Doty. She is an assistant teacher in the Carrollton school. A Mr. Fisk performed on the melodion. Miss Eldridge (Mrs. Temple, that is now) and her husband and a few others formed the choir. When the music commenced I could not help smiling. Lettie had written to me about Newton seeing a man playing an organ and had a monkey to dance. Newton went with his parents to the Catholic church. He heard the melodion. He whispered to his Pa, "Where de monkey?" I thought of what Lettie had written me about Newton.

Several of our servants went to hear the Bishop. The Bishop and Mr. Holstead put their gowns on in a room in the courthouse and came out by Washington [*slave*]. He was astonished and he said to Ritt, "Why Cousin Ritt, what sort of folks *dem*?" You would laugh to hear Ritt tell it. She says the bishop ought to wear a hoop with his gown that it hung down so straight it was nearly in his crease. Their performance was a perfect show for our servants.

Major and Mrs. Hawkins and their son John and their daughter Jennie dined here with the Bishop. Mrs. John Hawkins was sick that prevented her from coming. Major Hawkins' family were the only company that was invited here. I had a very nice dinner for them. The Bishop inquired about you[122] and said you were the hardest person to get to talk that he ever tried to make talk. He said he met with you at Washington and you had improved and that he got you to talk some. He sent his love to you. He went with Mrs. McIntire home from Carrollton after preaching Saturday night. Mr. and Mrs. McIntire, Bishop Green and some say Mr. Holstead were in Mr. McIntire's carriage with wild

122. Bishop Green had met Mary and her father when she was enroute to school at Holly Springs and took on the task of escorting her instead to the Patapsco Institute in Maryland. He evidently found Mary speechless.

horses. The horses got frightened near Judge Johnson's and ran away. The foot board broke off and the driver fell out and held to the reins until the wheels ran over him. The horses ran with the carriage until they got to the bridge. The post of the bridge caught the wheels and the tongue broke and the horses went on with the tongue.

Your very welcome letter of the 14 inst. was received Wednesday. You request me to give you a full description of Lizzie Whitehead's wedding. The bride was dressed in a white tarlton made double skirt and both skirts had one row of wide satin ribbon around it. White satin body with blond lace on it and the sleeve. The double skirt looped up with flowers on one side. The bridemaids were Sarah Collins, Laura Whitehead, and Miss Montgomery. They were dressed like the bride only they had blue satin bodices and their dresses trimmed with wide blue ribbon. Judge Oliver's waiters were Mr. Gordon, Shawl Stevens and Mr. Weir, son of Dr. Weir that lived at Shongalo. Lizzie was married Tuesday night and left Thursday. They went to New Orleans and from there to Eutaw in Alabama where Judge Oliver resides. Very few people were invited to the wedding besides the neighbors and relations. Octavia Palmer had on a purple silk. Lizzie Barrow had on a white dress. I have forgotten what I wrote you about the wedding. I can't think of anything that is interesting enough to write you about that occurred that night. I enjoyed myself very pleasantly.

I went to Bluff Springs to church three weeks tomorrow and saw Mrs. Davis, and Mary Elisa had a beau with her. I did not hear who he was. Mary Elisa was dressed in her plaid silk and she looked well. Price McLemore[123] was there. His cheeks looked like they were painted and his eyes looked like old Virginia chinquapins, they are so black. For all that, there is something lacking about him to make the refined gentleman.

You wrote to get permission to purchase your commencement and traveling dress in Washington City. I can't advise you to get them at Washington. You will have to wait until your Pa comes home and get his consent to get them there. Your report of the grade in studies and deportment for the quarter was received yesterday. It is very gratifying to see you are doing so well. Your marks are all of the very highest number. It seems to me that you are studying very few of the highest branches to graduate next June twelve months.

A letter came from Mr. and Mrs. Hillyer to your Pa lately. Mr. Hillyer sent your accounts for the articles you bought when you were in Washington. Mrs. Hillyer wrote to your Pa that he must not think you were extravagant for a young lady in Washington, if she goes in society she must dress like a gen-

---

123. Price McLemore's brother, Jeff, will in a few years become Mary's husband.

tleman's daughter. She said your Pa is able to do it and you are a nice, sweet, behaved girl so it was a great pleasure to your cousins to carry you to see the members of the cabinet[124] and other places that you attended with them. Therefore she knows his pride would be to have his daughter to appear as well as anybody there.

Cousin Henry Watkins is living at Little Rock. A letter came from him lately to your Pa. He says he is employed as an assistant with one of the state engineers and is getting on very well. I am very anxious to see you but if your Pa will consent for you to go to Virginia, I will not object to it as you had rather go there than to come home. I reckon he will return home shortly and write you which he prefers for you to come home or to go to Virginia. I think he will say come home.

Miss Montgomery had a party given to her at Judge Whitehead's three weeks last night. She is not pretty but good looking and a pleasant girl. She has very good sense. I don't know that she is intelligent. Last Monday week I went to Carrollton and called on Mrs. Barnes and Mrs. Richard Whitehead and went shopping. Had the good luck to meet with Mrs. E. Whitehead and Jennie Kennedy. Jennie bought a grenadine dress and gave twenty five dollars for the pattern and the mantuamaker charged eight dollars for making it.[125] She got it to wear at a party in Vaiden. It was to be made with a double skirt. Mrs. Temple and her husband is living in Carrollton. He has a cash store. They are boarding at one of the hotels. I can't write for making mistakes. You must excuse them.

Abram told me that an infant was found the other side of Carrollton Sunday week. It was naked and only a few hours old. Dr. Hart and Dr. Ladell went in search for the mother. It is said that its mother is a Miss Newel living on Pelusia and they made her take it. I don't know the truth of it. I have not seen any white person to hear about it. Tomorrow a hard shell Baptist is to preach at Concord near Major Neill's. There is to be feet washing. I do wish there was a way for the carriage to go from here there. I would go to the feet washing. It is well the weather is cool, it will prevent their smelling of each other's toes.

Write soon.

Your devoted mother,

S. E. Watkins

P.S. What is the name of the evergreen you sent in your letter? Ritter and America send love to you. Martha says I must tell you she is not a darky. No more than Patty. She was very indignant at you calling them darkys.

---

124. These would have been members of President James Buchanan's cabinet.
125. Thirty–three dollars for the finished dress would be perhaps two hundred dollars today.

To Letitia Walton from Sarah Watkins:

May 25, 1860
Carrollton, Mississippi

Mrs. L. A. Walton
Austin, Texas

My Dear Child,

It is five weeks today since the last letter I received from you was written. The time appears longer than that to me. I would be very uneasy about you if I did not think you were too busy to take time to write.

I am very busy making my dresses and I could get on faster with them if I only had somebody to fit them on me. Your Pa brought me a summer silk and organdy muslin. I don't like either of them. He got Miss Montgomery to chose them. I gave Mrs. White five dollars to make the silk. The body is made plain with a little point and the bosom padded. It is too large over the shoulders and one side of the neck higher than the other. The padding makes it very disagreeable for the summer. Mrs. White said it would add to my form as I am so flat. I do look better with a full bosom but she has put too much in. Four buttons in the form of a rosette and white and brown, the color of the dress, are put on the body down the front. The sleeves are cut the form of your silk sleeves and lined with white muslin silk and white gauze ribbon quilled inside of them. They are trimmed with two rows of narrow brown and white silk trimming that was gotten with the dress. There is a plain piece about a half finger long sewn in the armhole and the sleeve quilled on to that and a cap on top cut full and quilled in to the armhole that is lined with silk and has one row of the trimming put on. I will send you a piece of the silk in this letter. Dresses are worn here cut half high neck. The large bonnets are not worn here yet.

Your Pa went to Mr. Roberson's yesterday and he expects to be back tomorrow or the next day. In my last letter I wrote you that I would give you a full account of the negroes that he bought.[126] You must not say nothing about what I write you about them when you write to me. Your Pa would not like for anything to be said against them. He thinks that he has done finely in buying them. They all appear to be very good, humble servants but none of them has been used to hard work such as is required of them here. He bought one old woman named Sallie, about fifty-eight or nine years old. She was bought to come with her daughter. Her daughter is fifteen and one eye is crossed. She is sick this week with a rising finger[127] and today she has bowel

---

126. Dr. Watkins purchased new slaves in Missouri.
127. Boil or felon, probably at the fingernail.

disease and chills. Her name is Catharine.[128] One girl named Hannah, fourteen years old, she is laid up with a swelled ankle she says was sprained two years ago. Janie is twenty and has a white child four months old. Her master sold her for it. It was his son-in-law's child. She seems to be a very good woman and the best looking of all of the females. Jacob is nineteen and very likely looking. Bob is seventeen, very likely. He has come in with a breaking out on his neck. Two brothers, Dickson and Charles—Dickson is 13 and Charles is younger. Jim Moses eight years old, Anna is a yellow girl said to be twelve years old. She says she is in her fourteenth year. She says that she is sickly. She is half a head taller than Martha's Milly and big head and formed like Sally except the big belly. She is just as sleepy headed. She don't know how to do nothing. She never will be as useful as Sally has been. She can't stand the sun. She shows that she belonged to well-raised people. It will take someone that is strict to make her any account. I have spoken right sharp to her but she seems to have such a good disposition and knows so well how to get around a person to gain their good will that I hate to whip her. She had the measles when she got here. She took them after she started from St. Louis. We made her stay in the shed room until she got over them. She soon got well of them. Your Pa says that he bought her for me and calls it a present and says she is given for what he is owing me. If I have to pay for the present, I don't want her. I think it very hard after being kept out of money such a long time to have to receive pay in such a way as he chose to pay it. He has not given me a bill of sale for her yet. If she is sickly I don't want her. I want one that can stand any kind of work. I have enough sickly ones about me now. I told him that I did not care to buy no negro but America.[129] I have a great notion to tell him if my money has to go for Anna I do not want her. I could cry and can hardly keep from it when I think that is the way my money has to go. I have heard him say lately that he was owing you something and spoke of paying you when you come here. Do pray, don't say anything about what I have written you. I would not have him to know what I have written in regard to Anna and what was said about paying you.

Ritter has a rising on her finger. There is always something the matter with her at the very time that she is the most needed. Sally is yet suffering with her jaw. I heard her grunting from her house to the dining room door this morning, the pain was so severe. If the pains were lasting I think it would kill her. It is just at times they are so severe. She came in here just now and told

128. This mother and daughter, Sally and Catharine, figure in the letters for the next several years. Aunt Sally is not to be confused with another Sally, already a family servant, who has had an infected jaw for years.

129. America belonged to Letitia but did not want to move to Texas, so Sarah Watkins "hired" her from the daughter each year.

me to give her love to you and Newton and told Newton that she dreamed that she and him were carrying hickory nuts to Ritter. I asked her if she would not send howdy to Early too. She said she would like to see him but Newton was her favorite.

Mr. Joe Scruggs died last Friday with pneumonia. I went with your Pa in the buggy to see Mrs. Hemingway two weeks last evening. She has been sick with hemorrhage of the lungs. Mr. Hemingway was sick too. Margaret A. has been sick with chills. She don't stay with her mother much. She lives nine miles from here on Teoc, Jack Johnson's old place. We spent the day at Mr. E. Whitehead's this day week. Mr. E. Whitehead sends his respects to you and Mr. Walton.

There are few strawberries, raspberries, and cherries here this year. The plums are getting ripe. I received a letter from Baby this week. She said the kind manner in which I gave my consent for her to visit Virginia this summer turned her heart immediately towards home and greatly increased her desire to return home this summer. She has permission to go to Virginia or to come home and it is left to her to decide which she will do. I think her Pa would like for her to come home.

Give my love to Mr. Walton and the children. Kiss the boys for me. Write soon and oftener.

Your loving mother,
Sarah E. Watkins

To Mary Watkins from Sarah Watkins:

July 10, 1860
Winona, Mississippi [130]

Miss M. E. Watkins
Black's and White's, Virginia

Direct your letter to Winona. That is our P.O. office.

My Dear Child,

It has been some time since I have written you. It was not for the want of an inclination why I have not written you. Yesterday three weeks I got up in the morning with the bowel complaint. As Mrs. E. Whitehead and Miss Montgomery spent the day with me, I kept up all day. The next day I had dysentery but still continued with diarrhea and a very sick stomach until the next

---

130. The coming of the railroad meant that the mailing address was moved to Winona. The death of Middleton was under way.

Sunday. I had a large blister drawn on the left side of my abdomen.[131] Your Pa said I had an attack of fever. He thought me dangerous and sent for Mrs. Whitehead one day to come to see me. She was expecting Mrs. Phillips and Eppe Oliver [*Mrs. Phillips' granddaughter*] to see her and did not come until Sunday morning. Miss Montgomery and William Whitehead rode over last Friday evening to see me. Mrs. Whitehead said if I needed sitting up with, Miss Montgomery was to send to let her know and she would come and sit up with me. I did not need sitting up with. Ritt and America slept in the room with me. My health is not good yet. My bowels hurts me frequently and I have a weak stomach and am very feeble. I can walk to the weaving house and garden in the cool of the morning and evening.

A protracted meeting[132] is going on at Bluff Springs. I am not well enough to attend it, I wish I was. I would enjoy it very much. If I were well I could not go to it. Abram[133] is busy whitewashing my room. What good does wealth do a person when they cannot enjoy themselves in no way that they like, that is my unfortunate lot. It is not that people don't care for me why they do not visit me in sickness. On account of your Pa's eccentricity, I have to live so aloof from everybody that very few people feel welcome to come here.

Mrs. Phillips told Mrs. Whitehead to tell me if I needed her assistance and would let her know it, she would come and do all she could for me. Baby, it is very wrong to put off preparing for death until the last hours of our lives. I was so sick. I did not feel like using my tongue to pray, but my heart was and is always placed on my redeemer. He is my comforter in all my troubles in this world, and I pray when I die he will receive my soul in heaven. I hope the Lord will spare me to see my beloved children again and enjoy their sweet society. Oh the pleasure it will afford me if I live to see my dear beloved Baby in twelve months return home an accomplished lady. When I think of it, it revives my spirits. Then what a happy family ours would be if your Pa would become an affectionate father to his poor unfortunate child, Lettie. He seems to care very little about her and I don't think he does care anything for her. Take warning and do not give him cause to cast you off as your self-willed sister did. He idolizes you and none have a place above you in his heart. Oh, that I had somebody to love me as much as he does you.

He went to Grenada to meet you and thought perhaps you would come

131. The producing of a blister by the making of a small fire over the skin. Sometimes a moist slice of potato was placed over the area and a small flame built on top of the potato. Heat and blistering followed. Also, a drug such as cantharides was sufficiently irritating that when it was applied to the skin, a blister would form. This reaction was thought to be beneficial. Such therapy is still widely used in Asia.

132. Revival.

133. Abram drove the carriage, also.

with Miss Green. He saw Miss Green and her brother and came from Grenada to Winona with them. Miss Green spoke very highly of you to him and said that she thinks you will get an honor when you graduate. We are very anxious to get a letter from you and wonder why you do not write and let us know what has become of you. I am very anxious to see you but am not sorry much that you did not come home as you would have to go back and the parting with you would be so grievous to me. I think you will have better health in Virginia than you would have had here at home and will be more. I hope you will not be a trouble to them. I would like very much to see them all. Write me all about them [*the kinfolk in Virginia*]. Write soon and often.

Your loving mother,
S.E. Watkins

To Mary Watkins from Sarah Watkins:

July 31, 1860
Winona, Mississippi

Miss M. E. Watkins
Black's & White's, Virginia
My Dear Child,

Your very welcome letter of the 18th inst. was received last Saturday which gave us much joy to hear from you and my relations. My health is improving. I have been taking iron rust and Hostetters bitters that has given me a great appetite equal to a famished hound. If I could only have a heart free of distress and unhappiness I would be in good health again. The animosity your Pa still has against your dear sister causes grief to be so deeply seated in my heart that I cannot get over it. He seems not to like Lettie writing so much about you not coming home. I received a letter from her last week. He read it and made some remark about it. The next morning he said he did not mind a little extravagance in his children, that he dealt out to them freely, but he did not like disobedience in them and went on talking about Lettie as he usually does. I told him Lettie was always obedient to him in everything except marrying. He said it made him mad everytime he reads her letters. I said to him that he told Lettie that he had forgiven her. He said yes, I said so then, but it is not so. Oh Baby, it had added so much to my happiness when I thought he had forgiven my poor dear child. Since he had told me he had not forgiven her, it has kept my poor heart aching. When you write don't say nothing about what I have written respecting Lettie. I pray God will soften his heart towards her and we may yet be a happy family.

I did not think myself dangerously ill was the reason I did not comply with my promise to let you know it. Your Pa wrote to you when I was sick. I did not know when he wrote. He said he did not tell you I was sick. Mrs. E. and Mr. E. Whitehead and Mrs. Farmer spent the day here yesterday. Thursday week Mrs. Moore, Ella and Laura, Sally, Mollie and Bettie Collins were to see us. Ella and Laura Moore and M. Collins staid until Saturday evening. Your Pa sent for Jennie Wellons and Miss Hemphill Friday. They staid until Sunday morning. Mr. Hemphill lives at James Collins' place near Judge Wellons. I enjoyed the girls' company very much. You know I am a great lover of young people's company. Martha Jane Gary had a daughter last week. I promised to spend this day at Mr. E. Whitehead's. It rained this morning and is yet cloudy that prevents me going there today.

I have a great many good watermelons and muskmelons. I often wish my children had them. Some of the negroes are most always sick. Big Milly and Isham are sick. Isham is quite sick today. Every wet day Charlotte is sick with a wheezing. Sally's jaw is no better.

Give my love to all my relations, particularly to Aunt Mary Williams and cousin Fayette's family and tell them I am very much obliged to them for their kindness to you. You must get cousin Betty Irby to promise to come and spend some time with you when you return home. It would give me pleasure to have my relations to visit me. Write me about all my relations. Is cousin Mary Miller living in Texas? How many children has she? Inquire about cousin Polly Stith and her sister Elisa. Cousin Jack Fitzgerald, what has become of him? Who did Aunt Patsy Epes's daughters, Sally and Martha marry? Whose son is that smart lawyer Fitzgerald living at Farmville? Is Uncle Frank Fitzgerald and Aunt Sally Ward living? Which of the Epes's sons did cousin Jack Williams' daughter marry? Try and get a history of all my relations and write me all about them. I would like very much to hear from them all and would like to visit them if I thought a visit from me would be welcomed by them. Tell Aunt Mary I often think of her and Uncle David's kindness to me when I staid with them and went to school. I have always been thankful to them for their kindness to me and pray they will be rewarded in heaven for their kindness to me.

Martha and Ritter says you must inquire about their uncles Abram and Patrick and let them know who they belong to and where are they living. Tell all the old servants howdy for me. If Ritter, Caty, and Ann Elisa are living, give them a present for me. Write me which of the old servants you see that knew me. Martha, Ritter and America send their love to you. Write often. We are always anxious to receive a letter from you.

Your loving Mother,
Sarah E. Watkins

To grandson Early Walton from Sarah Watkins:

August 25, 1860
Carrollton, Mississippi

Master Early W. Walton
Care of Mr. Wm. M. Walton
Austin, Texas

My Dear Grandson,[134]

I will comply with my promise and write to you. It has been some time since I have written to your Mother. I have been busy that has prevented me from writing to you both. I have had so many watermelons, Early. I wish you all had some of them. I had a few good apples, they staid here in the house and rotted. We had no peaches except on the trees in the back yard. Some people had a plenty in their orchards.

Were you not afraid to stay on that mountain where there were so many wild animals? I would have been so uneasy, I could not have slept fearing they would catch me while I was sleeping. Did you see any of them?

Has not the sun burnt you and Newton's sweet and pretty skins most yellow this hot summer? We have had very hot dry weather until lately. It has rained some most every day this week. I went to preaching in Middleton two weeks ago and coming back it rained so hard Abram had to stop and get under the carriage out of the rain. It did not rain here enough to lay the dust.

I saw a tame raccoon last week at Mr. E. Whitehead's. It would get in the chair and go to sleep like a cat and knew its name when it was called "Coonie." At Mr. Hemingway's they have a pretty little fawn with white spots on it. Paten caught it with the dogs. I had rather have your kitten than the coon or fawn. The kitten will be useful to catch mice and the other pets will be mischievous.

Your mother says you are a sweet child. I am very glad to hear it. You must continue to be good and obey your parents and everybody will love you. Tell Newton he must be good too. Tell your mother I received her letter of the 8th inst. this week, and was very glad to hear from you all. I will answer her letter soon. Give my love to your parents and Newton. Kiss your mother and Newton for me and tell them to kiss you for me. You must answer my letter shortly. Tell your mother to write soon and often. Abram and Ritter send their

134. Newton Walton was born March 12, 1855 in Austin; his brother, Early, was born at the Watkins home, September 1, 1856. George Longstreet Walton will be born December 5, 1860, but Mrs. Watkins has not been told of this possibility.

love to you all. I want to see you all very much. I expect you are nearly as large as Newton. Are you not? I wish I could send you a long letter. I can't think of anything to write that will amuse you.

Your affectionate Grandmother,
Sarah E. Watkins

To Letitia Walton from Sarah Watkins:

September 5, 1860
Winona, Mississippi

My Dear Child,

I have put off too long answering your affectionate letter of the 8th ult. Writing to dear Early made me delay writing to you. I expect by this time the sweet child has received my letter. I imagine I can see him smile when it is handed to him.

I was very glad to hear that Mr. Walton has bought a place if it will not embarrass him to pay for it. Having a place of your own will make you so much better contented. You must not be too hard to please and worry your husband to death, it will make against the improvement in his health. A mind at peace and ease adds greatly to health and if a person can't have that at home, they can't enjoy themselves nowhere. A disagreeable husband or wife is enough to distract any man or woman. I know from experience when my heart is at ease, my mind is strong and my body feels so much better.

My health is better than it has been for some time. I have not swollen any this week. I look better than I did before I was sick. My hair has most all come out. I have used one bottle of Woods hair restoration and am using the second bottle, it does not prevent my hair from falling out, it has taken out the dandruff. Did you use yours on your head? How did you like it? Just as soon as I was able after being sick I took your advice and changed my feather bed to a mattress and find it much more pleasant than the bed. My back has been in less pain than it has been since Baby was born. Writing makes it hurt me at this time.

The weather has been excessively hot this summer and is yet very warm but more pleasant this morning. It rained several times lately. With the assistance of Ritt and America I dried some peaches enough to give you some. Wet weather came before I could get them dried. I reckon peaches will come again before you can get a chance to get these.

The Baptists had a meeting at Whitehead's school house all last week. Gus Bird was baptised Sunday morning in the creek near Echol's old place. Sunday was the only day I attended the meeting. I saw Mary Arnold there. She looks very badly. She has a baby about eight weeks old. Mary A., Mrs. Parmele and Mrs. Hines McCarroll [*Mrs. Parmele and Mrs. McCarroll were sisters-in-law*] went to the Artesian well last month for falling of their wombs. I don't know whether they were benefited any by going to the wells. Mrs. Allen Gary died several months ago. I did not hear of her death until lately.

We received a letter from Baby last week. She was enjoying herself finely at cousin Henrys father's in Prince Edward County. She will leave there for Washington City next Thursday. Cousin Henry's pa will go with her. I expect she has written to you and told you more news about Virginia than she had written to us. She wrote me that Aunt Patsy Epes died last spring. Ritt brought in a plate with six bunches of nice ripe grapes just now. I do wish you all had them. Cousin Frank Watkins has written twice to your Pa since Baby has been at his house. He speaks very highly of her and says his family is very glad to have her with them. I believe I wrote you that Judge Field was here last month. Judge Hillyer expects to move back to Georgia this month. That will kill Baby's joy.[135]

Mary Jones is very sick with fever. Our negroes come in every day with chills or biles. Martha went to church Sunday and that night she had a chill and has been right sick ever since with fever. Last month Charlotte was sick. She had a congestive chill and after the chill was off she wouldn't speak and was out of her head crying and raving as if she was scared. Three or four times she was that way after having chills. Mr. Pentecost was sick with a chill yesterday. He did not have chills until his watermelons got ripe. I think from that eating watermelons gives chills. America has had several biles. She bruised her breast with the whale bone in her dress body and caused it to rise which made her quite sick all last week. Her breast had to be lanced twice. She is able to be up this week. Sally is yet grunting with her jaw. She gets better, the pains do not last so long at a time as they did. She spins and helps to sew the negroes' clothes. Uncle Vivion gets sick now and then and thinks he is tricked by his having pains. He is well at this time and able to attend to the hogs.

Give my love to Mr. Walton and the children. Tell Newton and Early they must be good boys. Tell Early he must answer my letter. Newton must write to me too. America sends love to you all and says Newton and Early must write to her. Ritter sends love to you all. Write soon and often.

Your affectionate mother,
Sarah E. Watkins

---

135. She won't have anyone to visit in Washington City.

September 13th, 1860
Winona, Mississippi

Miss M. E. Watkins
Patapsco Institute, Md.

My Dear Child:

Your very welcome letter of the 6th inst. was received with gladness last Monday. The last letter I wrote to you I directed it to Black's & White's.[136] I expect you have not received it. Your Pa has written to you so frequently that it caused me to be more negligent in writing you and I thought it useless to write until you returned to Patapsco. I suppose you are there ready to commence your studies today. It was so much better for you to spend your vacation in a healthy place than to have come home and perhaps have chills and fevers that would have prevented you from returning to school and being qualified to graduate next summer. I do look forward with so much joy for the time to come when my dear daughter will return home an accomplished lady and be a comfort to her poor broken hearted Mother, that one beloved daughter has caused so much unhappiness.

Cousin Frank Watkins writes to your Pa that you are a great favorite with his family and they were pleased to have you to stay with them. He wrote that his wife says she never had a relation to stay with her that was as little trouble to her as you were.

What bridal party did you go with from Richmond to Washington City? Is cousin Fayette smart? Did he and his wife appear to like your visiting them? Your Pa wrote two or three times to cousin Fayette and he has not answered his letters. A man of his standing and property certainly can write.

Did you see cousin Tom & Emily Epes? How is cousin Tom getting on? Whose son is Sam Epes? Who did you go with to his house? I feel very sorry for cousin Dandridge Epes's daughter. Were I to be in her company or any of his families I would show them as much respect as I would any other relation if they act well. They ought not to be slighted for what their Father has done. [*An earlier letter indicated that he was sentenced to be hanged.*]

I am very glad that you have got my Mother's profile.[137] Take care of it. I had one but the moths ate it nearly up. I can't hear enough from you about old Va. Write all about every relation you saw. Every little circumstance is interesting to me.

I attended a protracted meeting last Sunday, Tuesday and yesterday at Chestnut Ridge, and it is yet going on. It is a real warm Methodist meeting,

136. Two rival tavern keepers in Nottoway County, Virginia, whose location grew into a settlement; the area was renamed Blackstone in 1885.
137. A cut–out silhouette.

there were several mourners and some converts. I dined at Mrs. Hemingway's Sunday and at Mr. Bryan's Tuesday.

Nothing has been done to our old house but white washing all the rooms except the dining room. That is yet to do when it is convenient to have it done. Your Pa says he will set you up with it thinking he will prepare the house for your reception. He is joking. It would be his delight to have two nice rooms put up if he could.

He has had a two story frame gin house put up near the old one. It is finished near enough for ginning to be done in it. The negroes are constantly with chills. Charlotte was taken with chills five or six weeks ago. She had a congestive chill and could not say anything but "Oh heaven" for most of the day. Two chills, she had after that. She was out of her head and would cry and look as if she was frightened. She got well.

Last Saturday I carried her with me to preaching riding up by Abram. The sun made her sick by the time I got to Mrs. Petty's. Since then she has been having chills. Martha was sick last week with fever, she is well this week. Tave had a chill today. Alfred has been quite sick all the week with chills and fevers. Tom, Polly and old Aunt Sally Missouri have chills. Charlotte has grown very much and is as fine looking as when you saw her and just as lazy.

The negroes all but three little boys live in Polly's house. The three boys live in Robin's house. Polly has staid with Ritter since Glasgow died. Aunt Sally and her daughter Catharine are black, Hannah, fourteen years old, is dark color. Jane is black[138] and her baby is white. Anna is yellow. She was bought for my maid. I could not make her do anything. She was sent to the field. She says she had rather be in the field. Pentecost[139] says she is a hard case. He has whipped her several times. She is a little taller than Martha's Milly. She shows in her manners to white people that she has been raised with genteel people. If I was a strict mistress, I could make a nice maid of her. Jacob and Bob are almost men, they are yellow. Dickson is thirteen, he is yellow. Charlie is younger, he is black. James Moses, said to be eight years old, he is black. They are all very well behaved negroes. Most of them have not been used to working as hard as they have to work here. Charlotte says I must tell you howdy and that she wants to see you mighty bad and you must save her a dress.

Your Pa gave all the women and the little girls a calico dress. I promised Charlotte to buy her one if she would be attentive to her business. Have you a dress like the piece of muslin you enclosed in your letter? It is pretty.

I have not heard from Lettie in about a month. I am getting uneasy and

138. The new slaves, purchased in Chillicothe, Missouri, in April 1860.
139. Overseer.

am very anxious to hear from her. In her last letter she mentioned that they had bought a place in Austin and she would commence keeping house next month. I expect you hear from her as often as I do. My health is good for one of my age. I pray I may live to welcome you home next July. Oh the happiness it will afford me to embrace my beloved Baby in my arms and rejoice and thank my God that he has permitted me to live to see my child return home as a well educated lady.

Martha, Ritter and America send their love to you and say they want to see you very much. I will write to you oftener. You must write often and soon. We are always anxious to hear from you. It puts your Pa in fine spirits to receive letters from you. He says it makes him mad every time he reads a letter from Lettie and told me not to show him her letters. It does hurt my feelings so much the way he treats poor Lettie. I pray the Lord will change his heart and make him an affectionate Father to his own child.

Your Affectionate Mother,
Sarah E. Watkins

To Mary Watkins from Sarah Watkins:

October 6, 1860
Winona, Mississippi

Miss Mary E. Watkins
Patapsco Female Institute
Ellicotts Mill, Maryland

My Dear Child,

Time passes off so swiftly that I cannot keep account of the last time I wrote to my children. I received your letter of the 21st ult. last week. It is useless to say I am always rejoiced to hear from you and wish I could write you letters to be as interesting to you as yours are to me.

Last Thursday your Pa and myself attended a barbecue given to Colonel Jeff Davis[140] in the woods near Winona. He delivered a very good speech against the abolitionists of the north and had something to say about all the candidates for presidency. I have not the intelligence to inform you what he said in regard to them. He is in favor of [*John C.*] Breckenridge for president[141]

---

140. On February 10, 1861, he was elected president of the Confederacy. In 1860 he was a United States senator.

141. The Democratic Party, of which Davis was a member, had now split into two factions. The southern faction supported incumbent Vice President Breckenridge, while the northern faction supported Stephen A. Douglas of Illinois.

Hoping to throw the election into the House of Representatives, a fourth party, the Consti-

and [*Joseph*] Lane, vice president. When he was speaking some man hollared out, "Hurrah for Bell." Someone answered by making a noise like an owl, "Who who who?" Governor [*John J.*] Pettus delivered a short speech after dinner. Several people attended, but not as many as I expected to see.

A very nice dinner was furnished. The tables were very long and formed a square. Some of the tables had nice iced cake on them. Mrs. Vaiden and I were together and got to a very poor table where there was nothing on it but mutton, light bread, corn bread, and sweet potatoes. There was one small cake at the foot of the table but by the time we got sight of it, it was taken off. I don't know what became of it. Mrs. Vaiden was wishing for some of the cake. I wanted to see it. I did not care for it to eat. I heard Mrs. Phillips tell Mrs. Palmer that she was up until eleven o'clock the night before dressing the cake. I had curiosity to see how it was dressed. I did not see it at all.

Salsbury went to carry the sheep that your Pa gave for the dinner and staid to assist in cooking and to help to do anything that was required of him. Salsbury said that Mrs. Palmer furnished most of the cake—that she had a box full and a basket half full. She sent three men last week to help to fix the place for the barbecue.[142] Mrs. Kennedy, Ophelia, Tom K. [*Kennedy*] and his wife, Dr. and Mrs. Vaiden[143] came up on the car to the barbecue.

Judge Collins has been very sick and he has sent here for ice three or four times. His servant was here this morning for ice. He said his master was mending slowly. Allen Gary is very sick, he sent for ice yesterday. Lizzie Oliver came to her father's last Sunday week, I spent the day with her at Pa's last Monday. She expects to return to Alabama in three weeks. Mr. Oliver has gone back and Eppe went with him. Lizzie looks very well and happy. I expect she has a good husband.

Baby if you had been in the carriage Thursday you would have been ashamed of the mules that was to it. We drove Mary and Jim. Abram was whipping them all the way and chucking to them. I thought, "Is Abram's mouth not tired." It had rained and the road was muddy that made it harder pulling. When we got most to Winona your Pa fretted at Abram for not getting Meaddy mule. Jake had to have her to work the wagon as she is the lead mule but he was done with her before we started. Abram asked your Pa if Mary and

---

tutional–Union, ran John Bell of Tennessee. As it would turn out, Abraham Lincoln, the Republican candidate (called the abolitionists by our correspondents) won enough electoral votes that the election did not go to the house. This "last straw" induced seven states to secede from the Union.

142. Usually a large, long pit.

143. Dr. C. M. Vaiden lived east of Shongalo. His son, Henry Merritt Vaiden, married Camilla Kennedy on March 22, 1882. Camilla was the daughter of Margaret Virginia (Whitehead) Kennedy.

Jim would do to work and he replied to Abram that they would do as well as any. He said to Abram you had *no business* to ask if they would do.

I go from home so seldom and see so few people that I do not know any news to write you. I am very glad to hear that you can cut and make your own dresses. I hope when you come home you will cut and make mine for me. The muslin and calico samples you sent are very neat dresses for every day.

I wrote to you only twice while you were in Virginia. Lawyer Fitzgerald of Farmville is my second cousin. I would be pleased to have his likeness and would like to know who his mother was. If his mother is living, he must be the son of his father's third wife. Is he very intelligent?

Some of the negroes are constantly sick with chills. Your Pa was sick last week, I think he had chills. America had a chill yesterday. She is not well today. Ritt has not been well for three days, they are about their business today and send their love to you. Sally is yet suffering with pain in her jaw. Your Pa says I must tell you that you must use large envelopes like such as he uses and you must, or he would like for you to write to Bishop Green and direct your letter this way.

Rt. Rev. Wm. M. Green
Bishop of the Diocese of Mississippi
Jackson, Mississippi

Write soon and often.

Your loving mother,
Sarah E. Watkins

To Letitia Walton from Sarah Watkins:

October 20, 1860
Winona, Mississippi

My Dear Child,

Your very welcome letter of the 7th inst. was received last Thursday. Your Pa was anxious to hear what you would agree to about swapping America for Catharine and her mother[144] opened your letter before I received it. I was very glad that you did not write anything that you would not like for him to see.

Major Neill is not at home. He has gone to Tennessee. When he comes back your Pa says that he will get him to value the negroes when he returns home. His price for the negroes is fifty dollars difference between them and America and if Major Neill says they are worth more than that, he will not charge you anymore than fifty dollars. He says send Bill Patton by here and very probably

144. Sally and Catharine were purchased by the doctor in Missouri.

it will be a trade. He says he hates parting with them mightily but to pleasure me to get America, he will make the swap if you are willing to do it. They were sold to him for sound healthy negroes both in body and mind and he believes them to be healthy and thinks Catharine has a better constitution than America. They have had chills since they have been here. He says that he thinks he was told that Aunt Sally is fifty-two. I think fifty-seven would come nearer to her age. He says she is not gray, I have never seen her without her cap. Last week and part of week before last America was quite sick with chills and fever. She is well now but looks pale. America says she had rather go to Texas to you and leave her mama than to be sold to anybody but me. I told Sally [*America's mother*] that she could go with America. She said she would never leave me, that you are not able for her to sit down and do nothing. She suffers enough with her jaw to kill her. She grunts and makes such a fuss that when your Pa sees her, he thinks she is deceitful. Anyone to look at her can see something is the matter with it. She spins and helps to make the negroes' clothes.

I spent the day at Major Hawkins' Thursday. Mrs. Hawkins had been sick eight weeks, she was getting well. She sits up part of the day. She did not leave her room only to go in a room joining hers that is called the nursery to lie down. Major Hawkins' brother and his wife that live in Texas were there. She had Cholera Morbus from eating ground peas the day before. You would like her, she is a very pleasant lady. Mrs. Kendel, Tom Purnell's aunt who lives with him was there and Mr. and Mrs. Foltz, and Mr. and Mrs. Baskerville.

I spent yesterday at Mr. Hemphill's. He lives at J. Collins' place near Judge Wellons'. Old Mrs. Ladell and Mrs. Dr. Ladell spent the day there. I was not acquainted with Mrs. Hemphill. Miss Hemphill was there this summer. I think I wrote you of her and Jennie Wellons being sent for to come here.

In writing to you and Baby I forget which of you I mention some things to. I attended a barbecue near Winona the fourth of this month given to Jeff Davis.[145] He spoke in the forenoon and Governor Pettus in the evening. Rebecca Sanders was married Wednesday night to a Mr. Weed. She had a large wedding and dancing. I don't know that she danced that night, I heard that she danced last winter. I don't expect she married much from what I have heard about him. Dr. Hudson staid here one night lately. He told me that he saw a Miss Miller that told him she saw you at Mr. George Walton's last fall and that you looked very young and well. Lizzie Oliver has been at her father's about four weeks. I went to see her the next week after she came. She has not been to see me. She said she expects to go back to Alabama in three weeks

---

145. Davis is U.S. senator from Mississippi, now campaigning around the state in behalf of the state rights Democrats, in the forthcoming federal election.

or as soon as her Pa could leave her mother after her confinement. He will go part of the way with her. I have not heard whether Mrs. Whitehead has been confined. Lizzie looks very happy. She looks not quite so fleshy and a little pale. She came to stay only a few days at her Pa's as Mr. Oliver could not stay longer but she said her Pa would not let her go back so soon.

21st, Sunday morning. As the sun set last evening before I could finish my letter, I will finish it today. Abram has a bile [*boil*] under his arm that prevents me from attending church today. It is very pleasant weather this morning. There has been several days of cold weather this week. Hannah came in sick with almost the croup last Monday night, she got a great deal better and Thursday she relapsed and has been very sick since. She is a good deal better this morning and able to sit up in bed. She told me that Chloe told her that Mrs. E. Whitehead had a daughter [*Ella Gertrude Whitehead*] Thursday and two of Mr. Freeman's negro cabins burned down Thursday night. His negro Antonette's child about five months old was so badly burnt that it died. The child was locked up in one of the cabins that was burnt.

I hope you and your family are enjoying yourselves at your own house and you may see more happiness than your poor mother has ever seen. Give my love to Mr. Walton and the children. Kiss the children for me. Tell Early it is time he was answering my letter. He and Newton must write to me how they employ their time. You must write soon and often.

Your affectionate mother,
S.E. Watkins

CHAPTER SIX

Gathering Storm Clouds

Life continued along its relatively placid pathway for the Watkinses, even as the nation careened down the disastrous track that led to civil war. Mr. Watkins began 1861 with a new contract between him and his plantation overseer. "Baby" Mary must have given some hint that she favored Abraham Lincoln for the presidency, for her mother wrote, "Your Pa says if he thought you were in favor of Lincoln, he would not let you come in this house." It is tempting to regard this as an exaggeration, since Mary was such a favorite, the very "apple" of her father's eye. But Mrs. Watkins expressed hope that Lincoln would not be elected, and in this she—and everyone else who dreaded the election of the abolitionist Republicans—were to be disappointed.

Mary completed her studies at the end of the school term in 1861 and returned home. She had expressed a desire to stay and do some postgraduate reading, but there was much excitement, and fretting, concerning her safety, as violence had broken out in Baltimore when Lincoln passed through the city on his way to Washington, D.C., for his inauguration. Although they were soberly concerned about the future, the Watkins family—like many other southerners—remained hopeful that no war would come.

This chapter contains one of the most remarkable of the letters, in which a number of the slave women dictated passages, transcribed by Mrs. Watkins, to Mary. The affection shown by the black people for their owners—at least for certain of them—is striking, as is the lack of any apparent discord on the plantation even as civil war loomed. It is particularly arresting that *these* slaves expressed an affinity for the song "Dixie" and also an affection for the South itself, as well as a happy resolution to the life which was their lot—all on the eve of their "jubilee of freedom dawning," which they may dimly, if at all, have perceived to be on the way.

To Mary Watkins from Sarah Watkins:

November 2, 1860
Winona, Mississippi

Miss M. E. Watkins
Patapsco Institute

My Dear Child,

It has been so long since I have written to you that I must lay aside my work and answer your very welcome letter of the 15th ult. that was received last Saturday with delight. Your letter of the 21st ult. to your Pa came at the same time. He had gone to Mr. Roberson's. He staid three or four days and returned home last Monday evening. I have been engaged over a week cutting out the negroes' winter clothes and have not finished yet but have to quit until more cloth is wove. It almost cripples me in my ankles, feet and arm cutting so much.

What a pity you could not attend the party given by Mr. Barksdale when you were in Washington City. He staid a night here last Monday two weeks and told us that he saw you and that the party was mostly given on you and the Misses Collins account. Colonel Strong and his two sons, they live near Aberdeen, spent a night here lately. Colonel Strong had been to Sunflower County and bought land to settle his sons on. Evening before last Mrs. Vaiden, Mrs. Herron and their nephew, Mr. Herron came here just as a hard rain came up. They left here yesterday between eleven and twelve o'clock. I had dinner preparing for them. I could not get them to wait for dinner and gave them a lunch. It was raining a little when they left here. It was a cold rainy day yesterday and today is cold and the wind blows very hard like a March day. The sun is shining very pretty. I was regretting having my young duck killed as the company did not stay to eat it and I have not many young ducks. America said to me why, "Why Miss Sarah, that is like Baby and the chicken."

Rebecker Sanders was married Wednesday night two weeks to a Mr. Weed, who stays about Carrollton. I don't expect he is much. She was married at her father's. They had dancing. John Fox gave them an affair. Weed, it is said, is a keen trader and does a good deal of J. Fox's trading for him. I dined at Major

Hawkins' Thursday two weeks. Mrs. Hawkins had been sick eight weeks. She is out of bed and recovering. Mr. John Hawkins and his wife from Texas are visiting them. Mrs. Kendel, Mr. and Mrs. Foltz, Mr. and Mrs. Baskerville spent the day there. John Hawkins and his wife are living at Major Hawkins'. She has two children. This day two weeks I went with your Pa to Mr. Hemphill's who lives at James Collins' place near Carrollton and spent the day. Old Mrs. Ladell who is a sister of Mr. Hemphill's dined there and Mrs. Dr. Ladell. Mrs. E. Whitehead has a daughter two weeks old. Lizzie Oliver expects to return to Eutaw, Alabama next week. She has not been to see me since she has come home. I staid all day at Mr. Whitehead's Tuesday and Lizzie had gone to Mrs. Phillip's to spend the day. Mrs. Barry, Cordelia Roy that was, has a baby. Mrs. J. O. Young and Mrs. Frank Pleasants have young babies.

Mr. Parmele's mother, Mrs. Townsend[146] had a house built just as the workman was driving in the last nail he saw it was afire and it burned down and the old house caught afire and burned up and most everything in the house was burnt. William Parmele pulled off his coat to assist in moving out the things and that got burnt and forty dollars was in his coat pocket and old Mrs. Townsend would have been burnt if she had not been taken out. She left her gold watch lying on the table and carried out an old book that was not worth a shuck. Mr. Freemon got two of his negro cabins burnt and a little negro baby burnt so badly that it died soon after it was taken out of the house.

Hannah has been very sick with pneumonia, I believe. She is getting well. At one time your Pa thought she would die. Chloe came home sick last Sunday. She is here yet with a rising in her ear. Patty has had a very sore leg for two or three weeks. She can scarcely walk. She sits down all the time and sews.

Your Pa says if he thought you were in favor of Lincoln, he would not let you come in his house. I hope Lincoln will not be elected. The democrats are very much concerned about it. If we should have war, I hope it will not commence before you return home. I think the north and south will just keep growling at each other like cats and dogs and that is all that will be done.

Your Pa says you may get a guitar. America and Ritter send their love to you. We all want to see you very much. Our sensible cousin Fitzgerald's mother was my third cousin. She was Catharine Campbell. Write soon and often.

Your affectionate mother,
Sarah E. Watkins

P.S. Did you see or hear from Mrs. Middleton who lives in Farmville? She is cousin Tom Epes' sister and my first cousin. SEW

---

146. Mrs. Lydia Townsend's first husband was Joseph Parmele.

To Mary Watkins from Sarah Watkins:

November 26, 1860
Winona, Mississippi

Miss M. E. Watkins
Patapsco Institute, Md.

My Dear Child,

I have been very remiss in writing to you. Before I commence my work this Monday morning I will answer your affectionate letter of the 10th inst. that was received last Saturday which gave me pleasure to hear from you. My memory is so bad that I can't recollect how long it is since I wrote you last. I mentioned in my last letter to you that your Pa said you could get a guitar at fifteen or twenty dollars. I have been busy cutting out the negroes' winter clothes that has prevented me from writing to my children oftener and I was so much in need of chemises I had to make me some.

Ritter and America are the only servants I have to wait in the house. Ritter is very slow and has to be sick every month you know and America is most always complaining of being sick. Sally suffers so much with neuralgia in her jaw that she has not done anything in the house for several months. We are trying to trade with Lettie for America. We proposed to swap Old Sally and her daughter Catharine for America. Your Pa charged fifty dollars to boot. Lettie said she was willing to swap even but if her Pa was not, we would get Major Neill to value the negroes and if he did not value S. and C. much higher than America, she would go by what Major Neill said. Major Neill came here last Monday and valued America three hundred dollars higher than Catharine. He put no value on the old woman. Your Pa says he will swap even and will not give any boot between them. I have written to Lettie that I think an even swap would be a fair trade between them. I am very anxious to hear how she will decide it. Bill Patton's wife has some negroes left her in Virginia and Patton was to start for them this month. Lettie said as he would be in Mississippi he could come by here and take her negroes with him to Texas. She speaks of selling America if we do not get her. America says she will go to Texas before she will be sold to anybody except us. Sally is very much disturbed in mind about it. She is welcome to go with America if she wants to go.[147] She can't make up her mind whether to go or stay as she is very much opposed to going to Texas to eat beef and can't take all her old lumber with her.[148] Your Pa says I must write you that he is having the ice house made ready to put up ice against you come home next summer. He says you can go

147. The Sally referred to here is America's mother.
148. "Lumber" refers to stored items or simply "belongings."

to keeping house when you come, that he has a potato house. You may live in it.

Bishop Green is expected to preach in Carrollton next Sabbath. If the weather is good we expect to go to hear him. It is very cloudy today and has sprinkled a little. There was some cold days last week. Friday morning the milk was frozed. I would be so glad to see you that I would let you eat all the cream if you had been here. I don't make much butter. I send a few pounds to Carrollton every week.

Lizzie Oliver has gone back to Alabama. She did not come to see me. I supposed her mother's being confined prevented her coming. Mrs. Whitehead has a daughter. I saw Martha Jane Gary and Octavia Palmer at church in Middleton Sunday week. They inquired about you. Martha J. sent her love to you. I said to her, "And tell her you have a fine daughter." She laughed and said yes. She looked better than I ever saw her.

Hannah has recovered from her sickness. She is not strong enough to go out to work. Patty is down with her leg yet. None of the negroes is sick today which has become very uncommon here, not to be sick. I forgot Harry Ann got her finger mashed in the mill. If they can't get sick, they will having risings or hurt of some kind to prevent them from work. I will write to you oftener, I am not out of work yet. Miss Giving, the teacher in Middleton, sent me a newspaper containing the obituary of Uncle Frank Fitzgerald's death. He died the 17th of September and Mrs. E.G. Booth, Sally Tanner Jones that was, she died in August. She is sister to cousin Dandridge Epes's wife.

Ritter and America send their love to you. Write often.

Your devoted mother,
Sarah E. Watkins

Dr. Watkins employed Mr. Pentecost as overseer during the year of 1861. The written agreement between the two men offers an example of the wages and rights of an overseer.

December 1860
Carroll County

Agreement between Thos. A. Watkins and James Pentecost. The former agrees to pay the latter four hundred dollars for his services as an overseer on said Watkins' place for the year 1861. Said Pentecost can ride a mule at any time in attending to said Watkins' business except when all the mules are very busy plowing. He can also ride a mule on Sunday. When either wishes the above contract cancelled, they can separate and said Watkins is to pay for the time, at said rates, that said Pentecost has been on the place attending to the business. For any of said Pentecost services the money will not be considered due until January 1st, 1862 . . .

Thos. A. Watkins
J. T. Pentecost

To Letitia Walton from Sarah Watkins:

December 17, 1860
Winona, Mississippi

Mrs. L. A. Walton
Austin

My Dear Child,

Your very welcome letter of the 6th inst. was received today. It gave me pleasure to hear from you and your family. I felt very uneasy about you as Mr. Walton wrote in your letter that you gave birth to a son the night before. I could not believe it so and thought he was quizzing [*teasing*] me or I had made a mistake in reading what he had written until I read his note enclosed in the bill of sale saying you were sick in bed. Why did you keep it from me that you were in the family way? I hope you are doing well and will not suffer for the want of attention. I wish I could be with you to wait on you and assist you in nursing your baby.

I am very much obliged to you for your accommodation swapping between America and Catharine and Sally. If I thought America was worth more than Catharine, I would not advise you to swap even. I don't think America is worth any more than Catharine. Your Pa don't want me to let them know that we have swapped. I am anxious to tell Sally and America but can't tell them yet. You thought Sally and America would rejoice to hear it. It is quite to be the contrary with America. She asked me just now if I had gotten a letter from you and what you agreed to do. I told her I could not tell her. She said I don't want Miss Lettie to swap me for Master's negroes. I had rather go to Texas to her than to belong to Master. I told her that he never had abused her and he would not treat her ill, that she ought to have said sooner that she did not want to stay here. She did say if I was not able to buy her that she'd rather go to Texas than to belong to the Dr. I hated for her to be parted from her mother, that was the only inducement for me to keep her. I could not get Sally to agree to go with her. America provokes me right much after I have put myself to trouble to keep her to be with Sally for her now to be so opposed to staying and willing to leave her old, afflicted mother that is not able to wash her own clothes. Your Pa will not agree to pay the expenses of Sally and Catharine to Texas. He says that he will send Sally and Catharine by

Mr. Patton to Texas if he comes by for them and will pay Mr. Patton one hundred dollars for America's hire this year. I thought I would have to pay America's hire. If I do not I will send you some money and if I do, I will send you a little, can't tell how much yet, by Mr. Patton.

Tell Newton I am mighty sorry he does not want to come back to stay with me. I love him and Early very much and would be so glad to see them. I am pleased to hear that Newton is spelling and Early is learning his letters. I want them to be smart boys and make intelligent gentlemen. I heard Bishop Andrews preach in Courtland [*Alabama*] and liked his sermon and looks very much. I wish he was a refined gentleman as he is our Methodist Bishop. Bishop Green and Dr. Adams spent a night with us last Friday two weeks. Bishop Green preached in Carrollton the next Sunday to a large congregation. He confirmed Mr. and Mrs. Temple, (Miss Eldridge that was), Jennie Wellons, Mrs. Joe Keys and Miss Georgia Moore and baptized George Wellons, Mr. and Mrs. Temple. Mrs. Temple was a Baptist you know. Dr. Adams is the stationed Episcopal preacher in Carrollton. I rejoice to hear that you have been baptized and taken in full membership in the Methodist church and determined to live a true Christian. I pray we may live faithful Christians and when we die we may live together in heaven where parting will be no more. Richard Whitehead[149] and his wife [*Mary Conkey*] spent a day here last week. He is looking in better health. She is a lovely lady. I don't think Richard could have done better than to marry her. She sent a great deal of love to you. They are staying at Judge Whitehead's until January. Mrs. Farmer[150] has gone to New Orleans to a doctor who thinks he can cure her. Mrs. Phillips went with her. When Mrs. Phillips was coming back, the car ran off the railroad. She did not get hurt. Martha had a big boy the ninth of this month.[151] She is doing well with the exception of sore nipples. Old Mr. Holeman died. I think last winter. His estate is very much in debt. I will send you a small bag of dried peaches by Sally and C. if they can carry them. I have no quinces, only two trees bore this year, one was quite full and I think they were stolen off. I did not have any to preserve.

When I was to see Mrs. Hawkins, she gave me some yeast, it is called magic yeast. I have had rolls made with it every day except Sundays. It is an excellent kind of yeast. I made some leaven with some of it and will send you some

149. Richard Whitehead was sickly most of his life, but lived to be an old man. He frequently attended spas and watering places. He recovered for a period and was a chaplain in the Confederate Army.

150. Mrs. Farmer was Mrs. Phillips's daughter, Julia Feliciana. Mrs. Parmele and William Oliver's first wife were Mrs. Phillips's other daughters.

151. Martha, a slave, named her son, born December 9, 1860, Jeff Longstreet. Lettie's son, born December 5, 1860, was named George Longstreet.

of the leaven. Every day I have to put a tea cup of flour and a tablespoonful of sugar to it to make the flour and sugar as thick as hop yeast and change the bottles every day. Make the bread up like hop yeast bread. To a quart of flour put a teacup of yeast. Make it up with cold water and a small piece of lard. I will send you some dried flour I got out of the bottom of the bottle of yeast. You must dissolve it in water and put to it a cup of flour and a tablespoonful of sugar and let it ferment and if it does, you can increase the quantity by putting flour and sugar to it every day. The leaven I expect would make yeast.

Uncle Vivion is calling hogs. It is most dark and raining. Give my love to Mr. Walton and if you are not able to write, ask him to write to me as soon as you get this. I am very anxious to hear from you. Kiss the children for me.

Your affectionate mother,
Sarah E. Watkins

P.S. Enclosed your Pa sends you bill of sale for America. America sends howdy to you all. I hope you and George are doing well. Kiss him for me.

P.S. Recipe for "magic yeast"

Magic yeast, dissolve this in cold water and then beat up a cup of flour and a tablespoonful of sugar in as much water as it will make it as thick as hop yeast and add it to the dissolved flour and let it ferment and then put a cup of flour and a tablespoonful of sugar to it make as thick as hop yeast with cold water. When you get enough of it try it if it will make bread before you waste much flour and sugar with it. I have tried the leaven. That made right good bread.

BILL OF SALE
December 18, 1860
Carroll Co., Mississippi

I have this day sold to Letitia A. Walton of Austin, Texas a negro woman named Catharine aged about sixteen years and of dark complexion—also a negro woman named Sally, aged between fifty and sixty and of dark complexion. I warrant said negroes be sound in body and mind and to be slaves for life. They were sold to said L.A. Walton in consideration of a bill of sale made to me by her for a certain negro slave named America of rather light complexion and aged twenty-two years. The word negroes interlined by me[152] on line seven [six] from the bottom before signing.

Thomas A. Watkins (Seal)

152. This refers to a caret added after the word "said" and an added word "negroes."

January 1, 1861
Winona, Mississippi

Miss M. E. Watkins
Patapsco Institute, Md.

My Dear Child,

Your letter of the 26 ult. was received last evening. I am very sorry that mark [*Mary has a sore place on her wrist*] is giving you pain. I cannot tell the cause of it. It makes me feel trouble about you. Were you with me I could know better what to do for it. If it appears to be rising a cornmeal poultice would be good for it, and if it is only sore and painful a linament made of spirits, turpentine, sweet oil, heartshorn and laudanum [*tincture of opium*] would be good to rub it with. Maybe it would be better not to do anything for it. Ask Mr. and Mrs. Archer's advice about it, they can judge better what ought to be done for it than I can inform you what to do. Your Pa says you must keep your hand in a sling and not let it hang down. He says maybe you are not regular in a monthly time that would cause that mark to be sore. Let me know in your next letter if you have no obstruction at a monthly time. I feel so uneasy about you that I can't compose my mind to write you correctly. If you cannot write yourself, get someone to write for you and let me hear how long it has been sore and if it pains and swells your arm and how it looks and all about it. I hope it will soon be well.

A man has come to sell your Pa some mules. He is sitting in here talking. Lettie wrote me the 3rd of December and before the letter was mailed Mr. Walton wrote in it that Lettie gave birth to a son the 5th of December, and he weighed ten pounds and is named George Longstreet Walton. I received a letter from Lettie Saturday written the 17th of last month. She had not been out of bed since the birth of her child. She said she was doing well. Her boy is a healthy, good and handsome baby. He has black hair and blue eyes. Lettie swapped America even with us for Aunt Sallie and her daughter Catharine. They are packing up their baggage today and expect to start to Texas tomorrow with Mr. Bill Patton.

I am glad you enjoyed yourself so finely at Christmas. We spent a very dull time. I spent my time making a shirt for your Pa and finished it today. I did not have a turkey nor any cake made and not even an eggnog for Christmas. The negroes were less merry than usual. There was a party at Winona Thursday night, I expect it was tag rag bobtail affair. I heard that Pentecost escorted Miss Mary Jones to it. I have not asked him about the party. He is employed here again this year. I am glad of it. Charlotte had the croup last night. We gave her a dose of tartar emetic this morning. She is better since taking it. Jack Turner, Old Mrs. Stevens, Ben Moore, and a negro man of old Mrs. Gering's died the week before Christmas. It is said that B. Moore was to have been married to Miss Lucas the night of the same that he died. She was sent for to see him. He died before she got to see him, so I heard.

It snowed here Saturday night enough to cover the ground. There has been some very cold weather, but none cold enough to put up ice yet. Patty's sore has nearly healed up and she sits enough to give her the dropsy. She came to the kitchen week before last to show Polly how to season the sausage meat. It is the first time I have seen her in the yard for several weeks. She is stuffing sausage meat yesterday and today. Sally is suffering with her jaw very much. I hope and pray your mark will be well when you receive this letter. Be sure to write soon. I will be uneasy about you.

Your Devoted Mother,
Sarah E. Watkins

P.S. Uncle Vivion is calling hogs.

To Letitia Walton from Sarah Watkins:

January 2, 1861
Winona, Mississippi

Mrs. L. A. Walton
Austin, Texas
My Dear Child,

Your very welcome letter of the 17th ult. was gladly received last Saturday. It was a great relief to my uneasy heart and mind to hear that you and your baby were doing so well. I felt very uneasy about you for fear you were not doing well. Your Pa wrote to Judge Longstreet the night of the same day I received your letter telling him that you had named your son after him.

Judge Wellons wrote to your Pa last week that Mr. William Patton was in Carrollton. He sent Abram immediately with a letter to Mr. Patton to inform him about carrying your negroes and to know of him when he expected to go to Texas. Mr. Patton wrote to us that he would have come here that day but the rain prevented his coming and that he would start from Grenada today on the cars. As it will be in the night when the cars get to Winona, your Pa thought it best to take the negroes to Grenada on the cars today. He and the negroes started this morning to Winona with their baggage all in the wagon. It has commenced raining since they left. I fear they will all get wet. I am glad for you to have Aunt Sally and Catharine but I could not keep from crying when they bid me farewell. I like them very much and think they are good, honest, obedient servants. They did not know they were going away until night before last, I believe. Catharine was very willing to go, she does not like to work out. Sally was willing to follow her daughter. I expect she was sorry at going away as she was living very comfortably. I never said anything to her about it until this morning. I told her you were a very feeling woman. She said that she will do everything she can to please you. I hope you will like them.

I sent by them a small bag of dried peaches and a bag with some leaven, pie melon seed and a pair of your stockings you left here. Your Pa told me to send you a dozen apples. I sent you about sixteen. We got a barrel of apples from St. Louis. I would have sent the children some cake and other eatables but Sally and Catharine had so much of their own things to carry I did not think they had room to put anything more. I sent you enclosed in an envelope by Mr. Patton one hundred and three dollars in gold. One hundred I send to you and one dollar apiece I send to Newton, Early and George Longstreet Walton. Your Pa don't know that I have sent you any money. I sent it to Mr. Patton when he was in Carrollton by Abram. He [*the doctor*] will pay for America's hire to Mr. Patton as you requested.

We had a very dull Christmas. I went nowhere nor saw nobody. I did not even have a turkey nor any cake and not so much as an eggnog made. It snowed here Saturday night enough to cover the ground. There has been some quite cold weather but not cold enough to put up ice. Your Pa said to me, "Tell Lettie when you write that I am a strong secessionist." I am too and most everybody about here is I believe. I am afraid of war. Are you not? I will be so glad when the excitement is over and we all can be at peace again. I expect it will be some time before there can be peace. You are one that always looks on the bright side so I expect you don't let such things trouble you much.

I received a letter from Baby Monday. She wrote me that that mark on her wrist was very sore and pained her so much that she was not able to use her pen to write. She got one of her friends to write for her. She wrote, not withstanding the above mentioned misfortune, she was spending a delightful Christmas. She spent the Saturday before with a number of the girls in Baltimore and enjoyed themselves to the highest degree. She writes, "Please don't be uneasy about me." Oh! How can I help being uneasy about my dear child. I am uneasy about her for fear that place may be something serious with her. It is so strange for a mark to be sore and painful. When I am uneasy about my children it affects my heart and mind. When I hear they are doing well it gives me such a happy feeling.

Mr. Wolfe would have given your Pa one hundred and twenty-five dollars for Aunt Sally if you had not taken her. Wolfe came and looked at her. She does not know that he would have bought her. I would have been sorry for her to been sold from Catharine. Ritter and America send their love to you all. Ritt is sick with her old pains. She says I must tell you she can't be smart like you to have children. She can only dream that she has them. She dreamed last night she had a child and was very proud of it . . . I expect your negroes will get home before you receive this letter. I will be very glad to hear that they arrived safe and sound and hope you will be pleased with them. America seems very well satisfied. The Dr. told her that she would belong to you again at our death. I have not seen Sally to talk to her since it was told that Sally and Catharine had to go. She has been suffering with her jaw several days. Give my love to Mr. Walton and the children. Kiss all three of the children for me. Write soon.

Your devoted mother,
Sarah E. Watkins

January 26, 1861
Winona, Carroll Co., Miss.

Miss Mary E. Watkins
Ellicotts Mill, Md.

My Dear Daughter,

Your very welcome letter of 7th inst. was received a few days ago. We are all well. I went to New Orleans some three weeks ago and returned several days since. I missed you very much while there. If I could have had you with me I could have enjoyed myself much better. I stopped at the St. Charles Hotel and thought many times of the merry times I and our company of friends had there then. But few lady visitors were at the hotel. By accident I found out that cousin Thomas M. Mathew's wife and son were boarding there. I renewed my acquaintance with them. I found my cousin's wife to be a very agreeable and intelligent lady and was sorry that I had to leave her so soon. Cousin Thomas had just left for home in Alabama, but was expected back in a few days so I had not the pleasure of seeing him. It was the youngest son of his that I saw. He appeared to be a modest well behaved boy. Cousin Thomas' daughter, Dora, was at school in New Orleans, but I did not see her. I expect she is a little younger than yourself. You must tell Cousin Martha Mathews about my seeing our relatives in New Orleans and also give my love to her.

I saw in Jackson, Mississippi Miss C. Green's father. He is quite a gentleman and I was anxious I should visit him, but I was pressed for time and could not go to his house.

The time is now drawing near when you will graduate and take your place among the young ladies, but I doubt if you will ever enjoy yourself as well as you have while a school girl. I shall hail you with much joy in your new sphere. I think and hope you will come up to the expectations of your parents and relatives and friends. I know you have studied and improved your time and think you will graduate with much credit to yourself and all interested in your welfare. We are counting the time when you will be one of our little family circle. We are anxious for that time to come along as fast as possible. It will soon be here and do not be too impatient.

I dined in New Orleans with Major Watt and family. They had a most excellent dinner and the way I made the good things disappear was a sight. Dr. Poindexter dined there also at same time. The first time I see Laura Witherspoon again I will plague her about the said gentleman. He is a first rate gentleman but possibly a little too old to suit Mrs. W.'s fancy.

I know of nothing new to write you. I and your mother are always glad to hear from you. We have just received two letters from Lettie, all well. She has a boy about seven weeks old called George Longstreet. Your mother will write you shortly.

Mollie Collins told Octavia Merriwether that you were a splendid woman. Please excuse inaccuracies in writing and spelling. By the by, you do not write now quite legible enough. Now is the time to form, while young, a habit of good readable writing. With that exception your letters are fine. I have just sent Mr. Archer some money for your schooling, board, etc. I shall have but little more to pay out for the schooling of my children. I do not mind expending anything in reason for this mental advancement.

> I have the honor to be
> Your affectionate father,
> Thomas A. Watkins

The following letter of January 27, 1861, to Mollie, at Patapsco, Maryland, is unusual. Mrs. Watkins acted as scribe for the women household servants, Martha, Chloe, Melia, Polly, and America. Note the reference to the song "Dixie Land."[153]

Dear Miss Mary:

. . . Martha has another boy seven weeks old tonight, named Jeff Longstreet. Alberta is very intelligent and as pretty as she was when you were here. All of my family are well. Charlotte is growing very fast, you ought to come home and put her to work. Aster has a girl named Hannah. She will not work no longer than she is looked over and she can outdance anything in the place and yet she can't work good for pain in her ankles.

We had a fine time last night with just our own people and Payton to play

153. Although the song was written as a minstrel "walk around," it is interesting to note the slaves not only like the song, but have an affection for it.

the violin and banjo, and Simon played on the tambourine. Susan had a quilting and after we got the quilt out they had to dance instead of a supper.

John's barrel of flour has not arrived from St. Louis. I have sent for a barrel too. I will have my quilting next Saturday night. I want my flour to come so I may have a supper. Harry Ann sit up in the corner clapping her foot and she wanted us to keep on singing to drown the noise of pots and ovens. She done that to keep us from thinking about having anything cooked. You must get the song of Dixie Land. I made my stand I live and die for Dixie Land. Learn to play it on the guitar and play it for me when you come home. Milly has not grown six inches since you went away. She sends a heap of howdy to you. Your mamma send a heap of love to you and says she want to see you mighty bad that you must make haste and come home. She has been off two Saturday nights hand running as a night sheriff [*meaning unclear*]. If she was here she would have a longer message to send you. Goodbye Baby. I have no more news to write you at this time.

Your affectionate servant,
Martha Watkins

Chloe, Baby, as Cousin Martha has written you, I will let you see I have not forgotten you. I am staying at home this year and am anxious for the time to arrive for you to home, so we may see happy times together like we used to have when we were little girls. [*Chloe had been hired out the previous year.*] I had a young gentleman lately to put me down so low as to give me a nail tooth brush to chew. Lower than he acted towards the rest of the ladies. Mr. Robert Watkins from Missouri was the gentleman. Mamma had the backache and laid before the fire a liked to burned her dress off behind. I enjoyed myself finely last night. The first set I danced with a married gentleman. Goodbye Baby, I hope to see you soon.

Your affectionate servant,
Chloe Watkins

Baby, I must send you a word or two to keep you from forgetting me as I often think of you. I enjoyed myself finely last night with the young men. Silla sends a heap of howdy to you and says she wants to see you very much. Daddy sends his love to you. Mamma has not been well since her child was born. She is always with the backache. Her child is a boy named Phillip Moore. I don't know no news Baby. Goodbye. Melia Watkins.

Baby, I am almost ashamed to write as I have not written to you before this. I enjoyed myself finely last night looking at the young folks dancing.

Uncle Vivion[154] came around this morning grumbling because the music gained so many soldiers last night. I am going to a quilting and I hope the young people will enjoy themselves as they did last night, while they have dancing in their heads they must take it as their supper. I am too poor to give us supper. I have a half barrel of flour coming, but I must keep it for my fatherless children. I write to you to let you see I have not forgotten you. I am so glad Master has children to leave me and my family to if I should be the longest liver. . . . I have a very pretty little girl for your maid named Dianah. Farewell my dear Mistress, I hope you will be at home soon. Accept my love for yourself. I want you to come home to write our letters for us to help your Mother from having the trouble of writing for us.

Your servant,
Polly Watkins

Dear Baby:

I set down to have a few lines written to you this evening to tell you what a dull Christmas I spent. This is new year. I hope I will spend it more pleasantly. The girls were enjoying themselves last night. I felt too bad to enjoy myself as I was sick with a gripeing and had to sit like an old woman in the corner and look at the others. I have the gripeing yet. I often go in shed room and wish I could have the pleasure of enjoying myself with you like I did before you were sent away. You can't think I have forgotten you when I have named Cousin Martha's child after your beaux Jeff McLemore. You must write to me all the news, let me know how you are getting along with your music and dancing lessons and playing of the guitar. You must learn some very pretty tunes to play for me when you come home. You must excuse my few lines. I have not been from home to hear any news to write you. I have had the pleasure of turning off both of Master's men he bought and brought here. They both offer their services to try it over again, but I will not accept it. The first time I get a chance to go to Middleton, I think I will get a call from a young gentleman named Matt. I will tell you about my other beau in my next letter.

Goodbye, I have no more news to write. The next letter I hope will fill it out myself. You must write to me soon. Mother sends howdy and says she hope the Lord will bless you for praying for her jaw to get well. She is suffering very much with it today. Uncle Joe sends howdy to you.

America Watkins

---

154. Uncle Vivion held steadfast against dancing, on religious principles.

The next letter is from the mother to Mary:

January 31, 1861
Winona, Mississippi

Miss M. E. Watkins
Patapsco Institute

My Dear Child,

Your letter of the 7th inst. was welcomely received two weeks ago. Your Pa received one from you this week. It is useless to say we were glad to receive them. We are always rejoiced to see them and sometimes get impatient for one to come. I suppose your examination is going on at this time. I didn't doubt but that you will acquit yourself well. You must have more confidence in yourself and not be so frightened. From your good marks you are as capable of doing well as any of the girls. Think that of yourself and you will overcome the timidness.

I received a letter from dear Lettie lately. She wrote that Occa Merriwether wrote her that Sally Collins said to her what a splendid woman Mary Watkins is. Lettie wrote "news that will make you proud my mother" Oh! yes, it does make me proud to hear my daughter so highly spoken of. I know you merit the praise that is given to you. What a pleasant feeling it gives me when I think in six months you will return home an accomplished lady and be a comfort to your loving parents in their old age. I expect you had rather read and hear what is going on at home and in this neighborhood.

Work is going on as usual here. All the hands are at home this year except Daniel and John Smith. We have a large new ground, most of the woods between Jenkins' place and the big road is cleared up.[155] The road from here the way we go to Middleton will be stopped up. I have just commenced gardening yesterday and today is fine weather for it. I intend to make Charlotte earn her bread with the sweat of her brow working in the garden if she does not have chills as she did last year when I put her to sweeping the yard. There have been three children born since you went away. Polly has a girl over a year old named Dianah, Becky had a boy named Phill, and Martha has a boy named Jeff Longstreet. Semira expects to have one in March. We have the finest looking young negroes I ever saw on one place and they seem so content and happy.

I have not been from home but twice this year. Mrs. Hemingway was sick week before last and I went to see her twice. I have not had a lady to see me this winter, Ritt and America say when Baby comes home then we will have

155. The earth, quickly exhausted from repeated cotton planting, had to be replaced with newly cleared land.

company. Dr. Adams stayed one night and till nearly dinner the next day last week. The rain prevented him from going away in the morning. Your Pa had a headache, I expect he spent a dull time here, he passed off his time reading the newspapers. He found out that I am a Methodist. I reckon he will not come here again soon. He is the Episcopalian minister in Carrollton.

It is said that Mr. Helm is to be married to Miss Prince tonight at her sister's in Claiborne County. Albert Keys is married to a Miss Hunter of Claiborne County. Ritter and America send their love to you. Ritter says she has five hens setting and she is going to raise a heap of chickens for you and your beaux to eat next summer.

The winter has been so mild we could not get any ice to put up. Sunday night Washington asked permission to marry Anna. I expect they will have a wedding. She is no more fit to marry than my Milly. She can't do as much work as Milly. Charlotte says I must tell you if that dress is yours that you wore to the fancy ball you must bring it home to her. You would laugh to see and hear her stuttering to tell me what to tell you. She says, "I want Baby come home, I want to see her." Sally has suffered day and night for the last week with her jaw. Patty's leg is better; she has a cold. Mingo got his little finger badly mashed rolling logs. Dick sprained his ankle getting over the fence Sunday. I wish cousin Bettie Irby would come home with you. Give my love to her when you write her and tell her I would be very glad to see her. Give my respects to your friend and tell her I am very much obliged to her for writing for you to come. I thought of thanking her for her kindness when I wrote you before but neglected doing so. Give my love to Miss Gunn, Miss Watt and your roommates. Is Sally Watt at Patapsco Institute? I am obliged to the girls for their kind offer to take care of you and hope you will do the same favor for them.

Is Mr. Archer a secessionist? Your Pa saw a circular yesterday of the Patapsco Institute for this year at Judge Wellons' that you sent Miss Wellons. He is anxious to get one of this year's date. Write soon and often. Do not regret writing about the pain and soreness of your mark. I am glad that you informed me of it and hope you will always let me know if anything is the matter with you. Ask cousin B. Irby who was cousin Washington Epes's father and mother.

Your affectionate mother,
Sarah E. Watkins

P.S. did you see Patrick's wife Ritter, and Caty when you were in Virginia last summer?

January 28, 1861
Winona, Mississippi

Mrs. L. A. Walton
Austin, Texas

My Dear Child:

Your very welcome letters of the 5th and 13th Inst. was gladly received the 22nd of this month. It has not been convenient for me to answer them until now. As I am alone this morning I will take time from my work and write you. It is with me as it is with yourself about work this winter behind, hand shirts for the Dr., chemise nightgowns, night caps, all needed at the same time and negroes clothes it seems to me I never will get done cutting out, before I can get the winter clothes wove and made the time draws near to cut and have made the summer clothes. I bought some of the yarn cloth, too. Martha has had so much hindrence by sickness in her family during last year that she would not get on fast with weaving and she was not in a situation to weave. Ritt has to wash and iron, do what Sally used to do in the house and attend to the fowls. When there are many clothes to wash I have one of the field women to help her. Our family is so small that I hate to take another one to assist in washing only when it is needed. Ritter does not get any faster about her work then she used to and is getting more sleepy headed when she is sewing and she complains of pains as much as ever. America is in the same way, always something the matter. So I never know when to expect a good day's work from them. This morning she is in a great deal of pain with it.

I am very glad to hear that your servants arrived safely to you and hope they will suit you. Your Pa went to New Orleans the next week after Sally and Catharine left here. It rained a great deal while he was gone and caused him to stay longer than he intended. When he got the other side of Canton the railroad was out of order. He had to get out of the warm car that he was in and walk to get on an open car. He did not put on his big coat and it gave him a very bad cold. He got home Saturday week. He has been very unwell ever since confined to the house most of the time. He went to Maj. Neill's Sunday and has gone to Carrollton today. I think he has been uneasy about war in the last week. Judge Hillyer wrote him that he thought there would be war. There was a mule driver here yesterday that told us that he heard that Jeff Davis had got to Grenada from Washington City and said all was peace and there would be no war.[156] Glorious news if it is true.

156. Davis had made his final speech in the U.S. Senate, and resigned from that body, exactly one week before, on January 21, 1861. He publicly expressed his hope that there might be no war.

The railroad has been impassable from Vaiden to Winona. I don't know how far above Winona. The ground has been so wet I have not gardened any yet. This is the most pleasant day we have had in some time. If I had a gardener at my command I would be busy at it today. Abram is like the old story Sally used to tell, about the hawk and some other bird staying behind, behind, always behind. I believe Abram is setting out peach trees that prevents him from working the garden today. I sent you some peach seed and three blue plum seeds in the bag of piemelon seed. The peach seeds are very fine late peaches. I have several piemelons yet and they make very good pies and a very convenient dessert. Write me how you make your cheesecake with four eggs.

I staid at home until I got so tired of my own victuals. I spent Saturday at Mr. Hemingway's. They had a turkey for dinner and well cooked rice. It ate mighty good to me. Mrs. Hemingway has been very sick. I was to see her twice during her sickness. It rained so much I could not see her when I first heard she was sick. Lynn has been sick with a cold. He always inquires about you. Mr. Hemingway is opposed to secession. It is said that Mr. Helm is to be married to Mrs. Prince the 31st of the month at her sister's in Claiborne County. I heard from Miss Lucas that B. Moore was engaged to live fourteen miles above Grenada.

I wish I could see your fine boy George Longstreet. I am rejoiced to hear that your health is good and you were so well attended to during your confinement. I want to see all more than can be expressed. It makes me happy to hear that my children are doing well. I have nothing to disturb my peace at this time. Oh! What a happy feeling! I do thank God for his mercies to me and my dear beloved children. I pray my dear child that we will be faithful Christians and if we cannot live together in this world we may have seats together in heaven where parting will be no more.

Your Pa said when he was coming from New Orleans he met with Gen. Thomas Green and his two little daughters from Austin. He was carrying his daughters to Nashville to school. They said they did not know you. Gen. Green said he knew Mr. Walton. He saw a Mr. Spindle, editor of a paper. Do you know anything of them?

I am anxious to know if you could make bread with the leaven and yeast from the dried yeast I sent you. My bread has not done well lately. Robin said it was cold weather that prevented its rising. I think he has got tired of making it. In the first place I think the yeast got sour. Mrs. Petty told me to take a little of the yeast and add it to a cup of flour and a teaspoonful of sugar made up with water. I did so and I have good yeast again. I wish I had your turn [*for*] cooking. I would be independent of a servant to cook nice things for me.

Give my love to Mr. Walton and the children. Kiss the children for me and tell them it makes me very proud to know I have such pretty sensible grand-sons. They must be good industrious boys and learn their books and every-body will love them.

Robin sends howdy to Newton and Early and says you must tell E. [*Early*] he must get a good education and come to see him that he wants to see him before he dies. America sends her love to you all and to Aunt Sally and C. and says tell Newton he must learn to read and come and read about the boy stealing apples to her. Becky's child is named Phil. America named Martha's child Jeff after Jeff McLemore, Martha has named it Jeff Longstreet. Tell Aunt Sally and Catharine howdy. Tell Aunt Sally I have just used the dried apples she gave me. They ate very good. Washington has asked to marry Anna. They expect to marry shortly. She has no more business with a husband than Martha's Milly and can't do as much as Milly. The servants would send their love to you all if they knew I was writing to you.

I have filled out the sheet and written nothing interesting. I wish I could write you an interesting letter as I have delayed writing you four weeks to-morrow. Four weeks today since I wrote to Baby. I received a letter from her last Tuesday week. She was well and in fine spirits as usual. Write soon and often.

Your Devoted Mother,
Sarah E. Watkins

P.S. Jan. 30th. We received a letter from Baby yesterday. She was well. Maj. Neill's Ann died two weeks ago. Wm. McMahon is dead. I admire Aunt Sally's cap, it reminds me of the old-time servants. Don't make her take it off.

To Letitia Walton from Sarah Watkins:

February 16, 1861
Winona, Mississippi

Mrs. L. A. Walton
Austin, Texas

My Dear Child,

One month has passed off since your last letter was written. I am anxiously expecting every mail to receive a letter from you. I think the breakage in the railroad prevents the mail from coming is the reason I have not received a letter from you before this. There has been three very hard rains this winter that injured the railroad below every time. We have a mailbox put upon the side of the road near T. Jones's house. The stage driver is very accommodating in bringing out papers and letters every day from Winona to that box. Abram has gone to the box now. I hope he will bring me a letter. Oh! He has come and brought no letter from my darling child. I said to Abram I am just writing to Lettie, that I hope you would bring me a letter from her. He said I must give his love to you. John W. was at the door. He sends his love to you, Aunt Sally and Catharine.

I spent the day very pleasantly with Mrs. Richard Whitehead. I sent her word that I would dine with her Thursday but the weather was too unlikely for me to go. Yesterday was a good day. Your Pa and I went in and dined with them. They are living a mile from Carrollton, the other side of old Mr. Nelson's on the right hand of the road in a white house with a flat top, perhaps you'll remember it. She had a good dinner for new beginners and for this time of the year. For dessert she had peaches put up in their own juice. We ate them in saucers with milk and sponge cake. On the table was the largest sausage I ever saw. It was cooked whole and had eggs boiled and cut in slices and put on the side around it. I think it a nicer looking way to have sausage than the little black sausage we have. They have only two servants, a woman and man. Richard looks very badly. She looks very well. I like her so much. She inquired about you and sent her love to you.

Mrs. E. and Mrs. Judge Whitehead and Jennie Kennedy [*Edmunds's second daughter*] spent the day there this day two weeks. Mrs. Whitehead has not named her baby. Mr. E. Whitehead calls it Gertrude.[157] Jennie's little girl is walking and talks very plain. It is pretty and sensible. Jennie has not weaned her yet. Mr. Helm was married to Mrs. Prince the 30th of June. He has bought Summerfield Fox's place and intends building. I don't remember writing you about Albert Keys's marriage. He was married this winter to Miss Hunt of Claiborne County. Mrs. Simmons' brother, Thomas Walton, is married to Miss Mary Longstreet, Judge Longstreet's adopted daughter. Do you and Mrs. Simmons visit each other? It is said that the Dr. that Mrs. Farmer went to in New Orleans has nearly cured her sores. She wears a wig. I have not heard of her returning home. Mrs. E. Whitehead told me that Mrs. Phillips traveled with Mrs. Patton up from New Orleans. She spoke very favorable of Mr. Walton and said you were doing very well. I heard that Mrs. Phillips is trying to catch Allen Gary. Don't say nothing about it to nobody.

I suppose you have commenced gardening. I have had peas, cabbage, lettuce, radishes and beets sowed. It rained last night and today is cold, windy and cloudy, now and then the sun shines out. It seems to me it rains every Saturday or Sunday. There has been no suitable weather this winter when

---

157. Ella Gertrude Whitehead, later to be Mrs. Alfred Cicero Dimond.

preaching days for me to attend church. I want to go tomorrow to Middleton to hear Mr. Pittman but expect bad weather will prevent my going.

Washington and Anna [*slaves*] are going to be married tonight. Anna has borrowed Ritter's wedding dress to wear. Ritter says Harry Ann is mad with her for lending Anna her dress. Washington's parents don't want him to have Anna so I hear from the negroes. Anna is too much of a child to marry but we think if they are not allowed to marry that they will be keeping each other and we had better let them marry. Washington got Abram to ask the Dr. for some flour and sugar today. I suppose the women will cook the supper for them this evening. They have given to them by their Master over twelve pounds of flour, five of sugar and five of coffee, a ham of bacon and some potatoes. They have not yet asked me for anything. I will give them some lard if they want it. Jane has come for it. I have given it out to her. I would not give Ritter a wedding. For that reason, I don't care to do much towards this marriage as Anna could have made me such a nice maid if she had been governable.[158] Jane says if it were her going to be married, I would be the first one she would come to ask for anything. I believe Jane to be a good girl and I would want her to have a nicer supper.

Give my love to Mr. Walton and Newton and Early and kiss all the children for me. Ritter and America send their love to you all. Tell Aunt Sally and Catharine howdy. I hope they are getting on well. They must send me word in your next letter how they like their home. Write soon and often and write like we were together talking. Everything would be interesting to me. Do you ever hear from Mr. James Watkins' family and Martha Peacock? Anna has been in to get some eggs. She said Martha is going to make her a cake.

Your affectionate mother,
Sarah E. Watkins

P.S. 17th—I went to preaching today and heard Mr. Pittman preach. There was a small congregation. It is a clear, windy, cold day. I saw Aunt Mary Cobbs. She said Mrs. Phillips has gone to New Orleans. Ritter went with me. Jane told her that Mrs. Parmele is in the family way. Mrs. Bennett died this day week with pneumonia. Sally sends love to you all and to Aunt Sally and Catharine. She suffers with pain in her jaw very much. I forgot to send my letter today by Salsbury as he went to Winona. He has returned and brought me no letter from you. I heard from Baby last week, she was well and happy as usual. SEW

---

158. Anna was bought by the doctor in Missouri to be Mrs. Watkins's house servant, but she was not willing and therefore worked in the fields. When bought, she was either twelve or fourteen; now she is thirteen or fifteen.

February 23, 1861
Winona, Carroll Co., Miss.

Miss Mary E. Watkins
Ellicotts Mill, Md.

My Dear Daughter:

Your letter of 17th inst. is just at hand—contents noted. I can see no cause for you being afraid to stay at school where you are. You are as safe there as you would be anywhere. I do not think there will be war, and if there should be, it will not be near Ellicotts Mill, Md. If there should be fighting anywhere it will be at sea, near Charleston, South Carolina or New Orleans, Louisiana.[159]

I am sorry that any man should come from Washington City and alarm you all so much. I do not expect he had good sense. Make yourself perfectly easy. It is so near time for you to graduate that I am very anxious for you to stay and became a well educated and highly accomplished young lady. It will add so much to your character and standing to be a graduate. I have paid Mr. Archer in advance nearly up to the time you will have to stay, and if I take you away I will have to lose all that money.

Give our best respects to Miss Sally Jones. Tell her if she goes home she will pass near us and that she must call and see us. We would be so glad to see her.

When you write to Miss Irby tell her that we hope that she will come on home with you next summer and that she must stay with us as long as she can. We will be glad to have as much of her company as possible.

No talk of any other of the negroes marrying at present. But I expect that some of them will have a wedding as soon as you get home.

Try and study hard and graduate with all credit. You stand very high at your school and I do not want you now in the eleventh hour to come up missing.

Your affectionate father,
Thos. A. Watkins

P.S. Your mother made some cake lately in honor of your birthday. T.A.W.

159. The doctor showed keen insight.

To Letitia Walton from Sarah Watkins:

March 9, 1861
Winona, Mississippi

Mrs. L. A. Walton
Austin, Texas

My Dear Child,

Oh! How delighted I was a week yesterday to receive your letter of the 14th ult. Your Pa and myself were in the buggy going to Mr. E. Whitehead's and met Abram in the road coming from meeting the stage that brought the letters. Your Pa stopped to read his. I could not get my spectacles out of my pocket to read mine and waited to get to Mr. E. Whitehead's. I had not been there many minutes before I read it. I was sorry to hear that Mr. Walton's health was not good and glad that you and the children were well. I hope Mr. Walton's health is restored by this time.

I have heard of several deaths about here in the last month, most of them died with pneumonia. They were none of them acquaintances of ours. Mr. Gee that married Miss Townsend and his brother died last month. It is a wonderful cure that physician has made with Mrs. Farmer. All of her sores have healed up except one little place. Mrs. Phillips has been down twice to see her. She may be down there yet, but she had not returned home last week. She and Mrs. Palmer went down together in February. Mrs. Phillips says Mrs. Farmer has fattened. The physician wants her to stay in New Orleans until April. Mrs. Gaden, Mrs. Lizzie Davis and a negro woman of Ophelia Kennedy's are in New Orleans for that doctor to attend them.[160] Mrs. Major Hawkins has been down to see him. She follows his prescription at home so I heard. Mrs. Gaden and Mrs. Farmer stay at Dr. Sykes's. Margaret Sykes had a child an hour before Mrs. Palmer got to New Orleans. Mrs. Phillips makes no more of going to New Orleans than I do of going to Carrollton it seems to me.[161]

The railroad is so often washed away between here and New Orleans that I would be afraid to travel on it. I would do as she does if I had a child there. I would go to see it if I could.

Lou Bingham has a baby at last. She has been married four years. Mr. Bingham was married four years to his first wife before she had a child. Mrs. Sally Whitehead [*Edmunds's daughter-in-law*] is pregnant the third time and threatened with abortion. Mrs. E. Whitehead is going to see Lizzie in two weeks to be with her during her confinement. Mrs. E. Whitehead sends her love to you and says as you want a daughter that you must come and see if

160. The new railroad had made New Orleans and special medical care available.
161. Mrs. Farmer was Mrs. Phillips's daughter.

you and she can't make a swap but she will charge you boot as her daughter is so pretty [*Ella Gertrude*]. From the description you gave me of George Longstreet, he must be beautiful. I wish I could see him. Martha says her Longstreet is smarter than yours, that she can hear him crow from her house to the weaving house. He was very sick yesterday, almost had the croup. I gave him a dose of oil in the morning and your Pa went down to see him and thought him very sick but not dangerous. He gave him some cough drops made of one grain of tartar emetic, a little laudanum, gum arabic and licorice put in a tolerable large vial and filled up with water and gave a teaspoonful every ten minutes until it vomited him. After that gave it every two hours. I went to see it late in the evening and it had gotten better and was breathing easy. Patty gave it indigo last night. This morning I went to see and it looked well but had some cough. Martha had a chill last Tuesday. She thought her breast that she gives milk from was rising, it was so painful. She rubs it well with liniment. She is well today. Several of the negroes have had colds. Becky is sick with a cold. Tom is sick a little. Ritter as usual is complaining. She ate turnip salad yesterday and it gave her bowel complaint. She has quit dipping [*snuff*] and taken to smoking.

We have a very early spring. The peach and plum trees are in bloom. I am afraid cold weather will come and kill the fruit. The weather is so changeable. There has been frost this week, Abram thinks it killed my cabbage plants. My peas look very pretty. It rained very hard last evening and today is cool and windy. Tell the children I wish they were here to eat my ground peas. I have had no one to eat them and it is nearly time to plant again. I made Ritt trim the rose bushes and work in manure for most of the flowers last week. The hyacinths are in bloom and the tulip roots you set out are up. I never go in the garden without thinking of you. The flowers remind me so much of you. I often think will I ever see you again. I trust in God that I may enjoy many happy days with my children.

I am rejoiced to hear that you are determined to live a Christian. It is my greatest desire to be a faithful Christian and I do try to serve my God and pray we may all be prepared to live together in heaven.

The last letter we received from Baby, she was uneasy about war and wrote to come home. We do not think there is any danger or any need of her coming so she was written to that she must stay until this session is out which will be the twenty-sixth of June.

Hannah is very much pleased at Mr. Walton sending howdy to her. She sends howdy to you all. She sends such a long message to Catharine and the children I can't write it. She is in a pucker with Isham and Jane. She says Jane says she would have Isham if it was not for her. She says Jane would just have Isham for a nest egg. Poor Jane, she is in hot ashes. Semira is jealous of her and Paten. Ritter came in just now to show me a strange looking hen's egg. It is three inches long and singular looking at the end. Ritter and America and Uncle Vivion send love to you all and say you must not let yourself be deceived but hold out faithful to the end. He says he wishes he could see the children before he dies. He says tell Aunt Sally if he never sees her on earth he hopes he will meet her on Canaan's shore. Most all of the negroes would send a message to you all if they knew I was writing. Sally is coming in, she will have a word to send. She sends love to you all and says she is bad off with her jaw and a cold.

Your Pa told me to write you that it is pretense in Catharine complaining so much.[162] That is the only fault he found of her. She came in once and said she was sick and he saw her under the hill at work. He got her and drove her to the field. He says if he had not considered her sound and healthy he would not have swapped her to you, that she is a healthy girl. I thought you would be very much pleased with her and am sorry she is so complaining. I expect she does have pains at a monthly time, if I were in your place if she has much pain at such a time I would have her bled. And if they do not suit you I would sell them and try to get one that would suit. It is impossible to get one without some fault.

Give my love to Mr. Walton and the children. Kiss the children for me. Tell Aunt Sally and Catharine howdy. I hope they will do well. Write soon and oftener.

> Your devoted mother,
> Sarah E. Watkins

To Mary Watkins from Sarah Watkins:

> March 11, 1861
> Winona, Mississippi

Miss M. E. Watkins
Patapsco Institute, Md.

My Dear Child,

Your last letter was received the 20th of Feb. Why have you not written to us since? The time appears so very long since I heard from you, I feel uneasy about you, fearing you are sick. Do write oftener. It has been three weeks today since I wrote to you but your Pa has written you since is the reason I have not written you in a shorter time. Having two children to write to prevents me from writing oftener to them. I have not written to Lettie but once

---

162. The traded daughter and mother have not pleased Lettie.

in three weeks. When I am not uneasy about one child, I am of the other. I had not received a letter from Lettie for some time until Friday week. Most of her family had been sick with bad colds. They were well when she wrote.

I have not seen anyone but Mrs. E. Whitehead since I wrote you last. I spent a day with her Friday week. She is going to see Lizzie Oliver [*Eutaw, Alabama*] in two weeks to be with her when she has a baby. Lou Bingham has a child at last. Mrs. Palmer went to New Orleans to see her daughter, Mrs. Dr. Sykes. She had a baby an hour before Mrs. Palmer arrived there. Mrs. Farmer has been staying in New Orleans several months for a physician to attend her. It is said that all her sores have cured up except one little sore. She has fattened and wears a wig.

Your Pa has just come in from meeting the stage and brought no letter. He says it is curious, that you must be sick is why you don't write. I hope you are not uneasy yet about war. There is no use of your being uneasy. If we thought there was any need of you coming home in case of war, we would certainly bring you home very quickly. We don't think there will be any war and if there is a war it would not hurt you or us. The time will soon arrive for you to come home, it would be a pity for you to quit school. I hope you will apply yourself closely to your studies and be prepared to graduate with credit. We received your marks last month, we were delighted to see you had the highest number for everything. Laura Whitehead saw one of your schoolmates in St. Louis last summer, Miss Thornburg. She told Laura that you stood high in all of your classes. You can't imagine how proud it makes us for you to be so highly spoken of and we know you merit all the praise that is given you. I had a cake made in honor of your birthday. I told Robin if he made it nice, I would write that you must bring him a present. He baked it very nice so you will have to bring him a pipe for it.

Patty sends a great deal of love to you and says the Lord has promised to take care of the fatherless and motherless children and now you are off from us you are like the fatherless and motherless and you must look to and trust in God for protection and he will let nothing trouble you.

I wish I knew some news to write you. Nothing is talked about but politics.[163] I took my seat to write this morning. I thought I would have a quiet time. I am so disturbed for first one thing and then another and so low-spirited at not getting a letter from you that I cannot compose my mind to write you as I want to do. Ritter and America send their love to you. We are always talking about the time and counting the months for Baby to come

163. The first seven states to secede had formed the provisional government of the Confederate States, adopted a constitution on February 8, 1861, and selected Jefferson Davis, on February 9, to be president. Abraham Lincoln was inaugurated exactly one week prior to this letter.

home. That day will be a great jubilee with us. Oh! I am so impatient for that day to come when I can embrace my dear child and thank the Lord for his goodness in sparing us to meet again. It would complete my happiness if my dear Lettie could be with us. I have no idea when I shall ever see that poor dear child again. It is a great consolation to me to hear that she is doing well. Becky is sick a little and Susan's finger is rising. My health is very good. Give my love to Mary Watt, Elba Gunn and your roommates. I hope Miss Sally Jones' parents were wise like us and did not send for her. I do think it is a folly taking the girls from school on account of the fear of war. You must be contented. If we see necessity for you to come home, we will be as anxious for you to come home as you are to come. Write soon and oftener.

Your affectionate mother,
Sarah E. Watkins

P.S. Your Pa sent you two dollars in a letter. He wants to know if you received it. He says he wrote to you to let him know if you got it. SEW

To Letitia Walton from Sarah Watkins:

March 25, 1861
Winona, Mississippi

Mrs. L. A. Walton
Austin, Texas

My Dear Child,

I will take this Monday morning and write to my dear children. I have just answered a letter I received from Baby yesterday. The first one I have read from her in several weeks. I had become provoked with her for not writing to me but her letter has put me in a good humor with her. She said it had been so long since she had heard from her dear sister that she was really uneasy about you. I received your very welcome letter of the 8th inst. last week. It gave me much pleasure to hear that you were all well and getting on well. I hope the cut worms will not destroy your vegetables. It is so much trouble to have a good garden unless there is a good gardener to attend it.

The spring was early, there has been several cold days and frost this month. I fear the peaches are killed. My peas look very well, cabbage and lettuce does badly, radishes are too thick. Abram says the cold weather injured the cabbage but I believe it is the way he plants things and works the ground why I don't have a better garden. He has such little idea about gardening. I am to blame too, I don't see to the planting enough. I trust too much to servants to do things. The best of them will do to suit their own convenience. I trusted to Ritter to attend to my hens. They went to setting very early and did not hatch very well. Three weeks ago I had 25 little chickens and Ritter told me last week that there were only eighteen. She let the cold weather kill several of the last hatchings. I asked her what had become of them and she said the cold weather killed them. Instead of putting them in coops she kept them in the henhouse. Robin told me today he went to the hen house one morning and eight or nine were lying on the floor dead and the hen was up in the nest. Ritter thought she was doing the best way with them. She is like Abram about gardening, it is for the want of knowledge. I think I will attend more to the garden and fowls too.

Baby asked what would I say to her staying at Patapsco until September for her to have an opportunity to read and improve her mind. We can't agree to that. She can come home and read from day to day if she wants to, and have to pay nothing for it. She is a queer genius. She has been from her mother so long and willing to stay off longer. Lizzie Oliver has come to her father's to have a baby. I heard last week that William Whitehead's wife had a child and was very sick. Mrs. Richard Whitehead has no child and no prospect of one. Richard Whitehead's health is very bad and he looks badly. Mrs. Hemingway's mother has come to see her. I have not seen Lynn to deliver your message to him. I have not been from home nor seen any person since I wrote you last. Your Pa received a letter from Judge Longstreet. He wrote in this way, "A bushel of love to my dear Lettie for the honor she has done me to name her son after me." The most of his letter was advising your Pa to become friendly with you and Mr. Walton. He is a warm friend of yours. He is in Columbia, South Carolina [*his new university presidency*]. He said nothing about his wife's health. She was not with her daughters last month in Oxford and her health was not good. Your Pa met with Dr. Conkey [*father of Richard Whitehead's wife*] and his daughter up here at the road. They were in the stage going on to see Mrs. R. Whitehead. He heard from them of Mrs. Longstreet's ill health.

We expect Bishop Green to dine with us the eighth of April and perhaps Dr. and Mrs. Stansbury. R. Whitehead does not live at the Russell place. He lives farther out of town in a flat top house on the right hand of the road to Blackhawk.

You did not mention Newton and Early in your last letter. You must always write something to them. Ask them if they don't care for me, why they do not send me some message in your letters to let me see they have not forgotten me. I wish I could see your fine son, I don't think he will be prettier than Newton was when I saw him, or sweeter than Early. Kiss all the children for me. Give my love to Mr. Walton. He never sends his respects to me, perhaps my love is not returned by him. Abram and John W. sends their love to all, America sends love to all and says you must mention the children when you write. My letter would be filled with love and messages if the negroes knew I was writing. I hope Aunt Sally and Catharine will get all their baggage. Tell them howdy for us all. I am glad to hear they are satisfied with their home and had good health. Catharine is very young. I reckon she will improve in her work as she gets older. I hope they will be very useful to you. Write soon and often, I am always anxious to hear from you and all your family.

Your affectionate mother,
Sarah E. Watkins

P.S. Enclosed you will see an announcement of Miss M. E. Cummings' marriage.

*"You have seen already
as happy days as ever you will see"*

II

Civil War Letters
1861–1865

Fort Sumter has been fired on during the previous night; the war has begun. Dr. Watkins writes Mollie on April 12, 1861, not knowing of the tragedy. With no sense of irony, he writes that she has already had her "happy days."

By the time she reads this letter, all concerned will know that the fort capitulated on April 13. On April 15, President Lincoln issued what amounted to a presidential proclamation of war and called for seventy-five-thousand militia. This action induced four more states to secede.

April 12, 1861
Winona, Mississippi
Carroll County

Mary E. Watkins
Ellicott Mills, Md.

My Dear Daughter:

We do not write you from home as often as it is our duty to do so but it is not from any want of affection that we seemingly neglect you. We are careless and besides have no news that would interest you.

Your mother is counting the days and hours that will elapse before it is time for you to come home.

The last of June will soon be here and then you will be a grown young lady. You think there will be so much fun in store for you after you graduate but I expect you have seen already as happy days as ever you will see. You must excuse this short letter—all I write for is to let you know that you are still near and dear to us.

There has been much sickness and some fatality in the county this spring and past winter. Mr. Jack Turner and Mr. Samuel Young have both died this year—also old Mrs. Steadman and old Mrs. Eubanks and also William White-head's wife who was before marriage Sally Tyson.[164] Our family has enjoyed remarkable good health this spring and past winter.

164. After two miscarriages, she died during the delivery of the third pregnancy.

I see you have a Miss DeGraffenreid in your class. The DeGraffenreids are of Swiss origin. They are descended from Baron DeGraffenreid who emigrated from Switzerland many years ago and settled in North Carolina. He was very wealthy but his descendants were swindled out of a great deal of their property by some bankers in Europe. I have a history of that family and if Miss D.G. wishes me to send her a copy of that part that relates to her family, I will do so.[165] Please ask her if she has not a relation who first married a Mr. Picket and afterwards James Blair Gilmer of Louisiana. What has become of her? Mr. Gilmer, her husband is dead. McLemore's sister married a Mr. D.G. [*DeGraffenreid*] of Tennessee who is very rich.

Your mother sends bushels of love to you.

Your affectionate father,
Thomas A. Watkins

P.S. Mr. Gilmer above mentioned usually made about three thousand bales of cotton. He was very enterprising and industrious. T.A.W.

---

165. The Whiteheads were very close to the DeGraffenreid family and both Edmunds and the judge used the name for sons. William DeGraffenreid Whitehead was listed in Mississippi Agricultural Census as owning 480 acres, 2 horses, 4 mules, 5 milk cows, 10 sheep, and 45 swine. The cash value of his farm was judged to be $4,320. His father's farm was valued in the same census at $15,000. It was William Whitehead's wife who had just died.

CHAPTER SEVEN

"I hope it is all talk"

Will, Lettie's husband, joined a volunteer company in Texas. This unit soon lay plans to walk the more than one hundred miles to Port Lavaca and to seize U.S. property at that place. Like many young mothers in the incipient Confederacy, as her husband prepared to go off to war Lettie fretted about her own well-being and that of her three small children.

Impending war affected the Watkinses' Mississippi neighborhood, too. On Monday, April 29, 1861, the first company of volunteers left Carrollton and went first to an assembly camp at Corinth. Soon thereafter, they entrained for Virginia. Many eager volunteers flocked to the colors at this early stage of hostilities. Not only those of the appropriate age, but also the very old and the very young seemed eager to get in on the expected adventure. Various lively social gatherings were held to honor the volunteers. The doctor joined the Home Guards.

Mary, now home from Patapsco, her schooling completed, writes letters that reflect a self-conscious charm. She commenced a romance, via correspondence, with her soon-to-be husband, Jeff McLemore. A sewing society was organized in Middleton to make clothes and other items for the Winona Stars, one of the many new military units, and for other soldiers mustering in Mississippi. Jeff saw action in the first Battle of Manassas. Although he was unscathed, he drew the sad duty of receiving the body of his first lieutenant, who had been killed in the action, and of overseeing the burial. Alas, the war was not going to be just "all talk."

To Letitia Walton from Sarah Watkins:

April 13, 1861
Winona, Mississippi

Mrs. L. A. Walton
Austin, Texas

My Dear Child,

As I had written to you a few days before I received your letter of the 19th ult. I delayed writing. I have so little to write that will interest you that I scarcely know what to write. There have been several deaths in this county lately. Mrs. Sally Whitehead had a child about three weeks ago. She and her child died. Old Mrs. Eubanks attended Sally's burying and was buried or died a week from that day. Sam Young died Sunday week and Mr. Nailer's negro woman died nearly the same time with pneumonia. Several others have died that were not our acquaintances.

We expected Bishop Green to dine with us last Monday. He did not come until Tuesday evening. He called a few minutes on his way to Carrollton. He was sick with a chill in Canton that prevented him from coming here Monday. He looks very feeble. Dr. Stansbury's family and Major Hawkins were invited to dine here last Monday. John Hawkins and his wife and Miss Halida, a relation of Mrs. Hawkins were the only persons that came. Mrs. Major Hawkins was not well enough to come. Mrs. John Hawkins said Mrs. Hawkins told her to be sure to inquire about you and to ask the name of your baby. In case Mrs. John Hawkins should not remember what I told about you, Miss Halida was to recollect to tell her. Mrs. Simmons' Octavia and Miss Simmons, a niece of Mr. Simmons, spent the night at Mr. E. Whitehead's two weeks last Thursday and intended to spend the next day at Judge Collins'. Charles came here at night to see Semira and told me that his mistress and Octavia said I must go to see them at Mr. E. Whitehead's the next morning. As they did not care to come to see me, I thought it useless to stop the mules from the plough to go over to see them. They might have come here the next morning if they only staid a few minutes.

Charles said Octavia had been up [*visiting*] two weeks and was uneasy about Dr. Merriwether as she had not received a letter from him and she said she would go back home the next Saturday if she did not get a letter from him. Mrs. Hawkins said the scarlet fever was in Charleston [*Mississippi*] was the reason Octavia came to her father's. Lizzie Oliver is staying at her father's to be confined. I heard that Margaret Ann Pleasants is in the family way. Semira had a large girl last Wednesday night two weeks, it is named Agnes after Paten's mother. Tell Aunt Sally that Green grows fast and can talk a little and holds his hand to us to beg for a biscuit. Washington and Anna have quit Jane's house and are living with Bob and the three little boys at her old house. Jane is ploughing. I made a pink calico dress for her last week that her beau, Bird, gave her for knitting for him.

I received a letter from Sarah A. Fitzgerald lately informing me that her sister, Lettie expected to be married in two weeks to a Mr. Hill from Arkansas. She said Lettie was staying with Mr. Alexander at Danville and his son had come to Moulton for her to go to Lettie's wedding. Sarah Ann said in her letter, "I want [not] to do as bad as sister Lettie. I will get your advice first, dear aunt. I'll have your consent *upon it*. There is a man coming to see me. He has not property but is a hard working man. His name is James B. Windham. I will not marry him unless you say so." I wrote to her that I did not know anything against Windham's family's character but they were not equal to her father's family in regard to respectability and high standing in society and if she would associate with people of high standing that she would be noticed by respectable people. I could not advise her to marry in a family that I would oppose my own daughter marrying in. I gave her a good deal of advice. I advised her as I would my own child. She thought Lettie was too young to marry. I think so too unless the poor child has married well.

My garden begins to look well. The pea vines are full of blooms and young peas on them. The weather has been changeable sometimes cold and rainy. There has been no frost this month to injure anything yet. I think some of the fruit was injured last month. The peach trees in the back yard have some peaches on them. This is a lovely day.

Mary did not write us anything about her fainting. I expect she wrote Laura Moore about it. Laura told your Pa that Baby had written to her and said something about her fainting. I could not understand what she meant. I have not seen any of Colonel Moore's family this winter. Baby has written to me very seldom lately. I don't know what to think of her. Her last letter written home was to Patty. Major Neill's mother-in-law does not live with him. His two daughters board with Mrs. Parker near Captain Binford's. Amanada goes to school at Mrs. Parker's. Mrs. Pink Scales died at her mother's in Jackson last month.

Give my love to Mr. Walton and the children for me. Tell them to kiss you for me. Tell Aunt Sally and Catharine howdy. America and Ritter send love to all. Robin says tell Newton and Early he has potatoes in the cellar yet. Write soon and often, I am always anxious to hear from you all. How did Mr. Walton's goats turn out?

> Your devoted mother,
> Sarah E. Watkins

To Mary Watkins from Letitia Walton:

> April 24, 1861
> Austin, Texas

My Dear Sister,

Your affectionate letter of 12th inst. was gladly received today which is two letters from you since I last wrote you. Will wrote to you for Newton some time lately is the reason your last letter is still unanswered. I thought you would hear from us by that letter and would not get uneasy—so I delayed writing.

Sister, these are indeed eventful times we are living in [166] and though I shall direct this to Patapsco, I hope you will be home when you receive it.

Will and self were speaking of you this morning. Hearing of the fighting at Baltimore occasioned the conversation. He said he reckoned you had gone home and, if you had not, he thought you ought to for shortly there might be some difficulty in getting there. Last night about 2 1/2 o'clock I awoke and heard a cannon fire—called Will and asked what it meant—he wanted to go right up town and see. I objected—in a little while it fired again—he got up, said he must go and see. He could not rest 'till he knew. I consented and off he went. I went to sleep again and Will did not return 'till after daylight. The news reached here last night that Virginia had seceded and had taken all the government property in that state. General [*Winfield*] Scott had resigned his office in the Federal army [*an untrue rumor*] and tendered his services to Virginia etc. Confederacy and that is why the cannon was firing.

Will has joined a volunteer company which is being organized now in this place. This company expects to start this week or next Monday to Port Lavaca, which is over one hundred miles from here and *walk*, too, to take possession of some property there now in possession of the United States troops. I hope it is all talk. They will not go for by the time they walk there they will not be fit for service. I cannot yet feel like Will is going, and hope there will be no need of any of them going, but oh: my sister, if he would go what

---

166. They certainly were. Fort Sumter had surrendered ten days earlier, Virginia seceded on April 17, there were riots in Baltimore on the eighteenth, and Lincoln had declared a naval blockade of the southern states.

will become of me—just imagine my situation away off here with three little helpless children and my husband who is as near and dear to me as my own heart—gone off to war. If I had no children I would go with Will. Oh, how I wish Pa's family and mine were near together; very soon perhaps the mouth of the Mississippi will be blockaded and we cannot even hear from each other. I would feel more secure in Mississippi than in this State if we do really have war, yet I would not be willing to go there and leave Will here. It does seem foolish for intelligent beings to involve their country in civil war, but I believe we will have war and it will only be fulfilling some of the prophecies in the Bible—that is my notion about it.[167] The Lord's will must be done.

Lincoln has called a session of Congress in July. I presume Congress has power to declare war; yes it has, Will told me so just now. I told Mother long ago about your fainting and received a letter from her last Sunday saying you had not mentioned it to them. Sister do hush talking and thinking about your parents being disappointed in you. You know they will be no such thing. I know it. You are their own flesh and blood. They will love you and be glad to see you even if you were a dolt. I know you are smart and accomplished and they know it, too, but they will not expect to see an angel in human form so do not rack your brain any more about the matter. Sister, don't talk so—it is wicked to say you wish your parents could never see you again. Think child before you speak, for you certainly did not mean that. If they should be disappointed (you *know* they will not be) but, just suppose such a thing, whose fault will it be? Not yours to be sure. You cannot be more than nature intended you should be. Then why distress yourself? Will says all this is affectation in you. You ought to feel thankful that you have parents to see and rejoice that the time is so near at hand for you to meet them and beg our Heavenly Father to spare them and you to meet once more. God has greatly blessed you my sister, but you do not yet know it or thank him for it, I fear.

I have seen a good many woolen shawls this year. Looked like they were crocheted, netted, or something of the kind. I think them very pretty, but did not feel able to buy one. I would prefer a shawl to a talma [*a cloak or cape*] (talmas are out of fashion are they not?) and be much more obliged to you for one to wear next fall if you feel like doing that sort of work on vacation. George is so plump, fat and sweet I feel like *biting* him nearly all the time and he is so good, too. Will's health is not good, children and self are well. All are asleep except myself, and I feel quite tired. I arose at 6 o'clock this morning

167. Lettie was far from alone in the belief. Actually, however, it was more of a typical phenomenon among northern Protestants (which now were officially separated from the southern churches). See James Moorhead, *American Apocalypse; Yankee Protestants and the Civil War* (New Haven: Yale University Press, 1978).

and it is now only a few minutes of 10 o'clock at night. Sister you are mean not to tell me your secrets.

I have a fine garden. Will soon have cabbage to eat, have had peas and beets for two weeks and snap beans last Sunday. I will answer your letters more fully shortly—am too tired stooping over now. Good night my own sweet sister.

Yours ever sincerely,
Lettie

To Mary Watkins from Sarah Watkins:

April 27, 1861
Winona, Mississippi

Miss M. E. Watkins
My Dear Child,

Your very welcome letters have been received. As usual I have procrastinated writing to you. Your Pa wrote to you last week that caused me to delay writing until now. I received a letter from you and your sister at the same time. I had been in the dining room cutting out the negroes' summer clothes, when I went in my room your Pa said to me, "Raise up the pillow and see what is under it." Nothing could have pleased me more. There was a letter from both of my beloved children that he had brought and put under it to surprise me.

We had a small mess of strawberries for dinner today. I would have enjoyed them much more if my children had been here to partake of them with us. I am rejoiced that the time is so near for you to come home. I think you were highly honored to have so many of the young ladies to assist in dressing you for the party. Why were they not dressing for the party too? You wrote to know if I would meet you in Virginia. I rather you would come home Baby. It does not suit me to leave home. You have been from home so long that you have gotten weaned from home.

Mrs. Frank Keys died week before last. She was only sick twenty-four hours with convulsions. Mrs. Bennett died last Saturday and was buried Monday morning in Middleton. Lizzie Oliver had a daughter Sunday week. I went to see her yesterday. She was sitting up dressed and looked as well as if she was not confined. Women having children, deaths and war is all that is talked about now. Mrs. John Davis is going to have a baby.

We expected Bishop Green here Monday two weeks to dinner and had a nice dinner prepared for him. He was sick in Canton with a chill and did not come until the next day. He called by a few minutes in the evening on his way to Carrollton. He married the Episcopal preacher of Carrollton to Miss Doty that assisted Mr. Holt in teaching school when he taught last year. He inquired about you. Mr. John Hawkins, his wife and Miss Halida, his cousin, dined here the day we expected the Bishop. Miss Halida graduated at Patapsco six years ago.

I attended church at the Methodist church in Middleton Sunday evening. I saw Colonel Moore's family but did not speak to them. Colonel Moore killed a large snake in church just as the preacher commenced singing. Abram heard the noise that was made killing the snake, he said he thought someone had got happy mighty quick. I received a letter from Miss Meady Eggleston yesterday. She said we must go to see them when you come home. I answered her letter today. Patty sends a heap of howdy to you and says you must not think of going nowhere this summer, that you must come on home. She wants to see you mighty bad. Ritter and America send their love to you. I feel as stupid as a jack looks, I can hardly write.

Brother's daughter, Lettie, is married to a Mr. Hill from Arkansas. I received a letter from Sarah Ann saying that Lettie was going to be married and that she [*Sarah Ann*] wanted to do so bad but she would get my advice about it and if I objected to it she would not marry the man. She said James Windham was going to see her. I wrote her that I would not advise her to marry in a family that I would oppose my own daughter marrying in and gave her the advice that I would my own child. I have not heard from her since. Your Pa says you must write every week by Adams express.

Your devoted mother,
Sarah E. Watkins

To Letitia Walton from Sarah Watkins:

May 2, 1861
Austin, Texas

My Dear Child,

I had the table brought in my room and intended writing you as soon as I finished reading the Memphis Avalanche, when your letter of the 21st ult. was brought in to me by our boy Robert who had been with your pa to bring his buggy back from Winona. Your Pa started this morning about day to Grenada expecting to meet Miss Green on her way home to Jackson from Patapsco. He wanted to hear from Baby by her, perhaps he may telegraph to Baby when or if he concludes to go for her. We have received two letters from Baby this week dated the 22nd and 24th of April. The one written the 24th was mailed from Yazoo City. I expect it was sent by the young ladies Misses Holt and Hyatt that live in Yazoo City and left Patapsco at that time. Mary wrote that the school was decreasing rapidly and two of the teachers had left, and

Mr. Archer told her that it was unreasonable to think of having a commencement. She said she hates having to come away after three years of labor without a diploma or any reward. She asked her Pa if he intends going for her to send her a telegraphic dispatch so she might have her trunks packed and be ready to start when he gets there. She said she was well and calm. She didn't fear any danger there, but she was afraid the Southern railroads will be torn up and she can't get home. I think your Pa will go for her next week. I am afraid he will take her to Virginia and stay a while there before he brings her home. If he does that I had rather she would stay at school until the session is out, which will be the 26th of June. I am more uneasy about my children than about myself. I trust in God he will bring all things right and peace will be made sooner than is expected.

A company of volunteers left Carrollton Monday. Frank Liddell was the Captain. Lynn Hemingway was one of the numbers. Several troops came from below and met them at Winona. They were all going to Corinth to stay until they receive orders where to go. There is another company made up in Carrollton. They are so anxious to go on that they want Major [*Gilbreth F.*] Neill to go to Montgomery to get Jeff Davis to let them go. There is a company of old men forming there that is called the home guards. They are to be ready to act in case of insurrection. Pentecost went to T. Jones's [*Jones's house was on the main road*] to see the soldiers pass. He said Dick Love, Cicero Wellons and Ben Wellons were very tight, and your Pa saw Ben at Winona and has said Ben was drunk. He did not know that Ben drank. I told him I had known for two years.

Dr. Fisher gave a large party to the volunteers last week. There is to be a party given to them at Winona tonight. Mrs. Hemingway and her mother spent the day with me yesterday. Mrs. Hemingway bears with Lynn going to war better than I thought she could. Lizzie Oliver had a daughter last Sunday two weeks. I was to see her Tuesday week. She was sitting up in a chair, dressed, and even had on her corset. She did not look like she had a child. I advised her not to sit up too much. She then laid down the balance of the day. She had a difficulty in passing off her water. Dr. Atkins drew it off after her child was born.

Her Aunt Morris told her the alum poultice was good and she had used the alum poultice. I told her balsam caperica was good for it and when I came home I asked the Doctor's advice about it. He said the caperica would be good for her. I sent her some that night. The next day I sent over to know if it relieved her. She sent me word that she took it as soon as she got it and one dose of it relieved her. Dr. Watkins said the poultice was good, but alum was too stringent and ought not to be used in it.

Octavia Merriwether expects to have a child in August. Mrs. Freeman has another daughter and has been quite sick since. Mrs. Frank Keys died with convulsions; she was sick only 24 hours. She was pregnant. Mary Tyson has been very low with rheumatism of the heart. One day she was blind. Mr. Bennett died Saturday week. Last week T. Jones got his fingers torn to pieces with a rope he was jerking about. One finger is off and the ends of two others. His family is to be pitied. He drinks too much yet. Mrs. Farmer, after being almost well, was taken very ill in New Orleans week before last. Mrs. Phillips went down to see her as soon as she heard it and had not come back last Sunday. I went to Whitehead's schoolhouse to preaching Sunday. Abram heard from Mrs. Phillips' man that Mrs. Farmer was better. We have had a wet spring— some people's cotton is dying. My garden is tolerable good. I had peas Tuesday and beets yesterday, snaps are not in bloom, cucumbers and watermelons looking badly.

No preparations are making for Mary's reception. Times are too hard to think of doing anything. We were fortunate to get our meat from St. Louis before the port was blockaded at Cairo. Mary Petty told Mr. Pentecost that she and the other ladies of Carrollton sewed all day last Sunday for the volunteers that had to go off. Your Pa thinks it was the cold country in Missouri that caused Aunt Sally's daughters to have consumption. I hope Catharine will be healthy and do you much service. I am sorry you are deceived in Lizzie. If her lewdness is the only objection you have to her, I would not part with her. It is very hard to get as smart a servant as she is and so few negro women or girls but what will take up with men and the more you try to keep them from it the worse they are. So I would put up with the tail business if that was her only fault. I would be afraid she would get the bad disorder and that would destroy her health. Has she never had the child she was pregnant with?

Tell the children I would have sent them some peas by Aunt Sallie if she had had room for them. I wish I had sent peas instead of apples as the apples rotted. Tell them they must come to see me next year and I will give them a plenty of peas. Times are too hard for them to come this year I reckon. I want to see them very much. I wish I could see your baby. It must be mighty pretty. I would persuade you to come to see me this year, but as the times are so hard I don't think you would be doing justice to yourself and family to come. Your Pa never reads your letters. Your aunt's name was Lucy Reese—I never heard of Bosworth. I see the name in a Georgia paper: W. Bosworth, captain of a company in Fayette County, Georgia.

Give my love to Mr. Walton and the children. Kiss the children for me. Driver died before C & S [*Catharine and Aunt Sally*] went away. Ritt and

America send their love to all. Tell C & S howdy for me. I received a letter from Miss Meady Eggleston last week.

She sent her love to you. Write soon and often.

Your loving Mother,
S.E. Watkins

P.S. I will enclose your letter to Sarah Ann.

To Letitia Walton from Mary Watkins:

May 20, 1861
Winona, Carroll County, Miss.

My Sweet Sister,

I fear you have ere this experienced a little or more anxiety about one who has been compelled by a multiplicity of reasons to neglect you longer than it was either her desire or intention of so doing.

I am now seated in the "New Room" writing on *the* work-stand, it seems to inspire me in this pleasant duty as my seat is one which I have so often had the pleasure of seeing Sister occupy, but in days gone by, days now soon throw a gloom over me on realizing that they have been borne too far in the past by "Time's rapid wing" ever to be recalled and repeated. But ah! let us cast aside such feelings and "look not mournfully into the past," but glance upon the light side of things.

Eighteen of the girls and myself left Patapsco today a week ago. Among the number were Mollie Watt, Elba Gunn, three or four other Mississippians and one Louisianan who were under the protection of Judge Schackleford of Canton, Mississippi. We were retained in Lynchburg from Tuesday evening until Wednesday afternoon during which time we met with several of our Mississippi friends, who, being in the army, were stationed for a short period in two miles of the above named city. The great kindness and attention of the soldiers rendered everything so agreeable that with a little pleading we prevailed upon the Judge to remain there another day. Jeff and Price McLemore, especially the former, were with us most of the time. Col. [*Frank*] Liddell and L. Hemingway and a few others frequently honored us with a visit. L. Hemingway spoke in very or the highest terms of you and also sent you his likeness. Must I forward it to you or wait and give it to you?

Jeff gave me his gold society badge [*fraternity pin*] and begged me for my daguerreotype, which I partly promised him. He asked to renew the correspondence that once existed between us. I told him I was willing if Pa had no objections. He went to the depot with me when I left—before the cars started he brought me (through my request), my bonnet box from which I took my prayer book that was nicely placed in the tray with all the stockings, night-caps, towels and underbodies that I possessed and gave him. I think he as-sisted me a little in finding the book. We were in such haste that I am consoled with the thought and hope of his not seeing any of the above mentioned articles. A few moments before the blow of the whistle severed us, I fear forever, he gave me his likeness and said, "Accept this Mollie, and when you become tired of it throw it away." I told him not to expect mine for I could nor would do nothing of the kind without the consent and admonition of my parents. He seemed to admire my view of it, but appeared anxious for the picture. I intend asking Pa about writing to him, and if he objects I am going to state the whole affair to J. and have my likeness taken and sent him. Do not think me conceited, but I do not care much for him. He left Lynchburg last Friday morning and I guess reached Harper's Ferry either Saturday eve-ning or Sunday. I hope to receive a letter from him next Saturday. He is First Lieutenant of his Company and having to fill such a conspicuous position, I'm very much afraid he will be among the first to be killed, but to have him die in such a glorious cause I would be willing to give him up.

I reached home last Sunday morning. Pa, not knowing that I would have such a good opportunity as I have had of returning South, started for me. But we missed each other on the way. He passed through Lynchburg, when I was there, but only stopped long enough to change cars. Our school is en-tirely broken up. The excitement became so great around us that Mr. A. was obliged to send all the girls home whose parents did not come for them. Mollie and Elba came home with me and are here now, but I do not know how long they intend remaining with us. Pa has not yet returned. I expect he is visiting his relatives and friends in Courtland, as that was his intentions when he left home.

I received a letter from you and Mr. Walton a few days before I left Pa-tapsco. I replied to it immediately but not having any stamps was compelled to wait several days before I could send it, and then I concluded to destroy it and delayed writing until tonight. All of the family are well, and Mother says she has laughed more in the past few days than she has done for many months. I appear to be happy but am not, as such a thing could never be the case during your absence from home or our separating. I regret very much being denied the pleasure of answering Mr. Walton's sweet interesting letter. He can little imagine how much I enjoyed it. Well, sister, I am so sleepy as you can see from the whole appearance of my letter, that I must close. Mother, the girls, and the servants join me in much love to you, and my dear Brother, and sweet nephews. How I wish you could be here now. Good night dear one. Write soon.

Baby

June 3; 1861 [168]
Winona, Carroll Co., Miss.

My Own Darling Sister,

Why is it dear one that you have allowed so long a time to elapse without writing to Mother or myself? I have for the last two mornings walked to the road to meet the stage, expecting to hear at least some news concerning your welfare, but have both times experienced that disappointment which is impossible to describe. I am not only pained by your silence but am also grieved at beholding the gloom which invariably darkens our sweet Mother's brow on learning that not even one line has been received from her beloved and fondly remembered daughter. Our anxiety was somewhat decreased yesterday by the perusal of Mr. Walton's letter of 13th ult. in the Carrollton Democrat. It was the first one of his that I had ever read in the paper and was so much pleased with it that I wish he could write more frequently. If I ever marry (which prospect is now very poor) I wonder if my husband will be as smart and approaching so near perfection as yours? Please do not allow Mr. Walton to call me a flatterer as you know I am too candid to be guilty of anything similar to flattery.

Oh! dear, notwithstanding it rained and so fortified the atmosphere that it is much cooler and more pleasant than it has been since my return home yet it is warm now. I can scarcely write a letter capable of being read much less sending it as far as Texas so without proceeding farther I must beg of you to excuse the numerous deficiencies with you which will find this letter filled as I have not now so great an excuse for them as I had while pursuing my scholastic course at Patapsco. Pa reached home several days since. He had not been here long before he inquired of Mother when she had heard from you!

I received a long and *nice* letter last Thursday from Jeff; Pa saw it. Oh! what's coming now? And at breakfast the next morning he asked me, "Well Baby, who was your letter from yesterday? *Is it a secret?* Was it from any of your schoolmates?" Of course Pa like, as many questions as usual. I said no sir, it was from Jeff McLemore; he (Pa) laughed (to tease me) and said he had *no objections* to our correspondence, provided I was particular in not making mistakes and also for the manner in which I wrote to him. Saturday night, near eleven o'clock I began answering it, and although I wrote until half past two, I did not write more than seven pages on small size commercial paper and last night I was up until half past twelve and finished it and this morning I gave it to Pa to mail but he went to Winona and learning from Mr. Pink Scales that he was on his way to Harper's Ferry where Jeff's company [*the University*

___

168. This letter was written on the same day the first land battle of the Civil War was fought at Phillipi, (later West) Virginia.

Grays][169] is now stationed; he gave it to him, as it will go more direct than if sent by mail. What do you think of that? As I have already written you all that occurred between Jeff and myself at Lynchburg I will not encroach upon your patience by repeating it. I do not love him nor do I think for a moment that he cares anything for me, so do not be too hasty in your prophecy as regards our future welfare. I almost lost my heart while in Lynchburg with Lieut. Stanley[170]—(how the mosquitoes do bite) of this state. He is the most handsome gentleman that I have ever seen. I know you are tired of hearing about the boys so I will say no more upon that subject. Polly's youngest child Dianah died last Thursday night and was buried Friday evening. She had the diarrhea, a complaint of which most of the negroes are subject.

Oh! who can imagine the delight with which your kind missive of the 14th ult. to Mother, was perused by she and myself. Pa has joined the "Home Guards," a company which consists of the older gentlemen of Middleton and its vicinity. Today he was compelled to go to the drill at that place and when he returned he brought your letter and one from Hebe[171] to me. The latter seemed anxious to know if I missed her so much as she did me and said that the night before she wrote, she began thinking of old Patapsco and myself and cried herself to sleep. Sweet girl. How I would love to see her. Laura did not go home today, but will start early Saturday and I will go with her and expect to remain two weeks during which time I will return Misses Collins', Palmer's, and Sykes's visit.

To Letitia Walton from Sarah Watkins:

June 6, 1861
Winona, Mississippi

Mrs. L. A. Walton
Austin, Texas

My Dear Child,

It gave Baby and myself joy to receive your letter of the 21st ult. last evening. We had not heard from you in such a long time that we were getting

169. The University Grays comprised 136 university students, average age, twenty-one; before the Grays were disbanded, 116 were killed or wounded. Dunbar Rowland, *Military History of Mississippi*, (Spartanburg, S.C.: The Reprint Company, 1978), 51; and Maud Morrow Brown, *The University Greys* (Richmond, Va: Garrett and Massie, 1940).
On March 1, 1862, Jeff resigned from the Grays and became a first sergeant, Company B, Dixie Rangers, Cavalry, 28th Regiment.
170. Probably James S. Standley, lieutenant, Co. K, Carroll County Rifles. Mentioned in letter of September 10, 1862.
171. Hebe Johnston, a classmate from Patapsco.

uneasy about you all. Baby got home two weeks last Sunday. She has written you since she returned home. I expect you have received her letter by this time giving you a description of her departure from Patapsco and her travel from that place home. She has not changed much in her manners and looks since you saw her. She is taller than I am and rather spare. She has not been alone more than two days since she came home. Mollie Watt and Elba Gunn came home with her and staid from Sunday to Saturday. Laura Moore came Monday week and left this morning. Baby went home with her, she will stay several days. She is fond of company, I don't know how she will content herself here. This day week Mollie Collins, Octavia Palmer and Ellen Sykes spent the day here. Day before yesterday Mr. and Mrs. E. Whitehead came over in the evening. Lizzie Oliver went home last week. Mr. Oliver came for her. His health is not good. Lizzie and Martha Young came over late in the evening before Lizzie left. Mrs. Whitehead speaking of Lizzie leaving her seemed grieved more so than when Lizzie married and went away. I truly sympathize with her. I know her feelings at parting with a loving daughter. Prayers to God is the only solace that can give relief to a mother's grieved heart. I wish you and your family could be with us. It would make Baby and I so happy to have you with us.

Major Neill intended having a fish fry at the creek near his place last Tuesday. We were invited to it. Baby would not go because she had no shoes suitable and a *hat to wear*, I did not know hats were the fashion for young ladies to wear to fish fries. I did not know that my hoop was not a fashionable shape until Baby laughed at it. She says I look like a chicken with the feathers pulled out of its tail.

You do work fast, your machine [*sewing machine*] must be a great deal of help to you. I am sorry Catharine is sickly and wish I had the money to give you to buy a healthy servant. Pains once a month is common on this place. The out negroes [*those working in the fields*] send or come for something to take and keep on at work. Ritter gets worse with her pains. She frequently lays up two days at a time. She was sick yesterday and the day before was bled for the pains. Bleeding would be good for Catharine at such a time now and then. Your Pa will not agree that Catharine is sickly. He says if he had have thought her sickly, he would not have sold her to you. He says it is all pretence in her and you ought to whip it out of her or get a reliable physician to examine her and see if she is sickly. I would rather sell a negro than to be always whipping them.

Diarrhea has been prevailing with our negroes for four or five weeks. Polly's youngest child had it and got better and was taken worse Sunday week and died Tuesday night week.

Your Pa got home that day from Patapsco, he went for Baby. She left Patapsco before he got there. One of the mules that he bought this year died in the night with the colic while he was gone. Semira's baby has blue eyes the color of her other daughter, Sarah Jane. I have two cucumbers today, the first I have had. Rain is needed here very much, I am glad you have such a good garden, plenty of rain and fine crops in Texas. Hardly anything is talked about but war, nearly all the nice beaux have gone off to war. I wish peace could be made without any fighting. It would be better for both sides. Near Duck Hill it was said that the negroes were going to have an insurrection.[172] I can't hear a full account of it. Colonel Top's negro was whipped to death. It was said they were to rise last Saturday night in Middleton. One of Hines McCarroll's negroes was whipped very badly. Lately somebody fastened Mr. Whitehead's overseer up in his house by putting something in the key hole. He had to call up to some of the negroes to go up to the house to get some tool to take the lock off of his door. Our negroes are as humble and well behaved as they have always been.

Frank Keys married Mary Griffith, Dr. Stansbury's niece. Lert Keys is dead.

You asked if the yeast I sent you was California yeast. It is called magic yeast. It is very different from the California yeast. I used the California yeast and the beer until it was said to be poisonous. You wrote of having beer from your yeast. How did you make the beer from it? If your yeast gets sour, take some of it and add to the flour and sugar and it will be good again. I am so sleepy I can scarcely hold my eyes open. I will make you some blackberry cordial if there are any blackberries. Do you like the juice stewed or made without stewing?

Your Pa has joined the company of Home Guards. They drilled yesterday in Middleton and he dined at Mrs. Phillips'. Give my love to Mr. Walton and the children. Kiss the children for me and tell them they must be good boys. I want to see them very much. Tell Aunt Sally and Catharine howdy. Tell Aunt Sally that Jim Moses is bad off with his old complaint. America sends her love to you all. Write soon and often.

> Your devoted mother,
> Sarah E. Watkins

---

172. Although there were no mass insurrections of blacks, whites much feared and expected there would be.

To Mary Watkins from Letitia Walton:

June 17, 1861
Austin, Texas

My Sweet Sister,

Two of your kind letters are before me, and oh! who can imagine my joy on recognizing your handwriting and the postmark Carrollton. Oh, my sister, it has been my constant prayer that God might bring you again to my mother's arms in safety. A letter was received from Sarah Ann at the same time, but before I read it I had to go and thank God that my prayer had been answered that you were again at our dear old home. My soul longeth to be there, too, but we cannot have all things as we wish and we cannot have perfect happiness in this life. Let not the thoughts of my absence mar your happiness. Sister, when I read that part of your letter about Pa calling you Lettie, it touched a tender cord of my heart and I wept. I was melancholy. It does seem too hard that we have to be separated, that mother has only two children and can rarely ever see one of them. Life is too short to waste in anger and hatred. It does no good but causes much unhappiness. Could you see my baby you would see the sweetest child you ever saw. I am really proud of him and am willing to show him in any crowd. You may know I am not ashamed of him for I sent him up to the Capitol this evening where a number of ladies were assembled sewing. The ladies of Austin have met at the Capitol daily for nearly two weeks to sew for a company of soldiers organized in this place. I took a real dress coat to make last week and finished it today. I never attempted to make one before but got along finely with this one considering it was the first.

I believe Jeff loves you, and you cannot be indifferent to him—if you think otherwise why do you encourage him by writing to him? I think Pa was making the matter right public, sending your letter by Mr. Scales. You spelt one word wrong, and you are distressed about it—poor child, you have very little to trouble you. Anyone is liable to make such mistakes, none of us is perfect. Just let it alone. I have no idea he ever noticed it and cannot spell as well as you do to save his life. Baby, you love Jeff, but you are not willing to admit it even to yourself. I was the same way about Will and tried my best not to love him and when I told Will yes it was not my intention to tell him so. I had made up my mind to do no such thing and I repeat it, if you do not love anyone else you love Jeff, and if you do not love him do not flirt with him. Trifling with one's heart is a serious thing; remember that my sister.

Bless Lynn's [Hemingway] soul; he sent me his likeness did he. He could not have sent me anything more acceptable or that which I would prize more highly. The mails are too irregular to send it now, keep it 'till I call for it if you please. When you write to Jeff, give my best love to Lynn—tell him he has my best wishes and my prayers.

Sister, I noticed one or two grammatical mistakes in your letter, which I feel it is my duty to point out to you so that you may guard against them in writing others. You say, "she and myself" it should be *her* and *myself* or—she and I. Do not think dear sister that I am criticizing your letter but am only fearful you will make such mistakes in writing to gentlemen. I know I make many mistakes, particularly in spelling, but I have no correspondents with whom I feel it necessary to be very particular, but your case is different.

I was sorry to hear of the death of Polly's little daughter. Tell Polly she has two children in heaven now. She must think of them pray faithfully and try to meet them there.

Do not be uneasy about Jeff. His being Lieutenant does not make him any more exposed to danger than others. Will says that he is not. How did the negroes know you were coming to meet you at the road? Did Pa go all the way to Patapsco? I felt some uneasiness about him 'till I heard he had reached home again. I did not think it was safe for a Southerner to go that far north. Mr. Baker, the Presbyterian preacher of this place, went to Philadelphia to attend synod some weeks ago and he and all the Southern ministers in attendance were burnt in effigy. He reached home last week. Mosquitoes are so troublesome we all sleep under bars [*mosquitos bars, nets*] this summer. Sister, you must not fear Pa as I used to. Do not keep your love affairs secret from him. It will do no harm to let him know all, and you will be happier by it. Obey him as far as possible, be tender, respectful and kind to your parents. I am so anxious to see you, to know how you look since you were grown. Mother and Pa are proud of you and love to look at you. The envelope on your last letter was the first of the kind I had seen. I gave it to a young lady who carried it to church where it was quite a show (before service commenced) all, or many, had to take a look. The company for whom we have been making clothes will start to Virginia in two weeks. The clothes are not finished yet. I am so anxious to see you all, but God only knows when I shall have the pleasure. If you all could just see my baby, fat and sweet as he is now, I know Mother would give it up [*would say*] that he beat all the babies she ever saw—her own not excepted. Even Pa could not help noticing him. He attracts attention, makes people notice him.

Will and the boys are asleep. Kiss my sweet precious mother for me. Give my love to all the negroes. How is Uncle Vivion getting along? Tell him to be faithful, that once lately while on my knees at church a thought of him came upon my mind and I have been and will continue to pray for him. I pray for all of them. Tell them they must help me to pray. Write often and long.

> Your sister,
> Lettie

To Letitia Walton from Mary Watkins:

> Saturday night
> June 22, 1861
> Winona, Carroll Co.,
> Mississippi

My Beloved Sister,

Notwithstanding a reply to my last two letters of the past few weeks are still owed me, yet I will not wait for it but write again, as I know from experience the great pleasure it affords one to hear, if only a few words from home and have decided to write you whenever I can.

I received a long and interesting letter from Jeff last week as regards the prayer book I gave him, he wrote as follows: (I told you all about our meeting at Lynchburg and also mentioned presenting the book to him, in my last letter.) "I will now tell you what effect reading the prayer book you gave me has produced. I think it almost sacrilege to read it because I believe anyone's whole heart and mind should be placed upon the prayers they repeat, or they will receive but little benefit from them. I frequently read them and try to give them my entire attention, but in spite of my efforts to the contrary my thoughts will naturally run in the most pleasant channel, consequently they will wander from the prayer to the *fair donor* (quite flattering) and after several vain efforts to bring my thoughts from such sweet themes, as will come crowding in my brain, back to the book which I had been reading. I generally close it or turn to the fly leaf and with eyes upon the name there inscribed, I yield to all the sweet and soul inspiring reveries of the past and hope for the future. If it is at night I seldom think of anything else until I am wrapped in the oblivion of Morpheus. If it should be in the day, seldom do I suffer my thoughts to be interrupted until the drum calls me to the charge of my squad (he is second Lieutenant of the "University Grays" of Oxford) then the anxiety I feel for the improvement of my men and self compells me to banish all other thoughts and devote my whole attention to the company."

What do you think of it? Please don't criticise him too sincerely for he wrote while surrounded by a great many noisy boys. I expect another letter from him next Monday and will be very much uneasy and greatly disappointed if I do not. "Hark! me think I hear sweet music, so gently o'er me stealing that my soul is lifted above all earthly treasures and soars to the mighty realms above from which beams the Queen of Night's bright face"—but oh! dear, all poetry has fled from me, and I am brought from the great sphere in which I so recently imagined myself and I must now descend from the sublime to the ridiculous, for a rotten egg has exploded under Mother's room, and I can tell you the odor is enough to drive away all other thoughts—but that of holding one's nose, especially one so unfortunate as myself in having the disadvantage of so many in having such a tremendous nose (as mine), as to inhale, more than a share of the very delightful perfume. Oh! Poor me, I am almost suffocated.

I was very much surprised day before yesterday by a visit from cousin John Powell and Dr. Collins of Issaquena County of this state. I traveled with the latter gentleman summer before last from Lynchburg to the Natural Bridge. He is very wealthy, handsome, good, right intelligent and is indeed quite a nice gentleman. They spent last Thursday here and left yesterday morning. It is right singular that one of your first beaux should have been a Collins and the second gentleman (Ras was the first) who called on me, after I left school, was one of the same name. [*The young lady, home from finishing school, is attracting possible swains.*]

Pa left home last Monday on a fishing excursion at Robinson's and has not yet returned, but he (Pa) saw Dr. Collins summer before last and was *very much pleased* with him. Dr. Collins told some of the boys at Corinth (some of the Carroll companies are stationed there) that he was coming to see me and challenged him in a jest of course. Some time ago a gentleman commenced making a "speech" to me, but did not seem at all experienced in the art, and after blundering out a few nonsensical love words, there came a dead pause in the conversation, he at length raised his head, as if to determined to proceed, to get through as soon as possible, drawled out in the most pitiful manner imaginable, "Miss Mollie did you ever here the *ah* song called *Mollie,* wo-wo-won't you ma-marry!" Oh! Sister I liked to have laughed in the man's face! I do wish you could have heard the *doubting* manner in which he said it, and observed the expression of his countenance. Oh! that egg, *that* egg will kill me before morning.

Mother and I attended the Presbyterian church this morning at Middleton. It commenced last night and will continue until tomorrow evening. We spent last Tuesday at Colonel Moore's. When we left home it was our intention to return Mollie Collins' visit, but no one was there so we continued our ride to Colonel Moore's. We were over to see Mrs. E. Whitehead last evening. She told me that everybody said Ras would not go to war but was staying home on my account. I contradicted it and told her that he knew my sweetheart had gone to Harper's Ferry [173] and if the report was true, he had just as well go on for it would avail him nothing remaining here.

Laura, Mrs. Moore and myself spent one day last week at Judge Palmer's. I met Mrs. Dr. Sykes there, it was the first time I had seen her for five or six years. She is very ugly. Ellen Sykes is quite pretty, delicate and a very sweet girl. Occa [*Palmer*] has improved a great deal. All of the family, especially Mrs. Connelly *is courting Jeff* for *Occa.* But he seems to understand it all.

Mother has received yours of 4th inst., she sends much love and says she will write very soon. America and Ritt send much love to you, Mr. Walton and the boys. Semira and Becca have been quite sick this week but are now a great deal better and will be able to go to the field Monday. The crops are very good but suffering much for rain. It is very warm and exceedingly dusty. America is snoring, Mother is killing bed bugs. I am almost suffocated by the spoiled egg. There! another one has bursted. I think if they keep on at this rate we will be minus a house tomorrow morning.

Much love to my sweet brother and darling nephews. Do write soon a very long letter to your devoted sister, Molly. The chickens are now crowing for midnight. The music I mentioned in this letter was a serenade made from Payton and Simon on the tambourine and fiddle. Good night, I am not at all sleepy. I expect my "lover" is on night guard. Poor fellow. How I pity him.

Sunday night, June 22, 1861;

Cousin John went to Jackson the morning he left here and on his return home, he came again this evening but will leave tomorrow. He sends his best love to you and says you may expect him *if your vegetables* continue to do so well. He inquired after you the other day.

Mother attended church this morning but it was too warm for me to go so I remained at home and had a Sunday school among several of the little negroes. I taught them the prayer "Now I lay me down to sleep" and many other little things. I had turning down in the class which seemed to have amused them very much. I told them to come every Sabbath and the one who stayed the longer, from now until Christmas should have a flounced silk of mine, and the one whose conduct was the better would receive a worsted dress. Margaret, Millie and Lucinda are my smartest scholars. The former is very ambitious and the latter quick. Francis too is very good. I asked Tave of what was Eve made? She replied "Adam's rib *bone*." I am very much interested in my class and hope it will do well.

---

173. In western Virginia, at the confluence of the Shenandoah and Potomac Rivers. The U.S. had long had an arsenal there, which the Confederates had captured. The place changed hands several times.

To Letitia Walton from Sarah Watkins:

July 9, 1861
Winona, Mississippi

Mrs. L.A. Walton
Austin, Texas

My Dear Child,

I have been very busy lately that made me very remiss in writing you and answering your affectionate letter of the fourth ult. This morning your Pa, Baby, Abram and America started to Mrs. Eggleston's. Baby and America went in the carriage. She expects to stay until next Monday. Your Pa went in his buggy, he will return in two or three days. It is too warm and dusty to travel. Rain has been very partial in this county. There has not been a good rain here since May, only a few showers. Our corn crop is ruined by the drought and several people's crops are suffering as much or more than ours. I am very glad to hear that the season is fine in Texas and hope fine crops will be made there. I heard it thunder just now. It often thunders and lightnings but brings no rain.

Sally and Betty Collins promised to stay some day with me this week. Yesterday a company of soldiers started from Carrollton. Dan Russell, Mr. George, Frank Keys and William Whitehead[174] were in the company. I don't know the name of the company nor what place they are going to. They had a nice dinner given them yesterday at Tobin's Spring by the people of this neighbourhood. The Dr. was at it. He said several ladies attended it, Baby and I did not go. I was anxious to finish a pair of pants that your Pa needed to carry with him today. Baby and Martha undertook to make a silver cake to send to the dinner. Martha took Robin to show her how to bake it. When it was taken out of the oven, it had burnt almost to a coal at the bottom and split open and not cooked. We did not send it. We did not hear until late Saturday of the dinner and we had only yesterday morning to cook anything for it.

The negroes had Saturday given them in place of the fourth of July. They had a big dinner and Susan and Bob were married at night. Baby married them by reading the Episcopal ceremony and Paten repeating after her. They were married in the front passage. The ceremony wound up by one of the crowd letting an awful stink just as she was repeating the Lord's prayer. The supper was set in Harry Ann's house. She would not let the eatables go far off from her. They danced before Semira's door. I don't know whether the fault is

---

174. Recently widowed son of Edmunds Whitehead.

in the paper or my pen why I write so badly. My mind is wandering, I can't collect my ideas to write correctly.

Laura Whitehead and Emma spent the day with us Saturday. Dr. Moore [*Ras*] visited Baby in the evening. Baby had not gotten up out of bed when Laura came late Saturday morning. She sits up at night writing and sleeps half the day. She sleeps in the new room and keeps her clothing in the shed room so both rooms are occupied by her and not kept in order. If company was to come and want a private room, I would not have a nice room to ask them in. I will have to put a stop to it and make her keep one room. She has taken possession of Charlotte and will not let her do anything but what she chooses for her to do. Charlotte is as trifling as Caroline.

Baby would not let me read your letter to her. She read it to me. It seems strange to me that a mother is not allowed to see letters that is written by one child to the other. I believe she tells you everything about herself. Very little she communicates to me about herself. She is very lively and can make herself very agreeable when she chooses.

Several of the ladies have joined to have a sewing society in Middleton to make up clothing for the troops. Baby and I have joined it. We are to meet every Wednesday at the Methodist church. We went in last Wednesday and there was no sewing done. Subscription was made to purchase clothing to make up.

Mrs. Farmer was at the dinner given at Tobin's Spring yesterday. I have not seen her since she returned from New Orleans. Mrs. Parmele expected to be confined last month. I have not heard whether she has been or not. Kendall that married John Purnell's sister died lately in the neighborhood of Tom Purnell's. Mrs. Kendall lives with Tom. She went to Kendall's burial. I heard that she said they were going to live together the day he died.

Hardly anything is talked of but the war.[175] I do wish peace could be made before so many lives are taken unnecessarily. I received a letter from Aunt Elizabeth[176] lately. She wrote mostly about the eccentricity of the Early's. It was the old devil reproving of sin. She is as eccentric as any of them.

As Catharine does not suit you I am sorry you have not got America. America to her age is not smarter about work than Catharine and has not as good of a disposition as Catharine. If Catharine does not suit you, I advise you to sell her and get one to suit. Some of the negroes have been sick a little. Jane's child has been quite sick with diarrhea. It is well though to come to the door for a biscuit just now.

175. Numerous small skirmishes had erupted at many places here and there, and the day before this letter was written, the Confederate War Department sanctioned an expedition from Texas aimed at seizing New Mexico.

176. Dr. Watkins's sister. Their mother was Mary "Polly" Early Watkins.

Baby and I are very anxious to see you and your family. I am afraid it will be a long time before we have the pleasure of enjoying that happiness. It does my heart good to hear you are enjoying religion and pray that you may gain a crown in heaven. Remember your poor broken-hearted mother, my dear child, in your prayer. I need the prayers of the righteous. If I never see you again I pray we will meet in heaven. I think Baby will be an Episcopalian. She is now in principle. She gave her prayer book to Jeff McLemore and was delighted at getting another one last week. She is anxious to stay at Mrs. Eggleston's to attend the Episcopal church next Sabbath [*in Lexington, Mississippi*].

Give my love to Mr. Walton and the children. Kiss the children for me. Tell Sally and Catharine howdy for me. Becky sends her love to you and says you must pray for her, that she intends never to give up trying to get religion. All of the servants would send their love if they knew I was writing.

Your loving mother,

P.S. This letter is written so badly I would write it over. It is so warm and my eyesight is so bad you must excuse it. Write soon. Sarah E. Watkins

From Mollie to Lettie:

Mon. Night
July 22, 1861
Winona, Carroll Co., Miss.

My Very Dear Sister,

Having taken a very long nap this evening and not feeling at all sleepy tonight, I have concluded to employ a few hours writing to my absent and devoted sister who tho severed by many long miles from those that love her yet is often and fondly remembered.

We returned home last Thursday from our visit to Mrs. Eggleston's and Mr. Helm's and Mr. Berry Prince's all of which we enjoyed very much, especially the one to Mrs. Eggleston's. I was at first unwilling to go to Mr. Prince's but Pa insisted upon my so doing saying that as he was such a great friend of yours, he (Pa) wished me to become acquainted with him. We spent a day and night there and when we started home the next morning Pa said, "Well, Baby, how did you enjoy your visit to Mr. Prince's?" I replied very much indeed. He said, "Yes, oh! Yes, I knew you would. They are very fine people, and then Mr. Prince was such a great friend of your sister's was one reason I wanted you to go see him." Oh! dear one it made me so happy to hear him speak even thus of you. Whilst at Mrs. Eggleston's Willie Eggleston who is very bashful and scarcely goes before girls, taught me how to hold a gun, load and shoot a pistol. We also took a nice horseback ride one evening. Miss

Fannie's and Meady's (Eggleston) riding dresses were not at home so I pulled off my hoop and rode in one of Miss Meady's old traveling dresses. When Willy saw I had on no hoops he laughed at me. I did not care but mounted the horse and off we went in a rapid pace and had the exquisite, romantic pleasure of riding for a short time by moonlight.

When we reached Mr. Helm's no one was at home. So we started to Mr. Prince's, but a few yards from Mr. Helm's house one of the front carriage wheels broke all to pieces, just as we commenced descending a long and steep hill but no one nor anything else was at all hurt. I was not in the least alarmed but got out of the carriage, into the buggy and we returned to Mr. Helm's. The family came soon afterwards and we remained there until the next morning. During Mrs. Helm's absence, some of the negroes stole one of her new tablecloths and she promised them a *grand whipping frolic* as soon as we left.

Not long since I received a letter from J. [*Jeff*] containing the following, "I have always thought it the best policy for everyone to keep their own secrets, for there are so few in whom we can confide. I have never been so blessed to have a sister old enough to know how to appreciate a secret or to know how sacred one should be kept. The only persons to whom I ever unbosomed myself are Price and two of my college chums. Frequently have I wished for a sister or some lady friend that I could approach as a sister and one that could feel some grief, one who would be able to brighten my path and dispel many of the dark clouds which so often cut out the light of hope from my heart and by the soothing influence she can exert over me, render my course through life as smooth and easy as possible. I know of no one I would choose sooner (to fill that place) than yourself. Would you grant me a brother's place in your affections and allow me to write to and confide in you like a sister?"

I replied to his letter a few nights ago and granted him that privilege. No, sister, you are vastly mistaken. I do not love Jeff but wish I could for he seems to love me and he is among the few now my parents would be willing for me to marry. I believe he thinks I love him and it distresses one. He writes me every week, has written me seven letters, six of which were eight pages long, the other one was four. I have written him only five. In his last letter he wrote that the Colonel of the 11th Regiment of Mississippi volunteers was sick with the *flux*. He might well have omitted the name of the Colonel's disease.

It is late, I must close until tomorrow night. Mother, America and Ritt send much love to Mr. Walton, yourself and the dear boys.

Thursday night: A very severe and nervous headache deprived me of the pleasure of finishing this letter last Tuesday night. While sewing on one of mother's dresses, I was taken that evening with pain in my right eye and could see nothing for several minutes except a few black specks. I then retired to my room and sometime afterwards was awakened from my sleep by my own crying and Pa's asking, "What was the matter?" He then gave me two doses of morphine which eased the pain to some degree but my sleep was unsound during the night. I feel very well now except a sore forehead caused by the mustard plaster.[177]

I suppose you have heard or will hear before this letter reaches you of our great victory gained at Manassas Junction. All of my friends from this State and I expect most of our Virginia relatives were engaged in it. The brigade to which Lynn and Jeff belong was in the hardest part of the battle. We have not yet heard who were the killed and wounded. Only that their Brigadier General (Gen. Bernard E. Bee) was killed, General [*Joseph E.*] Johnston is their other general. I am daily expecting a letter from Jeff and if I do not receive one next week, I will certainly go crazy. Oh! Suppose he is killed. If it should be so I believe mother would regret it more than I would.

Joe Eggleston was also engaged in the contest at Manassas. His mother and all of that family sent much love to you.

There has been a sewing society organized in Middleton for the benefit of the "Winona Stars"[178] and other soldiers. Mother and myself are very punctual members. At our last meeting which was yesterday we saw Mrs. Farmer and Mrs. Phillips. They inquired very particularly after you. Mrs. Phillips says the reason Mrs. Parmele hasn't written to you is she has a very fine boy. I think Mrs. Farmer is looking very badly but everyone thinks her health is improving. Mrs. Phillips has told it in one or two families that Ras Moore was staying at home on my account. She would oblige me very much by keeping *such reports* to her *busy old self*. I wonder how she knows so much about his affairs. He has only been twice to see me and how I do wish he would come again. Pa received a letter from Cousin Powell yesterday saying that his two sisters, himself and two nieces, Bill and Mary Porrance would come down on the train next Friday evening to see us.

Write soon and often my own darling sister.

Baby

---

177. A classic description of a migraine headache.

178. Winona Stars were Co. B., 15th Mississippi Infantry. (See William Amann, *Personnel of the Civil War*, 2 vols. (New York: Yoseloff, 1961), vol. 1, 165.

To Mary Watkins from Letitia Walton:

August 5, 1861
Austin, Texas

My Dear Sister,

After seating myself to write I discovered there was no letter paper in the house and concluded this paper would answer this time.

Your interesting letter of 22nd June was received three days ago. I wrote to Mother last week and answered your letters sometime before that. It was a great pleasure to hear from you all once more even if your letters had been a long time on the way—it was sweet to me. Your letter was both interesting and amusing. I asked Will if that was not funny about the rotten eggs—"yes," said he, "but funnier about that big nose of hers—nobody will ever plague her much about that nose."

My sister, let me tell you one thing which perhaps you will not own even to yourself—you love Jeff right hard. When I was about your age I loved Dick Collins and thought I could never love another. Jeff no doubt loves you. It was very wicked for him to tell or write that way about the prayer book. What he said was flattering, is true. He is young and light-hearted and doubtless felt what he said. Just to think when he should be thinking of the great and merciful Creator, he was thinking of a human being. Poor child, he had better be thinking of his soul's salvation. Sister, you ought to be good and pray for him. Can't you, oh! won't you repent and believe in the Lord Jesus Christ? It is not hard to do.

It is raining a little now and thundering and lightening a great deal tonight. We need rain very much. I have not more than two or three kinds of vegetables now.

How does Wash and Anna get along together? That is a good idea, teaching the little negroes on Sundays. I think it is right and ought to be done. I do not believe that God gave us negroes just for our ease and comfort, but some good is intended for the negro—by association with us, and what can be that good if it is not religious instruction? As I heard our minister say a short time ago, "slavery is right if used righteously, otherwise it is not."

The election came off today [*for district judge*]. Though all the precincts have not been heard from, Will says he is beaten by Townes. Had it not been for wire workers and liars, Will would have been elected. I am truly sorry if he is beaten. I do not like for my husband to fail in what he attempts. It is raining—good night to sleep. I will have more to say to my sweet sister tomorrow night—goodbye.

7th—Will was beaten sure enough and Townes elected. I am truly sorry and do not feel like I even want to see Townes for he did not act right in the matter nohow.

I have seen some peaches this year such as you all would not eat for 25 cents per dozen and $4.00 per bushel. Watermelons and muskmelons are in abundance.

We had news this morning that an attempt had been made by the blockading fleet to burn Galveston—fired sixteen big shells but all the damage done was the killing of one man and wounded two more. Our guns were better than they thought, and we made them run.[179]

Oh! me how I do wish I was with you all. The U.S. troops stationed in New Mexico (about five hundred) attempted to take El Paso and three hundred Texans killed 33 of them and took the others prisoner, then went on and took possession of the fort [*Fort Fillmore*].

George is fat and well and I think will walk in a short time if he keeps well. When lying down he can get up and sit up and can stand up well by anything. He is a fine baby and no mistake—such beautiful black eyes and so full of life. Newton and Early are out at Mr. Gray's, went yesterday—Newton I believe would be willing to stay a month. It is the second or third time they have been there with me.

I wonder if Lynn and Jeff were in that great battle at Manassas and also if they were injured. I do wish I could get Lynn's likeness, but it will not do to send it—"them rotten Yankees" might get it. Keep it 'till I ask for it or come after it.

I have heard something of the correspondence between Dr. Watkins and Daniel S. Dickerson and have anxiously wished to find the publication in some paper but have been disappointed. What was it about? We have had no good rain yet. Catharine has been sick four or five days, but went to work today. She is not much account—awful slow—but is a good negro I think.

The candle flies are so troublesome, I am anxious to quit writing. Give my love to Pa and Mother. Tell all the negroes howda—tell them I think about them and pray for them all and I want them to pray for themselves. Tell Simon he was mighty wicked and I thought kept others from getting religion, and he must quit that—think of his father and pray to meet him in heaven.

Oh! that I could see you all once more. Will sends love to you and Mother.

Your sincere sister,
Lettie

179. It was an episode of lesser import: a few shots had been fired by blockaders and were answered by Confederate shore batteries.

To Letitia Walton from Sarah Watkins:

August 8, 1861
Winona, Mississippi

Mrs. L.A. Walton
Austin, Texas

My Dear Child,

Your very affectionate letter of the 24th ult. was received today. I am always delighted to hear from you and your family and am very sorry that the irregularity of the mails prevents us from hearing from each other more frequently. I came in Baby's room for my inkstand. She proposed for me to stay and write to you. I agreed to her proposal but cannot write as well in any place as in my own room. I expected to enjoy her company while writing but she has left, no telling how long she will be out and where she will ramble to with the little negroes before she comes back. She intended going to Judge Collins' today and stay until Sunday. It commenced raining last evening and has been raining too much today for her to go.

We had rain last month that helped the crops some since then it has been dry until now. It is needed but came in a bad time as the hands are pulling fodder. I commenced drying peaches for you and myself. As I have to keep them in the house. I am afraid they will rot. We have very few peaches. If it was not that I am drying them for you I would not dry any. I will put up damsons [*plums*] for us both as soon as the weather gets good. I have so much blackberry cordial that I did not make any. I saved the best cordial I have for you.

Baby and I attend the sewing society every Wednesday but have done no work until now. Baby is knitting a pair of socks and I have a pair of casnet pants to make. Mrs. Barrow has promised to do that stitching for me on her machine. I am going to her house Monday for her to do it for me. She said if I could not come she would make the pants. It is very kind of her to do it. I am very thankful to her but rather assist in making them.

Baby and I spent the day at Mrs. Phillips' this day week. Mrs. Parmele has a fine, fat boy[180] five weeks old today. Mrs. Parmele looked well. She has not been out of bed since her child was born. Dr. Atkins advised her to lie in bed six weeks to prevent a falling of the womb. Mrs. Phillips said yesterday that Mrs. Parmele was not well, that she had taken cold and it gave her a fever. Mrs. Farmer had gone to George McLean's the day we visited Mrs. Phillips. Mrs. Farmer does not look well, her face has boils and is swollen. All of them

180. James Jefferson Parmele. Later, as a young man, he moved to Austin, Texas, and, in 1889, married Sarah Walton, Letitia and Will Walton's daughter.

send their love to you. Mrs. Parmele said she thought of naming her child Lettie if it had been a girl.

It is so warm and the flies so troublesome, I have scarcely patience to write. Mrs. John Davis has a baby and Rebecca Weed has one. Rebecca's was three pounds. Abbey Eubanks was married Tuesday night to Mr. McCain, a widower. I received a letter from Sarah Ann. She wrote that Lettie had married badly. The man is a drunkard and dissipated and worth nothing. She had been told that Lettie went barefooted and her husband's sister wore her dresses. Sarah says she likes the man her mother married, that he is smart. He has no property and has been clerking two years. Her mother has a daughter.

Abram received a letter from Joe today. He wrote that Lucy was with her mother in Memphis.

Mr. and Mrs. E. Whitehead spent the day here Tuesday. Last week Mrs. E. Whitehead's baby had spasms. She thought they were caused from eating fruit. Two or three drops of balsam capenia given to your child would relieve him of the gravel, it is a good purgative. Tell Newton I wish he could come to see me. I am very glad he is not a man, if he was he would go to war and I would be so uneasy about him. I do wish you and your family could be with us but can't advise you to leave your good husband to come and I know you could not be happy to be away from home.

It is so warm it makes me sick to write. You must write soon and often. Give my love to all your family. Ritter and America send their love to you all.

Your loving mother,
Sarah E. Watkins

P.S. A note from Mary . . .

Dear Sweet Sister,

Although it has passed ten o'clock tonight, I have a letter to write to Jeff before retiring. I have concluded as Mother did not fill this page to add a little of my nonsense but as she writes so neatly I am almost ashamed to enclose any of my scrawl in the same envelope. I received a letter today from Jeff written Tuesday after the Manassas battle whilst he was waiting for the body of his 1st Lieutenant to be brought and buried. The Lieutenant was killed in the battle. I expect I was the first he wrote to, after the fight. He also wrote me the following Thurday and gave a very long description of the battle but I will not repeat it here as you have no doubt read as good accounts of it in the newspapers. He closed his letter with these words (*don't let my dear brother laugh at me*) "No more *my dear sweet friend* not that I have nothing to write, but have not time, as we are not allowed to mail our letters here and I will send this one by a gentleman who will start in a few minutes to Corinth, Mississippi."

If it does not rain I will go to Judge Collins' tomorrow and remain until Wednesday. I will write to Newton the night after I return home. Give my love to my own darling brother and kiss the children for me. Write soon and tell us all about your family and self.

Good night my precious Sister.

Baby

CHAPTER EIGHT

"War fever is raging high here"

In Texas, Lettie's church could not pay the preacher, so he joined the army as a chaplain. In Mississippi, Mary is enormously busy— entertaining company, knitting and sewing for soldiers, and helping to raise money. Soon, too, she and her mother will commence teaching school. In this chapter we have another marvelous—and this time, a long—letter dictated by a slave, as well as another interesting letter from Lettie in which she addresses fond passages to each of several slaves in Mississippi. The doctor continues his role as a planter and, to stymie an undesirable neighbor, buys more land—at fifty cents an acre. Even as early as the fall of 1861, the family is becoming aware of short-ages, of shockingly high prices, and of the growing illiquidity of Missis-sippi state bank notes. How little did they perceive that the worst was still to come.

The arrival of a new year, and perhaps the reality of ongoing war, brought to an end the doctor's hostility to his elder daughter and her husband. In early 1862, eight years after the marriage, he finally found forgiveness in his heart, expressing his new openness in a letter but quickly changing the subject.

As winter wore on, the war clearly already had invaded the lives of our entire cast, though they tended to express that impact in differing degrees of intensity. Nevertheless, in everyone's correspondence there was no more serious issue than life and death, as gradually the young men began to disappear from the community, going off to war. People shared too the sad news of those who were killed in action.

To Mary Watkins from Letitia Walton:

                                    August 27, 1861
                                    Austin, Texas

My Dear Sister,

I have a letter from you and one from Mother and your letter and Mother's together on same sheet all unanswered, and I cannot tell which I wrote to last, you or Mother, but I think it was to Mother, and I wrote to both of you a short time before the reception of your letters and some of the letters had been a long time on the way. We have now a direct mail route from New Orleans to Houston, so you need not direct via Alexandria [*Louisiana*] any more.

I am out of snuff and am trying to quit using it. It is such an ugly, inconvenient and injurious practice. I hope you never will indulge in the filthy habit. Do my sister, take the advice of one who knows the evils of such practice. There is none that I like at but at one place in town, and (owing to the blockade) they ask 35 cents for it, and I do not feel like encouraging men who rise on their goods these days. Perhaps I will quit—can't tell yet.

My poor back aches now, aches nearly all the time.

Sister, you ought not to keep anything secret from Mother. It would be a great pleasure to her for you to make her your confident, and it will do you no harm. She was my confident and I never had cause to regret it. Our Mother can keep a secret, you know that—then why not tell her all? Tell Pa all you can too, it will make him love you and have more confidence in you.

28th—The war fever is raging high here. I fear I cannot keep my husband with me much longer. Oh! how can I give him up to go and stand up and be shot at, one that I love so dearly? Some men wish Will to get up a company and have him for Captain. I hope he will do no such thing yet a while, no how. Will says he is ashamed to be at home and can never die satisfied unless he has a hand in this fight and all such talk as that.

30th—George stopped me from writing night before last, and last night I went visiting and tonight I expect company, so I will try to finish this this evening. I paid several calls this morning, among them was Mrs. Haralson of Georgia. She said she had been anxious to know me ever since she found out I was Dr. Tom Watkins' daughter, but circumstances had prevented her visiting me until recently. I was also to see Mrs. Clark (mother of our present Governor). She knew Pa's grandmother and grandfather, also his father and mother—went to school with Polly Early and talked about Guss Longstreet [*Augustus B. Longstreet*]. Mrs. Clark's maiden name was Margaret Long. Oh!

how I do wish Pa could see her and talk to her. I thought about him and wished for him while talking to the old lady. She also spoke of Peter Early and what a smart man he was. Tell Pa about it. Perhaps it will revive pleasant recollections. Mrs. Haralson is a very genteel looking woman but looks like she has seen much trouble, and I expect she has had her share since she came to Texas.

Our church could not pay the preacher, so he is Chaplain in company soon to start to Virginia. He is going to carry his family to his relatives in Georgia. They leave this evening. I am so sorry to part with them. I thought a great deal of them and loved to hear him preach.

Has any of Aunt Jane's sons joined the army? I expect many of our Virginia relatives are in the army. Sister, you did not tell me a word about Lynn. Don't you know I was anxious to hear whether he came out of the great battle safe or not? I think a great deal of him and want you to keep me posted as to his welfare. I was rejoiced to hear that Jeff came out uninjured. Has Jeff addressed you yet? I think if he loves you that that was a strange request he made—for you to be as a sister to him. I don't care what you say, I believe you love Jeff. Sister, I suppose it is Mrs. Phillips' private opinion publically expressed, that Ras is staying at home on your account.[181] It does no one any harm for it to be so reported. She has a right to express her opinion and you ought not to care for it. Mother acted hurt that you would not let her see my letters to you. Sister, tell your mother your most sacred thoughts and secrets. It will give her much pleasure.

Will is going to start to San Antonio Sunday on business—will be absent about a week perhaps, I expect to go out to Judge Sneed's tomorrow and remain some days.

Tell Mother I will answer her letters before long. What did Robin say to Susan's marrying?

Are you subject to such headache? I hope not. Pa does not suffer with it as he used to, does he? Who was that gump that asked you about the song "Mary won't you marry?" Tell me how many gentlemen have addressed you and who they were. You expected a visit from the Misses Powell and Co. They were the dryest girls I almost ever saw—good and nice tho. I have not answered your letters as fully as I wish but will do so at another time. Kiss my Mother for me. Love to all. Tell Becky I am trying to help her to pray and she must be faithful.

Write often to your

Sister Lettie

P.S. Have you heard anything from Occa Merriwether lately? I am anxious to hear from her.

181. Dr. Ras (Erasmus) Moore, son of Col. O. J. Moore.

To Letitia from Mary:

September 11, 1861
Winona, Carroll, Miss.
Wednesday Night

My Very Dear Sister,

Can your kind and forgiving heart pardon the neglect which circumstances have forced me to show towards you! I commenced a letter to Newton and Early last Sunday but was suffering so much with the headache that I was compelled to postpone the pleasure of finishing my letter until I was able to write which I thought would be the next night. Having to remain in Middleton all day Monday making arrangements for a concert which the young ladies of our Military Aid Society will give next Friday night so fatigued and worried me that on my return home I found much to my disappointment another headache to prevent completing my letter. And yesterday, (Tuesday), it was the same as the day before, and last week I was too busy entertaining company and knitting for the soldiers to think of writing to anyone. So you see dear one it has not been my fault in not writing before.

The object of our concert is to collect money for the purpose of purchasing winter clothing for the two companies for which we are sewing, namely the "Winona Stars" [182] and "Carroll Guards." [183] The girls who will give the concert are to represent the different Confederate States with each girl having the name of the state which she is to represent printed distinctly on the white sash which she wears pinned on the right shoulder, extending across her breast and back and tied in a bow on the left hip. I am going to wear my last summer's commencement dress with a white and blue bertha [a large collar]. My hair will be braided and narrow blue ribbon, run in the shape of small diamonds in each braid. I shall appear no less then seven or eight times on the stage, one of my pieces (Maid of the Nile) I will sing alone, another (Wanita) I accompany Laura Moore on the piano with the guitar, another (Touch Again That Sweet Guitar), Laura Whitehead and I will play and sing on two guitars. The concert will be in the large study hall at the Seminary in Middleton. The room will be decorated with evergreens and brilliantly lighted, but what is most interesting, Martha Jane Palmer that was, is going to perform several pieces with nothing so prominent as a very large stomach, thereby verifying the old saying, "Coming events cast their shadows before." Don't you think we can very well dispense with her assistance?

182. Company B, Winona Stars, of Carroll County, Mississippi, mustered into state service at Winona, March 22, 1861, of 15th Mississippi Infantry.

183. Company C, Carroll Guards, of Carroll County, Mississippi, mustered into state service at Carrollton, April 19, 1861, of the 20th Regiment–Infantry.

I don't know what is coming over the dreams of the women, it seems that all of them are bent on having children these hard times. There are at least four baby girls in this immediate neighborhood that have been born in the past few weeks, among which is Mrs. Hemingway's little granddaughter that is a week and a few days old. It is not yet named. Mother rode over to Mr. Hemingway's last Sunday, said Margaret Pleasants appeared very well and was quite cross, as to express it in Mother's words, very snappish.

Sun. night. I commenced this letter a few days ago but was unable to finish it until tonight. Mother and I attended church today at Chestnut Ridge (near the place Ritt was married), heard a very poor sermon delivered by Mr. Applewhite. We saw Mr. and Mrs. Baskerville, who told us that Maj. Hawkins' family were well. Occa Merriwether has a son. Mrs. Simmons is now in Charleston with Miss Occa. Margaret Pleasant's baby is named Mary Ella. I received a letter from Jeff the other day stating that his health was so bad, he was afraid he could not stand the camp life. Oh! sister, Jeff writes me such affectionate and interesting letters that half the pleasure I now have is writing to and receiving letters from him. He writes me at least every ten days. He was in the thickest of the fight at Manassas and his company was the first to advance upon Sherman's Battery. Compliments are constantly paid him and Price [*his brother*] in almost every letter that the soldiers write to their friends here. Lynn and the rest of the Carroll Rifles did not reach the battle ground until the enemy began their retreat.

Tues. Night. I was so sleepy last Sun. night that it was impossible to finish this letter as I expected. Dr. Holeman and his brother Andy came here late this evening. I take Andy's visit to myself. He is not at all intelligent and he is in no respect equal to Jeff. Mrs. and Mrs. Helms and Miss Helms spent a few days with us last week.

Mother Ritt, America and all the negroes join me in much love to you, your darling boys and Mr. Walton. Excuse a short letter my dear sister, for it is too late to write more and I am anxious to send this by
tomorrow's mail. Do write often to your loving
                                        Sister
P.S. Ras Moore started last night to the war. Dr. Holeman requested me to add a post script and give his kindest regards to you. M.E.W.

The following letter was written by Mollie to "Miss Lettie," acting as the scribe for the slaves at the Watkins homestead. The words are America's.

October 1, 1861

Dear Miss Lettie:

I have chosen tonight to write you a few lines in order to hear how you is getting along. I am well and enjoying the blessing of very good health. The times are getting so hard that we stay at home so much, I haven't any news to write, but it is only my desire to talk wid you that has prompted me to begin this letter. I went down to Mrs. Eggleston's with Baby and had a delightful time and captivated many young hearts among whom was Mrs. Eggleston's Henry. I think the love was mutual on both sides. I am afraid to place my heart on any young man as I might be disappointed like I was once before. Semira is quite sick, has a high fever all day but is somewhat better tonight. Isham has been waiting on Jane ever since she has been here, but she will not have him and expects to be confined in December. Although it is not his baby, he yet shows her attention.

Don't think of hard of my not writing to you as I have not had an opportunity of so doing before tonight. My best love to Newton and Early. Tell them to send me some message, even if it is not more than two words. My best love to Mas. William, and tell him to bring you and the children to see us. . . . Uncle [*Vivion*] sends much love to you all. Mama sends a heap of howdy. Her jaw is still very painful. Uncle John Smith sends love and says remember him in your prayers.

I am not thinking of marrying yet, but intend remaining single as your maid. I discarded one of my beaux the other day and he told me that if I did not marry soon the gloss would be off of me and then I could not get married at all. Tell Aunt Sally and Catharine howdy. Write soon, my much loved Mistress, to your servant, America.

In the same envelope Mollie included a letter dictated by servant Martha. Martha has named her son Jeff Longstreet Watkins. She dictates:

I bet you that Jeff Longstreet is smarter den George Longstreet. He can stand alone, got four teeth and has made one step and is de prettiest and de best baby I ever had. Siah has been sick but is now much better. Milly was very sick last week but is now well. De chillen gather so many chinquapins that I often wish Newton and Early was here to get dem. Some of us went after turnips salad yesterday and it reminded us so much of the old walks we used to have on the creek and oh! Miss Lettie, we did wish you could have been here. Please come soon and stay wid us all de war last and bring every one of your chillen. Simon sends howdy to all and says come to see us. Milly picks 150 pounds of cotton most every day. Patty sends heaps of howdy and says kiss the children for her. Tell Aunt Sally and Catharine howdy and that Jeff is a great big boy. Ask Catharine if she has found a sweetheart yet. Give my love to Master William and the children.

Goodbye, write soon to,
Martha Watkins
Your good and faithful servant

To Letitia Walton from Sarah Watkins:

October 3, 1861
Winona, Mississippi

Mrs. L. A. Walton
Austin, Texas

My Dear Child,

I have put off too long writing you. It has not been for the want of an inclination why I have not written, business prevented me and Baby writing you made me slower in writing you. I received your affectionate letter of the 13th ult. this week. It was a pleasure to hear that you were well and doing well. The war causes us all to feel grieved and sad, those that have not husbands and sons to be distressed about have son-in-laws and, Baby says, sweethearts. I think Mr. Walton ought to go to war for the sake of his country and his children. If he does go, I wish very much you and your children could come and be with us. As it is such a long journey from Texas here and expensive, I cannot insist upon your coming unless you could come without embarrassing your husband. Your Pa says he thinks Mr. Walton ought to go to war. He thinks it is the duty of every man that has youth and health to go. He says if you were to be left a widow he would have you near him and do the best he could for you. He says as you are comfortably situated in Austin, he advises you not to break up keeping house. If you want to visit us do box up your most valuable articles and get someone you could rely upon to take care of them for you and let someone take care of your house and lot and come and visit us as long as you please. Baby and I would be delighted to have you and the children with us.

I have never known for the times to be so hard and provisions to be as scarce as they are now in this state. I hear of wealthy people being out of meat. I don't know what any of us will do for coffee in a short time from now. We have commenced having coffee made for supper from the grounds left of breakfast. As much as I want to see you and your dear sweet children my heart prompts me to be candid and say to you if you are doing well in Texas you are happier there than you would be here. Do not let what I say keep you from coming if you desire to come. Do the way you and Mr. Walton think best. Mr. Hugh Davis'[184] son Hugh is in the army at Knoxville, Tennessee. He was taken very sick. His father went to see him. He was sick himself when he left home and was not at Knoxville long before he died the 26th of last month. His son, Hugh was too sick to know of his father's death. Hugh was very sick when I heard from him last.

Cousin John Powell is in the army at Knoxville too. The last I heard of cousin Henry Watkins he was at Little Rock. I saw Mrs. Baskerville two weeks ago at Chestnut Ridge church. She told me that Octavia Merriwether had a son and was doing well. Mrs. Foltz has one and Mrs. Richard Whitehead. I saw Mrs. Richard Whitehead two weeks tomorrow at Judge Whitehead's. Richard W. looks very badly. Three weeks ago I spent the day at Mr. Arnold's. He and Mr. Parmele were talking of making up a company. Mary [Arnold] was violently opposed to her husband going to war. Tom Kennedy and Dr. Hudson are in a cavalry company called the Carroll Rangers.[185] They are in Missouri. Mr. E. Whitehead's son William and Eugene Whitehead are in Judge Drake's company. They are in Trenton, Tennessee. Several married men have gone to war from this county. I often hear of the corpses of soldiers being brought down on the railroad to be carried to their homes to be buried. Mary Thomson had two brothers to die at Corinth last spring. Lynn Hemingway was not in the Manassas battle. An accident happened to the car he was on prevented him from being in it. We have several sick negroes, they are none dangerous. Semira has been very sick with the fever. She is getting better. Siah has had a fever all day. He came in yesterday had a chill the night before. Tom Purnell's health is too bad for him to be to the war.

Baby joins me in love to you and Mr. Walton. Kiss the dear sweet children for us. Write soon and let me know if Mr. Walton is going to war and what place he will go to. Tell Aunt Sally and Catharine howdy. Washington and Anna had a fight this week in the field, she cut him on the face with her hoe.

Your affectionate mother,
Sarah E. Watkins

Mrs. Watkins takes on the serious task of writing the son-in-law regarding military duty.

---

184. Brother of Elizabeth Davis Whitehead, Judge W. W. Whitehead's wife. The son also died.

185. Carroll Rangers became Co. A, 1st Mississippi Cavalry (see Amann, *Personnel of the Civil War*, vol. 1., 25).

October 4, 1861
Winona, Mississippi

Mr. Wm. M. Walton
Austin, Texas

My Dear Son-in-law,

Your very welcome letter of the 13th ult. was received this week, Dr. Watkins and I think you ought to go to war, I would dislike for it to be thrown up to my grandchildren that their father did not fight for his country. As you are comfortably situated in Austin, we cannot advise you to break up keeping house there to move here during the war. Dr. Watkins says it would cost you a great sum to do so. The houses in Middleton are in a very dilapidated state and most of them occupied by very poor people that cannot support themselves. Provisions are scarcer than I have ever known them to be in this state. The drought this summer injured the corn crops very much and the many rains that fell the latter part of summer injured the cotton crops. I hear that some wealthy people are out of meat. Dr. Watkins says if Lettie wants to visit us he thinks it would be better for her to box up her most valuable articles and put them in care of someone that could be depended on and leave someone to take care of the house and lot and get a two-horse wagon and come and stay with us as long as she pleases. Give yourself no uneasiness about your family being taken care of in case of your death. The doctor says were you to die he would have Lettie to live near him and do the best he could for her. My beloved child and her family should never suffer while I have a cent of my own. It would afford me great happiness to have her and her family with me and hope she will visit us if it will not be too great an expense to you. It would be much more pleasant to me and perhaps to Lettie for us to be together these troublesome times but cannot insist upon it if it will prove at all disadvantageous to you. If you think it is best for her to come I would be delighted to have her with us as soon as possible.

Judge Drake, Mr. George, and Mr. Dan Russell and several other married men have gone to war. If you go I pray God will protect and guide you and permit you to return to your much beloved family and enjoy peace and happiness with them again. I will be anxious to hear from you often.

Give my love to Lettie and a kiss to the dear sweet children for me.

Your affectionate Mother,
Sarah E. Watkins

To Letitia Walton from Sarah Watkins:

November 4, 1861
Winona, Mississippi

Mrs. Lettie A. Walton
Austin, Texas

My Dear Child,

Your affectionate letter of the 18th ult. was gladly received last Wednesday. Baby has received a letter from you since that was written before you wrote mine. I don't know why you do not receive letters from me sooner.

I wrote you a few days before Baby sent you that extract from the Gilmer book. I answered Mr. Walton's letter the same day. I do not write you as often as I should, it is not the want of love nor that I do not think often of you. Why I do not I am so slow about my work and have such slow servants to assist me that I'm always kept busy and having to assist the sewing society makes me have more to do that prevents me from writing oftener to you. I have knit five pair of socks, made three pair of pants, and have a coarse linsey coat to make for the soldiers. I have all of the negroes clothes to cut out.

Tomorrow, Baby and I expect to go to Carrollton to buy some articles for winter. I expect the high price of the goods will prevent me from buying what I need, Judge Wellons has just received new goods. Coffee is fifty cents a pound here and scarce at that. Bacon is 25 cents a pound, corn one dollar a bushel. Mr. Prince gave $2500 for 50 barrels of pork lately in New Orleans. Some people will have to quit feeding their negroes meat unless the war closes. I have heard of some people's hogs dying. We use parch wheat mixed with our coffee. To one tablespoon of coffee, put two tablespoonsful of wheat. Parch the wheat separate from the coffee and grind the coffee and wheat together when the coffee is to be made. The rich people that have not given anything for the war are Col. LeFlore, Dr. McLean and the Garys. Your Pa has given something, I do not know how much besides three pairs of blankets and I believe he promised 50 bales of cotton. He gave 5 pounds of wool and two pounds of yarn to the sewing society in Carrollton. I gave three pounds of yarn to the society in Middleton.

Martha Young's oldest and youngest child died lately with diphtheria. Mary Arnold's oldest child Charles and her daughter Betty died with the same disease. Charles died last Tuesday. Mary fainted when he died. It was sometime before she could be brought to. [*Judge Whitehead's family*].

Else had a stillborn child over two weeks ago. She said it was caused by lifting her basket heavy with cotton. She was taken in the field and just got to her house to have it on the floor by herself. She said she would have had it this month. Jane expects one this month. Semira's baby Agnes died two weeks tonight. She was cutting teeth and had a violent cold. It suffered very much for several days and the day it died it had spasms. Semira had been very sick. Jesse has been very sick and has fevers yet, Becky has been staying with him over two weeks. Patty and Siah have been very sick. Siah is well now and Patty is well, all to weakness. I had a very bad cold and cough for four weeks. I have got well of the cold and nearly well of the cough. Joe is sick a little. Mrs. Hugh Davis' son Hugh died week before last at Knoxville, Mrs. Davis thought him recovering and expected him home this week. Jones that married Pentecost's sister died last week. He lived near Mrs. Estell's old place. Mr. Gouch that bought Mrs. Estell's place has been anxious to move to Texas. He wanted to sell his place to your Pa. I don't know why he did not get it. Baby says she got a good letter from Jeff yesterday. It is reported that she and Jeff will be married as soon as he returns from war.

Martha says Jeff[186] has four teeth and can walk. He is bigger than Becky's child that is older. Hannah and Uncle Vivion send love to you. I wish very much you could be with us. We are very anxious to see you all. Baby joins me in love to you, Dr. Walton and the children. Kiss the children for us. Do you think Mr. Walton will go off to war? Patten started to Virginia Friday with Mr. Ray. He is going on to Manassas to Lynn. George and Shaler Hillyer are in the war. I do not know where Cousin Henry is. You must not wait for me to answer your letters. I will write as often as I have time. I am always anxious to hear from you and your family and will be uneasy about you if Mr. Walton goes to war. I wish you and the children could be with me. Write soon.

Your loving Mother,
Sarah E. Watkins

P.S. Your Pa is not acquainted with Mrs. Clark. He does not know whether she is the Margaret Long mentioned in the Gilmer book. He would like to know if she is. I am very much obliged to you and the boys for the pecans and wish I could have the pleasure of receiving them from your dear hands.

Letitia writes to the old family servants at Forest Place:

November 20, 1861
Austin, Texas

My Good Old Friend Ritt:

I was highly gratified a short time ago by the reception of a letter from you. Ritt, tho' we are far apart (and may never meet again) I often think of you (a

---

186. Martha, a family servant, named her son Jeff in honor of Mary's fiance.

cat has come right before my nose and puked. I am holding my nose while Catharine hunts a rag to wipe it up), and the happy hours we have spent together. Those were good old days, Ritt, when we were young. We are getting old now and stepping onto the grave. It is time now for us to be thinking not of worldly pleasures but our soul's salvation. Are you thinking of that or have you determined to go head-long down eternity? Oh! Ritt, stop, look and see the awful pit that is open before—will you step into it or will you turn to the Savior? He alone can save you.

I am very glad you can yet call Jackson your "good old man" and hope you and he get on lovingly together. Tell him howda. I had a good laugh about Polly and that thing beside her so black that it could not be told from "the very darkness itself."

She and Robert must have had a fine time. My family are all well now but some days such grunting among the darkies. Sally has such a pain in her hip and her back, Catharine has fluttering at the heart, and likely such a pain in the belly. Then I scarcely can get anything done. I do wish I could see you and talk to you but I must quit writing now as I have others to write, too. Will sends howda to you.

Ever your friend,

Mrs. Vanity Martha,

Your kind letter was gladly received a short time ago. Talking about Jeff Longstreet being smarter than George—why George Longstreet is the smartest child I know of. He is running all about, was stepping when he was nine months old, can wave his hand and say bye and will soon be talking, I think.

I am sorry Siah is sick so much and I hope he will outgrow those spells. Martha, I do wish you were young and belonged to me. Money could not buy you.

Two young ladies took dinner with me today. I had bacon and cabbage, roast beef, fried chicken, Irish potatoes, sweet potatoes, beets, tomatoes, and onions, bread, butter and milk. Sally gave us dinner at 3 o'clock, fashionable she was, and Lizzie picked the chicken for her too and no dessert. I raised all the vegetables except sweet potatoes and could have had four other kinds of vegetables. The Irish potatoes come up themselves where I had potatoes dug in the summer.

Milly is mighty smart to pick so much cotton. I thank you for the wish to have myself and children visit you all and would most willingly go if I could.

Tell Simon howday and that I want to hear of his seeking religion. Give my love to mamma and tell her Early often speaks of her and seems glad and proud to say "my mamma," he always puts *my* to it.

I do not think Catharine has caught a beau yet. I will ask her tomorrow. 25th—Sally says howda and she hopes you are all trying to seek the Lord and will keep on trying until you find peace. Catharine says "howda and kiss your baby for her, as to beaux that is the last thing that I am thinking about. There has been a wedding here every Saturday night for the last two months. One half of them have parted already and that has put me out of heart."

My Highly Esteemed Polly,

It was a great pleasure to me to see that some of you thought enough of me to write to me and cannot say that I did not feel somewhat jealous when I knew that some of you had written to sister and not one had ever done so to me. I am glad to hear that you enjoy preaching and have joined the church. I pray for you, Polly, and pray that you may never turn back. The Lord will not turn his back on you if you seek him faithfully. You must give yourself up wholly into the hands of the Lord. Let him do the work. Be willing for him to do anything with you. Don't expect to do too much yourself. You are a poor condemned lost sinner unless the Lord will have mercy on you. Feel that and trust in him. Oh! That I could bring poor sinners to the foot of the cross and help them to find the Savior! I try to be a Christian and I hope I am one but at times I have my doubts and fears.

Why is Chloe going to marry Pa's Daniel? That old man. Tell her she had better take Joe, an old grandfather at once. I am proud of the invitation you all have given me to come home. I would love to go but it does not suit me to do so just now for if I were to go home my good husband would go off to the war and I intend to keep him from going as long as I can. Give my love to Abram, Becky, Melia, Tilly, Elsie, Milly, Big Milly, and everybody. Sally and Catharine want to write to all but I do not feel like writing for them tonight. They would send love if they knew of my writing. Will sends howda to you all. I am glad to hear that your children are going to Sunday School and learning so well.

Letitia Walton

Miss America Indiana,

Your kind letter was received a few days ago. I am sorry you do not belong to me now. True you have pains and aches, but you can hardly beat Catharine at that. She has fattened and grown very much. Looks healthy and well but I reckon she has been in the habit of complaining and does not know how to leave it off. For my part I do not know what she knows how to do or what she is good for. Has very little sense and is a poor hand at any sort of work.

You have plenty of beaux and are not married yet. Well, if you ever intend to marry, you ought to marry soon and not put it off until you get so old—for then it will go much harder with you to have children. Look at Ritt. I believe if she had married young she would have had children and been happy and healthy now.

Judge Dillahunty is a member of the Legislature and is now in town. If Will thinks of it tomorrow he will ask him about your father. Yes you will stay single—'til you get so old and ugly no young man will want you. Then you will take some old grandfather like Chloe is about to do. Mrs. Eggleston's Henry is too far off. Love somebody near home.

Who is the father to Jane's child? Tell Isham he is too good looking to notice Jane after her misbehavior and he must hold his head higher than that.

Give my love to Sally, Joe and John Smith. Tell him I do and will remember him in my prayers. He must hold out faithful. Newton and Early call the baby George. They think a great deal of him but Early cannot understand how George can hurt or strike him and he not hit him back. He is sure to strike George back every time and say, "Well, Mudder, George hit me." He is a funny child yet.

I will now write a few lines for Sally and Catharine.

"Tell sister Sally, Patty, brother Bibin, and all howda, howda . . ."

November 20, 1861
Winona, Carroll Co., Mississippi

Mr. John Hall
Columbus, Mississippi

My Dear Friend,

I wish to have a piece of land entered near me to keep off a man I and all of my neighbors are vastly opposed to. Please, if possible, let the receiver at the land office have some money enough to enter some eighty acres of land. It will take some forty-five or forty-eight dollars ($45.00 or $48.00).

Confederate bonds or Confederate notes will do. I presume that as you are well known even your note would do, or the common currency of the country. I hope it will put you to no inconvenience to make the above arrangement.

I have the honor to be your obedient servant,

Thomas A. Watkins

Rec'd $40.00 on above November 30, 1861 and $5.00 March 1, 1861, in all $45.00. F. G. Baldwin.

Dr. Thomas Alexander "Pa" Watkins

Sarah Epes Fitzgerald Watkins

Mollie Early Watkins McLemore and husband Jeff McLemore

Letitia Ann Watkins (Letty Walton) ca. 1853, age 16

Right: William Martin
Walton ca. 1853, 21 years
old; *below:* William Martin
Walton in his 20s.

Newton Samuel Walton ca. 1874, age about 18

Early Watkins Walton,
age about 17

George Longstreet Walton
ca. 1870, 10 years old

Sarah Walton ca. 1870, about 5-6 years old

From Mrs. Watkins to Lettie:

December 9, 1861
Winona, Mississippi

Mrs. L. A. Walton
Austin, Texas

My Dear Child,

My mind has been so burdened with work for the last month that I have neglected writing you longer than I ought to have done. Baby received your letter of the 15th ult. mentioning Newton being sick and Early's ear. I feel uneasy about them and I am very anxious to hear from them. I dreamed of suckling Newton a short time before Baby received your letter. He was very pale.

I am very glad Mr. Walton has not left you and the children to go off to war and hope he will not have to go. When I told your Pa that Mr. Walton was private secretary for the Governor he said, "That is better than Lettie breaking up in Texas" and moving here.

Mr. Hemingway's old man Prince was here yesterday. He told your Pa that Mrs. Hemingway told him to tell us that Mr. Walton was doorkeeper in the legislature. I did not see Prince, I would have sent word to Mrs. Hemingway that she was mistaken. We saw it mentioned in the Vicksburg Weekly Sun, last night, "Governor's private secretary W.—. Walton." I saw in another paper that he was assistant clerk in the legislature. Does Mr. Walton hold both offices?

Baby has had girls to stay with her for the last three or four weeks. She is alone today. She is ripping up a dress body to cut another body of a dress she is making. She has two calico dresses to make. I have one calico and one worsted to make. We gave fifty cents a yard for the calico. It is wider than common calico. We meet every Wednesday in Middleton yet. We have not had any work to do for the soldiers in several weeks except knitting. The next Wednesday every member has to report to the society how much work they have done. Last Wednesday, Sally Collins was elected secretary, Mrs. Phillips corresponding secretary, and Baby treasurer. You guessed very true about Baby. She writes to Jeff more frequently than to anyone else and gets letters from him oftener than she does from any other person. She pretends she don't love Jeff and when she receives a letter from him it always puts her in a fine humor.

Davy Turner that lives at John McLane's old place had a little daughter to die with croup a week tonight. The next night Mrs. Turner's sister Miss Clark was married to John Money of Carrollton. Mr. Parmele, Mrs. Parmele, and Mrs. Farmer dined with us a few weeks ago. Mrs. Parmele spoke of you and sent her love to you and was anxious to receive an answer to her letter to you. Octavia Merriwether came her father's two weeks ago and intends staying some time. I have not seen her. I heard her boy has red hair. Hardly anything is talked about except war and working for the soldiers. I would rejoice if peace could be made. I see no prospects of peace. Abram saw Mrs. Simmons in the stage on her way from Texas and going to her father's at Greenwood. She inquired of him about you. She thought you were here. Abram thought she would have called by here to see if you had been here. Abram said he thinks it was said Simmons had gone to war. I thought of Simmons' old coat you gave Salsbury. If she should call for it, Salsbury would have to produce it.

T. Jones intends moving shortly to the Tallahatchee swamp. There is no house on the place. He proposes hiring Mingo. We can't agree for Mingo to live in that swamp.

Isham Scruggs has bought the Wadlington place that Jones is living on.

It is so long since I wrote to you that you will expect a long letter. I wish I could, my dear beloved child, not disappoint you and write you a long letter. The times are so dull that I can't think of anything to write about. Your Pa said to me just now, who are you writing to? To Lettie? Tell her about Mrs. Hemingway sending us word about Mr. Walton being doorkeeper. He thought Prince made a mistake or Mrs. Hemingway didn't know what she was talking about. He said tell Lettie it is better to be a doorkeeper in the House of the Lord than to dwell in the tents of wickedness. I do not think he is as bitter towards you as he used to be. He speaks of you oftener and in a more affectionate way. Frequently he laughs about what you said and done when you were a child. I do want to see you and your family more than can be expressed and pray that we may be spared to meet again. Which of Mr. Watkins' son-in-laws is dead? Baby joins me in love to you, Mr. Walton and the children. Kiss the children for us and tell them to kiss you for us.

Uncle Vivion sends much love to you and says he knows you are on the right way to heaven. Hannah sends love to you. Becky has dysentery today. America has it but has not laid by for it yet. Martha had it all last week badly. Tell Aunt Sally and Catharine howdy. Jane is expecting to increase every day.

Write soon and often.

Your loving mother,
Sarah E. Watkins

P.S. I would syringe Early's ear with castile soap suds with a small syringe.

From Baby:

I began a letter to you last night but was too sleepy to finish and have been too busy today. If company does not come in I will send it off next Saturday. I have almost finished my eighth pair of socks for the soldiers.

January 12, 1862
Winona, Carroll County, Miss.

Mrs. Letitia A. Walton
Austin, Texas

My Dear Daughter,

Mr. Walton's proposition to "bury the hatchet" is accepted. There is no need of members of the same family being at variance. I would be pleased at any time to receive letters from you and Mr. Walton. Whenever it suits the convenience of you both, I would be glad to see you and your children: but "business first and pleasure afterwards" is my motto.

We are all well. No news but what you see in the papers. The weather is very warm and there is danger of much pork spoiling.

Your affectionate father,
Thos. A. Watkins

To Dr. Thomas A. Watkins from Lettie:

January 24, 1862
Austin, Texas

Doct. T. A. Watkins
Winona, Carroll Co., Miss.

My Dear Father,

Words can scarcely express my surprise and gratitude on the reception of your very kind letter of 12 inst. which was gladly received this morning. Accept many thanks for the contents of that letter. It has been a matter of rejoicing to me all day. I thank God that you once more feel kindly towards me and mine.

Nothing would give me more pleasure than to be with you all and I can assure you when time and opportunity will permit I will avail myself of your kind invitation and again mingle in scenes and association in which I have spent many of the happiest days of my life.

Father, I have been, to say the least, comparatively happy since I have resided in this State: but I must confess that a cloud as it were has hung over and in various ways—sometimes lightly at other times heavily, oppressed me because of your displeasure, and often time I have doubted the propriety of a child's disobediance to a Father under any circumstances and as often have I prayed that the light of your affection might scatter this, my only gloom, and we again be united in the happy family circle—thus bringing blessings upon you and your family and upon me and mine.

Permit me again, Father, to express my pleasure at the relations hereafter to exist between us.

So far the winter in Texas has been unprecedented both in dryness and warmth. It has not rained here for months and for most of the time we have had Spring like weather. As the crop-making rains as a rule fall here in winter and as the planting season is near at hand serious doubts are entertained for the well of the farmer during the present year.

My children have been sick with the epidemic sore throat with which many children have died in this City recently, but I am glad to say that my boys are all convalescent and I think soon they will be enjoying their usual good health. My own health is very good.

The present war has borne hard on Texas up to this time. She has lost some of her best most trusted and honored men. Terry Lubbock, McLeod, and Hemphill have all laid down their lives. The bodies of Judge [*John*] Hemphill[187] and Gen. [*Hugh*] McLeod[188] are now enroute for this City to receive in the sepulchre at the State [*Austin*] burial grounds. While we mourn their untimely death and deplore the country's loss, yet we know that they could not have fallen any more glorious, righteous cause.

Your friend Charles S. West is Secretary of State. He is a man of talent, ability and well deserves the position.

Mr. Walton desires me to say that he feels much gratified at your acceptance of his proposition to resume amicable and friendly relations and that he will take advantage of the first opportunity to so express himself to you.

I hope you will write to me often. Give my love to Mother and sister. Say to sister that her letter of 12th inst. was received this morning and will be answered soon.

> Your affectionate daughter,
> Lettie A. Walton

Will Walton writes directly to the doctor:

> Feb'y 4, 1862
> Austin, Texas

Doct. Thos. A. Watkins
Winona, Mississippi

My Dear Sir,

Your very kind letter under date of 12th ult. addressed to Mrs. Walton was received some days since. I had the pleasure of perusing it.

---

187. Judge John Hemphill had been a U.S. senator and chief justice of the Texas Supreme Court.

188. "General" Hugh McLeod was colonel, First Texas Infantry, CSA. He was possibly a general in the state militia.

The letter written by me to Mrs. Watkins several months ago was penned in sincerity and truth with the hearty desire that it might result in good, even in happiness to those who merited it. I mean sir, my wife, her parents and sister.

Need I say that I was gratified in a high degree, at the open, frank, and sincere manner of the acceptance on your part of the propositions made by me.

I trust that I may entertain that hope that nothing but *good* will spring from the peaceful relation between us.

It would not probably be profitable to recur to the past. With your consent let it be a sealed book between us. I shall live for the future, live toward and in new events, hoping however to be benefitted by experience.

The letter was the source of much joy to my wife. It is for what she has long hoped. She has written to you and did circumstances permit, would visit you in the spring: but of this I see no present prospect. The pending war together with the legislative action of this state in passing a "stay law"[189] have closed down on me very suddenly: but the war is in defense of principle and the action of the State for the anticipated security, benefit and advantage of the mass of her citizens. So I have no right to nor do I murmur at existing facts, still I am necessitated to greater economy than heretofore.

The general cotton crop of this state finds a market in Mexico. It is being transported there and disposed of for return cargos, of arms, munitions of war, and other articles of prime necessity for the use of the army, as well as to supply the wants of the people. The major part of the cotton is transported by railroad to the bay of Matagorda, thence down that bay and through the Bays, Espiritu Santo, Arkansas, and Corpus Christi and then the Laguna de la Madre, to the City of Brownsville, from whence, it is carried into Mexico by carts. By looking to the map and observing the southern coast you will see that we have all the advantages of an inland sea, from the east end of Matagorda Bay to the west end of the Laguna de la Madre. It is unapproachable by the enemy save through the passes, one at Powderhorn, one at Corpus Christi and still another at Brownsville. All these passes are fortified and believed to be impregnable to the blockaders.

The price paid for cotton, which keeps up this trade, ranges from eight to ten cents the pound, according to the distance of transportation to water communication. The better price being of course paid for the staple when

189. "Stay Law: An act suspending all laws for the collection of debts and liabilities on bonds, promissory notes, bills of exchange, and contracts for the payment of money until the 1st of day of January, 1864, or until six months after the close of the present war should it terminate before the date named, or otherwise provided by law." General Laws of the Ninth Legislature of the State of Texas [legislature met November 4, 1861, through January 14, 1862].

delivered nearest the Bay of Matagorda. The trade is a difficult and dangerous one, and is sustained in its present proportions only by the great necessity of procuring the needful articles before mentioned from that direction.

Individual traders engage in the trade also, incited by the prospect of amassing great gains. Staple goods are becoming very scarce, and as a consequence command enormous prices. While these traders demand the most unconscionable prices for their imported stuffs, yet, even at fabulous prices, they are a relief to the entire community.

Our beef cattle are being driven for market, to New Orleans, and to other points under contract, both army and private, thus throwing a good deal of money into circulation.

Much gloom was cast over the *minds and hearts of all* our patriotic men and women, by the news of our defeat at Somerset[190], and the death of the gallant [*Gen. Felix K.*] Zollicoffer. I say, "all our patriotic men and women" because we have an element amongst us which is neither southern in sentiment nor gladsome at heart when success attends the efforts of our brave men. I am sorry to make such an admission, but it is truth.[191] If as rigid measures were adopted as ought to be, perhaps these incipient traitors might be hindered from doing us at no future day a mass of injury. I have combatted them in every shape that my abilities will permit, so much so, that every unsound man and woman is my enemy. He who is not for us, is against us. He who is against us cannot and shall not, be on any other terms with me than those of enmity. The friendship of such persons brings ruin upon the true southern man.

The bodies of Judge Hemphill and General McLeod were buried on the 1st Inst. They lay in state at the Capitol [*Austin*] and were then buried with civil demonstrations and military honors. These men were staunch friends of the state and of the whole Confederacy.

I am happy to say that my wife and children are well at this time tho my children have all suffered from the sore throat which has been epidemic for some months and from which many children have died.

In conclusion I will say that if circumstances ever permit, I will take great pleasure in visiting you and your family. I know of nothing which would give me more pleasure but my affairs are so that they are absolutely necessary that every able bodied man shall take his place in the army. I fear that that time is fast approaching: when it comes, I have no choice. I must fill my place.

---

190. January 19, 1862, most commonly called Battle of Mill Springs, at Logan's Cross Roads, Kentucky; also called Battle of Fishing Creek and Beech Grove.

191. Anti–secessionists were active in various places in the South — even Texas.

My desire is to be there now, but, duty to my family has thus far kept me at home.

Receive sir my kindest wishes for your continued prosperity and health.

Letters from you will be received with pleasure. I shall at all times attempt to respond.

> I am sir with high respect
> Your friend,
> Wm. M. Walton

To Letitia Walton from Octavia Merriwether (Mrs. Charles Merriwether): [192]

> February 9, 1862
> Charleston, Mississippi

Mrs. W. M. Walton
Austin, Texas

My Dear Lettie,

Your ever kind letter reached me last week. It gave me both pain and pleasure. I know you think I have treated you badly and so I have but not to the extent you accused me of. Your last letter only remains unanswered, that not unanswered for I answered it and laid it away to mail it and neglected it. I do not blame you for the rebuke you gave me for I feel I deserve it. I should have written to you several times. Lettie, I am becoming too careless about letter writing since I have had a family, but I can assure you with sincerity I have never ceased to love you. I often think of you and talk to those who know you and even those who do not, about our love for each other. Lettie, I was sick in bed when your letter came and my poor Charlie was in the war. He returned the next day and don't you know I was rejoiced. Yes indeed I was for I had looked upon him almost as lost. He left here in a sixty day company as a private, pledging himself to stand by his friends in sickness and in health. But against all entreaties on his side, [*Gen. James L.*] Alcorn had him appointed surgeon of the regiment. From that time on he had a hard time of it. He was left at Union City, Kentucky with two hundred and forty sick men to take care of, and his company the only well company in the regiment, were ordered back to Columbus. The poor sick creatures were suffering from measles and pneumonia. He was ordered to take them from there to Jackson, TN as the enemy were supposed to be advancing, they were carried on open cars and

---

192. Octavia and Letitia were childhood friends and schoolmates in Carroll County.

in the rain. Several died before reaching Jackson and on reaching there in the night no arrangement had been made for them and they had to stay on the damp cold ground until next morning. The consequence was a good many died that day.

Charlie had a very valuable negro boy with him, one that he prized very highly on account of his faithfulness. He was among the sick and died in a few days after reaching Jackson. Two or three years ago he could have sold him for three thousand dollars. He was a splendid house carpenter. But I feel that we should be reconciled to any bad luck these times if we can only conquer in the end. Yet it looks very gloomy at present, having been whipped in last attempts. I hope though they will have nothing else to exult over soon.

Jimmy Smith was in the Fishing Creek Battle under Colonel [*Winfield S.*] Statham.[193] His regiment in battles in Tennessee you know did all the fighting. A good many of our Carroll County boys were killed or taken prisoner. Tom Booth, Phil Palmer, Hugh and Phil Freeman, George Weisinger, Tom Allen from Duck Hill and many others you do not know were missing, either killed or prisoners. John and Jimmy Binford, Jimmy and Charlie Campbell, Tom Collins, Jimmy Smith and many others fought through it without a scratch. Those who were left had to march eight days almost without food or clothing. Jimmy says they had to make up what little flour they had with them in their handkerchiefs. Poor creatures. They had a hard time of it. Oh, Lettie! What awful times we are passing through now, so different from what it was when we last saw each other. It is just as much as we can do here to get enough to eat. I feel thankful for anything to live on. Bread and meat is all we can get. I have been out of flour ever since September and don't expect to have any more until wheat comes in. At first it went very hard with me but now I feel we are doing well to live at all. Charlie could not collect ten dollars hardly to save his life when he went to the war. He had to borrow money to get clothing. I don't know whether times are as hard with you, Lettie, but they are awful here and still worse in the invaded States. Mississippi has called for ten thousand more troops. Charlie speaks of going again. Oh, how I dread his having to leave again, I suffered so much when he was gone, constantly dreading to hear for fear I would hear he had been killed, but thank God he has been spared to me. Oh Lettie no one knows but those who have had such trials, how dreadful it is. I hope your husband is still with you and will be able to

193. Fifteenth Regiment, Infantry. This regiment, 854 strong in December 1861, suffered 44 killed and 153 wounded at Fishing Creek, almost 25 percent of the command. (Rowland, *Military History of Mississippi*, 231.)

remain with you. This is a cruel, cruel uncalled for war and I hope it will fall severest on those who brought it about.

Your spoke of your children having sore throats. I hope ere this the little creatures are well. It is an awful disease, we had had it in our family and I have been uneasy for fear my precious little babe would have it but so far, Lettie, he has been very healthy and as fat as a pig. He is just a few days over five months and weighed over 18 pounds six weeks ago. I have not weighed him since. You directed your letter to Duck Hill. Pa sent it up to me but did not send those little shoes you sent. I am very much obliged to you for making them for my little boy and will get them home as soon as possible or I fear he will not be able to wear them, he has such a tremendous foot. And a red head, Lettie, I wish you could see him. In spite of his little red head you would say he is a fine looking little fellow. He is very fond of his Pa and will go from me anytime to his Pa who is so proud of him as a dog with two tails, some think him like me, others like Dr., and some like Mittie,[194] but I think him more like Tom than anyone else. Only he is prettier. Tommy says he is glad Sister thinks the baby like him because Sister used to think he was so ugly. He and Mittie and Read think there never was such a baby in the world. He has been sleeping a long time and has just woke up. He is so much company for me and a heap of trouble too. I don't know what will become of our poor little children. No one ought to grieve for the loss of little ones now.

I received a long letter from Aunt Ann last night. Her health is very bad. Also John's wife Sallie, she has three children. She is quick, isn't she? Oh, I wish I could see you. I would not tire for a long time talking to you and telling you all of my ups and downs. We all have them in this world. Give my love to Mr. Walton and a number of kisses to the little boys. I wish I could see them. I will close now. Lettie, don't think I love you less.

Your affectionate Occa

To Letitia Walton from Sarah Watkins:

February 24, 1862
Winona, Mississippi

Mrs. L. A. Walton
Austin, Texas

My Dear Child,

I received your very affectionate letter of the 23rd ult. the 4th inst. and would have answered it before this time if Baby had not written to you soon

194. Occa's sister; Read (Reid) and Tom are her brothers.

after its reception. It is gloomy times with us all in the neighborhood. I expect you have heard of the defeat of the Confederates at Fort Donelson after fighting hard four days.[195] Their loss is said to be twelve thousand.[196] Judge Drake and his company and Dan Russell's company were taken prisoners. Russell escaped by not being in the fight. He had his ankle hurt some weeks ago. He has returned to Carrollton to get up another regiment. Mr. George and Mr. Barnes, George Wellons, Robert Palmer and William Whitehead [*Mr. Edmunds Whitehead's son*], Judge Drake and Joe Gee are missing and thought to be taken prisoners. Eugene Whitehead was in Drake's company. He was at the hospital sick. I don't know what became of him. His brother William was with Russell's company. John Palmer was sick and has come home. I have not heard the name of any that were killed. General Acee[197] left here this morning. He is trying to get up a regiment. One of the soldiers that was captured at Fort Donelson got away by running and jumped on a boat as it was starting off. His name is [*Henry W.*] Williford, he lives near the plank road this side of Greenwood. I feel very much alarmed. I fear the federals will get here and deprive us of all we have. If they are successful in the next battle as they were in the last battles, the south had as well give up, I think.

We have had a very wet winter. The ground has not been in order to garden any. Peas are the only seed I have sown. Today is very pretty and the wind blowing it will dry the ground enough for me to have my other seeds sowed. I hope you received the four papers of cabbage seed I enclosed in my last letter to you. Your Pa received your letter to him last week and one from Mr. Walton Saturday night. Mr. Walton's reminded me of some of Baby's to Jeff as to size. She sews hers like a book. Laura Moore came here Saturday, she is with us yet. I expect Mrs. Moore and Mrs. Lay[198] tomorrow. Laura and Baby intend to commence teaching school this day week, Laura will teach for a family living above Grenada. Baby will teach at Mr. E. Whitehead's school

195. "Ft. Henry was so badly located it could not be defended . . . after the naval attack compelled the surrender of Ft. Henry of February 6, Drake and Hyman retreated to Ft. Donelson . . . the surrender followed and the regiment became prisoners of war . . . until exchanged. Nearly 100 died in military prison, mainly at Indianapolis . . . after the exchange, 279 of the Fourth were reported on duty at Ponchatoula, Louisiana, in October 1862 . . . in the latter part of November the regiment was transferred to Vicksburg." The combat was February 13–16. From Rowland, *Military History of Mississippi*, 159, 1803–98.

196. Estimates ranged from five thousand to twenty thousand. E. B. Long, *Civil War Day by Day* (Garden City: Doubleday, 1961), suggested that twelve thousand was probably the best bet.

197. No General Acee appears in roster of CSA. As early as 1856, Acee is identified in the letters as a general.

198. Mrs. J. T. Lay was Mrs. Moore's eldest daughter and married to a young businessman from Grenada.

house and walk from home every morning. I am glad that she will have something to make her get up early in the morning. She sits up late at night and
sleeps until nine or ten o'clock in the morning. She has breakfast carried in
her room every morning. Laura rode from her father's on horseback here and
caught Baby in bed asleep. (Mother is telling tales out of school.)[199]

Paten returned home Saturday. He has been in Virginia with Lynn Hemingway.[200] He says Lynn has re-enlisted. Since our sewing society has adjourned,
I seldom see anybody or hear any news. I believe nothing is thought or talked
of but the war. Goods are very scarce and dear. Change is so scarce that a
five dollar bill is cut in half to make two and a half dollars. We need some
articles for summer. We have no way to make money now, only by my selling
butter. Very little specie I get for it. The merchants in Carrollton sell their
goods for cash. Our cotton is ginned and baled and put away in the pickroom
of the gin house. Some of our negroes have been sick with sore throats. Tilla
has it now. I am very glad your children have recovered. I was uneasy about
them. I am very anxious to see you all and am afraid it will be a long time
before we will be together again. I pray God will protect us from the Yankees
and spare us to meet again. If we should not meet in this world let us try to
meet in heaven where parting will be no more. Sometimes I see Uncle Vivion.
He asks me when I heard from you. I tell him that you are well and he says,
"Thank God for that, bless my mistress." John Smith is the only one of the
servants hired out this year. He is hired to the same man that hired him last
year. There is some talk of Daniel and Polly marrying. Give my love to Mr.
Walton and the children. Kiss the children for me and tell them to kiss you
for me. Write soon and often. America sends love to you all. Tell Aunt Sally
and Catharine howdy.

Your loving mother,
Sarah E. Watkins

A note from Baby:

P.S. Mother has just asked me if I had a message to send. I at first thought
of nothing but after a little thinking, and seeing she had not filled this sheet, I
concluded to add little nonsense at any rate. Laura Moore is now paying us
her last visit for long months. Oh! lonely ones they will be to me without her.
What do you think of our teaching a school? A very good idea is it not. No
doubt we will make the finest teachers in the Southern confederacy. Oh! yes,
old gal, I know something about you, don't I.[201] Oh? Well give *it* a pretty name

199. Written by Mollie, the younger sister.
200. Paten is a slave who had, as many did, accompanied his young master to war.
201. Mollie teases her sister about a suspected pregnancy.

or after your Sister—Mollie—I wrote you quite a long letter last week and shall soon expect a reply—Pa received your very nice letter a few days ago. Well I believe that's all. My love to the family. Do write *soon* and a long letter too.

Your loving sister,
Mollie.

Laura and I commence teaching the first Monday in next month.

March 18, 1862
Winona, Carroll Co, Mississippi

Mrs. L. A. Walton
Austin, Texas
Dear Daughter,

I am in receipt of two letters from Mr. William Walton and one from you. I think it would be bad policy of you to break up housekeeping in Texas. Provisions are very scarce here and high and will continue to be so. Besides the enemy is at Corinth on Memphis and Charleston R.R. about 70 miles east of Memphis.[202] You must excuse this short letter as I am low spirited and in haste.

If the enemy comes much nearer I will take all my volatile negroes to Wood County, Texas. We are all well.

Your affectionate father,
Thos. A. Watkins

29th March 1862
Winona

Dr. Thos. A. Watkins at home
Dear Sir:

Your kind favor per servant enclosing two fifty dollar Miss. cotton notes is at hand and I regret exceedingly that they will not answer my purposes.

I hope that you will not think hard of me for not receiving it, they are of no practical use to me. I enclose and return them by the Servant.

Hoping that it will not be any disappointment to you, I remain your Friend and Obt. Servt,
W.W. Marshall

202. The doctor overstates. The enemy was moving south along the Tennessee River, but Corinth was still secure and would become CSA headquarters for the Battle of Shiloh.

Letter from Mrs. Watkins in Winona to Lettie:

March 31, 1862

Mrs. L. A. Walton
Austin, Texas

My Dear Child,

Before this you have been expecting an answer to your letters. Expecting you would be here by this I delayed writing you no longer than I should have done. We received your letter and nice presents that were sent by Judge Terrell, Saturday. We are very much obliged to you for them and prize them very highly. Judge Terrell did not come to see us. He gave the articles you sent to us to Dr. Moore who came on from Virginia with him. As we were going to Middleton Saturday to attend our sewing society we met Dr. Moore coming here to bring us the articles. He handed them to us and he went on to Carrollton, I expect he was so glad of an excuse to come here and was sorry to meet us. He said Judge Terrell spoke very highly of Mr. Walton. I would be delighted to have your and Mr. Walton's and the children's likeness. Baby has taken the ring from me, she insisted so much on wearing it that I could not refuse her. She takes everything that is mine, my watch, ink stand, pens, pencil, sometimes my thimble. She does not take care of anything.

We dined at Dr. Sykes's Saturday. Margaret Sykes had a very nice dinner. Mr. Conley's family is living with them. Mrs. Palmer, Octavia Palmer, and Mrs. Farmer dined there also. Mrs. Farmer came in our carriage to Mrs. Phillips'. Mrs. Parmele came to the carriage to see us. She inquired about you, so did Mrs. Farmer and said they were glad you were coming to see us. Mrs. Phillips was busy in her garden. Mr. Parmele expects to go off to war this week and also Mr. Arnold.

Hugh Freeman was wounded and taken prisoner at Somerset. He got away and came home last week. Phillip Freeman was wounded in his thigh and was confined to his bed when Hugh left him. The Yankees intended sending them north and Phil persuaded him to come off [*escape*]. Phil Palmer is with Phillip Freeman. Phillip Palmer is on parole and has a fine time visiting the girls [*paroled by the Union forces with the agreement that he would not rejoin the Confederate military*].[203] There are several secessionists living there and they are very kind to the prisoners.

Judge Whitehead and Mrs. Edmunds Whitehead have not heard from their sons since they were taken prisoners at Fort Donelson. Virginia Kennedy

---

203. The parole arrangement, a bit haphazard in function but more or less formal, continued until the latter part of the war.

[*Whitehead*] has a son, it is four weeks old next Wednesday. Mrs. Judge White-head had a daughter four weeks old Thursday.

Baby has written you about our teaching school. She is very fond of it. I think she will get tired of it after a while. She often wishes Newton and Early were here for her to teach them.

My garden is very backward. My peas look better than anything else. After so much wet weather it is now very dry and warm, fine weather for planting seed. Abram is called on to do so many other things that he has not much chance to work in the garden. He is fixing up the string to the cow bell in my room. It reminds me of the time Newton said, "Uncle Abram's foot does stink." Pentecost has gone to war. We have no overseer, Prince is put to look after the other negroes. I never thought my negroes would have a black grand devil as Prince is over them. It makes my blood boil, but I can't help myself. Else miscarried two weeks ago. Your Pa's health has improved. The war makes him low spirited. It is enough to make us all so. Unless the Lord assists us I think the South will be whipped. What do you think about it?

Baby and I are very anxious to see you and your family and were expecting you every day until we received your last letter saying you did not know when you would come. I am sorry Mr. Walton has to go to war and hope the Gov-ernor [*of Texas*] will insist on him not to go. Give my love to Mr. Walton and the children and kiss the children for me. Martha and America send love to you all. Martha says her child is smarter than yours. Write soon.

Your Loving Mother,
Sarah E. Watkins

To Letitia Walton, Austin, from Sarah Watkins, Carroll County:

April 13th, 1862
Winona, Mississippi

Mrs. L. A. Walton
Austin, Texas

My Dear Child,

Your welcome letter of the 29th ult. was received today. Baby and I have been anxiously expecting you and your family every day, that prevented me from answering your last letter. I wrote you first before its reception. I do not know the contents of your Pa's letter nor did not know he had written to you. I am very anxious to see you and your family. I think it best my dear child for you not to come until the times are more peaceable and provisions more plentiful as you have a comfortable home and provisions are plentiful in Texas. You will be happier at your own home than you would be here with us. Your Pa says provisions are scarce, very high, and hard for him to get. Political troubles disturb his mind so much that he could not bear the noise of children. He did not mean for me to write you what he said. He is opposed to your coming. That has caused me to write advising you not to come. It would be a great pleasure to me to have you and children with me if I had only had half a loaf I would willingly divide it with yours.

I am very much obliged to you for your kind invitation to go to your house if the Yankees should come near us. Your Pa says he will not move. It would be impossible for me to go unless he would too. I pray and trust in God that we will not have our property taken from us. I could not live without it. If I thought you would be more contented to be here while your husband is in the war, I would insist on your coming. I know you will be happier to be at your own home where your children can enjoy themselves better than if they were here. I feel very much for you, my beloved child, and wish you could be with me all the time. Before you receive this letter I expect you will hear of the battle 25 miles from Corinth. The confederates were victorious, Gen. [*Albert*] Sidney Johnson was killed.[204]

Bishop Greene came by here yesterday from Mrs. Phillips and went on to Carrollton in our carriage. He expected to preach at Carrollton but he had no congregation. Baby went with him. She returned and went to Col. Moore's. She will return home this evening. Old Mrs. Ludell and Mrs. Escrige, Martha Fox that was died lately. Maj. Hemphill, brother of old Mrs. Luddell died last week with sore throat. America has been sick most of the week with dysentery. She has sore throat today. The negroes frequently have it. My garden begins to look better. Give my love to Mr. Walton and the children. Kiss the children for me and tell them to kiss you for me. Ritter sends her love to you all. In my last letter I wrote about Prince[205] being put head over the hands. Don't write nothing about it in your letter to me. Your Pa might see it and he would not like it. Write soon and often.

Your Loving Mother,
Sarah E. Watkins

P.S. During the battle John Binford was pulling his pistol out of his belt, shot himself through the hand. James Binford heard that his brother was shot and attempted to go to him and struck himself against a man's bayonet and it stuck in him. Their wounds roiled them too much for them join in the fight. Mr. Jay was slightly shot in the thigh, he pulled the bullet out himself.

204. The Battle of Shiloh, April 6–7, 1862. The Confederates were victorious only on the first day; the fighting on the second day reversed the fortunes of both sides. The Confederates withdrew to Corinth, while the Federals massed strength at Pittsburg Landing, on the Tennessee River.
205. This is the same Prince who had run away in 1851.

Tom Booth was wounded. Tom Collins got lost from his Company and laid down behind a log, a Yankee came to him said he was his prisoner. Tom pretended to be wounded and said to him, "Oh don't make me get up, here take my gun." The Yankee was so intent to fire at the other soldiers that he went off from Tom. Tom waited until his company came up. He then joined his company and recharged up his gun.

CHAPTER NINE

"This looks ominous, don't it?"

Mary's beau, Jeff, daringly infiltrates Union lines and conducts a successful spying mission. Lettie thinks that Mary is actually in love with their cousin, Shaler, but that is a false suspicion: a love affair between Mary and Jeff is gestating.

A conscription act, which had been passed by the Confederate Congress, was approved by President Jefferson Davis on April 16, 1862. The law required three years of military service by all white males between ages eighteen and thirty-five. During the first year of the war, enlistments had been accepted for only ninety days, evidence of how brief many had expected the conflict to be. By September 1862, however, the draft age was raised to forty-five, and later, as the manpower shortage grew more serious, the draft ages were extended from seventeen to fifty.

The conflict seemed to be closing in upon the homeland of the Watkinses. One of the doctor's friends, John Hall, feeling safer in Columbus, Mississippi, offered the Watkins family sanctuary. They chose not to relocate, but Mary did go to Columbus for an extended visit. Following the fall of New Orleans, new constraints were imposed upon communications. Federal gunboats began patrolling the lower Mississippi River, and mail became erratic.

To Letitia Walton, Austin, from Dr. Thomas A. Watkins, Winona, Mississippi:

April 19th, 1862
Winona, Carroll Co., Miss.

Mrs. L. A. Walton
Austin, Texas

Your kind letter of 1st inst. just at hand—contents noted. I shall not move to Texas. If the enemy comes near here I shall take to that state some of my negroes—such as I can best trust.

We all would at any time be glad to see you all on a visit. I still think it bad policy to break up housekeeping in Texas. We are all well.

Your affectionate father,
Thos. A. Watkins

May 3, 1862
New Orleans [206]

Doct. Thos. A. Watkins
Winona, Mississippi

Dear Sir:

Yours of 22nd came to hand the 25th with contents noted. On the occupation of the City by the Federal Navy and Troops and to the absence of communication to the interior by rail or otherwise, we have not as yet attempted to procure the articles you order. Should we find an opportunity to forward the articles you want, we will send them, if possible to procure them. But we suppose that communication with the interior will not be permitted.

Yours truly,
Carroll Hoyt

June 21, 1862
Columbus, Mississippi

Dr. Thomas A. Watkins
Carrollton, Mississippi

My Dear Friend,

I send you this to let you know I paid $45.00 for the land I entered for you. Mr. Thomas Jones came through here and spent several days with me on his way to Corinth. He said that the Yankees had his father in custody some ten days and had his own plantation and servants. He left a mule with me to sell for him which I did for $140.00. I name it to you in case of death that I hold in

---

206. Bombardment of New Orleans began April 18, 1862; the forts surrendered April 28, 1862. Gen. Benjamin Butler officially took over the city May 1, 1862.

my hands $140.00, his money. I am uneasy for fear the Yankees might come down on you. I wish you could come and bring your family to my house and stay with me. I will give my house up to you and your family. They are fortifying this place. The Confederates are putting up immense works here, have already put good many. There are a great many wounded and sick soldiers here, some five or six thousand and many soldiers camped all around this place.[207]

The enemy went to Holly Springs a few days since and they killed General Bradford of that place.[208]

It is immensely dry here, I shall make no corn, peas, or potatoes. Bacon is selling at 50 cents here, butter one dollar a pound.

I am anxious to see you and have contemplated a pleasant visit to you this summer. Let me hear from you and let me know when you hear from my friend General Acee. I have not heard one word from him since he left here. My respects to your family and Mr. Helms and to Mr. Prince.

>Yours sincerely,
>John Hall

June 27, 1862
Winona, Mississippi

Mrs. L. A. Walton
Austin, Texas

My Dear Beloved Child:

I cannot express the joy it gave me to receive a letter from you yesterday of the fifth inst. It has been so long since I received a letter from you that I had come to the conclusion that we could not get letters from each other until the war ended. That prevented me from writing to you before this time.

I saw Mrs. Richard Whitehead last Sunday. She told me her husband wrote her the Indians were getting troublesome. He went to Texas last fall or winter for his health and has not returned to Mississippi yet. He has been very sick, he is attending the springs [*Thorpe Springs, near Granbury, Texas*] . . .

Mr. Parmele[209] was taken sick at Corinth and stayed there two weeks. He came home remained sick several weeks and died last Friday night. I attended

207. As it turned out, Columbus was indeed a relatively safe place. The town was never captured; hence, many of its antebellum structures still stand, spared from the flames that devastated other nearby towns. It was the Tombigbee River, however, that provided the real protection, not the fortifications.

208. No General Bradford killed at Holly Springs is identified in the CSA records. Perhaps he had a pre-war service.

209. Lt. James Parmele, whose son married Will and Lettie's daughter.

his burying last Sunday in Middleton. Mrs. Parmele's health is very bad with womb disease. Sam Wilson was killed in the battle at Chickahominy, Virginia [*Battle of the Seven Pines, May 31, 1862*]. Wm. Hamilton had three fingers on his left hand shot off.[210] Price McLemore was slightly wounded in the head. He fought on until his gun was struck and bursted and stunned him. Jeff had come to join a cavalry company. He heard Price was badly wounded and went to Virginia to see about him expecting to bring his corpse home. Price has nearly recovered. Jeff returned home last Saturday. He speaks of joining [*John Hunt*] Morgan. Six weeks tomorrow Mrs. Sam McLemore and Jeff spent the day here. Jeff was here the Saturday before. He brought Baby a pretty horn cup of his own make.

The Federals have possession of Memphis and Holly Springs and are trying to take Vicksburg.[211] The papers say many depredations were committed by them during their stay at Holly Springs. The growing crop of Judge Clayton was destroyed and his son taken prisoner. They had an engagement near Tallachatchee bridge. The Confederates whipped them back, seven Federals were killed and seven wounded. Two of the wounded were taken prisoners. Your Pa received a letter from Dr. Hall. He wrote that Tom Jones came to his house on his way to join the army. He told him the Federals had taken all his negroes and land and taken his father, Col. Dick Jones, prisoner. There are hospitals for the sick soldiers at Grenada and Winona. Several families near Winona have taken soldiers to their houses. I had a room prepared expecting some would come here but none came. I send buttermilk to those at Winona every Saturday. We were called on to send servants to Grenada to attend the hospital. Ned was sent in April, he stayed three weeks, was taken sick and sent home. He was taken with the mumps after he came home, several of the servants have them now. I expect they will go through the family. Ann and Hannah Missouri were carried to Grenada week before last to wash for the soldiers at the hospital for a month.[212]

Great many soldiers from above passed Winona Wednesday going down to

210. William Hamilton became sheriff of Carroll County from 1876 to 1884, principal of a college in Carrollton in 1898, and the author of a useful reference: *History of Carroll County*, 1905.

211. The Federals also now had Corinth, which the Confederates excavated on May 30, 1862.

212. The Confederate Army, short of manpower, impressed slaves for military labor. For example: a slave owned by W. W. Whitehead, "Twenty years old, 155 pounds, height 5'7", worth $3,000, conscripted March 24, 1864"; a slave owned by E. G. Whitehead, "Orange, 21 years old, 155 pounds, 5'6", value $3,000, March 24, 1864." From *Register of Slaves Impressed*, chap. 1, vol. 25, National Archives.

Vicksburg.[213] A fight is expected there. Gen. [*Earl*] Van Dorn has ordered the women and children to be carried out of the city. Mrs. Whitehead received a letter lately from her son William. He and Eugene were at Indianapolis as prisoners. His servant Joe was with him. Provisions and goods are very scarce and high and hard to be got here. I heard some people have no salt to salt their food. We have salt enough to last a while. We have meat, molasses, sugar, and coffee yet. I don't know what we will do for more when what we have gives out. We are using flour from wheat of our own raising. It makes very black flour. Our corn is promising and would be fine if we could have a plenty of rain which is very much needed. I have not got vegetables as plentiful as I would like to have them.

Susan has a boy nearly five weeks old, it is named Robert Moten. Mr. Parmele told his family that he saw Mr. Walton's brother at Corinth. He did not know his given name. He asked him where his brother was. He told him he was there. It must have been some other Walton he took to be Mr. Walton's brother. I thought it strange if Mr. Wm. Walton was there and he did not write to me and was sorry I had advised you not to come to Mississippi.

I wish very much we could be together. It would add very much to my happiness. If we can receive letters from you it will be a great comfort to me. I am very glad Mr. Walton has not left Texas and hope he will not have to leave the State so you can hear from him and be with him in case he should be sick. You say I must look on the bright side. Every side is dark to me. We are almost whipped. I put my trust in God, his will must be done. If the South is subdued it is the will of the Lord for it be done and we must be resigned to his will and trust in him to take care of us. I pray God will hear my prayers for you and your family and if we never see each other again in this world may we meet in heaven where parting will be no more.

Baby says she wishes she could stay with you. She is teaching school yet and gets on very well with it and is fond of teaching. She has not got a new bonnet nor dress this summer. I can't get her to go from home only to preaching at her school house. Tell Newton I am pleased to hear he is going to school. He must learn fast and be a smart boy. Baby joins me in love to you and the children. Kiss them for us.

Lynn Hemingway answered your letter. I did not send it to you as it was received since New Orleans was taken. Sam Hemingway is with Lynn in Virginia and has been very sick. I expect you received the last letters your Pa and I wrote you. I think in April or May. I would have written you often since

---

213. This letter was written June 27, 1862; at 2 A.M., June 28, Federal boats did run south past the Vicksburg batteries.

had I not thought it impossible for you to receive them as I had not received one from you since April.

Abram, Ritter, and America send love to you all. Polly Early and Sarah Jane say I must give their respects to Miss Lettie, Master Newton, Master Early, and Master George. Baby could not govern Charlotte. She put her in the field and took Lucinda.[214] Write soon and often.

Your Affectionate Mother,
Sarah E. Watkins

P.S. I have Frances [*Milly's daughter*] in the house. She sends howda to you and the children.

July 31, 1862
Winona, Mississippi

Mrs. L. A. Walton
Austin, Texas

My Dear Beloved Child:

Your very welcome letters of May and 29th of June were received last week and would have been answered immediately if Baby had not commenced a letter to you. I do not know whether she has sent it off as she went to Col. Moore's Tuesday to spend the week with Laura. She and I spent the day at Judge Collins' and she went to Col. Moore's in the evening. The day before we spent the day at Mrs. Hemingway's. Lynn was wounded in his shoulder in the battle at Chickahominy,[215] an ounce ball went in his shoulder and had not been taken out when his parents last heard from him and was not thought dangerous. Sam is with Lynn.[216] He has been sick most of the time Sam was at Mr. Elam's in Farmville. He wrote to his parents that Cousin Henry Watkins had been to see him and cousin Henry's grandmother sent him a bowl of strawberries. Margaret Ann is staying with her parents while Mr. Pleasants is in the war. He is in Virginia.

Baby and I spent last Friday at Mrs. Phillips'. Mrs. Parmele's health is still bad. She is very sad . . . she sits up in the chair half of the day. She told me to give her love to you and tell you you must write to her. She has not been able to write to you. She said she had rather see you than any relation she has.

---

214. Charlotte was able to thwart Mrs. Watkins and Mary and ultimately was removed from house duty and sent to the fields. Lucinda was Becky and Abram's daughter.

215. While this could have been on June 27 during the just-concluded Seven Day Campaign in Virginia, it more likely was on June 1, the Battle of Fair Oaks or Seven Pines.

216. Lynn Hemingway survived the war and later became state treasurer. Sam Hemingway, son of William Hemingway, died in the war.

Mrs. John Fox died two weeks ago. Henry Purnell and his daughter Eliza Alice (she married a Dr. Fitzgerald) died last month. Tom Purnell's tongue is paralyzed so much he can scarcely speak.

Richard Whitehead has returned from Texas looking well. He has bought land and speaks of moving to Texas next fall. Mrs. Edmunds Whitehead has just sent me a basket of peaches. I do wish you and your children had them. We have a few ripe soft peaches. We have had good rains in the last three weeks that has helped our crops very much. The drought had almost ruined them.

If the war continues I don't know what we will do for meat and salt another year. I have faith in the Lord that he will provide for us. Nothing hardly is talked about here but the war. I see no prospect of peace. I think the South will be badly used up before there is peace. I see from the paper that Col. Giddings of Carter's Texas Cavalry Brigade arrived at Munroe, Louisiana. It made me think Mr. Walton is in that company. I am very sorry if he has left Texas.[217] I feel very much for you and your dear children. I pray the Lord will spare him to return to his family again. Do not give up to grief my dear child. Try to bear with it and put your trust in the Lord. He will provide for you. I wish you were with us.

Last Sunday six weeks we were called on to send two women to Grenada to wash for the sick soldiers. Anna and Hannah Missouri were sent, Hannah was taken sick in two weeks after she left here and was almost dead before we heard she was sick. Your Pa went for her and had her brought home last Friday week. She died Monday week.[218] Anna had the mumps while there. Ned was sent there and he came home sick and brought the mumps. Every week since the negroes are coming in with the mumps. Mingo is sick and Charlotte with the fever. Mingo was very ill Sunday and Monday, he is better today.

Your Pa says I must tell you he would write to you but he does not write much now and he has no news to write you. He has been very unwell with diarrhea and a cold for four weeks. He is well and looking better.

Uncle Vivion sends his love to you and Aunt Sally and says you are on the straight road to heaven, that you must hold out faithful, and he hopes to meet you in heaven if he never sees you on earth again. Ritter and America send love to you and the children. Give my love to the children and kiss them for me. I want to see you very much and hope we will meet again. I wrote to you

217. He had left Texas and gone to Louisiana. His regiment was Company B, 21st Texas Cavalry, commanded by Carter and Giddings.

218. Hannah Missouri's death was the first ominous sign of the toll that fatigue and malnutrition was taking among the Negroes. As are the soldiers, they are being exposed to communicable diseases.

the 27th of June as I have received two letters from you since. I expect you have received mine.

We are out of envelopes and paper is getting scarce with us. We heard Miss Fanny Eggleston was very sick. Abram was sent to Mrs. Eggleston's to see how Fanny was. She was better. Mrs. Steven Eggleston told Abram to tell me to give her love to you when I wrote to you.

Write often. I am always anxious to hear from you all.

Your Loving Mother,
Sarah E. Watkins

August 18, 1862
Oxford, Mississippi

Doct. Thomas A. Watkins
Winona, Mississippi

Dear Cousin Thomas,

The man I employed as a substitute[219] failed to come so I am still in want of one. I would like to get the favor of you to see Townsend's clerk and say to him that I think that there is no chance for him and me to trade but I think he could get me a substitute with but little trouble. Say to him I will give $1,500 for one. He can get him as low as he can and keep the balance of the money.

I see by a Kentucky paper that Kentucky has named her quota of Lincoln's "call for 300,000 volunteers." This looks ominous, don't it? Our army which was at Baton Rouge has come up to Jackson and I understand are coming this way and I think I will wait until they come through here. It is my calculation to be at your house in about a week and take a trip over to Choctaw. I have written to ABC [*meaning not known*] over at Carrollton.

I see that the Yanks are fortified at Courtland [*Alabama*]. Mrs. J. Thompson and her mother are going to her place on the river to see if they can't bring off some of the negroes as it is believed that they are still on the place. Rather a hazardous adventure. I think the Yanks are destroying property to an unlimited extent in the Bottoms.

Very truly yours,
Your relative
Thos. H. Jones[220]

219. Refers to substitute for military service, a legal practice.
220. Col. Richard Jones of Courtland, Alabama, was married to a relative of Dr. Watkins's mother (they were Earlys). This Thomas Jones was Colonel Richard Jones's son.

August 30, 1862
Oxford, Mississippi

Thomas A. Watkins
Winona, Mississippi

Dear Cousin Thomas:

I did not call at your house as I expected. The cause was that I had employed a substitute above and was desirous of consumating the matter as soon as possible. He was accepted and I start home this evening via Columbus.

I have received several letters from home since I saw you but they were all of old date, the latest being the 29th of July. The Yanks had not up to that time done much harm in our neighborhood but since then I learned that they have been very destructive. Some five or six of my father's negroes had gone to the Yankees. Our cavalry had burned our cotton and while doing it burned my father's gin house and my press.

I think our prospects are brightening since I saw you if the reports about taking Nashville, Donaldson, and Clarksville are so.

I think this army of Van Dorn's will go north very soon.

I had to give a very high price for the substitute, $1,900.00.

Give my love to Cousin Sarah and Cousin Molly. I must bring my letter to a close on account of starting on the cars [*train*]. Will write you more fully soon.

Very truly,
Your relative
Thos. A. Jones

September 10, 1862
Winona, Mississippi

Mrs. L.A. Walton
Austin, Texas

My Dear Child,

Your very welcome letter of the 3rd ult. was received yesterday with delight to hear from you again. I do not know why you do not receive my letters and Baby wrote you a short time ago. Shaler Hillyer came here last Friday and insisted so much that Baby should go with him to Columbus to visit Judge Field's family and said his sister was very anxious for her to visit her. Baby went off with him Saturday morning to Winona and left at night on the car for Columbus. She expects to stay a month. Henry Hillyer and Dr. Tom Field were here about four weeks ago. Henry wanted Baby to go with him to Judge

Field's [*Mrs. Field is Dr. Watkins's niece*]. Her excuse was her wardrobe was not nice enough. I will be uneasy about her until she returns to me. Shaler is quartermaster in the army. Henry assists him.

Baby expects to have a nice time. Shaler told her he was going to Lagrange, Georgia and carry Mrs. Bacon and Jane Reece to Judge Field's. Dr. Bacon and Mr. Todd's oldest sons were killed at battle in Virginia.[221] Lynn Hemingway has been home for four weeks and speaks of going back soon. He was wounded in his left shoulder. The ball has not been taken out. He can't use his hand much. He looks very well. He spent a day with us week before last and would have come here Saturday with Captain Stanley[222] who was wounded in the arm the same time Lynn was if Baby had not gone away. In my last letter to you I told you of Mr. Parmele's death and Hannah Missouri. I expect you have received my letter by this time.

Mrs. Jenkins died last month. We have a great deal of sickness with our negroes. Nine sick, some with chills and some with the fevers, four with risings. Polly's Moses was sick nearly four weeks and died Monday week. Jane was very low several weeks with the fever. She is recovering. Harry Ann and Hannah had to wait on her all the time. Hannah is staying with her yet. Times are very hard here. Everything is very high. Meat can't be bought. We have very little bacon, none to give the negroes. We have to kill a beef for them every week and feed them on molasses. We will not raise meat enough for next year. We made about 30 bushels of wheat that is not used up yet. We have made the coffee hold out by using potatoes with it. We have plenty of sugar yet. I have not preserved anything but tomatoes and peaches. It was not convenient for me to have any peaches dried.

Cousin Tom Jones stayed several days with us last month. He left the army on account of sickness and employed a substitute. Major Neill's two daughters were here at the same time, they stayed two weeks. They are living at Major Hawkins'. Amanda is going to school in Middleton.

We are making salt from the dirt of the floor of the smoke house. We have made about a bushel of nice salt. Your Pa thinks he will make two barrels of salt.

I am very glad Mr. Walton has not crossed the river [*Mississippi*] and you have it in your power to hear from him. I feel very much uneasy for him and always remember him in my prayers. I am surprised about your saying you were cold hearted and loved but few. My dear child, that is not a Christian spirit. We are commanded to love everybody. You must try to love your enemies and pray for them if you want the Lord to be merciful to you. Baby is

221. Second Manassas, August 29–30, 1862.
222. Probably James S. Standley. See letter, June 3, 1861.

very cold hearted, she cares for very few people. Sometimes I doubt her love for me. I think you love me more than she does and treated me with more respect when you were a girl than she does.

I do wish the war would end and let us have the pleasure of being together again. I am very anxious to see you all. I am sorry Catharine is so trifling and wish you would sell Catharine and buy one to suit you.

Dr. Hall left here this day week. He stayed over a week with us. He has altered in his looks. He has a long white goatee and moustache and sits about the house as much as ever. He said every person he's heard speak of Mr. Walton spoke well of him. He said he saw Mrs. Stringer who told him you boarded with her. She spoke very well of you and Mr. Walton.

Give my love to Newton and Early. Kiss all the children for me and tell them to kiss you every day for me. Ritter, America and Frances send love to you all. Your Pa is looking well. Write soon and often. Is Jane Watkins in Alabama yet?

> Your loving mother,
> Sarah E. Watkins

> September 21, 1826
> Gerenton, Mississippi

Dr. Watkins

Dear Sir;

I send you the boy Jack. My price for building the chimney is 50 cents a foot for single and 75 cents for double chimneys. I hope the price and boy will suit you.

> Yours truly,
> John D. McLemore [*Jeff's father*]

> October 7, 1862
> Winona, Mississippi

Mrs. L. A. Walton
Austin, Texas

My Dear Beloved Child,

Your affectionate and highly appreciated letter of the 1st ult. was received last Saturday week. It seems useless for me to write to you as I have written you frequently since April and you have not received not one of my letters. I hope you have received some of them by this as I received one from you Saturday that was written the 26th of April.

I wish I could write you cheerful letters. The dreadful war keeps us gloomy. Nothing is talked about but the war. My sympathy for Mrs. Hemingway has made me feel very sad the last two days. She received news Saturday that her son Sam was killed on the battlefield at Sharpsburg, Maryland.[223] It made her very sick, she had spasms Saturday. The family thought she would die. I went to see her Sunday evening and set up with her the last part of the night. She was better yesterday morning. I sent Semira over this morning to see how she was and to carry her a piece of light bread. She is better this morning. Mr. Hemingway sent me word that Lynn telegraphed home that Sam was not killed but badly wounded and the same surgeon had him in charge that attended him when he was wounded. Mr. Hemingway has not told Mrs. Hemingway that Sam was not killed for fear that it might make her worse if the report is not true about his not being killed. Lynn started Friday as soon as he heard that Sam was wounded to go to him. He expected to start tomorrow night to Virginia to join his company again. He has not recovered from his wound. It is healing up, he can't use his hand much yet. Frank Liddell was wounded badly and taken prisoner. Baby went with Shaler Hillyer 6th of September to Judge Field's in Columbus. She wrote us that she will be home the 11th of this month. I am so lonely. I am glad the time is near for her to come home.

In my letters to you I mentioned the deaths of several of our acquaintances. Mr. James Parmele and Mrs. Jenkins. Mrs. Parmele said she had rather see you than anybody she knew and sent a message to you, I can't remember it now. She said you must write to her. Her health is very bad and she is the saddest looking person I ever saw. I have not seen or heard from any of the family lately as I have been at home very closely for several weeks. We have had so much sickness with our negroes this summer and some are yet sick. Hannah Missouri died in June, Polly's Moses, Jane's infant and Louisa have died in the last five weeks. Jane has been at the point of death. She is well all to weakness. Bob had a child by Susan and he could not get along well with her father and mother. He parted from her. Anna and Washington are always quarreling and fighting. Times are hard. We can't buy any meat and have not more than one shoulder and one middling. The rats are worse in eating the meat this year and destroyed more for us than they ever have done. A beef is killed every week, but that is not enough to last all the week. The negroes have a plenty of molasses given them every week. When the molasses is gone I can't tell when we can get more. Our hogs have died mightily this year. We will not raise meat enough for next year and we will have to kill some as soon as the weather is cold enough. I never felt as warm weather in October as we have this month. We have sugar, flour and coffee yet. I make enough butter for my family but have not made enough to sell for some time. Now everything sells

---

223. Battle at Sharpsburg, Maryland, September 17, 1862—the bloodiest single day in all American military history.

high, butter sells for less. We have been making salt from the dirt dug out of the smoke house floor. We have made nearly a barrel full and expect to make more. Henry Echols was shocked with a shell at the battle of Iuca lately.[224] He is at Mr. Freeman's. His wife is in Arkansas. I heard that Phil Freeman had gone for her. Phil Freeman was one of the exchanged prisoners. He has lately come home. He and Hugh were wounded and taken prisoners at the Battle of Fishing Creek.[225] Hugh made his escape as soon as he was able and came home. Mrs. T. Jones died last Saturday with a congestive chill. Her corpse was buried at Mr. Hemingway's graveyard yesterday. Her Rose died a month ago with a congestive chill. Mr. Jones moved his family to a swamp last winter. Mr. and Mrs. Whitehead have gone to see Lizzie [*Elizabeth Oliver in Alabama*]. William and his servant came home after he was exchanged [*William Whitehead*]. He stayed only a few days and went to Jackson to join his company. Their old woman Hannah died Saturday with congestive chill. Martha is not in a condition to weave. I have put Semira to weaving that the negroes may have clothes before the winter is gone. We have to buy their shirting and give 60 cents a yard for towels. I can't get any nice shoes nor stockings nor calicos. Abram has gone to day to bring me a pair of shoes from the tan yard. Your Pa went to Vaiden last evening. He is not returned yet. When I wrote to you some months ago he told me to tell you that he would write to you if he had any news to write, that I would write you all the news.

I wish my dear child we could be together. It would be a great source of happiness to us both. Let us pray faithfully to God. I hope he will bless us to meet again with peace and happiness. Tongue cannot express my feeling and love for you and your family. I pray God will hear my prayers for you all. I am anxious to hear from Mr. Walton and dread to hear of his being in battle. I pray God will be his shield and deliver him from danger. Give my love to the children and kiss them for me. Tell them to kiss you every day for me. How does Newton get on at school? Tell him he must be a good boy and learn fast. Tell Aunt Sally and Catharine howda. Semira, America, Ritter and Francis send their love to you all. Francis and Lucinda are sitting in here knitting. They keep so much talking I can't write correctly. They keep me scolding at them to make them hush. I had to put Lucinda on the other side of the room to prevent their disturbing me. Baby changed Charlotte for Lucinda. She had to whip Charlotte. She has never whipped Lucinda. Write often and soon. I'm always anxious to hear from you.

Your loving mother,
Sarah E. Watkins

224. Battle of Iuca, September 19, 1862.
225. Somerset, Kentucky, January 19, 1862.

October 12, 1862
Columbus, Mississippi

Dr. T. A. Watkins
Carrollton, Mississippi

Very Dear Father,

A few days since Dr. Hall gave me a hundred dollars ($100.00) to take home to you and I now write to know if it would not be well to use it in paying my expenses here and bearing my expenses from here home.

Please write immediately and tell me as there is a great probability of my returning home the last of next week. I am very anxious to see you all and I think I shall never leave you for so long a time again.

I went last night to see Mrs. Colonel Billups. My resemblance to mother was to her so apparent that it recalled the days of her girlhood and caused her to almost shed tears. She could not realize that mother wore spectacles and caps and possessed an older appearance than herself. She seemed to love to talk about you and mother. I enjoyed my visit to her immensely and will try to go again to see her. She looks no older than Mrs. Edmunds Whitehead.

It is now quite cool here though not cold enough to require winter apparel.

Aunt Jane wrote Cousin Eben that she was having chills and fever. Cousin Eben has been conscripted.

The people here are expecting the arrival of the Federals in a short time. They are making arrangements to throw up entrenchments in the middle of the town which I regard as being perfectly useless. Mother not writing to me is very wounding to my feelings; how I would appreciate a letter from her.

My love to her, Mama and all of the servants. Write very soon my dear Pa to

Your Loving Daughter,
Mary E. Watkins

October 1862 [not dated]
Columbus, Mississippi

Mrs. L. A. Walton
Austin, Texas

My Own Sweet Sister,

A few weeks since I received a letter (22nd of Aug.) from my dear Brother, requesting or rather begging me to write to you and enclose the letter in an envelope addressed to Captain W. H. Russell at Vicksburg. I immediately wrote to Brother and also to you which epistles I hope have reached their place of destination. Mr. Walton wrote me from Pine Bluff, Arkansas. His letter was so affectionate, so interesting and so highly appreciated that it was with the greatest delight I replied to it. I left home last month (11th ult.) under Cousin Shaler Hillyer's care (and arrived here the next day) with the intention of returning home after an absence of six or eight weeks, but after the Confederate defeat at Corinth[226] it was thought that the government works here would induce the Federals to attack this place; therefore it was reported that a force of 150,000 strong was marching for this place which report reached Pa's ears, whereupon, he concluded to come after me, with a baggage wagon and the carriage and arrived here today. So I will leave for home tomorrow morning after spending a most delightful time.

Cousin Emily and Judge Fields have contributed every way in their power to my happiness. Although I am anxious to get home, yet I am really sorry Pa came for me as Cousin Shaler would have taken me himself in a few weeks and I anticipated such a nice trip with him. Oh! How I do wish he wasn't my cousin. He seems to love me a great deal which I am sure is more than reciprocated. I received quite a cool letter from Jeff today in reply to one in which I expressed great admiration for Cousin Shaler. Sam McLemore was wounded, captured and paroled at Jackson, Tennessee and long since. He is now at home. Sam Hemingway was killed at the Battle of Sharpsburg,[227] also Colonel Frank Liddell of Carrollton, Colonel Drake's son was shot in the jaw. Lynn Hemingway was wounded at the Battle of Seven Pines[228] and came home for a short time, spent a day with us before I left. He and Captain Standley were to have called me on the very day I left.

J. Sam Nelson was killed at the Battle of Seven Pines, also Aunt Emily Todd's eldest son Fontleroy.

Phil Palmer was wounded at the Battle of Corinth. Poor fellow, he has had a rough time of it.

Polly's little Moses, Hannah Missouri, Jane's baby and Louisa have died within the past three months. Mingo's wife Rose is also dead.

Mr. James Parmele died a few months ago. Mrs. Parmele could scarcely survive her loss. How much that family is to be pitied.

I have gotten me a beautiful drab colored silk bonnet trimmed with blue, cost $14.00. A brown and white silk, made gored, trimmed with large blue cord; a lavender colored berage, five flounces, bound with green silk, puffed sleeves and body, trimmed to correspond with the silk, and a black berage with four colored flounces are the dresses which I purchased this fall. Do wish you could see them, they are so pretty.

You must miss Mr. Walton so much. My dear Sister, words are inadequate

226. Battle of Corinth, October 3–4, 1862.
227. Sharpsburg, September 17, 1862.
228. Battle of Seven Pines, May 31, 1862.

to express my sympathy for you. Would that you and yours were with us, but let us not dispair. "He doth all things well," and time may yet bring us together.

How is Newton getting on at school? Tell him to learn fast and write me the first letter he attempts to write. I have a good many plans laid off for his improvement which I intend carrying into execution after the war is over. Bless his dear heart, no one knows how much his Aunt loves him. Teach them to call me "Aunt" without the Mary or Molly.

I expect to send this letter by a Mr. Carrington from Austin. He is here but will leave in a few days for Texas. I do wish I could go with him.

Pa's health is excellent and he is looking better than he has for a long time. He seemed so glad to see me.

Cousin Emily is expecting to be confined every day. I am very glad; she will not be before I leave. Her only child is a girl ten years old.

Aunt Jane has four sons in the army and soon will have five. Cousin George is Captain of a Company. Cousin Shaler is quartermaster, stationed at Canton. Carlton is in the quartermaster department and Cousin Eben has some office but I don't know what.

I received a letter from Cousin Frank Watkins in which he sent his love to you and stated that Cousin Henry was ward master in a hospital in Lynchburg, not by any means a very desirable situation.

Joe Davis was wounded in the Battle of Chickahominy and died in a month afterwards, also Plez Peoples. Price McLemore was wounded but would not give up until his gun was shattered in his hand.

Oh! I am so thankful that Jeff was not in any of the engagements. He is a member of Captain Scales's Company and Colonel Stark's. (In Captain Scales's company and Colonel Stark's cavalry regiment and he is now in Bolivar County, Mississippi.)

How I do wish, my sweet one, that I could write more, and I would do so but having no fire in my room feel very cold and I am tired from packing my trunks and besides it is nearly twelve o'clock and I will have to rise very early in the morning.

Oh! May God's greatest and richest blessings rest upon you and each of your family. Give my love to Mr. Walton and kiss the children for me. Write when you can to

Your devoted Sister,
Mollie

P.S. Mother has received five letters from you since the fall of New Orleans. We write you very frequently but have no idea that you receive our letters. Good night, sweet darling.

November 4, 1862
Winona, Mississippi

Mrs. Lettie A. Walton
Austin, Texas

My Dear Child,

I am very glad to hear from your letter of the 28th of September that you had received two of my letters and hope you will receive the others that I have written you. I am sorry Galveston[229] is captured and I am afraid it will prevent us from receiving letters from each other. Baby returned home from Columbus yesterday two weeks. She received a letter from Mr. Walton with two of yours to him enclosed in it. She wrote to you from Columbus and sent it by a gentleman. I have not received a letter from Mr. Walton, would like very much to hear from him. I am all alone. Baby went to Mrs. Eggleston's this day week. She intended visiting Mr. Helm's family. I expect her home this evening. Your Pa went to Mr. Robinson's yesterday. Expects to be gone two or three days. I can't remember the last time we had no sickness with our servants. Seven are sick and Susan has a rising on her foot. Martha thinks she is in labor. Wash, Moses, and Van Buren are recovering from the fever. Van can't sit up yet. Your Pa and several others have sent their wagons to Lake Bisto towards Vicksburg for salt. I feel uneasy until Salsbury gets back for fear the Yankees will take him.

Miss Fanny Eggleston and her aunt Mrs. Jones came to see us this day three weeks and stayed until the next Saturday. They sent their love to you. Miss Fanny's hair came out from having fever. She had it shingled off and she is getting gray. Mrs. Parmele has gone to a doctor in Macon, Georgia. Mrs. Farmer went with her. I think I wrote you that Sam Hemingway was killed in battle at Sharpsburg and Frank Liddell was wounded. He has since died. Price McLemore has received a flesh wound in the arm. Mr. Atlas Johnson died last week. Sally Collins was married two weeks ago at 11 o'clock in the morning to Dr. Dauny. He has a plantation in the swamp. She is his fourth wife. His third wife was such a drunkard, he got a divorce from her. She is living in Texas.

We have made a very good corn crop, I don't know what we will do for meat another year. We kill two hogs a week. That is all the meat we have for ourselves and negroes to eat. I have a few chickens and not many turkeys. Shoes and clothing are hard to be got. I am having my ground peas dug. I wish Newton and Early were here to eat them. I do wish the war would end so I could see you and your dear children. I pray God will spare us to meet

---

229. A premature observation. Galveston fell October 15, 1863.

again. Give my love to the children and kiss them for me. Write soon and often. Tell Aunt Sally and Catharine howda.

Your loving mother,

Sarah E. Watkins

P.S. Letter is very short. I have no news to write. My pen is so bad I can scarcely make it mark.

P.S. November 5—I spent another lonely night. My letter is so short, I left it unclosed expecting Baby would come home and fill this page. Martha had a large daughter this morning. Semira sends her love to you and says I must tell you she has named Martha's child Laura. Patty and Ritter and Martha send love to you all. Patty says kiss your boys for her. Martha says Jeff is larger than your son George. Jeff is a spritely child but tall and slim. He has had chills most all this Fall. Else's Epes is quite sick with a cold. Monday he seemed to be choked with phlegm. I gave him an emetic. He has fever and can't speak out of a whisper. I hope he is not dangerous.

November [*not dated*] 1862

Winona, Mississippi

My Dear Sister,

Mother received your welcome missive of the 21st a few days since. Words are inadequate to express our delight in learning your intention of visiting us . . .

Pa says, "It is best for you to remain in Texas as far as escaping the Yankees for weeks. But if you come this must be your home until Spring when it will be time enough for you to look elsewhere for a home." Oh! Sister please come. Things here are not molested by Federals. To have you with us will be one of our greatest consolations, my parents and your society, I believe it would prolong Mother's life a good many years. It would relieve her of the greatest anxiety which she continually feels for you. If you do come which I pray will be the case it will afford me the greatest pleasure to teach Newton and Early thereby saving this expense of sending them to school. I wish you could have seen the negroes' joy when I told them you were coming. Mamma[230] was in one of her angry tantrums and when she heard your intentions she seemed to cool down immediately and exclaimed, "Thank God my chile coming . . ." Mother thinks she would take $16.00 for Catharine and Aunt Sal and bring Denmark and Lizzie whether they want to come or not. Pack up and come before the roads get too bad.

John Purnell died last week of colic and Wm. McCain of a congestive

230. A senior slave woman who had been Lettie's baby nurse.

chill. Jeff is now at home. I went last Friday to Miss Givens burying, he was there. I haven't seen him since. Mrs. John McLean told Dr. Ward he told Jeff that the reason Laura Moore and I were so intimate was Laura thought she would marry Price and I thought I would marry Jeff. Jeff told me about it. I reached home a few days ago from a visit to Mrs. Eggleston's of a week's duration. I went to see old Mrs. Mead, Mr. Helms, Mrs. Harriet Eggleston and Mrs. Dr. Jones and Mrs. Sessions. Everywhere I went everybody inquired and seemed interested about you. It made me like them so much more. Margaret Pleasants and Wilson Hemingway spent last Wednesday here. We enjoyed their visit very much. Meady Eggleston and Sophia Dabney went with me to Mrs. Helms'. Mr. Helms is in the army, belongs to Berry Prince's cavalry company. Mrs. Prince has lost four of her oldest children this year. She is now in Claiborne County.

While in Columbus, I wrote you two letters, one of which I enclosed as directed by Mr. Walton to Capt. Russell in Vicksburg, and the other I sent by a Mr. Carrington which lives in Austin. Have you received either of them?

Mother and I expect to attend the Baptist Association in Middleton tomorrow. I intend knitting a yarn shirt for Mr. Walton as soon as I have the material spun. I now have Lou and Fanny picking up rabbit fur which mixed with wool or cotton will make beautiful socks. Today I dyed some cotton a right pretty scarlet with poke berries, crab apples and alum. I am going to have it spun and crochet Jeff a bridle which will be bordered with black. Mother says she has received two letters from you this month and would have answered the first but just had written you when it was received and the last one she would also reply to but I have written. She sends much love to you and a kiss to the children. Charlotte, Tave, Lou, Fanny, Letty, send "a heap of love" and say do make haste to come. They want to see you mighty bad. Martha has a fine daughter named Laura.

I expect to spend next week with Occa Palmer, return her visit to me last November 1861. I can think of nothing else but your coming. Oh! Sister I do want to see you so much. My happiness would be almost complete if you all could be here. Pa has sent Salsbury to Lake Bistineau in company with some of Mr. Freeman's and Judge Whitehead's negroes for the purpose of making salt. Phil Freeman went with them, he having been so wounded at Fishing Creek as to render him so unfit for military service as to procure a discharge.

As I have to write to Cousin Shaler Hillyer tonight, I must close.

November 29, 1862
Canton, Mississippi

Dr. T. A. Watkins
Winona Station

Dear Uncle,

I got through my business at Durant this evening and came straight on to Canton, the train waiting for me at the former place. I have just seen the proprietors of the "Dixie works."

They request me to state that they will give you $100.00 per month for six negro men including the blacksmith and the striker and the two carpenters and two fieldhands averaging all at $16.66 a piece.[231] They are to board them and you clothe them. This they inform me is what they are paying and as provisions are so high, I suppose it is pretty fair wages, better at any rate than their doing nothing. Says you can take them away whenever you wish to. Be sure if you accept this proposition to add on one more boy to hire to me at $18.50. I will also buy six good mules. You might let the boys ride them to Canton, saving railroad fare. If they are good mules, I will give $200.00 for them. If you accept, manage to get here by Wednesday.

Yours,
Shaler [232]

December 1, 1862
Winona, Carroll Co., Mississippi

Mrs. Wm. M. Walton
Austin, Texas

Much Loved Sister:

I replied to yours of the 30th Oct. on the 19th of last month but have not yet received a reply to my letter. As I have an opportunity of sending this letter by hand to Texas, I will write again tonight which mother would do if she could see how to write by candlelight.

Pa rode out this evening and met a gentleman, Lt. Murry, from Texas who belongs to General Kirby Smith's command and who, being on his way, has kindly offered to take this letter.

We heard this morning that the Yankees were at Grenada. Mother was cutting out the negroes clothes and the news so alarmed her she became sick turned pale and could scarcely finish her cutting. Fanny went to the mailbox

---

231. The price offered, $16.66 a man per month, is a useful index as to slave labor value in late 1862.

232. Shaler Hillyer, the son of Dr. Watkins's sister, in the Confederate quartermaster corps.

and brought a confused account of Jeff's being in the Yankee's camp which, with the above news, excited me no little! That about Jeff turned out to be nothing more than his disguising himself as a Federal and going as a spy in their camps and obtaining a great deal of important information which with the news of the Federals being at Grenada were false reports. You can imagine our happiness and composure tonight compared to the turmoil and excitement that prevailed today. Pa started to Carrollton and on hearing the above mentioned news, turned back, came home and began preparations to start tomorrow with Big Simon, Isham, Bob, Jake, Dickson, Jane, Frank, Daniel, Mingo, Washington, Dick and Annie to Canton, Georgia or West Point, Alabama. We do not know how long he will be absent. The war has afflicted his mind considerably. His eyes have a very unnatural expression. Don't mention this in your letters. We so much wish all we had were in Texas. Pa regrets not having moved there this Fall. Oh! How we wish you were with us. From your last letter we can but hope that you will come as soon as possible. Though we think you will be much safer in Texas than here. Innumerable families are now moving or have moved to that state, numbers having left Holly Springs and vicinity.

A few days ago while I was at Colonel Moore's, I received a note from Cousin Shaler Hillyer stating that he was at the hotel and if the carriage wasn't in town, he would hire a conveyance and go out home with me. I replied that the carriage wasn't there so he got a hack and we came home. He spent the night here and left in the morning. He is very handsome and one of the best men I ever saw. He seems to love me so much but only as a cousin.

Price McLemore was wounded in the Battle of Sharpsburg and he is now at home. Laura is much grieved at his not visiting her. I heard the other day that Colonel McLemore had told Jeff to return my letters and ask for his letters and ambrotype [*photograph*] but I don't believe it.

It is now reported that 5,000 Federal cavalry, having crossed at Helena, Arkansas were in seven miles of Grenada. We may expect them any time down here. Mother is in a great dilemma as to where she will hide her money. I have no money but my greatest treasures are a horn cup beautifully carved which Jeff made while in winter quarters at Dumfries [*Virginia*] and his gold badge [*fraternity pin*]. The former I will bury and the latter I will break the pin off and swallow. What do you think of my plans?

Prince is quite sick with rheumatism. Pa sent Salsbury in company with Mr. Freeman's, Judge Whitehead's, and Mr. E. G. Whitehead's negroes to Lake Bistineau, Louisiana after salt. They returned last Friday after an absence of four weeks. Pa's mules look dreadfully, also Salsbury who was sick all the time he was gone and now by no means well.

Pa sent for seven sacks but got only four which with the traveling expenses cost him over $200.00. The above mentioned gentlemen (except Mr. Freeman) sent their money by Alex McCarroll who was to have gone on, bought the salt, had the sacks all filled and everything ready by the time the wagons got there but through some mistake went to different salt works from the wagons. He has bought salt where he is but cannot get it here. It was thought for some time that he had run off with the money. I am glad it was not so.

While at Colonel Moore's I visited the hospital at Winona and had the pleasure of relieving the wants of several poor sick Texans and Missourians by carrying them a broiled chicken, sweet and butter milk, preserves and biscuits, etc. though Pa has prohibited my going in the wards. I intend going to the doors tomorrow or the next day and carry them some other little luxuries. They seem to be so grateful for the least attention paid them by the ladies. I saw one of them, a Texan, dying last Saturday. They are dying very rapidly. Oh! It is a sad sight to behold. They look so badly and so sad, would that it were in my power to relieve them and comfort them.

John and Green Bledsoe spent yesterday week with us. John Bledsoe belongs to Wall's Legion.[233] He was sick and came to his brother's. He married a widow, formerly a Miss Justice and niece of Mrs. John Glass. He looks dreadfully. The march from Texas to Holly Springs made him and many others sick and killed several. One or two died as soon as they reached Vicksburg. A great many that are in the hospital are from Freestone County, Texas.

My hair was so thin and not very long, that I have had it cut off. It is not more than a finger long. I now wear it back with a round comb. Cousin Shaler thought it very becoming. Mother speaks of cutting hers.

John Purnell died of colic a few weeks ago. Also William McCain of congestive chill.

As soon as Lucinda heard that John Bledsoe was from Texas she exclaimed in a most anxious tone, "Oh! I do wonder if he can tell me anything about my sweet mistress and marse Newton!"

The negroes seem to sympathize with you a great deal and are constantly inquiring about you.

I have written all I could think of. I write you repeatedly but never receive a reply—guess you do not get my letters. Mother, Pa and the negroes send love. Mother says she will write soon if the Yankees don't come and destroy her. Do, dear sister, write soon. It would afford me so much pleasure to receive a letter from you. My love to Mr. Walton and the dear children.

Lovingly your sister,
Molly W.

233. Col. T. N. Waul's Texas Legion.

To Lettie from Mollie:

December 15, 1862

Much Loved Sister:

Yesterday for the first time in many months I was pleased with one of your long expected eagerly perused letters . . . I wrote you quite a long letter several weeks ago and sent it by Lieutenant Murry of Kerby Smith's division who was on his way to Texas. In it I mentioned Pa's intention of removing some of his negroes which he did the morning after I wrote. He carried them to Shelby County, Alabama, and hired them on the Northern and Southern Alabama Railroad. Daniel hired for $300.00. I have never witnessed as much distress and so many tears as was shown and shed the morning they left. There was not a dry eye on the place, even the negro men cried like children.

Pa returned home last night after an absence of two weeks. He said parting with the negroes liked to have killed him and he has not recovered from its effect. They are hired for 12 months, will not come home until 11th of next December, 1863. Prince would have gone too, but near the time for Pa's departure he was suddenly attacked by a violent rheumatism and was not able to turn himself in bed and required Else and Hannah's attendance all of the time Pa was absent. His legs and hands and shoulders were immensely swollen. He now is able to walk to the fields with the assistance of a stick. I can't help believing a little of it was feigned because he seriously objected to leaving home.

I wrote and informed Cousin Shaler of Pa's absence, and as soon as his business permitted he came to see us but couldn't spend one night. How I do wish you knew him. He is so pious, so conscientious, so noble, so handsome and ever respected as perfect that you could not help loving him. After my dear Brother [*her brother-in-law, Will*], I love him better than any gentleman I have ever seen. He is as far superior to Jeff as the heavens are above the earth. No, Sister, Jeff and I are not engaged nor will ever be. I still retain the same affection for him that I ever had, which was but friendship. I once regarded him as my true friend, and one in whom I placed the most implicit confidence. I think he does not love as of yore, his letters are small, seldom, and continually grow colder . . . so they may continue, for I am almost too misanthropic which has been increased by him to grieve for the loss of any man's love. No indeed not I—the Jackasses may just go for ought it concerns me. He spent several days at home last week but did not deign to visit me.

Willie Whitehead [*son of E. G. Whitehead*] died last week in Vicksburg of a congestive chill. Mrs. Whitehead was with him only three days before his death. She was informed of his illness and went down immediately and came home with his corpse last Saturday morning. He was buried by torch light. Tom Purnell died about the same time. He with paralysis.

The week before last Jeff went as a spy into the Federal camp, claiming to be a citizen and wishing to purchase salt. By some means he was detected and imprisoned for a day and a half when he made his escape by riding a night and half day over the distance of a hundred miles and killing two mules in so doing. He says he suffered himself to be captured in order to obtain more information. His achievement proved to be of great value to Generals [*Earl*] Van Dorn and [*John C.*] Pemberton for it gave a good deal of important information. No doubt he thinks it was the most wonderful, greatest act of the war . . .

. . . The negroes of this vicinity seem to know all about the Yankees but are as submissive and respectful as ever. I do not think we have one at home now that would follow them. I have heard of some of Mr. Whitehead's expressing their determination to go the first opportunity . . .

Pa has the blues most dreadfully, looks pale and retchedly, has been inside all day. I can't bear to see him, it makes me feel dreadfully. Mother and I take great pride in telling Pa of Mr. Walton's heroic and daring deeds. He is a man that anyone may be proud to claim as a relative.

P.S.: 17th

I neglected sending my letter today and as it is such a pleasure to write to you, I will scribble off a few more lines. Ritt fell down today and knocked her leg out of place, but it slipped back again. It was very much swollen and she is unable to walk.

Mother and I spent today at Mr. Whitehead's. He was very sad and has been sick for the past two weeks. Mrs. Whitehead was very much distressed, looked dreadfully, has changed a good deal in her appearance.

Jenny Kennedy's two children are very smart and pretty. Her youngest is named Thomas Benjamin . . .

To Letitia Walton from Sarah Watkins:

December 25th, 1862
Winona, Mississippi

My Dear Child:

I received your affectionate letter of the 7th Inst. last evening and one of the 19th recently. I would have written you before this if Baby had not written you twice lately and wrote all the news. She wrote you that I received a letter from Mr. Walton on the 17th about the contents of his letter. I was very glad to hear from him. He was in Clarendon, Arkansas.

We are spending a lonesome Christmas morning. Not even the servants are merry. Jesse, Moses and Ned are at Grenada working on the fortifications. Your Pa carried several of his men and Jane and Anna to Alabama and hired them on the North and South railroad. The Yankees took off negroes in Yalobusha. I heard some of cousin Powell's went off with them. I am uneasy fearing the Federals will get here. They destroy as they go. News came to Winona yesterday that Van Dorn had'taken fifteen hundred prisoners at Holly Springs and destroyed several of their government stores. I hope the news is true.[234]

Mr. Walton wrote that he left it to you to decide whether you would come to Mississippi or not, that he would rather you should be with us in case he should be killed. He said he could not come with you but would have friends to come with you to Vicksburg. Now the Yankee gunboats are there. You could not cross the river on that account with safety. I don't know what way you could come not to be molested by the Yankees. It would be great pleasure to me, my dear child, for us to be together. I do not know what to advise you to do. Provisions, clothing, and everything is very hard to get in this county. I don't know what we all are to do for meat. The hogs have died, a great many with cholera. If our army is whipped up above or falls back to Jackson, this part of the State will be taken. At this time I think you are safer in Texas than you would be here.

Your Pa read your letter, he noticed what you said in regard to him. He did not like it, he said you went off without his consent, he said he still thinks you are better off in Texas than you would be here. I am sorry I showed him your letter. I have showed him all of them for some time. He speaks more affectionately of you and cares more to hear from you than he used to do. When you write to me don't say nothing about my writing to you that he did not like it. Keep friendly with him. It will add to my happiness and yours too.

Salsbury has been back three or four weeks and brought us four sacks of salt. He was sick and looked very badly when he came back. He has recovered. Prince is suffering with rheumatism. Susan is sick with headache. Polly had a son last Friday night. Daniel is the father to it. His wife has been living in Carrollton part of this year and he visited her every week. Ritter scoured out my room this day week and was carrying out the tub. Her foot slipped and she fell with her weight on her lame leg and crippled her so she can't walk without a crutch. She is confined to her house but able to sew. I miss

---

234. On December 20, 1862, General Van Dorn's forces successfully raided the Federal forces at Holly Springs and took approximately 1,500 prisoners. Mrs. U. S. Grant, though not herself taken into custody, was in Holly Springs at the time.

her very much. Martha has to attend to Ritt's business and that hinders her from weaving. Semira can weave some but has to do the spinning. America was sick last week and apart from this, she is up now.

Wm. Whitehead died today two weeks with congestion of the brain in Vicksburg. Mrs. Whitehead went to see him. He just did not know her. She was with him two days before he died. Mr. Whitehead was sick and could not go with her. His corpse was brought up and buried at his father's last Saturday night week. I spent this day week with Mrs. Edmunds Whitehead. She is very much distressed. Baby called on Eppe Oliver the same day. She said Mrs. Parmele was looking better. You ought to write to Mrs. Parmele. She is a true friend to you and would appreciate a letter from you very much.

I rejoice to hear you are enjoying religion and pray you may continue to enjoy such a great blessing. It is the greatest comfort anyone can have in any situation they are placed in. I try to live as a Christian and wish I enjoyed religion more than I do. Pray for me, my dear child, that I may make my way to heaven and if we never meet again in this world we may meet in heaven where parting will be no more. I do want to see you and your children more than can be expressed.

Becky nor none of the servants have professed religion. Abram has been having chills a week. Baby joins me in love to you and the children. Kiss them for us. Tell Newton I am pleased to hear he is going to school and learning fast. Tell Early he must learn his book too and be a smart boy. Tell Aunt Sallie and Charlotte howda. Martha and America send love to you all.

Write soon and often.

> Your Loving Mother,
> Sarah E. Watkins

> January 12, 1863
> Austin, Texas

My Sweet Sister:

. . . Sister, what on earth is the matter with you and Jeff. You want me to tell you? Well, you love Cousin Shaler. You did not desire to do so but have, I expect grown cold toward Jeff and unintentionally manifested such a feeling (coldness) in your letters to Jeff and he thinks you do not care for him. Take my advice, don't follow Laura Moore's example. If you have ceased to love him, let him know it. If you still love him, wait for him to make the first advances, and if he comes to his senses again and visits you, treat him as though nothing had happened. But Sister, never stoop to living man (except Pa, of course).

Perhaps Jeff's head is a little swelled after performing that great act of going in disguise into the Abolitionist ranks. If it was swelled, one should have no more to do with him ... Sister, I am opposed to cousins marrying cousins. Watch out. Don't let Cousin Shaler steal your heart. Give my love to him and tell him I love him from your description of him ...

> Your devoted Sister,
> Lettie

March 20, 1863
Winona, Mississippi

Miss Lettie A. Walton
Austin, Texas

My Dear Child,

... The Federals came down in two or three miles of Greenwood Wednesday week and commenced shelling the fort called Pemberton that has lately been put up. They came through Yazoo Pass, Coldwater and Tallahatchee rivers with the intention of going on to Vicksburg this way. Our guns have prevented their passing the fort yet. The enemy has twenty seven transports and two boiler clad and two iron clad boats. It is said that our guns have disabled one or two of their boats. Three men were killed in the fort by a ball exploding and struck the ammunition boxes.[235] If they do not succeed in passing the fort I have no idea what they will do. The high water between here and Greenwood will prevent their getting here just now ... If they take Vicksburg we are gone, if they do not succeed I think that will be the turning point in our favor.

... Judge Palmer was taken sick last Saturday night two weeks and died Sunday at ten or eleven o'clock. He was buried in Middleton Tuesday evening.

... I have had so much hindrance from sickness with my weaving that I have not finished giving winter clothes to all yet and now it is time to commence summer clothes. I will have to have all the clothes woven at home. We are having another loom made; Semira will weave on one and Martha on the other ...

Martha's baby was taken with spasms, Thursday two weeks and had them until the next Wednesday. The first day it had twelve and had them through the night, the next days and nights. It had a great many. Calomel and pink root was given it. Ned cupped it. A blister was drawn on the back of its neck. The spasms left after the blister drawed. She did not seem to be sick only when the fits came on. She has not been as lively since. America will be as great a nodder as Sally. She has just taken her seat to knit. I looked around and she is asleep. Ritter is able to walk without her crutch, sitting constantly

---

235. Fort Pemberton, near Greenwood, successfully blocked the Yankee attempt to push past on March 11, 1863.

has made her fleshy. For a week she has taken exercise attending to the fowls and trimming the rose bushes . . .

> Your loving mother,
> Sarah E. Watkins

From Mollie to Lettie:

> April 13, 1863
> Geronton,
> Carroll Co., Mississippi

Dear Darling Sister:

. . . I am at Major Hawkins' employed as governess. My reason for taking this situation is to obtain some means of assisting the poor and one or two other charitable purposes. I am perfectly delighted with the situation, came here the second week of February and will remain until the second of July. The family seems devoted to me. I am fond of teaching and have comparatively no trouble with any pupils. Mrs. Simmons brought Mittie yesterday to commence school today. She is a very obedient sweet little girl and will be quite a fine looking lady. Miss Occa wrote to you five days ago. She was here three weeks since and talked a great deal about you. She did not bring her baby. She and Read came on horseback. Last Friday two weeks, Mary E. and Alice Davis came to see Retta Nutall (cousin of Major Hawkins) and me, remained until Sunday evening when Retta, Mrs. Martin Purnell and I accompanied them home on horseback, but returned that eve and Martin spent the night here, last Friday week. He came over in the carriage with us to Mr. Davis' where we remained until Saturday evening, which day we attended a fish fry and had a delightful time. Willy Hamilton was my escort. Last Thursday night Willy and Martin came here and remained until 11 o'clock. The next evening, Retta, Martin, Willy, Eliza and Emma Hamilton went home with me. The two first named went in our carriage and remained until yesterday morning. The others remained until Saturday evening.

I think I have written you of Jeff and my engagement. He addressed me by letter Wednesday the 21st of January . . . I answered in the affirmative. I never had anything of this kind to frighten me as much as this did. I almost idolize Jeff but I'm afraid I am not worthy of him, think perhaps he is mistaken in me and some day will be so disappointed in me. We will not marry until the War ends. He is now with Van Dorn.[236] I have read five letters from him since he left which was in February. His health is dreadful, he has been sick ever since he left. He was opposed to my teaching and requested me not to stop wearing

---

236. Jeff is now a sergeant in G. C. Wood's Co., 28th Regiment of Mississippi Cavalry. He enlisted at Jackson, July 15, 1863, for three years.

hoops, or cut off my hair, the last of which I have done . . . and wear it with a comb. I wish you knew him, "to see him is to love him."

Everyone believes we are engaged, but I carry on with other gentlemen and I do all I can to convince them of the contrary.

(16 April) I have just heard of Van Dorn's defeat at Franklin, Kentucky [*Tennessee*] and am uneasy about Jeff. Oh I shall be so wretched until I hear from him. . . . Pa was absent while I was at home. He had gone in search of meat. If not successful, he intends carrying more of his negroes to Alabama. Dick, Ned, and Moses are now at Greenwood working on the fortifications. The Yankees seem at last convinced of the impossibility of passing that place and have at last left. It is impossible to number the depravations they committed on the Yazoo and Tallahatchie Rivers. They took nearly all of Maj. Hawkin's cows, burned several of his negro cabins, his gin house and carried off five of his best mules.

(April 21) Not having any ink is the cause of my not finishing this. There is to be quarterly meeting at Gerenton this Friday, Saturday and Sunday. Retta and I will attend the dinner at Mrs. Kendall's. Mother will be down Sunday. It is supposed by many that Willy Hamilton has or will address me. Although I believe he loves me, he will never attempt such a thing. Mr. Purnell told me yesterday that he thought Jeff and I were engaged and was somewhat under the impression that I would flirt. Jeff and they being such intimate friends, he had a great notion of acting a friendly part and informing him of my intentions. I positively denied any engagement existing between us, I intend telling Jeff of the whole circumstances . . .

May 6th—I have not had time before this evening to finish this letter. Last Saturday, Retta and I went to Mr. Davis' and remained until Sunday evening.

Abe Davis rode with Retta, and Willy H. with me. We were on horseback. While on the way here Willy addressed me. I, of course, will discard him but have not yet given him an answer but will do so the first good opportunity.

Martha Jane Gary died last Sunday from childbirth. She left three little girls. Phil Palmer and Alice Davis are very much pleased with each other. Frank Campbell had all of his fingers on the right hand except the fourth and thumb and most of his right hand shot off in the firing in Franklin, Tennessee. Hernando Money and Maj. E. P. Jones were taken prisoner. The latter was seriously wounded. Lynn [*Hemingway*] was examined by the medical board in Carrollton four weeks ago and sent to Brookhaven. Not having heard from him I fear he was captured by the Feds during their recent raid in that vicinity and destruction of that place. He is unfit for military service and I think it was cruel to send him there.

> . . . your loving sister,
> Mollie

CHAPTER TEN

"I am afraid Mississippi will be gone"

Between the previous letter, from Mollie on April 13, 1863, and the ensuing one, from Sarah, June 11, 1863, there occurred the battles of Port Gibson, Raymond, the fall of Jackson, Champion's Hill, and the commencement of the siege of Vicksburg. But—despite the bitter reality of Vicksburg's fall on July 4, 1863, and the subsequent extension of Federal control along all of the Mississippi River—family life moved on. Occasional attempts were made bravely to continue at least a modicum of social life. The mails between Mississippi and Texas, however, were much constrained, and the volume of correspondence between Austin and Carroll County noticeably decreased. The family seized every opportunity it could to impose upon each traveller heading west to carry a letter or two. On October 7, 1863, Jeff proposed marriage to Mary. Her response was a "yes," and Jeff secured furlough, so the wedding could take place while he was home on Christmas leave.

The doctor, obviously stressed, worried, and seeking to regain control over his affairs, fretted about having hired some of the Watkinses' slaves to his nephew, Shaler Hillyer, who himself had become a major in the Confederate quartermaster service. But the Confederate army's ever-increasing needs continued to make escalating demands on the planters, and the doctor strove mightily to comply. Too, he tried to oblige his friends, who knew that he stacked his ice house each winter, and also that he sometimes was a generous man. The doctor also corresponded with his elder son-in-law about the serious question of the welfare of the doctor's grandchildren, should Will be killed in the war.

It was not Will, however, but Jeff who sustained a wound in combat. Jeff was shot during the Battle of Ezra Church, near Atlanta, Georgia, on July 28, 1864. In August, Mollie went to him. The doctor, needing money to help pay for her trip, tried to secure payment from the South and North Alabama Railroad, to which he had hired out several of his slaves. But skyrocketing inflation was eroding the value of all Confederate money.

The war ran to its unhappy—and bitter, from the southerners' perspective—end. But, for the Watkins family, a far more tragic event also accompanied the downfall of the Confederacy. Mrs. Watkins became deathly ill and died in late March 1865.

To Lettie from Sarah Watkins:

June 11, 1863
Winona, Mississippi

Mrs. L. A. Walton
Austin, Texas

My Dear Child:

It has been so long a time since we received a letter from you that I thought it useless to write you. I heard a few days ago that there is a direct mail by Natchez and on to Little Rock that induced me to write you hoping my letter will reach you. Baby said she wrote you a long letter lately. She is at Major Hawkins teaching school and enjoys herself finely. She comes home every two or thee weeks. Her school will be out the 12th of July. She says she will not teach again. I think she will be so lonesome staying at home alone that she will change her mind and continue to teach. She is so much pleased with Major and Mrs. Hawkins.

When I wrote you last, the Federals were at Greenwood. Our army whipped them away. The Federals on their return from Greenwood destroyed some things on the plantations on the river [*Yazoo River*]. Major Hawkins had brought most all his negroes from the river. The few he left did not go with the Yankees. They burnt his gin house and took off some of his mules. Dr. Ewing's and Major Neill's negroes had been brought away. They took off Greenwood Sharkey's fine furniture and took him prisoner and carried him to Helena, Arkansas.

Mrs. Sharkey had lost her baby a short time before that. They attempted to dig it up. She told them the first one that stuck a spade in that grave, she would shoot them. So I heard. They came up with some of their boats as far as Mr. Southworth's lately. Mrs. and Mrs. Southworth were away from home. They ordered the negroes to get breakfast for them. Next morning they came out on their boats to wash and Captain Morgan fired on them, killed some, and that frightened them and they put back down the river. They were trying to destroy our steamboats and our government stores at Greenwood. Some of the boats had been sunk to prevent their coming. The Governor had wagons impressed to haul the government stores from Greenwood to Winona. Our team has been hauling two weeks or more. The Federals took Jackson last month, they did not keep it. They burned Green's factory and the penitentiary and some other houses and sacked Bishop Green's house.

There was a fight at Big Black Bridge. Eugene Whitehead is missing, it is not known whether he was killed or captured. The Yankees have taken one hundred and forty of Berry Prince's negroes. They took two hundred and forty of Col. McGee's. He is a very rich man living in Boliver County. He has forty-three negroes left. He is carrying them to Georgia. The Yankees uniformed and armed his negroes and forced them off.

They are trying very hard to get Vicksburg, and if they do I am afraid Mississippi will be gone. Your Pa often wishes he had moved to Texas last fall. We can't get there now. He frequently wishes you were with us. The gloves you gave him—he brought them to me last week and asked if I had not better put them away. I told him the moths might eat them and he had better keep them. He said when he looked at them sometimes it almost made him cry. Don't mention it when you write to me. I don't want him to know I wrote you about what he said.

I am so tired of this dreadful war, I do wish peace could be made. It is distressing to be parted from you and your children, it makes it more so not getting letters from you. I am always uneasy about Mr. Walton and would like very much to hear from him.

The crops and gardens have needed rain very much. Night before last and yesterday we had a good rain which will benefit my garden very much.

Your Pa went up in some of the northern counties of Mississippi and bought flour, lard, and some meat. He was not far from the Yankee lines.

I am expecting Mrs. Whitehead and Lizzie Oliver to see me this week. Lizzie has fallen off very much. She has just weaned her child. She came very unexpectedly to her father's the last of April. Nancy [*slave at Simmons's plantation*] came to see Semira Saturday week, she said Mr. Simmon's family were well, Octavia is staying at her father's. I have not seen her. Nancy says Octavia wrote to you by Tom Pender and expects him to bring her an answer to her letter from you.

The Baptists had a meeting at the Whitehead school house last Sunday week. Mrs. Green Bledsoe saw Baby. She said to me Mary [*Baby*] is not as pretty as Lettie. She looks courser. She said she ought not to say it to me. She thought you very pretty.

The mules are so busy plowing, I have not been from home lately nor seen anyone only at church. The war makes we old people low-spirited. Most of the young ones I have seen are cheerful, particularly Baby. As Jeff has gone on to Vicksburg, I expect it will make her sad.

As usual, some of the negroes are sick. Becky, Tilla, Tom, and Moses. Moses was taken with chill and fever. He has pains and swelling in his legs and feet that prevents him from walking. Semira is in the family way and Else is expecting to be confined.

I had Irish potatoes for dinner today as large as small eggs. I am so anxious to see you and the children. I fear we will never see each other as long as the war lasts. Give my love to the children and kiss them for me. Give my love to Mr. Walton when you write to him and tell him I will always be glad to hear from him. Ritter and America send their love to you all. Ritt is lame yet and most always something the matter with her. America was sick all last week with diarrhea. She is as tender a plant as ever.

Write soon and often. I am always anxious to hear from you and your family.

Your Loving Mother,
Sarah E. Watkins

From Mollie's suitor, Jeff McLemore:

October 7, 1863
Camp near Clinton, Miss.

Dear Miss Mollie,

You will no doubt be greatly astonished at receiving this style of a letter from me. (I would not have written such a month ago.) You know I have always combatted the policy of marrying during the present unhappy condition of our oppressed and bleeding country and could not at that time be induced to believe this war could possibly long continue. I can at this time see no possible chance of its closing for a considerable time—I was opposed to marrying now because I thought it might in some way lessen one's ardor to serve in the field when everyone's strength should be exerting themselves to their utmost to advance our cause. I have since learned to look upon it in a different light. I can see no reason why a married man can't make as good if not a better soldier than a single one for if he has the proper love for his wife he will strive to do his duty so as to make his officers to give a good report to her of him.

Enough of this . . . I know a patriot will let neither something nor another prevent him doing his duty when called upon. My object in writing this letter is to persuade you to consent to terminate our engagement by being joined in wedlock sometime between this and Christmas or soon as I can get furlough for that purpose. I understand I can very easily obtain one for fifty or sixty days for that purpose. If we could see any possible chance for this unholy war to cease within any reasonable time I should not object to waiting. From present indications it may last from three to seven years.[237]

Another reason for not wishing to postpone it any longer than necessary is I know not at what time I might be taken very ill and might accidentally receive a wound and then it would be such a *great pleasure* to have you near me. So it is now you would feel a delicacy in even calling on me much less would you think of staying with me. I have never mentioned it to your father. You told me you had informed your mother of our engagement and she of course told your father. It is not at all in the regular mode of asking a father through the daughter, but owing to circumstances I shall have to request you to hand this note in your letter to the Dr. You can read it before delivering. My father is opposed to marriages at this time but will raise no serious objection of anything of the kind I might do and even if he should I am old enough to act for myself and in such cases intend to do so. *Do give me an answer to this as soon as possible.*

My regards to Miss Retta.[238]

> Yours and
> Very affectionately,
> J. H. McLemore

Soldier's Furlough

To All Whom It May Concern:

The Bearer hereof J. W. McLemore, a Sergeant of Captain G. C. Woods's Company, 28th Regiment of Mississippi Volunteers, Cavalry, age 23 years, 5 feet 7 inches high, born in County of Yalobusha, Miss. and enlisted at Jackson, in the State of Mississippi on the 15th of July, 1862 to serve a period of three years is hereby permitted to go to Carrollton in the County of Carroll, State of Mississippi, he having received a Furlough from the 1st day of December 1863 to the 10 day of January, 1864 at which period he will rejoin his

---

237. This remarkably tenacious attitude in the face of the severe adversity that Confederate soldiers in the western theater had faced by this point in the war is impressive—even amazing!

238. Mollie's friend at Major Hawkins's. She was a Hawkins relative, a "refugee" from Corinth, Mississippi.

Company at Camp Raymond, Mississippi or wherever it may be or be considered a deserter.

Give under my hand, at Camp Raymond, Mississippi
21st day of Nov. 1863
G. C. Woods Capt. Co. B. 28th Miss. Regiment

January 8, 1864
Winona, Carroll County, Miss.

Maj. S. Hillyer
Selma, Alabama

My Dear Nephew:

As there is no writing between us concerning the hire of my negroes, I wish you would send me some instrument of writing stating the terms upon which they were hired. They commenced with you on 29th last October. For John you were to give forty dollars, for Martha twenty-five dollars each per month. All to be fed at your expense. All to have clothes at government prices. The expense of the clothing is to be paid by me at above rates. Pay must be made me monthly. I know you are much pressed for time but I hope you can answer this letter or just endorse it and forward it back to me by mail . . .

Your affectionate uncle,
Thos. A. Watkins

Jeff's new mother-in-law reports to Letitia:

January 9, 1864
Winona, Mississippi

Mrs. L. A. Walton
Austin, Texas

I received your letter of the 22nd of Oct. last week and your letters of the 20th and 30th of November last evening. It gave me unspeakable pleasure to hear from you and your sweet children and to hear Mr. Walton has recovered his health. Baby received a letter from him last month written in November with two of your letters to him enclosed in it. We are always glad to receive letters from him and would write to him if our letters could be conveyed to him.

Baby was married to Mr. Jeff H. McLemore the 23rd of December. There were about forty people invited to the wedding. We had a nice supper. Mrs. Phillips assisted me in preparing for it. You know everything was nice if she managed it. Baby was married in the same tarlton dress that she wore when she waited on Ellen Moore. She tried but could not get a new dress. We wished very much you could have been here. Baby and Jeff left here the next morning. She went in a buggy with Jeff to Col. McLemore's. Ritt and her trunk were carried in our carriage.

Mary Elisa Davis was married the night after Baby to Mr. Robert Perkins, a nephew of Col. McLemore's. Mary Elisa Davis and Mr. Perkins waited on Baby and Jeff, and the next night Baby and Jeff waited on them. Ritter went to wait on Baby at Mary Elisa Davis' wedding. I attended the dining given them at Col. McLemore's Christmas day. Baby and Jeff returned here Thursday week and left here last Wednesday. Jeff wrote to you while he was there. They are very loving and make as free before each other as if they had been married a long time. He has but one week more to stay with her. I wish you could see him, you would like him. Baby says I must love you better than I do her and must love Jeff better than I do Mr. Walton. I told her I would love the one that treats me with the most respect the best.

Thursday week it sleeted and snowed some and turned very cold and has been freezing cold ever since. We commenced putting up ice last Saturday and have continued putting it up to this time. The ice house is nearly full.

A Yankee raid passed though Winona last summer—it did very little injury and it went on through Grenada. Some of them called at Mr. Simmons' and got breakfast, and went to Mrs. Kennedy's and took some of her meat and paid her in greenbacks. I was very uneasy of fearing they would come here. I buried my silver, my money and my watch. It ruined my watch. They have done a great deal of injury on the river plantations. I am afraid they will get here. It would frighten me very much to see them coming.

Your Pa carried several more of his negroes to Alabama last fall. Chloe, Melia, Tilla, and Letty are hired near Mr. Todd's [*a brother-in-law of Dr. Watkins*]. John Watkins, Moses, Van, Tom, Dick, are hired to Shaler Hillyer at Selma, Alabama. Prince, Else and her four children are in Montgomery, Alabama. Your Pa wrote to you from Montgomery and sent it by a man who was going to Texas. Charlie and Jim Moses are hired in Montgomery. Jane and Anna have had a child since they went to Alabama. Wash and Anna have parted. Mingo died in Alabama. America will have a baby shortly. She is not married.

Mary Arnold died last fall. Mrs. Judge Whitehead's oldest son died nearly the same time. About six weeks ago Grey Whitehead was badly wounded in his knee in a battle between Holly Springs and Memphis [*Moscow, Tennessee*].[239] Mr. and Mrs. Whitehead went up to see him. They have not returned home yet. Dr. Davis and Richard Whitehead did not go to Texas. Tom Jones

239. Probably the skirmish on December 3, 1863, at Wolf River Bridge, near Moscow, Tennessee.

went last fall and I don't know to what part. I heard the Yankees caught him, and his negroes would not leave him and the Yankees let him pass on. It is seldom the Yankees are so good.

Lynn Hemingway got home this week from the army in Virginia. He looks well. Ellen Lay has a son. Sally Dauny has a daughter. Laura Moore was married in the summer to a nephew of Jack Turner's, Dr. Turner. His wife had been dead one year. He had one child.

Provisions and goods are very scarce and dear. We have a little coffee. We use potatoes with the coffee. All our white sugar was used in cake, the icing was made of your sugar you left here that I had put away for you. Necessity compelled me to use it. I will replace it or pay you for it. We have nothing plentiful but corn. Mrs. Hawkins gave Baby two hams of bacon and sent me some loaves of light bread. I called a few minutes to see her on my way home from Col. McLemore's. She and Major Hawkins were both sick. They were invited to the wedding but were not well enough to attend it. Their daughter Jennie was here. She is a nice looking girl. I have not seen Octavia Merriwether since Lizzie Whitehead was married. I have heard of her passing the road near me, but she will not call to see me. Phil Palmer was married to Miss Sue Brown near Canton the 23rd of December. Mrs. Palmer gave them a dinner Christmas day. The company was invited to dine at three o'clock. There was a tea party at Mrs. Phillips' Friday night a week ago. Baby and Jeff were invited. It was so cold they would not go to it. Semira had a daughter in November. Else had one in the summer. Susan had a boy the night after she started to Alabama and had to be left thirty miles from here and brought home three weeks after the birth of the child. It was born before the time. It died a few days after she got home. It is said Salsbury is father to it.

I do feel very much for you my dear child and wish you could be with us. None but a mother can know my feelings for you and your dear children and husband. I pray God will provide for you all and spare us to meet again on earth. If we should not meet on earth let us strive to meet in heaven where parting will be no more.

My health is very good. Your Pa's health is better than I have ever known him to have. Your Pa says he sends the message to you and Mr. Walton that Mr. Jefferson sent to Col. Mathews who was afterwards Governor of Georgia and whose son married your aunt. During the Revolution Col. Mathews was made prisoner and sent to the British prison ship in the harbor of New York where he was confined for a long time and suffered cruelties and deprivations which British officers never impose except upon offending rebels. He appealed to his government for relief. Mr. Jefferson, then Governor of Virginia, wrote to him: "We know that the ardent spirit and hatred of tyranny which brought you into your present situation will enable you to bear up against it with the firmness which has distinguished you as a soldier, to look forward with pleasure to the day when events shall take place against which the wounded spirits of your enemies will find no comfort even from reflections on the most refined of the cruelties with which they have glutted themselves."

Give my love to the children and kiss them for me and tell them to kiss you for me. I wish I could send them some of the wedding cake. Tell them they must be good boys and love their book and make smart men like their Pa. Tell Aunt Sally and Charlotte howda. Sally, America, Ritt and Frances send love to you all. I hope your husband is with you, if he is, give my love to him and tell him to write to me. My hand is so cold I can scarcely write.

Your affectionate Mother,
Sarah E. Watkins

P.S. I am much obliged to you for the wafers. We had none. After Baby was dressed to be married, she favored you so much that I liked to look at her. Her large nose spoils her beauty. She is coarser looking than you are. Jeff and Baby left here last Wednesday morning on horseback. It was very cold. They went off in a lope. I heard they loped their horses all the way to Col. McLemore's.

To Dr. Watkins from Edmunds Whitehead:

At Home
February 7th, 1864

Dr. Watkins

Dear Friend:

Yours of yesterday's date has just reached me. Be assured, I do highly appreciate the kind feelings expressed therein—it is always consoling to receive such evidences of friendship, especially so from those we highly esteem.

I got a report yesterday that the Yankees had been driven back below Canton,[240] I do trust to God that this may be so for it would prolong our safety here. Grey seems to be still improving and asks for the favor of borrowing your crutches, thinks he will try and walk some. Please send me a late paper or two, if you have read them yourself and oblige.

Yours truly,
E. G. Whitehead

---

240. This "victory" was of little consequence. Gen. William T. Sherman's devastating Meridian expedition (February 3–14, 1864) was a forewarning in Mississippi for the soon-to-come "march to the sea" in Georgia.

The doctor, who is in Selma trying to find out the condition of his property, writes his wife:

February 24, 1864
Selma, Alabama

My Dear Wife:

I have not been up to see my negroes yet. I have heard from them. They are all well. I have been down to see my cousin Joel Mathews. I had a very pleasant visit there. I saw there Miss Mattie Mathews and Mrs. M. Cahal. I shall start to see my negroes tomorrow and return home in about 10 days. I saw Miss Adelaide [*Jeff's sister*] McLemore at Summerfield. She was well. I did not see Jennie Hawkins as she was on a visit to Cahaba. I paid over Col. McLemore's money to the proper place and took a receipt. I paid at Summerfield $500 to pay for Miss Jenny Hawkins' schooling. I let Miss Adie McLemore have $20 for pocket money. She did not ask me for it but I asked her if she wanted any and she said she would take a little.

I regret very much that I did not take her to see my cousin, Joel Mathews. She would have enjoyed the visit very much.

The cows must not run over the rye longer than first of March, nor the sheep on the wheat.[241]

Love to Baby and best respects to her husband.

Your affectionate husband,
Thos. A. Watkins

A letter to Dr. Watkins:

April the 4th, 1864

Dr. Watkins:

Dr. Stansbury is in Grenada, and will not be at home before tomorrow evening. I know that it would afford him great pleasure to accept your kind invitation were he at home. I would come with pleasure myself, but the "Yankees" have left us without horses for our carriage.

With kind regards for yourself and family,

I am your friend,
E. A. Stansbury
Carrollton

241. The planter speaks with authority about the crops and husbandry.

June 1, 1864
Jackson, Mississippi

Mr. William Walton
Austin, Texas

Sir:

. . . Her husband (Jeff) left for Dalton, Georgia some two months ago. He has been slightly wounded in the arm in a recent battle near last mentioned town. He is, however, not disabled so as not to be able still to do cavalry service. My daughter is living with us and as yet no prospect of an heir.

With regard to the education of your sons in case of your decease, please give yourself no uneasiness. In that event I will see that they are properly educated—proved the vandals do not rob me. If I die my wife will do all in her power to "train up a child in the way he should go."

Dr. McClure died suddenly lately, Mrs. Helm Prince lately died. Virginia Williams lately married a very sick man who died two days after marriage. Mrs. Jerry Robinson's son died last winter. Our man Jesse is dead. I am in haste and scarce of paper.

Your ob't servant,
Thos. A. Watkins

June 4, 1864
Austin, Texas

Dr. T. A. Watkins
Winona, Mississippi

My Dear Father:

I was much gratified a short time since by the reception of your kind letter of 18th Oct. It was mailed at Shreveport on 8th Dec. Although it was not very late news from home, it was a great consolation to me to hear that you all were alive and well and I was much pleased that my father thought of writing to me. I wish very much your pen and paper had been better so you could have written a longer letter.

I was sorry to hear of Mingo's death, not only because it was a loss to you, but because he was the only brother of my old mama and I know she was greatly distressed. Did he die at home or in Alabama?

My husband is with me now—reached home on 28th ult.—has a furlough for sixty days. He had two severe spells of sickness last fall and is not in good health now . . .[242]

Your affectionate daughter
Lettie Walton

June 19, 1864
Sunday
Canton, Mississippi

Dr. Watkins
Near Winona, Mississippi
Dear Sir:

I am now collecting the cotton that has been heretofore donated for the relief of the Mississippi soldiers in camps & hospitals in the army in Georgia & Virginia. Our great object is to relieve the wants of those brave men promptly—as large numbers of them—are without a pair of ducks [*cotton pants*] to their names or a second shirt—or a pair of drawers. If their kind benevolent friends at home will act promptly in delivering the cotton promised then we can be prompt in our relief of them.

Please forward to the railroad agent at Winona the three bales of cotton which you donated. I *would* like to get it at that place by next Friday 24th—as I will call for it then.

I am very respectfully,
C *Lombard*
Agent for C. K. Marshall

July 10, 1864
Southerland

Dr. Watkins:

At the request of Mr. Hawkins I write to ask the favor of you to send him a little ice. He has been very sick, is quite indisposed at this time. If you have any brandy or whisky will you be so kind as to send him a very little. Present me kindly to Mrs. Watkins and Mollie, would be much pleased if you would bring them to see us soon.

With much respect,
Mrs. A. C. Hawkins

---

242. Will Walton's leave of January–February 1864 was followed nine months later (October 4, 1864) by the birth of Sarah, whose descendants are the holders of these letters.

From Sarah to Lettie:

July 25, 1864
Carrollton, Mississippi

Mrs. L. A. Walton
Austin, Texas

My Dear Child:

A man has just stopped here to get his dinner. He is on his way to Texas. I have time to write you only a few lines as it is now after twelve o'clock. Baby wrote you lately and wrote you all the news. We're all well. Susan's child [*slave*] died two weeks ago with bowel complaint. The Yankees have not disturbed us yet. I expect you hear as much about the War as we do. There has been some fighting at Atlanta lately. The enemy was driven back and the Federal General McPherson killed.[243] I do hope this cruel war will soon end so we may meet again. I have not heard from you since Mr. Walton wrote to Baby in February and that letter was several months coming. Jeff McLemore is in Georgia near Atlanta. We have not heard from him since the fighting has been going on.

Major Watts' family have moved to Alabama. Mary Elisa Watt is staying with us. She is going on to Alabama in few days with Dr. McLane and his daughter. Mrs. Jack Moore, Mrs. Watts' sister died in Alabama lately. Baby and I spent the day at Mrs. Phillips' last month. The family were well. Mrs. Parmele is looking to be in better health. She said she had rather see you than any lady in the world. Dug Stevens, that was, her husband was killed in the army. She has had a child by a married man. Price McLemore was badly wounded in the hip in one of the last battles in Virginia.

. . . Baby sends her love to you and Ritt sends her love to you. Our dinner is ready. I must close my letter. If I had time I would write you a long letter. My eye sight is so bad I can hardly see how to write. I have been sewing this weather and it has inflamed my eyes.

Your affectionate Mother,
Sarah E. Watkins

---

243. Gen. James B. McPherson, killed in action July 22, 1864.

August 12, 1864
Carrollton, Mississippi

Mr. Frank M. Gilmer
President of South and North Alabama railroad
Montgomery, Ala.

Sir:

I am sorry to trouble you but these war times unsettles everything. My daughter makes a sudden and unexpected trip to Atlanta, Ga. to see her husband, Mr. McLemore who has been severely wounded. She may need money while absent and if so please let her have some three to six hundred dollars. The South and North Ala. R.R. are now owing and by middle of December next will be owing me some sixteen hundred dollars. Should she or her father-in-law, Col. J. D. McLemore, or her husband Mr. J. H. McLemore draw on you or Mr. Hopper, please honor the amount they draw from and it shall be good in my settlement with said R.R. If you are not now President of the R.R. please hand this over to the President. My negroes are still in the employ of said R.R.

> I am, Sir with great respect,
> Your ob't. servant,
> Thos. A. Watkins

P.S. Any amount the above mentioned parties may draw for I will cheerfully pay, even if it is for the whole of the sixteen hundred dollars above mentioned. Thos. A. Watkins

The doctor strives to meet his responsibility to the Confederate military:

Written from home, September 9, 1864, to Col. W. T. Townsend.

Sir:

I send three packages of cotton for use of Mississippi soldiers who may be sick in the hospitals in Georgia and Virginia. Please see that it is deposited in the railroad depot at Winona subject to the order of Mr. Lombard, Agent, for the above mentioned sick soldiers. I wish you to be witness that it is so deposited.

I am Sir, with great respect,

> Your ob't servant,
> Thos. A. Watkins

Addressed to Mrs. L. A. Walton, Austin, Texas, from the mother:

September 13, 1864

Mrs. L. A. Walton
Austin, Texas
My Dear Child,

I cannot express the great joy it gave me at receiving your letter from you dated the 5th of August. It is the first time we have heard from you since you wrote to Jeff that was received last month. We sent it on to Georgia to him. He came home before he received it. He was wounded, shot through the hip the 28th of July near Atlanta, Georgia. As soon as he was able he went to Fort Valley and staid with an acquaintance of his and wrote for Baby to go on to see him. She started this day four weeks. Grey Whitehead went with her as far as Selma. There she met with Col. McLemore and he went with her to Jeff and went on to see his wounded son Price who is in Virginia.

Jeff and Baby returned home last Thursday. I received your letter the same day. Jeff's wound is doing well. He has to walk with crutches. He and Baby went to his Pa's this morning and expect to be back here tomorrow . . .

The Yankees have not interrupted us yet. I reckon our time will come after a while. A raid came to Carrollton last winter. Several of them were negroes.[244] They carried off all the negroes they could get and forced off some. Jim Harris has gone to the Yankees. He came up on the boat with them, carried his negroes to Louisiana and is cultivating Mr. John McLane's sister's plantation, a widow that had to forsake her home and move to Choctaw out of the way of the Yankees.

We don't know anything about Mrs. Bush. The Yankees have been very destructive north of Grenada. Cousin Patsy Powell and Tom Powell have had several of their negroes to go off. It is said that Col. Booth has taken the oath [*allegiance to the Union*]. I don't know that is so. The Yankees took 27 negroes from him. Dr. Fisher has taken the oath, left his wife on his plantation and he is gone off with the Yankees.

Mr. Perkins, a cousin of Jeff's, he was married to Mary E. Davis the night after Baby was married, was killed 22nd of last month in a battle in Georgia. He was shot in his throat and bled to death.[245]

Nothing hardly is talked about here but the war. It seems that it never will

244. Since mid–1863, the Federals had been using increasing numbers of black troops.
245. This could have been either the skirmish at Jonesborough, or the one at Canton, Georgia, small but lethal actions leading to the fall of Atlanta, which had occurred before this letter was written.

end. If it lasts much longer I do not know what Baby and I am to do for clothes. We are both very needy. Some people run the blockade and get things. I believe your Pa would go in rags before he would trade with the enemy. I would not go in their lines but if I had money or cotton and could get the chance, I would supply myself with clothes. We have no coffee but make out very well without it. We use potato coffee. We have some sugar yet. We have one ham of meat. We had to let the government have some and we have to kill a hog every week for the servants. We have plenty of vegetables. Most of my cows went dry, milk only two now, three have calves, will be to pail in three weeks. Our wheat turned out well. There was a good deal of rain at the time was cut. I believe the corn crop is good. I am afraid we will make no sweet potatoes. I have not raised many turkeys, I have some ducks, have done tolerably well raising chickens.

In four months we have had three deaths in the family. Jesse died in May, Susan's child in July, and a week yesterday Becky's youngest child Phil died with the fever. Sarah and Semira's son Willie is very sick with fever. We used to be so fortunate in not having our negroes to die. In the last five years we have lost thirteen counting Susan's child that was born before the time. Now when any of them are sick much I lose most all hope of their recovery. I am not complaining. God does all things well. I mention it just to let you know how many we have lost since you were here. Polly has chills. America's child has had chills a month or more. It first had the whooping cough. All our little negroes have had it, took it last spring, and some of them cough yet. Most all of the last negroes that were carried to Alabama and Georgia have been brought home. Melia married while there. She is with child. Uncle Vivion is living, does nothing but shuck corn . . .

Joe attends to the hogs. We will have plenty of meat for next year if no accident happens. Hannah made me very uneasy just now. She said she thought Sarah was dying. I went down to see her. She was asleep and I called her and it was some time before she spoke. She was sweating and her pulse was weak. I don't think she is dying. Becky is staying with her and got uneasy because she would not talk and slept so much. Milly had a son last Sunday. Jesse is said to be the father of it.

There was nothing the matter with Baby two weeks ago. She and Jeff are very loving. If he stays some time from the army I am afraid she will be caught [*pregnant*]. I think it will be sometime before he will be able to return to the army. I hope Mr. Walton will be with you during your confinement. I'll be very uneasy about you and I wish I could be with you at that time. I am very thankful that Mr. Walton has not been killed nor wounded and pray he may go through the war safely. In writing to us about the price of things you put in figures and made mistakes. Your Pa told me to tell you to write it in words and not in figures. My mind is so troubled about the sick, I can't write without making mistakes . . .

Mrs. Keys married last month a brother-in-law of Albert Keys, Mr. Hunter. He is several years younger than herself. Albert Keys was wounded in battle and some time ago was taken prisoner and died.[246] Eugene Whitehead has been captured twice. The guard went to sleep and he went got away and returned home last week.

Baby has written to you twice and I once and I sent them with men that were going across the river. If Baby and Jeff had known I was going to write, they would have sent you a message. They came home before he received your letter that was sent on to him . . .

September 14th, 1864 [*letter continues*] Sarah and Willy appear better this a.m. We are making molasses from the sugar cane and have made some very good molasses. We have a small sugar mill put up near the yard. If Newton and Early were here, they would amuse themselves riding the mule around that works the mill.

My health and your Pa's are very good. He never has headaches now. We both show age. I have lost nearly all my upper teeth. I am balder than ever. [*She is now fifty.*] Give my love to Mr. Walton, tell him it is always a pleasure to hear from him. I am very anxious to see you all. I am afraid the war will last so long I will never see you all again. Tell Aunt S & C howda.

Your Loving Mother,
Sarah E. Watkins

September 20, 1864
Carrollton, Mississippi

Mr. William M. Walton
Austin, Texas

My Dear Son:

Your very welcome letter of the 17th ult. was joyfully received here last Friday. Not hearing from you and my dear child since February until I received her letter of the 5th of August week before last. It caused me to be very uneasy about you. I imagined you were killed or wounded as we could not hear from you. Am glad to hear you have not been killed or wounded. I pray the Lord will spare you to return to your family safely.

You need not apologize for calling me Mother. I wish you to look upon me

---

246. The reader will remember the letter of July 4, 1855, when Albert Keys was a young suitor at the Whitehead home. He now becomes a casualty.

as your mother. It would be a pleasure to me to act the part of a mother towards you and hope if life lasts I will be able to do so.

If this war lasts much longer, I fear I will never see you and your dear family again. I am getting old, begin to show my age, my health is very good for one of my age. I had a shaking chill. It lasted some time yesterday. Am taking quinine and feel nearly well today. July, 12 months, a Yankee raid passed through Winona, did very little injury [*Grierson*].[247] Stopped at Mrs. Kennedy's on their way up and took some of her meat. Last winter a raid came to Carrollton, most of them were negroes. They took all the horses and negroes they could get. Went to Maj. Watts' in search of him. He just had time to get out of their way. Maj. Watt was a conscription officer. They have never troubled us yet. I'm afraid our time will come after a while. Jeff McLemore was wounded the 28th of July shot through his hip. The battle was near Atlanta, Georgia. He went to an acquaintance of his near Fort Valley, Georgia. Baby went on to see him. They returned home tomorrow two weeks. Jeff's wound is doing well, he has to use crutches. The same day he was wounded his hat was shot through the crown and took off a lock of his hair.

Our corn and wheat crop are good. We will have plenty of meat for next year if no accidents happen. We are making our own molasses. From what you write about the boys I am very proud of them and hope they will when grown be an honor to their parents and an ornament to society. I wish very much I could be with them and their dear mother and yourself. Do try and be with dear Lettie during her confinement. It would be a great relief to my feelings if I know you will be with her at the time. I will be so uneasy about her. It is so seldom that I can hear from her. Some of your letters and hers that were written last year have been received lately.

Jeff and Baby have gone to Winona today. If she was here she would send a message to you. I will be very glad to see you whenever you can have an opportunity of coming to see us. Write often, I am always glad to hear from you. I forgot to mention I received Lettie's letters enclosed with yours and read them with pleasure. Excuse this short letter as I am not very well today.

Your affectionate mother,
Sarah E. Watkins

The following short note to Lettie is added:

My Dear Child:

As I do not know where to direct my letter to Mr. Walton, I will direct it to Austin and you can send it to him. I wrote to you last week and mentioned

---

247. D. Alexander Brown, *Grierson's Raid* (Urbana: University of Illinois Press, 1954).

the illness of Sarah and Willie. Sarah is getting better and Willie is nearly well. Polly has been very low for several days. She is better than she has been. Don't be uneasy about me. I will soon be in health again. Jeff has a letter written to you to send off with mine. I expect he wrote you all the news. Margaret Hemingway, daughter of Collins Hemingway, has been staying at her Uncle William Hemingway's and expects to start Arkansas tomorrow. We will get her to carry our letters across the river. Give my love and kisses to the children. America and Ritt send love to you all.

Your loving mother,
Sarah E. Watkins

Lettie to her husband:

September 26, 1864

My Precious Boy:

In the event you cannot come home as early as the time I appointed, I will write a few lines to you tonight but hope and think by the time this letter gets there you will be here. I did not rest well at all last night and have not been well today but feel better tonight. My supper disagreed with me last night and gave me the colic. It was a simple diet too and ought not to have hurt me. I have been careful about eating today and have been halfway starving.

Why do you censure yourself darling for my being here instead of on the other side of the river? It is no more your fault than my own. I have never been willing to leave you on this side of the river since the War and do not think I will ever be. You are more to me, my love, than all the world besides, and if I cannot be with you I must be where I can hear from you.

Amelia Hutchins and Adelia spent last night with me and Amelia is with me again tonight. I rest so badly that I dislike exceedingly to remain alone at night.

Adelia has come to go to school again. She received your letter. I received a note Saturday from Mrs. Carrington saying she would sell a negro woman for $600 or the woman and child for $700.[248] She is said to be a splendid servant. Mrs. Randolph was here this evening, came to see me about buying Lizzie. Carrington bought the woman she has for sale from Randolph. Mrs. Randolph said she liked the negro so well that she had been trying to buy her back but Mrs. Carrington would not let her have her. She said that she went to Mrs. Carrington's Saturday morning and offered to buy the woman

248. Life continues its long-accustomed pattern; within six months, slavery ends. Lettie seeks better domestic help.

back again and Mrs. Carrington told her she did not wish to sell her, so she must be a smart negro. I want her but must dispose of Lizzie first. I wrote a note to Chandler today and asked him to buy the woman and child for me and take Lizzie to sell. I told him perhaps I was asking too great a favor of him but if he thought so he could decline and I would not be the least offended. He was busy in court when Newton gave him the note but said he would be down this evening or in the morning. So I hope to get the negro but must confess it is a faint hope because I am generally disappointed in everything.

You must excuse this scratching for I am hurrying to get through and entertain Amelia and the wind is blowing the light in every direction. We are all well. I feel well now, but if you don't hasten home I fear you will not find me well when you come. Oh, you must be with me, my own one, by middle of October.[249] That time will soon be here and how anxiously, how longingly I will await your coming. Fate will be cruel indeed if this one desire of my heart is not granted. I believe you will be here and know that you will do all in your power to come. Good night my own sweet boy. May God bless you and bring you safely to us soon.

Your devoted Lettie

heading: Slave Business

October 8th, 1864
E. G. Whitehead

Doctor T. A. Watkins
at home

Dr. T. Watkins
  Sir:

In reply to you of this date, will say that my hands were last Spring required to work in the Mipi. C.R. Road [*Mississippi Central Railroad*] for one month *or more,* or get out, for said Road, 500 cross ties.

Respectfully
Yours,
E.G. Whitehead

The doctor then queried the agent in Grenada as to the specifics of the authorization. This letter came in reply:

---

249. Her expected date of confinement. Will was not able to come home in time for the baby's arrival.

October 20th, 1864
Grenada, Mississippi

Dr. Thos. A. Watkins

Dear Sir:

I called on Col. Goodman and requested a copy of the order of impressment issued by him to press negroes. He told me he had no copy of the order and did not recollect the wording now, but he told me to say to you to go and see Mr. Spivey and get the original from him. He was perfectly willing for you to have the order. And he thought it was better than a copy. He also said he was satisfied your negroes were prepared to work on the Rail Road. He also said he was perfectly willing to give you a copy, but he thought the original copy much the best. He did not now remember the wording of the order.

I remain yours,
C. H. Guy

The following is an account of Grierson's last raid[250] December 19, 1864 to January 5, 1865) written by Mrs. Margaret Virginia Whitehead Kennedy, Edmunds Whitehead's daughter living near Vaiden. Although not one of the Watkins letters, it is included for completeness.

The raid passed through our neighborhood on January 1, 1865. Miss Wendol, a visitor in our home from Oxford, Mississippi, advised to put on our best clothing and hide whatever was of any value as Grierson's raid had previously been to Oxford [*Mississippi*] and she knew of their ungentlemanly behavior. We had been informed the night before by my uncle, Judge W. W. Whitehead, that the Yankees were encamped at old Middleton on their way to Vaiden. Our slumbers were not very sweet that night. We arose quite early "New Year's morning" and prepared ourselves to meet our unwelcomed guests. We sent off and hid everything of value. I was trying to hide a nice shawl on top of the teaster of my bed when I heard 'The Yankees are coming, the Yankees are coming!' In my haste to get down from my high position, I fell and tore my nice black silk dress. I was so excited the fall didn't hurt me.

I suppose the raid numbered about 1,000 men, white and black. My dear mother asked an officer to please not let the negro soldiers come into her house, which request was granted. Some of the officers and soldiers asked, 'Why are you all so dressed up? You must be expecting company!' Mother

---

250. Col. Benjamin H. Grierson's first raid was in April 1863 in support of Grant's attack on Vicksburg. His cavalry continued to be active, and on December 19, 1864, struck out from Memphis, east, to break the Mobile, Ohio Railroad. The doctor describes the route through Mississippi. The raid ended at Vicksburg on January 5, 1865.

replied, 'I think we have company.' In a few moments, soldiers occupied the house. They took everything that was of value with them and they destroyed a great deal they could not take. They robbed us of our mules, horses, bed-clothing and provisions. Went into our trunks; they said they were looking for clothing. Mother had carefully tied packages which one soldier anxiously un-tied. You ought to have seen his countenance change when he found only dried rose leaves instead of money. He inquired, 'What do you want these for?' 'To make tea for the little negro babies,' mother answered.

They went into Uncle Cicero Kennedy's tool box, breaking the lock, and scattered the tools, for which they had no earthly use. I gave Mr. Kennedy's wedding suit, locked in a carpet bag for which I paid $30 in Confederate money to an old negro (Uncle Mark) to hide for me from the Yankees. Uncle Mark said, "I show will bring the suit back, Miss Jennie.' What was my surprise the next day, Uncle Mark came up with the carpet bag but all in pieces and the suit gone.

From our home they went to grandmother's, where they acted in a similar manner. They didn't leave her anything to eat, took her chickens, threw them up in the air, and cut them with their sabers as they came down. Why they showed such hatred to an old lady 70-years old I can't tell unless they knew she had three noble sons in the Confederate Army.

They went from here on the Shongalo Road to Major Kopperl's about where Mr. McClellen lives. Major Kopperl was killed by a negro soldier. When I think of such deeds, the flames awaken my heart of passionate rebellion. We can forgive but we cannot forget.

The affect of his march can hardly be overestimated in damage to the South. Before this raid there was terror, and behind them there was death and ashes.[251]

February 4, 1865
Carrollton, Mississippi

Mrs. Lettie Walton
Austin, Texas

My Dear Daughter,

I have time only to write a few lines. We are all well. Your mother has received three letters from you in the last two months. Amelia has a son a few days old. No prospect of Baby having an heir. About two months ago she was thrown from a horse and has had her ankle dislocated and the small bone of her leg broken near the foot. She had to keep to her bed about a month.

---

251. Margaret Virginia Kennedy was born on the Whitehead plantation in 1839 and died in 1936, having seen the entire course of life in Carroll County for almost a century.

She can now walk about the yard. Jeff's wound is still suppurating. He will stay with us until he gets well.

We were all much excited at the Grierson's raid[252] which passed rapidly through a part of this county about 1st last month. It spread desolation as it went, burning corn cribs, gin houses, stealing negroes, horses, and mules. It started out at Memphis—went on near Aberdeen and then turned and came on by Houston, Greensboro, Lodi, Winona, Middleton, Shongalo, Lexington, and then on to Vicksburg. It came with in about two miles of me, but did no damage. It ruined Judge Collins in the way of mules and negroes—also Mrs. Judge Kennedy—also a good many others in the eastern part of this county. It took four negroes from Col. McLemore, his horses and mules, and all his blankets and the clothes of his family. It took all the provisions of old Mrs. Pleasant's. It burned the gin house near me, and several cribs of corn. It served Col. O. J. Moore very badly. This letter will not tell half of the thieving, meaness and rascality of Grierson and his men. They took all of Maj. Hawkins' mules—also the mules and four negroes from Judge Whitehead, but they took nothing from E. G. Whitehead or Hemingway. They stole clothes, blankets, money wherever they went.

Jeff, though not well of his wound, attacked the rear guard and killed some stragglers. Had a spirited resistance been made, much damage would have been prevented. Every person except Jeff and 9 or 10 men with him seemed to be paralyzed.

Mrs. Joe Keys and Mrs. Albert Keys have lately married. Not many marriages or deaths among your acquaintances here. This country is very much altered since the war. The population is somewhat changed and most persons look sad, badly dressed, and many look prematurely old. The people visit about on wagons and horseback.[253] All of my family send their best love to you and family. Jeff and Baby appear to be very happy in their marriage. Joe Eggleston died in Bermuda[254] having escaped from being a prisoner. The Yankees did not go near Mrs. Eggleston's. Please excuse this very hasty letter as the bearer is about to start. My family have plenty to eat which is a great thing these times, but we all are bare of store clothes, sugar and coffee.

Tell Mr. Walton to kiss you and the children for me. My respects to him.

Your affectionate Father,
Thos. A. Watkins

252. By this stage of the war, the South could offer little resistance.

253. The grand days of carriages and cotton have begun to pass. Life in Carroll County moves into decline.

254. Joe Eggleston had been a prisoner–of–war, but escaped to Bermuda where he died of yellow fever. His family was from near Lexington, Mississippi, and is mentioned frequently in the letters.

This note is from Sallie McLemore, Jeff's stepmother. The M.C.P. is Martha Cobbs Phillips (Mrs. Phillips) from Middleton, whose grandson in later years marries Lettie's daughter. It is the first mention of Mrs. Watkins's fatal illness.

Dear Jeff:

I will come up in the morning, will go by for M.C.P. I regret so much to hear of Mrs. W. severe illness. I deeply sympathize with Mollie and hope in many days her mother will be out of danger.

Mrs. Allen will come with me if well enough.

> Your affectionate Mother,
> Sallie McLemore

As the war comes to an end, death comes for Mrs. Watkins. Among the letters is the announcement, ribboned in black:

The funeral services of Mrs. Dr. Watkins will be held at the residence of Dr. Watkins, Friday 24th, March, 10 o'clock A.M., 1865.

The man who sold the coffin writes the doctor:

> March 23, 1865
> Carrollton

Dr. Watkins

Sir:

I have sent you the best coffin I have but am sorry to say that I have no lumber suitable for making the case and it is impossible to get any. If you have any lumber on the plantation, have the grave curbed up about 15 inches high as that is the plan I have had to adapt in several instances on the account of the scarcity of lumber. You can have the coffin by 3 o'clock this evening. Please send two mules as I have tried and can't provide any in town.

> Yours Respectfully,
> P. W. Johnson

"How lonely and almost objectless seems future life"

III

Post-War Letters
1865–1881

Nothing would ever again be quite the same for Lettie and her sister Mary, now that their dear mother was gone. Adjustments, including even accepting the reality of Sarah's death, were difficult. When he recovered from his wound, Jeff took over management of Forest Place. He found it a struggle to organize a pattern of labor and to reopen the marketing of cotton.

From Lettie to her sister in Carrollton:

July 23, 1865
Austin, Texas

My Dear Sister:

Your letter dated 11th April was received by Will many weeks ago but its contents and even its reception was kept from me by him until yesterday when I had sat down to write to my mother he handed me the letter and said he had shielded me from the blow as long as he could. The reason that the letter had been kept from me was the condition of my health which has been extremely critical balancing me between life and death.

Oh! sister I cannot realize, I cannot feel that our dear Mother is dead—that I shall never see her again on earth, that all her tenderness and devotion towards her children will be known no more. How lonely and almost objectless seems future life. The darling object of my life for the last few years has been to see my mother once more, to place my arms tenderly around her and impress her with the truth and devotion of my love . . . How pure and good she was, how just and true and loving—a model which her daughters might well and profitably take as their guide and pattern. In her, we lost much that was dear to us on earth . . .

We have not yet decided [to] what point we will go but feel almost certain that we will go either to New Orleans or to the coast of Texas. It may be a year however before we move, but I designed spending the intervening time with you all. Is a serious matter to us to break up now, established here by 11 years, residence, a good and comfortable home and with the prospect under ordinary surroundings for Will to do well in the practice of the law. But still the reasons for a change are insuperable and must prevail. Will has a strong inclination to leave this country altogether and says should you and Jeff manifest a willingness to go with us to Brazil or to New Grenada, we will not be long in preparing to go. We are at present, however, in very straightened circumstances and must make sales of real estate before we can go anywhere.

. . . Mr. George Walton [*Will's brother*] has at last been relieved from the prison at Johnson's Island and is at home broken in fortune as is every slave holder.

I expect he would join with us in an expedition to Brazil.

Our little daughter is said by many to be pretty. I do not consider her pretty much yet, but her features are good and have no fears that they will not make a pretty woman. I named her Sarah after our loved and now sainted mother. I'm afraid that Mother never knew her name. Will preferred the name of Mary, but insisted on my naming her what my affections prompted.

. . . How are the negroes doing? Have they all left? Mine all wanted to set up for themselves except Denmark. I told them at first they might go and afterwards concluded to keep them until the arrival of the Yankees. They are still here notwithstanding the Yanks have been in town for some days and I do not know how long they intend remaining. Lizzie [*former slave*] has to suckle my baby. I not only have not milk but have not even any breast so you can form some idea of how low I have been and how poor I am now. My baby was sick and I scarcely able to walk and my negroes were all ready to leave me after all my kindnesses to them. It makes me have no kind feeling for them. I have been too indulgent and too kind and thereby the fault.

I do so much wish to visit my old home again and earnestly pray that we may be spared to meet again on earth. How is my father? Does he seem very lonely without our precious mother? Oh that I could have seen her once more.

. . . Remember me to all who were kind to our mother during her illness. Some of them I do not know but they too have my lasting gratitude. Kiss Mrs. E. Whitehead. I loved her before but she is dearer to me now. Tell her what I say . . . Give my love to Pa and Jeff.

To all the negroes who are at home and behaving well, I wish to be remembered . . .

Your devoted Sister,
Lettie A. Walton

The comments about setting up life in Brazil or elsewhere were not unusual. Though most were glad just to have the war over, defeat was not an acceptable fact to many southerners.

A popular book printed in 1866, *Brazil, The Home for Southerners*, by Ballard Dunn, may have influenced some of them.[255]

255. See Andrew F. Rolle, *The Lost Cause,* (Norman: University of Oklahoma Press, 1965); Eugene C. Harter, *The Lost Colony of the Confederacy* (Jackson: University Press of Mississippi, 1985).

CHAPTER ELEVEN

A "confused and unsettled condition of affairs"

In the fall of 1865 the entire South was in a state of uncertainty and disarray. Federal troops governed under martial law, but some areas were much more lawless—hence dangerous—than others. Austin, Texas, was in an especially unsettled condition. Mr. Walton realized that his wife and family would be better off in the relative security that prevailed in the vicinity of Forest Place. They moved there, Lettie and the children departing from Austin late in October 1865, and remained in Mississippi for a year.

But there was great tension at Forest Place. Jeff's role as plantation manager proved to be a difficult one for him. Worse perhaps, Lettie soon discovered that her father seemed to have a drinking problem. The plantations were without their former labor supply. Families of great tradition and former wealth now were destitute. Indeed, the doctor painfully learned that he no longer had certain prerogatives. When he chose to order a former slave from his property, he learned that Federal authorities would prevent that from happening.

The men of Carroll County essentially knew how to do but one thing to make a living, and that was to raise cotton. Jeff rounded up labor as best he could, and he did raise cotton, as well as corn, on Dr. Watkins's plantation. Jeff kept a diary, and his words lend insight to the routine chores of farming at that time and under the extant conditions. Throughout the South there were experiments with new ways to keep cotton flowing to the market and with working out new ways to secure and use adequate hired labor. Eventually, "sharecropping" became a standard arrangement.

August 23, 1865

W. L. Tyson

Dear Will:

I have gotten permission to ship twenty-five or thirty bales in Wm. A. Gayden's name and five in your own. The permit for your five is now at Capt. Dyches—send them immediately and Henry Payne promised to ship forthwith. He will ship Monday next if you can get it down by that time. Send the Gayden cotton to Dr. Henry with written instruction from you for it's to be sent to McLemore, Ryburn & Co. by first steamers.

Respectfully yours,

Jeff H. McLemore

August 23, 1865

Dr. T. A. Watkins:

I went down to find out about the seizure of your cotton and found it to be a mistake. The cotton has been shipped. Send me by the box a pound or two of rice if you have it convenient. Also a pair of clock stockings and a cotton chemise for Mollie.

Please forward the above note in a sealed envelope to Tyson immediately as it is important and I wish no one to see it. I have no envelope. Mollie and I are well—will be at home by the last of the week.

Respectfully and Aff. yours,

Jeff H. McLemore

From Mr. Walton to the doctor:

September 10, 1865

Austin, Texas

Dr. Thomas A. Watkins

Carrollton, Mississippi

My Dear Sir:

The confused and unsettled condition of affairs in this state, particularly on the Rio Grande requires the precautionary step from me to remove my family to a place of great safety at least for the present. It is very natural for my mind to point to you for the temporary asylum but I am fearful of throwing a greater charge upon you than your affairs will permit you to bear. If you are as entirely broken up as we are out here, I am inside of the fact when I state that nine/tenths of the planters here are ruined. For this reason I have hesitated to send my family to Mississippi until we had heard from you. There are other reasons why I wish for my wife to visit you and why she wishes to go and among these are that she realizes that you are growing old and she wishes to receive from you full forgiveness for all the past. She wishes to see you again. She desires to see her sister and the grave of her mother. All the impulses of her nature demand that she shall go. On my part I am anxious for her to go because she wishes to go and I most earnestly desire that a complete reconciliation may take place which can be done in sight of the grave of the wife and mother and, besides this, my affairs at this time are so uncertain that I am not free from doubt that if my family remains here they will be subjected to hardship, unexpected and disagreeable. If the country can recover from the almost fatal measure of the Federal authorities and that of our own military regime it will begin the recuperation within a given number of months. Until those months pass, I am anxious to feel that my wife and children are secure and to myself to be free to remain and go as circumstances may determine. I can myself undergo any degree of hardship, but for me to do so with silence and stoicism, my family must not be subjected to the same measures.

I shall await word from you as to your condition until the approach of cool weather, when, if no word is sent the venture must be made tho' at a hazard. I hope however that I may hear from you at an early day. It is not possible for me to accompany wife. Neither my duty to the future nor my present pecuniary condition will permit it. My earnest undivided and constant attention is demanded to enable me to even reasonably hope for competence in the future. It gives me pleasure to say that the health of my wife is strengthening daily and that I may presently see her completely restored. Her illness has been long and almost fatal. Our children are well grown, going to school (2 older boys) and learning rapidly.

Wife writes by this mail to Mary which it is hoped that she will receive.

If the condition of things should ameliorate here, I shall advise you.

Hope for life, health, and prosperity to attend you.

> I am truly and obediently
> your friend,
> W. W. Walton

Office of the Sub Commissioner Freedmen's Bureau
Winona, Mississippi
October 9, 1865

Dear Watkins:

Sir:

You must keep this family or provide them with a home or pay them sufficient to support themselves until New Years. It will not do to turn them off
now that it is coming on cold weather.

They are of course expected to work when they are able and they must
do it.

L. D. Patterson, Lt.
Sub Com. Freedmen's Bureau

[written in pencil by the doctor on the envelope of this letter is the
comment: "Dammed Yankee Negro (unreadable)"]

From Lettie in Winona, Mississippi, to her husband:

March 14, 1866

My Dear Husband:

I was glad to hear you sold the parlor furniture so well. You sold everything
better than I did. Remember Bowers owes you for the crib [baby crib] and
two ovens. Make old Judy pay up. Did Lizzie [freed slave] ever get any of her
children with her? Is Catharine [freed slave] with Mrs. Bowers yet?

It has been raining nearly all day and is still raining. Daughter has five teeth
and so many sweet winning ways. I so much wish you could be with her now.
You member the negro Nancy that Pa sold to Mr Simmons? I hire her, she
cleans up my room, attends to the baby and sews for me. I don't know exactly
what I will pay her. She's a very smart negro. What do women hire for there?
Since the baby commenced walking I have a little girl about eight years old
to walk after the baby and am to give her two dresses and a chemise for her
pay. So you see I am right well fixed for a while at least. Nancy is very high
tempered and if she gets too much above herself I will not have her about
me. The nurse I had first I only engaged until March and her father has hired
her to some lady else after that time so I could not get her. I paid her two
dollars per month for January and February. I got her for nothing before
Christmas as Baby and Jeff kindly furnished me with a nurse. Baby read your
letter in which you said you would meet me at Umbra's.[256] She said, "I think

256. "Umbra" was Will's name for his brother, George Walton. George's plantation was
on the Mississippi River in Louisiana, in Concordia Parish. George's nickname for Will was
"Buck," and Will was known throughout Texas as Major "Buck" Walton.

Mr. Walton might come here. I felt right hurt when I read the letter." Jeff spoke up, "I was right mad when I read the letter but never said anything then. I want to see him." You must come here, I want my friends to see you. I am proud of my husband and Jeff came to my door just now and said, "Writing to your old man?" "Yes." "Tell him buss my toenail." He is a case [*slang manages to bridge 130 years*].

Everytime Pa goes to town he gets whiskey, brings it home and drinks but he has not taken a real spree in a long time. He drank last night and this morning but was up this evening. I would not have you in Jeff's place for a great deal. He gives as an excuse for drinking the selling of his place and Jeff has let him have the place back again twice, and then he begged Jeff to take it off his hands again and today he has been after Jeff to let him have it again. I believe myself that it is the loss of the property and remorse of conscience that makes him drink.

I would like to live on the Mississippi River if we could all leave there in summer. My cotton sold for only 4.2 cents per pound. The money has not yet come but I have Jeff's note for $369.37 currency.

Goodnight my own darling. I long to see my precious boy. Love to all my friends.

Your Lettie

The following is from Jeff's diary, March 1, 1866:

Saturday, March 10th—commenced planting corn with two plows, ran a bulltongue (plow) on top of the ridge and covered with a harrow.

Monday, March 12th—finished breaking up corn ground and commenced planting corn with four plows in same manner as Saturday.

Thursday, 15th—tremendous rain, washing away fences, put a stop to planting. Hauled wood and rails—put up some fences—ground meal.

Monday, March 19th—recommenced planting corn.

Saturday, March 24th listing up [*prepared soil*]

Wednesday, April 4th—commenced bedding out cotton land, still planting corn.

Monday, April 9th—heavy frost [*Each diary entry contained a comment about the weather, but only a sampling is included here.*]

Tuesday, April 12th—commenced planting cotton.

Monday, April 15th—warm and showers of rain, broke up cotton ground, commenced working corn, buffalo gnats very bad.

Tuesday, April 24th—clear and cool, planted cotton with three plows did more work than I ever saw done with same force in same length of time.

Wednesday, May 9th—hoed and thinned corn, set out potatoes, repaired circle ditches.

Thursday, May 10th—did first cotton scraping [*hoe work*]

Thursday, May 17th—commenced hilling up my corn for the first time.

Monday, May 21—very pleasant and clear, finished planting cotton, continued working corn and cotton.

Thursday, June 7th—cut wheat

Monday, June 18th—finished hoeing cotton for first time, commenced laying by of corn.

Monday, July 9th—hoed, hilled, and plowed cotton. Tuesday, July 15th—got press timber [*probably to support the giant screw of the cotton compress*].

August 1st—commenced raising press, shocked up corn, hoed cotton.

Wednesday, August 25th—cleaned gin house and sowed turnips.

Tuesday, September 4th—commenced picking cotton and building cotton scaffold.

Monday, September 10th—made cotton sacks, made baskets, cleaned under gin house [*sacks and baskets were used in the fields by hands picking cotton*].

Monday, September 24th—commenced ginning.

Saturday, September 29th—finished picking over cotton for 2nd time.

Monday, October 1st—hoed turnips, baled and picked cotton.

A letter to Dr. Watkins from Col. Richard Jones in Alabama, a kinsman of Dr. Watkins and father-in-law to Gen. Joe Wheeler of the Confederate Army, describes what is happening in Alabama:

April 22, 1866

Dear Cousin:

I want to hear from you and should have written before this but thought by waiting a while I would probably receive a letter from you and I had a little advantage of you. Good luck and chance threw me into the company of Col. McLemore, the father of your son-in-law. He I found to be a very nice gentleman, social and frank in conversation. He gave me your whereabouts and position and satisfactorily answered such questions about you and yours as I thought proper to ask, so you see I got the start of you in that way.

I rented my plantation and this year for $3,456 payable in gold and we are now living with Tom at a cheap convenient tavern.

This course I took as I had no confidence in hired labor and wanted a year's rest which gives me opportunity to observe the system, results of laborers, at the end of this year I shall resume planting or rent again as best befitting my interest.

Tom is planting on shares with a part of his old gang of negroes, say 32 hands. Both of us are in debt but think we will work out without a sacrifice, but be left free with but little besides our land. The war pretty much used us up, however escaping as well as our neighbors and probably in some respects a little better . . .

The negroes are working and behaving well except stealing everything they can lay hands on. I think I see a tendency in them to run back into barbarism. The most of them are like brutes and have no idea of elevating themselves further than to supply absolute wants and not at all scrupulous in and about the way they do that . . . We hope and trust the President's policy of restoration of the representation of the southern states will prevail, his Proclamation of Peace gives some hope and satisfaction, but we're not safe yet and must not "holloo" before we are out of the woods.[257] The hateful radicals will use their power to ruin every citizen in the South and as far as they can to effect that object.

I should like to see you very much to confirm ideas and hear that full gush of laughter you used to indulge in when a good idea well told was presented to you.

Now let us keep up a pleasant equanimity of mind under all circumstances and not be cast down by trifles. We have well learned the lessons of toleration and will we not profit by it? Yes, and when we can stand on our feet, will we forget the law "an eye for an eye."

> With consideration
> Your Cousin,
> Richard Jones

P.S. Plague on these steel pens. Always give me the green goose [*quill pens*].

Will Walton writes Lettie a love letter—and a frank message:

> May 29, 1866
> Austin, Texas

My darling—my wife,

. . . If circumstances permitted me to place you all in a position where comfort and convenience would surround you, I should be very nearly a happy man. With my wife, I am fully satisfied and love her as she wishes to be loved by the man whom she loves and who is the father of her children—

257. President Johnson attempted, unsuccessfully, to ease the readmission of the southern states to the Union. On April 2, 1866, he officially proclaimed "that the insurrection which heretofore existed" was ended.

the children I love—and the wife and mother would have them loved. But few persons have ever lived as happily as we have—notwithstanding the doubts and prophecies that were made about us, when we together started up the hill of life. Up the hill we have traveled, wifey darling, and when the shades of night and death come, we will lay "tigither"[258] at the foot, like John Anderson and his deary.

Did you ever think, darling, how much we have been absent from one another since we've been married? Think of it—full five long years have we not pleased the sight of each other, and that too of twelve years. Have we been less happy because of these divergences? Are not our meetings gifted with more zest because of them? Tell me about it.

You speak of there being so much rain there [*Mississippi*] during the spring, so it has been here [*Austin*] but we have not had too much but an abundance. Crops are as fine as you ever saw them, even in Mississippi. Vegetables of every kind are in market and very cheap. Roasting ears, cabbage, peas, beans, Irish potatoes, beets, indeed everything that is due at this season. The wheat crops are splendid. The corn crops are about made, at least so far advanced that a large yield will be gathered. If we could always have as much rain as we have had this year, there would be no grander country than this, but I may say what I please, you will have a prejudice against the State, not an undue one because you have cause and your feeling of distaste towards the State will remain unless some lucky things happens by which or through which our circumstances shall be greatly changed for the better.

. . . You speak of my settling at Winona. What could I do there? Can you tell me? Sue the people about there in a Justices Court and draw up contracts between the Planters and the negroes? If a man could get enough of business in justice court, he might make money, but whenever you find the inferior court full of business, you may know that *that* is an embarrassed community and that the earth is yielding badly or the people lazy. If people can't pay their *little* debts, there must be something wrong. But suppose I could collect $10,000, a large amount to pass yearly through a man's hands by practicing in justice courts, and what would it make me? At most $500 according to the fees charged by lawyers in Mississippi. What good would $500 do me, I mean as a result of my efforts for a year's work?

. . . While I am not vain, darling, and while I greatly lack self-esteem and am devoid of egotism I may yet truthfully say that it would be a prostitution of the talent God has given me to bury it in a justice court in an interior village unless by doing so I could see certain results of great advantage by

258. Evidently, this is a literary quote from something they both knew about, John Anderson (a Scotsman?) and his "deary."

which I could reap benefit to last us through life. How am I to do that at Winona? While I see no bright sunshine here, which by work I can certainly reach, still it does seem to me that the sunshine here is closer to us than back in Mississippi. I do not deny the close association with your father and sister would be very grateful to you, indeed nothing could add so much (at least of a personal kind) to my own pleasure as to see you thus associated. But my darling, we have very grave duties to perform, we cannot look to what will give personal satisfaction but to that which will bring ultimate results, the which we so much wish to bring about and by bringing them about advance ourselves and enable us to do by our children as we wish to do. I am by no means limited to Texas. The wide world is open to us. The only question is where should we strike in order that success may attend us and attending us, give our children position and advancement.

. . . The children need not fear of worrying me by repeating the same word to me. Bless their hearts, I only wish to know that they think of me and are willing to be taught by me. If they can't with their young heads find different messages to send, tell them to talk with their hearts and say to me what their hearts say to them about me.

George does not need much whipping. He is too easily cowed, anyhow. I see that and sometimes regret that I ever whipped him at all. I know you will not whip him unnecessarily, and when you hit him a little it will be when an ordinary child would need it. But you must take into consideration the nature of George. I want the children to feel free, intelligent, bold, that they are as good as the highest and best in the land and fear the frown of no one because they, in conscious honesty and truth, feel full strength and that in that strength, they have power.

You all are certainly having very fine health. It does me good to know of it. I hope you will continue well and get good and fat before I see you. You'll have to fatten fast if you keep up with me. I am slipping along increasing at a rate of 30 pounds every six months. I'll be a bully boy by the time you see me. People say I am a large man now, I did not use to be so. Wonder what makes me grow so, do you know?

. . . If I were not a candidate [*for attorney general of Texas*] I should be able I believe to relieve myself of all debt and be entirely free once more, but I am compelled to spend what money I have and maybe a good deal more to run the race in proper style. I told you that I had withdrawn from the race for judge or rather that I "had been withdrawn," but as luck seems to light on me very much like one of these lightning bugs light up the darkness around them, so luck has presented me another ray of light and through the efforts of friends who work with a will, my name has been placed before the people for Attorney General of the State. This is a much more lucrative office than the other. The salary being $3,000 a year with fees of office amounting from 1 to 3 thousand dollars more—besides I can keep up my practice at the Bar, save in criminal actions, but the State is a very large one and the time in which to concentrate the vote very short. But I am working myself and working everybody else who is about me . . . think I will succeed—shall try, to say the least. There are many other things I would say to you but I am not at liberty to write longer now. God bless you.

Your boy—
Will

Lettie's husband has been elected attorney general of Texas. Mrs. Simmons, Octavia Simmons Merriwether's mother, writes Lettie:

September 18, 1866
Valley Cottage, Mississippi

. . . Mr. Simmons and myself congratulate you on the success of Mr. Walton and wish him every success in his new and distinguished position which he hopes he will fill with honor to himself and entire satisfaction to the people . . .

Now for cholera in Duck Hill, I learned from the only citizen himself who recovered that had the disease that 21 persons died during the prevalence of the disease, 14 cases were cholera, the balance from other causes, the population of Duck Hill including 1/2 mile each way from the depot is or was about fifty. Twenty of that number died, men and women and children and negroes. But all is now quiet. Mr. Simmons was there last week. The merchants have all resumed their business and are about as before as none of the most prominent citizens died (I refer to the Gentlemen) . . .

Love from the children and myself to yourself and Mollie.

Ever your friend,
L. M. Simmons

An old Alabama friend of the doctor's writes, sharing the same sad story heard throughout the South:

October 12, 1866
Montgomery, Ala.

Doct. T. A. Watkins

Dear Sir:

When I left you I intended to have written you before this, but the day before I reached home, I was taken with fever and most of the time I have been in bed and I am still very feeble tho up and about. I had a wet time after I left you nearly all the way home and when I reached Ala. I met with the Army worm which pretty much destroyed the late crop of cotton.[259]

I have seen your friend Frank Gilmer and Crawford Bibb, they were both very glad to hear from you. They are very well, but very gloomy. Bibb has 2,500 acres planted in cotton and won't make 200 bales. I never have seen people as gloomy. Many crops are almost entire failures.

Will you do me the favor to let me know how the prospect is with you now. How much will Mr. McLemore make on your place? [*Jeff was planting Dr. Watkins's land.*] I would be glad to hear from you or him how those crops in the swamp are turning out which we visited.

I found my family all well. Many thanks to your family for your kindness during my visit. I hope someday to have the pleasure of reciprocating. Present my kind regards to both your daughters and to Mr. McLemore.

Yours very respectfully,

W. T. Hatchett

P.S. I told my wife of our visit to Mr. Fox. How I was *struck*.

To Lettie, who is in Carroll County, from Will:

November 28, 1866

My Darling Wife:

I am still well and still love you. However quickly I may cease to be the former I shall never cease to do the latter.

. . . Enclosed you will find the memorandum in regard to proper marking of your boxes—so mark them and they will come safely if not sunk in the gulf.

I have ordered bedroom and dining room furniture here. Carpets and parlor furniture may be bought in New Orleans—or you may defer and buy here.

I am still very busy and shall have a great mass of work on my hands when I get back but the trip after you will give me needed recreation.

I shall leave here between the 15th and 20th of December and push straight for you unless something I know nothing of now intervenes to stop me.

Kiss children. Love to old folks. I love you, believe it. Goodbye my darling. I hope soon to have you in my arms.

Your boy

---

259. The larvae of any of numerous moths, which travel in multitudes.

CHAPTER TWELVE

"The seasons and prices . . .
are always uncertain"

Dr. Watkins was a stiff, opinionated man, but ultimately the burdens of widowerhood, loss of estate, and other realities caused him to decide, late in 1866, to sell his place in Mississippi. The breaking up of his home of some twenty years—selling furniture, packing up keepsakes, clearing the way for the new owners—all were complicated and traumatic undertakings.

Early in 1867 Mr. Walton travelled to Mississippi to retrieve his family. Lettie had been visiting Forest Place, attempting to assist in the disposal of household effects. Will, however, also found it expeditious to travel to Washington, D.C., on state business.

Mollie and Jeff, meanwhile, decided to remain in Mississippi, and they settled into planting on one of Colonel McLemore's places on the Yazoo River, near Greenwood, using "hired hand" labor. One ensuing letter tells about the new lives now being enjoyed by the former slaves as "Freedmen."

The year 1867 proved to be a painful one for Mr. Walton. The office of attorney general of Texas was taken from him, as indeed not only he but also other elected state officials were removed from office when Congress commenced a new phase of Reconstruction, dissolving former governments. Will returned to full-time private law practice.

Gradually the families adjusted to the realities of living under new circumstances. The old ways of life were now part of a bygone era. One last letter details what had become of the former family slaves; interestingly, it also reflects the existence of some lingering affection between former mistress and former bondspeople.

The years pass, and letters begin to appear from Lettie's children, for now they are growing into young adulthood and going off to school. Those members of the family who have moved away from Mississippi gradually adjust to their new circumstances; and only scant and infrequent correspondence keeps them in touch with the news of Carroll County. Life on the plantation fades, for the Watkinses and the Waltons, into ever-more-dimly recalled memories. Now, it is only the letters that remain.

Home
January 23, 1867

Mrs. L. A. Walton

Dear Daughter:

I wish you and Mary would come over in the morning—also Mr. McLemore.

Your affectionate father,
Thos. A. Watkins

From Dr. Watkins in Winona to Maj. William Walton, in care of the St. Charles Hotel in New Orleans, Louisiana:

January 28, 1867

Dear Sir:

Maj. Watt has not yet returned and I cannot leave for Texas until I see him. You need not wait in New Orleans for me. I will come as soon as I can settle my business with Major Watt. I shall ship in a day or two some things to you such as various articles of crockery, glassware, blankets, brass kettle, books, etc. I have put up the shot gun for Newton. You may expect me shortly. I am much obliged to you and Lettie for your kind invitation to visit and stay with you. I know that a visit to Austin will improve my health.

My respects to Lettie and the children.

I am, Sir, with great respect
Your Obt. Servant,
Thos. A. Watkins

From Lettie Walton in Austin, Texas, to Dr. Watkins in Winona:

Feb. 16, 1867

My Dear Father,

We were much disappointed in not meeting you in New Orleans, but after we reached here I was glad you did not come when we did as our house was being repaired and will not be ready for us to go in before the middle of next week, if then. But you must not disappoint us again—be sure to come as soon as possible. You will find a comfortable room ready for you and we will be so glad to have you with us.

Pa, if you have not disposed of the pickle jars and salt-cellers, I would like very much to have half of them. That is one of the glass pickle jars and three of the little salt-cellers. I reckon sister will want the others. I wish I had thought to speak for the coffee pot too, but I bought one today, tho' it is not as nice as yours. Crockeryware is very high here.

We are staying with a friend—reached here on morning of 14th inst. after two nights and a day traveling in the stage. The hack we expected did not meet us.

Give my kindest regards to Major Watts' family. I really love them all and don't know when I ever became so much attached to a family in so short a time.

Give my love to Mrs. Whitehead and family and tell her that I left two dresses in New Orleans to be sent to her and Emma. Hope they have received them.

Tell them I intended sending nicer presents but did not have time to do anything as I wished.

Love to all my friends. Tell Miss Mollie and Elba [*Mollie Watt and Elba Gunn*] to write to me. Received two letters from you. Hope to see you soon. It is late at night and I have another letter to write tonight. Tell all the servants howday.

Your affectionate child,
Lettie Walton

To Lettie Walton from Martha Jennett Whitehead, wife of Edmunds Grey Whitehead:

June 8, 1867
Magnolia

My Dear Lettie,

Your kind and long looked for letter I had the pleasure to receive a few days ago. We all are very glad to hear from you. It is the second time that I have . . . [*illegible, torn manuscript*] New Orleans. I am glad to be able to say to you that it found us all well and getting along as well as we can expect. I think from what you say of the Freedmen, they are doing much better here than with you. I have heard no complaints in this neighborhood of their misbehaving, those I have about the house are doing pretty well, did not succeed in getting as good a house woman as I wished, but after hearing how they are acting with you, I think I ought to feel very well satisfied.

You inquired of me if I went to see Lizzie. I did not, but am pleased to say to you that Mrs. Phillips [260] was with her during her confinement, she has a fine boy [*William Bacon Oliver*]. Mrs. Phillips wrote me that it weighed 12 lbs. with his clothes on, had a fine head of black hair and that they were both doing well. I shall always feel under lasting obligation to Mrs. Phillips for her kindness to Lizzie during her confinement. My health was not good enough for me to leave home to be with her and hearing that Mrs. Phillips would be with her reconciled me in regards to being with her for I knew she was a much better nurse at such times than I was. I cannot tell you how Mrs. Phillips is making out but I expect rather badly. She mentioned in her letter that Mrs. Farmer's health and Mrs. Parmele's health had improved much lately. It was thought a few weeks ago that Mrs. Farmer had dropsy of the chest and would not live long but Mrs. Phillips mentioned in her letter that she expected to leave in a few days for Mississippi, so she must have improved very rapidly. I do truly sympathize with Mrs. Phillips,[261] and if I was able [*illegible, torn manuscript*] . . .

Her cup of trouble has been full to overflowing, but also how changed our times and things with us. It is now all we can do to make a support. Say to your Pa that Mr. Whitehead has turned out to be a real worker. He plows, hoes, or anything else that is necessary to be done (that is in the garden and for the tasks about the house) and, I believe, he is getting quite fond of it. Your Pa gave us all the dodge, and did not even come by to say goodbye. I am glad to hear that he is pleased with Texas and so well pleased with Mr. Walton. Not flattering you, Lettie, for I'm not one of the flattering sort, from the short acquaintance I have with Mr. Walton, I think he is a son-in-law your Pa may very well feel proud of. I have not seen Jeff and Mollie since

260. Mrs. Phillips's deceased daughter, Elizabeth, had been Mr. Oliver's first wife. All in the Phillips–Parmele family were particularly fond of Mr. Oliver and of Lizzie. "Eppie" was Mr. Oliver's daughter by Elizabeth. Lizzie was Elizabeth Oliver, Mrs. Whitehead's daughter.

261. Eppie was living with her father and Lizzie at this time in Alabama, and the three widows, Mrs. Phillips and her daughters, Julia Farmer and Mariah Parmele, and the five little Parmele children had moved to Alabama to be near Mrs. Phillips's brother. They had lost their plantation in Mississippi after Lieutenant Parmele's death.

you left. I have heard of her being in the neighborhood of Carrollton and Mr. McLemore's once or twice.

Virginia [*her daughter who married Captain Kennedy*] was up a short time ago and spent some two weeks with us, she and her family are well. I have not been to see Mrs. Watt [*who bought Watkins's place*] since you left. She came over and spent the evening with me. I was very much pleased with her. I intend going to see her soon. I leave home so seldom that it has gotten to be quite a task to visit.

I have not spent the day from home more than three or four times this year. They have quite a large family at Major Watts. Mr. [*illegible*] and family are living there. I think they have some 18 or 20 in all in family. Our children are all going to school and we have some three or four boarders, so you can see we have a pretty large family ourselves.

Patsy, as you call her, is still right fussy about her dinner. Ella Gertrude [*age seven*] has asked me when I am writing to say, "Give my love to Miss Lettie and all of them and tell her to kiss little Sarah [*Lettie's daughter*] for her and say to George that she is going to school and is nearly through her Second Reader."

Very little of interest has taken place in the neighborhood since you left. I believe there has been some three or four weddings. Captain Sanford to Miss Mildred Talliferro; John Turner to Miss Newell,[262] and Captain Rather of Louisville to Alice Davis. They were married in the morning, dined in Winona, and left on the Cars that evening. They had no one at the wedding. Not even their relations. Dr. Davis and Mrs. Perkins went with them to Louisville. Rumor says that she has married quite wealthy. There have been no deaths among your acquaintances since you left. Old Mrs. Gooch died a few weeks ago. Mrs. Weisinger had her youngest child scalded to death, or at least died the next day, after the accident happened. I did not hear any of the particulars.

You inquired of me if we had received some linen lawn that you left at Haggerties to be sent up. We have not even heard of it until I received your letter, also mentioned that it was your intention to have gotten several nice presents for my family. You ought not to have gotten what you did. You had already given me and the children several presents which are appreciated very much. You spoke of the kindness you received while here at my house, rest assured, Lettie, that all I did was cheerfully done, the only regret was that I was not able to have given you better accommodations and fare than I did

262. The daughter of Col. Camp P. Newell, an early lawyer of the county and several times mayor of Carrollton.

while you were here. It will, I do hope, always be a pleasure to me and my family. It may not, Lettie, be our fortune to meet any more in this wicked world, let us try and act so as to meet in Heaven where we both have loved ones awaiting us.

I saw Salsbury [*freed slave*] this morning, delivered your message to him, he says they are all well and doing pretty well and that he will get someone to write a letter for him soon to you.

Puss [*Mary L. Whitehead*] says she is going to write to Miss Lettie soon. I will not vouch for the truth of what she says. Mr. Whitehead and all the family join me in love to you and family including your Pa. You must excuse this uninteresting letter, will try and do better next time. I never write letters unless it is to my children and am very much out of practice. This is the first letter I have written to a friend for a long time. You must write as often as you can find time. We will always be glad to hear from you and family.

May health and happiness attend you and yours is the wish
of your sincere friend
M. J. Whitehead
I will deliver your message to Mrs. Watt when I see her. M.J.W.

Mollie writes to her sister:

September 21, 1867

. . . Last Thursday Addie and I went to Winona shopping and spent the day at Captain Edwards' and that night at Mr. John Davis' who is now living at John McLean's old place in Middleton. We met Mrs. Captain Rather and Mrs. J. Davis (wife of Brigadier General [*Joseph R.*] Davis) there and had quite a pleasant time . . . Addie and I spent last Friday at Judge Collins' and had a mighty good dinner, enjoyed ourselves finely, and we went to Mr. E. G. Whitehead's that night. All the family seemed very glad to see us and inquired there as they do everywhere also, only more so about Pa and you all. Gertie [*Ella Gertrude Whitehead*] said, "Miss Mollie, how is Sarah? Does Sarah ever talk about me?" After awhile she asked, "How is George? Is George forgot me?"

Dr. Brooks is boarding at Mr. Whitehead's and he told Gertie if she would have him for a sweetheart he would give her a fine house and a horse. She told him she didn't want them, that George Walton was her sweetheart and she intended never to have another. Tell George to send Gertie his photograph.

John Hawkins, Jr. died a few weeks ago with something like yellow fever, a disease contracted in the swamps. He was perfectly resigned to death. Before he died he asked his wife what clothes he would be shrouded in, and told them not to shave him but comb his whiskers nicely and be sure to brush his teeth. Mrs. Hawkins will return to her mother in North Carolina. Jennie Hawkins graduated last summer in Jackson, Tennessee. She is quite a sweet and pretty young lady.

. . . Colonel McLemore was so upset at the probability and so much opposed to Jeff leaving him to go so far as Texas that Jeff formed a partnership with Murril and Colonel Townsend and will merchandise in Winona next year.[263]

. . . Alice Davis and her "rich husband" will come in a few weeks to spend this winter at Mrs. Davis'. I don't know how they get along together, but well I bet, as long as he has enough money for her to spend according to her notion. I could but notice Mrs. Davis the other day in speaking of Rafter, she spoke of him with so much pride and emphasized the *Captain,* but in speaking of Rebecca's husband it was Weed did so, no Mr. or any other title. . . . Mrs. Whitehead has a good deal of her work to do herself. Emma frequently does the ironing.

I saw Aunt Hanna [*slave*] in Carrollton last week. She looked very badly. None of our negroes are pleased with Major Watts. Daniel told Jeff that they know the Major wouldn't pay them anything this year. Polly has been very sick. I am in hopes I can get Polly next year as a house servant . . ."

Mollie writes Lettie, detailing what has become of the family slaves, three years after the end of slavery. Mollie is boarding with the Whiteheads for the summer. Jeff has a place in the "swamp," i.e., the Delta.

From Mollie Watkins McLemore to sister Lettie Walton [first page of letter is missing]:

Fall 1868

. . . Polly is living with Mr. Barry on Mrs. Estill's old place. Ritt, Abram's family, Martha's family are living at Colonel Neill's. Robin stays at Petits Hotel in Carrollton. He doesn't work but superintends it [*the work*]. Polly does my washing for which I pay her $3.00 a month. Margaret is married, she had a baby very soon afterwards but it's dead. Early will marry in a month. Hannah heard Jeff [*McLemore*] was sick and last Saturday came to assist in nursing him. She and Chloe are living on a place two miles from Middleton which Chloe's husband bought. Chloe has two children and will soon be confined. John W., his wife Susan and Mitchell are near Courtland, Alabama and are anxious to get back here but have not the money to bear their expenses on the trip. Semira is living with the Blalocks near Winona. Henry is married and lives near Blackhawk.

263. Nevertheless, Jeff and Mollie did eventually move to Texas.

None of our negroes are faring as well as they would were they not so lazy.

Hannah says please send her one of the Baby's pictures. She begged me for one of those I have. Please send me one of those you have recently had taken of Baby [*Sarah*] and George and yours too if you had it taken. The last picture of Baby you sent me was not good. She is much better looking and not near so large. Oh how I would love to see her. Jeff talks about her all the time and is so anxious to see her. Jeff returned two weeks ago from the swamp. A few days afterwards he went to Carrollton and on his way there was taken with vertigo, came near fainting and falling from his horse and was too sick to return here for two days and a night. He went to bed after reaching here and had an attack of bilious fever. Dr. Ward said there was considerable congestion accompanying the fever. He started day before yesterday to the swamps and will be absent one or two weeks. I'm so miserable about him it almost crazes me. I can't sleep at night and rise every morning with headache and tired aching feeling in all bones.

Dromgoole bitters had none but the happiest effect on me. Perhaps your dose is too large which produces a sick stomach and your snuff dipping causes the strange feeling in your breast.

You ask why I didn't consult Dr. Ward as he once relieved me. I don't do it because Dr. Ben Ward never attended on me for the gravel or whatever it is and Dr. Ward is in Arkansas and did me no good when he was here. Kept me in bed three weeks while Dr. McEachern relieved me in one week. I don't suffer now like I did and I'm taking no medicine but bath every night in hot weather.

Mrs. Whitehead and all of her family were very kind and attentive to Jeff while he was sick. Mrs. Whitehead could not have been more attentive to one of her children. I do feel so grateful to them for this kindness to Jeff and me this summer and am so much more satisfied here than at Pa's [*Pa McLemore*]. Some people are very busy trying to find out why I came here instead of going there. Let them talk on just as I'm blessed in not being there.

A few weeks ago Sister Marion's [264] father arose perfectly well in the morning, was very lively during breakfast, arose from the breakfast table, walked to the water bucket, took a drink of water, and fell dead. No negroes or servants were on the place. The family do all of their own work. I'm so glad that Sister Marion visited them this summer although her trip partly prevented mine to you all. I expect her sister and mother will live next year with her. One thing's certain, I'm not going to keep house for them.

Cousin Sallie is staying with her sister Mrs. Doctor Wall in Panola County. She has discarded Dr. McEachern.

264. Jeff's sister–in–law, Sam McLemore's wife.

Gertie [*Ella Gertrude Whitehead*] is one of the sweetest children I ever saw. She often speaks of George and thinks he ought to send her his photograph as she sent him hers. She was much amused at Baby's nervousness on being left alone and seems interested when I talk about George and my little angel. She reminded me of a little old woman waiting on Jeff while he was sick. I am taking the Bazaar [*women's magazine*]. Have received two copies. Will appreciate and enjoy them fully when I go to the swamp. Sister Etta will be confined very soon. She beats me clearly in that line . . .

Your devoted sister,
Mollie W. McLemore

A letter written by Judge W. W. Whitehead from Hazelgreen in 1869 to his son, Eugene:

Hazelgreen
September 4, 1869

Dear Eugene:

Yours of the 22nd ult. reached me in due time as also Jennie's to your Ma. I am truly sorry to learn your crop has been cut-off for want of rain. It is a great misfortune to lose a crop at any time, but particularly so now when you are just setting out and when from the high price of cotton that portion of the crop is so valuable. The seasons and prices per cotton are always uncertain, and if you create a debt for land you might fail another year which would be ruinous. If you will take advice from me, don't go in debt for land. As you very well know, I am unable to assist you so far as money is concerned, but am entirely willing to give you land enough to make you a good little farm. You can have 160 acres in the southwestern part of my tract which will give you as much land (and that is as good) as you will need for cultivation, and by buying some 20 or 25 acres of the Holeman tract, you can make a good and comfortable settlement. This I think will be much the best for you in the end. This is a good part of the country, more healthy than Panola, and where any man is industrious and economical can get along and do well. I give you this opinion and advice and leave you to determine for yourself. The crops here that have been well worked are all good. My early corn was somewhat injured by the five-week drought but is a very fair crop. Cotton is doing as well as I ever saw it up to the present time. There are no insects interfering with it and it is very heavily bolled. I shall make up much when the few hands can get it.

Gertie and Charles [*children*] were both quite sick last week but are now well as are also the balance of the family. Martha Young [*daughter by first marriage*] has been unwell for the past week, but is better now and I hope will be well in a few days.

Since I commenced writing, she sent for me to go over and see Mattie who broke her arm again this morning, so I must come to a close. All send much love to you and Jennie. Write to me and let me know what you intend doing, as ever your affectionate father,

W. W. Whitehead

On January 17, 1875, Letitia's second son, Early, writes to his aunt in McLemore Bend, Mississippi:

How does George seem to like his new home? Does he like Gertie as well as ever, and did he enjoy his stay at Mrs. Whitehead's? . . .

By January 30, 1875, Letitia's son, Newton, is in school at the University of Virginia, and he writes his brother (Master George Walton) at Greenwood, Mississippi, where George is visiting Aunt Mollie and Uncle Jeff.

. . . Have you seen Gertie yet? Was she glad to see you? Do you love her much, George? Come, tell me, I won't tell on you. Is she pretty and sweet? Kiss her for me. What of old Ed and the rest of the family? Give my love to them all.

February 7, 1875, George Walton writes from Lone Star Bend, Tallahatchee River, Mississippi, to his brother, Newton, at the University of Virginia:

. . . You asked me if I love Gertie as well as ever. Yes, but she went back on me to find another one . . .

[This childhood romance between Ella Gertrude Whitehead and George Walton fortunately ended. Ella Gertrude's marriage to Alfred Dimond was important to the well-being of the co-editor.]

In July 1879, John D. McLemore writes to Dr. Thomas Watkins in Austin:

. . . I have just heard from Mr. Edmunds Whitehead. All seems well there but there has been more sickness in the neighborhood than usual. Mostly pneumonia has been the case all over the country. When I last saw Jeff, I felt very uneasy about him for he had a terrible cold bordering pneumonia. . . . All of your old friends in and around Carrollton are well as far as I know and getting along about as usual. Times are terrible here. Money was never as scarce since I have been in the States as it is now, and everybody or nearly everyone seems to be pressed and no one has any money to loan, but a plenty of borrowers.[265]

To Newton Walton from Edward D. Whitehead:

December 27, 1881

Newton Walton
Austin, Texas

My Dear Sir,

Gertie received a letter today from you from your mother asking her to see that your Grandmother's grave was all fixed up and I went over immediately on receipt of your letter to me and had the grave all nicely fixed up. Should have written to you immediately but saw Jeff McLemore and told him what I had done and he promised me he would write you and tell you. I had fixed the grave all up, you can say to your mother the grave is all nicely fixed up. Gertie is now in Alabama visiting our sister, Mrs. Oliver, and will be absent several weeks. I will forward your mother's letter to her.

I have nothing new to write. Time very full, crops, etc.

Hope you're getting along nicely. Wishing you a merry Christmas and all a happy New Year, I am your friend,

Eddie Whitehead[266]

December 30, 1881
Eutaw, Alabama

Dear Mrs. Walton,

You will see from the above I am now in Eutaw, have been here with Sis Lizzie for three weeks. I received your letter this morning (it was forwarded from Winona). I was so glad to hear from you all and hope I may have the pleasure of getting letters from you often. I heard from home a few days since all were well. I am getting quite anxious to see them all, will return home the first of February.

We regretted so much your not coming back to see us before you left Mississippi. Expected you to spend several weeks with us, would be so glad to have you and Sarah [*Lettie's daughter*] spend some time with us.

Since I left, bud Tommie [*brother*] and his wife have moved over home, he

265. The nagging economic depression following the Panic of 1873.
266. Edward DeGraffenreid Whitehead

has sold his place and will stay with us until he buys another. He speaks of going to the swamp, though we are very much opposed to it. I was glad they moved over to our home, will be so much company for us. Bud Grey [*brother*] is still merchandising in Winona. Eddie is clerking for him.

I saw Mr. McLemore about two months ago. He said Miss Mollie would be out the next week to spend some time with us but she hadn't come when I left. I suppose you have heard ere this of Cousin Martha Young's[267] death. She died about two months since. Sis Puss and I miss her very much as she visited us quite frequently, *and we loved her very dearly.*

Yes, Miss Lettie, I will take pleasure in seeing your mother's grave attended to and as soon as I go home will get Eddie to go over and see if the tomb needs mending and that the railing is put up right.

Sis Puss and I are *so much* obliged to you for the tie and fichu.[268] Will deliver your message to Polly [*freed slave*] when I see her. Where are Early and George now? You don't mention them in your letter at all.

Sis Lizzie sends her love and says she would be so glad if you would write to her.

Sis Jennie[269] spent a day or two with us before I left home. She and her family were well.

As I have written all the news will close. With much love for yourself and family. (Write soon)

Affectionately,
Gertrude W.

267. Martha Louise Whitehead, Judge Whitehead's daughter, who married John Ossian Young.

268. A shawl-like scarf of lace or thin material, tied in front.

269. Margaret Virginia Whitehead married Thomas Benjamin Kennedy.

EPILOGUE

In our cast of characters, William M. Walton, Lettie's husband, was almost the last survivor. He maintained his military title, major, and was addressed as Buck Walton. He lived on until 1915. Lettie died in 1914. Only one of their children, Sarah, survived them. The three sons died at ages twenty-six, thirty-two, and thirty-nine. Dr. Watkins died in 1884 in Austin.[270]

Jeff died at age forty-five in Chicago while delivering sheep to market. Stepping down from a street car, he was struck by another car. Mollie never remarried and lived in Austin, remaining close to the family, until her death at age ninty-one, in 1935—she was truly the last of the Watkinses of Carroll County, Mississippi.

After Lettie's death, "Buck" wrote an "epitome" of his life. The manuscript was in pencil on yellow legal-size paper and was not published until 1965. The manuscript came down through his daughter, Sarah [Mrs. Sarah Walton Parmele], to her daughter, Mrs. Louise Parmele Johnson.[271]

Buck Walton's story is the appropriate summary for this book. Through his children, the Watkins family line was continued, while Mollie and Jeff were childless. Because the central theme of the letters is Lettie's rebellion, her father's hostility and denigration of her husband, and the slow but ultimate healing of the wound, it seems only fair to let the old survivor, the final player on the stage, tell his side of the story. In the letters, Mrs. Watkins and the doctor have their time, repeatedly, to castigate the groom. Now, in his epitome, the groom, no

270. The *Austin Daily Statesman*, upon his death, wrote: "No ordinary man passed from the stage of action when Dr. Watkins died. He played a prominent and useful part in the drama of life, and died at the ripe age of eighty–two beloved and respected by a host of friends. He was a man of most varied scholarship, possessing a fund of knowledge on almost every subject."

271. The manuscript now belongs to the Austin–Travis County Collection, Austin Public Library.

longer an unproved, poor youth, but a secure man with honors, family, and a wife of sixty-one years, tells of the love affair—for the Watkins letters are a love story with a happy ending.

In this epitome, we learn for the first time that there was almost a different story. Just as Lettie had her other swains, Mr. Walton had his "moment." Here is the story in his words:

After returning from the University of Va., I visited the ladies—attended parties and balls—frequently—and half way fell in love with a girl—and the thing was working toward matrimony, although I never told her that I loved her & she did not tell me that she loved me—but all the same—the thing was patent that she thought a great deal of me, as I did of her. Knowing that I ought not to marry—common sense told me that—& she not being the woman I should marry, I formed the resolution to absent myself from the country for a while. I went to see her the morning I was to start & told her that I was on the eve of starting to Texas. The tears made her face look very sweet. She was a beautiful woman—the tears also blinded my eyes. Thus we parted.

. . . The whole time I was absent, I had written no letter home and had received no word from there. I wrote to my old sweetheart from Shreveport and told her I was coming home—but I had been absent too long. She had married and had been a bride for more than three months when I arrived.

Soon after that I became acquainted with my wife. I loved her truly and alone from the first time I saw her. The sequel will prove my love and the persistency with which I pursued her. In about eighteen months from the time I met her, I told her that I loved her, and wanted her to be my wife. She kicked me—or mittened me. I, a university man cut up and cut down, was a strange idea. I thought she was mistaken—that she did not understand herself. I made a new start—and thought I would teach her to understand herself. I was particularly polite and attentive. In my association with her I said nothing of love, nor intimated a word of marriage. I sought to make myself indispensable to her. A few months passed—with my heart seething and burning—but sternly repressed. The time at last came—and I opened the subject again. She was astonished and told me so—and not having forgot her privilege of kicking, kicked me again, and gave me the second mitten. I was nearly ready to come to Texas—and bade her an eternal good bye—and started for the wilds of that state on my good steed, Frank Pearce.

. . . I started on a rainy day—and traveled about forty miles—and stopped at Lexington for the night. I found there a fortune teller—a fakir—but I consulted her— . . . She bowed her head and thought for some time as if in a trance. She waked up & told me that a young woman loved me—and that some misunderstanding existed between us—and that I was running away from fortune—that if I would return, the sky would clear and the misunderstanding would pass away. I wanted to go back any how. I felt deep down in my heart that she loved me—and that there [*was*] some obstruction in the way. I had told all my friends good bye—and I hardly had the moral courage to return. I had my horse saddled the next morning however—and resolved to let him choose what I would do. I mounted & he without any hesitancy started for home.

. . . The next day I went to see her. I had suffered so much at the idea of leaving her forever—that its effects were plainly visible in my appearance. She was very glad to see me—and before I left her, I put my fate to the test once more, and she agreed to marry me—provided her parents would consent. I was not long in seeing her father. I was sure of her mother—one of the noblest and kindliest women in the world—but the father was of sterner stuff. He at first said that he would consult with his wife and daughter and let me know the result—all very kindly and courteous. The consultation must have been very short—for the very next day I received a note of a few lines from him—in which he declined the alliance which I offered to make with his family—Respectfully declined. I was but twenty years old—and his action confounded me. We had quite a correspondence over the subject—but it wound up, with the statement—that Dr. Watkins (my wife's father) never changed his written opinions and conclusions. I went to see her, Miss Lettie A. Watkins, once again—and then we solemnly engaged ourselves to marry, that I should come on to Texas and make provision for her reception—and in a year or two, she would let me know when to return for her . . .

I came on to Austin, the place I had long before selected as my home. I arrived here on the 19th day of February, a month after I was twenty one years old . . .

During the year 1853 brother George had charge of the Negroes and attended all outside business. He employed some of them on a farm, some in brick making, & hired some of them out. We had a good many ups and downs—but generally came out even. My fees, made at law, were thrown into the general hotch potch and left for George to manage. He was ten years in advance of the time—and expended the most of our money in land—until we became land poor—and had to sell at a loss—and we became embarrassed—and we had to sail close to shore for several years—but we never sold any negroes. They were negroes that we had inherited from our parents—and we would not think of parting with them . . .

In the winter of 1854, I received a letter from Miss Watkins. We had corresponded all the time, secretly—but in this letter she told me to come, and that she would marry me, no matter what opposition might be made. Her father during 1853 had carried her on a long trip north & she had visited most of the cities, trying & her father helping her, to forget me—but there was a fatality about it. I had landed in her heart, as she had rode in mine—and our destinies were fixed. I was soon ready and rode horseback to Shreveport, La. where I took boat—and was with her as soon as the boat could get there. I got there on a Monday—and we fixed the time for marrying on the next Thursday. Her father was still opposed—violently so. I told him I had come to marry his daughter—but that I did not intend to steal her—that I should come in a carriage at 10 o'clock—and would take her off, & be married at the County Judge office. He made some threats, if I came to his house for that purpose. I said to him that I could not die in a better cause, & that I would come as I said I would. It may be that I was a fool to brave Dr. Watkins that way—but I was young, warm blooded and hot headed. On the night before I was to go out, I received a note from him—in which he consented for us to be married at his house, but saying that he would not see us married. I felt greatly relieved—for I had expected bloodshed. I went out with a few friends—and the ceremony was quickly over—and I took my wife away—and I never saw Dr. Watkins again until 1867.

We came to Texas at once. When we arrived here I advised my wife that it was [a] child's duty to make the first step toward a reconciliation, where there was an estrangement between it & its parents—to write to her father a kind letter—but not to mention me in the letter nor say anything about being married. She did so, and in due time received the letter back unopened, but endorsed on the back "I have no correspondent in Texas"—and signed his name. Now I said to wife, "You have done your duty and we will pursue your way, as best we can—loving one another—doing our duty—and trusting in God." Her mother corresponded with wife all the time. In 1855, we had a baby boy Newton—and wife wanted to see her mother. I sent her back, not to her father's house—but to one of his neighbors [Edmunds Grey Whitehead's home]—where she could meet her mother—but her father's heart relented and he sent his carriage for her. She remained away the whole of that year—and during her absence brought me another baby boy, Early. Then we had two babies. I met her at Galveston where I first saw my new baby boy. He was a homely little thing and I asked permission of wife to throw him out of the window in the ocean. No sir she could not dispose of him that way. He soon was a fine looking boy and grew up to be one of the finest—and handsomest men—in the country, with the sweetest disposition and noblest heart that was ever seen or known among men. He died in New York in Sept. 1888, and at the time of his death was House Surgeon of the Manhattan Eye, Ear & Throat Institution.

Wife went again to see her parents in 1858—staying about a year—and I went after her in 1859. Those trips to Miss. were memorable, for it was a stage coach to Houston—Buffalo Bayou Steamer to Galveston—a steamer over the Gulf to N.O.—by boat to Greenwood on the Yazoo River, and thence by horse or mule back out to the hills where Dr. Watkins lived.

Wife did not go to Miss. any more for six years—not until 1865 and then her mother was dead. She had had a terrible spell of sickness when our daughter Sarah was a baby. She went to her father's house & there met him & her sister Mary—while I remained at Austin to try to build up my fortune after the war. We then had four children—George had come in 1860. He grew up to be a manly man—very much like me in person, more so than any of the children. He was accidentally shot when he was twenty five years old— lingered and died after three months of suffering.[272]

Sarah, our only girl, married J. J. Parmele in 1890—and now lives—being the mother of eight children. She is a splendid mother & woman—none better on earth. She lives very happily with her husband, who is a splendid husband & father. May they live many years, after I have passed over the River.

I was elected Atty. Genl. of Texas in 1866—but did not serve the term out, being removed by the military authority of the United States as an obstruction to reconstruction, a very arbitrary exercise of power—destructive of states' rights and local self government—but we were then under the heel of despotism, helpless, and we had to submit to innumerable outrages. It was a good thing for me however. It forced me back to my profession of the law which I followed with diligence and profit for many years afterwards.

Of course, the central figure in the letters was the patriarch, Dr. Thomas Alexander Watkins: born in Georgia, schooled in Philadelphia, a doctor in Alabama until the age of forty-five, then a planter in the new country for twenty years. He was sixty-three when his wife, Sarah, died and sixty-five when he sold the plantation and joined his daughter and her husband in Austin, living with them for seventeen years. His bitter intransigence was a shadow over the lives of Sarah, of Lettie, of Buck and, of course, over his own. From the time of the marriage in 1854 until 1867, the two men did not see each other. Lettie was welcomed

---

272. He was accidentally shot when an inebriated man shot wildly during a Christmas tree celebration in Granger, Texas—the small town near the Walton sheep ranch owned by the three Walton sons and managed by George.

back into the home in 1856, 1859, and 1865, and she and the grand-children—as well as her husband's successful career, in both war and peace—served to quiet and eventually remove the doctor's hostility.

Stern, stubborn, imperial, educated, mannered—he was perfectly cast for the role he played in this small saga of life as it was lived on a plantation in Carroll County, Mississippi. In truth, they all were: Sarah, Lettie, Mollie, Jeff, the servants—and, the doctor.

APPENDIX

CAST OF CHARACTERS

(compiled by Eugenia Richards)

The following pages list people and locations mentioned in the letters. Included are the dates of letters in which each entry appears and, when possible, a brief identification.

A second list follows providing information about the Forest Place slaves.

A

Aberdeen, Mississippi
Sept. 2, 1854
Acee, General
Mar. 8, 1854
Feb. 24, 1862
June 21, 1862
1) spelled "Acey" in letter of Mar. 8, 1854. We are unable to verify initials or source of his title.
Acklin, Mr.
May 30, 1851
Sept. 2, 1854
1) of Ala.
2) bought Uncle Billy Fitzgerald's slave, Lucinda
Adams, Dr.
Dec. 17, 1860
Nov. 26, 1860

Jan. 31, 1861

April 27, 1861

1) Episcopal minister at Carrollton, Ms.

2) m. Miss Doty, 1861

3) Mrs. Adams taught at Middleton Female Seminary for a time in 1861–62

Alford, Hon. Julius C.

Dec. 28, 1857

1) living in Texas

2) boyhood friend of Dr. Thomas Watkins

Allen, Mrs.

March 20, 1865

Allen, Tom

Feb. 9, 1862

1) of Duck Hill

American Courier

1) a newspaper Dr. Watkins sent to Lettie while she was in school at Columbia, Tn.

Anderson, Martha

Dec. 24, 1851

1) niece of Richard Anderson; school friend of Lettie Watkins at Holly Springs, Ms.

Anderson, Richard "Dick"

Dec. 29, 1848

Jan. 13, 1849

1) uncle of Miss Ann Watkins of Huntsville, Ala.

2) uncle of Martha Anderson

Andrews, Bishop

Dec. 17, 1860

1) Methodist bishop

Applewhite, Mr.

Sept. 11, 1861

Archer, Mr.

Nov. 1, 1858

Mar. 15, 1859

Nov. 2, 1859

Dec. 16, 1859

Feb. 10, 1860

April 4, 1860

Jan. 26, 1861

Jan. 31, 1861

1) headmaster of Patapsco Institute in Ellicotts Mill, Maryland, where Mary "Mollie" Watkins attended school.

Armstrong, Mrs.

Mar. 31, 1849

Arnold, Charles A.

Oct. 3, 1861

1) m. Mary S. Whitehead (daughter of Judge WilliamWhitehead), May 8, 1856
2) see Arnold, Mary

Arnold Martha W.

Sept. 2, 1854

Arnold, Mary S. (Formerly Mary Whitehead)

Mar. 11, 1857
July 30, 1857
Dec. 2, 1857
April 5, 1858
Dec. 20, 1858
Dec. 5, 1860
Oct. 3, 1861
Nov. 4, 1861
Mar. 31, 1862
Jan. 9, 1864
1) m. Charles A. Arnold, May 8, 1856
2) 1860 census:

Charles Arnold	30	Ms.
Mary	25	Ms.
John	2	Ms.
Sally	6/12	Ms.

Ascue (Askew), Dr.

April 4, 1851
1) doctor in Carrollton

Atkins, Dr. H. B.

May 2, 1861
Aug. 8, 1861
1) physician in Middleton
2) 1860 census:

H. P. Atkin	35	physician	S.C.
N. E.	29		Ms.
M. A.	6 f		Ms.
W. T.	3 m		Ms.
Margaret	1 f		Ms.

Austen, Miss

Feb. 23, 1852
1) child born out of wedlock

Austin, Dr. T. A.

Dec. 28, 1857
1) m. Jane (Jennie) Sykes, Dec. 20, 1857

Austin, Texas

1) Lettie and William M. Walton's home from their marriage until their deaths

Avery, Mr.

April 4, 1854
1) lived on the way to the Egglestons

Ayres, Joe
   Sept. 2, 1854

B

Bacon, George Ann Merriwether (Mrs. Thomas J.)
   Sept. 10, 1862
   1) Dr. Watkins's niece
   2) daughter of Dr. Watkins's sister, Lucy, and her first husband, George Merriwether
   3) husband killed in action, Battle of Seven Pines, May 31–June 1, 1862
   4) Jane Reece was her half-sister

Bailey, Ann*
   Sept. 23, 1855
   Jan. 12, 1856
   1) m. West Gary, Nov. 25, 1855
   2) daughter of Alden S. Bailey and Evaline
   (A. Bailey was head professor of boys' school in Middleton and a Baptist preacher, Judson Institute)
   3) 1850 census:

Alden S. Bailey	50	Bapt. minister	Vt.
Evaline	38		Ga.
Joshua	19	merchant clerk	Ga.
Thomas	17		Ms.
*Ann	13		Ms.
Mary	11		Ms.
Simeon	4		Ms.

Bailey, Joshua
   Mar. 11, 1857
   1) son of A. S. Bailey
   2) m. Minerva Barrow

Bailey, Tom
   Sept. 23, 1855
   Mar. 26, 1860
   1) m. Mary L. Barrow, Oct. 11, 1855
   2) Mary and Tom moved to California

Baker, Mr.
   Dec. 28, 1856
   1) had a storm party which Mary Watkins attended
   2) lived around Middleton

Bamburg, Mr. George
   May 15, 1857
   1) lived six miles from Dr. Watkins, Middleton area
   2) hired servant, London
   3) m. Julia A. Swift, Oct. 13, 1836

4) 1850 census:

George Bamburg	38	farmer	S.C.
Julia Ann	33		S.C.
William	12		Ms.
Robert	9		Ms.
Thomas	7		Ms.
Joseph	6		Ms.
George	3		Ms.
Mary	1		Ms.

Barbee, John
May 15, 1857
June 8, 1857
Dec. 28, 1857
June 14, 1858
1) Ala. resident
2) his son, John Barbee, also mentioned

Barker, Charles
Dec. 1, 1848
1) killed, Moulton, Ala.

Barkdsale, Mr.
Feb. 21, 1853
Nov. 2, 1860

Barksdale, Miss
Mar. 19, 1850
1) schoolmate of Lettie's at Capt. Binford's at Grenada

Barnes, Mr.
Feb. 24, 1862

Barnes, Garbriella (Gabe)
Mar. 16, 1860
Mar. 17, 1860
1) parents: Henry P. and Mary Barnes of Carrollton
2) 1850 census: age 12, b. Ms.

Barnes, Mr. and Mrs. Henry P.
Dec. 28, 1850
1) 1850 census:

Henry P. Barnes	48	merchant clerk	N.C.
Mary	30		N.C.
Orrin	17		N.C.
Augustina	15		N.C.
Gabriella	12		Ms.

Barnes, Mrs. Mary
April 26, 1860
1) of Carrollton
2) 1850 census: age 30, b. N.C.
3) 1850 census: her husband, Henry P. Barnes, listed as a merchant in
Carrollton, age 48, b. N.C.

Barrow, Lizzie
Mar. 17, 1860
April 28, 1860
1) daughter of William Barrow
2) see Barrow, Mary
3) m. Shaw Stevens
4) 1850 census: age 8

Barrow, Mary L.*
Sept. 23, 1855
Mar. 26, 1860
1) m. Tom Bailey, Oct. 11, 1855; moved to California
2) daughter of William Barrow
3) (Narcissa) Mrs. Barrow's father was Warner Wadlington; they came from Madison Co., Ms., in 1834
4) 1850 census:

William Barrow	43	farmer	Tn.
Narcissa	37		Ky.
*Mary	13		Ms.
Isabella	11		Ms.
Minerva	10		Ms.
Eliz	8		Ms.
James	7		Ms.
George	6		Ms.
John	3		Ms.
Margaret	9/12		Ms.

Barrow, Minerva
Mar. 11, 1857
1) daughter of William Barrow
2) m. Joseph Baily; going to California

Barry, Mrs.
Mar. 26, 1860

Barry, A.B.
Nov. 2, 1860
Fall 1868
1) m. Cordelia Roy, Dec. 1, 1859
daughter of Alexander Roy (see Roy, Alexander)
2) 1860 census (Carroll Co., Ms.):
A. B.　24　Cordelia　19

Barry, Mrs. Cordelia (Roy)
Nov. 2, 1860
1) new baby, 1860
2) Cordelia Roy m. A. B. Barry, Dec. 1, 1859

Baskerville, Mr. and Mrs. John W.
Oct. 20, 1860
Nov. 2, 1860
Sept. 11, 1860

Oct. 3, 1861

1) 1860 census:

John W. Baskerville	37		Va.
Sallie A.	36		N.C.
Wesley	11		Va.
John	9		Va.
Ann	7		Va.
Sallie	5		Va.
Mary	3		Va.

Bee, General Barnard

July 22, 1861

Bennett, Miss M. W.

Sept. 2, 1854

1) m. J. W. Holeman (Dr.), Sept. 6, 1854

2) older daughter of E. W. Bennett

Bennett, Minerva, Jr.

Dec. 28, 1856

1) m. T. B. Coopwood of Chickasaw Co., Jan. 25, 1859

2) older daughter of E. W. Bennett

Bennett, Mrs. Minerva* (Mrs. E. W.)

Feb. 16, 1861

April 27, 1861

May 2, 1861

1) lived in Middleton

2) 1860 census:

E. W. Bennett	58	farmer	N.C.
*Minerva	46		N.C.
E. W., Jr.	23		Ms.
McComb	16		Ms.
John	14		Ms.
Barton	10		Ms.
Julia	6		Ms.
F. B.	3		Ms.
William Rush	10		Ms.
George Rush	8		ms.

Bently, Fanny

Dec. 1, 1848

1) m. Mr. Houston of Courtland, Ala.

Bibb, Algernon S.*

Jan. 18, 1849

Feb. 20, 1849

Mar. 9, 1849

Mar. 26, 1849

1) marriage to Miss Mary Carroway described

2) son of John Dandridge Bibb, state senator of Ala.

3) b. Jan. 1829

4) lived in Montgomery Co., Ala.

5) 1850 census (Montgomery Co., Ala.):

*Algernon S. Bibb	21	Ala.
Mary A.	19	Ms.
Mary C.	1/2	Ala.
Dandridge	22	Ala.
Terry, Mary	39	N.C.

Bibb, Mr. and Mrs.

Mar. 26, 1849

1) friends of Dr. and Mrs. Thomas Watkins

2) probably Algernon S. Bibb and his new bride, who married shortly before

Bibb, Governor Thomas, of Alabama

Mar. 26, 1860

1) uncle of Algernon S. Bibb

Bibb, Crawford

Oct. 12, 1866

1) brother of Dandridge and Algernon Bibb

2) b. Jan. 1, 1820

Bibb, Dr. Dandridge Ashbury

Jan. 13, 1849

Feb. 20, 1849

1) brother of Algernon Bibb

2) called "deaf" Dr. Bibb by Dr. Watkins

3) son of John Dandridge Bibb, state senator of Ala.

4) b. Nov. 10, 1827

5) 1850 census (Montgomery County, Ala):

listed age 22, b. Ala. and living with A. S. Bibb (his brother)

Billings, Miss Amanda

Mar. 26, 1849

April 25, 1849

1) teaching school at the academy at Middleton

2) 1850 census: age 21, b. N.Y., boarding with the Hogarth family

Billups, Mrs. Col.

Oct. 12, 1862

1) old friend of Dr. and Mrs. Watkins

2) living in Columbus, Ms. in 1862

Binford, Capt. John A.

Jan. 13, 1849

July 23, 1849

Feb. 9, 1850

Mar. 9, 1850

April 20, 1850

April 13, 1861

1) had a school on his place near Grenada, Ms.

2) Lettie Watkins in school there, spring 1850

3) Adelaide Geren in school there, 1849

Binford, John and Jimmy
April 13, 1861
Feb. 9, 1862
April 13 1862
1) sons of Captain John Binford

Binford, Miss Margaret
Mar. 19, 1850
June 7, 1850
Jan. 30, 1852
1) school friend of Lettie's.
2) only daughter of Capt. Binford, Grenada
3) m. Solon Skyes, Dec. 27, 1852
4) 1850 census: age 16, b. Tn.

Bingham, Lou (Mrs. Robert) (See Gee)
Mar. 9, 1861
Mar. 11, 1861
1) 2nd Mrs. Bingham
2) formerly Lou Gee (Mary Louise Gee, daughter of Peter and Mary A. Gee)
3) 1850 census: shows Catherine (first wife)

Bingham, Robert Leroy
Mar. 9, 1861
1) m. Cathrin Terry, July 30, 1845
2) second wife, m. Mary Louise "Lou" Gee
3) he appears with his first wife on 1850 census
4) had a mercantile firm in Carrollton for many years
5) 1850 census:

Robert Bingham	34	farmer	Tn.
Catherine	23		Ala.
Thomas	1		Ms.
Robert Sr.	75		N.C.

Bingham, Tom
Mar. 2, 1852
1) Dr. Watkins's former overseer, killed on another place by his Negroes

Bird, Gus
Sept. 5, 1860
1) A. J. Bird m. Margaret Wright, Dec. 15, 1852
2) 1860 census:

Augustus Bird	35	farmer	N.C.
Margaret	25		Tn.
James	7		Tn.
Henry	5		Tn.
Laura	3		Tn.
Ella	8/12		Tn.

Bird, Mr. and Mrs.
Nov. 7, 1851
Jan. 30, 1852

April 4, 1852
April 19, 1852
July 4, 1855
Sept. 23, 1855
Jan. 12, 1856
1) overseer on Dr. Watkins's place (and later on E. Whitehead's place)

Blackhawk, Mississippi
Oct. 8, 1857 and other repeated mentions

Black's and White's Virginia
July 31, 1860
1) old Virginia town named for two taverns at either end of town run by
Mr. White and Mr. Schwartz ("black" in German)

Blalock, Mr. and Mrs.
1) fall, 1868, near Winona

Bledsoe, Green
May 15, 1857
June 14, 1858
Dec. 1, 1862
June 11, 1863
1) brother of Mary Bledsoe Fitzgerald, who was Sarah Watkins's sister-in-law
2) 1850 census:

Green Bledsoe	29	farmer	N.C.
Sarah	23		Ala.
Mary	1		Ms.

Bledsoe, John
Dec. 1, 1862
1) brother of Mary Bledsoe Fitzgerald, Sarah Watkins's sister-in-law
2) brother of Green Bledsoe of Carroll Co., Ms.
3) member of Wall's Legions in Civil War
4) from Tx., had moved there with mother and brother, Henry
5) wife a widow, formerly Miss Justice, niece of Mrs. John Glass

Bledsoe, Mrs. Winnie Murphy
Feb. 14, 1849
Sept. 2, 1854
1) Sarah E. F. Watkins's brother's mother-in-law in Ala.
2) widow of Joseph Bledsoe
3) daughters were Mary A., who m. Sarah Watkins's brother, William Fitzgerald,
and Sallie
4) four known sons who lived to adulthood: Calvin; Henry and John, who
moved to Tx. with their mother; Green, who lived in Carroll Co., Ms.

Bluff Springs, Mississippi (Church)
June 8, 1857
April 10, 1860
April 28, 1860
July 10, 1860

Blunt, Mr. David
Dec. 28, 1859
Feb. 10, 1860
1860 census:

David Blunt	52	N.C.
Sina	37	Ms.
L. J.	20 f	Ms.
I. W.	18 m	Ms.
Suzanna	16	Ms.
Benjamin	13	Ms.
E. A.	11	Ms.
James	9	Ms.
Charles	7	Ms.
Alfred	4	Ms.
L. M.	4	Ms.
Paralee	2	Ms.

Blunt, Miss Laura Jane
Feb. 3, 1860
Feb. 10, 1860
1) m. to W. E. Duke, Feb. 2, 1860
2) daughter of David Blunt
Boling, L. S.
Nov. 2, 1859
1) m. Lala Shaw (Sarah B. Shaw), Oct. 18, 1859
Booth, Ad.
Mar. 11, 1857
Booth, Mrs. E. G.
Nov. 26, 1860
1) Sally Tanner Jones formerly
2) sister to "cousin" Dandridge Epes's wife
3) Sarah Watkins's kin in Va.
Booth, Colonel
Sept. 15, 1864
Booth, Tom
Feb. 9, 1862
April 13, 1862
1) Carroll Co. soldier
2) probably son of William Booth
Booth, Mr. William
Nov. 7, 1851
June 1, 1855
1) family mentioned
2) the Mr. Booth mentioned was no doubt William Booth, sheriff of Carroll Co.,
and close neighbor to Dr. Watkins

3) 1850 census:

William Booth	47	N.Y.
Matilda	38	Ky.
DeWitt C.	20	Ms.
William	18	Ms.
John M.	13	Ms.
Thomas J.	11	Ms.
Henry H.	9	Ms.
Julia	4	Ms.
Matilda	3	Ms.
Sally	10/12	Ms.

Bowen, Ann
Dec. 29, 1849
Feb. 14, 1849
Mar. 9, 1849
Mar. 31, 1849
1) Lettie's school friend at Columbia, Tn.
Bowers, Mr. and Mrs. (Judy)
May 14, 1866
1) Austin residents
Bradley, Mrs.
Mar. 26, 1860
1) her daughter was in school at Patapsco
2) Mrs. Bradley, the granddaughter of Gov. Thomas Bibb of Ala.
Branch, Babe Watkins
Jan. 12, 1856
1) See Wingfield, Mary
Brian, Mrs. James (Bryan)
Mar. 16, 1860
Mar. 17, 1860
1) has a niece, Miss Shackleford
Bridges, Mr. and Mrs.
July 23, 1849
Bridges' Tavern
June 7, 1850
1) in Middleton
Broadwell, Mr.
March 26, 1849
1) visited Dr. Watkins's home
Brooks, Dr.
Sept. 21, 1867
1) boarding at Mr. Whitehead's
Brown, Mr.
Jan. 30, 1852
Jan. 8, 1864
1) of Carrollton, Mississippi

Brown, Mr.
  July 23, 1849
  1) of Grenada, Mississippi
Brown, Sue
  1) m. Phil Palmer
Bryan (Bryant, Briant), James A. S.
  July 23, 1849
  Jan. 12, 1856
  1) half-brother of Elizabeth N. Davis (Mrs. Judge William Whitehead)
  2) m. first Felicita Bell, Aug. 19, 1845
  3) 1850 census: age 28, farmer in La., and Felicitas, age 3, Ms.
Buchanan, Mary
  Sept. 2, 1854
  1) letter says she was to marry Jimmy Davis but evidently she didn't
  2) daughter of Thomas E. Buchanan
  3) 1850 census:

Thomas E. Buchanan	37	farmer	Ga.
Sarah A.	37		Ga.
Catherine	17		Ga.
Virginia	15		Ga.
Mary A.	12		Ga.

  plus other younger children
Burleson, Mrs.
  Sept. 2, 1854
  1) died in June 1854; Ala. resident
Burrows, Mr.
  Nov. 7, 1851
Burt, Ann
  March 16, 1860
  1) reported to be ill
  2) See Pratt, Abraham
  3) 1860 census: age 22
Burt, "Old" Mr. Harry
  Oct. 24, 1857
  1) dead
Burt, Mr. and Mrs. S. M.
  Mar. 16, 1860
  1) dead of pneumonia
  2) see Pratt, Abraham
  3) 1860 census (Carroll Co.):
  A. F. Pratt (admin. of estate of S. M. Burt, deceased)

A. F. Pratt	30	farmer	Ga.
Mary Pratt	20		Ms.
John Pratt	1		Ms.
Ann Burt	22		Ms.
Eugenia Burt	16		Ms.
James Burt	12		Ms.

Bush, Mrs.
   Sept. 15, 1864
Butt, Ellen D.*
   July 30, 1857
   1) m. to Green Summerfield Fox, July 10 1857
   2) 1850 census:

John W. Butt	36	physician	Va.
Francies	36		N.C.
Benjamin	13		Ms.
*Ellen	11		Ms.
Henry	11		Ms.
John	7		Ms.
Nancy	6		Ms.
Virginia	4		Ms.
Charles	2		Ms.
Leander	5/12		Ms.

C

Campbell, Mr.
   Sept. 2, 1854
   1) of Mountain Home, Ala.
Campbell, Catherine
   Nov. 22, 1860
   1) Virginia resident, third cousin of Sarah Epes Fitzgerald Watkins
Campbell, Frank
   April 13, 1863
Campbell, Jimmy and Charlie
   Feb. 9, 1862
Campbell, Miss Sarah
   April 9, 1851
   May 30, 1851
   Oct. 16, 1851
   Nov. 7, 1851
   1) school friend of Lettie's of Middleton
   2) boarded with Mrs. Phillips and Mr. Holt
   3) 1850 census: age 14, b. Ms., boarding with Benjamin Holt
Campbellites
   Nov. 7, 1851
   June 8, 1857
   1) disputing with Methodists in Middleton
Caperton, Lucy Ann
   Mar. 26, 1849
   1) ran away, m. Mr. Rowe at Parson Neal's
   2) 1850 census:

Washington Rowe	29	farmer	S.C.
Lucy A.	19		Ms.

Marianna	4/12	Ms.
Caperton, Maria C.	53	N.C.

Caroway, Miss Mary
Dec. 29, 1848
Feb. 14, 1849
Mar. 9, 1849
1) m. Algernon S. Bibb on Mar. 7, 1849
description of bridesmaids: Elisa Terry and Martha Whitehead
Carrington, Mr.
Oct. _____, 1862
Nov. _____, 1862
1) of Austin, Tx.
Carrington, Mrs.
Sept. 26, 1864
1) of Austin, Tx.
Carrollton, Mississippi
July 4, 1855
Sept. 23, 1855
numerous other mentions
1) county seat of Carrollton
2) six miles from Dr. Watkins's home
Carter, George Washington
July 31, 1862
Company B, 21st Texas cavalry
Cathren, Mr.
Feb. 10, 1860
Mar. 16, 1860
1) incorrect spelling, see *Kettering*
Caudle, Mary (Cardle)
April 4, 1851
Sept. 26, 1864
Chandler, Mr.
July 4, 1855
1) of Austin, Tx.
Chestnut Hill, Mississippi
Nov. 2, 1859
1) new church
Chevalier, Mr. and Mrs.
Oct. 8, 1857
Oct. 24, 1857
Nov. 30, 1857
Dec. 28, 1857
Jan. 18, 1858
1) principal of Mary's (Mollie) school at Holly Springs
Chylibeate Springs
Sept. 2, 1854
1) Mountain Home, Ala.

Clapp, Mr. and Mrs.
Dec. 15, 1851
Dec. 24, 1851
Mar. 2, 1852
Mar. 12, 1852
1) friends of Dr. Watkins at Holly Springs, Ms.
Clark, Miss
Dec. 9, 1861
1) m. John Money of Carrollton
Clark, Mr.
Dec. 24, 1851
1) the dancing master at Lettie's school in Holly Springs
Clark, Mrs.
Aug. 27, 1861
Nov. 4, 1861
1) maiden name was Margaret Long
2) mother of Gov. Edward Clark of Texas
Clayton, Judge
Oct. 15, 1851
April 11, 1852
June 27, 1862
1) lived near Holly Springs
Cobbs, "Aunt Mary"
Nov. 7, 1851
Mar. 11, 1857
Feb. 16, 1861
1) Martha M. Phillips's sister
2) 1850 census: listed as Mary Cobbs, age 30, b. Va.
Collins, Dr.
June 22, 1861
1) of Issaquena Co., Ms.
2) friend of Mollie's
Collins, Dick
Aug. 5, 1861
1) old friend of Lettie's
Collins, Elizabeth (Bettie)
Dec. 28, 1857
Nov. 1, 1858
Mar. 17, 1860
July 31, 1860
Nov. 2, 1860
July 9, 1861
1) daughter of Judge William Y. Collins
2) m. second Reuben Baskin
3) 1850 census: age 10

Collins, James
July 31, 1860
Nov. 2, 1860
Collins, Mary (Mollie)
Dec. 28, 1857
Nov. 1, 1858
Mar. 17, 1860
July 31, 1860
Nov. 2, 1860
Jan. 26, 1861
June 6, 1861
June 26, 1861
July 9, 1861
1) daughter of Judge William Y. Collins
2) m. Dr. Washington Stovall
3) 1850 census: age 8
Collins, Sarah (Sally)
Dec. 28, 1857
Nov. 1, 1858
Dec. 20, 1858
Nov. 2, 1859
April 10, 1860
July 31, 1860
Jan. 31, 1861
July 9, 1861
Dec. 9, 1861
Nov. 4, 1862
1) daughter of Judge W. Y. Collins
2) 1850 census: age 15
3) m. Dr. Dauney (Downey), his fourth wife
Collins, Tom
Feb. 9, 1862
Mar. 13 1862
1) Carroll Co. resident
2) probably son of Judge William Y. Collins
Collins, Judge William Y. and Mrs.
Dec. 28, 1856
Oct. 24, 1857
Feb. 16, 1858
June 14, 1858
Oct. 26, 1858
Dec. 20, 1858
Jan. 27, 1860
Mar. 16, 1860
July 31, 1860
Oct. 6, 1860

Oct. 20, 1860
Aug. 8, 1861
July 31, 1862
Feb. 4, 1865
Sept. 21, 1867
1) second wife, Mary Hill, Copiah Co.
2) 1850 census:

William Y. Collins	60	farmer	S.C.
Mary	45		Ms.
Thomas	12		Ms.
Elizabeth	10		Ms.
Mary	8		Ms.
Catherine Holt	55		N.C.
Mary M. Newman	16		Ms.
Sarah Collins	15		Ms.

3) 1860 census:

William Collins	69	farmer	S.C.
Sarah	24		Ms.
Bettie	20		Ms.
Mollie	18		Ms.
Thomas	22		Ms.
*Mary	60		Va.

f., mulatto, washer woman
*This Mary must have been "free" to appear on the 1860 census.

Columbia Female Institute
Columbia, Tn.
1) Judge Whitehead's daughters attended school there
2) Lettie Watkins went to school at Columbia

Compton, Martha
April 4, 1851
1) m. Green Summerfield Fox
2) d. by Sept. 23, 1855

Cone, Mr.
Dec. 28, 1857
1) nephew of Julius Alford of Tex.

Conkey, Dr. Z.
Dec. 28, 1859
Mar. 25, 1861
1) physician in Oxford, Ms.
2) daughter Mary m. Richard Whitehead
3) 1850 census (Lafayette Co., Ms.):

Z. Conkey	51	physician	N.Y.
Jane E.	16		Tn.
Mary A.	14		Tn.
Clara Z.	7		Ms.
Helen S.	5		Ms.
A. H. Conkey	26		N.Y.

Conley, Mr. and Mrs. Middleton (Connerly, Connelly)
Jan. 14, 1852
April 26, 1854
May 15, 1854
Sept. 2, 1854
June 1, 1855
Dec. 28, 1857
Mar. 16, 1860
June 22, 1861
Mar. 31, 1862
1) Middleton "Mid" Conley m. Ellen C. Palmer, July 9, 1851
2) intended having a store at Middleton; used storehouse that Parmele and Farmer had owned
3) moved to Greenwood, Ms., to merchandise
4) money stolen from him
5) new son
6) See Palmer, Ellen

Cooper, Mr.
July 30, 1857
1) minister in Mountain Home, Ala.
2) with Aunt Letty Fitzgerald in her last illness and preached her funeral

Cothron, Judge William (Major Cothron)
April 26, 1858
June 14, 1858
Dec. 20, 1858
Dec. 28, 1859
1) m. Francis M. Young (sister of Elizabeth Young, Mrs. James Z. George) on July 11, 1839
2) also 1873 m. Sally Tennessee Young Sanders, whose first husband was Dr. John W. Sanders
3) 1850 census:
William Cothron   40,   lawyer,   b. Tn.
listed with James Z. George family
4) 1860 census:
William Cothron   45   circuit judge,   b. Tn.

Couch, Miss
Jan. 12, 1856

Courtland, Alabama
1) where Dr. and Mrs. Watkins had married and lived before moving to Carroll Co., Ms.
2) where Sarah and her brother, William Fitzgerald, grew up (they were born in Nottoway Co., Va.)

Craft, Mr.
Nov. 30, 1857
1) lived at Holly Springs, Ms.

Cummings, Dr. and Mrs.
   Dec. 15, 1851
   Dec. 24, 1851
   Mar. 2, 1852
   Mar. 12, 1852
   April 11, 1852
   Mar. 25, 1861
   1) Lettie stayed with his family while in school in Holly Springs
   2) his wife's brother was one of Lettie's beaux
Cummings, Miss M.E.
   Mar. 25, 1861
   1) m. to Mr. William Griggs Hartsfield
   2) Lettie's old school friend

D

Dabney, Sophia
   Nov. _____, 1862
   1) of Holmes County
Dale, W. I.
   Oct. 23, 1848
   Dec. 29, 1848
   July 16, 1849
   July 23, 1849
   1) merchant in Columbia, Tn.
Dandridge, Dr. H. B.
   July 23, 1849
   1) left to go to California to Gold Rush, 1849–50, then came back to Panola Co.
   to live
   2) living in Middleton area in 1849
Davis, Abram
   April 13, 1863
   1) son of John Davis
Davis, Alice
   April 13, 1863
   June 8, 1867
   Sept. 21, 1867
   1) daughter of John Davis
   2) m. Capt. Rather of Louisville
Davis, A. M.
   Mar. 9, 1849
   1) m. Elizabeth M. Newman, Feb. 22, 1849
   sister of Mrs. John D. LeFlore
Davis, Anna (Feliciana)
   Jan. 12, 1856
   April 13, 1863
   1) daughter of Hugh Davis

Davis, Evvie
Mar. 29, 1849
July 23, 1849
Nov. 7, 1851
April 15, 1854
1) m. John C. Stevens, April 10, 1854
2) daughter of Hugh W. Davis (see Davis, Hugh)
Davis, Hugh
April 10, 1860
Oct. 3, 1861
Nov. 4, 1861
1) son of Mr. Hugh W. Davis
2) died in 1861 during war
3) 1850 census: age 9
Davis, Mr. and Mrs. Hugh W.
Mar. 26, 1849
July 23, 1849
Jan. 12, 1856
April 10, 1860
Oct. 3, 1862
Nov. 4, 1861
1) Margaret Davis was sister of Martha Jennett,
Edmunds Grey Whitehead's wife
2) 1850 census:

Hugh W. Davis	38	farmer	La.
Margaret	36		La.
Robert J.	16	student	Ms.
Margaret E.	14		Ms.
Hugh W.	9		Ms.
Lewis	7		Ms.
Felicianna	5		Ms.
Joseph	7/12		Ms.

Davis, Mrs. J.
Sept. 21, 1867
1) wife of Brigadier General Davis
Davis, Col. Jeff
Oct. 6, 1860
Oct. 20, 1860
May 2, 1861
Davis, R. "Jimmy" James
May 30, 1851
Jan. 12, 1856
1) m. Oct. 3, 1855 to Mary Jenkins
2) son of Hugh W. Davis (see Davis, Hugh)
3) lived in Water Valley in 1905
Davis, Joe
Oct. 1862

Davis, John H.
  Jan. 19, 1860
  1) Miss Gipson's uncle
  2) see census on Davis, Rebecca
Davis, Mrs. John H.
  April 28, 1860
  April 28, 1861
  Aug. 8, 1861
  1) see Davis, Rebecca
Davis, Mrs. Lizzie (Mrs. Miranda)
  Mar. 9, 1861
  1) Lizzie Taylor m. Miranda Davis, Mar. 8, 1855
Davis, Mary (Mrs. James)
  Mar. 11, 1857
  1) formerly Mary Jenkins
Davis, Mary Elisa
  Oct. 24, 1857
  Dec. 28, 1857
  April 28, 1860
  April 13, 1863
  Jan. 9, 1864
  Sept. 15, 1864
  1) friend of Mollie's
  2) daughter of John H. Davis
  3) 1850 census: age 9
  4) m. Robert Perkins, killed in the war
Davis, Miranda
  April 15, 1854
  1) m. Lizzie Taylor
  (M. G. Davis m. E. W. Taylor, Mar. 8, 1855)
  2) son of John H. Davis (see reference)
Davis, Mr.
  June 1, 1855
  1) once boarded at Uncle Billy Fitzgerald's in Ala.
  2) once editor of newspaper in Columbus, Ms.
Davis, Orren
  Dec. 1, 1848
  1) Alabama resident
  2) kept tavern on road to Columbus
Davis, Rebecca
  Nov. 7, 1851
  Mar. 2, 1852
  April 19, 1852
  1) in school in Middleton
  2) boarding with Dr. Davis's family
  3) m. Dr. Sanders

4) 1850 census:

John H. Davis	43	farmer	N.C.
Hetty	36		N.C.
Miranda	18	student	N.C.
Rebecca	14		N.C.
Joseph	11		Ms.
Mary	9		Ms.
Alice	7		Ms.
Abram	4		Ms.
Aurelia	2		Ms.

Dauny, Dr. and Mrs. (Downey?)
Nov. 4, 1862
Jan. 9, 1864
1) name not clear
2) Sally Collins's husband

Degraffenreid, Miss Jennie
April 12, 1861
1) of Chester, South Carolina
2) family history mentions Baron DeGraffenreid
3) Several of the Whitehead families used the name DeGraffenreid. An early Mississippi lawyer of some fame was M. F. DeGraffenreid, practiced in Woodsville where William Whitehead studied law. DeGraffenreid was a state legislator in 1827, 1829, 1831. A son of Edmunds Grey Whitehead was named Edward Degraffenreid, b. Mar. 27, 1858.

Delap, Mr.
Nov. 7, 1848
Feb. 14, 1849
April 25, 1849
1) Dr. Watkins's overseer

Denmark
Oct. 24, 1857
1) One of the Walton family servants who came to William Martin Walton from his father's estate. Walton's father, Samuel Walker Walton, died in Carroll Co. (near Shongalo) in 1838.
2) William Martin Walton and his brother, George Loe Walton, took all their combined Walton slaves to Texas in 1853. When George's wife, Amanda Moore/Miller, inherited a place in Concordia Parish, La., all the servants were turned over to George, who took them to La., except Denmark.
3) Denmark remained in Austin, helped support Lettie and her children while Maj. Walton was gone to war.

Dennis, Caro
Mar. 16, 1860
1) niece of Mrs. Martha M. Phillips

Devine, Daniel
May 15, 1850
1) Ala. resident, dead

Dickerson, Daniel S.
  Aug. 5, 1861
Dillahunty, Judge
  Nov. 20, 1861
  1) of Tex.
Dismuke, Bennet C.
  Sept. 23, 1855
  1) m. to Fanny Nelson, Aug. 5, 1855 (Nelms?)
  2) 1860 census:

Bennet Dismuke	33	farmer	Ga.
Sarah F.	22		Ms.
Mary	4		Ms.
Elizabeth	1		Ms.

Donaldson, Mr.
  Dec. 24, 1851
  1) m. Jennie Watson
Doty, Miss
  April 28, 1860
  April 27, 1861
  1) m. Dr. Adams, Episcopal minister of Carrollton
Drake, Judge Joseph
  Oct. 3, 1861
  Oct. 4, 1861
  Feb. 24, 1862
  Oct. 1862
  1) 1860 census:

Joseph Drake	53	planter	Ky.
Martha	45		Va.
Albert	21	student	Ms.
J. B.	19		Ms.
Andora	17		Ms.
William	8		Ms.
Mary	6		Ms.

Dudley, Dr. Benjamin
  June 26, 1846
  1) physician in Lexington, Ky.
  2) performed operation on Judge Whitehead's son
Duke, W. E.
  Feb. 3, 1860
  Feb. 10, 1860
  1) Mr. Edmunds Grey Whitehead's overseer
  2) m. Miss Laura Jane Blunt
Durram, Mr. (Durham)
  Jan. 18, 1858
Dyches, Capt.
  Aug. 23, 1865

E

Early, Aunt Sarah
Feb. 23, 1852
1) had seen Mary Wingfield
2) Dr. Watkins's kin

Early, Joel
Mar. 26, 1849
Feb. 20, 1849
Mar. 31, 1849
1) Dr. Watkins's uncle
2) of Greensboro, Ga.
3) brother to Mary "Polly" Early Watkins, Dr. Watkins's mother

Early, Family
July 9, 1861
1) Dr. Thomas Watkins's mother was an Early

Early, Mary "Polly"
Aug. 26, 1861
1) Dr. Thomas Watkins's mother

Early, Peter
Aug. 27, 1861

Echols, Henry
Oct. 7, 1862
1) son of Obadiah Echols
2) 1850 census: age 13

Echols, Judson
Jan. 12, 1856
1) son of Obadiah Echols (see Echols, Mrs.)
2) 1850 census: age 16

Ecols (Echols), Mrs. Obadiah
Jan. 30, 1852
Mar. 6, 1854
April 4, 1854
April 26, 1854
May 15, 1854
Sept. 5, 1860
1) neighbor of the Watkinses
2) 1850 census:

Obadiah Echols	64	farmer	Ga.
Elizabeth	59		Ga.
Judson	16		Ga.
Henry	13		Ga.

Edmundson, Miss
Nov. 7, 1851
Jan. 14, 1852
1) ass't. teacher in Dr. Smith's school in Middleton

Edwards, Captain
 Sept. 21, 1867
Eggleston, Mrs. Charles S. (Harriet Elizabeth)
 April 4, 1854
 Nov. _____, 1862
 1) widow of Charles S. Eggleston, who died 1847, family in Holmes Co.
 2) see Eggleston, Fanny Tabb
Eggleston, Fanny Archer
 Dec. 29, 1848
 Feb. 20, 1849
 Dec. 15, 1851
 May 15, 1857
 Nov. 2, 1859
 Mar. 26, 1860
 April 4, 1860
 July 22, 1861
 July 31, 1862
 Nov. 4, 1862
 1) Holmes Co., Ms.
 2) good friends of the Watkinses
 3) daughter of Fanny P. Eggleston and William Eggleston
 4) see Eggleston, Fanny Tabb
 5) 1850 census (Holmes Co.): age 24, b. Va.
Eggleston, Mrs. Fanny P. (Mrs. William)
 Feb. 14, 1849
 April 4, 1854
 Nov. 2, 1859
 April 4, 1860
 July 9, 1861
 July 22, 1861
 Oct. 1, 1861
 July 31, 1862
 Nov. 4, 1862
 Nov. _____, 1862
 Feb. 4, 1865
 1) Holmes Co., Ms.
 2) home called "Wanalaw"
 3) Mrs. Fanny P. Eggleston m. in 1821 to William Eggleston
 4) 1850 census (Holmes Co.):

Fanny P. Eggleston	48	Va.
Fanny A.	24	Va.
Sarah Meade	23	Va.
Stephen	20	Va.
Marianna Peyton	14	Va.
Charles Joseph	11	Ms.
William	7	Ms.

Eggleston, Fanny Tabb
Dec. 2, 1857
1) Fannie Tabb Eggleston m. Stephen Archer Eggleston on April 12 1855
(Eggleston m. an Eggleston)
2) Fannie Tabb Eggleston, daughter of Mrs. Harriet Eggleston, Holmes Co., Ms.,
and Charles S. Eggleston (d. 1847)
3) 1850 census (Holmes Co.):

Harriet Elizabeth Eggleston	50	Va.
Everard Meade	25	Va.
Signiora	23	Va.
Fanny Tabb	15	Va.
Mary	8	Ms.

Eggleston, Joe
Mar. 15, 1859
July 22, 1861
Feb. 4, 1865
1) son of William and Fanny P. Eggleston

Eggleston, Marianna
Oct. 24, 1857
Nov. 30, 1857 April 4, 1860
1) Holmes Co., Ms.
2) daughter of Fanny P. and William Eggleston
3) see Eggleston, Fanny P.

Eggleston, "Meady" Sarah Meade
Oct. 24, 1857
Nov. 30, 1857
Dec. 2, 1857
Jan. 18, 1858
April 4, 1860
April 27, 1861
May 2, 1861
July 22, 1861
Nov. _____, 1862
1) b. July 10, 1827
2) daughter of Fanny P. and William Eggleston
3) resident of Holmes Co., Ms.
4) see Eggleston, Fanny P.

Eggleston, The Misses
July 23, 1849
1) Holmes Co, Ms.
2) see Eggleston, Fanny P.

Eggleston, Seneora (Signiora)
April 4, 1860
April 10, 1860
1) Holmes Co., Ms.

2) daughter of Mrs. Harriet Eggleston
3) 1850 census: age 23, b. Va.

Eggleston, Stephen
July 31, 1862
1) son of William and Fanny P. Eggleston
2) Miss Fanny Eggleston's brother

Eggleston, Willie
July 22, 1861
1) son of William and Fannie P. Eggleston

Elam, Mr.
July 31, 1862
1) at Farmville, Va.

Eldridge, Miss Marley
Dec. 28, 1856
Mar. 11, 1857
April 28, 1860
1) Middleton school teacher of Mollie's
2) m. Levi Temple

Elliot, Mrs. Billy
Dec. 1, 1848
1) Ala. resident, died

Elliot, Bob, and Wife
Sept. 2, 1854
1) Ala. residents
2) she stabbed him and they parted

Epes, "Aunt" Patsy, daughters Sally and Martha Epes
July 31, 1860
Sept. 5, 1860
1) Va. resident
2) dead (Sept. letter)

Epes, Dandridge
Oct. 21, 1848
Nov. 26, 1860
1) of Va.
2) condemned to be hanged in Dec.

Epes, Tom
Nov. 2, 1860
1) Mrs. Watkins's cousin

Epes, Washington
Jan. 31, 1861

Eppes, Capt.
Mar. 2, 1852
Mar. 12, 1852
1) tavern owner in holly springs, ms.

Eskridge, Mrs.
April 13, 1862

Estel (Estill), Charles
Feb. 3, 1860
Feb. 10, 1860
1) son of Mrs. Nancy Estill (see Estill, Nancy)

Estel (Estill), Mrs. Nancy
Feb. 14, 1849
Mar. 9, 1849
Feb. 9, 1850
May 15, 1857
Dec. 28, 1859
Nov. 4, 1861
Fall 1868
1) widow, neighbor of Dr. and Mrs. Watkins
2) 1850 census:

Nancy Estill	44	Ky.
Thomas	24	Tn.
Maria	18	Tn.
Harriet	16	Ms.
Semira	14	
Charles	11	
Margaret	8	
Allis	7	

Estel (Estill), Semira
April 19, 1852
1) m. Joe Money on April 17, 1852; Mary and Susan Jenkins were her waiters
2) see Money, Joe

Estel, Tom
April 19, 1852

Eubanks (Youbanks), Abbey
Mar. 16, 1860
Mar. 17, 1860
Aug. 8, 1861
1) daughter of Joseph Eubanks
2) m. Mr. McCune
3) 1860 census:

Joseph Eubanks	60	hotelkeeper	S.C.
Harriet	57		S.C.
William	27		Ms.
Abigale	22		Ms.
Elizabeth	18		Ms.
Sarah	13		Ms.
Samuel	12		Ms.
Ellen	9		Ms.

Eubanks, "Old" Mrs.
April 12, 1861
April 13, 1861
1) dead

Ewing, Betty
April 4, 1851
Mar. 6, 1860
Mar. 16, 1860
1) m. to Dr. Tyson of Tn.
2) daughter of Dr. William Ewing (see Ewing, William)

Ewing, Fannie
April 4, 1851

Ewing, Dr. William
Mar. 18, 1846
Jan. 14, 1852
Mar. 11, 1857
June 11, 1863
1) brought his daughters home from Columbia, Tn.
2) 1850 census:

William Ewing	49		Tn.
Frances	40		S.C.
Samuel	23		Tn.
Andrew	20	med student	Tn.
Mary	17		Tn.
Elizabeth	13		Tn.
Frances	12		Tn.
William	10		Tn.
Amanda	8		Ms.
Thomas	6		Ms.
Worth	4		Ms.
Sarah	2		Ms.

Ewing, Mrs. William
Nov. 2, 1859
1) mother died

F

Farmer, Jack (Joseph J.)
Jan. 30, 1852
April 19, 1852
1) wife was Julia F. Phillips Farmer

Farmer, Mrs. Dr.
Mar. 9, 1849

Farmer, Julia Phillips
Dec. 1, 1849
Jan. 13, 1849
Feb. 14, 1849
Mar. 9, 1849
July 23, 1849
Feb. 9, 1850
June 1–3, 1855

May 15, 1857
June 8, 1857
Oct. 7, 1858
Mar. 16, 1860
July 31, 1860
Dec. 17, 1860
Feb. 16, 1861
Mar. 9, 1861
Mar. 11, 1861
April 13, 1861
May 2, 1861
July 22, 1861
Aug. 8, 1861
Dec. 9, 1861
Mar. 31, 1862
Nov. 4, 1862
June 8, 1867
1) daughter of William Henry and Martha Mumford Cobbs Phillips
2) sister to Mariah Louise Phillips Parmele
3) 1850 census:

Joseph J. Farmer	35	merchant	N.C.
Julia F.	24		N.C.
*William J.	4		Ala.

*this child died

Farmer, William B.
Mar. 26, 1849
1) William B. Farmer m. Mary C. T. Matthew, Mar. 15, 1849
2) 1850 census:

William B. Farmer	40	farmer	N.C.
Mary	18		Ms.
Ross	6/12		Ms.

Fearn Family
Mar. 26, 1860
1) Miss Fearn of Patapsco Institute, friend of Mollie's
2) Dr. Thomas Fearn of Huntsville, Ala.
3) George Fearn of Jackson, Ms.
4) Lee Fearn of Mobile, Ala.

Felts (Phelps), Miss
Oct. 8, 1857
1) William Gooch m. Frances Felts, Sept. 25, 1857

Field, Eldon
April 4, 1854
1) killed a man

Field, Emily Eliza Foster
(Mrs. Judge Field)
Sept. 10, 1862

Oct. 1862

1) Dr. Watkins's niece, daughter of his sister, Jane, and her first husband, Daniel Foster

2) half-sister to all the Hillyer group

Field, Judge J.

Sept. 5, 1860

Sept. 10, 1862

Oct. _____, 1862

Oct. 7, 1862

1) Dr. Watkins's nephew-in-law

2) wife, Emily Eliza Foster Field, daughter of Daniel and Jane Watkins Foster

Field, Dr. Tom

Sept. 10, 1862

Finney, Ellen (Phinney)

Jan. 27, 1860

1) daughter of Prof. Finney (see Finney, Prof.)

Finney, Mrs. Francis (Phinney)

Mar. 31, 1849

1) husband, Prof. Finney, died; taught at the Female Institute in Middleton for several years before his death

Fisher, Dr.

Sept. 15, 1864

Fisher, Mr.

Feb. 23, 1852

Fisk, Mr. (Fish)

April 28, 1860

Fitzgerald, Catherine Campbell

Nov. 2, 1860

1) Mrs. Watkins's kin

Fitzgerald, "Uncle" Frank

July 31, 1860

Nov. 26, 1860

1) Sarah Fitzgerald Watkins's Va. kin, her uncle

2) he was brother to "Uncle Billy" Fitzgerald and Sarah's father, Thomas Fitzgerald

3) d. Sept. 17, 1860

4) his wife, Frances Jones Fitzgerald, d. 1823

Fitzgerald, Frank

Dec. 28, 1859

1) Sarah Watkins's cousin

Fitzgerald, Freeman

Dec. 28, 1859

1) Sarah Fitzgerald Watkins's uncle

2) lived in Lawrence Co., Ala., where he had gone from Va., and then moved to Florida

3) his wife was Elizabeth Williams's (Irby) niece of Aunt Letty and Sarah's mother

Fitzgerald, Henry

May 15, 1854

1) son of Col. William and Mary Bledsoe Fitzgerald

Fitzgerald, Jack

July 31, 1860

1) Sarah Watkins's "cousin" in Va.

Fitzgerald, "Lawyer"

Oct. 6, 1860

1) Sarah Watkins's second cousin of Farmville, Va.

Fitzgerald, Lettice "Aunt Letty"

July 23, 1849

May 30, 1851

Mar. 12 1852

April 4, 1852

May 15, 1854

Sept. 2, 1854

June 1, 1855

Mar. 11, 1857

May 15, 1857

June 8, 1857

July 30, 1857

Oct. 24, 1857

Dec. 28, 1857

1) daughter of Thomas Roper Williams and Catherine Greenhill Williams

2) see Fitzgerald, Capt. William

Fitzgerald, Letty

Feb. 6, 1858

Feb. 10, 1860

April 13, 1861

April 27, 1861

Aug. 8, 1861

1) niece of Sarah Watkins

2) daughter of Col. William and Mary Bledsoe Fitzgerald

3) Lawrence Co., Ala.

4) m. Mr. Hill from Arkansas in 1861

Fitzgerald, Lucy

Aug. 8, 1861

1) Sarah Watkins's niece

2) daughter of Col. William and Mary Bledsoe Fitzgerald

Fitzgerald, Mary Bledsoe

June 8, 1857

July 30, 1857

Dec. 28, 1857

June 14, 1858

Feb. 10, 1860
Aug. 8, 1861
1) wife of Col. William Fitzgerald, Sarah's brother
2) m. second Jeff Kettering (see ref.)
3) daughter of Joseph and Winnie Bledsoe (see ref.)
Fitzgerald, Mary and Fanny
Dec. 28, 1859
1) old maid cousins of Sarah Watkins
Fitzgerald, Sarah Ann
July 30, 1857
Dec. 28, 1857
Feb. 6, 1858
Feb. 10, 1860
April 10, 1860
April 13 1861
April 27, 1861
June 17, 1871
Aug. 8, 1861
1) niece of Sarah Watkins
2) daughter of Col. William and Mary Bledsoe Fitzgerald
3) Lawrence Co., Ala.
Fitzgerald, Sarah Epes
1) m. Thomas Alexander Watkins, M.D.
2) daughter of Thomas Fitzgerald and Ann Roper Williams
3) see Watkins reference
Fitzgerald, Thomas
June 8, 1857
1) Sarah Watkins's nephew
2) son of Col. William and Mary Bledsoe Fitzgerald b. _____, d. May 3, 1857
3) Lawrence Co., Ala.
Fitzgerald, Virginia
Dec. 28, 1859
1) Freemon Fitzgerald's daughter, Sarah Watkins's cousin
Fitzgerald, Capt. William ("Uncle Billy")
Jan. 13, 1849
Feb. 14, 1849
April 25, 1849
Feb. 9, 1850
Feb. 23, 1852
Mar. 21, 1852
1) Wife, Lettice Greenhill Williams Fitzgerald (Aunt Letty), was b. Jan. 4, 1791, and d. July 6, 1857. A sister to Sarah Watkins's mother, Ann Roper Williams Fitzgerald (who m. 2nd Col. Savage), Lettice married Capt. William Fitzgerald Feb. 8, 1809, by Rev. John Jones.
2) "Uncle Billy," b. Feb. 8, 1786, and d. Feb. 9, 1852, was brother to Sarah Watkins's father, Thomas Fitzgerald.

3) These family members were from Nottaway Co., Va., and lived in Lawrence Co., Ala.

4) 1850 census (Lawrence Co., Ala):

William Fitzgerald	63	Va.
Lettice G.	59	Va.

Aunt Letty and Uncle Billy had no children of their own. They were second parents to Sarah Epes Fitzgerald and her brother, William Fitzgerald. The children's real father (brother of Uncle Billy), Thomas Fitzgerald, died in 1816 when Sarah Epes was only about two years old. Aunt Letty was sister to Ann Roper Williams Fitzgerald (wife of Thomas and mother of the two young children). Therefore, Aunt Letty and Uncle Billy were actually double aunt and uncle—two sisters married two brothers.

Fitzgerald, Col. William (Brother William)

Nov. 7, 1848

Feb. 9, 1850

May 15, 1850

Mar. 6, 1854

May 15, 1854

Sept. 2, 1854

Nov. 9, 1854

1) Sarah Watkins's brother

2) son of Thomas and Ann Roper Williams Fitzgerald

3) lived for much of his youth with "Uncle Billy" and "Aunt Letty" Fitzgerald

4) Lawrence Co., Ala.

5) wife was Mary A. Bledsoe

6) 1850 census (Lawrence Co., Ala.):

William Jr.* Fitzgerald	38	Va.
Mary	23	Ala.
Thomas	7	Ala.
Sarah Ann Roper	5	Ala.
*Lettice Greenhill, Jr.	4	Ala.
Mary E.	2	
William	2/12	

*Jr. did not mean son necessarily—it sometimes was nephew, etc.—just distinguished family members.

Flournoy, Miss

Jan. 12, 1856

1) mother was half-sister to the Mrs. Early who died at the Watkins home and cousin to Mrs. Hawkins of Carroll Co.

Foltz, Mr. and Mrs. E. E.

Sept. 23 1855

Feb. 6, 1858

Oct. 20, 1860

Nov. 2, 1860

1) Mrs. Foltz was (Eliza) Helen Purnell; m. Sept. 29, 1853

2) daughter of Micajah Purnell

3) the Purnells were from N.C.

4) Mr. Foltz was from Salem, N.C.

Forest Place

1) name of Dr. T. A. Watkins's plantation home six miles east of Carrollton in Carroll Co., Ms.

Fort, James

Mar. 9, 1849

1) son of Jethro B. Fort (see ref.)

Fort, Mr. Jethro B.

Nov. 7, 1848

Feb. 14, 1849

July 23, 1849

Mar. 9, 1849

1) taking son, James, and servants to Tex.

2) rest of family staying with Mrs. Jenkins

3) 1850 census: the whole family is in Bowie Co., Tex.

Jethro Fort	44	planter	N.C.
Sarah	44		N.C.
Tempe	20		Tn.
James	16		Tn.
Cochilla (?)	13		Tn.

Fort, Temperence

Feb. 14, 1849

Mar. 9, 1849

July 23, 1849

Nov. 7, 1851

1) daughter of Jethro B. Fort (see reference)

2) m. to widower named Reynolds

Foster, Sarah

Oct. 24, 1848

1) some sort of family kin to Watkins family, called her "cousin"

2) resident of Nashville, Tn.

Fox, Green Summerfield

July 30, 1857

Feb. 16, 1861

1) m. first Martha Jane Compton, Dec. 19, 1851; she had died by Sept. 23, 1855

2) m. second Ellen Butt, July 10, 1857

3) 1860 census:

Summerfield Fox	30	Ala.
E. B.	21	Ms.
E. C. m	8	Ms.
F. N. m	2	Ms.

Fox, Mr. and Mrs. John

Nov. 2, 1860

July 31, 1862

1) 1860 census:

John A. Fox	50	farmer	N.C.
Ann T.	48		Ms.
Margaret	18		Ms.
William	12		Ms.
Ben	14		Ms.
Les	10		Ms.

Fox, Martha
  April 26, 1858
  April 13, 1861
  April 13, 1862
Freeman, Mr.
  Oct. 20, 1860
  Nov. 2, 1860
  Oct. 7, 1862
  Nov. _____, 1862
  Dec. 1, 1862
Freeman, Mrs.
  May 2, 1861
  1) has a new baby
Freeman, Hugh and Phil
  Feb. 9, 1862
  Mar. 31, 1862
  Oct. 7, 1862
  Nov. _____, 1862
  1) Carroll Co. soldiers
Frierson, Miss
  Oct. 21, 1848
  1) niece of Mrs. Wingfield (Tn.)
  2) m. Mr. Macuin (McCune, McEwen?) Nashville, Tn.
Frierson, S. D.
  Oct. 23, 1848
  July 16, 1849
  1) Columbia, Tn.
  2) one of the trustees of Columbia Female Institute

G

Gant, Mr.
  Jan. 1, 1856
Gary, Allen
  Oct. 6, 1860
  Feb. 16, 1861
  1) m. Judith Scurlock, June 16, 1842
  2) 1850 census (Carroll Co.):

Allen Gary	48	farmer	Ky.
Judith	28		Va.
West	13		Ms.

Eliza	11	Ms.
Julia	6	Ms.
Allen	3	Ms.
John	1	Ms.

Gary, Dr. Allen W.*

1) m. Martha Jane Palmer, May 11, 1859
2) Dr. Gary was son of West Gary
3) practiced medicine at Winona
4) 1850 census (Carroll Co.):

West Gary	51	farmer	Ky.
Elizabeth	47		Ky.
*Allen	20	med student	Ms.
Marvel	15		Ms.
Margaret	10		Ms.
Ophelia	8		Ms.
Elizabeth	6		Ms.

Gary, Julia

Sept. 23, 1855

1) school friend of Mollie's at Middleton
2) daughter of Allen Gary and wife, Judith Scurlock Gary
3) see Gary, Allen

Gary, Judith Scurlock (Mrs. Allen)

Sept. 5, 1860
Feb. 16, 1861

1) m. Allen Gary, June 16, 1842
2) d. Sept. 5, 1860
3) see Gary, Allen

Gary, Martha Jane Palmer (Mrs. Dr. Allen W.)

Mar. 17, 1860
April 4, 1860
July 31, 1860
Sept. 5, 1860
Nov. 26, 1860
Sept. 11, 1861
April 13, 1863

1) m. A. W. Gary, May 11, 1859
2) daughter of Judge John E. Palmer

Gary, William West

Sept. 23, 1855
Jan. 12, 1856

1) m. Ann Bailey, Nov. 25, 1855
2) son of Allen Gary (see ref.)
3) 1860 census:

West Gary	23	Ms.
Ann	20	Ms.
Judy	3	Ms.
Allen	8/12	Ms.

Gayden, Mr.
Nov. 7, 1851
1) probably Reuben Gayden
Gayden, Mrs.
Feb. 23, 1852
Mar. 9, 1861
Gayden, Mrs. Jane Hearn (Widow)
Nov. 7, 1851
April 26, 1858
1) second husband Reuben Gayden, m. March 16, 1843
2) m. third, William Mattox, Sept. 10, 1857
3) 1850 census:

Reuben Gayden	52	farmer	S.C.
Jane	32		Ga.
Virginia	6		Ms.
Emma	5		Ms.
Julia	1		Ms.

Gayden, William A.
Aug. 23, 1865
Gee, "Joe" Joseph James
Mar. 16, 1860
Mar. 17, 1860
Feb. 24, 1862
1) son of Peter and Mary Ann Moore Gee
2) m. Miss Charlie A. Kimbrough
3) his sister was Lou Bingham
4) see Gee, Lee
Gee, Mr. Joseph L.
Mar. 9, 1861
1) m. Sarah Townsend, Dec. 8, 1846
2) son of William J. Gee, lived east of Middleton
3) he and brother died Feb. 1861
Gee, Lou (Mrs. Robert Bingham)
April 15, 1854
July 4, 1855
Mar. 9, 1861
1) despite rumors of engagement elsewhere, Mina Louise Gee m. Robert Bingham, Feb. 1, 1857
2) daughter of Peter Gee and wife, Mary Ann Moore Gee; they had two children: Mina Louise and Joseph J.
3) 1850 census:

Peter Gee	46	Va.
Mary	43	Va.
Joseph	15	Va.
Louise (Mina)	13	Va.
Elizabeth Nalley	63	Va.

George, James Z. (Senator)
Dec. 28, 1859
July 9, 1861
Oct. 4, 1861
Feb. 24, 1862
1) m. Elizabeth B. Young, May 30, 1847
2) stepfather was Seaborn Durham; they lived around Shongalo when J. Z.
George was a child
3) 1850 census:

James Z. George	23	lawyer	Ga.
Elizabeth	22		Tn.
Fanny	2		Ms.

Geren, "Old" Mrs. (Gering)
Jan. 1, 1861
Geren (Gerin, Gearing), Adelaide
Jan. 13, 1849
April 4, 1854
April 26, 1854
Sept. 2, 1854
1) died by Sept. 2, 1854
Geren, Dr. Simon
Nov. 7, 1848
Jan. 13, 1849
Feb. 14, 1849
1) living at Mr. Phinney's lot at Middleton; says the cholera is fifty miles from
Greenwood on Honey Island
2) his father was Abram Geren
3) he was a brother of Sally McLemore, Col. McLemore's second wife. Another
sister was Mrs. John H. Davis.
4) 1850 census:

| Simon Geren | 42 | physician | N.C. |
| Mary A. | 34 | | |

Giddings, Dewitt Clinton
July 31, 1862
1) Capt., Co. B, 21st Texas cavalry
Gilmer, Frank
Aug. 12, 1861
Oct. 12, 1866
1) President of the South and North Ala. RailRoad
Gilmer, James Blair
April 12, 1861
Gipson, Miss
Jan. 19, 1860
1) John Davis's niece
2) m. Sam McLemore

Givens, Miss Isabella
Dec. 28, 1859
Jan. 27, 1860
Nov. 26, 1860
Nov. _____, 1862
1) bought female school in Middleton in 1860
2) died in 1861
3) 1860 census:
    Isabella Given   48   teacher   Scotland*
    *other sources say Virginia and Florida

Glassock, Mr.
Mar. 8, 1854
1) of Austin, Tx.

Gooch, "Old" Mrs.
June 8, 1867

Gooch (Gouch), Miss Julie E.
Jan. 12, 1856
April 10, 1860
1) m. James Woods, Dec. 27, 1855

Gooch (Gouch), Mrs. William B.
April 10, 1860
Nov. 4, 1861
1) Julia Gooch Wood's (Mrs. James Wood's) mother
2) 1860 census:
    William B. Gooch   51   farmer   S.C.
    with children
    wife is dead

Gooch (Gouch), Mr. William
Oct. 8, 1857
Nov. 4, 1861
1) m. Frances Felts, Sept. 25, 1857
2) 1860 census:
    William S. Gooch   25   farmer   S.C.
    Frances   17   Ms.
    Georgiana   1   Ms.

Gordon, Mr.
April 10, 1860
April 28, 1860
1) one of the "waiters" (groomsmen) at William Oliver and Lizzie Whitehead's wedding

Gould, Mr.
June 9, 1851

Graham, Judge
July 30, 1857
1) Mrs. Baskerville Vaughan m. to Judge Graham
2) Ala. residents

Green, Miss Clara
Mar. 26, 1860
July 10, 1860
Jan. 26, 1861
May 2, 1861
June 11, 1863
1) of Jackson, Ms.
2) friend of Mollie's at Patapsco Institute
3) daughter of J. Green of Jackson, Ms.
Green, Mr.
Nov. 7, 1851
1) pastor of Methodist church at Middleton
Green, Rt. Rev. William Mercer
(Bishop Green of Mississippi)
Oct. 26, 1858
Mar. 26, 1860
April 4, 1860
April 10, 1860
April 28, 1860
Oct. 6, 1860
Nov. 26, 1860
Dec. 17, 1860
Mar. 25, 1861
April 13, 1861
April 27, 1861
April 13, 1862
June 11, 1863
1) long and dear friend of the Phillips family and of Dr. Watkins's family
2) had been Rector of St. Matthews Church (Episcopal) in Hillsborough, N.C.
when Mr. and Mrs. Phillips and their daughters lived there
3) later was professor at Chapel Hill, N.C.; bishop of diocese of Mississippi;
and finally president of University of the South at Sewanee, Tn.
Grey, Mrs. (Gregg)
June 8 1857
1) sister to Eggleston Townes
2) maiden name Frances Townes
Griffith, Dr. George R.
Oct. 26, 1858
Nov. 1, 1858
Feb. 10, 1860
1) 1860 census:
   George R. Griffith   24   physician   Md.
Griffith, Mary
June 6, 1861
1) Dr. Stansbury's niece

2) m. Frank Keys
3) d. by April 27, 1861
Gunn, Mr.
May 15, 1854
1) Mr. Watts's family living with him
Gunn, Elba
Jan. 31, 1861
Mar. 11, 1861
May 20, 1861
June 6, 1861
Feb. 16, 1867
1) at Patapsco with Mollie
2) a Mississippi girl

H

Halida, Miss
April 13, 1861
April 27, 1861
1) Hawkins's cousin
Hall, Dr. John
April 20, 1850
Dec. 15, 1851
Jan. 30, 1852
Nov. 20, 1861
June 21, 1862
June 27, 1862
Sept. 10, 1862
Oct. 12, 1862
1) old friend of Dr. Watkins
2) of Columbus, Ms.
Hale, Mr.
May 15, 1857
1) killed by two Negro men who were hung
Hale, Mrs.
Jan. 12, 1856
1) had a baby, to have another
Hamilton, Willie
April 13, 1863
Haralson, Mrs.
Aug. 27, 1861
1) of Austin, Tx., formerly of Georgia
Harris, Mrs. James Clark
Dec. 2, 1857
1) James Harris m. Rebecca Leflore, Dec. 27, 1855
2) on this same date, a double wedding: Martha Halsey m. Green Davis

Harris, Mr. James Clark
   Feb. 6, 1858
   1) master builder in Carroll Co., Ms.
   2) b. in Ga.
   3) m. daughter of Greenwood Leflore
Harris, Buckner
   Oct. 7, 1858
   1) family connection of Dr. Watkins
Harris, Early
   Oct. 7, 1858
   1) family connection of Dr. Watkins
Harris, Eugenia
   July 8, 1849
Harris, Jim
   Sept. 15, 1864
Harris, Louisa "Cousin"
   Oct. 21, 1848
Hart, Emily S.
   Mar. 26, 1860
   1) m. J. R. Tuston, Mar. 22, 1860
   2) daughter of Samuel Hart
   3) 1860 census:

John L. Tustin	23	silversmith	S.C.
Emma	17		Ms.

Hart, Samuel, Sr.
   Mar. 26, 1860
   1) probate clerk
   2) father of Emily Hart Tustin and Dr. Hart
Hart, Dr. William
   April 28, 1860
   1) 1850 census:

Dr. William C. Hart	23	physician	Tn.

   no wife or family listed
   boarding with Orman Kimbrough family in Carrollton area
Hastings, Misses
   Oct. 15, 1851
Hatchett, W. T.
   Oct. 12, 1866
Hawkins, Mr. and Mrs.
   Oct. 20, 1860
   1) from Texas
Hawkins, Mrs. Frank (Ann)
   Sept. 23, 1855
   Oct. 8, 1857
   Dec. 2, 1857
   1) Mrs. Sarah Watkins says she likes Mrs. Hawkins very much

Hawkins, Maj. and Mrs. Frank
   June 1, 1855
   Jan. 12, 1856
   Mar. 11, 1857
   July 30, 1857
   Oct. 8, 1857
   Oct. 24, 1857
   April 5, 1858
   April 10, 1860
   April 28, 1860
   Oct. 20, 1860
   Nov. 2, 1860
   Mar. 9, 1861
   April 13, 1861
   Sept. 11, 1861
   Sept. 10, 1862
   April 13, 1863
   June 11, 1863
   Jan. 9, 1864
   July 10, 1864
   Feb. 4, 1865
   1) lived around Gerenton
   2) fall of 1857 bought the Stedman place
   3) there was a kinship between some of the Purnells, Simmonses, and
   Hawkinses (see Simmons, Joseph)
   4) 1850 census:

Frank Hawkins	31	farmer	N.C.
Ann C.	29		N.C.
John D.	11		N.C.
(?)Rhesn	5		N.C.
Jane B.	11/12		Ms.
Read, Mary B.	67		N.C.

Hawkins, Jennie
   April 28, 1860
   Jan. 8, 1864
   Sept. 21, 1867
   1) Maj. Hawkins's daughter
   2) see Hawkins, Frank
   3) 1850 census: 11/12 years

Hawkins, Dr. John and Mrs. ("Young" Dr. Hawkins)
   Oct. 8, 1857
   Nov. 30, 1857
   Dec. 2, 1857
   April 26, 1858
   Mar. 16, 1860
   April 28, 1860

Nov. 2, 1860
Dec. 17, 1860
April 13, 1861
April 27, 1861
1) m. in N.C.
2) son of Frank Hawkins (see ref.)

Hays, Miss
Mar. 9, 1849
1) a classmate of Lettie's in Columbia, Tn. who died

Hazelgreen
1) name of Judge William Whitehead's home and plantation in Carroll Co., Ms.

Helm, Mr. William Brook
Dec. 2, 1857
Jan. 31, 1861
Feb. 16, 1861
July 22, 1861
June 21, 1862
Nov. _____, 1862
Nov. 4, 1862
June 1, 1864
1) m. Mrs. Martha Prince
(marriage record in Claiborne Co. says 12-14-1860)
2) partner of Judge Wright in Carrollton in 1857
3) he m. second, Sally Meade Eggleston, Nov. 13, 1873, a sister of Fanny
Eggleston (Holmes Co.)
4) 1850 census:
    William B. Helm   28   lawyer   Va.
    boarding with Dr. Joseph Askew and family in Carrollton area

Helms, Mr. and Mrs. and Miss
Sept. 11, 1861

Hemingway, "Old" Mrs.
Feb. 14, 1849
1) has died

Hemingway, Collins
Jan. 13, 1849
May 15, 1850
Jan. 12, 1856
Dec. 28, 1859
Sept. 20, 1864
1) m. Agralina (Agripina?) Bell, April, 22, 1840
2) 1850 census:

Collins F. Hemingway	33	farmer	S.C.
Agrippina	26		Ala.
Wilson	9		Ms.
Martha	7		Ms.
Margaret	5		Ms.

| William | 3 | Ms. |
| James C. | 1 | Ms. |

Hemingway, Lynn
Sept. 23, 1855
Dec. 28, 1856
Dec. 28, 1859
Mar. 25, 1861
May 20, 1861
June 17, 1861
July 22, 1861
Aug. 5, 1861
Aug. 28, 1861
Sept. 11, 1861
Oct. 3, 1861
Nov. 4, 1861
Feb. 24, 1862
June 27, 1862
July 31, 1862
Sept. 10, 1862
Oct. 7, 1862
Oct. _____, 1862
April 13, 1863
Jan. 9, 1864
1) good friend of Lettie and her mother
2) son of William Hemingway
3) 1860 census:
   Lynn Hemingway   21   trader   Tn.
   boarding with David Meredith and family

Hemingway, Margaret
Sept. 20, 1864
1) daughter of Collins Hemingway

Hemingway, Margaret
Dec. 28, 1856
June 8, 1857
April 5, 1858
Mar. 6, 1860
Mar. 16, 1860
Mar. 17, 1860
Mar. 26, 1860
May 25, 1860
1) daughter of William Hemingway
2) m. Gus Pleasants, Mar. 15, 1860

Hemingway, Sam
July 31, 1862
Oct. 7, 1862
Oct. _____, 1862

Nov. 4, 1862
1) son of William Hemingway

Hemingway, Mr. William
Jan. 13, 1849
May 15, 1850
April 5, 1858
Mar. 15, 1859
Dec. 28, 1859
Jan. 19, 1860
Mar. 2, 1860
April 10, 1860
May 25, 1860
Aug. 25, 1860
May 2, 1861
Dec. 9, 1861
Oct. 7, 1862
Sept. 20, 1864
1) 1850 census:

William Hemingway	40	farmer	S.C.
Sarah W.	31		N.C.
Margaret	13		Tn.
William Lynn	11		Ms.
Samuel	5		Ms.
Wilson	5/12		Ms.
Mary Ivy	60		N.C.

Hemingway, Mrs. William H.
April 4, 1852
April 5, 1858
June 14, 1858
Jan. 27, 1860
Mar. 16, 1860
Mar. 17, 1860
Jan. 31, 1861
Mar. 25, 1861
May 2, 1861
Sept. 11, 1861
Dec. 9., 1861
July 31, 1862
Oct. 7, 1862

Hemingway, Mr. and Mrs. Wilson
Nov. _____, 1862
1) son of William Hemingway

Hemphill, Judge John
Jan. 24, 1862
Feb. 4, 1862
1) chief justice, Texas Supreme Court

2) senator from Texas

3) died Jan. 1862

Hemphill, Mr. and Mrs. and Miss

July 31, 1860

Oct. 20, 1860

Nov. 2, 1860

1) living at James Collins's place

2) 1860 census:

Phillip W. Hemphill	55	farmer	S.C.
Narcissa	38		Ga.
Cynthia	19		Ga.
Mary	18		Ga.
Sarah	6		Ms.
Charles	3		Ms.

Hemphill, Major

April 13, 1862

1) brother of "old" Mrs. Liddell

2) died lately

Henry, Mr.

Dec. 28, 1856

Aug. 23, 1856

1) cotton burned

Herring, Mr. Lewis W.

Jan. 18, 1858

1) 1850 census:

Lewis W.	28	farmer	N.C.
*Emily	26		Va.
Elizabeth	1		Ms.
**Vaiden, Sarah	35		Va.

    *Dr. Vaiden's sister

    **Emily Vaiden Herring was Dr. C. M. Vaiden's sister; married Herring in 1845

Herring, Mrs. Lewis W. (Herron)

Dec. 2, 1857

Nov. 2, 1860

1) relative of Dr. and Mrs. C. M. Vaiden

2) maiden name Emily *Vaiden* (Vaidens b. in Va.)

3) see Herring, Mr.

Hill, "Old" Mrs.

June 1, 1855

1) dead

Hillyer, Eben

Oct. 12, 1862

Oct. _____, 1862

1) Dr. Watkins's nephew

2) son of Judge Junius and Jane Watkins Hillyer

Hillyer, George, Shaler, Henry and Carlton
  Nov. 4, 1861
  Sept. 10, 1862
  Oct. ————, 1862
  Oct. 7, 1862
  Nov. ————, 1862
  Nov. 29, 1862
  Dec. 1, 1862
  Jan. 12, 1862
  Jan. 8, 1864
  Jan. 9, 1864
  Mar. 20, 1865
  1) nephews of Dr. Watkins
  2) son of Judge Junius Hillyer and his wife, Jane Watkins Hillyer, Dr. Watkins's sister

Hillyer, Jane Watkins
  Nov. 1, 1858
  Dec. 27, 1858
  April 28, 1860
  Aug. 27, 1861
  Oct. 12, 1862
  Oct. ————, 1862
  1) Dr. Watkins's sister; husband was Junius Hillyer

Hillyer, Judge Junius
  Dec. 20, 1858
  Dec. 27, 1858
  Mar. 17, 1860
  April 28, 1860 Sept. 5, 1860
  1) Dr. Watkins's brother-in-law
  2) wife was Jane Watkins Hillyer

Hines, Miss
  Oct. 8, 1857

Hines, Miss Lizzie
  April 10, 1860

Holly Springs, Mississippi
  July 23, 1849, and many other references
  1) both Lettie and Mollie at school in Holly Springs

Holeman, Mr. David
  "Dr. David Holeman's fine new house burnt up," Jan. 24, 1855

Holeman, "Old" Mr.
  April 10, 1860
  Dec. 17, 1860
  1) has died by Dec. 17

Holeman (Holman), Dr. James. W.
  Sept. 2, 1854
  Sept. 11, 1861

1) J. W. Holeman m. M. W. Bennett (older daughter of E. W. Bennett) Sept. 6, 1854
2) 1850 census:
   James W. Holman   20   med. student   Ala.
   boarding with Dr. Dabney Lipscomb and family

Holmes, Miss
Feb. 9, 1850
April 20, 1850
1) school friend of Lettie's at Capt. Binford's in Grenada, Ms.

Holstead, Rev.
April 28, 1860
1) Episcopal minister at Holmes County, Ms.

Holt, Mr. Benjamin
Dec. 1, 1848
April 20, 1850
April 27, 1861
1) at Middleton Female Seminary until 1848
2) has a school in Blackhawk
3) was from Vicksburg, a Methodist minister
4) 1850 census:
   Benjamin Holt   51   teacher   S.C.
   Julia   49   N.C.

Holt, Mrs. Benjamin
Mar. 9, 1849
1) attends wedding

Holt, "Old" Mrs.
Oct. 24, 1857
1) dead

Homer, Miss
1) school friend of Lettie's at Capt. Binford's in Grenada

Honey Island
Jan. 13, 1849
1) fifty miles from Greenwood, Ms.

Honeycutt, Mr.
April 4, 1854
1) killed by Mr. Field in Lowndes Co., Ms.

Hooker, Miss
April 4, 1854
1) of New Orleans

Horses, Watkins Place
Mar. 26, 1849
April 25, 1849
1) names of some of the horses: Sam, Bill, Felton, Bob

Hudson, Dr. C. L.
April 4, 1854
Dec. 28, 1856

Dec. 2, 1857
Oct. 20, 1860
Oct. 3, 1861
1) m. Sue Davis, Jan. 6, 1855
2) wife died by Dec. 28, 1856

Hunter, Miss Georgie S.
Jan. 31, 1861
Feb. 16, 1861
1) of Claiborne Co., Ms.
2) m. Albert Keys, Dec. 14, 1860

Huntsville, Alabama
May 15, 1850
1) disastrous fire

Hutchins, Amelia
Sept. 26, 1864
1) Austin resident
2) Will Walton's kin, later Mrs. Glenn
3) in later years, Amelia's younger sister, Susie, m. Jeff McLemore's younger brother, Johnny

Hyatt, Nannie
May 2, 1861
1) of Yazoo City, Ms.
2) at Patapsco with Mollie

I

Irby, Betty
Dec. 28, 1859
July 31, 1860
Jan. 31, 1861
1) Mrs. Sarah Watkins's cousin

Irby, Edmund
Dec. 28, 1859
1) Sarah Watkins's cousin

Irby, William
Dec. 28, 1859
1) Sarah Watkins's cousin

Iva, Polly (Ivey?)
June 8, 1857
1) 1850 census:
    Mary Ivy   60   N.C.
    living with William Hemingway family

J

Jay, Mr.
April 13, 1862

Jefferson, Thomas
Jan. 9, 1864
Jenkins, Elizabeth
June 1, 1855
1) teaching school near Middleton, Ms.
Jenkins, Mr.
Feb. 14, 1849
1) had a dance at his home, Christmas, 1848
Jenkins, Mrs. Dr.
Sept. 2, 1854
1) Ala. resident
2) "died last month with milk leg"
Jenkins, Mrs. Mary
Nov. 7, 1848
Feb. 14, 1849
Mar. 9, 1849
April 4, 1852
May 15, 1854
Jan. 31, 1861
Sept. 10, 1862
Oct. 7, 1862
1) neighbor of Dr. and Mrs. Watkins
2) 1850 census:

Mary Jenkins	54		N.C.
Green	26	farmer	Tn.
John	24		Tn.
Mary	20		Tn.
Susan	18		Tn.

Jenkins, Mary A.
Nov. 7, 1848
April 25, 1849
May 15, 1850
April 4, 1852
April 19, 1852
Jan. 12, 1854
1) m. R. J. "Jimmy" Davis, Oct. 3, 1855
(Mrs. Davis not pleased)
Jenkins, Susan
Nov. 7, 1848
April 4, 1852
April 19, 1852
1) daughter of Mrs. Mary Jenkins; neighbor of Dr. Watkins
2) 1850 census: age 18
Johnson, Atlas
April 19, 1852
Jan. 12, 1856

Nov. 4, 1862
1) m. Martha L. Wood, April 15, 1852
2) son of John Johnson
3) 1850 census:

John Johnson	67	N.C.
Mary	63	N.C.
*Atlas	26	N.C.
Louisa	19	N.C.

Johnson, Jack
May 25, 1860
Johnson, Judge
April 28, 1860
Johnson, Misses
Dec. 28, 1857
1) school friends of Mollie's, Holly Springs, Ms.
Johnson, P. W.
Mar. 23, 1865
Johnston, Gen. Albert Sidney
July 22, 1861
April 13, 1862
1) Confederate general from Texas; killed in Battle of Shiloh
Johnston, Hebe G.
June 3, 1861
1) of Paducah, Ky.
2) at Patapsco with Mollie
Jolly, Mr.
May 15, 1854
1) has died
Jones, Fanny Cook
Nov. 2, 1859
Jones, Mrs.
April 25, 1849
Jones, Mrs. Dr.
Nov. _____, 1862
1) of Holmes Co., Ms.
Jones, Major E. P.
April 13, 1863
Jones, Mary
Sept. 5, 1860
Jan. 1, 1861
Jones, Mr. (Col.) Richard
Mar. 6, 1854
Sept. 2, 1854
June 1, 1855
June 21 1862
June 27, 1862

April 22, 1866
1) Lawrence Co., Ms.
2) old and respected friend of family; connection of Dr. Watkins
3) his wife was Lucy Early, daughter of Gov. Peter Early of Georgia; Lucy was Dr. Watkins's first cousin
4) Lucy and Richard Jones's daughter Daniella m. second, Joseph Wheeler ("Fighting Joe" Wheeler: general in the Confederate Army)
5) 1850 census (Lawrence Co., Ala.):

Richard	57	Va.
Lucy	57	Ga.
Thomas H.	30	Ga.
Daniella	9	Ala.

Jones, Sally
Feb. 16, 1861
Mar. 11, 1861
1) at Patapsco with Mollie Watkins

Jones, Sally Tanner (Mrs. E. G. Booth)
Mar. 16, 1860
Jan. 2, 1861
Feb. 16, 1861
May 2, 1861
Dec. 9, 1861
Oct. 7, 1862
1) 1860 census:

Z. T. Jones	46	N.C
E. H.	39	Tn.
M. E.	16	Ms.
J. T.	14	Ms.
A. M.	12	Ms.
M. E.	11	Ms.
William	9	Ms.
J. M.	8	Ms.
Nancy	6	Ms.
Frank	4	Ms.
Sally	2	Ms.

Jones, Thomas A. (cousin)
June 21, 1862
June 27, 1862
Aug. 18, 1862
Aug. 30, 1862
Sept. 10, 1862
April 22, 1866
1) son of Col. Richard Jones of Ala.

Jones, Tom
Jan. 9, 1864

Jorden, Robert

Dec. 1, 1848

1) Ala. resident; has died

Judson Institute

Nov. 7, 1851

Justice, Miss

1) m. John Bledsoe of Tx. as her second husband

2) niece of Mrs. John Glass

K

Kendall, Mrs.

Oct. 20, 1860

Nov. 2, 1860

July 9, 1861

April 13, 1863

1) "Mrs. Kendall, Tom Purnell's aunt who lives with him"

2) Mrs. Kendall was John Purnell's sister (also Micajah Purnell's sister)

Kennedy, Mrs. Benjamin (Francis A.)

April 4, 1854

Mar. 11, 1857

July 30, 1857

April 10, 1860

Oct. 6, 1860

Jan. 9, 1864

Sept. 20, 1864

1) she was a daughter of Thomas Pleasant

2) lived around Shongalo

3) 1850 census:

Capt. Benjamin Kennedy	49	farmer	Ky.
Frances A.	39		Ga.
Eugene A.	20	student	Ms.
Thomas B.	13		Ms.
Camilla	10		Ms.
Ophelia	8		Ms.
DeGraffenreid	7		Ms.
Emma	5		Ms.
Walter	3		Ms.
Arthur	7/12		Ms.

Kennedy, Camilla

May 15, 1854

Sept. 23, 1855

Dec. 2, 1857

1) m. Tom Purnell, Nov. 24, 1855

2) dead by Dec. 2, 1857, age 17

3) daughter of Benjamin Kennedy

4) 1850 census: age 10

Kennedy, Emma
June 14, 1858
1) daughter of Benjamin Kennedy (see ref.)
2) 1850 census: age 5
Kennedy, Eugene
April 4, 1854
July 4, 1855
Sept. 23, 1855
1) m. Sarah Smith
2) dead by Nov. 8, 1855, age 25
3) son of Benjamin Kennedy
4) 1850 census: age 20
Kennedy, (Jennie, Ginny, Mary, Virginia Whitehead, Mrs. Tom)
June 14, 1858
Mar. 15, 1859
April 4, 1860
April 28, 1860
Feb. 16, 1861
Mar. 31, 1862
Dec. 15, 1862
Dec. 30, 1881
1) m. Thomas B. Kennedy, Dec. 27, 1857
2) daughter of E. G. Whitehead (see ref.)
3) her letters re: Grierson's Raid are cited in text
Kennedy, Mrs. Judge
Feb. 4, 1865
Kennedy, Ophelia
Oct. 24, 1857
Dec. 28, 1857
Oct. 6, 1860
1) daughter of Benjamin Kennedy (see ref.)
2) 1850 census: age 8
Kennedy, Tom B.
May 15, 1854
Mar. 11, 1857
Oct. 8, 1857
Dec. 28, 1857
Jan. 18, 1858
Mar. 15, 1859
Oct. 6, 1860
Oct. 3, 1861
1) m. Mary Virginia Whitehead, Dec. 23, 1857 daughter of Edmunds Grey
Whitehead
2) son of Benjamin Kennedy (see ref.)
3) 1850 census: age 13

Kettering, Jeff T.
April 10, 1860
Aug. 8, 1861
1) of Memphis, Tn.
2) second husband of Mary Bledsoe Fitzgerald,
sister-in-law of Sarah Watkins

Keys, Albert and Mrs.
July 4, 1855
Oct. 8, 1857
Dec. 28, 1857
Jan. 18, 1858
April 26, 1858
Jan. 31, 1861
Feb. 16, 1861
Sept. 15, 1864
Feb. 4, 1865
1) m. Miss Hunter of Claiborne Co., "in the winter" says letter of Feb. 1861
2) Albert and Frank Keys are brothers of Joe Keys, sons of Dr. Joseph M. Keys, whose plantation was west of Coila
3) Claiborne Co. records: Georgie S. Hunter to Albert G. Keys, Dec. 14, 1860
4) 1860 census:

A. G. Keys	26	planter	Ala.

Keys, Frank
Jan. 18, 1858
April 26, 1861
May 2, 1861
June 6, 1861
July 9, 1861
1) m. Mary Griffith, Dr. Stansbury's niece
2) April 27, 1861, Mrs. Frank Keys died
3) 1860 census:

Frank Keys	24	lawyer	Ala.
Mary G.	20		Md.

Keys, Mr. Joe
July 30, 1857
1) died while visiting the McLemores, 1857
2) see Keys, Mrs. Joe

Keys, Mrs. Joe
Dec. 17, 1860
Sept. 15, 1864
Feb. 4, 1865
1) m. Mr. Hunter, brother-in-law of Albert Keys
2) 1860 census:

Ann E. Keys	26	Ala.
Zella	8	Ms.
Lettie	6	Ms.

Keys, Lert
June 6, 1861
1) is dead
2) 1860 census:

J. J. Keys	32	planter	Ala.

Kirkwood, Mr.
June 8, 1857

L

Lake Bistineau, Louisiana
Dec. 1, 1862
Lagrange, Tennessee
Sept. 2, 1854
Latham, Mary Ann
April 4, 1851
Lay, Mrs. J. T.
Feb. 24, 1862
Jan. 9, 1864
1) Col. Moore's oldest daughter
husband in business in Grenada (Ella Moore)
Lee (Leigh), Mr. Charles C.
Oct. 24, 1857
1) new Baptist minister at Middleton in 1857
2) pastor there, 1858–59
3) moved to another church in area
4) 1860 census:

Charles Lee	37	Baptist minister	Ala.
Francis	36		Ga.
and children			

Leflore, Mrs. Jack
Dec. 2, 1857
Leflore, Mr. (Col.) Greenwood
Feb. 20, 1849
Nov. 4, 1861
1) 1850 census:

Greenwood Leflore	50	Ms.
Priscilla	32	Tn.
Jane	18	Ms.
Rebecca	12	Ms.
Greenwood	9	Ms.

Leflore, John D. "Jack"
Mar. 9, 1849
1) son of Greenwood Leflore
2) m. Miss Frances S. Newman, Feb. 22, 1849
3) 1850 census:

John D. Leflore	24	Ms.
Frances	18	Ms.

Leigh, Mrs. Richard
June 8, 1857
1) sister to Eggleston Dick Townes
2) maiden name, Polly Townes
Leigh, Patty "Cousin"
Sept. 2, 1854
1) m. to cousin Paschal Ligon
2) Ala. resident
Leigh, Randolph
Oct. 24, 1857
Leigh, William
Oct. 21, 1848
Feb. 10, 1860
1) used to live at the "crossroads" in Ala.
2) daughter Betsy Leigh m. "cousin" Dick Townes
3) resident of Florence, Ala.
Levert, Mrs. Octavia Walton
Mar. 26, 1860
1) granddaughter of George Walton, signer of the Declaration of Independence from Georgia
2) George Walton's sister, Sally Walton, who married "Thomas Watkins of Powhatan," Dr. Watkins's grandfather
3) Mrs. LeVert was Dr. Watkins's second cousin and a resident of Mobile, Ala.
Lexington, Mississippi
April 4, 1854
1) in Holmes Co.
Liddell (Ladel), "Old" Mrs.
Oct. 20, 1860
Nov. 2, 1860
April 13, 1862
1) sister of Mr. Hemphill
2) her husband was James Liddell
Liddell, Col. Frank
May _____, 1861
May 2, 1861
Oct. 7, 1862
Oct. _____, 1862
Nov. 4, 1862
1) Col. Frank Liddell of Carrollton
Liddell (Ladel), Dr. and Mrs. W. W.
April 28, 1860
Oct. 20, 1860
Nov. 2, 1860
April 13, 1861
1) 1850 census:
　　William W. Liddell　　30　　　physician　　Ga.

*Elizabeth A.	24	Tn.
Mary A.	7/12	Ms.
*Elizabeth Small		

Ligon, Dr.
Sept. 2, 1854
June 1, 1855
1) Ala. resident

Ligon, Pascal "Cousin"
Sept. 2, 1854

Lilly, Mr.
June 9, 1851

Lincoln, Abraham
Nov. 2, 1860
April 24, 1861

Lipscomb, Dr. Dabney M.
July 9, 1846
Jan. 30, 1852
1) bought some books from Dr. Watkins
2) doctor in Middleton
3) m. Miss Milicent Scrivner, Jan. 16, 1838
4) 1850 census:

Dabney M. Lipscomb	44	physician	Va.
Milicent	32		Tn.
Mary	12		Ms.
Curier	10		Ms.
Joseph	8		Ms.
Ann D.	6		Ms.
Frances R.	4		Ms.
Jenner	2		Ms.
John S.	2/12		Ms.

and boarders

Little (Lytle), John
Jan. 19, 1860
Jan. 27, 1860
Mar. 16, 1860
1) 1860 census: estate of John Little

Lockhart, L. Tine
April 15, 1854
May 15, 1854
1) Middleton school friend of Mollie's

Lombard, Mr.
Sept. 9, 1864

Long, Margaret
Nov. 4, 1861

Longstreet, Mrs. A. B.
Mar. 26, 1861

Longstreet, Judge A. B. (Augustus B. "Gus")
   Oct. 8, 1857
   Oct. 24, 1857
   Dec. 28, 1857
   Jan. 2, 1861
   Feb. 16, 1861
   Mar. 25, 1861
   Aug. 27, 1861
   1) old friend of Dr. Watkins and of his father
   2) president of the University of Mississippi at Oxford
   3) 1850 census (Holmes Co., Ms.):
       A. B. Longstreet   60   Ga.
       Francis C.   57   N.C.
Lott, Dr.
   June 8, 1857
   1) resident, Austin, Tx.
Love, "Buck"
   April 4, 1851
Love, "Dick" R. B.
   Feb. 10, 1860
   Mar. 6, 1860
   Mar. 16, 1860
   May 2, 1861
   1) B. B. Love m. Mary E. Sanders, Feb. 18, 1860 (daughter of William Sanders)
   2) see Sanders ref.
Lubbock, Thomas S.
   Jan. 24, 1862
   1) member of Terry's Texas Rangers
   2) d. Jan. 1862
Lucas, Miss
   Jan. 2, 1861
Lum, "Old" Mrs.
   Jan. 13, 1849

Mc

McBride, Mr.
   Jan. 30, 1852
McCain, William
   Nov. _____, 1862
   Dec. 1, 1862
McCarroll, Elic (Alex)
   July 4, 1855
   Dec. 1, 1862
   1) his brother, Hines, m. to James Parmele's sister, Mary "Mollie" Parmele
   McCarroll

McCarroll, Mr. and Mrs. Hines

Sept. 5, 1860

June 6, 1861

1) Milton Hines McCarroll m. Mary N. Parmele, Nov. 18, 1847

2) called her "Mollie"; James Parmele's sister

3) 1850 census:

Milton H. McCarroll	27	farmer	Ms.
Mary N.	22		Ms.
Thomas A.	2		Ms.
Nora P.	5		1/2 Ms.

McCarroll, Laura Parmele (widow)

Mar. 9, 1849

1) second m. to Isaac Curtis, Feb. 4, 1852

2) James Parmele's sister

3) first m. to John H. McCarroll, brother to Laura's brother-in-law, Hines McCarroll

4) 1850 census:

Laura A. McCarroll	26	Ms.
Felece E.	6	Ms.
John H.	4	Ms.

McClure, John

July 30, 1857

June 1, 1864

1) m. Mrs. Sarah Norwood, July 5, 1857

2) 1850 census:

John McClure	26	dental surgeon	Ohio

boarding with Newell family in Carrollton

3) 1860 census:

John B. McClure	35	dentist	Ohio
Sarah A. McClure	32		N.C.
Aletha Norwood	12f		Ms.
C. C. Norwood	10f		Ms.
L. M. McClure	2f		Ms.

McConnell, Mrs.

July 16, 1849

McConnell & Brothers

June 26, 1846

Mar. 31, 1849

1) merchants of Greenwood, Ms.

2) Richard McConnell, one of the first merchants at Greenwood, with interests at Carrollton as well

McCray, Ellen

Mar. 9, 1849

1) goes to school at Mr. Holt at Blackhawk, Mar. 1849

McCuin, Mr. (Meewen) (McCune) (McCain)

Aug. 8, 1861

1) m Abbey Eubanks (Youbanks)

McCune, Mr.
  Oct. 21, 1848
  1) of Nashville
  2) m. Miss Frierson
McDonel (McDonald), Mr.
  July 4, 1855
  Oct. 24, 1857
McGee, Col.
  June 11, 1862
  1) of Bolivar Co., Ms.
McGhee, Martha
  Sept. 2, 1854
  1) boarder at Aunt Letty's home in Mountain Home, Ala.
  2) parents lived in Moulton, Ala.
McIntire, Mr. and Mrs. J. C.
  Dec. 28, 1859
  Jan. 27, 1860
  April 28, 1860
  1) 1860 census:

J. C.	39	planter	N.C.
M. G.	31		Ala.
A.	13		Ala.
M. G.	11		Ala.
Innis	9		Ms.
J. M.	7		Ms.
Gordon	3		Ms.

McKenzie, Hugh
  April 4, 1851
McKenzie, Mr. John C.
  Feb. 6, 1858
  1) wife is Margaret
McLane, John
  Dec. 9, 1861
  Nov. _____, 1862
  Sept. 15, 1864
McLean, Dr.
  Nov. 4, 1861
McLean, George D.
  Aug. 8, 1861
  1) m. Eliza Alzade Parmele (James Parmele's sister), Jan. 10, 1843
  2) 1850 census:
    George D. McLean   44   Ky.
    (wife dead)
McLean, Mrs. Geo. D.
  Dec. 1, 1848
  Dec. 28, 1849
  1) died

2) this was Eliza Alzade Parmele, sister of James Parmele

3) her husband's (George McLean's) sister was Martha M. McLean who m. Nathaniel S. Neal, Nov. 14, 1837

McLemore, Adelaide

Feb. 27, 1864

1) Jeff's younger sister

McLemore, Jefferson H.

March 11, 1857

Jan. 27, 1861

May 20, 1861

June 3, 1861

June 17, 1861

June 22, 1861

July 9, 1861

July 22, 1861

Aug. 5, 1861

Aug. 8, 1861

Aug. 27, 1861

Sept. 11, 1861

Nov. 4, 1861

Dec. 9, 1861

June 27, 1862

Oct. _____, 1862

Nov. _____, 1862

Dec. 1, 1862

Dec. 15, 1862

Jan. 12, 1863

April 13, 1863

Oct. 7, 1863

Jan. 9, 1864

July 25, 1864

Aug. 12, 1864

Sept. 15, 1864

Sept. 20, 1864

Feb. 4, 1865

Mar. 14, 1866

Jan. 30, 1875

July _____, 1879

1) m. Mary Early "Mollie" Watkins, Dec. 23, 1863

2) son of Col. John C. McLemore

McLemore, Mr. John D. (Col.)

Feb. 9, 1850

July 30, 1857

Dec. 1, 1862

Jan. 9, 1864

Feb. 27, 1864
Aug. 12, 1864
Sept. 15, 1864
Feb. 4, 1865
Mar. 20, 1865
April 22, 1866
Sept. 21, 1867
1) child died with smallpox
2) m. Sarah A. Geren, Jan. 8, 1844 (second wife)
3) son, Jeff, m. Mollie Watkins
4) Sarah Geren McLemore was the daughter of Abram Geren and sister to Mrs. John H. Davis
5) 1850 census:

John D. McLemore	36	farmer	Tn.
Sarah W.	24		N.C.
Samuel	12		Ms.
Price D.	10		Ms.
Jefferson	9		Ms.
Adelaide	1		Ms.

McLemore, Price
April 28, 1860
May 20, 1861
July 22, 1861
Sept. 11, 1861
June 27, 1862
Oct. _____, 1862
Nov. _____, 1862
Nov. 4, 1862
Dec. 1, 1862
July 25, 1864
Sept. 15, 1864
1) son of Col. John D. McLemore
2) brother of Jeff, Mollie's husband
McLemore, Sam
Jan. 19, 1860
June 27, 1862
Oct. _____, 1862
Fall 1868
1) m. to Miss Gipson, John Davis's niece
2) son of Col. John C. McLemore
McLeod, Gen. Hugh
Jan. 24, 1862
Feb. 4, 1862
1) Colonel of 1st Texas Infantry, CSA
2) died Jan. 1862

McMahon, Ethelbert

Oct. 24, 1848

1) resident of Nashville, Tn.

2) of Courtland, Ala.; son of Robert G. McMahon; brother of John J. McMahon

McMahon, Harriet Shackelford

Dec. 1, 1848

1) Mrs. John J. McMahon

2) see McMahon, Trotter, Pearsall ref.

McMahon, John J.

Dec. 1, 1848

1) see McMahon, Trotter, Pearsall ref.

McMahon, Trotter & Pearsall

1) commission merchants in New Orleans

2) John J. McMahon m. Harriett Shackelford (both of Courtland, Ala.) whose father, Dr. Jack Shackleford, was an old friend and once a partner with Dr. Watkins in Courtland, Ala.

3) John J. McMahon's father was William

1) Joseph Trotter came to Courtland, Ala. from Tenn. (Pulaski)

2) moved to Caddo Parish, La. and opened commission house in New Orleans: Trotter & Pearsall

3) second wife returned to Pulaski and died there

McMahon, Wm. P.

Feb. 23, 1852

Mar. 16, 1860

1) practiced law in Courtland, Ala.

2) brother of John J. McMahon

3) wife was Laura Chafee

McPherson, Gen.

July 25, 1864

McWilliams, Professor H. F.

Mar. 6, 1854

Jan. 12, 1856

1) resident of Middleton

2) had charge of Female Seminary in Middleton until he retired in 1857

3) Mrs. McWilliams (daughter of Dr. Allen Gary) had charge of the dormitory building

M

Maddox (Mattox), Miss

April 26, 1858

1) daughter of William Maddox

Maddox (Mattox), Mr. William

Dec. 28, 1857

April 26, 1858

1) m. Jane Gayden (the widow Gayden) 1857

2) also Heans and Gaydens living with them in 1860

3) 1860 census:

William Mattox	60	farmer	Ga.
Jane	40		Ga.
Charles	21		Ga.
Mary	18		Ga.

Martin, Miss
June 9, 1851

Martin, Mrs.
Dec. 15, 1851
Dec. 24, 1851
1) resident of Holly Springs, Ms.

Mason, Mr.
Dec. 15, 1851
Feb. 23, 1852
Mar. 12, 1852
1) resident of Holly Springs, Ms.
2) merchandising business

Masterson, Mr.
Dec. 28, 1857
1) Tex. resident

Matthews, Col.
Jan. 9, 1864
1) one-time governor of Georgia

Matthews, Dora
Jan. 26, 1861
1) daughter of Thomas M. Matthews

Matthews, Dr.
Mar. 9, 1849

Matthews, "Cousin" Joel
Feb. 24, 1864

Matthews, Mary
Mar. 26, 1849
1) m. William Farmer

Matthews, Martha "Cousin Mattie"
Feb. 10, 1860
Mar. 26, 1860
Jan. 26, 1861
Feb. 24, 1864
1) her grandmother, Lucy Early Matthews, was Dr. Watkins's aunt
2) Mollie's classmate at Patapsco

Matthews, Thomas M.
Jan. 26, 1861
1) Dr. Watkins's cousin

Mayes, Bradley
Oct. 23, 1848
July 16, 1849
1) resident, Columbia, Tn.

Mead, Mr.
April 4, 1860
1) m. Signiora Eggleston (Holmes Co.) (her cousin)
Measles Outbreak
Jan. 13, 1849
Feb. 14, 1849
1) Mollie had it but Lettie didn't because she was away at school
2) Lettie got it in Texas right after she married and moved there in 1854
Mead, Mrs.
April 4, 1854
Nov. _____, 1862
1) friend of the Egglestons (Holmes Co.)
Merriwether, C. J. F. (Charles) M.D.
Nov. 2, 1859
Feb. 9, 1862
1) m. Octavia Simmons, Nov. 17, 1859
2) lived at Charleston, Ms., Tallahatchie Co.
3) 1860 census (Tallahatchie Co., Ms.):

| Charles J. F. | 28 | physician | Ky. |
| Octavia D. | 25 | | N.C. |

Merriwether, Octavia Simmons (Mrs. C. J. F.)
April 10, 1860
Jan. 26, 1861
Jan. 31, 1861
May 2, 1861
Aug. 27, 1861
Sept. 11, 1861
Oct. 3, 1861
Dec. 9, 1861
Feb. 9, 1862
April 13, 1863
Jan. 3, 1864
1) see Simmons and Merriwether ref.
Methodists
Nov. 7, 1851
1) disputing with the Campbellites in Middleton
Middleton, Mrs.
Nov. 2, 1860
1) of Farmville, Va.
Middleton, Mississippi
Mar. 26, 1848 (and repeated mentions)
1) old town now completely gone—closest post office to Watkinses and
Whiteheads at one time
2) Parmeles and Phillips lived quite close
Middleton Female Academy
Mar. 31, 1849

Miller, "Cousin" Mary
  July 31, 1860
  1) relative of Mrs. Watkins
Miller, Miss
  Oct. 20, 1860
  1) relative of Mrs. George Loe (Amanda) Walton, Lettie's sister-in-law
Mississippi Central Railroad
  Feb. 3, 1860
  Feb. 10, 1860
  Mar. 26, 1860
Money, Hernando
  April 13, 1863
Money, James
  April 4, 1851
Money, Joe
  April 19, 1852
  Mar. 16, 1860
  1) m. Semira Estel, April 17, 1852
  2) son of James Money
  3) Semira d. by May 15, 1854
  4) Joe m. second, Margaret Estel, on May 24, 1858
  5) wife has a new baby
  6) 1850 census:

| James Money | 72 | landlord | Va. |
| Joseph | 20 | merchant's clerk | N.C. |

Money, John
  Dec. 9, 1861
  1) of Carrollton
  2) m. Miss Clark
Money, Semira Estel (Mrs. Joe)
  May 15, 1854
  1) has died
Montgomery, Charlotte
  Mar. 16, 1860
  Mar. 17. 1860
  April 4, 1860
  April 10, 1860
  April 28, 1860
  May 25, 1860
  July 10, 1860
  Oct. 3, 1861
  1) daughter of Dr. and Mrs. Edward Montgomery
  2) formerly of Middleton area, before 1854, now of St. Louis
Montgomery, Dr. and Mrs. Edward
  Mar. 16, 1860
  Mar. 17, 1860

May 25, 1860
1) uncopied letter of Aug. 29, 1854 lists children:
Charlotte, two young boys, youngest daughter as Hannah Maria Jeanette
2) good friend of Martha M. Phillips
3) formerly of Middleton, had medical practice there, now of St. Louis (1860)
4) sold medical practice in Middleton to Dr. Liddell in 1850
5) very prosperous practice in St. Louis

Moore, Miss
Mar. 17, 1860
1) from Baltimore
2) cousin of Laura Moore's

Moore, Ben
Jan. 2, 1861
1) has died
2) son of Col. O. J. Moore

Moore, Ella
July 31, 1860
Feb. 24, 1862
Jan. 9, 1864
1) daughter of Col. O. J. Moore
2) m. J. T. Lay, young businessman from Grenada

Moore, Miss Georgia
Dec. 17, 1860

Moore, Mrs.
July 7, 1849
July 8, 1849
July 16, 1849
July 23, 1849
July 31, 1860
June 22, 1861
Feb. 24, 1862

Moore, Mrs. Jack*
July 25, 1864
1) Ala. resident
2) Mrs. Watt's sister
*probably the same as Mrs. O. J. Col. Moore

Moore, Laura
Dec. 28, 1857
Feb. 10, 1860
Mar. 6, 1860
Mar. 17, 1860
July 31, 1860
April 13, 1861
June 3, 1861
June 6, 1861
June 22, 1861

Sept. 11, 1861
July 31, 1862
Nov. _____, 1862
Feb. 24, 1862
Dec. 1, 1862
Jan. 12, 1863
Jan. 9, 1864
1) daughter of Col. O. J. Moore
2) m. Dr. Davie B. Turner (brother of Capt. W. T. Turner, who m. Octavia Palmer, see ref.), nephew of Jack Turner

Moore, Col. Osbourn J.

Dec. 28, 1856
Nov. 1, 1858
Mar. 6, 1860
April 13, 1861
April 27, 1861
June 22, 1861
April 13, 1862
July 31, 1862
Dec. 1, 1862
Feb. 4, 1864
1) m. Rebecca Gee in Mecklenburg Co., Va. and came to Carroll Co. in 1846, age 33
2) 1850 census:

Osbourn	37	farmer	Va.
Rebecca W.	37		Va.
Benjamin	14		Va.
Erasmus	12		Va.
Ella A.	10		Va.
Laura J.	8		Va.

Moore, Mrs. Osbourn J.

1) she was Rebecca Gee
2) m. Col. O. J. Moore in Mecklenburg Co., Va.
3) came to Carroll Co. in 1846

Moore, Dr. Ras

June 22, 1861
July 9, 1861
July 22, 1861
Aug. 27, 1861
Sept. 11, 1861
Mar. 31, 1862
1) son of Col. O. J. Moore

Morey, Miss Kate P.

Mar. 26, 1849
April 25, 1849
1) teaching school at the academy at Middleton

Morgan, Capt.
June 11, 1863
Morris, "Aunt"
May 2, 1861
1) Lizzie Whitehead Oliver's aunt
Morrison, Mr.
Feb. 14, 1849
April 25, 1849
Nov. 7, 1851
1) former teacher in Middleton
2) preached at Methodist church at Middleton
3) teaching singing school at Middleton
4) a Morrison was pastor at Shongalo Presbyterian Church at one time
5) 1850 census: 3 Morrisons in Carroll Co. in the Middleton area:

Adrean	37 m	Pres. minister	N.C.
Robert	41 m	Pres. minister	N.C.
Elizabeth	31 f		Tn.

Moseley, Sarah
May 30, 1851
1) Ala. resident, dead
Mountain Home, Alabama
Sept. 2, 1854
1) where "Aunt Letty," "Uncle Billy," Sarah's brother William Fitzgerald, and family all moved in 1854
Mules on the Watkins Place
Oct. 6, 1860
May 15, 1854
1) names of some of Dr. Watkins's mules were: Mary, Jim, Meady, Jenny
Mumford (Munford), Amelia Antoinette (Mrs. Edward)
June 1, 1855
1) daughter of Paul J. Watkins of Lawrence Co., Ala.
2) died winter 1854
Murry, Lt., CSA,
1) in Gen. Kirby Smith's command
Dec. 1, 1862
Dec. 15, 1862
1) Confederate soldier in Gen. Kirby Smith's command
Murry, Mrs. Judge and Daughter
April 4, 1854
1) from Natchez

N

Neal, Mrs.
May 15, 1850
Neal, Mr. and Mrs. Nat (Martha)
Dec. 1, 1848

Jan. 13, 1849
Oct. 7, 1858
1) Nathaniel S. Neal m. Martha N. McLean (George D. McLean's sister),
Nov. 14, 1837
Neal, Parson
Mar. 26, 1849
Nov. 1, 1858
Neill, Amanda
April 13, 1861
Sept. 10, 1862
1) daughter of Maj. G. F. Neill
Neill, Mrs. Caroline (Mrs. G. F.)
1) new baby named Amanda
Neill, Major (G. F.) Gilbreth F.
Dec. 28, 1856
May 15, 1857
April 26, 1858
June 3, 1859
Jan. 19, 1860
Feb. 3, 1860
April 28, 1860
Oct. 20, 1860
Nov. 26, 1860
April 13, 1861
May 2, 1861
June 6, 1861
Sept. 10, 1862
June 11, 1863
Fall 1868
1) neighbor and friend of Dr. Watkins
2) Mississippi state senator
3) lawyer
4) 1850 census:

G. F. Neill	39	farmer	Tn.
Caroline	24		Tn.
Robert	4		Ms.
Henry "Ha"	2		Ms.
Amanda	1/2		Ms.

Nelson, "Old" Mr. Richard
Feb. 16, 1861
1) living about one mile from Carrollton
Nelson, Fanny (Nelms)
Aug. 23, 1855
1) m. B. C. Dismuke, Aug. 8, 1855
2) see Dismuke, Bennet

Nelson, J. Sam
  Oct. _____, 1862
Newell, Miss
  April 28, 1860
  June 8, 1867
  1) m. John Turner
  2) daughter of Col. Camp P. Newell
Newland, Mary
  Jan. 12, 1856
  1) 1850 census: Mary M. Newland, 16, Ms., living with William Y. Collins
Newman, Elizabeth M.
  Mar. 9, 1849
  1) m. A. M. Davis, Feb. 22, 1849
  2) daughter of Josiah Newman, lived a few miles west of Shongalo
Newman, Frances S. ("Fannie")
  Mar. 9, 1849
  1) m. John D. "Jack" Leflore, Feb. 22, 1849
  2) daughter of Josiah Newman, lived a few miles west of Shongalo
Norman, Miss
  June 9, 1851
Norwood, Mrs. Sarah A.
  July 30, 1857
  1) m. John McClure (McClun), July 5, 1857
  2) first husband was Frank Norwood
  3) 1850 census:

Frank Norwood	35	farmer	S.C.
Sarah	24		S.C.
Lelha	2		Ala.
Clarace	1		Ala.

Nunry, Mrs. John
  Mar. 16, 1860
  1) 1860 census:

John Nunnary	57	farmer	S.C.
C.	35		Va.
J. W.	7/12		Ms.

Nutall, Retta
  April 13, 1863
  Oct. 7, 1863
  1) cousin of Maj. Hawkins
  2) of Corinth, Ms.

O

Oliver, Elizabeth Phillips (Mrs. Wm. Carter)
  April 25, 1849
  July 23, 1849
  1) resident of Eutaw, Ala.; b. in Hillsborough, N.C.

2) daughter of William Henry and Martha M. Phillips

3) Judge Oliver's first wife

4) Mrs. Parmele and Mrs. Phillips are her sisters

5) one surviving child, Martha Epes Oliver, "Eppy"

Oliver, Lizzie (Elizabeth) Whitehead

Oct. 6, 1860

Oct. 20, 1860

Nov. 2, 1860

Nov. 26, 1860

Mar. 11, 1861

Mar. 25, 1861

April 13, 1861

April 27, 1861

May 2, 1861

June 6, 1861

June 11, 1863

Dec. 27, 1881

Dec. 30, 1881

1) daughter of E. G. and Jenette Whitehead

2) m. Judge Oliver, Mar. 27, 1860. First wife was Elizabeth Phillips

Oliver, Martha Epes ("Eppie")

Oct. 7, 1858

Jan. 19, 1860

July 10, 1860

Oct. 6, 1860

Dec. 25, 1862

1) daughter of William C. and Elizabeth P. Oliver

2) granddaughter of Mrs. Martha Phillips

Oliver, Judge William Carter

Oct. 7, 1858

Jan. 19, 1860

Feb. 10, 1860

Mar. 26, 1860

April 4, 1860

April 28, 1860

Oct. 6, 1860

Oct. 20, 1860

1) first wife was Elizabeth Phillips, daughter of W. H. and Martha Phillips

2) second wife was Elizabeth "Lizzie" Whitehead, daughter of E. G. and Jenette Whitehead

3) Judge Oliver lived in Eutaw, Ala. His son, Will (Buck), was dean of University of Ala. School of Law; U.S. congressman

Oury (Ory), Mr.

June 1, 1855

1) 1850 census:

John M.   34   tailor   Va.

Elizabeth   35   S.C.
and children
Oxford, Mississippi
June 24, 1852
1) home of the University of Mississippi

P

Palmer, Ellen C.
Mar. 26, 1849
1) m. Mid Conley,* left county after the war
*(Middleton Conley)
Palmer, Mrs. Judge John E. (Martha M. "Patsy")
April 4, 1852
May 15, 1854
Dec. 28, 1856
Mar. 17, 1860
Oct. 6, 1860
Mar. 9, 1861
Mar. 11, 1861
Mar. 31, 1862
Jan. 9, 1864
1) Martha M. "Patsy" Davis (sister of Mrs. William W. Whitehead, whose maiden name was Elizabeth N. Davis) m. John E. Palmer in La.
2) 1850 census: age 45
Palmer, Judge John E.
April 26, 1854
Sept. 2, 1854
June 1, 1855
July 4, 1855
Dec. 28, 1856
June 22, 1861
Mar. 20, 1863
1) wife Martha M. "Patsy" Davis, sister of Elizabeth Davis who m. Judge William W. Whitehead—all came to Carroll County together: Whitehead brothers, Hugh Davis, John E. Palmer
2) 1850 census:

John E. Palmer	53	farmer	Ga.
Martha M.	45		La.
Ann C.	20		La.
Ellen C.	18		La.
Margaret	16		La.
John W.	14		Ms.
Martha J.	12		Ms.
Phillip H.	9		Ms.
Octavia V.	7		Ms.
Hugh	1		Ms.

Palmer, John W.
> June 1, 1855
> Feb. 24, 1862
> 1) son of Judge Palmer

Palmer, Margaret (See Margaret Sykes)
> Nov. 7, 1848
> April 25, 1849
> 1) daughter of Judge John E. and Mrs. Martha M. Palmer
> 2) m. Dr. William Sykes, Dec. 22, 1852, age 18
> 3) 1850 census: age 16

Palmer, Martha Jane
> April 15, 1854
> May 15, 1854
> Dec. 28, 1856
> Sept. 11, 1861
> 1) see Gary, Martha Jane
> 2) daughter of John E. and Martha M. Palmer
> 3) 1850 census: age 12

Palmer, Octavia
> Mar. 17, 1860
> April 4, 1860
> April 28, 1860
> Nov. 26, 1860
> June 6, 1861
> June 22, 1861
> Mar. 31, 1862
> Nov. _____, 1862
> 1) m. William T. Turner, moved to Tn. after War
> 2) daughter of Judge John E. and Martha M. Palmer
> 3) friend of Mollie's
> 4) 1850 census: age 7

Palmer, Phil
> April 4, 1860
> Feb. 9, 1862
> Mar. 31, 1862
> Oct. _____, 1862
> Jan. 9, 1864
> 1) of Canton, Ms., area
> 2) m. Sue Brown
> 3) son of Judge John E. and Martha M. Palmer
> 4) Carroll Co. resident
> 5) 1850 census: age 9

Palmer, Robert
> Feb. 24, 1862

Parker, Mrs.
> April 13, 1861

Parmele, Mr. James
Jan. 14, 1852
Mar. 16, 1860
Nov. 2, 1860
Oct. 3, 1861
Dec. 9, 1861
Mar. 31, 1862
June 27, 1862
Sept. 10, 1862
Oct. _____, 1862
Oct. 7, 1862
1) son of Joseph Parmele and Lydia McGinty Parmele (who m. second A. M. Townsend)
2) m. Mariah Louise Phillips, Dec. 23, 1846
3) son, James, m. Sarah Walton, daughter of Maj. and Mrs. William M. Walton
4) 1850 census:

James Parmele	24	merchant	Ms.
Maria L.	20		N.C.
Martha M.	3		Ms.
*Joseph J.	3/12		Ms.
John C. Stevens	25	merchant	N.C.
**Mary Cobb	30		Va.
***Martha E. Oliver	6		Ala.

*this child died in 1851
**Martha Mumford Cobbs Phillips's sister
***"Epie"

Parmele, James Jefferson
Aug. 8, 1861
1) son of James and Mariah Phillips Parmele

Parmele, Mrs. Mariah Louise Phillips (Mrs. James)
Mar. 26, 1849
Oct. 15, 1851
Nov. 7, 1851
April 4, 1852
April 4, 1854
May 15, 1857
June 8, 1857
Dec. 28, 1857
April 5, 1858
Oct. 7, 1858
Mar. 16, 1860
Sept. 5, 1860
Feb. 16, 1861
July 22, 1861
Aug. 8, 1861
Dec. 9, 1861

Mar. 31, 1862
June 27, 1862
July 31, 1862
Oct. 7, 1862
Nov. 4, 1862
Dec. 25, 1862
July 25, 1864
June 8, 1867
1) daughter of William Henry and Martha Mumford Cobbs
2) m. James Parmele on Dec. 23, 1846
3) see Parmele, James

Parmele, Julia
Oct. 7, 1858
1) daughter of James and Mariah Louise Phillips Parmele

Parmele, Martha
Mar. 16, 1860
1) daughter of James Parmele and Mariah Louise Phillips
2) granddaughter of Mrs. Phillips

Parmele, William J.
Nov. 2, 1860
1) James Parmele's brother

Parrish, Joe
Oct. 21, 1848
1) Tn. resident (Nashville)

Patapsco Female Institute
Repeated references after fall 1858
1) at Ellicotts Mill, Md.
Mollie Watkins's finishing school; she began there in the fall of 1858 and was there when the war began; came home by train.

Patton, William "Bill" D.
April 4, 1851
Sept. 23, 1855
Oct. 20, 1860
Nov. 26, 1860
Dec. 17, 1860
Jan. 2, 1861
Feb. 16, 1861
1) moved to Austin about the same time as William Martin Walton—they were friends in Ms. and Tex.
2) 1850 census:
age 21 merchant clerk Tn.
working for Judge James Wellons, merchant

Payne, Henry
Aug. 23, 1865

Peacock, Martha Watkins
Aug. 15, 1854

Feb. 16, 1861

1) Lettie's "cousin" and good friend

2) daughter of James C. Watkins of Texas (formerly of Ala.) and his second wife, Lettie Williams, a cousin of Mrs. Sarah Epes Watkins

3) m. Capt. James Peacock of San Antonio, Tx.

Peck, George W.

Jan. 12, 1856

1) m. Hulda Petty, Dec. 23, 1855

Pemberton, General (John C.)

Dec. 15, 1862

Pentecost, Mr.

Jan. 12, 1856

April 26, 1858

April 4, 1860

April 28, 1860

Sept. 5, 1860

Dec. 1860

Jan. 1, 1861

May 2, 1861

Nov. 4, 1861

Mar. 31, 1862

1) Dr. Watkins's overseer

Peoples, Plez

Oct. _____, 1862

Perkins, Mary Eliza Davis

June 8, 1867

1) widow of Robert Perkins

Perkins, Robert

Jan. 9, 1864

Sept. 15, 1864

1) nephew of Col. McLemore

2) m. Mary Eliza Davis on Dec. 24, 1863

Perry, Mr. John D.

Mar. 26, 1860

1) of St. Louis

Petits Hotel

Fall 1868

1) in Carrollton, Ms.

Pettus, Gov. John Jones

Oct. 6, 1860

Oct. 20, 1860

1) elected governor of Mississippi, Oct. 1859, as a representative of the movement for southern independence

2) governor during the war years

Petty Family

July 23, 1849

1) there were several Petty families on 1850 census

Petty, Hulda*

Jan. 12, 1856

1) m. George W. Peck, Dec. 23 1855

2) daughter of Hilliard Petty

3) 1850 census (Carroll Co.):

Hilliard	51	farmer	S.C.
Hannah	30		Tn.
Rebecca	13		Tn.
*Hulda	13		Tn.
Lucy	11		Ms.
Martha	9		Ms.
Mary	7		Ms.
Rufus	4		Ms.
Hilliard	1		Ms.

Petty, Mildred

Jan. 12, 1856

1) daughter of Abner Petty

2) 1850 census:

Abner	45	farmer	S.C.
Malvina	39		N.C.
Gayden	19		Ala.
Cynthia	17		Ala.
William	16		Ala.
Philemon	14		Ala.
Mildred	13		Ala.
James	12		Ala.
Sally	10		Ala.

Petty, Mrs. Abner (Malvina)

Dec. 2, 1857

1) from Carrollton

2) wife of Abner Petty

3) see Petty, Mildred

4) 1850 census: age 39

Petty, Mary

May 2, 1861

Petty, Sally

Dec. 2, 1857

1) of Carrollton

2) daughter of Abner Petty

3) see Petty, Mildred

4) 1850 census: age 10

Phillips, Mrs. Martha Mumford Cobbs (Mrs. William Henry)

Jan. 13, 1849

Feb. 14, 1849

Mar. 26, 1849

July 23, 1849

Oct. 15, 1851
Nov. 7, 1851
Jan. 30, 1852
April 15, 1854
June 3, 1855
Dec. 28, 1856
Mar. 11, 1857
May 15, 1857
June 8, 1857
Dec. 28, 1857
April 5, 1858
Oct. 7, 1858
Dec. 20, 1858
April 28, 1860
July 10, 1860
Oct. 6, 1860
Nov. 2, 1860
Dec. 17, 1860
Feb. 16, 1861
May 2, 1861
June 6, 1861
July 22, 1861
Aug. 8, 1861
Aug. 27, 1861
Dec. 9, 1861
Mar. 31, 1862
April 13 1862
July 31, 1862
Jan. 9, 1864
July 25, 1864
Mar. 10, 1865
June 8, 1867
1) b. Mecklenburg Co., Va.
2) daughter of Thomas Cobbs and Elizabeth Phillips Cobbs
3) moved to Raleigh, N.C. with parents
4) m. William Henry Phillips, son of James Phillips and Nancy Lockhart Phillips of Hillsborough, N.C.
5) moved to Ala.
6) three daughters:
    Elizabeth, who m. William C. Oliver;
    Julia F., who m. Joseph Farmer;
    Mariah Louise, who m. James Parmele
7) see husband's ref. for census

Phillips, William Henry
April 25, 1849
April 4, 1852

April 19, 1852
1) m. Martha Mumford Cobbs
2) daughter of Thomas Cobbs and Elizabeth Phillips Cobbs
3) he was son of James Phillips and Nancy Lockhart Phillips and was b. in Hillsborough, N.C.
4) moved to Ala. and then to Ms.
5) 1850 census:

| William H. Phillips | 50 | merchant | N.C. |
| Martha | 43 | | Va. |

Phinney—See Finney

Pierce, Mr.
Mar. 16, 1860
1) Ala. resident

Pigeon named Polly on Watkins Place
July 23, 1849

Pillow, Gen. Gideon J.
Jan. 13, 1849

Pinchback, Mr.
Feb. 14, 1849
1) sale of Negroes in Holmes Co., Ms.

Pittman, Henry
June 8, 1857
Oct. 24, 1857
Mar. 17, 1860
Feb. 16, 1861
1) m. Mary F. Nelms, Jan. 4, 1844
2) m. Isabella D. Wadlington, Nov. 1, 1854
3) pastor at Middleton 1847–57 and again 1860–65
4) 1850 census:

Henry	33	Baptist minister	N.C.
Mary	35		Ga.
Catherine	4		Ms.
Harriet	2		Ms.

Pleasant, Augustus "Gus"
Jan. 18, 1858
Mar. 6, 1860
Mar. 16, 1860
Mar. 17, 1860
Nov. 2, 1860
1) m. Margaret Hemingway, Mar. 15, 1860
2) his father was Thomas Pleasant
3) grew up in Shongalo area

Pleasant, Frank
Mar. 11, 1856
Mar. 16, 1860
Nov. 2, 1860

1) his father was Thomas Pleasant; grew up in Shongalo area
2) 1860 census:

Frank	37	sheriff	Ms.
Mary E.	26		Md.
Mattie E.	7		Ms.
Thomas	3		Ms.
Frank P.	1		Ms.

Pleasant, Margaret Hemingway (Mrs. Gus)
April 13, 1861
Sept. 11, 1861
July 31, 1862
Nov. _____, 1862

Pleasant, Mary F.
Nov. 30, 1857
Dec. 2, 1857
April 26, 1858
1) m. William Stewart April 24, 1858 (Sarah Epes Watkins says "Dr. Stuart" of Sidon)

Pleasant, Mrs. Thomas
July 30, 1857
Feb. 4, 1865
1) she knew William M. Walton's parents, who lived near Shongalo, Ms.
2) lived in Shongalo area
3) 1850 census:

Thomas	64	farmer	Va.
Mary	56		Ga.
Augustus	23		Ms.
Mary	15		Ms.

Poindexter, Dr.
Jan. 26, 1861

Poindexter, Mr. J. T.
Mar. 11, 1856
Mar. 20, 1865

Powell, "Cousin" John
Dec. 28, 1857
June 22, 1861
July 22, 1861
Aug. 27, 1861
Oct. 3, 1861
Dec. 25, 1862
1) of Yalobusha Co., Ms.

Powell, "Cousin" Patsy
Oct. 21, 1848
Oct. 15, 1851
July 30, 1857
Sept. 15, 1864

Powell, "Cousin" Tom

Sept. 15, 1864

Pratt, Mrs. Abraham

Mar. 16, 1860

1) "Mr. Burt's daughter, Mrs. Pratt, expected to die."

2) One of Mr. and Mrs. Pratt's children, Florence, born after 1860 census, was reared by Jeff and Mollie McLemore, who were childless, and moved with them to Texas. Florence's parents, A. F. and Mary Burt Pratt, had died. Florence died unmarried.

3) Abraham Pratt m. Mary W. Burt, June 9, 1858

4) 1860 census:

A. F. Pratt	30	farmer	Ga.
(admr. of estate of S. M. Burt deed)			
Mary Pratt	20		Ala.
John Pratt	1		Ms.
Ann Burt	22		Ala.
Eugenia Burt	16		Ala.
James Burt	12		Ms.

Prince, Mr. and Mrs. Berry W.

April 20, 1850

July 22, 1861

Nov. 4, 1861

June 21, 1862

Nov. _____, 1862

June 11, 1863

1) cousin of William Brook Prince

2) m. Eliza Terry (see reference)

3) 1860 census:

Berry W.	34	planter	Ms.
Eliza	30		Ms.
Robert	9		Ms.
Charles	7		Ms.
W. B., Jr.	5		Ms.
S.	3 f		Ms.
Martha	1		Ms.

Prince, Mrs. Wm. B. (Martha Terry)

April 26, 1854

Jan. 31, 1861

Feb. 16, 1861

June 1, 1864

1) Martha Terry m. William B. Prince May 8, 1844, Carroll Co.

2) m. to Mr. Helm on Jan. 30, 1861; her second husband called the "widow Prince" in uncopied letter dated Feb. 20, 1855 (Mr. Prince dead by April 26, 1854)

4) 1850 census (Claiborne County) (shows first husband):

William Brook Prince	27	planter	La.

Martha	23	Ms.
R. C.	6	m Ms.
W. T.	4	m Ms.
R. B.	2 m	Ms.
C. S.	6/12 f	Ms.

Pulliam, Misses

Mar. 26, 1860

1) of St. Louis

2) went to Patapsco Institute with Mollie Watkins

3) Mr. Perry, their stepfather

Purnell, Camilla Kennedy (Mrs. Tom)

Dec. 2, 1857

Purnell, Ellen

Nov. 2, 1859

1) daughter of John G Purnell and wife, Suzanna

2) 1850 census: age 14; b. N.C.

Purnell, Henry

Mar. 11, 1857

July 31, 1862

1) daughter Eliza m. Fitzgerald

Purnell, John G.

Mar. 11, 1857

July 9, 1861

Nov. _____, 1862

Dec. 1, 1862

1) uncle of Tom Purnell

2) John's brother was Micajah Purnell; they were from N.C.

3) 1850 census:

John G. Purnell	45	farmer	N.C.
Suzann	27		Tn.
Ann E.	15		N.C.
Ellen	14		N.C.
Victoria L.	12		N.C.
Sarah E.	10		N.C.
William	1		Ms.

Purnell, Mr. and Mrs. Martin

April 13, 1863

1) son of Micajah Purnell

Purnell, Mrs. Micahjah

(spelling varies in letters, sometimes Micajah)

Jan. 13, 1849

1) Helen (m. Foltz), Eliza (m. Sturdivant), Martin, Tom, James C. (m. Jane Hawkins—cousin)

2) she was dead by Jan. 1849

3) her brother-in-law was John G. Purnell

Purnell, Tom
  Jan. 13, 1849
  Mar. 2, 1852
  Sept. 23, 1855
  July 30, 1857
  Dec. 28, 1857
  April 26, 1858
  Jan. 19, 1860
  Oct. 20, 1860
  July 9, 1861
  Oct. 3, 1861
  July 31, 1862
  Dec. 15, 1862
  1) in Jan. 1849 letter "Mrs. Purnell, Tom Purnell's mother, died last month"
  2) m. Camilla Kennedy, Nov. 24, 1855
  3) wife dead by Dec. 2, 1857
  4) farmed six miles from Vaiden
  5) died in 1863
  6) see Micajah Purnell's ref. for Tom's brothers & sisters
  7) 1860 census:

M. T. Purnell (Tom)	Tn.
M. A. Purnell (brother Martin)	Ms.
M. E. Kendall (aunt)	N.C.

R

Rafter, Mrs. Captain
  Sept. 21, 1867
Randolph, Fannie Hutchins
  1) Austin resident
  2) Will Walton's kin
Ransom, Mrs.
  Nov. 7, 1851
  1) 1850 census:

Isa P. Ransom	45 f	Ga.
Elliott	18	Ms.
Robert	15	Ms.
Andrew	11	Ms.
Susan	6	Ms.

Rather, Capt.
  June 8, 1867
  1) of Louisville
  2) m. Alice Davis
Ray, Mr.
  Nov. 4, 1861
Reece, Jane
  Sept. 10, 1862

1) Dr. Watkins's niece

2) daughter of Dr. Watkins's sister, Lucy, and her second husband, Dr. Charles Milton Reece

3) her half-sister was Mr. Bacon (George Ann Merriwether)

Reece, Lucy

May 2, 1861

1) Dr. Watkins's niece (see Jane Reece ref.)

Reed, Sarah

April 4, 1860

1) friend of the Egglestons of Holmes Co.

Reeves, Mr.

Oct. 24, 1857

1) died of cramp colic

Robinson (Roberson), Alfred

Feb. 14, 1849

June 7, 1850

Oct. 15, 1851

Nov. 7, 1851

May 15, 1854

Mar. 11, 1857

Oct. 26, 1858

May 25, 1860

1) Yazoo River up to his door

2) living on the river

3) died Oct. 10, 1858

4) 1850 census:

Alfred Roberson	42	farmer	Ms.
Nancy			Canada

Robinson (Roberson), Jeremiah "Jerry"

Feb. 14, 1849

April 26, 1854

May 15, 1854

Sept. 2, 1854

Mar. 11, 1857

May 25, 1860

Nov. 2, 1860

Nov. 4, 1862

June 1, 1864

1) new baby, fall of 1848, living on the Yazoo

2) lost youngest child with measles

3) lived near Sidon

4) 1850 census:

Jeremiah Roberson	42	Ms.
Adele	23	Ala.
J.	1 f	Ms.

Rogers, Wells
July 30, 1857
1) in Holmes Co., Ms.
2) health treatment spa

Rosco, Miss Sylvia M.
April 25, 1849
1) teaching school in Carrollton
2) 1850 census:
Sylvia M.   50   N.Y.
boarding with George Brown, editor, and family

Rose, Mrs.
April 20, 1850
May 15, 1850
1) made a dress for Lettie; in school in Grenada

Ross, Miss Frances
Feb. 14, 1849
1) attended a dance at the Jenkins
2) daughter of Riley W. Ross
3) 1850 census:

Washington	29	farmer	S.C.
Lucy A.	19		Ms.
Marianna	4/12		Ms.
Maria Caperton	53		N.C.

Roy, Cordelia
Nov. 2, 1860
1) m. A. B. Barry, Dec. 1, 1859
2) 1850 census:

Alexander	47	b. Scotland
Margaret	46	Scotland
Barbara	11	Ms.
Alexander	10	Ms.
Barry, A. B.	24	Ms.
Cordelia	19	Ms.

Russell, Capt. W. H.
Oct. _____, 1862 (letter not dated)
Nov. _____, 1862 (letter not dated)

Russell, Dan R.
July 9, 1861
Oct. 4, 1861
Feb. 24, 1862
1) m. Mary E. Booth, Feb. 29, 1848 (oldest daughter of William Booth)
2) 1850 census:

Dan R.	28	lawyer D.C.	(Mo?)
Mary E.	21		Ms.
Kate	1		Ms.

S

Sanders, "Cousin" Mary
Oct. 21, 1848
1) Tn. resident (Nashville)

Sanders, Mary E. (Mrs. Dick Love)
Feb. 10, 1860
Mar. 6, 1860
1) to m. Dick Love that month
2) P. B. Love m. Feb. 18, 1860
3) this William Sanders's father and grandfather both named Hardy Sanders—his grandfather m. Lucy Utley in New England—came to Wake and Anson Co., N.C. in 1743; a lt. col. in the revolution
4) 1850 census:

William	50	merchant	N.C.
Margaret	46		Va.
John	19	med student	Tn.
Mary	12		Tn.
James	9		Ms.
Henry			
Summerfield	7		Ms.
Julia	4		Ms.

Sanders, Rebecca
Oct. 20, 1860
Nov. 2, 1860
1) first m. Dr. J. Y. Sanders
2) second m. T. B. Weed, Oct. 17, 1860

Sanford, Capt.
June 8, 1867
1) m. Mildred Talliferro

Saunders (Sanders), Dr. J. Y.
April 25, 1849
Mar. 2, 1852
April 19, 1852
1) m. Sarah Rebecca Davis, April 5, 1852
2) first wife lost a baby (in Middleton) and d. 1849

Saunders, James
May 15, 1850
1) has bought Major Robert H. Watkins's homeplace and land, Lawrence Co., Ala.
2) author of "Early Settlers of Alabama"
3) friend of Dr. Thomas Watkins
4) resident of Courtland, Ala.

Saunders (Sanders), Mr. Thomas
Dec. 29, 1848
1) of Carrollton, has died

Savage, George
> June 8, 1857
> 1) living at Little Rock, Ark.

Scales, Capt.
> Oct. _____, 1862

Scales, Mrs. Pink
> April 13, 1861
> 1) has died
> 2) 1860 census:

J. Pinkney	29	lawyer	N.C.
Kate S.	22		Ms.

Scales, Pink
> June 3, 1861
> June 17, 1861
> 1) see Pink, Mrs. ref.

Scruggs, Mrs. Isham
> April 19, 1852
> Dec. 9, 1861
> 1) Isham Scruggs m. Susan Wood, Dec. 18, 1845
> 2) sister to Martha Wood, who m. Atlas Johnson
> 3) 1850 census:

Isham P.	26	farmer	Tn.
Susan	23		Tn.
William	4		Ms.
Jane	3		Ms.

Scruggs, Joe
> May 25, 1860
> 1) dead
> 2) 1850 census:

Joseph	37	farmer	Tn.
Louise	23		Va.
Sarah	4		Ms.
John	3		Ms.
William	1		Ms.

Sessions, Mr. (and family)
> April 4, 1854
> Nov. _____, 1862
> 1) Holmes Co. friends of the Egglestons

Sewanee House
> Oct. 21, 1848
> 1) hotel in Nashville, Tn.

Shackleford, Judge
> May 20, 1861
> 1) daughter Helen a Patapsco classmate of Mollie's

Shackleford, Miss
> Mar. 16, 1860

Mar. 17, 1860
1) Mrs. Brian's niece
Shackleford, Mr. and Mrs. Jack (Dora)
April 26, 1854
Aug. 15, 1854
Mar. 16, 1860
1) to visit Texas
2) Ala. residents, Mrs. Shackleford dead
Sharkey, Greenwood
June 11, 1863
1) m. Elizabeth Williams on Jan. 31, 1855
2) uncopied letter Feb. 20, 1855, says she was "a niece of Mrs. Alfred Roberson's. Miss Rose and Mary A. Hicks and his cousin Allen Hicks were waiters."
3) 1850 census:
> Greenwood   16   student   Ms.
> boarding with Joel Pate
Shaw, Sarah B. "Lala"
Nov. 2, 1859
1) m. to Mr. L. S. Boling of Kansas City, Oct. 18, 1859
Shepherd, Mr.
Mar. 26, 1849
Sherrod Brothers (Sam, Frederick, and Maj. Felix)
Dec. 29, 1848
Jan. 13, 1849
1) all died of "winter fever"
2) sons of Col. Benjamin Sherrod of Cotton Garden Plantation, Lawrence Co., Ala.
Sherrod, Sarah
Oct. 21, 1848
1) in Nashville, Tn.
Shongalo, Mississippi
July 4, 1855
July 30, 1857
1) now absorbed by Vaiden, Ms.
Sidon, Ms.
1) formerly named Marian
2) built on the land of Alfred Robinson, near to Jeremiah Robinson with Major Terry, Berry Prince, Sharkey, William B. Prince, Alfred Murdock, and Reuben Gayden nearby (near present Sidon, Ms.)
Sill, Rev. G. Y.
Oct. 16, 1851
Dec. 24, 1851
Jan. 14, 1852
1) head of Lettie's school at Holly Springs, Ms.

Simmons, Mrs.

Feb. 16, 1861
Dec. 9, 1861
Mar. 14, 1866
Sept. 18, 1866
1) Tx. resident, formerly of Ms.
2) father lives in Greenwood

Simmons, Mr. Joseph L.

Jan. 13, 1849
Dec. 2, 1857
April 26, 1858
Jan. 9, 1864
Sept. 18, 1866
1) father of Octavia Simmons
2) lived between Middleton and Duck Hill
3) also a son named Reed, medical student, not listed on the census, and younger children, Tom and Mittie
4) he was said to be brother-in-law of the Purnells and also a Hawkins connection; they all came from N.C. in the late 1840s
5) 1850 census:

Joseph L	46	farmer	N.C.
Lydia	38		
Joseph	20		
Octavaia D.	14		
Augusta	8		

Simmons, Mrs. Joseph L. (Lydia)

July 30, 1857
April 28, 1858
Sept. 11, 1861
April 13, 1863
June 11, 1863
1) Octavia Simmons's mother

Simmons, Marion

June 9, 1851

Simmons, Tommie and Mittie

Feb. 9, 1862
April 13, 1863
1) younger brother and sister of Octavia Simmons Merriwether

Simmons, Octavia Dallas

April 4, 1851
June 9, 1851
Jan. 30, 1852
Feb. 23, 1852
Mar. 2, 1852
Mar. 12, 1852

April 4, 1852
April 19, 1852
April 15, 1854
May 15, 1854
July 4, 1855
Sept. 23, 1855
Dec. 28, 1856
Dec. 28, 1857
April 5, 1858
April 26, 1858
June 14, 1858
Dec. 20, 1858
Nov. 2, 1859
April 13, 1861
1) m. C. J. F. Merriwether, Nov. 17, 1859
2) Lettie's best friend in Carroll County
3) daughter of Joseph L. Simmons (see ref.)
4) 1850 census:
   Octavia, age 14, b. N.C.

Simmons, Reed
Dec. 28, 1856
Feb. 9, 1862
April 13, 1863
1) Octavia's brother
2) son of Joseph L. Simmons
3) medical student

Smith, Al
Mar. 16, 1860
Mar. 17, 1860
1) groomsman at Gus Pleasant's wedding

Smith, Dr.
June 7, 1850
1) Rector Franklin G. Smith's brother

Smith, Dr.
Nov. 7, 1851
1) teaching school and music in Middleton, Judson Institute
2) keeping house in Middleton

Smith, General Edmund Kirby
Dec. 1, 1862
Dec. 15, 1862
1) Confederate general

Smith, Fanny
Nov. 2, 1859
1) daughter of Mrs. N. D. Smith of Middleton
2) taught at Middleton, Shongalo, and Gerenton

Smith, Jimmy
> April 4, 1851
> Feb. 9, 1862

Smith, Mrs. N. D.
> Mar. 6, 1854
> 1) resident of Middleton

Smith, Rev. Franklin G.
> Mar. 26, 1848
> Oct. 23, 1848
> Oct. 31, 1848
> Dec. 1, 1848
> Dec. 29, 1848
> Mar. 9, 1849
> 1) director of Columbia Female Institute in Columbia, Tn., where William W. Whitehead's daughter was in school in 1846 and where Lettie went by March 1848

Smith, Miss Sarah
> April 15, 1854
> July 4, 1855
> Sept. 23, 1855
> 1) will not teach music anymore; gone to visit uncle Dr. Smith in Monticello
> 2) m. Eugene Kennedy, Sept. 13, 1855

Sneed, Judge Sebron Graham
> 1) Austin attorney, family friend of the Waltons

Southworth, Mr. and Mrs. Hunter H.
> Nov. 7, 1851
> May 15, 1854
> June 11, 1863
> 1) her mother died in Vicksburg in 1854
> 2) m. in 1851 to H. H. Southworth; she was Mary Morgan
> 3) they lived on the Yazoo below Sidon
> 4) 1850 census:
>> Hunter H. Southworth   27   lawyer   Ms.
>> boarding in Carrollton
>> served in legislature

Spivey, Mr.
> Sept. 26, 1864

Stanley, Captain, Lieutenant
> May 20, 1861
> Sept. 10, 1862
> 1) Probably James S. Standley, first lieutenant, Company K, Carroll County Rifles

Stansbury, Dr. and Mrs. Washington
> Nov. 30, 1857
> Dec. 2, 1857

Mar. 25, 1861
April 13, 1861
April 4, 1864
1) of Carrollton
2) 1850 census:

Washington	36	physician	Md.
Emily A.	26		Ky.
Thomas	1		Ms.
George Griffith	14	(nephew)	Md.

Stark (Starke), Col. (Peter B.)
Oct. _____, 1862 (letter not dated)
Steadman, "Old" Mrs.
April 12, 1861
Stedman Place
1) bought by Mr. Hawkins
Steele, Dr.
June 8, 1857
1) of Austin, Tx.
Stevens, Dug
July 25, 1864
Stevens, John C.
May 30, 1851
June 9, 1851
Mar. 6, 1854
April 15, 1854
Sept. 2, 1854
Sept. 23, 1855
1) m. Evvie Davis, April 10, 1854
2) old beau of Lettie's
3) 1850 census:

John C.	25	merchant clerk	N.C.

Stevens, "Shaw" Marshall Wright
April 10, 1860
April 28, 1860
1) brother of John C. Stevens
2) half-brother to the Farmer boys: James, Henry, William, Joseph J.
3) m. Elizabeth Barrow (Lizzie), daughter of William Barrow
4) 1860 census:

Marshall Stevens	22	clerk	N.C.

Stevens, "Old" Mrs.
Jan. 2, 1861
Stevens, "Old"
Sept. 2, 1854
Stevens, Winny (Winey)
Sept. 2, 1854

Stewart, Dr. William (Stuart)
April 26, 1858
1) m. Mary F. Pleasant
Stith, "Cousin" Polly; "Cousin" Eliza; Mrs. Stith: "Cousin"
April 26, 1858
July 31, 1860
1) Sarah Watkins's kin in Va.
Stovall, Mrs.
Mar. 26, 1849
1) resident of Columbia, Tn.
Stovall, Simon
April 4, 1851
Jan. 14, 1852
1) rumor is his business is going bad and rumor is he will marry
Miss Edmundson
2) his wife, Lucy (Louisiana) Jenkins Stovall, came with him to county in
early days
3) Middleton resident
4) 1850 census:
   Simon   44   farmer   Ca.
   wife not listed, apparently dead
   large family of children
Strictlin, Mr.
April 11, 1852
Stringer, Mrs.
Sept. 10, 1862
Strong, Col. and Sons
Mar. 2, 1852
Nov. 2, 1860
1) of Aberdeen, Ms.
Sturdivant, Mrs. Benjamin W.
July 30, 1857
Oct. 24, 1857
1) she was Eliza R. Purnell, m. Aug. 14, 1853
2) daughter of Micajah Purnell
3) Tom Purnell was her brother
Sturdivant, John
Jan. 18, 1858
Summerville, Mr. and Mrs. James
May 15, 1854
Mar. 11, 1857
Oct. 24, 1857
1) Carrollton residents
2) 1850 census:
   James   28   lawyer   Va.
   boarding with another lawyer, Samuel B. Jones, and his family

Swoope, Cynthia Early (Mrs. John M.)
Dec. 1, 1848
July 30, 1857
1) Dr. Watkins's kin of Courtland, Ala.; first cousin
2) daughter of Gov. Peter Early of Georgia and sister of Lucy, Col. Richard
Jones's wife
3) dear friend of the Watkins family and of the Ala. Fitzgeralds

Swoope, Mary, Emma, and Virginia
Dec. 1, 1848
May 30, 1851
April 11, 1852
1) daughters of Cynthia Swoope in Courtland, Ala.
2) Mary d. 1852; Emma m. Dr. Andrew J. Sykes; and Virginia m. Hon. E. C. Betts
(see Saunders)

Sykes, Ellen
June 6, 1861
1) 1850 census:

William	35	farmer	Va.
Mary	23		N.C.
Ellen	6		Ala.

Sykes, Jane
Dec. 28, 1857
1) m. to Dr. T. A. Austin of Grenada, Ms. on Dec. 20, 1857

Sykes, Margaret Palmer (Mrs. Dr. William)
April 26, 1858
Dec. 20, 1858
Mar. 15, 1859
Mar. 9, 1861
Mar. 11, 1861
June 22, 1861
Mar. 31, 1862
1) see Palmer, Margaret
2) m. William Sykes, Dec. 22, 1852
3) daughter of Judge Palmer
4) in 1858 she and Dr. Sykes were living out of the state

Sykes, Mrs. Solon M. (Margaret Binford)
Oct. 24 1857
Dec. 20, 1858
1) m. Solon Sykes, Dec. 27, 1852
2) only daughter of John A. Binford, Sr.; lived near Duck Hill

Sykes, Dr. William
April 26, 1858
Mar. 26, 1860
Mar. 9, 1861
Mar. 31, 1862
1) wife: Margaret Palmer

T

Tab, Fanny
Dec. 2, 1857
1) see Fanny Tab Eggleston

Talliferro, Mildred
June 8, 1867
1) m. Capt. Sanford

Taylor, Dr.
July 4, 1855

Taylor, Miss Elizabeth
April 15, 1854
1) Lizzie Taylor m. Miranda Davis in March (M. G. Davis m. E. W. Taylor, March 8, 1855)
2) see Davis ref.

Temple, Mr. and Mrs. Levi
April 28, 1860
Dec. 27, 1860
1) cash store in Carrollton
2) m. Miss Marley Eldridge
3) 1860 census:

| Levi W. Temple | 30 | merchant | Vt. |
| Marley L. | 25 | | N.Y. |

Terrell, Judge Alexander W.
Mar. 31, 1862
1) Austin, Tx. attorney
2) district judge 1857–62
3) brigadier general—CSA
4) served sixteen years as state legislator
5) minister to Turkey 1893–97 under President Cleveland
6) good friend of Major Will Walton

Terry, Major and Mrs.
Dec. 29, 1848
Feb. 14, 1849
Mar. 9, 1849
Mar. 26, 1849
Mar. 31, 1849
1) rented out his place and moved near Yazoo Valley

Terry, Benjamin F.
Jan. 25, 1862
1) Terry's Texas Rangers (8th Texas cavalry, CSA)
2) d. Dec. 1861

Terry, Miss Eliza
Dec. 29, 1848
Feb. 14, 1849
Mar. 9, 1849
Mar. 26, 1849

Mar. 31, 1849
April 25, 1849
April 20, 1850
April 26, 1854
1) daughter of Major Terry
2) rumor has it "she is to be married to Mr. Prince, a cousin to her brother-in-law," April 1850
3) 1850 census (Claiborne Co., Ms.)

Prince, Berry W.	23	planter	Ms.
Prince, Eliza	19		Ms.
Terry, Joseph B.	31		Ms.
Terry, William	56		Ms.

Thomas, Mr.
Mar. 11, 1857
Thompson, Mrs. Jacob (Catherine Jones)
Oct. 21, 1848
Aug. 18, 1862
1) father was Peyton Jones, brother of Col. Richard Jones (see ref.)
2) husband, Hon. Jacob Thompson, member of Congress from Ms. and member of President Jefferson Davis's cabinet
3) 1850 census (Lafayette Co., Oxford, Ms.):

J. Thompson	39	member Congress	Va.
Catherine	27		Ga.
C. Macon	11		Ms.

Thompson, Dr. James M.
Oct. 21, 1848
1) moved to Ark.
Thompson, Mary
Oct. 3, 1861
Thompson, Mr.
Feb. 23, 1852
1) Baptist minister who preached "Uncle Billy" Fitzgerald's funeral in Ala.
Thornburg, Miss
Mar. 11, 1861
Tobin's Spring, Carroll Co., Mississippi
July 9, 1861
Todd, Emily Watkins
Feb. 20, 1849
Mar. 31, 1849
Oct. _____, 1862
1) Dr. Watkins's sister
2) Lettie's "Aunt Emily"
Todd, Fauntleroy
Oct. _____, 1862
1) son of Emily Watkins Todd
2) nephew of Dr. Watkins

Todd, Mr. Henry Waring
> Oct. 8, 1858
> Oct. 26, 1858
> Sept. 10, 1862
> 1) Dr. Watkins's brother-in-law

Todd, Lucy
> Oct. 7, 1858
> 1) Dr. Watkins's niece
> 2) Emily's daughter

Top, Colonel
> June 6, 1861

Townes, Cousin "Betsy"
> June 8, 1857
> July 30, 1857
> Oct. 24, 1857
> 1) maiden name, Betsy Leigh (Lee)
> 2) daughter of William Leigh (Lee) (see ref.)
> 3) wife of Judge "Dick" Richard Townes of Austin, Texas

Townes, Judge Eggleston Dick
> June 8, 1857
> Oct. 24, 1857
> Dec. 28, 1857
> April 28, 1858
> 1) in Tx., said to be moving back to Ala. (they did not)
> 2) sisters are Mrs. Grey and Mrs. Leigh
> 3) said to be pleased with Texas
> 4) parents were John Leigh Townes and Polly Eggleston

Townes, Judge
> Aug. 5, 1861
> 1) of Austin, Tx., area

Townes, Cousin Dick
> Oct. 21, 1848
> Oct. 15, 1851
> July 30, 1857
> 1) wife was Betsy Leigh, whose father was William
> Leigh who used to live at the crossroads (near Courtland, Ala.)
> 2) living in Austin, Tx., area

Towneses and Leighs
> intermarried more than once. They had come from Va. and northern Ala. and
> then to Ms. and Tx. Several families, all kin, came to the Austin area about
> 1854. The kinship of these families with Mrs. Watkins was through her Green,
> Hill and Claiborne lines back in Va.

Townsend, Mrs. Lydia McGinty Parmele (Mrs. A. M.)
> Nov. 2, 1860
> 1) first husband was Joseph Parmele

2) their children:
  James Parmele
  William Parmele
  Laura McCarroll Curtis
  Dianna Beler
  Mollie McCarroll
  Hannah Trotter
  Huldah Alsworth
  Caroline Alsworth

Townsend, Col. W. T.
  Sept. 9, 1864

Trotter, Mr. and Mrs. Joseph
  June 26, 1846
  1) merchant in Courtland, Ala., from Pulaski, Tn.
  2) opened a commission house in New Orleans: McMahon, Trotter, and
  Pearsall

Trousdale, Mr.
  Mar. 26, 1849

Turner, Davy
  Dec. 9, 1861

Turner, Jack
  Jan. 1, 1861
  Jan. 2, 1861
  April 12, 1861

Turner, John
  June 8, 1867
  1) m. Miss Newell

Turner, Mr.
  June 8, 1857
  1) slave named Burt
  2) 1850 census:

John J.	46	N.C.
Jane	38	Tn.
Mary	20	Tn.
Susan	18	Tn.
Martha	17	Tn.
James	15	Tn.
Virginia	14	Ms.
Irene	12	Ms.
John T.	10	Ms.
Jane	8	Ms.
Lucy	4	Ms.
Evelyn	2	Ms.
Sally	11/12	Ms.

Turyan, Mrs.
   Dec. 28, 1857
   1) Lawrence Co., Ala.; bought Aunt Lettie's desk
Tuston, John L.
   Mar. 26, 1860
   1) Emily S. Hart m. John Tuston Mar. 22, 1860
   2) see Hart, Emily S.
   3) 1860 census:

John L.	23	silversmith	S.C.
Emma	17		Ms.

Tyson, Dr.
   Mar. 6, 1860
   1) of Tn.
Tyson, Mary
   May 2, 1861
Tyson, Sally
   Dec. 20, 1858
   Dec. 27, 1858
   1) m. William Whitehead (Edmunds Grey Whitehead's son), Dec. 22, 1858
   2) see Whitehead, William

V

Vaiden, Mrs. Dr. (Elizabeth)
   Nov. 30, 1857
   Dec. 2, 1857
   Oct. 6, 1860
   Nov. 2, 1860
   1) see Vaiden, Dr.
Vaiden, Dr. Cowles Meade
   Oct. 6, 1860
   1) 1812–80; lived east of Shongalo
   2) 1850 census:

Vaiden, Cowles	38	farmer	Va.
*Elizabeth W.	28		N.C.

   *Mrs. Elizabeth Vaiden (1818–86) was Elizabeth Herring, sister of Lewis W.
   Herring
Vaiden, Miss Sally
   Dec. 2, 1857
   1) 1808–57; sister of Dr. Vaiden
   2) 1850 census:

Vaiden, Sarah	35	Va.

   living with Lewis Herring family
Van Dorn, Gen. Earl (CSA)
   June 27, 1862
   Aug. 30, 1862
   Dec. 25, 1862
   April 13, 1863

Vaughn, Mr. Baskerville
  Mar. 6, 1854
  1) Ala. resident; has died
Vaughn, Mrs. Baskerville
  July 30, 1857
  1) widow; m. to Judge Graham
  2) Ala. residents

W

Wade, Miss Georgianna
  April 4, 1854
  July 4, 1855
  1) ward of Mr. Jesse B. Walton of Lexington, Holmes Co., Ms.
  2) very wealthy; accompanied Dr. Watkins and Lettie and Jesse Walton on a trip to New York World's Fair, 1853
  3) m. a Mr. Johnson (a mule trader) from Kentucky at 9:00 A.M., April 10, 1855
Wadlington, Isabella (Mrs. Henry Pittman)
  June 8, 1857
  1) m. Henry Pittman, Nov. 1, 1854
  2) daughter of Warner W. Wadlington
  3) 1850 census:

Warner W.	65	farmer	S.C.
Mary	60		Ky.
Margaret	30		Ky.
William Kelly	27		Ky.
Isabella	22		Ky.
Mercer	13		Ms.
Elizabeth	6		Ms.
Rachael Thompson	55		Va.
Charles Thompson	50	carpenter	Va.

Wadlington, Mr. and Mrs. James A.
  July 23, 1849
  Dec. 9, 1861
  1) 1850 census:

James M.	39	landlord	Ky.
Amanda	35		Va.
James C.	10		Ms.
Mary	8		Ms.
Ann V.	5		Ms.
Thomas R.	3		Ms.
*William L.	1		Ms.

  *letter of 1849 says W.'s son had a son last week. census of 1850 says he is one year old.
Walton Family
  1) of Major William Martin Walton
  2) see material before letter of Feb. 21, 1853

Walton, Early Watkins

Sept. 6, 1856

Dec. 28, 1856

May 15, 1857

Aug. 25, 1860

Jan. 17, 1875

and repeated references

1) second son of Lettie Watkins and William M. Walton, b. at the Watkins home place in Carroll Co., Ms. and named after she got him home; calling him "Johnny" was a joke. Named Early Watkins for Dr. Watkins's parents.

2) was a physician, died young, unmarried

Walton, George

Sept. 2, 1854

1) grandfather of William Martin Walton

2) b. in Franklin Co., Ga. (or N.C.)

3) m. Rebecca Isaacs in Franklin Co. (probably)

4) moved to Lincoln Co., Tn. then to Lawrence Co., Ala.

5) moved to Panola Co., Tx. and died there

Walton, George Loe (Lowe)

Oct. 24, 1857

Oct. 20, 1860

July 23, 1865

Mar. 14, 1866

1) brother of William Martin Walton

2) grew up in Carroll Co., Ms.

3) m. Miss Amanda Moore (Miller); moved to her family plantation in Condordia Parish, La.

4) family nickname "Umbra" (from Spanish *hombre*)

Walton, George Longstreet

Dec. 17, 1860

Jan. 1, 1861

Mar. 9, 1861

June 8, 1867

Sept. 21, 1867

Feb. 7, 1875

Jan. 30, 1875

1) third son of Lettie and William Martin Walton

2) b. Dec. 6, 1860; 6:00 A.M., 10 1/2 lbs., Austin, Tx.

3) named George for his great-grandfather; Longstreet was for Judge A. B. Longstreet

4) died unmarried in his twenties

Walton, Mr. Jesse B.

April 4, 1854

1) friend of Dr. Watkins

2) resident of Lexington, Holmes Co., Ms.

3) guardian of Miss Georgiana Wade

Walton, Newton Samuel
Sept. 6, 1856
Dec. 28, 1856
July 30, 1857
Aug. 25, 1860
Dec. 27, 1881
and repeated references
1) Lettie and William Walton's first son, b. in Austin
2) named Newton for a deceased uncle; Samuel for his grandfather Walton
3) practiced law in Austin, Tx.; m. 1st Annie Hicks; 2nd May Patrick
Walton, Sarah
July 23, 1865
June 8, 1867
Sept. 21, 1867
1) fourth child of Lettie Watkins and William Martin Walton
2) b. Oct. 24, 1864 while her father was in La. in the Confederate Army
3) named for her grandmother Watkins
4) m. James Jefferson Parmele
Walton, Thomas
Feb. 16, 1861
1) brother to Mrs. Simmons of Austin, Tx.
2) m. Mary Longstreet, adopted daughter of Judge A. B. Longstreet
Walton, William Martin
Feb. 23, 1853
April 14, 1854
and repeated references
1) son of Samuel Walker Walton and Mary Wilkerson Lowe
2) m. Letitia Ann Watkins, Feb. 9, 1854; daughter of Dr. Thomas A. and Sarah
Epes Fitzgerald Watkins
3) lawyer in Austin, Tx.—nickname "Buck"
4) attended University of Virginia; read law in Judge Cothron and J. Z. George's
office in Carrollton
William Walton's great-grandfather, Jesse, was the son of William and
Susannah Cobbs Walton of Goochland Co., Va., born about 1740. Major Jesse
Walton was an officer in the revolution, Indian fighter, founder of the town of
Jonesborough, Tn., and political leader living in Surry and Wilkes Cos., N.C.
during the Revolutionary War. His wife was Mary, family tradition has her Mary
Walker, and both Jesse and Mary died in Franklin Co., Ga., where they had
taken up bounty land in 1785.
The son, George, William's grandfather, left Ga. early in the 1800s and bought
land in Lincoln Co., Tn., where he lived until about 1817 when he moved into
Ala. and then on through Ms. and into Tx. during the days of the Republic of
Texas. George and his wife, Rebecca Isaacs, had a number of children, one of
whom, Samuel Walker Walton, married Mary Wilkerson Lowe, Ala., and moved
first to Madison Co., Ms., and then to Carroll Co., Ms. in the 1830s where he
died. He left land and slaves in Carroll Co. which came to his sons. By 1852,

all of the family in Carroll Co. were dead except for William and his brother, George, who were drawn to Tx., partly because their grandfather and several uncles lived there, one uncle in Austin itself.

Ward, Aunt Sally

July 31, 1860

1) Sarah Watkins's Va. kin

Ward, Dr.

Nov. _____, 1862

Fall 1868

Washington City

Nov. 1, 1858

1) Washington, D.C.

Washington, J. S.

July 15, 1862

Watkins, Anderson

Dec. 28, 1858

1) "cousin" of Dr. Watkins, first cousin once removed

2) son of Judge George C. Watkins of Little Rock, Ark.

Watkins, Miss Ann

Dec. 1, 1848

Dec. 29, 1848

Feb. 20, 1849

1) daughter of William and Harriet Anderson Watkins

2) "cousin" and classmate of Lettie's at Columbia, Tn.

3) niece of Richard Anderson

4) lived in Huntsville, Ala.

Watkins, Uncle Bob and Aunt Prudence (Major and Mrs. Robert H.)

Oct. 21, 1848

Feb. 20, 1849

May 15, 1850

1) Nashville, Tn.

2) probably not really kin to Dr. Watkins

3) Robert H. Watkins and Prudence Oliver Watkins

4) sold out to James Saunders and his sons and moved to Nashville

Watkins, "Cousin" Frank

Sept. 5, 1860

Oct. _____, 1862

1) father of "cousin" Henry (see ref.)

2) of Prince Edward Co., Va.

Watkins, Judge George Claiborne

June 8, 1857

Feb. 10, 1860

1) resident of Little Rock, Ark.

2) Dr. Watkins's first cousin; son of his father's brother, Isaac Watkins

Watkins, "Cousin" Henry

Jan. 19, 1860

Feb. 3, 1860
Feb. 10, 1860
April 4, 1860
April 10, 1860
April 28, 1860
Sept. 5, 1860
Oct. 3, 1861
July 31, 1862
Oct. _____, 1862
1) son of "cousin" Frank Watkins; Prince Edward Co., Va.

Watkins, James Coleman
Feb. 14, 1849
Aug. 15, 1854
Feb. 16, 1861
Dec. 9, 1861
1) though probably not really Watkins's kin, close family connection of
Dr. Watkins from Lawrence Co., Ala., and later Tx.
2) living in Tx. by Feb. 1849
3) second wife was Lettie William (Sarah Epes Watkins's cousin)

Watkins, Jane
Sept. 10, 1862

Watkins, Jennie
Dec. 24, 1851
1) m. Mr. Donaldson

Watkins, Letitia Ann ("Lettie")
repeated references
1) daughter of Dr. Thomas Alexander Watkins and Sarah Epes Fitzgerald
2) m. William Martin Walton, Feb. 9, 1854
3) children:
 Newton Samuel Walton
 Early Watkins Walton
 George Longstreet Walton
 Sarah Walton

Watkins, Martha and Mary
Oct. 15, 1851
1) daughter of Paul Watkins of Ala.

Watkins, Mary Early ("Mollie")
repeated references
1) called Baby in early letters
2) daughter of Dr. Thomas A. and Sarah Epes Fitzgerald Watkins
3) Lettie's sister
4) m. Jefferson H. McLemore, Dec. 23, 1863
5) no children

Watkins, Dr. Miles S.
Mar. 26, 1830
1) Jackson, Ms.

Watkins, Milton

May 30, 1851

1) son of James C. Watkins of Lawrence Co., Ala. and Tx. (see Watkins, James C. ref.)

2) m. Ann E. L. McGehee, Nov. 1850 (there was an aunt with an Acklin connection)

Watkins, Paul J.

Sept. 2, 1854

June 1, 1855

Dec. 28, 1857

1) first wife: Elizabeth Watt

2) m. second (1857), Mary Morrison Lowe, widow of General Bartley Lowe of Huntsville, Ala.

3) resident of Lawrence Co., Ala.

4) had a daughter named Amelia Mumford

5) 1850 census (Lawrence Co., Ala.):

Paul	55	planter	Ga.
Elizabeth	45		N.C.
Martha	17		Ala.
Mary E.	15		Ala.

Waktins, Mrs. Paul J. (1st) (Elizabeth Watt)

Sept. 2, 1854

1) dead, Lawrence Co., Ala.

Watkins, Robert

Feb. 14, 1849

1) brother of Dr. Watkins

2) black sheep of the family

Watkins, Dr. Robert

June 8, 1857

1) Little Rock, Ark.

2) Dr. Watkins's first cousin; son of his father's brother, Isaac Watkins

Watkins, Sam

Feb. 6, 1858

1) Petersburg, Va.; kin of Dr. Watkins

Watkins, Sarah Epes Fitzgerald

repeated references

1) m. Thomas Alexander Watkins

2) daughter of Thomas Fitzgerald and Ann Roper Williams

3) lived with Uncle Bill and Aunt Letty Fitzgerald in Lawrence Co., Ala., after her father's death and mother's remarriage

Watkins, Susan

May 30, 1851

1) daughter of James C. Watkins of Lawrence Co., Ala., and later Tex.

2) m. Arthur Acklin of Ala.

Watkins, Dr. Thomas Alexander ("Pa," "Grandpa")

repeated references

1) son of George Watkins and Mary "Polly" Early

   2) m. Sarah Epes Fitzgerald
   3) 1850 census:

Thomas A.	48	farmer	Ga.
Sarah	36		Va.
Letitia	15		Ala.
Mary	6		Ala.

   4) 1860 census:

Thomas A.	58	planter	Ga.
Sarah E.	46		Va.
Mary E.	16		Ms.

Watkins, William
   April 26, 1854
   1) Ala. resident

Watt, John M.
   May 15, 1854
   Oct. 8, 1857
   Oct. 24, 1857
   Jan. 26, 1861
   July 25, 1864
   Sept. 20, 1864
   Jan. 28, 1867
   June 8, 1867
   1) sold land and many slaves
   2) 1850 census:

John M.	37	farmer	Tn.
Mary	38		N.C.
Laura	14		N.C.
John	12		Ala.
Robt.	10		Ala.
Alfred	8		Ala.
Mary	6		Ala.
William	4		Ms.
Sarah	3		Ms.

Watt, Mrs. John M.
   May 15, 1854
   July 25, 1864
   1) moved to Greenwood, Ms.

Watt, Laura
   May 15, 1854
   1) returned from school
   2) daughter of John M. Watt, 37, farmer, Tn. (1850 census)
   3) 1850 census: age 14; b. in N.C.

Watt, Mary Elisa "Mollie"
   Jan. 31, 1861
   Mar. 11, 1861
   May 20, 1861
   June 6, 1861

July 25, 1864

Feb. 16, 1867

1) at Patapsco with Mollie Watkins; family living in New Orleans in 1861

2) daughter of John M. Watt, 37, farmer, Tn. (1850 census)

3) 1850 census: age 6; b. in Ms.

Watt, Sally

Jan. 31, 1861

Watts, Major

Sept. 21, 1867

Wear, Ben

Mar. 9, 1849

1) son of music school teacher, George W. Wear

Wear (Ware), Mr. and Mrs. George W.

Mar. 9, 1849

1) gave Lettie piano lessons in Middleton in 1846

2) teacher in Middleton; first music teacher there

3) came to U.S. from England as a boy, age 14

4) very talented musician

5) married Julia Holt, daughter of Benjamin Holt, teacher

6) see Wear's Hotel for 1860 census

7) ambushed and slain by Negroes near Carrollton

8) 1850 census:

George W.	33	music teacher	Engl.
Julia	27		S.C.
Benjamin	5		Ms.
Mary	3		Ms.
Catherine	1		Ms.

Wear's (Ware's) Hotel

Jan. 19, 1860

1) proprietor was George W. Wear, teacher and tavern keeper in 1860

2) hotel was in Carrollton

3) 1860 census (Carroll County):

George	57	tavern keeper	England
Julia	40		S.C.
and family			

Weed (Wied), Thomas B.

Oct. 20, 1860

Nov. 2, 1860

Aug. 8, 1861

1) trader for John Fox in 1860

2) m. S. R. (Rebecca) Sanders, Oct. 17, 1860

3) 1860 census:

Thomas B.	26	trader	N.C.
living with:			
Pearson Money & family	50	merchants	N.C.
Hernando	21		Ms.

Sarah F.	16	Ms.
Ladora	12	Ms.
William B.	10	Ms.
James D.	7	Ms.
Martha	4	Ms.

Weir, Mr. Rob

April 10, 1860

April 28, 1860

1) son of Dr. Weir of Shongalo and Mrs. Jane Weir

2) his father dead by 1860

3) 1860 census:

Jane Weir	43		Va.
Robert	24	medical student	Ms.
William	18		Ms.
Cornelius	17		Ms.
Rush	10		Ms.

Weisenger, George

Feb. 9, 1862

June 8, 1867

1) Carroll Co. soldier

Wellons, Ben

Feb. 21, 1853

May 2, 1861

1) son of Judge James Wellon

Wellons, Cicero

May 2, 1861

Wellons, Ed

Oct. 15, 1851

1) son of Judge and Mrs. James Wellons

Wellons, George

April 28, 1860

Dec. 17, 1860

Feb. 24, 1862

1) son of Judge and Mrs. James Wellons

2) 1850 census: age 13

Wellons, Judge James

July 4, 1855

Oct. 20, 1860

Jan. 2, 1861

Jan. 31, 1861

Nov. 4, 1861

1) of Carrollton, friend of the Watkins boys after their father died and mother remarried

2) a merchant in Carrollton

3) 1850 census:

James	51	merchant & lawyer	N.C.

Cynthia	49		N.C.
Benjamin	22	clerk	N.C.
Edward L.	20		N.C.
George W.	13		Ms.
Virginia	11		Ms.
William O. Patton	21	clerk	Tn.

Wellons, Jennie (Virginia)
July 31, 1860
Oct. 20, 1860
Dec. 17, 1860
1) daughter of Judge and Mrs. James Wellons
2) 1850 census: age 11
Wells, Narcissa
Mar. 11, 1857
West, Charles S.
Jan. 24, 1862
1) secretary of state, Texas
2) Austin resident
White, Mr. and Mrs.
April 10, 1860
May 25, 1860
1) Carrollton dressmaker and husband
Whitehead, Edmunds Grey
Mar. 26, 1849
April 20, 1850
May 15, 1854
Mar. 8, 1855
June 1, 1855
Nov. 17, 1855
Dec. 28, 1856
May 15, 1857
June 8, 1857
Oct. 8, 1857
Nov. 30, 1857
Jan. 18, 1858
June 14, 1858
Feb. 7, 1859
Mar. 15, 1859
Jan. 27, 1860
Feb. 3, 1860
Mar. 16, 1860
May 25, 1860
Aug. 25, 1860
Oct. 20, 1860
Nov. 2, 1860
Mar. 9, 1861

June 6, 1861
Feb. 4, 1862
Oct. 2, 1862
Oct. 7, 1862
Dec. 1, 1862
Dec. 25, 1862
Feb. 7, 1864
Oct. 8, 1864
Jan. 23, 1867
June 8, 1867
Sept. 21, 1867
July 1879
1) June 1855: "has built near schoolhouse where Elizabeth Jenkins taught"
2) m. Martha Jennett Scott, May 17, 1836
3) respected friend and neighbor to Watkins family
4) 1850 census:

Edmund G.	44	farmer	N.C.
Jennett	32		La.
Elizabeth	13		Ms.
Virginia	11		Ms.
William	7		Ms.
Grey	4		Ms.
Thomas	2		Ms.
Emma	5/12		Ms.

Whitehead, Mrs. Edmunds Grey (Martha Jennett Scott)
Mar. 26, 1849
July 23, 1849
Feb. 9, 1850
April 20, 1850
June 9, 1851
Nov. 7, 1851
Jan. 30, 1852
April 4, 1852
April 4, 1854
April 15, 1854
May 15, 1854
July 4, 1854
Sept. 2, 1854
Sept. 23, 1855
Mar. 11, 1857
May 15, 1857
June 8, 1857
Oct. 8, 1857
Oct. 24, 1857
April 5, 1858
Oct. 7, 1858

Nov. 1, 1858
Dec. 27, 1858
Nov. 7, 1859
Mar. 6, 1860
April 28, 1860
July 10, 1860
July 31, 1860
Oct. 20, 1860
Nov. 2, 1860
Nov. 26, 1860
Feb. 16, 1861
Mar. 9, 1861
Mar. 11, 1861
June 6, 1861
June 22, 1861
Aug. 8, 1861
Mar. 31, 1862
June 27, 1862
July 30, 1862
Oct. 7, 1862
Oct. 12, 1862
Dec. 15, 1862
Dec. 25, 1862
June 11, 1863
July 23, 1865
Feb. 16, 1867
June 8, 1867
Fall 1868
July 1879
1) born in La.
2) kind and beloved friend to Watkins family

Whitehead, Elizabeth (Lizzie)
April 25, 1849
Feb. 9, 1850
Nov. 7, 1851
April 15, 1854
July 4, 1855
Sept. 23, 1855
Feb. 6, 1858
Oct. 7, 1858
Nov. 2, 1859
Jan. 19, 1860
Mar. 6, 1860
Mar. 16, 1860
Mar. 26, 1860
April 4, 1860

April 28, 1860
Oct. 7, 1862
Jan. 9, 1864
June 8, 1867
1) Edmunds Grey Whitehead's daughter
2) m. William Carter Oliver of Eutaw, Ala., March 26, 1860
3) see Oliver, William Carter
Whitehead, Edward D.
Dec. 27, 1881
Dec. 20, 1881
1) son of E. G. Whitehead
Whitehead, Emma
Mar. 11, 1857
Mar. 17, 1860
Juy 9, 1861
Feb. 16, 1867
1) Edmunds Grey Whitehead's daughter
Whitehead, Eugene
April 4, 1860
Oct. 3, 1861
Feb. 24, 1862
June 27, 1862
June 11, 1863
Sept. 15, 1864
Sept. 4, 1869
1) Judge Whitehead's son
Whitehead, Gertrude (Ella Gertrude)
Feb. 16, 1861
Aug. 8, 1861
June 8, 1867
Fall 1868
Sept. 21, 1867
Jan. 17, 1875
Jan. 30, 1875
Dec. 27, 1881
Dec. 30, 1881
1) Edmunds Grey Whitehead's daughter
2) m. Alfred Cicero Dimond
Whitehead, Grey
Jan. 9, 1864
Feb. 7, 1864
Sept. 15, 1864
Dec. 30, 1881
Whitehead, Laura C.
Sept. 23, 1855
Oct. 24, 1857

Dec. 28, 1857
Feb. 6, 1858
Dec. 20, 1858
April 4, 1860
April 10, 1860
April 28, 1860
Mar. 11, 1861
July 9, 1861
Sept. 11, 1861
July 15, 1862
1) Judge Whitehead's daughter
2) m. Dr. G. Werter Drake in 1873

Whitehead, Martha

April 25 1849
Nov. 7, 1851
May 15, 1854
1) Judge Whitehead's daughter
2) m. John O. Young, Aug. 27, 1856
3) 1860 census:

John O. Young	46	Va.
Martha	28	Ms.
David	16	Ms.
John	12	Ms.
William	3	Ms.
Samuel	1	Ms.

Whitehead, Mary

Jan. 13, 1849
April 25, 1849
Nov. 7, 1851
Jan. 30, 1852
Feb. 21, 1853
April 26, 1854
May 15, 1854
June 1, 1855
Jan. 12, 1856
1) Judge Whitehead's daughter
2) m. Charles Arnold, May 8, 1856

Whitehead, Mary L. "Puss"

June 8, 1867
Dec. 30, 1881
1) daughter of Mr. and Mrs. E. G. Whitehead

Whitehead, Richard

Dec. 28, 1859
Jan. 19, 1860
Dec. 17, 1860
Mar. 25, 1861

Oct. 3, 1861
July 31, 1862
Jan. 9, 1864
1) Judge Whitehead's son
2) m. Mary Conkey at Lagrange, Tn., in 1859
Whitehead, Mrs. Richard (Mary Conkey)
April 4, 1860
April 10, 1860
April 28, 1860
Dec. 17, 1860
Feb. 16, 1861
Mar. 5, 1861
Oct. 3, 1861
June 27, 1862
1) Mary A. Conkey (Judge Whitehead's daughter-in-law)
2) living at Carrollton in 1860
Whitehead, Sally Tyson
Mar. 9, 1861
Mar. 5, 1861
April 12, 1861
April 13, 1861
1) died; wife of William Whitehead, the son of Edmunds Grey Whitehead
Whitehead, Tom
Jan. 27, 1860
Dec. 20, 1881
1) Edmunds Whitehead's son
Whitehead, Virginia
April 25, 1849
Feb. 9, 1850
Nov. 7, 1851
April 15, 1854
July 4, 1855
Sept. 23, 1855
Jan. 12, 1856
Mar. 11, 1857
Oct. 8, 1857
Oct. 24, 1857
Dec. 28, 1857
June 14, 1858
Oct. 7, 1858
April 28, 1860
1) Edmunds Grey Whitehead's daughter
2) m. Thomas B. Kennedy, Dec. 27, 1857
Whitehead, William
Dec. 20, 1858
Dec. 27, 1858

Mar. 17, 1860
July 10, 1860
Mar. 9, 1861
Mar. 25, 1861
April 12, 1861
July 9, 1861
Oct. 3, 1861
Feb. 24, 1862
June 27, 1862
Oct. 7, 1862
Dec. 15, 1862
Dec. 25, 1862
1) Edmunds Grey Whitehead's son
2) died at Vicksburg, Civil War

Whitehead, Judge William W.

May 4, 1856
June 26, 1846
Feb. 28, 1848
Dec. 29, 1848
Mar. 26, 1849
Jan. 13, 1849
Mar. 31, 1849
Dec. 15, 1851
Jan. 30, 1852
June 24, 1852
Feb. 21, 1853
April 26, 1854
May 15, 1854
Sept. 2, 1854
Mar. 8, 1855
June 1, 1855
Sept. 23, 1855
Jan. 12, 1856
June 8, 1857
July 30, 1857
Oct. 24, 1857
Nov. 30, 1857
April 5, 1858
Mar. 15, 1859
April 4, 1860
April 28, 1860
Dec. 17, 1860
Mar. 31, 1862
Dec. 1, 1862
Feb. 4, 1865
Sept. 4, 1869

1) b. 1799 in N.C.

2) first probate judge of Carroll County

Whitehead, Mrs. Judge Wm. (Elizabeth Davis, 1st Mrs.)

Sept. 2, 1854

Sept. 23, 1855

Mar. 11, 1857

July 30, 1857

Feb. 16, 1861

Mar. 31, 1862

1) William Whitehead "has gone to Tn. to marry one of the teachers at the Middleton School" Sept. 2, 1854

Williams, Uncle David and Aunt Mary

Feb. 6, 1858

July 31, 1860

1) Va. kin of Sarah Watkins

Williams, Fayette

July 31, 1860

1) Va. kin of Sarah Watkins

Williams, "Cousin" Jack

July 31, 1860

1) Sarah Watkins's kin in Va.

2) Sarah Watkins's mother's maiden name was Ann Roper Williams

Williams, Virginia

June 1, 1864

Williford, Mr. Henry W.

Feb. 24, 1862

1) from around Greenwood

2) 1860 census: 17, b. in Ill., farm laborer

Wilson, Sam

June 27, 1862

Windham, James B.

April 13, 1861

Wingfield, Albert M. and family

Oct. 21, 1848

Oct. 23, 1848

Dec. 29, 1848

Jan. 13, 1849

July 7 and 8, 1849

July 16, 1849

July 23, 1849

1) lived at Columbia, Tn.

2) Lettie visited them in the summer of 1849

Wingfield, Ellen

Jan. 12, 1856

1) possibly the daughter of the Wingfield family of Columbia, Tn., where Lettie stayed

Wingfield, Mary
July 16, 1849
Feb. 23, 1852
Jan. 12, 1856
Mar. 16, 1860
1) m. to Mr. Martin, very pretty
2) neighbor of Babe Watkins Branch in Ark.
3) is dead in 1860 (Babe Watkins Branch was probably the youngest daughter of Paul J. Watkins and her husband, James Branch
4) the daughter of the Wingfield family of Columbia, Tn., with whom Lettie stayed

Winona, Mississippi
July 10, 1860
1) grew up on Col. Moore's land around the railroad station for Mississippi Central Railroad

Wise, Mr.
Dec. 28, 1857
1) of Moulton, Ala.
2) at one time, guardian of Sarah Epes Watkins's niece and nephew, children of her deceased brother, William Fitzgerald

Witherspoon, Laura
Jan. 26, 1861

Witty, Bill
Nov. 7, 1851
Mar. 6, 1854
July 4, 1855
1) Ritt says he has more hair on his mouth than anybody she ever saw
2) 1850 census:
   Bill Witty   21   merchant's clerk   N.C.
   boarding in Middleton with Prof. Alden S. Bailey and his family

Witty, Miss Mary
Nov. 7, 1851
1) boarding in Middleton
2) 1850 census:
   Mary Witty   27   Ms.
   boarding with Dabney Lipscomb, M.D., and family

Wolfe, Mr. Jacob B.
Jan. 2, 1861
1) 1850 census (Carrollton area):

Jacob B.	36	grocer	S.C.
Maria S.	25		S.C.
Augustus	8		S.C.
Pauline E.	6		S.C.
Walter B.	2		S.C.
George Wills	28	grocer	Germany

2) 1860 census: Jacob was a postmaster

Wolfe, Mrs. Jacob B. (Maria S.)
Mar. 26, 1849
1) sister of Mr. Washington Rowe
2) 1850 census: age 25 (see Wolfe, Jacob)
Woods, Captain and Mrs.*
April 10, 1860
*not known which Mr. Woods was called Capt. Wood
Woods, Green (Grem)
Dec. 28, 1857
Jan. 19, 1860
1) son of Andrew Wood
2) brothers Peter and James
3) lived west of Middleton at Bluff Springs Church
4) 1860 census:

Green C.	37	farmer	Tn.
Nancy P.	32		Tn.
Josephine	12		Ms.
Charles	11		Ms.
William P.	4		Ms.
H. H.	1		Ms.

Woods, James ("Jim")
Jan. 12, 1856
1) m. Julia E. Gooch, Dec. 27, 1855
2) father was Andrew Wood
3) brothers, Peter and Green
4) 1860 census:

James	24	farmer	Tn.
Julia	22		S.C.
Francis	4		Ms.
Leroy	2		Ms.
James	3/12		Ms.

Woods, Mrs. "Jim" (Julia Gooch)
April 10, 1860
1) brothers-in-law were Green and Peter
Woods, Martha L.
April 19, 1852
1) sister of Susan Woods who is now Mrs. Isham Scruggs
2) m. Atlas Johnson, April 15, 1852
Woods, Peter
Jan. 12, 1856
1) son of Andrew Woods
2) 1850 census:

Andrew	57	teacher	Ky.
Huldah	49		Ky.
Peter	17		Tn.
James	14		Tn.
Louisa	12		Ms.

3) 1860 census:

P. Woods   26   farmer

Wright, Judge

Dec. 2, 1857

1) lives two miles from Carrollton (in 1857)

2) m. a cousin of Mr. Helms

3) is a partner of Mr. Helms

Y

Yazoo River, Mississippi

Feb. 14, 1849, and repeated references

Young, John Ossian

July 30, 1857

Nov. 2, 1860

1) brother of Samuel and Lucien Young, all came as young men to the county

2) first wife was Margaret Jane Marr

3) m. second, Martha Whitehead (daughter of Judge William Whitehead), Aug. 27, 1856

Young, Mrs. John O. Young (Martha Whitehead)

Mar. 11, 1857

July 30, 1857

Nov. 2, 1860

June 6, 1861

Nov. 4, 1861

Dec. 20, 1881

1) daughter of Judge William W. Whitehead

2) see Whitehead ref.

3) m. John O. Young, Aug. 27, 1856 (his second wife)

Young, Mr. Samuel H.

April 12, 1861

April 13, 1861

1) brother of Lucian and John Ossian Young

2) m. Catherine Small, July 10, 1845

3) 1850 census:

Samuel	29	farmer	Va.
Catherine	23		Ms.
John	4		Ms.
Mary	2		Ms.
Samuel	2/12		Ms.

Z

Zollicoffer, General Felix

Feb. 4, 1862

1) Confederate general; died early in the war

2) his niece, Cornelia Zollicoffer, married Edmunds Grey Whitehead; her father was Dr. Frederick Zollicoffer, brother of Gen. Zollicoffer

THE SLAVES

Much of plantation life involved slaves. The mistress of the plantation was often isolated, separated from friends by the vastness of the land and bad roads, so at times the slaves were her only contact. Therefore, almost every letter tells of illness, births, sickness, deaths, and doings of the Watkinses' slaves. Identification of these slaves gives substance and depth to the letters.

Servants of Dr. and Mrs. Thomas A. Watkins
at Carroll County Plantation

The first list was gleaned from wills, deeds, letters, and an old account book showing births kept by Mrs. Watkins. It is not complete. A second, abbreviated list was made from memory in 1900 by the two Watkins daughters, Lettie and Mollie. The two lists vary some, but in the main, match.

1. *Mingo.* Married to Rose, who belonged to the Hemingways on a neighboring plantation. Mingo came into the family as a young boy (bill of sale, 1822). He came from Mrs. Watkins's grandfather, William Fitzgerald's family, to Mrs. Watkins's mother, Ann Roper Williams Fitzgerald (widow of Thomas Fitzgerald) after her husband's death. Mingo died in 1862. Mrs. Watkins's mother deeded Mingo to her in a deed of gift in 1824 when Mingo was six years old. Mingo had been with the family forty years. Mingo's sister [unknown] was Lettie's "mama," her baby nurse.

2. *Pompey.* Came from Dr. Watkins's family in 1840, when he was 40 years old.

3. *Sally.* Willed to Mrs. Watkins by her mother in 1840; America, her child, was willed to Lettie at the same time.

4. *America.* Born June 11, 1838. America actually belonged to Lettie Watkins Walton but didn't want to leave Mississippi, so she did not go to Texas with the Waltons. America's first child was Sally Epes, born Jan. 27, 1864. Sally Epes married a Curtis and was still in the Kilmichael, Mississippi, area in 1913. America married one of the Hemingway servants and was named America Hemingway.

5. *Harry Ann* (Harriet Ann). Her children were:
Washington born 1839, married Anna
Susan born 1841

Moses born April 1844
Van Buren born May 1847
Amos born Jan. 22, 1849
Louisa born Jan. 10, 1851; died Sept. 28, 1862
Mitchell born October 1854; died at four weeks of age

  6. *London*. Died Dec. 9, 1859. London and his mother [unknown] came to Dr. Watkins from his mother, Polly Early Watkins, when she divided her Negroes among her heirs in 1839.

  7. *Glasgow*. Born 1826; died Dec. 22, 1859. He was willed to Mrs. Watkins by her mother in 1840.

  8. *Josiah*. Died Jan. 3, 1843.

  9. *William*. Died Jan. 6, 1860.

  10. *Becky*. Married to Abraham. She is referred to as Becca and Rebecca in the letters. Her children were:

Melia (Amelia) born March 9, 1843
Tilla (Matilda) born Jan. 18, 1845
Tom (Thomas) born September 1847
Abram born Dec. 16, 1849
Lucinda born July 3, 1855
Charles born July 3, 1855
Jackson born May 3, 1858; died 1894
Phill born Sept. 14, 1860; died Sept. 5, 1864

  11. *Martha*. Born in 1830. Her father was Moses Fitzgerald; her mother was Peggy. Martha was willed to Mrs. Watkins by her mother in 1840. Sometimes she is called Martha Ann. Old Peggy Fitzgerald, her mother, came to Mississippi to live after the war and is listed on the 1870 census of Carroll County. She had lived with the Fitzgeralds in Alabama before that. Martha's children were:

Siah born July 7, 1847
Milly born Oct. 31, 1848
Charlotte Ann born July 19, 1850
Henrietta born Feb. 27, 1853
Alfred born July 16, 1858
Jeff Longstreet born Dec. 9, 1860
Laura born November 1862

  12. *Semira*. Born November 1831. Her children were:

Henry born May 21, 1850
Paten born September 1852
Willie born June 1855
Sarah Jane born Feb. 21, 1858
Agnes born March 27, 1861

13. *Else.* Born 1826. Her children were:
Letty born Feb. 12, 1851
George A. born Nov. 26, 1852
Robin born Dec. 1, 1854
Epes born June 26, 1858
Becky born July 1863

14. *Milly.* Married to Tom. Her children were:
Simon born in the spring of 1849; still living near Carrollton, Mississippi, in 1911.
Sarah born June 30, 1851
Frances born Dec. 30, 1853
Preston born Sept. 1854
Elisa born Sept. 3, 1856

Milly and two children not listed here were bought from Uncle Billy Fitzgerald in 1849.

15. *Polly* (another daughter of Peggy). Called "Polly Baby," she was bought from "Uncle Billy" Fitzgerald in 1849. Her sister was Martha, another Watkins servant. Her children were:
Margaret born March 31, 1851
Phill born Feb. 11, 1853; died Oct. 1854
Moses born Oct. 10, 1855; died 1862
Mary Early born Nov. 5, 1857
Dianah born Nov. 21, 1859; died May 28, 1861
Shaler Walter born Dec. 19, 1862

16. *Anna.* Bought as a young girl by the doctor in Missouri.

17. *Jane.* Her children were:
Green born 1860
Mary Ella born Dec. 16, 1861; died September 1862

18. *Susan.* Her child was:
Robert Moten born May 25, 1862; died July 1864

19. *Patty.* Did some of the cooking. Her child was:
Frank born April 12, 1847

20. *Salsbury.* Born April 1829.

21. *Hannah.* Sometimes the cook.

22. *Agnes.* Died October 1861.

23. *Uncle Vivion.* Born about 1788; came from the Fitzgerald family. He was still alive in 1864.

24. *Robin.* Born about 1804; came from Aunt Lettie Fitzgerald's family after her death; was a good cook.

25. *Abraham* (or Abram). The carriage driver and gardener. His wife was Rebecca (*supra vide*).

26. *Ritter* (or Ritt). Seems to be the same person as Henrietta; willed to Mrs. Watkins by her mother in 1840. She, along with America, was Mrs. Watkins's personal servant in later years.

27. *John W.* The carpenter, whose full name was John Watkins. He came to Dr. Watkins from his mother Polly Early, in 1833.

28. *Isham*

29. *Chloe*

30. *Simon*

31. *Daniel*

32. *Polly*

33. *Nancy*

34. *John Smith*

35. *Aunt Sally**

36. *Caroline**

*These are a mother and daughter who went to Texas in 1860 in trade for America, who did not want to leave Carroll County and move to Texas. Sally and Caroline had come from Missouri and had not grown up in the family.

37. *Prince.* Head of the field hands in 1862 (during the war) when the overseer went into the army.

38. *Jake*

39. *Jane*

40. *Jesse*

41. *Hannah Missouri.* Died July 21, 1862.

The following census, made from memory about 1900 by Lettie Walton and her sister Mollie McLemore, is a list of the Negroes with the Watkins family in about 1865. Some names differ on these two lists because of the time-frame; this list represents those with the Watkinses at about the time of the Civil War, while the other list includes individuals active in earlier decades.

1. John Watkins
2. Harriett Ann
3. Moses
4. Mitchell
5. Van Buren
6. Amos
7. Jake
8. Biddy
9. Washington
10. Anna
11. Tommie
12. Washington
13. Hannah
14. Prince
15. Letty
16. George
17. Epps
18. Big Jane
19. Mollie
20. Mollie
21. Becky
22. Abram
23. Meally
24. Lilly (Matilda)
25. Tomerta
26. Little Abram
27. Vivion
28. Isham
29. Chloe
30. Patty
31. John Smith
32. Salsbury
33. Frank
34. Mingo
35. Martha
36. Simon
37. Milly
38. Charlotte
39. Tave
40. Jeff
41. Alberta
42. Laura
43. Big Milly
44. Ned
45. Sarah
46. Francis
47. Eliza
48. Buster
49. Semira
50. Henry
51. Peyton
52. Willie
53. Sarah Jane
54. Lealia
55. Else
56. Lucinda
57. Jack
58. Phil
59. Bob
60. Susan
61. Little Bob
62. Polly
63. Daniel
64. Margaret
65. Polly Early
66. Shaler
67. Dick
68. Little Simon
69. Sally
70. America
71. Joe
72. Ritt
73. Sally Epps (America's daughter)
74. Armistead
75. Robin

INDEX